Excel® 2007 All-in-One Reference For Dummies®

BESTSELLING BOOK SERIES

P9-DCH-818

Excel is rampant with shortcut keys as these Cheat Sheet tables point out. Keep these tables handy, because their hot keys can really help speed up your work and make using Excel 2007 a much more enjoyable, and a lot less fatiguing, experience.

Hot Keys for Common File Commands

Hot Keys	Excel Ribbon Command	Function
Alt+FN	Microsoft Office Button | New	Displays the New Workbook dialog box where you can open a blank workbook or one from a template
Alt+FO	Microsoft Office Button | Open	Displays the Open dialog box where you can select a new Excel workbook to open for editing or printing
Alt+FS	Microsoft Office Button | Save	Saves changes to a workbook. When you first select this command for a new workbook, Excel displays the Save As dialog box
Alt+FA	Microsoft Office Button | Save As	Display the Save As dialog box where you can modify the filename, location where the file is saved, and format that the file is saved in
Alt+FP	Microsoft Office Button | Print	Displays the Print dialog box to send the current worksheet, workbook, or cell selection to the printer
Alt+FD	Microsoft Office Button | Send	Sends the current workbook as an e-mail attachment or fax it using Internet Fax
Alt+FC	Microsoft Office Button | Close	Closes the current workbook without exiting Excel
Alt+FI	Microsoft Office Button | Excel Options	Displays the Excel Options dialog box where you can change default program settings and modify the buttons on the Quick Access toolbar
Alt+FX	Microsoft Office Button | Exit Excel	Quits the Excel program and closes all open workbooks after prompting you to save them

Hot Keys for Common Editing Commands

Hot Keys	Excel Ribbon Command	Function
Alt+HVP	Home | Paste | Paste	Pastes the currently cut or copied cell selection or graphic objects in the worksheet
Alt+HX	Home | Cut	Cuts the cell selection or selected graphic objects out of the workbook and places them on the Windows Clipboard
Alt+HC	Home | Copy	Copies the cell selection or selected graphic objects to the Windows Clipboard
Alt+HFP	Home | Format Painter	Activates the Format Painter
Alt+HFO	Home | Clipboard Dialog Box Launcher	Displays and hides the Clipboard task pane
Alt+HII	Home | Insert | Insert Cells	Opens Insert dialog box so you can indicate the direction in which to shift existing cells to make room for the ones being inserted
Alt+HIR	Home | Insert | Insert Sheet Rows	Inserts blank rows equal to the number of rows in the cell selection
Alt+HIC	Home | Insert | Insert Sheet Columns	Inserts blank columns equal to the number of columns in the cell selection
Alt+HIS	Home | Insert | Insert Sheet	Inserts a new worksheet in the workbook
Alt+HDD	Home | Delete | Delete Cells	Opens Delete dialog box so you can indicate the direction in which to shift existing cells to replace the ones being deleted
Alt+HDR	Home | Delete | Sheet Rows	Deletes rows equal to the number of rows in the cell selection
Alt+HDC	Home | Delete | Sheet Columns	Deletes columns equal to the number of columns in the cell selection
Alt+HDS	Home | Delete | Sheet	Deletes the current worksheet after warning you of data loss if the sheet contains cell entries
Alt+HEA	Home | Clear | Clear All	Clears the contents, formatting, and comments from the cell selection
Alt+HEF	Home | Clear | Clear Formats	Clears the formatting of the cell selection without removing the contents and comments
Alt+HEC	Home | Clear | Clear Contents	Clears the contents of the cell selection without removing the formatting and comments
Alt+HEM	Home | Clear | Clear Comments	Clears all comments in the cell selection without removing the formatting and contents

For Dummies: Bestselling Book Series for Beginners

Excel® 2007 All-in-One Desk Reference For Dummies®

Cheat Sheet

Hot Keys for Common View Commands

Hot Keys	Excel Ribbon Command	Function
Alt+WL	View | Normal View	Returns the worksheet to normal view from Page Layout or Page Break Preview
Alt+WP	View | Page Layout View	Puts the worksheet into Page Layout View showing the page breaks, margins, and rulers
Alt+WI	View | Page Break Preview	Puts the worksheet into Page Break Preview showing page breaks that you can adjust
Alt+WE	View | Full Screen	Puts the worksheet in full-screen mode which hides the Microsoft Office Button, Quick Access toolbar, and Ribbon — press the Esc key to restore previous viewing mode
Alt+WVG	View | Gridlines	Hides and redisplays the row and column gridlines that form the cells in the Worksheet area
Alt+WYG	View | Zoom to Selection	Zooms the Worksheet area in or out to the magnification percentage needed to display just the cell selection
Alt+WN	View | New Window	Inserts a new window in the current workbook
Alt+WA	View | Arrange All	Opens the Arrange dialog box where you can select how workbook windows are displayed on the screen
Alt+WF	View | Freeze Panes	Opens the Freeze Panes drop-down menu where you select how to freeze rows and columns in the Worksheet area: Freeze Panes (to freeze all the rows above and columns to the left of the cell cursor); Freeze Top Row; or Freeze First Column
Alt+WS	View | Split	Splits the worksheet into four panes using the top and left edge of the cell cursor as the vertical and horizontal dividing lines — press hot keys again to remove all panes
Alt+WH	View | Hide	Hides the current worksheet window or workbook
Alt+WU	View | Unhide	Opens the Unhide dialog box where you can select the window or workbook to redisplay
Alt+WB	View | View Side by Side	Tiles two open windows or workbooks one above the other for comparison — press hot keys again to restore the original full windows
Alt+WW	View | Switch Windows	Opens the Switch Windows drop-down menu where you can select the open window or workbook to make active

Hot Keys for Common Formula Commands

Hot Keys	Excel Ribbon Command	Function
Alt+MF	Formulas | Function Wizard	Opens the Insert Function dialog box (same as clicking the Function Wizard button on the Formula bar
Alt+MUS	Formulas | AutoSum | Sum	Selects the occupied range above the cell cursor and inserts SUM formula to total the range
Alt+MUA	Formulas | AutoSum | Average	Selects the occupied range above the cell cursor and inserts AVERAGE formula to calculate the average of total in the range
Alt+MUC	Formulas | AutoSum | Count Numbers	Selects the occupied range above the cell cursor and inserts COUNT formula to count the number of values in the range
Alt+MI	Formulas | Financial	Opens a drop-down menu listing all Financial functions — click name to insert function into current cell
Alt+ME	Formulas | Date & Time	Opens a drop-down menu listing all Date and Time functions — click name to insert function into current cell
Alt+MN	Formulas | Name Manager	Opens Name Manager dialog box showing all range names in workbook where you can add, edit, and delete names
Alt+MMD	Formulas | Define Name	Opens New Name dialog box where you can assign a name to the cell selection or define a new constant
Alt+MS1	Formulas | Use in Formula	Displays drop-down menu with range names in workbook that you can insert into current formula by clicking
Alt+MC1	Formulas | Create from Selection	Opens Create Names from Selection dialog box where you indicate which rows and columns to use in naming cell selection
Alt+MH	Formulas | Show Formulas (Ctrl+`)	Displays and then hides all formulas in cells of the worksheet

For Dummies: Bestselling Book Series for Beginners

Excel® 2007
ALL-IN-ONE DESK REFERENCE
FOR
DUMMIES®

Excel® 2007
ALL-IN-ONE DESK REFERENCE
FOR
DUMMIES®

by Greg Harvey

Wiley Publishing, Inc.

Excel® 2007 All-in-One Desk Reference For Dummies®

Published by
Wiley Publishing, Inc.
111 River Street
Hoboken, NJ 07030-5774
www.wiley.com

Copyright © 2007 by Wiley Publishing, Inc., Indianapolis, Indiana

Published by Wiley Publishing, Inc., Indianapolis, Indiana

Published simultaneously in Canada

For general information on our other products and services, please contact our Customer Care Department within the U.S. at 800-762-2974, outside the U.S. at 317-572-3993, or fax 317-572-4002.

For technical support, please visit www.wiley.com/techsupport.

Wiley also publishes its books in a variety of electronic formats. Some content that appears in print may not be available in electronic books.

Library of Congress Control Number: 2006934843

ISBN-13: 978-0-470-03738-6

ISBN-10: 0-470-03738-5

Manufactured in the United States of America

10 9 8 7 6 5 4 3

1B/QX/RS/QW/IN

WILEY

About the Author

Greg Harvey has authored tons of computer books, the most recent being *Excel 2007 For Dummies, Windows Vista For Dummies Quick Reference,* and *Excel Workbook For Dummies.* He started out training business users on how to use IBM personal computers and their attendant computer software in the rough-and-tumble days of DOS, WordStar, and Lotus 1-2-3 in the mid-80s of the last century. After working for a number of independent training firms, he went on to teaching semester-long courses in spreadsheet and database management software at Golden Gate University in San Francisco.

His love of teaching has translated into an equal love of writing. *For Dummies* books are, of course, his all-time favorites to write because they enable him to write to his favorite audience, the beginner. They also enable him to use humor (a key element to success in the training room) and, most delightful of all, to express an opinion or two about the subject matter at hand.

Dedication

To Kelly — a best friend, sorely missed . . . Semper Fidelis.

Author's Acknowledgments

I am always so grateful to the many people who work so hard to bring my book projects into being, and this one is no exception. If anything, I am even more thankful for their talents, given the size and complexity of an All-in-One.

This time, special thanks are in order to Andy Cummings and Katie Feltman for giving me this opportunity to write and write and write about Excel in this great All-in-One format. Next, I want to express great thanks to my project editor, Beth Taylor, and, to my partner in crime, Christopher Aiken (I really appreciate all your encouragement on this one). Thanks also go to Gabrielle Sempf for the great technical edit, Adrienne Martinez for coordinating the book's production, and everybody at Wiley Publishing.

Publisher's Acknowledgments

We're proud of this book; please send us your comments through our online registration form located at www.dummies.com/register/.

Some of the people who helped bring this book to market include the following:

Acquisitions, Editorial, and Media Development

Project Editor: Beth Taylor

Senior Acquisitions Editor: Katie Feltman

Copy Editor: Beth Taylor

Technical Editor: Gabrielle Sempf

Editorial Manager: Jodi Jensen

Media Development Manager: Laura Carpenter VanWinkle

Editorial Assistant: Amanda Foxworth

Cartoons: Rich Tennant (www.the5thwave.com)

Composition Services

Project Coordinator: Adrienne Martinez

Layout and Graphics: Claudia Bell, Stephanie D. Jumper, Barbara Moore, Barry Offringa, Heather Ryan, Rashell Smith, Ronald Terry

Proofreaders: Laura L. Bowman, Jessica Kramer, Christine Pingleton

Indexer: Julie Kawabata

Anniversary Logo Design: Richard Pacifico

Publishing and Editorial for Technology Dummies

    Richard Swadley, Vice President and Executive Group Publisher

    Andy Cummings, Vice President and Publisher

    Mary Bednarek, Executive Acquisitions Director

    Mary C. Corder, Editorial Director

Publishing for Consumer Dummies

    Diane Graves Steele, Vice President and Publisher

    Joyce Pepple, Acquisitions Director

Composition Services

    Gerry Fahey, Vice President of Production Services

    Debbie Stailey, Director of Composition Services

Contents at a Glance

Table of Contents

Introduction

The *Excel 2007 All-in-One Desk Reference For Dummies* brings together plain and simple information on using all aspects of the latest and greatest version of Microsoft Excel. It's designed to be of help no matter how much or how little experience you have with the program. As the preeminent spreadsheet and data analysis software for the personal computer, Excel offers its users seemingly unlimited capabilities too often masked in technical jargon and obscured by explanations only a software engineer could love. On top of that, many of the publications that purport to give you the lowdown on using Excel are quite clear on how to use particular features without giving you a clue as to why you would go to all the trouble.

The truth is that understanding how to use the abundance of features offered by Excel is only half the battle, at best. The other half of the battle is to understand how these features can benefit you in your work, in other words, "what's in it for you." I have endeavored to cover both the "how to" and "so what" aspects in all my discussions of Excel features, being as clear as possible and using as little tech-speak as possible.

Fortunately, Excel is well worth the effort to get to know because it's definitely one of the best data processing productivity tools that has ever come along. Its all new Ribbon user interface, Live Preview feature, and tons of ready-made galleries make this version of the program the easiest to use ever. In short, Excel 2007 is a blast to use when you know what you're doing, and my great hope is that this "fun" aspect of using the program comes through on every page (or, at least, every other page).

About This Book

As the name states, *Excel 2007 All-in-One Desk Reference For Dummies* is a reference (whether you keep it on your desk or use it to prop up your desk is your business). This means that although the chapters in each book are laid out in a logical order, each stands on its own, ready for you to dig into the information at any point.

As much as possible, I have endeavored to make the topics within each chapter stand on their own. When there's just no way around relying on some information that's discussed elsewhere, I include a cross-reference that gives you the chapter and verse (actually the book and chapter) for where you can find that related information if you're of a mind to.

Use the full Table of Contents and Index to look up the topic of the hour and find out exactly where it is in this compilation of Excel information. You'll find that although most topics are introduced in a conversational manner, I don't waste much time cutting to the chase by laying down the main principles at work (usually in bulleted form) followed by the hard reality of how you do the deed (as numbered steps).

Foolish Assumptions

I'm only going to make one foolish assumption about you and that is that you have some need to use Microsoft Excel in your work or studies. If pushed, I further guess that you aren't particularly interested in knowing Excel at an expert level but are terribly motivated to find out how to do the stuff you need to get done. If that's the case, then this is definitely the book for you. Fortunately, even if you happen to be one of those newcomers who's highly motivated to become the company's resident spreadsheet guru, you've still come to the right place.

As far as your hardware and software go, I'm assuming that you already have Excel 2007 (usually as part of Microsoft Office 2007) installed on your computer, using a standard installation running under either Windows Vista or Windows XP. Although most of the figures in this book all show Excel 2007 happily running on Windows Vista, you will see the occasional figure showing Excel running on Windows XP in the rare cases (as when opening and saving files) where it does make a difference as to which operating system you're using.

This book is intended *only* for users of Microsoft Office Excel 2007! Because of the deep and significant changes to the user interface in Excel 2007, if you're using any previous version of Excel for Windows (from Excel 97 through 2003), the information in this book will only confuse and confound you, as your version of Excel works nothing like the 2007 version this book describes.

So, please put this book down slowly and instead pick up a copy of *Excel 2003 All-in-One Desk Reference For Dummies,* published by Wiley Publishing.

How This Book 1s Organized

Excel 2007 All-in-One Desk Reference For Dummies is actually eight smaller books rolled into one. That way, you can go after the stuff in the particular book that really interests you at the time, putting all the rest of the material aside until you need to have a look at it. Each book in the volume consists of two or more chapters consisting of all the basic information you should need in dealing with that particular component or aspect of Excel.

In case you're the least bit curious, here's the lowdown on each of the eight books and what you can expect to find there.

Book 1: Excel Basics

This book is for those of you who've never had a formal introduction to the program's basic workings. Chapter 1 covers all the orientation material including how to deal with the program's new Ribbon user interface. Of special interest may be the section on migrating to Excel 2007 from earlier versions of Excel: This section is intended to ease users who have some experience with earlier versions of Excel (97 through 2003) through the initial meeting and the first moments of getting used to Excel's new way of doing business.

Chapter 2 is your place to go to find out how to get online help in Excel. Believe it or not, after you have the All-in-One basics down, some of the online help topics actually start making sense!

Chapter 3 is not to be missed, even by those of you who do not consider yourselves beginners by any stretch of the imagination. This chapter covers the many ways to customize Excel and make the program truly your own. It includes information on customizing the Quick Access toolbar as well as great information on how to use and procure add-in programs that can greatly extend Excel's considerable features.

Book II: Worksheet Design

Book II focuses on the crucial issue of designing spreadsheets in Excel. Chapter 1 takes up the call on how to do basic design and covers all the many ways of doing data entry (a subject that's been made all the more exciting with the addition of voice and handwriting input).

Chapter 2 covers how to make your spreadsheet look professional and read the way you want it through formatting. Excel offers you a wide choice of formatting techniques, from the very simple formatting as a table all the way to the now very sophisticated and super-easy conditional formatting.

Chapter 3 takes up the vital subject of how to edit an existing spreadsheet without disturbing its design or contents. Editing can be intimidating to the new spreadsheet user because most spreadsheets not only contain data entries that you don't want to mess up but formulas that can go haywire if you make the wrong move.

Chapter 4 looks at the topic of managing the worksheets that contain the spreadsheet applications that you build in Excel. It opens the possibility of going beyond the two-dimensional worksheet with its innumerable columns and rows by organizing data three-dimensionally through the use of multiple worksheets (each Excel file already contains three blank worksheets to which you can add more). This chapter also shows you how to work with and organize multiple worksheets given the limited screen real estate afforded by your monitor and how to combine data from different files and sheets when needed.

Chapter 5 is all about printing your spreadsheets, a topic that ranks only second in importance to knowing how to get the data into a worksheet in the first place. As you expect, you find out not only how to get the raw data to spit out of your printer but also how to gussy it up and make it into a professional report of which anyone would be proud.

Book III: Formulas and Functions

This book is all about calculations and building the formulas that do them. Chapter 1 covers formula basics from doing the simplest addition to building array formulas and using Excel's built-in functions courtesy of the Function Wizard. It also covers how to use different types of cell references when making formula copies and how to link formulas that span different worksheets.

Chapter 2 takes up the subject of preventing formula errors from occurring, and, barring that, how to track them down and eliminate them from the spreadsheet. This chapter also includes information on circular references in formulas and how you can sometimes use them to your advantage.

Chapters 3 through 6 concentrate on how to use different types of built-in functions. Chapter 3 covers the use of date and time functions, not only so you know what day and time it is, but actually put this knowledge to good use in formulas that calculate elapsed time. Chapter 4 takes up the financial functions in Excel and shows you how you can use them to both reveal and determine the monetary health of your business. Chapter 5 is concerned with math and statistical functions (of which there are plenty). Chapter 6 introduces you to the powerful group of lookup, information, and text functions. Here, you find out how to build formulas that automate data entry by returning values from a lookup table, get the lowdown on any cell in the worksheet, and combine your favorite pieces of text.

Book IV: Worksheet Collaboration and Review

Book IV looks at the ways you can share your spreadsheet data with others. Chapter 1 covers the important issue of security in your spreadsheets. Here, you find out how you can protect your data so that only those to whom you give permission can open or make changes to their contents.

Chapter 2 takes up the subject of building and using hyperlinks in your Excel spreadsheets (the same kind of links that you know and love on Web pages on the World Wide Web). This chapter covers how to create hyperlinks for moving from worksheet to worksheet within the same Excel file as well as for opening other documents on your hard disk, or logging onto the Internet and browsing to a favorite Web page.

Chapter 3 introduces Excel's sophisticated features for sending out spreadsheets and having a team of people review and make comments on them. It also covers techniques for reviewing and reconciling the suggested changes.

Chapter 4 is concerned with sharing spreadsheet data with other programs that you use. It looks specifically at how you can share data with other Office 2007 programs such as Microsoft Word, PowerPoint, and Outlook. This chapter also discusses the role of Smart Tags in enabling you to automatically bring information into your spreadsheets from outside sources such as your Outlook Address Book and special Web sites on the Internet, how to save Excel files in a bunch of other easily-accessed file formats (PDF, XPS, and HTML), and how to publish them to shared spaces.

Book V: Charts and Graphics

Book V focuses on the graphical aspects of Excel. Chapter 1 covers charting your spreadsheet data in some depth. Here, you find out not only how to create great looking charts but also how to select the right type of chart for the data that you're representing graphically.

Chapter 2 introduces you to all the other kinds of graphics that you can have in your spreadsheets. These include graphic objects that you draw as well as graphic images that you import including clip art included in Microsoft Office as well as digital pictures and images imported and created with other hardware and software connected to your computer.

Book VI: Data Management

Book VI is concerned with the ins and outs of using Excel to maintain large amounts of data in what are known as databases or, more commonly, data lists. Chapter 1 gives you basic information on how to set up a data list and add your data to it. This chapter also gives you information on how to reorganize the data list through sorting and how to total its numerical data with the Subtotal feature.

Chapter 2 is all about how to filter the data and extract just the information you want out of it (a process officially known as querying the data). Here, you find out how to perform all sorts of filtering operations from the simplest, relying upon the AutoFilter feature, to the more complex that use custom filters and specialized database functions. Finally, you find out how to perform queries on external data sources such as those maintained with dedicated database management software for Windows such as Microsoft Access or dBASE as well as that run on other operating systems such as DB2 and Oracle.

Book VII: Data Analysis

Book VII looks at the subject of data analysis with Excel; essentially how to use the program's computational abilities to project and predict possible future outcomes. Chapter 1 looks at the various ways to perform what-if scenarios in Excel. These include analyses with one- and two-input variable data tables, doing goal seeking, setting a series of different possible scenarios, and using the Solver add-in.

Chapter 2 is concerned with the topic of creating special data summaries called pivot table reports that enable you to analyze large amounts of data in an extremely compact and modifiable format. Here, you find out how to create and manipulate pivot tables as well as build pivot charts that depict the summary information graphically.

Book VIII: Excel and VBA

Book VIII introduces the subject of customizing Excel through the use of its programming language called Visual Basic for Applications (VBA for short). Chapter 1 introduces you to the use of the macro recorder to record tasks that you routinely perform in Excel for later automated playback. When you use the macro recorder to record the sequence of routine actions (using the program's familiar menus, toolbars, and dialog boxes), Excel automatically records the sequence in the VBA programming language.

Chapter 2 introduces you to editing VBA code in Excel's programming editor known as the Visual Basic Editor. Here, you find out how to use the Visual Basic Editor to edit macros that you've recorded that need slight modifications as well as how to write new macros from scratch. You also find out how to use the Visual Basic Editor to write custom functions that perform just the calculations you need in your Excel spreadsheets.

Conventions Used in This Book

This book follows a number of different conventions modeled primarily after those used by Microsoft in its various online articles and help materials. These conventions deal primarily with Ribbon command sequences and shortcut or hot key sequences that you encounter.

Excel 2007 is a sophisticated program with a whole new and wonderful user interface, dubbed the Ribbon. In Chapter 1, I explain all about this new Ribbon interface and how to get comfortable with its new command structure. Throughout the book, you'll find Ribbon command sequences using the shorthand developed by Microsoft whereby the name on the tab on the Ribbon and the command button you select are separated by vertical bars as in:

```
Home | Copy
```

This is shorthand for the Ribbon command that copies whatever cells or graphics are currently selected to the Windows Clipboard. It means that you click the Home tab on the Ribbon (if it's not already displayed) and then click the Copy button (that sports the traditional side-by-side page icon).

Some of the Ribbon command sequences involve not only selecting a command button on a tab but then also selecting an item on a drop-down menu. In this case, the drop-down menu command follows the name of the tab and command button, all separated by vertical bars, as in:

```
Formulas | Calculation Options | Manual
```

This is shorthand for the Ribbon command sequence that turns on manual recalculation in Excel. It says that you click the Formulas tab (if it's not already displayed) and then click the Calculation Options command button followed by the Manual drop-down menu option.

Although you use the mouse and keyboard shortcut keys to move your way in, out, and around the Excel worksheet, you do have to take some time to enter the data so that you can eventually mouse around with it. Therefore, this book occasionally encourages you to type something specific into a specific cell in the worksheet. Of course, you can always choose not to follow the instructions. When I tell you to enter a specific function, the part you should type generally appears in **bold** type. For example, **=SUM(A2:B2)** means that you should type exactly what you see: an equal sign, the word **SUM**, a left parenthesis, the text **A2:B2** (complete with a colon between the letter-number combos), and a right parenthesis. You then, of course, have to press Enter to make the entry stick.

When Excel isn't talking to you by popping up message boxes, it displays highly informative messages in the Status bar at the bottom of the screen. This book renders messages that you see on-screen like this:

```
Calculate
```

This is the message that tells you that Excel is in manual recalculation mode (after using the earlier Ribbon command sequence) and that one or more of the formulas in your worksheet are not up-to-date and are in sore need of recalculation.

Occasionally I give you a *hot key combination* that you can press in order to choose a command from the keyboard rather than clicking buttons on the Ribbon with the mouse. Hot key combinations are written like this: Alt+FS or Ctrl+S (both of these hot key combos save workbook changes).

With the Alt key combos, you press the Alt key until the hot key letters appear in little squares all along the Ribbon. At that point, you can release the Alt key and start typing the hot key letters (by the way, you type all lowercase hot key letters — I only put them in caps to make them stand out in the text).

Hot key combos that use the Ctrl key are of an older vintage and they work a little bit differently as you have to hold down the Ctrl key as you type the hot key letter (though again, type only lowercase letters unless you see the Shift key in the sequence as in Ctrl+Shift+C).

Excel 2007 uses only one pull-down menu (the File pull-down menu) and one toolbar (the Quick Access toolbar). You open the File pull-down menu by clicking the Office Button (the four-color round button in the upper-left corner of Excel program window) or pressing Alt+F. The Quick Access toolbar with its four buttons appears to the immediate right of the Office Button.

All earlier versions of this book use *command arrows* to lead you from the initial pull-down menu, to the submenu, and so on, to the command you ultimately want. For example, if you need to open the File pull-down menu to get to the Open command, that instruction would look like this: Choose File⇨ Open. This is the equivalent of Office Button | Open and Alt+FO. Commands using the older command arrow notation rather than the vertical bar notation occur only in the tables in Chapter 1 for people upgrading to Excel 2007 from older versions of Excel.

Finally, if you're really observant, you may notice a discrepancy between the capitalization of the names of dialog box options (such as headings, option buttons, and check boxes) as they appear in the book and how they actually appear in Excel on your computer screen. I intentionally use the convention of capitalizing the initial letters of all the main words of a dialog box option to help you differentiate the name of the option from the rest of the text describing its use.

Icons Used in This Book

The following icons are strategically placed in the margins throughout all eight books in this volume. Their purpose is to get your attention, and each has its own way of doing that.

This icon denotes some really cool information (in my humble opinion) that if you pay particular attention to will pay off by making your work a lot more enjoyable or productive (or both).

This icon denotes a tidbit that you ought to pay extra attention to; otherwise, you may end up taking a detour that wastes valuable time.

This icon denotes a tidbit that you ought to pay extra attention to; otherwise, you'll be sorry. I reserve this icon for those times when you can lose data and otherwise screw up your spreadsheet.

This icon denotes a tidbit that makes free use of (oh no!) technical jargon. You may want to skip these sections (or, at least, read them when no one else is around).

Where to Go from Here

The question of where to go from here couldn't be simpler — why, off to read the great Rich Tennant cartoons at the beginning of each of the eight books, of course. Then, go to Chapter 1 and find out what you're dealing with. And, if you're someone with some experience with earlier versions of Excel, I want you to head directly to the section, "Migrating to Excel 2007 from Earlier Versions" in Chapter 1, where you find out how to stay calm as you become familiar and, yes, comfortable with the new Ribbon user interface.

Which book you go to after that is a matter of personal interest and need. Just go for the gold and don't forget to have some fun while you're digging!

Book I
Excel Basics

The 5th Wave   By Rich Tennant

Contents at a Glance

Chapter 1: The Excel 2007 User Experience

In This Chapter

✓ Getting familiar with the Excel 2007 program window

✓ Selecting commands from the Ribbon

✓ Starting and quitting Excel

✓ Getting around the worksheet and workbook

✓ Quick start guide for users migrating to Excel 2007 from earlier versions

*I*n Excel 2007, Microsoft introduces its brand-new Ribbon user interface to everybody's favorite spreadsheet program. This new interface is so called because of its reliance on a new on-screen element called the Ribbon as the means by which the vast majority of Excel commands are selected. A testament to this fact is that this latest version of Excel now supports just a single pull-down menu (the Office menu with common file commands) and toolbar (the Quick Access toolbar) along with a handful of task panes (Clipboard, Clip Art, and Research), a far cry from its earlier versions like Excel 2003 with its 9 pull-down menus, over 20 built-in toolbars, and 10 standard task panes.

As part of the new and improved Excel 2007 user interface, the program includes all sorts of graphical improvements. First and foremost is the Live Preview feature that shows you how your actual worksheet data would appear in a particular font, table formatting, and so on before you actually select it. In addition, Excel now supports an honest to goodness Page Layout view that displays rulers and margins along with headers and footers for every worksheet and that has a zoom slider at the bottom of the screen that enables you to zoom in and out on the spreadsheet data instantly. Last but not least, Excel 2007 is full of pop-up galleries that make spreadsheet formatting and charting a real breeze, especially in tandem with Live Preview.

Meet Excel's Ribbon User Interface

When you first launch Excel 2007, the program opens up the first of three new worksheets (named Sheet1) in a new workbook file (named Book1) inside a program window such as the one shown in Figure 1-1.

The Excel program window containing this worksheet of the workbook is made up of the following components:

✦ **Office Button:** When clicked, this button opens a pull-down menu containing all the file-related commands including Save, Open, Print, and Exit as well as the Excel Options button that enables you to change Excel's default settings.

✦ **Quick Access toolbar:** You can click the Save, Undo, and Redo buttons to perform common tasks to save your work and undo and redo editing changes. You can also click the Customize Quick Access Toolbar button to the immediate right of the Redo button to open a drop-down menu containing additional common commands such New, Open, Quick Print, and so on as well as to customize the toolbar, change its position, and minimize the Ribbon.

✦ **Ribbon:** Most Excel commands are contained in the Ribbon. They are arranged into a series of tabs ranging from Home through View.

✦ **Formula bar:** The address of the current cell along with the contents of that cell appears in this bar.

✦ **Worksheet area:** This area contains all the cells of the current worksheet identified by column headings, using letters along the top, and row headings, using numbers along the left edge with tabs for selecting new worksheets. You use a horizontal scroll bar on the bottom to move left and right through the sheet and a vertical scroll bar on the right edge to move up and down through the sheet.

✦ **Status bar:** This bar keeps you informed of the program's current mode and any special keys you engage, and enables you to select a new worksheet view and to zoom in and out on the worksheet.

Making the most of the Office Button

At the very top of the Excel 2007 program window, you find the Office Button (the round one with the Office four-color icon in the very upper-left corner of the screen) followed immediately by the Quick Access toolbar.

When you click the Office Button, a pull-down menu similar to the one shown in Figure 1-2 appears. This menu contains all the commands you need for working with Excel workbook files, such as saving, opening, and closing files. In addition, this pull-down menu contains an Excel Options button that you can select to change the program's settings and an Exit Excel button that you can select when you're ready to shut down the program.

Ribbon

Office Button

Quick Access toolbar

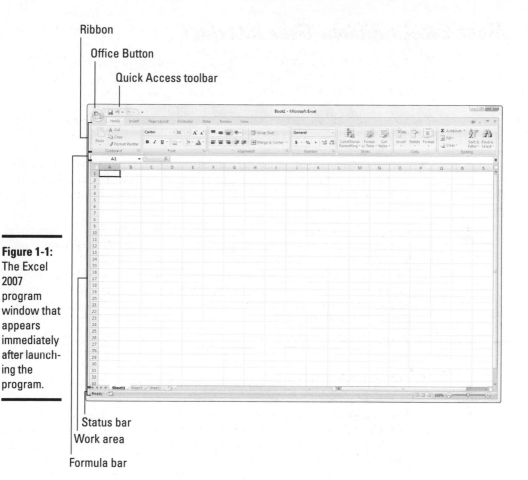

Figure 1-1:
The Excel 2007 program window that appears immediately after launching the program.

Status bar
Work area
Formula bar

Figure 1-2:
Click the Office Button to access the commands on its pull-down menu, open a recent workbook, or change the Excel options.

Ripping through the Ribbon

The Ribbon (shown in Figure 1-3) radically changes the way you work in Excel 2007. You no longer need to memorize (or guess) which pull-down menu or toolbar contains the command you want to use. The designers and engineers at Microsoft came up with the Ribbon, which always shows you all the most commonly used options needed to perform a particular Excel task.

Figure 1-3:
Excel's
Ribbon
consists of
a series
of tabs
containing
command
buttons
arranged
into different
groups.

Tab

Group   Dialog Box Launcher

The Ribbon is made up of the following components:

✦ **Tabs:** Excel's main tasks are brought together and display all the commands commonly needed to perform that core task.

✦ **Groups:** Organize related command buttons into subtasks normally performed as part of the tab's larger core task.

✦ **Command buttons:** Within each group that you select to perform a particular action or to open a gallery from which you can click a particular thumbnail, you find command buttons. Note that many command buttons on certain tabs of the Excel Ribbon are organized into mini-toolbars with related settings.

✦ **Dialog Box launcher:** This button is located in the lower-right corner of certain groups and opens a dialog box containing a bunch of additional options you can select.

To get more of the Worksheet area displayed in the program window, you can minimize the Ribbon so that only its tabs are displayed — simply choose Minimize the Ribbon on the menu opened by clicking the Customize Quick Access Toolbar button, double-clicking any one of the Ribbon's tabs, or pressing Ctrl+F1. To redisplay the entire Ribbon and keep all the command buttons on its tab displayed in the program window, click Minimize the Ribbon on the Quick Access Toolbar's drop-down menu, double-click one of the tabs, or press Ctrl+F1 a second time.

When you work in Excel with the Ribbon minimized, the Ribbon expands each time you click one of its tabs to show its command buttons, but that tab stays open only until you select one of its command buttons. The moment you select a command button, Excel immediately minimizes the Ribbon again so that only the tabs display.

Keeping tabs on the Excel Ribbon

The very first time you launch Excel 2007, its Ribbon contains the following seven tabs, proceeding from left to right:

✦ **Home:** Use this tab when creating, formatting, and editing a spreadsheet. This tab is arranged into the Clipboard, Font, Alignment, Number, Styles, Cells, and Editing groups (see Color Plate 1).

✦ **Insert:** Use this when adding particular elements (including graphics, PivotTables, charts, hyperlinks, and headers and footers) to a spreadsheet. This tab is arranged into the Tables, Illustrations, Charts, Links, and Text groups (see Color Plate 2).

✦ **Page Layout:** Use this tab when preparing a spreadsheet for printing or reordering graphics on the sheet. This tab is arranged into the Themes, Page Setup, Scale to Fit, Sheet Options, and Arrange groups (see Color Plate 3).

✦ **Formulas:** Use this tab when adding formulas and functions to a spreadsheet or checking a worksheet for formula errors. This tab is arranged into the Function Library, Defined Names, Formula Auditing, and Calculation groups (see Color Plate 4). Note that this tab also contains a Solutions group when you activate certain add-in programs, such as Conditional Sum and Euro Currency Tools — see Book I, Chapter 3 for more on Excel add-ins.

✦ **Data:** Use this tab when importing, querying, outlining, and subtotaling the data placed into a worksheet's data list. This tab is arranged into the Get External Data, Connections, Sort & Filter, Data Tools, and Outline groups (see Color Plate 5). Note that this tab also contains an Analysis group if you activate add-ins, such as the Analysis Toolpak and Solver Add-In — see Book I, Chapter 3 for more on Excel add-ins.

✦ **Review:** Use this tab when proofing, protecting, and marking up a spreadsheet for review by others. This tab is arranged into the Proofing, Comments, and Changes groups (see Color Plate 6). Note that this tab also contains an Ink group with a sole Start Inking button if you're running Office 2007 on a Tablet PC.

✦ **View:** Use this tab when changing the display of the Worksheet area and the data it contains. This ta is arranged into the Workbook Views, Show/Hide, Zoom, Window, and Macros groups (see Color Plate 7).

Although these seven tabs are the standard ones on the Ribbon, they are not the only tools that can appear in this area. Excel can display contextual tools when you're working with a particular object that you select in the worksheet, such as a graphic image you've added or a chart or PivotTable you've created. The name of the contextual tools for the selected object appears immediately above the tab or tabs associated with the tools.

For example, Figure 1-4 shows a worksheet immediately after I selected the embedded chart. As you can see, doing this causes the contextual tool called Chart Tools to be added to the very end of the Ribbon. Chart Tools has its own three tabs: Design (selected by default), Layout, and Format. Note too that the command buttons on the Design tab are arranged into groups: Type, Data, Chart Layouts, Chart Styles, and Location.

The moment you deselect the object (usually by clicking somewhere on the sheet outside of its boundaries), the contextual tool for that object and all of its tabs immediately disappears from the Ribbon, leaving only the regular tabs — Home, Insert, Page Layout, Formulas, Data, Review, and View — displayed.

Contextual tab

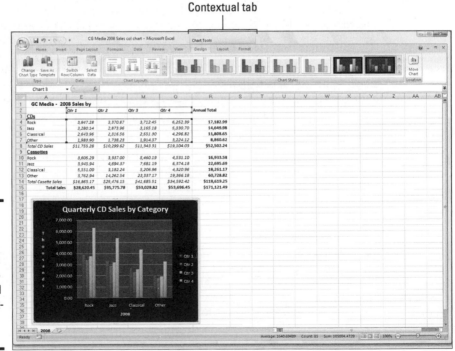

Figure 1-4: When you select certain objects in the worksheet, Excel adds contextual tools to the Ribbon.

If you do a lot of work with macros (see Book XIII, Chapter 1) and XML files in Excel, you'll want to add the Developer tab to the Ribbon. This tab contains all the command buttons normally needed to create, play, and edit macros as well as to import and map XML files. To add the Developer tab to the Excel Ribbon, follow these steps:

1. **Click the Office Button to open its pull-down menu.**

2. **Click the Excel Options button at the bottom of the File pull-down menu to open the Excel Option window.**

3. **Click the Show Developer Tab in the Ribbon check box in the Top Options for Working with Excel section of the Popular tab and then click OK.**

Selecting commands on the Ribbon

The most direct method for selecting commands on the Ribbon is to click the tab that contains the command button you want and then click that button in its group. For example, to insert a piece of Clip Art into your spreadsheet, you click the Insert tab and then click the Clip Art button to open the Clip Art Task pane in the Worksheet area.

The easiest method for selecting commands on the Ribbon — if you know your keyboard at all well — is to press the Alt key and then type the letter of the hot key that appears on the tab you want to select. Excel then displays all the command button hot keys next to their buttons along with the hot keys for the dialog box launchers in any group on that tab (see Figure 1-5). To select a command button or dialog box launcher, simply type its hot key letter.

Figure 1-5:
When you press Alt plus a tab hot key, Excel displays the hot keys for selecting all of its command buttons and dialog box launchers.

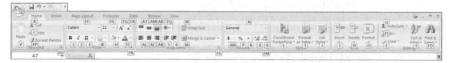

If you know the old Excel shortcut keys from versions Excel 97 through 2003, you can still use them. For example, instead of going through the rigmarole of pressing Alt+HC to copy a cell selection to the Windows Clipboard and then Alt+HV to paste it elsewhere in the sheet, you can still press Ctrl+C to copy the selection and then press Ctrl+V when you're ready to paste it. Note, however, that when using a hot key combination with the Alt key, you don't need to keep the Alt key pressed while typing the remaining letter(s) as you do when using a hot key combo with the Ctrl key.

Adjusting to the Quick Access toolbar

When you first begin using Excel 2007, the Quick Access toolbar contains only the following few buttons:

✦ **Save:** Saves any changes made to the current workbook using the same filename, file format, and location.

✦ **Undo:** Undoes the last editing, formatting, or layout change you made.

✦ **Redo:** Reapplies the previous editing, formatting, or layout change that you just removed with the Undo button.

The Quick Access toolbar is very customizable because you can easily add any Ribbon command to it. Moreover, you're not restricted to adding buttons for just the commands on the Ribbon; you can add any Excel command you want to the toolbar, even the obscure ones that don't rate an appearance on any of its tabs. (See Book I, Chapter 3 for details on customizing the Quick Access toolbar.)

By default, the Quick Access toolbar appears above the Ribbon tabs to the right of the Office Button. To display the toolbar beneath the Ribbon above the Formula bar, click the Customize Quick Access Toolbar button (the drop-down button to the direct right of the toolbar with a horizontal bar above a down-pointing triangle) and then click Show Below the Ribbon on its drop-down menu. Doing this helps you avoid crowding out the name of the current workbook that appears to the toolbar's right.

Fooling around with the Formula bar

The Formula bar displays the cell address and the contents of the current cell. The address of this cell is determined by its column letter(s) followed immediately by the row number as in cell A1, the very first cell of each worksheet at the intersection of column A and row 1, or cell XFD1048576, the very last of each Excel 2007 worksheet at the intersection of column XFD and row 1048576. The contents of the current cell are determined by the type of entry you make there: text or numbers if you just enter a heading or particular value, and the nuts and bolts of a formula if you enter a calculation there.

The Formula bar is divided into three sections:

✦ **Name box:** The left-most section displays the address of the current cell address.

✦ **Formula bar buttons:** The second, middle section appears as a rather nondescript button displaying only an indented circle on the left (used to narrow or widen the Name box) with the Function Wizard button (labeled *fx*) on the right until you start making or editing a cell entry, at which time its Cancel (an *X*) and its Enter (a check mark) buttons appear in between them.

✦ **Cell contents:** The third, right-most white area to the immediate right of the Function Wizard button takes up the rest of the bar and expands as necessary to display really, really long cell entries that won't fit in the normal area.

The Cell contents section of the Formula bar is really important because it *always* shows you the contents of the cell even when the worksheet does not. (When you're dealing with a formula, Excel displays only the calculated result in the cell in the worksheet and not the formula by which that result is derived.) You can edit the contents of the cell in this area at any time. By the same token, when the Cell contents area is blank, you know that the cell is empty as well.

Assigning 26 letters to 16,384 columns

When it comes to labeling the 16,384 columns of an Excel 2007 worksheet, our alphabet with its measly 26 letters is simply not up to the task. To make up the difference, Excel first doubles the letters in the cell's column reference so that column AA follows column Z (after which you find column AB, AC, and so on) and then triples them so that column AAA follows column ZZ (after which you get column AAB, AAC, and the like). At the end of this letter tripling, the 16,384th and last column of the worksheet ends up being XFD so that the last cell in the 1,048,576th row has the cell address XFD1048576.

What's up with the Worksheet area?

The Worksheet area is where most of the Excel spreadsheet action takes place because it's the place that displays the cells in different sections of the current worksheet and it's right inside the cells that you do all your spreadsheet data entry and formatting, not to mention the majority of your editing.

Keep in mind that for you to be able to enter or edit data in a cell, that cell must be current. Excel indicates that a cell is current in three ways:

✦ The cell cursor — the dark black border surrounding the cell's entire perimeter — appears in the cell.

✦ The address of the cell appears in the Name box of the Formula bar.

✦ The current cell's column letter(s) and row number are shaded (in an orange color on most monitors) in the column headings and row headings that appear at the top and left of the Worksheet area, respectively.

Moving around the worksheet

Each Excel worksheet contains far too many columns and rows for all of its cells to be displayed at one time. (It's true, 17,179,869,184 cell totals equal an illegible black blob, regardless of the size of your monitor.) Excel offers many methods for moving the cell cursor around the worksheet to the cell where you want to enter new data or edit existing data:

✦ Click the desired cell — assuming that the cell is displayed within the section of the sheet currently visible in the Worksheet area.

✦ Click the Name box, type the address of the desired cell directly into this box, and then press the Enter key.

✦ Press F5 to open the Go To dialog box, type the address of the desired cell into its Reference text box, and then click OK.

✦ Use the cursor keys, as shown in Table 1-1, to move the cell cursor to the desired cell.

✦ Use the horizontal and vertical scroll bars at the bottom and right edges of the Worksheet area to move the part of the worksheet that contains the desired cell, and then click the cell to put the cell cursor in it.

Keystroke shortcuts for moving the cell cursor

Excel offers a wide variety of keystrokes for moving the cell cursor to a new cell. When you use one of these keystrokes, the program automatically scrolls a new part of the worksheet into view, if this is required to move the cell pointer. In Table 1-1, I summarize these keystrokes and how far each one moves the cell cursor from its starting position.

Table 1-1	Keystrokes for Moving the Cell Cursor
Keystroke	*Where the Cell Cursor Moves*
→ or Tab	Cell to the immediate right.
← or Shift+Tab	Cell to the immediate left.
↑	Cell up one row.
↓	Cell down one row.
Home	Cell in Column A of the current row.
Ctrl+Home	First cell (A1) of the worksheet.
Ctrl+End or End, Home	Cell in the worksheet at the intersection of the last column that has any data in it and the last row that has any data in it (that is, the last cell of the so-called active area of the worksheet).
PgUp	Cell one screenful up in the same column.
PgDn	Cell one screenful down in the same column.
Ctrl+→ or End, →	First occupied cell to the right in the same row that is either preceded or followed by a blank cell. If no cell is occupied, the pointer goes to the cell at the very end of the row.
Ctrl+← or End, ←	First occupied cell to the left in the same row that is either preceded or followed by a blank cell. If no cell is occupied, the pointer goes to the cell at the very beginning of the row.
Ctrl+↑ or End, ↑	First occupied cell above in the same column that is either preceded or followed by a blank cell. If no cell is occupied, the pointer goes to the cell at the very top of the column.
Ctrl+↓ or End, ↓	First occupied cell below in the same column that is either preceded or followed by a blank cell. If no cell is occupied, the pointer goes to the cell at the very bottom of the column.
Ctrl+Page Down	Last occupied cell in the next worksheet of that workbook.
Ctrl+Page Up	Last occupied cell in the previous worksheet of that workbook.

Note: *In the case of those keystrokes that use arrow keys, you must either use the arrows on the cursor keypad or have the Num Lock key disengaged on the numeric keypad of your keyboard.*

The keystrokes that combine the Ctrl or End key with an arrow key (listed in Table 1-1) are among the most helpful for moving quickly from one edge to the other in large tables of cell entries. Moving from table to table in a section of the worksheet that contains many blocks of cells is also much easier.

When you use Ctrl and an arrow key to move from edge to edge in a table or between tables in a worksheet, you hold down Ctrl while you press one of the four arrow keys (indicated by the + symbol in keystrokes, such as Ctrl+→).

When you use End and an arrow-key alternative, you must press and then release the End key *before* you press the arrow key (indicated by the comma in keystrokes, such as End, →). Pressing and releasing the End key causes the END indicator to appear on the Status bar. This is your sign that Excel is ready for you to press one of the four arrow keys.

Because you can keep the Ctrl key depressed as you press the different arrow keys that you need to use, the Ctrl-plus-arrow-key method provides a more fluid method for navigating blocks of cells than the End-then-arrow-key method.

You can use the Scroll Lock key to "freeze" the position of the cell pointer in the worksheet so that you can scroll new areas of the worksheet in view with keystrokes such as PgUp (Page Up) and PgDn (Page Down) without changing the cell pointer's original position (in essence, making these keystrokes work in the same manner as the scroll bars).

After engaging Scroll Lock, when you scroll the worksheet with the keyboard, Excel does not select a new cell while it brings a new section of the worksheet into view. To "unfreeze" the cell pointer when scrolling the worksheet via the keyboard, you just press the Scroll Lock key again.

Tips on using the scroll bars

To understand how scrolling works in Excel, imagine the worksheet is a humongous papyrus scroll attached to rollers on the left and right. To bring into view a new section of a papyrus worksheet that is hidden on the right, you crank the left roller until the section with the cells that you want to see appears. Likewise, to scroll into view a new section of the worksheet that is hidden on the left, you crank the right roller until that section of cells appears.

You can use the horizontal scroll bar at the bottom of the Worksheet area to scroll back and forth through the columns of a worksheet. Likewise, you can use the vertical scroll bar to scroll up and down through its rows. To scroll one column or a row at a time in a particular direction, click the appropriate scroll arrow at the ends of the scroll bar. To jump immediately back to the originally displayed area of the worksheet after scrolling through single columns or rows in this fashion, simply click the black area in the scroll bar that now appears in front of or after the scroll bar.

You can resize the horizontal scroll bar making it wider or narrower by dragging the button that appears to the immediate left of its left scroll arrow. When working in a workbook that contains a whole bunch of worksheets, in widening the horizontal scroll bar, you can end up hiding the display of the workbook's later sheet tabs.

To scroll very quickly through columns or rows of the worksheet, hold down the Shift key and then drag the mouse pointer in the appropriate direction within the scroll bar until the columns or rows that you want to see appear on the screen in the Worksheet area. When you hold down the Shift key as you scroll, the scroll button within the scroll bar becomes really narrow, and a ScreenTip appears next to the scroll bar, keeping you informed of the letter(s) of the columns or the numbers of the rows that you're currently whizzing through.

If your mouse has a wheel, you can use it to scroll directly through the columns and rows of the worksheet without using the horizontal or vertical scroll bars. Simply position the white-cross mouse pointer in the center of the Worksheet area and then hold down the wheel button of the mouse. When the mouse pointer changes to a four-point arrow, drag the mouse pointer in the appropriate direction (left and right to scroll through columns or up and down to scroll through rows) until the desired column or row comes into view in the Worksheet area.

The only disadvantage to using the scroll bars to move around is that the scroll bars bring only new sections of the worksheet into view — they don't actually change the position of the cell cursor. If you want to start making entries in the cells in a new area of the worksheet, you still have to remember to select the cell (by clicking it) or the group of cells (by dragging through them) where you want the data to appear before you begin entering the data.

One good reason for adding extra sheets to a workbook

You may wonder why on earth anyone would ever need more than three worksheets given just how many cells each individual sheet contains. The simple truth is that it's all about how you choose to structure a particular spreadsheet rather than running out of places to put the data. For example, say you need to create a workbook that contains budgets for all the various departments in your corporation; you may decide to devote an individual worksheet to each department (with the actual budget spreadsheet tables laid out in the same manner on each sheet) rather than placing all the tables in different sections of the same sheet. Using this kind of one-sheet-per-budget layout makes it much easier for you to find each budget, print each one as a separate page of a report, and, if ever necessary, consolidate their data in a separate summary worksheet.

Surfing the sheets in a workbook

Each new workbook you open in Excel 2007 contains three blank work-sheets, each with its own 16,384 columns and 1,048,576 rows (giving you a truly staggering total of 51,539,607,552 blank cells!). But that's not all, if ever you need more worksheets in your workbook, you can add them simply by clicking the Insert Worksheet button that appears to the immediate right of the last sheet tab (see Figure 1-6).

Figure 1-6:
The Sheet tab scroll buttons, sheet tabs, and Insert Worksheet button enable you to activate your work-sheets and add to them.

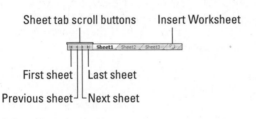

On the left side of the bottom of the Worksheet area, the Sheet tab scroll buttons appear followed by the actual tabs for the worksheets in your work-book and the Insert Worksheet button. To activate a worksheet for editing, you select it by clicking its sheet tab. Excel lets you know what sheet is active by displaying the sheet name on its tab in boldface type and making its tab appear to be on top of the others.

Don't forget the Ctrl+Page Down and Ctrl+Page Up shortcut keys for select-ing the next and previous sheets, respectively, in your workbook.

If your workbook contains too many sheets for all their tabs to be displayed at the bottom of the Worksheet area, use the Sheet tab scroll buttons to bring new tabs into view (so that you can then click them to activate them). You click the Next Sheet button to scroll the next hidden sheet tab into view or the Last Sheet button to scroll the last group of completely or partially hidden tabs into view.

Taking a tour of the Status bar

The Status bar is the last component at the very bottom of the Excel program window (see Figure 1-7). The Status bar contains the following areas:

✦ **Mode:** This button indicates the current state of the Excel program (Ready, Edit, and so on) as well as any special keys that are engaged (Caps Lock, Num Lock, and Scroll Lock).

✦ **Macro Recording:** This button (the red dot on a tiny worksheet) opens the Record Macro dialog box where you can set the parameters for a new macro and begin recording it (see Book XIII, Chapter 1).

✦ **AutoCalculate:** An indicator that displays the Average and Sum of all the numerical entries in the current cell selection along with the Count of every cell in the selection.

✦ **Layout:** A selector that enables you to select between three layouts for the Worksheet area: Normal, the default view that shows only the worksheet cells with the column and row headings; Page Layout View, which adds rulers and page margins, and shows page breaks for the worksheet; and Page Break Preview, which enables you to adjust the paging of a report.

✦ **Zoom:** A slider that enables you to zoom in and out on the cells in the Worksheet area by dragging the slider to the right or left, respectively.

Figure 1-7:
The Status bar displays the program's current standing and enables you to select new worksheet views.

Mode button

Autocalculate indicator   Zoom slider

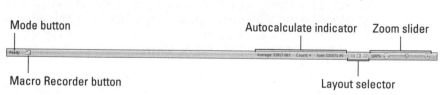

Macro Recorder button

Layout selector

The Num Lock indicator tells you that you can use the numbers on the numeric keypad for entering values in the worksheet. This keypad is often separate on the right side of a stand-alone keyboard connected to a desktop computer, and embedded into the regular typing keys on almost all laptop computers.

Launching and Quitting Excel

Excel 2007 runs under both the older Windows XP operating system and the brand-new Windows Vista operating system. Because of changes made to the Start menu in Windows Vista, the procedure for starting Excel from this version of Windows is a bit different from Windows XP.

Starting Excel from the Windows Vista Start menu

You can use the Start Search box at the bottom of the Windows Vista Start menu to locate Excel on your computer and launch the program in no time at all:

1. **Click the Start button on the Windows taskbar to open the Windows Start menu.**

2. **Click the Start Search text box and type the two letters** ex **to have Vista locate Microsoft Office Excel 2007 on your computer.**

3. **Click the Microsoft Office Excel 2007 option that now appears in the left Programs column on the Start menu.**

If you have more time on your hands, you can also launch Excel from the Vista Start menu by going through the rigmarole of clicking Start | All Programs | Microsoft Office | Microsoft Office Excel 2007.

Starting Excel from the Windows XP Start menu

When starting Excel 2007 from the Windows XP Start menu, you follow these simple steps:

1. **Click the Start button on the Windows taskbar to open the Windows Start menu.**

2. **With the mouse, highlight All Programs on the Start menu and then click Microsoft Office on the Start continuation menu before clicking the Microsoft Office Excel 2007 option on the Microsoft Office continuation menu.**

Pinning Excel to the Start menu

If you use Excel all the time, you may want to make its program option a permanent part of the Windows Start menu. To do this, you pin the program option to the Start menu (the steps for doing this are the same in Windows XP as they are in Windows Vista):

1. **Start Excel from the Windows Start menu.**

In launching Excel, use the appropriate method for your version of Windows as I outline earlier in this chapter.

After launching Excel, Windows adds Microsoft Office 2007 to the recently used portion on the left side of the Windows Start menu.

2. **Click the Start menu and then right-click Microsoft Office Excel 2007 to open its shortcut menu.**

3. **Click Pin to Start menu on the shortcut menu.**

After pinning Excel in this manner, the Microsoft Office Excel 2007 option always appears in the upper section of the left-hand column of the Start menu. You can now launch Excel simply by clicking the Start button and then clicking this option.

Creating an Excel desktop shortcut for Windows Vista

Some people prefer having the Excel Program icon appear on the Windows desktop so that they can simply double-click the program icon to launch Excel. To create an Excel program shortcut for Windows Vista, follow these steps:

1. **Click the Start button on the Windows taskbar.**

The Start menu opens where you click the Start Search text box.

2. **Click the Start Search text box and type** excel.exe.

Excel.exe is the name of the executable program file that runs Excel. After finding this file on your hard drive, you can create a desktop shortcut from it that launches the program.

3. **Right-click the file icon for the** excel.exe **file at the top of the Start menu and then highlight Send To on the pop-up menu and click Desktop (Create Shortcut) on its continuation menu.**

A shortcut named excel.exe - Shortcut appears on your desktop. I suggest renaming the shortcut to something a little more friendly, such as Excel 2007.

4. **Right-click the excel.exe - Shortcut icon on the Vista desktop and then click Rename on the pop-up menu.**

5. **Replace the current name by typing a new shortcut name, such as** Excel 2007 **and then click anywhere on the desktop.**

Creating an Excel desktop shortcut for Windows XP

If you're running Excel 2007 on Windows XP, use the following steps to create a program shortcut for your desktop:

1. **Click the Start button on the Windows taskbar.**

The Start menu opens the Search item.

2. **Click Search in the lower-right corner of the Start menu.**

The Search Results dialog box appears.

3. **Click the All Files and Folders link in the panel on the left side of the Search Results dialog box.**

The Search Companion pane appears on the left side of the Search Results dialog box.

4. **Type** excel.exe **in the All or Part of the File Name text box.**

Excel.exe is the name of the executable program file that runs Excel. After finding this file on your hard drive, you can create a desktop shortcut from it that launches the program.

5. **Click the Search button.**

Windows now searches your hard disk for the Excel program file. After locating this file, its name appears on the right side of the Search Results dialog box. When this filename appears, you can click the Stop button in the left panel to halt the search.

6. **Right-click the file icon for the** excel.exe **file and then highlight Send To on the pop-up menu and click Desktop (Create Shortcut) on its continuation menu.**

A shortcut named Shortcut to excel.exe appears on your desktop.

7. **Click the Close button in the upper-right corner of the Search Results dialog box.**

After closing the Search Results dialog box, you should see the icon named Shortcut to excel.exe on the desktop. You should probably rename the shortcut to something a little friendlier, such as Excel 2007.

8. **Right-click the Shortcut to excel.exe icon and then click Rename on the pop-up menu.**

9. **Replace the current name by typing a new shortcut name, such as** Excel 2007 **and then click anywhere on the desktop.**

After creating an Excel desktop shortcut on the Windows XP desktop, from then on, you can launch Excel by double-clicking the shortcut icon.

Adding the Excel desktop shortcut to the Windows Quick Launch toolbar

If you want to be able to launch Excel 2007 by clicking a single button, drag the icon for your Excel Windows Vista or XP desktop shortcut to the Quick Launch toolbar to the immediate right of the Start button at the beginning of the Windows taskbar. When you position the icon on this toolbar, Windows indicates where the new Excel button will appear by drawing a black, vertical I-beam in front of or between the existing buttons on this bar. As soon as you release the mouse button, Windows adds an Excel 2007 button to the Quick Launch toolbar, which enables you to launch the program by a single-click of its icon.

When it's quitting time

When you're ready to call it a day and quit Excel, you have several choices for shutting down the program:

✦ Click the Office Button followed by the Exit Excel button.

✦ Press Alt+FX or Alt+F4.

✦ Click the Close button in the upper-right corner of the Excel program window.

If you try to exit Excel after working on a workbook and you haven't saved your latest changes, the program beeps at you and displays an alert box querying whether you want to save your changes. To save your changes before exiting, click the Yes command button. (For detailed information on saving documents, see Book I, Chapter 2.) If you've just been playing around in the worksheet and don't want to save your changes, you can abandon the document by clicking the No button.

Migrating to Excel 2007 from Earlier Versions

If you're a brand-new Excel user, you're going to take to the program's new Ribbon User Interface like a duck to water. However, if you're coming to Excel 2007 as a dedicated user of any of the earlier Excel versions (from Excel 97 all the way through Excel 2003), the first time you launch Excel 2007 and take a gander at the Ribbon, you're probably going to feel more like someone just threw you into the deep end of the pool without a life preserver.

Don't panic! Simply use this section of the chapter as your Excel 2007 floatation device. It's intended to get you oriented, keep your head above water, and have you swimming with the new interface in no time at all. Just give me five minutes of your precious time and I promise I'll have you up and running with Excel 2007 and maybe even smiling again.

First, the bad news: There is *no* Classic mode in Excel 2007 that will magically turn that fat, screen real estate-stealing Ribbon back into those sleek and tried-and-true pull-down menus (thanks Microsoft, I needed that)! After the wonderful designers and engineers at Microsoft got through dumping all the pull-down menus and toolbars that you worked so diligently to master, there was just nothing left for them to hang a Classic mode onto.

Now, for the good news: You really don't need a Classic mode — you just need to find out where those scoundrel engineers placed all the stuff you used in the versions of Excel you used before the Ribbon User Interface. After all, you already know what most of those pull-down menu items and toolbar buttons do; all you have to do is locate them.

Cutting the Ribbon down to size

The first step is to get that busy Ribbon out of your face. At this point, it's just taking up valuable work space and probably making you crazy. So, please double-click any one of the tabs or press Ctrl+F1 right now to cut the Ribbon display down to only its tabs (single-clicking a tab temporarily redisplays the Ribbon until you select one of its command buttons, and pressing Ctrl+F1 immediately redisplays the Ribbon and keeps it open).

When only the tabs — Home through View — are showing at the top of the Excel program window, you should feel a whole lot more comfortable with the screen. The Excel 2007 screen is as clean and uncluttered as the earlier version of Excel that you were using with only the Quick Access toolbar, Ribbon tabs, and Formula bar displayed above the Worksheet area.

Now, you're probably wondering where those pesky Microsoft engineers moved the most important and commonly used pull-down menu commands. Table 1-2 shows the Excel 2007 equivalents for the menu commands you probably used most often in doing your work in the earlier versions of Excel.

When a particular command is assigned to one of the tabs on the Ribbon, Table 1-2 lists only the tab and command button name without naming the group because the group name plays no part in selecting the command. So, for example, the table lists the tab+command button equivalent of the View⇨Header and Footer command as Insert | Header & Footer without regard to the fact that the Header & Footer button is part of the Text group on the Insert tab.

Table 1-2	Excel 2007 Equivalents for Common Pull-Down Menu Commands in Excel 2003		
Excel 2003 Command	*Excel 2007 Equivalent*	*Common Shortcut Keys*	*Excel 2007 Shortcut Keys*
File Menu			
File⇨New	Office Button⇨New	Ctrl+N	Alt+FN
File⇨Open	Office Button⇨Open	Ctrl+O	Alt+FO
File⇨Save	Office Button⇨Save or Save button on the Quick Access Toolbar	Ctrl+S	Alt+FS
File⇨Save As	Office Button⇨Save As	F12	Alt+FA
File⇨Print	Office Button⇨Print	Ctrl+P	Alt+FP
File⇨Send To⇨Mail Recipient	Office Button⇨Send⇨Email		Alt+FDE
File⇨Send To⇨Recipient Using Internet Fax Service	Office Button⇨Send⇨ Internet Fax		Alt+FDX
File⇨Close	Office Button⇨Close	Ctrl+W	Alt+FC
Edit Menu			
Edit⇨Office Clipboard	Home | Dialog Box launcher in the Clipboard group		Alt+HFO
Edit⇨Clear⇨All	Home | Clear (eraser icon) | Clear All		Alt+HEA
Edit⇨Clear⇨Formats	Home | Clear (eraser icon) | Clear Formats		Alt+HEF
Edit⇨Clear⇨Contents	Home | Clear (eraser icon) | Clear Contents	Delete key	Alt+HEC
Edit⇨Clear⇨Comments	Home | Clear (eraser icon) | Clear Comments		Alt+HEM
Edit⇨Delete	Home | Delete		Alt+HD
Edit⇨Move or Copy Sheet	Home | Format | Move or Copy Sheet		Alt+HOM
Edit⇨Find	Home | Find & Select | Find	Ctrl+F	Alt+HFDF
Edit⇨Replace	Home | Find & Select | Replace	Ctrl+H	Alt+HFDR
View Menu			
View⇨Header and Footer	Insert | Header & Footer		
View⇨Full Screen	View | Full Screen		

(continued)

Table 1-2 *(continued)*

Excel 2003 Command	Excel 2007 Equivalent	Common Shortcut Keys	Excel 2007 Shortcut Keys
Insert Menu			
Insert⇨Cells	Home | Insert | Insert Cells		Alt+HII
Insert⇨Rows	Home | Insert | Insert Sheet Rows		Alt+HIR
Insert⇨Columns	Home | Insert | Insert Sheet Columns		Alt+HIC
Insert⇨Worksheets	Home | Insert | Insert Sheet		Alt+HIS
Insert⇨Symbol	Insert | Symbol		Alt+NU
Insert⇨Page Break	Page Layout | Page Breaks | Insert Page Break		Alt+PBI
Insert⇨Name⇨Define	Formulas | Define Name | Define Name		Alt+MMD
Insert⇨Name⇨Paste	Formulas | Use in Formula		Alt+MS
Insert⇨Name⇨Create	Formulas | Create from Selection		Alt+MC
Insert⇨Name⇨Label	Formulas | Name Manager		Alt+MN
Insert⇨Comment	Review | New Comment		Alt+RC
Insert⇨Picture	Insert | Picture		Alt+NP
Insert⇨Hyperlink	Insert | Hyperlink	Ctrl+K	Alt+NI
Format Menu			
Format⇨Cells	Home | Format | Format Cells	Ctrl+1	Alt+HOE
Format⇨Row⇨Height	Home | Format | Row Height		Alt+HOH
Format⇨Row⇨AutoFit	Home | Format | AutoFit Row Height		Alt+HOA
Format⇨Row⇨ Hide/Unhide	Home | Format | Hide & Unhide | Hide Rows/ Unhide Rows		Alt+HOUR/ Alt+HOUO
Format⇨Column⇨Width	Home | Format | Column Width		Alt+HOW
Format⇨Column⇨ Hide/Unhide	Home | Format | Hide & Unhide | Hide Columns/ Unhide Columns		Alt+HOUC/ Alt+HOUL
Format⇨Column⇨ Standard Width	Home | Format | Default Width		Alt+HOD
Format⇨Sheet⇨Rename	Home | Format | Rename Sheet		Alt+HOR

Excel 2003 Command	Excel 2007 Equivalent	Common Shortcut Keys	Excel 2007 Shortcut Keys
Format Menu			
Format⇨Sheet⇨Hide/ Unhide	Home | Format | Hide & Unhide | Hide Sheet/Unhide Sheet		Alt+HOUS/ Alt+HOUH
Format⇨Sheet⇨ Background	Page Layout | Background		Alt+PG
Format⇨Sheet⇨ Tab Color	Home | Format | Tab Color		Alt+HOT
Format⇨AutoFormat	Home | Format as Table		Alt+HT
Format⇨Conditional Formatting	Home | Conditional Formatting		Alt+HL
Format⇨Style	Home | Cell Styles		Alt+HJ
Tools Menu			
Tools⇨Spelling	Review | Spelling	F7	Alt+RS
Tools⇨Research	Review | Research		Alt+RR
Tools⇨Error Checking	Formulas | Error Checking		Alt+MK
Tools⇨Speech⇨Show Text to Speech Toolbar	*Available only as custom Speak Cells, Speak Cells - Stop Speak Cells, Speak Cells by Columns, Speak Cells by Rows and Speak Cells on Enter buttons added to Quick Access toolbar*		
Tools⇨Track Changes	Review | Track Changes		Alt+RG
Tools⇨Protection⇨ Protect Sheet	Review | Protect Sheet		Alt+RPS
Tools⇨Protection⇨Allow Users to Edit Ranges	Review | Allow Users to Edit Ranges		Alt+RU
Tools⇨Protection⇨ Protect Workbook	Review | Protect Workbook		Alt+RPW
Tools⇨Protection⇨ Protect and Share Workbook	Review | Protect and Share Workbook		Alt+RO
Tools⇨Macro	View | Macros	Alt+F8	Alt+WM
Tools⇨Add-Ins	Office Button⇨ Excel Options⇨Add-Ins		Alt+FIAA and Alt+G
Tools⇨AutoCorrect Options	Office Button⇨Excel Options⇨Proofing⇨ AutoCorrect Options		Alt+FIPP and Alt+A
Tools⇨Options	Office Button⇨Excel Options		Alt+FI

(continued)

Table 1-2 *(continued)*

Excel 2003 Command	Excel 2007 Equivalent	Common Shortcut Keys	Excel 2007 Shortcut Keys
Data Menu			
Data⇨Sort	Data | Sort or Home | Sort & Filter | Custom Sort		Alt+AS or Alt+HSU
Data⇨Filter⇨AutoFilter	Data | Filter		Alt+AT
Data⇨Filter⇨Advanced Filter	Data | Advanced		Alt+AQ
Data⇨Form	*Available only as a custom Form button added to Quick Access toolbar*		
Data⇨Subtotals	Data | Subtotal		Alt+AB
Data⇨Validation	Data | Data Validation | Data Validation		Alt+AVV
Data⇨Table	Data | What-If Analysis | Data Table		Alt+AWT
Data⇨Text to Columns	Data | Convert Text to Columns		Alt+AE
Data⇨Consolidate	Data | Consolidate		Alt+AN
Data⇨Group and Outline	Data | Group/Ungroup		Alt+AG/Alt+AU
Data⇨PivotTable and PivotChart Report	Insert | PivotTable | PivotTable/PivotChart		Alt+NVT/ Alt+NVC
Data⇨Import External Data	Data | From Other Sources		Alt+AFO
Window Menu			
Window⇨New Window	View | New Window		Alt+WN
Window⇨Arrange	View | Arrange All		Alt+WA
Window⇨Compare Side by Side	View | View Side by Side (two-page icon in Window group)		Alt+WB
Window⇨Hide, Unhide	View | Hide/Unhide		Alt+WH/ Alt+WU
Window⇨Split	View | Split		Alt+WS
Window⇨Freeze Panes	View | Freeze Panes		Alt+WF

For the most part, the pull-down menu commands listed in Table 1-2 are logically located. The ones that take the most getting used to are the Header & Footer PivotTable/PivotChart commands that are located on the Insert tab rather than the View tab and Data tab as might be expected given that they inhabited, respectively, the View and Data pull-down menus in earlier Excel versions. In addition, the worksheet background command ended up all by its lonesome on the Page Layout tab rather than going to the Home tab with all its fellow formatting commands.

Finding the Standard Toolbar buttons equivalents

If you're like me, you came to rely heavily on the buttons of the Standard toolbar for doing all sorts of everyday tasks in earlier versions of Excel. Table 1-3 shows you the Excel 2007 equivalents for the buttons on the Standard toolbar in Excel 2003. As you can see from this table, most of these Standard toolbar buttons are relegated to one of the following places in Excel 2007:

✦ **File pull-down menu,** which is activated by clicking the Office Button or pressing Alt+F (New, Open, Save, and Print Preview)

✦ **Quick Access toolbar** (Save, Undo, and Redo)

✦ **Home tab** in the Clipboard group (Cut, Copy, Paste, and Format Painter) and Editing group (AutoSum, Sort Ascending, and Sort Descending)

Table 1-3   Excel 2007 Equivalents for the Standard Toolbar Buttons in Excel 2003

Toolbar button	Excel 2007 Equivalent	Common Shortcut Keys	Excel 2007 Shortcut Keys
New	Office Button⇨New	Ctrl+N	Alt+FN
Open	Office Button⇨Open	Ctrl+O	Alt+FO
Save	Office Button⇨Save or Save button on Quick Access toolbar	Ctrl+S	Alt+FS
Permission	*Available only as a custom Permission button added to Quick Access toolbar*		
E-mail	Office Button⇨Send⇨Email		Alt+FDE
Print	Office Button⇨Print or Quick Print custom button on Quick Access Toolbar	Ctrl+P	Alt+FP
Print Preview	Office Button⇨Print⇨Print Preview		Alt+FWV
Spelling	Review	Spelling	F7	Alt+RS
Research	Review	Research		Alt+RR
Cut	Home	Cut (scissors icon in Clipboard group)	Ctrl+X	Alt+HX

(continued)

Table 1-3 *(continued)*

Toolbar button	Excel 2007 Equivalent	Common Shortcut Keys	Excel 2007 Shortcut Keys
Copy	Home | Copy (double-sheet icon in Clipboard group)	Ctrl+C	Alt+HC
Paste	Home | Paste	Ctrl+V	Alt+HV
Format Painter	Home | Format Painter (brush icon in Clipboard group)		Alt+HFP
Undo	Undo button on Quick Access toolbar	Ctrl+Z	
Redo	Redo button on Quick Access toolbar	Ctrl+Y	
Insert Ink Annotations	Review | Start Inking		Alt+RK
Insert Hyperlink	Insert | Hyperlink	Ctrl+K	Alt+NI
AutoSum	Home | Sum ((- Sigma icon)		Alt+HU
Sort Ascending	Home | Sort & Filter |Sort A to Z		Alt+HSS
Sort Descending	Home | Sort & Filter |Sort Z to A		Alt+HSO
ChartWizard	*Not available except as specific chart type command buttons in the Charts group on the Insert tab*		
Drawing	*Not available except as command buttons in the Shapes, Illustrations, and Text groups on the Insert tab and as custom buttons added to Quick Access toolbar*		
Zoom	View | Zoom		Alt+WQ
Microsoft Excel Help	Microsoft Office Excel Help button to the right of the Ribbon tabs	F1	

Because Excel 2007 supports only the Quick Access toolbar, the Drawing toolbar disappears completely from Excel 2007 and thus the Drawing button on the Standard toolbar has no equivalent. Most of its main features, including Clip Art, inserting graphics files, and creating diagrams and WordArt are now found on the Insert tab. Also, keep in mind that Excel 2007 doesn't have an equivalent to the ChartWizard button on the Standard toolbar because you can create a chart in a split second by clicking the Column, Line, Pie, Bar, Area, Scatter, or Other Charts command button on the Insert tab (see Book V, Chapter 1 for details).

Finding the Formatting Toolbar buttons equivalents

Finding the Excel 2007 equivalents for the buttons on the Formatting toolbar in earlier versions of Excel couldn't be easier. Every one of the buttons on the Formatting toolbar is prominently displayed on the Home tab of the Excel 2007 Ribbon. They're all easy to identify as they use the same icons as before and are located in the Font, Alignment, or Number group on the Home tab (refer to Figure 1-3).

In addition to the Font, Font Size, Bold, Italic, Underline, Borders, Fill Color, and Font Color buttons from the Formatting toolbar, the Font group also contains the following two buttons:

✦ **Increase Font:** Use this button to bump up the current font size a point.

✦ **Decrease Font:** Use this button to reduce the current font size by a point.

In addition to the Left Align, Center, Right Align, Decrease Indent, Increase Indent, and Merge and Center buttons, the Alignment group also contains the following buttons:

✦ **Top Align:** Click this button to vertically align the data entered into the current cell selection with the top edge of the cell.

✦ **Middle Align:** Use this button to vertically center the data entered into the current cell selection.

✦ **Bottom Align:** Click this button to align the data entered in the current cell selection with the bottom edge of the cell.

✦ **Orientation:** Use this button to open a pop-up menu of orientation options. You can change the direction of the text entered into the current cell selection by angling it up or down, converting it to vertical text, rotating it up or down, as well as opening the Alignment tab of the Format Cells dialog box.

✦ **Wrap Text:** Click this button to apply the wrap text function to the current cell selection so that Excel expands the row heights as needed to fit all of its text within the current column widths.

In addition to the Percent Style, Comma, Increase Decimal, and Decrease Decimal buttons from the Formatting toolbar, the Numbers group contains the following buttons:

✦ **Accounting Number Format:** This button enables you to select among several different currency formats from U.S. dollars to Swiss francs as well as to open the Number tab of the Format Cells dialog box with the Accounting number format selected.

✦ **Number Format:** This button opens a drop-down menu of different number options from General through Text, as well as opens the Number tab of the Format Cells dialog box when you select its More Number Formats option.

Putting the Quick Access toolbar to its best use

Figure 1-8 shows you the Excel 2007 program window with the Ribbon mini-mized and a completely customized Quick Access toolbar that's moved down so that it appears under the tabs and immediately above the Formula bar. This completely custom version of the Quick Access toolbar should seem very familiar to you: It contains every button from the Standard and Formatting toolbars in Excel 2003 with the exception of the Permission, Zoom, and Help buttons in the original order in which they appear on their respective toolbars. The Permission button is so esoteric and seldom used that I didn't bother to add it, and neither the Zoom button nor the Help button is really needed, as the Zoom slider that enables you to quickly select a new screen magnification percentage is always displayed in the lower-right corner of the Excel 2007 Status bar and the Help button is always displayed on the right side of the bar containing the Ribbon tabs.

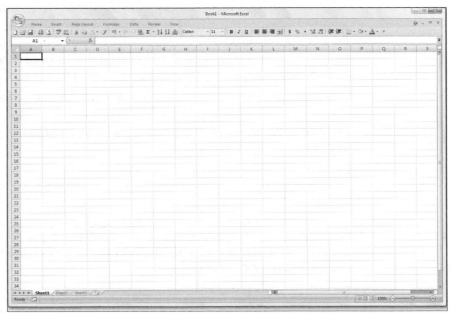

Figure 1-8: Excel 2007 window after minimizing the Ribbon and adding all but three of the buttons from the Standard and Formatting toolbars to the Quick Access toolbar.

To customize your Quick Access toolbar so that it matches the one shown in Figure 1-8 with every button from the Standard and Formatting toolbars except the Permission, Zoom, and Help buttons, follow these steps:

1. **Click the Customize Quick Access Toolbar button at the end of the Quick Access toolbar and then click the Show Below the Ribbon option.**

   When filling the Quick Access toolbar with buttons, you need to place the bar beneath the Ribbon so that it won't crowd out the name of the current workbook file.

2. **Click the Customize Quick Access Toolbar button again and this time click the More Commands option.**

   Excel opens the Excel Options dialog box with Customize Tab selected. The Customize Quick Access Toolbar list box on the right side of this dialog box shows all three default buttons in the order in which they now appear on the toolbar.

3. **Click the New option in the Popular Commands list box and then click the Add button.**

   Excel adds the New command button at the end of the toolbar; you can see the New button in the Customize Quick Access Toolbar list box on the right.

4. **Click the Move Up button (with the triangle pointing upward) three times to move the New button to the top of the Customize Quick Access Toolbar list box and the first position on the Quick Access toolbar.**

   Note that the New button is now in front of the Save button on the toolbar.

5. **Click the Open option in the Popular Commands list box on the left and then click the Add button.**

   Excel inserts the Open button in the Customize Quick Access Toolbar list box in between the New and Save buttons, which is exactly where it appears on the Standard toolbar.

6. **Click the Save button in the Customize Quick Access Toolbar list box on the right to select this button. Then, click the Quick Print option near the bottom of the Popular Commands list box on the left and then click the Add button.**

   Excel inserts the Quick Print button after the Save button.

7. **Click the Print Preview button near the bottom of the Popular Commands list box and then click the Add button.**

Excel inserts the Print Preview button after the Quick Print button in the Customize Quick Access Toolbar list box.

Now, you need to add the Spelling and Research buttons. They are located on the Review tab in Excel 2007. Before you can add their buttons to the Quick Access toolbar, you need to replace Popular Commands with Review Tab by selecting this option on the Choose Commands From drop-down list.

8. **Click the Choose Commands From drop-down button and then click Review Tab in the drop-down list.**

Excel now displays all the command buttons on the Review tab of the Ribbon in the list box.

9. **Add the Spelling and Research buttons from the Review Tab list box to the Customize Quick Access Toolbar list box and position them so that they appear one after the other following the Print Preview button.**

Next you need to add the Cut, Copy, Paste, and Format Painter buttons to the Quick Access toolbar. These command buttons are on the Home tab.

10. **Click the Home Tab option on the Choose Commands From drop-down list and then add the Cut, Copy, Paste, and Format Painter buttons from the Home Tab list box to the Customize Quick Access Toolbar in this order in front of the Undo button.**

Note when adding the Paste button that Choose Commands From displays two Paste buttons. The first is the regular Paste button that was on the Standard toolbar. The second is a Paste button with a drop-down button that, when clicked, opens a drop-down menu with all the special Paste options. You can add either one, although the second Paste button with the drop-down menu is much more versatile.

11. **Click the Format Painter option in the Insert Tab list box and then click the Add button.**

Excel adds the Format Painter button after the Paste button in the Customize Quick Access Toolbar list box on the right.

12. **Click the Redo button in the Customize Quick Access Toolbar list box to select it and then click Insert Tab on the Choose Commands From drop-down list and add the Insert Hyperlink button from the Insert Tab list box to the Customize Quick Access Toolbar list box.**

13. **Add the remaining Standard toolbar buttons, AutoSum, Sort Ascending, Sort Descending, and Create Chart, to the Quick Access toolbar.**

The AutoSum, Sort Ascending, and Sort Descending buttons are available in the Home Tab list box and the Create Chart button (the closest thing to the Chart Wizard in Excel 2007) is available in the Insert Tab list box.

14. **Add the buttons on the 2003 Formatting toolbar to the Quick Access toolbar in the order in which they appear.**

The Formatting toolbar contains these tools (all found in the Home Tab list box): Font, Font Size, Bold, Italic, Underline, Align Left, Center, Align Right, Merge and Center, Accounting Number Format (corresponding the Currency Style button), Percent Style, Comma Style, Increase Decimal, Decrease Decimal, Decrease Indent, Increase Indent, Borders, Fill Color, and Font Color.

15. **Click the OK button to close the Excel Options dialog box and return to the Excel program window.**

Your Quick Access toolbar should now have the same buttons as the one shown in Figure 1-8.

After adding all the buttons on the Standard and Formatting toolbars (with the exception of the Permission button that almost nobody uses, the Drawing button that has no equivalent in Excel 2007, and the Zoom and Help buttons that are always available in the Excel 2007 program window), the Quick Access toolbar fills the entire width of the screen on many monitors. Keep in mind that if you need to add extra buttons that can no longer be displayed on the single row above the Formula bar, Excel automatically adds a More Controls button to the end of the Quick Access toolbar. You then click this More Controls button to display a pop-up menu containing all the buttons that can no longer be displayed on the toolbar.

To add vertical bar separators to divide the buttons into groups as you see in the original Standard and Formatting toolbars and as shown in Figure 1-8, click the <Separator> option located at the top of each Choose Commands From list box followed by the Add button.

Coming up to speed with Excel 2007

The version of the Excel 2007 program window shown in Figure 1-8, with the Ribbon minimized to just tabs and the Quick Access toolbar displayed above the Formula bar with all but a few of the buttons from the Standard and Formatting toolbars, is as close as I can get you to any sort of Excel 2003 Classic mode.

Combine this simplified screen layout with the common shortcut keys (see Table 1-2) that you already know, and you should be pretty much good to go with Excel 2007. You need to keep in mind that in the course of using the program, the Ribbon can't always stay reduced to just its tabs. As you find out as you explore the features covered in the remaining chapters of this book, there'll be times when you need the tools (especially in the form of those fantastic galleries) that a particular tab has to offer.

The only other issues that should be of any concern to you right now are the new Excel 2007 file formats and running all those Excel macros on which you've come to rely.

Dealing with the new Excel file formats

Yes, it's true that Excel 2007 introduces yet another new native file format in which to save its workbook files (although Microsoft insists that this one is truly an "open" XML file format and not at all proprietary like all the previous ones).

Fortunately, Excel 2007 has no trouble opening any workbook files saved in the good old .XLS file format used by versions 97 through 2003. More importantly, the program automatically saves all editing changes you make to these files in this original file format.

Therefore, you don't have a worry in the world when it comes to making simple edits to existing spreadsheets with Excel 2007. Simply open the workbook file and then make all the necessary changes. When you finish, click the Save button on the Quick Access toolbar to save your changes in the good old .XLS file format that everybody in the office who is still using a previous version of Excel can open, edit, and print. Excel also warns you if you ever add a new 2007 element to the existing workbook that's not supported by its earlier versions.

The challenge comes when you need to use Excel 2007 to create a brand-new spreadsheet. The program automatically wants to save all new workbooks in its fancy new .XLSX file format (see Book I, Chapter 2 for a complete rundown on this new workbook file format and the pros and cons of using it). If you don't want to save your workbook in this format, you need to remember to click the Save as Type drop-down button and then click the Excel 97-2003 Workbook (*.xls) option on its drop-down menu before you click Save.

If you're working in an office environment where all the workbooks you produce with Excel 2007 must be saved in the old 97-2003 file format for compatibility sake, you can change the program's default Save setting so that the program always saves all new workbooks in the old file format. To do this, open the Save tab of the Excel Options dialog box (Office Button ‖ Excel Options or Alt+FIS) and then click Excel 97-2003 Workbook in the Save Files in This Format drop-down list box before you click OK.

Making the most of your macros

The good news is that Excel 2007 supports the creating and running of macros, using the same Microsoft Visual Basic for Applications of earlier versions. It even enables you to edit these macros in a version of VBA Editor, if you're sufficiently skilled to do so.

The biggest problem with macros comes about if you have a tendency, like I do, to map your global macros (the ones you save in the PERSONAL.XLS workbook so that they're available when working in any Excel workbook) onto custom pull-down menus and toolbars. Because Excel 2007 retains only the single pull-down menu and Quick Access toolbar, none of the custom menus and toolbars to which you've assigned macros comes over to Excel 2007. Therefore, although the macros are still a part of their respective workbooks and continue to run, you must now run all macros either using keyboard shortcuts you assigned to them or via the Macro dialog box (click View ‖ Macros ‖ View Macros or press Alt+WMV or Alt+F8).

You can assign macros to buttons on the Quick Access toolbar and then run them by clicking their buttons. The only problem is that all macros you assign to this toolbar use the same generic macro button icon so that the only way to differentiate the macros is through the ScreenTip that appears when you position the mouse over the macro button.

To assign a macro to a generic macro on the Quick Access toolbar, open the Customize tab of the Excel Options dialog box (Office Button ‖ Excel Options or Alt+FIC) and then select Macros in the Choose Commands From drop-down list. Excel then displays the names of all the macros in the current workbook (including all global macros saved in the PERSONAL.XLS workbook) in the Macros list box on the left. To assign a macro to a macro button, click its name in this list box and then click the Add button. You can then move the macro button to the desired position on the Quick Access toolbar with the Move Up and Move Down buttons and, if you so desire, make it part of a separate section on the toolbar by adding a <Separator> before and after its button.

Chapter 2: Getting Help, Tips, and Updates

In This Chapter

✔ Browsing Excel's help topics in the Help Viewer

✔ Looking up help topics in the Help Viewer's Table of Contents

✔ Searching for help information in the Help Viewer

✔ Getting online updates and diagnosing problems with Excel

There's nothing quite like the feeling of getting just the help you need when you need it. That's where the program's extensive and completely modified Help Viewer comes in. You can use it to get help on almost any aspect of using the program and, provided you have Internet access, it can supply you with the most up-to-date information on using Excel.

In this chapter, you find out just how helpful the Excel 2007 Help feature can be as you use its Help Viewer to get answers to your immediate questions on using Excel features. You also gain access to the latest tips and articles on mastering the program along with links to online goodies such as workbook templates, training, and other downloads.

Browsing Excel 2007 Help

When you first open the Excel Help window — either by clicking the Help button (the one with the question mark to the right of the last tab on the Ribbon) or by pressing F1 — the Help Viewer appears in the window (see Figure 2-1).

To display information on any topic in the Browse Excel Help list, simply click its link. For example, to get help on charting data in Excel, you click the Creating Charts link under Charts in the list.

Excel then replaces the list of browsing topics with a list of articles related to creating a chart. To display the actual help information in this pane, click the name of the article you want to see (Create a Chart, in this example).

Home

Refresh | Print

Stop | Change Font Size

Forward | Hide/Show Table of Contents

Back | Keep on Top/Not on Top

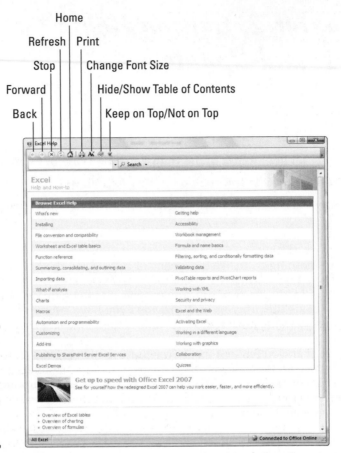

Figure 2-1:
Browsing
help topics
in the Help
Viewer in the
Excel Help
window.

Excel displays the text of the article in the Help Viewer (see Figure 2-2). You can read the article in the Help Viewer. Or you can print a copy. Click the Print icon on the Help toolbar to open the Print dialog box and then click the Print command button in this dialog box to send the article to the default printer.

You can click the Show All link at the top right of an article to expand all the subtopics throughout the article before printing it. If you don't want to expand all the subtopics throughout the article, you can click individual links to expand just those sections in which you're interested.

You can find links to related articles in the See Also section at the very bottom of each article. Be sure to check these links out whenever you feel that you need more information about a topic than the article you selected gives you.

Figure 2-2:
Displaying
the text of
the Create a
Chart help
article in the
Help Viewer.

Using the Table of Contents

When you click the Show Table of Contents button on the Help Viewer tool-bar (the one with the closed book), a Table of Contents pane appears on the left side of the window. The Table of Contents pane contains a list of all Excel 2007 help topics arranged hierarchically in topical categories.

When you first open the Table of Contents pane, only the main help categories are shown — the subtopics are collapsed beneath the main categories, as Figure 2-1 shows. To display a subcategory, click the closed book icon in front of the topic's name. As soon as you do this, the closed book icon becomes an open book icon, and all the subtopics for that section of pane are displayed, indented below the main topic.

After you've displayed the subcategories beneath a main help topic, you can start burrowing deeper into a particular category by clicking its closed book icon. All main categories have subcategories, and some subcategories have their own subcategories. Regardless of the number of nested levels, how-ever, you'll eventually come to a list of help pages, indicated by the blue question mark icon.

When you click a link with a blue question mark icon in the Table of Contents pane, Excel displays the help article in the right pane of the Help Viewer (see Figure 2-3). You can then expand all the information in the article by clicking the Show All link, and print the text by clicking the Print button.

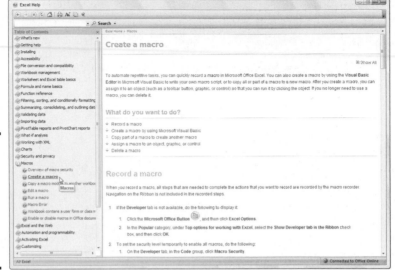

Figure 2-3:
Displaying a
help article
in the Help
Viewer by
clicking it in
the Table of
Contents.

Searching Office Online for Help

When you can't readily find the help information you need in the Browse
Excel Help topics or the Table of Contents pane of the Help Viewer, you can
search for the information you need on Office Online, a Microsoft Web site
that supplements the help topics copied onto your computer as part of the
Office or Excel 2007 installation.

To get help from Office Online, all you have to do is follow these three easy
steps:

1. **Click the Microsoft Office Excel Help button (the one with the ques-
    tion mark) or press F1.**

    Excel opens the Help Viewer in the Excel Help window, similar to the one
    shown in Figure 2-1. Notice that this window opens as a less than full-
    size window that is floating on top of the Excel program window.

2. **Type the keywords describing the topic that you want help with in the
    Search text box.**

    Note that Excel automatically places the insertion point in the Search
    text box of the Help Viewer whenever you first open the Excel Help
    window.

3. **Click the Search button or press Enter to display a list of possible help
    topics in the Search Results Task pane (see Figure 2-4).**

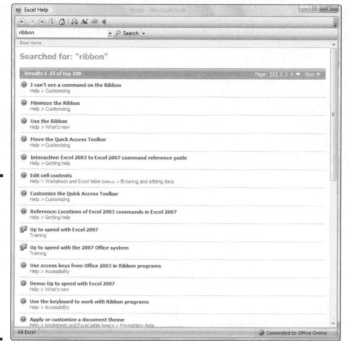

Figure 2-4:
Searching
Office
Online for
help topics
related to
printing
headings in
an Excel
worksheet.

If your computer doesn't have access to the Internet at the time you're searching for help topics, Excel then automatically displays only local help topics on your computer related to the search text you use (indicated by the Offline indicator in the lower-right corner of the Help window).

Displaying a help topic in the Search Results

After searching Office Online for help, Excel displays the results of the search in the main pane of the Help Viewer. If the key words you search for bring up more than one page of results, Excel adds Page buttons at the top of the pane along with a Go to Previous Page and Next buttons you can click to advance to later pages and revisit previous ones.

Excel identifies each item listed in the Search Results with an icon, such as a blue question mark icon to denote a text article or a green XL icon to denote an Excel template file. To display the text of one of the listed articles in the Help Viewer, click its link with the blue question mark icon. Whenever you click a link to an article when the Table of Contents pane is open in the Excel Help window, Excel automatically displays the article's name in the Table of Contents hierarchy in the left pane as it displays the article's information in the pane on the right.

To return to the previous page of search results after displaying a particular help article in the Help Viewer, click the Back button on the toolbar at the top of the Excel Help window.

To download an Excel template file listed in the search results, click its link with the XL icon. Excel then launches your Web browser and opens the Microsoft Office Online Template Web page from which you can download that template file simply by clicking its Download Now button. After you finish downloading a template file, close your Web browser's window by clicking its Close button to return to Excel where the program automatically opens a new workbook generated from the template. Then, to return to the Excel Help window, simply click the Excel Help button on the Windows Task pane.

Tiling the Excel Help and program windows

When you first open the Excel Help window, it opens as a less than full-size window that floats over the Excel program window. By default, the program selects the Keep on Top button so that the Excel Help window always appears on top of any other windows you have open along with it.

You can easily reposition the Excel Help window so that it's side by side with the Excel program window, assuming that you're not running any other programs. This window configuration enables you to peruse the help information in the Help Viewer and then immediately try applying it to the worksheet you have open (see Figure 2-5).

To set up this side-by-side window arrangement, you right-click the Windows taskbar and then, if you're running Excel on Windows Vista, you click the Show Windows Side by Side option on the taskbar's shortcut menu. (If, however, you're running Excel on Windows XP, you have to click the Tile Windows Vertically option on its shortcut menu, instead.)

Close the Table of Contents pane in the Excel Help window by clicking the Close button in the upper-right corner of its pane or the Hide Table of Contents button (the one with the open book icon) on the Help toolbar before you tile it side by side with the Excel program window. Closing this pane gives you a lot more room in which to read the help information — you can always use the Search text box to look up the topic on which you need help and with which you want to experiment in the Excel program window.

After you finish using the help information in the Excel Help window, you can manually resize the window by dragging its sizing handle in the lower-right corner before you close it by clicking its Close button. Then, maximize the Excel program window by clicking its Maximize button, the middle one of the three in the upper-right corner of the window.

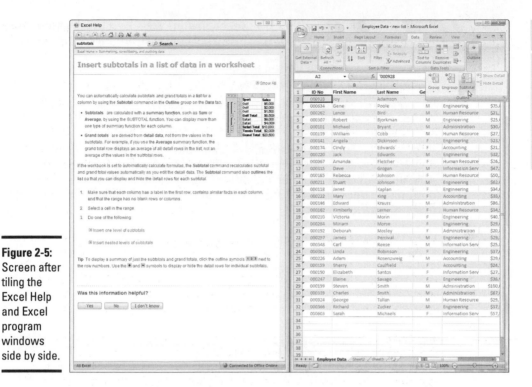

Figure 2-5:
Screen after
tiling the
Excel Help
and Excel
program
windows
side by side.

Using Microsoft Update Service

The Microsoft Update service enables you to check for any critical Windows updates, updates to Microsoft Office, as well as new drivers for the hardware connected to your computer.

If you've turned on Automatic Updates for your computer using the Install Updates Automatically (Recommended) setting on Windows Vista or the Automatic (Recommended) setting on Windows XP, Windows automatically downloads and installs all critical system and program updates on your computer usually while you're home in your bed fast asleep. (See my *Windows Vista For Dummies Quick Reference* or my *Windows XP For Dummies Quick Reference,* both published by Wiley Publishing, for details on setting up Automatic Updates.)

To manually check for updates when you don't use Automatic Updates, you open the Excel Options dialog box by clicking Office Button | Excel Options or pressing Alt+FI and then clicking the Resources tab. At the top of the Get Updates section of the Resources tab, you then click the Check for Updates button.

When you click this button, Windows launches your Web browser and opens the Microsoft Update Web page. This page contains two buttons:

+ **Express:** Click this button to check for higher-priority updates to the system and your Office programs.

+ **Custom:** Click this button to check for lower-priority updates for your system software and Office programs.

After you click one of these buttons and Windows finishes checking for higher- or lower-priority updates, the Review and Install Updates Web page lists all the updates you need to download and install. Click its Expand button (the one with the + sign) to expand a particular update to include a description along with the download size and estimated download time.

Click the Install Updates button to install all the high- or low-priority updates. Keep in mind that you may have to accept one of those obscure license agreements before downloading and installing the updates, and that you may have to reboot your computer to complete the installation of some system and program updates.

Using the Microsoft Office Diagnostics

As computer application programs, such as Excel, and the operating systems that run them, such as Windows Vista and Windows XP, become ever more sophisticated and complex, you run a greater and greater risk that something will suddenly start running amok at some point in their usage, and they will — how can I put this delicately — come unglued and go absolutely berserk on you (or at least won't work like you know they should). In the past, when this kind of thing happened in Excel, you had no choice but to completely reinstall the program.

Fortunately, Excel 2007 offers an alternative to complete reinstallation in the form of the new Microsoft Office Diagnostics command. When you click Microsoft Office Button | Excel Options | Resources or press Alt+FIR and then click the Diagnose button, Excel opens the Microsoft Office Diagnostics dialog box, shown in Figure 2-6.

To have the Microsoft Office Diagnostics utility begin its work, click the Continue button in the dialog box. Excel then runs the diagnostics (which can take up to 15 minutes or more, so be prepared). At the end of running the diagnostics, your Web browser opens a Results of Microsoft Office Diagnostics Tests Web page on the Microsoft Office Web site.

Figure 2-6:
Using the
Microsoft
Office
Diagnostics
dialog box
to try to fix
a broken
Excel.

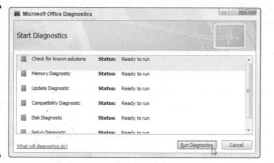

This Web page then lists all the problems that the diagnostic test found,
including computer memory, Windows and Office updates, program compatibility, as well as hard drive and setup errors. It also has links to click to get
more information on each of these problems and their possible solutions
along with links to Microsoft Update, Security, and Office Product Support
Web pages where you can go for more help.

Close the Web browser after you finish perusing the information about your
problems with Excel and perusing suggested solutions from the Results of
Microsoft Office Diagnostics Tests Web page to return to Excel 2007.

Chapter 3: Customizing Excel

In This Chapter

✓ **Customizing the Quick Access toolbar**

✓ **Changing various and sundry Excel program settings**

✓ **Extending Excel's capabilities with add-in programs**

$\mathbf{C}$hances are good that Excel, as it comes right out of the box, is *not* always the best fit for the way you use the program. For that reason, Excel gives an amazing variety of ways to customize and configure the program's settings so that they better suit your needs and the way you like to work.

This chapter covers the most important methods for customizing Excel settings and features. The chapter looks at three basic areas where you can tailor the program to your individual needs:

✦ The first place ripe for customization is the Quick Access toolbar. Not only can you control which Excel command buttons (on and off the Ribbon) appear on this toolbar, but you can also assign macros you create to this toolbar, making them instantly accessible.

✦ The second place where you may want to make extensive modifications is to the default settings (also referred to as options) that control any number of program assumptions and basic behaviors.

✦ The third place where you can customize Excel is in the world of add-ins, those small, specialized utilities (sometimes called *applets*) that extend the built-in Excel features by attaching themselves to the main Excel program. Excel add-ins provide a wide variety of functions and are available from a wide variety of sources, including the original Excel 2007 program, the Microsoft Office Web site, and various and sundry third-party vendors.

Tailoring the Quick Access Toolbar to Your Tastes

Excel 2007 enables you to easily make modifications to the Quick Access toolbar, the sole toolbar remaining in this newest version of the program. When you first launch Excel, this toolbar appears above the Ribbon with the three most commonly used command buttons: Save, Undo, and Redo.

Adding command buttons on the Ribbon to the Quick Access toolbar

Excel 2007 makes it super easy to add a command from any tab on the Ribbon to the Quick Access toolbar. To add a Ribbon command, simply right-click its command button on the Ribbon and then click Add to Quick Access Toolbar on its shortcut menu. Excel immediately adds the command button to the very end of the Quick Access toolbar, immediately in front of the Customize Quick Access Toolbar button.

If you want to move the command button to a new location on the Quick Access toolbar or group it with other buttons on the toolbar, you need to click the Customize Quick Access Toolbar button and then click More Commands on its drop-down menu.

Excel then opens the Excel Options dialog box with the Customize tab selected (similar to the one shown in Figure 3-1). Here, Excel shows all the buttons currently added to the Quick Access toolbar with the order in which they appear from left to right on the toolbar corresponding to their top-down order in the list box on the right side of the dialog box.

Figure 3-1:
Use the buttons on the Customize tab of the Excel Options dialog box to customize the appearance of the Quick Access toolbar.

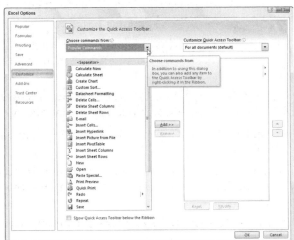

To reposition a particular button on the bar, click it in the list box on the right and then click either the Move Up button (the one with the black triangle pointing upward) or the Move Down button (the one with the black triangle pointing downward) until the button is promoted or demoted to the desired position on the toolbar.

You can add separators to the toolbar to group related buttons. To do this, click the <Separator> selection in the list box on the left and then click the Add button twice to add two. Then, click the Move Up or Move Down button to position one of the two separators at the beginning of the group and the other at the end.

If you've added too many buttons to the Quick Access toolbar and can no longer read the workbook name, you can reposition it so that it appears beneath the Ribbon immediately on top of the Formula bar. To do this, click the Customize Quick Access Toolbar button at the end of the toolbar and then click Show Below the Ribbon on the drop-down menu.

Adding non-Ribbon commands to the Quick Access toolbar

You can also use the options on the Customize tab of the Excel Options dialog box (refer to Figure 3-1) to add a button for any Excel command even if it's not one of those displayed on the tabs of the Ribbon:

1. **Click the type of command you want to add to the Quick Access toolbar in the Choose Commands From drop-down list box.**

   The types of commands include the default Popular Commands, Commands Not in the Ribbon, All Commands, Macros, the Office Menu, as well as each of the standard and Contextual tabs that appear on the Ribbon. To display only the commands that are not displayed on the Ribbon, click Commands Not in the Ribbon near the top of the drop-down list. To display a complete list of all the Excel commands, click All Commands near the top of the drop-down list.

2. **Click the command option whose button you want to add to the Quick Access toolbar in the Choose Commands From list box on the left.**

3. **Click the Add button to add the command button to the bottom of the list box on the right.**

4. **(Optional) To reposition the newly added command button so that it's not the last one on the toolbar, click the Move Up button until it's in the desired position.**

5. **Click the OK button to close the Excel Options dialog box.**

Adding macros to the Quick Access toolbar

If you've created favorite macros (see Book XIII, Chapter 1) that you routinely use and want to be able to run directly from the Quick Access toolbar, click Macros in the Choose Commands From drop-down list box and then click the name of the macro to add in the Choose Commands From list box followed by the Add button.

Adding commands lost from earlier Excel versions to the Quick Access toolbar

Although certain commands such as Data⇨ Form and File⇨Save as Web Page from earlier versions of Excel did not make it to the Ribbon in Excel 2007, this does not mean that they were entirely eliminated from the program. The only way, however, to revive these commands is to add their command buttons to the Quick Access toolbar after choosing the Commands Not in the Ribbon category on the Choose Commands From drop-down list on the Customization tab of the Excel Options dialog box.

Excel 2007 then adds a custom macro command button to the end of the Quick Access toolbar whose generic icon displays the branching of a programming diagram. However, you can change the icon that displays on a macro button. On the Customize tab of the Excel Options dialog box, click the macro name in the list box on the right. Then, click the Modify button, select the picture you want to use in the Modify Button dialog box, and click OK.

Exercising Your Options

Each time you open a new workbook, Excel makes a whole bunch of assumptions about how you want the spreadsheet and chart information that you enter into it to appear on-screen and in print. These assumptions may or may not fit the way you work and the kinds of spreadsheets and charts you need to create.

In the following five sections, you get a quick rundown on how to change the most import default or *preference* settings in the Excel Options dialog box. This is the biggest dialog box in Excel, with a billion tabs (nine actually). From the Excel Options dialog box, you can see what things appear on-screen and how they appear, as well as when and how Excel 2007 calculates worksheets.

Nothing discussed in the following five sections is critical to your being able to operate Excel. Just remember the Excel Options dialog box if you find yourself futzing with the same setting over and over again in most of the workbooks you create. In this situation, it's high time to get into the Excel Options dialog box and modify that setting so that you won't waste any more time tinkering with the same setting in future workbooks.

Changing some of the more universal settings on the Popular tab

The Popular tab (shown in Figure 3-2) is the first tab in the Excel Options dialog box. This tab is automatically selected whenever you first open this dialog box by clicking Microsoft Office Button | Excel Options or by pressing Alt+FI.

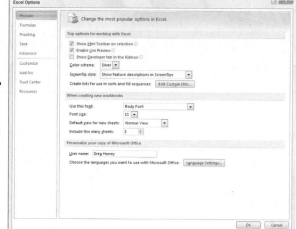

Figure 3-2:
The Popular tab's options enable you to change many universal Excel settings.

The options on the Popular tab are arranged into three groups: Top Options for Working with Excel, When Creating New Workbooks, and Personalize Your Copy of Microsoft Office.

The Top Options for Working with Excel group contains the following check boxes and buttons:

✦ **Show Mini Toolbar on Selection:** Disables or re-enables the display of the Mini Toolbar containing essential formatting buttons from the Home tab above a cell selection or other object's shortcut menu when you right-click it.

✦ **Enable Live Preview:** Disables or re-enables the Live Preview feature whereby Excel previews the data in the current cell selection using the font or style you highlight in a drop-down list or gallery before you actually apply the formatting.

✦ **Show Developer Tab in the Ribbon:** Displays or hides the Developer tab on the Excel Ribbon containing tools that you can use when working with macros (see Book VIII, Chapter 1) and XML files (see Appendix: Using XML File Formats).

✦ **Color Scheme:** Selects a new color scheme for the Excel 2007 screen: Silver (the default color scheme), Blue, or Black.

✦ **ScreenTip Style:** Changes the way ScreenTips (that display information about the command buttons you highlight with the mouse) are displayed on-screen. Click Don't Show Feature Descriptions in ScreenTips on the ScreenTip Style drop-down list to display a minimum amount of description in the ScreenTip and eliminate all links to online help, or click Don't Show ScreenTips to completely remove the display of ScreenTips from the screen.

✦ **Edit Custom Lists:** Opens the Custom Lists dialog box where you can create a new custom AutoFill list (see Book II, Chapter 1 for details).

The options in the When Creating New Workbooks section of the Popular tab of the Excel Options dialog box include only these four combo and text boxes:

✦ **Use This Font:** Select a new default font to use in all cells of new worksheets (Arial is the default font for Excel running on Windows XP, and Body Font, which is actually Calibri in the worksheet, is the default font when running it on Windows Vista) by entering the font name in the combo box or selecting its name by clicking it on the drop-down list.

✦ **Font Size:** Select a new default size to use in all cells of new worksheets (10 points is the default size for Excel running on Windows XP, and 11 points is the default size when running it on Windows Vista) by entering the value in the box or selecting this new point value by clicking it on the drop-down list.

✦ **Default View for New Sheets:** Select either Page Break Preview (displaying page breaks that you can adjust) or Page Layout (displaying page breaks, rulers, and margins) as the default view (rather than Normal) for all new worksheets.

✦ **Include This Many Sheets:** Increase or decrease the default number of worksheets in each new workbook (3 being the default) by entering a number between 1 and 225 or selecting this new number by clicking the spinner buttons.

The final section, Personalize Your Copy of Microsoft Office, enables you to change your user name or to select new languages to use in Microsoft Office 2007 applications such as Excel:

✦ **User Name:** In this text box, you can enter the new name to be used as the default author for new Excel workbooks you create.

✦ **Language Settings:** Use the command button to open the Microsoft Office Language Settings 2007 dialog box where you enable available foreign languages by adding them to the Enabled Editing Languages list box on the Editing Languages tab, or you can review an alphabetical listing of information about all foreign languages available for Office 2007.

Changing common calculation options on the Formulas tab

The options on the Formulas tab (see Figure 3-3) of the Excel Options dialog box (Office Button | Excel Options | Formulas or Alt+FIF) are divided into Calculation Options, Working with Formulas, Error Checking, and Error Checking Rules.

Figure 3-3:
The Formulas tab's options enable you to change how formulas in the spreadsheet are recalculated.

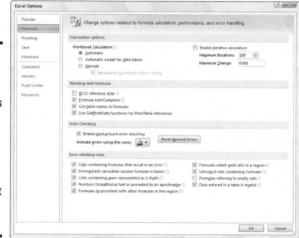

The Calculation options enable you to change when formulas in your workbook are recalculated and if and how a formula that Excel cannot solve on the first try (such as one with a circular reference) is recalculated. Choose from the following items:

✦ **Automatic** option button (the default) to have Excel recalculate all formulas immediately after you modify any of the values on which their calculation depends.

✦ **Automatic Except for Data Tables** option button to have Excel automatically recalculate all formulas except for those entered into what-if data tables you create (see Book VII, Chapter 1) — to update these formulas, you must click the Calculate Now (F9) or the Calculate Sheet (Shift+F9) command button on the Formulas tab of the Ribbon.

✦ **Manual** option button to switch to total manual recalculation whereby formulas that need updating are only recalculated when you click the

Calculate Now (F9) or the Calculate Sheet (Shift+F9) command button on the Formulas tab of the Ribbon.

✦ **Enable Iterative Calculation** check box to enable or disable iterative calculations for formulas that Excel finds that it cannot solve on the first try.

✦ **Maximum Iterations** text box to change the number of times (100 is the default) that Excel recalculates a seemingly insolvable formula when the Enable Iterative Calculation check box contains a check mark by entering a number between 1 and 32767 in the text box or by selecting by clicking the spinner buttons.

✦ **Maximum Change** text box to change the amount by which Excel increments the guess value it applies each time the program recalculates the formula in an attempt to solve it by entering the new increment value in the text box.

The Working with Formulas sections contains four check box options that determine a variety of formula-related options:

✦ **R1C1 Reference Style** check box (unchecked by default) to enable or disable the R1C1 cell reference system whereby both columns and rows are numbered as in R45C2 for cell B45.

✦ **Formula AutoComplete** check box (checked by default) to disable or re-enable the Formula AutoComplete feature whereby Excel attempts to complete the formula or function you're manually building in the current cell.

✦ **Use Table Names in Formulas** check box (checked by default) to disable and re-enable the feature whereby Excel automatically applies all range names you've created in a table of data to all formulas that refer to their cells (see Book III, Chapter 1).

✦ **Use GetPivotData Functions for PivotTable References** check box (checked by default) to disable and re-enable the GetPivotTable function that Excel uses to extract data from various fields in a data source when placing them in various fields of a pivot table summary report you're creating (see Book VII, Chapter 2 for details).

The remaining options on the Formulas tab of the Excel Options dialog box enable you to control error checking for formulas. In the Error Checking section, the sole check box, Enable Background Error Checking, which enables error checking in the background while you're working in Excel, is checked. In the Error Checking Rules, all the check box options are checked with the exception of the Formulas Referring to Empty Cells check box that indicates a formula error when a formula refers to a blank cell.

To disable background error checking, click the Enable Background Error Checking check box to remove its check mark. To change the color used to indicate formula errors in cells of the worksheet (when background error checking is engaged), click the Indicate Errors Using This Color drop-down button and click a new color square on its drop-down color palette. To remove the color from all cells in the worksheet where formula errors are currently indicated, click the Reset Ignored Errors button. To disable other error-checking rules, click their check boxes to remove the check marks.

Changing correction options on the Proofing tab

The options on the Proofing tab (see Figure 3-4) of the Excel Options dialog box (Office Button | Excel Options | Proofing or Alt+FIP) are divided into two sections: AutoCorrect Options and When Correcting Spelling in Microsoft Office Programs.

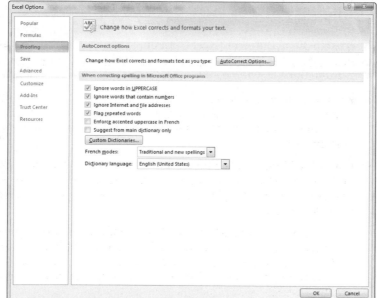

Figure 3-4:
The Proofing tab's options enable you to change AutoCorrect and spell-checking options.

Click the AutoCorrect Options button to open the AutoCorrect dialog box for the primary language used in Microsoft Office 2007. This dialog box contains the following three tabs:

✦ **AutoCorrect** with check box options that control what corrections Excel automatically makes, an Exceptions button that enables you to indicate what words or abbreviations are not to be capitalized in the AutoCorrect Exceptions dialog box, and text boxes where you can define custom replacements that Excel makes as you type.

✦ **AutoFormat As You Type** with check box options that control whether or not to replace Internet addresses and network paths with hyperlinks, and to automatically insert new rows and columns to cell ranges defined as tables and copy formulas in calculated fields to new rows of a data list.

✦ **Smart Tags** with various options for enabling and controlling Smart Tags that automatically link particular cell entries in the workbook with other data sources (see Book IV, Chapter 4 for details on using Smart Tags).

The options in the When Correcting Spelling in Microsoft Office Programs section of the Proofing tab control what type of errors Excel flags as possible misspellings when you use the Spell Check feature (see Book II, Chapter 3). It also contains a Custom Dictionaries command button that opens the Custom Dictionaries dialog box where you can specify a new custom dictionary to use in spell checking the worksheet, define a new dictionary, and edit its word list.

Changing various save options on the Save tab

The options on the Save tab (see Figure 3-5) of the Excel Options dialog box (Microsoft Office Button | Excel Options | Save or Alt+FIS) are divided into four sections: Save Workbooks, AutoRecover Exceptions for the Current Workbook (Book1), Offline Editing Options for Document Management Server Files, and Preserve Visual Appearance of the Workbook.

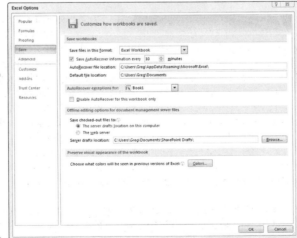

Figure 3-5: The Save tab's options enable you to change the automatic backup and recover options.

The settings in the Save Workbooks section on this tab include the program's AutoRecover settings. The AutoRecover feature enables Excel to save copies of your entire Excel workbook at the interval displayed in the Minutes text box (10 by default). You tell Excel where to save these copies in the AutoRecover File Location text box by specifying a drive, a folder, and maybe even a subfolder.

If your computer should crash or you suddenly lose power, the next time you start Excel the program automatically displays an AutoRecover pane. From this pane, you can open a copy of the workbook file that you were working on when this crash or power loss occurred. If this recovered workbook (saved at the time of the last AutoRecover) contains information that isn't saved in the original copy (the copy you saved the last time you used the Save command before the crash or power loss), you can then use the recovered copy rather than manually reconstructing and reentering the otherwise lost information.

You may also use the recovered copy of a workbook, should the original copy of the workbook file become corrupted in such a way that Excel can no longer open it. (This happens very rarely, but it *does* happen.)

Don't disable the AutoRecover feature by selecting the Disable AutoRecover for This Workbook Only check box on the Save tab, even if you have a battery backup system for your computer that gives you plenty of time to manually save your Excel workbook during any power outage. Disabling AutoRecover in no way protects you from data loss if your workbook file becomes corrupted or you hit the computer's power switch by mistake.

If your company enables you to share the editing of certain Excel workbooks through the Excel Services offered as part of the new SharePoint Services software), you can change the location where Excel saves drafts of the workbook files you check out for editing. By default, Excel saves the drafts of these checked-out workbook files locally on your computer's hard drive inside a SharePoint Drafts folder in the Documents (Windows Vista) or My Documents (Windows XP) folder. If your company or IT department prefers that you save these draft files on the Web server that contains the SharePoint software, click the Web Server option button to deselect the Server Drafts Location on This Computer option button and then enter the network path in the Server Drafts Location text box or click the Browse button and locate the network drive and folder in the Browse dialog box.

If you share your Excel 2007 workbooks with other less fortunate workers who are still using older versions (97 through 2003) of Excel, use the Colors command button to determine which color in the Excel 2007 worksheet to preserve in formatted tables and other graphics when you save the workbook file for them using the Excel 97-2003 file format option (see Book II, Chapter 1).

Changing a whole lot of other common options on the Advanced tab

The options on the Advanced tab (see Figure 3-6) of the Excel Options dialog box (Office Button | Excel Options | Advanced or Alt+FIA) are divided into 11 sections: Editing Options; Cut, Copy, and Paste; Print; Display; Display Options for This Workbook; Display Options for This Worksheet; Formulas; When Calculating This Workbook; General; Lotus Compatibility; and Lotus Compatibility Settings.

The various and sundry options in these 11 sections of the Advanced tab actually fall into four somewhat distinct areas: options for editing in the worksheet; options controlling the screen display; a potpourri area of formulas, calculating, and general options; and Lotus compatibility options for old Lotus 1-2-3 users (assuming that there are still some of you left) who are just now upgrading to Excel to make the transition easier.

Working the worksheet editing options

As you can see in Figure 3-6, the options in the Editing Options and Cut, Copy, and Paste sections at the top of the Advanced tab control what happens when you edit the contents of an Excel worksheet.

Figure 3-6:
The Editing and Cut, Copy, and Paste options at the top of the Advanced tab control how Excel behaves during editing.

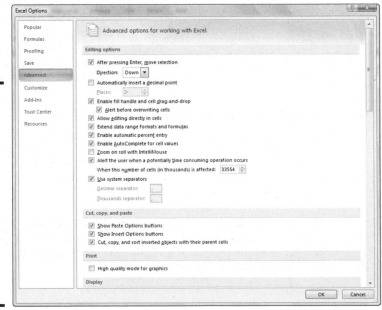

When you first open the Advanced tab of the Excel Options dialog box, all of the check box options in the Editing Options and Cut, Copy, and Paste sections are checked with the exception of these two:

✦ **Automatically Insert a Decimal Point** to have Excel add a decimal point during data entry of all values in each worksheet using the number of places in the Places text box (see Book II, Chapter 1 for details).

✦ **Zoom on Roll with IntelliMouse** to have Excel increase or decrease the screen magnification percentage by 15 percent on each roll forward and back of the center wheel of a mouse that supports Microsoft's IntelliMouse technology — when this option is not checked, Excel scrolls the worksheet up and down on each roll forward and back of the center wheel.

Most of the time you'll want to keep all the check box options in the Editing Options and Cut, Copy, and Paste sections checked. The only one of these you might want to disengage is the Use System Separators check box when you routinely create spreadsheets with financial figures expressed in foreign currency that don't use the period (.) as the decimal point and the comma (,) as the thousands separator. After removing the check mark from the Use System Separators check box, Decimal Separator and Thousands Separator text boxes become active and you can then enter the appropriate punctuation into these two boxes.

By default, Excel selects Down as the Direction setting when the After Pressing Enter, Move Selection check box option is checked. If you want Excel to automatically advance the cell cursor in another direction (Right, Up, or Left), click this direction on its drop-down list. If you don't want Excel to move the cell cursor outside of the active cell upon completion of the entry (the same as clicking the Enter button on the Formula bar), click the After Pressing Enter, Move Selection check box to remove its check mark.

Playing around with the display options

The display options in the middle of the Advanced tab of the Excel Options dialog box (see Figure 3-7) fall into three categories: general Display options that affect the Excel program, Display Options for This Workbook that affect the current workbook, and Display Options for This Worksheet that affect the active sheet in the workbook.

Most of the options in these three categories are self-explanatory as they either turn off or on the display of particular screen elements such as the Formula bar, ScreenTips, scroll bars, sheet tabs, column and row headers, page breaks, (cell) gridlines, and the like.

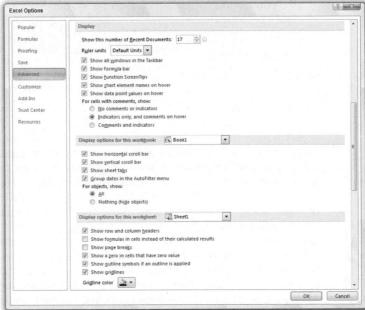

Figure 3-7:
The various display options in the center of the Advanced tab control what's shown on the screen.

When using these display options to control the display of various Excel screen elements, keep the following things in mind:

✦ The Ruler Units drop-down list box automatically uses the Default Units for your version of Microsoft Office (Inches in the U.S. and Centimeters in Europe). These default units (or those you specifically select on the drop-down list: Inches, Centimeters, or Millimeters) are then displayed on both the horizontal and vertical rulers that appear above and to the left of the column and row headings only when you put the Worksheet area display into Page Layout View (Alt+WP).

✦ Click the Comments and Indicators option button under the For Cells with Comments, Show heading when you want Excel to display the text boxes with the comments you add to cells at all times in the worksheet (see Book IV, Chapter 3).

✦ Click the Nothing (Hide Objects) option button under the For Objects, Show heading when you want Excel to hide the display of all graphic objects in the worksheet, including embedded charts, clip art, imported pictures, and all graphics that you generate in the worksheet (see Book V, Chapters 1 and 2 for details).

✦ Click the Show Page Breaks check box to remove its check mark whenever you need to add the dotted lines indicating page breaks in Normal (Alt+WN) view after viewing the Worksheet area in either Page Break Preview (Alt+WI) or Page Layout View (Alt+WP).

✦ Instead of going to the trouble of clicking the Show Formulas in Cells Instead of Their Calculated Results check box to display formulas in the cells of the worksheet, simply press Ctrl+` or click the Show Formulas button on the Formulas tab of the Ribbon — both the keystroke shortcut and the button are toggles so that you can return the Worksheet area to its normal display showing the calculated results rather than the formulas by pressing the Ctrl+` shortcut keys again or clicking the Show Formulas button.

✦ Instead of going to the trouble of removing the check mark from the Show Gridlines check box whenever you want to remove the column and row lines that define the cells in the Worksheet area, click the Gridlines check box in the Show/Hide group on the View tab or the View check box in the Gridlines column of the Sheet Options group on the Page Layout tab to remove their check marks.

Use the Gridline Color drop-down list button immediately below the Show Gridlines check box to change the color of the Worksheet gridlines (when they're displayed, of course) by clicking a new color on the color palette that appears when you click its drop-down list button. (I find that navy blue is rather fetching.)

Caring about the Formulas, Calculating, and General options

At the bottom of the Advanced tab of the Excel Options dialog box (see Figure 3-8), you find a regular mélange of options in five sections. The first three sections, Formulas, When Calculating This Workbook, and General, contain a veritable potpourri of options.

The settings of most of the options in these three sections won't need changing. In rare cases, you may find that you have to activate the following options or make modifications to some of their settings:

✦ **Set Precision as Displayed:** Click this check box *only* when you want to permanently change the calculated values in the worksheet to the number of places currently shown in their cells as the result of the number format applied to them.

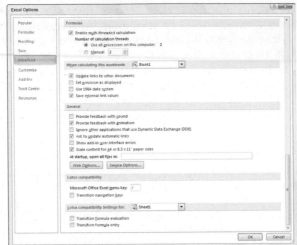

Figure 3-8:
The options at the bottom of the Advanced tab control various calculation, general, and 1-2-3 compatibility settings.

+ **Use 1904 Date System:** Click this check box when you're dealing with a worksheet created with an earlier Macintosh version of Excel that used 1904 rather than 1900 as date serial number 1.

+ **Web Options:** Click this command button to display the Web Options dialog box, where you can modify the options that control how your Excel data appears when viewed with a Web browser, such as Internet Explorer.

+ **Service Options:** Click this command button to display the Service Options dialog box, where you can modify various settings regarding when and how Excel gets online content from Microsoft.com, privacy settings that determine whether or not Microsoft can automatically collect information about your hardware configuration, and settings for Excel spreadsheets that are part of a SharePoint Team Services Web site.

Laying on the Lotus 1-2-3 compatibility

The last two sections on the Advanced tab, Lotus Compatibility and Lotus Compatibility Settings For (see Figure 3-8), are only of interest to Lotus 1-2-3 users who are just now coming to use Microsoft Excel as their spreadsheet program.

If you're a dyed-in-the-wool 1-2-3 user, you'll definitely want to put a check mark in all three check boxes, Transition Navigation Keys, Transition Formula Evaluation, and Transition Formula Entry, in both the Lotus Compatibility and Lotus Compatibility Settings For sections. That way, you'll be able to start formulas with built-in functions with the @ symbol — which Excel will dutifully convert to an equal sign (=) — as well as use all the keys for navigating the worksheet to which you've become so accustomed.

Keep in mind that you can activate the hot keys on the Excel Ribbon by pressing the forward slash (/) key even when none of the Lotus compatibility options are selected. When I want to use the program's hot keys to select an Excel command, I find pressing the forward slash, which activated the pull-down menus in Lotus 1-2-3, much easier than pressing the Alt key — this is because / is part of the QWERTY keyboard. This means that whenever you see a keyboard shortcut such as Alt+WP in the book, you can just press /WP (which in this particular case puts the Worksheet display area into Page Layout View).

Add-In Mania

Add-ins are small, specialized programs that extend Excel's built-in features in some way. Most of the add-in programs created for Excel offer you some kind of specialized function or group of functions that extend Excel's computational abilities. Before you can use any add-in program, the add-in must be installed in the proper folder on your hard drive, and then you must select the add-in in the Add-Ins dialog box.

There are three different types of add-in programs you can use to extend the features in Excel 2007:

✦ Built-in add-ins available when you install Excel 2007

✦ Add-ins that you can download for Excel 2007 from Microsoft's Office Online Web site (`www.office.microsoft.com`)

✦ Add-ins developed by third-party vendors for Excel 2007 that often must be purchased

When you first install Excel 2007, the built-in add-in programs included with Excel are not loaded and therefore are not yet ready to use. To load any or all of these built-in add-in programs, you follow these steps:

1. **Click the Office Button, then click Excel Options or press Alt+FI to open the Excel Options dialog box, and then click the Add-Ins tab.**

   The Add-Ins tab lists all the names, locations, and types of the add-ins to which you have access.

2. **Click the Go button while Excel Add-Ins is selected in the Manage drop-down list box.**

   Excel opens the Add-Ins dialog box (similar to the one shown in Figure 3-9) showing all the names of the built-in add-in programs you can load.

3. **Click the check boxes for each add-in program that you want loaded in the Add-Ins Available list box.**

Click the name of the add-in in the Add-Ins Available list box to display a brief description of its function at the bottom of this dialog box.

4. **Click the OK button to close the Add-Ins dialog box.**

As soon as you close the Add-Ins dialog box, an alert dialog box asking you if you want to install each selected add-in appears.

5. **Click the OK button in each alert dialog box to install its add-in.**

Figure 3-9:
Activating built-in add-ins in the Add-Ins dialog box.

After loading add-ins in this manner, Excel automatically places an Add-Ins tab at the end of the Ribbon. This Add-Ins tab displays the names of all the add-in programs that you've loaded. To then use any of these add-ins, click the Add-Ins tab (or press Alt+X) and then click the name of the particular add-in you wish to use.

If you end up never using a particular add-in you've loaded onto the Add-Ins tab, you can unload it (and thereby free up some computer memory) by following the previously outlined procedure to open the Add-Ins dialog box and then clicking the name of the add-in to remove the check mark from its check box before you click OK.

Excel add-in programs are saved in a special file format identified with the .XLA or .XLAM (for Excel Add-in) filename extension. These files are normally saved inside the Library folder (sometimes in their own subfolders) that is located in the Office 12 folder. The Office 12 folder, in turn, is located in your Microsoft Office folder inside the Program Files folder on your hard drive (often designated as the C:\ drive). In other words, the path:

```
c:\Program Files\Microsoft Office\Office 12\Library
```

After an add-in program has been installed in the Library folder, its name then appears in the list box of the Add-Ins dialog box.

If you ever copy an XLA add-in program to a folder other than the Library folder in the Office 12 folder on your hard drive, its name won't appear in the Add-ins Available list box when you open the Add-Ins dialog box. You can, however, activate the add-in by clicking the Browse button in this dialog box and then selecting the add-in file in its folder in the Browse dialog box before you click OK.

Add-Ins included with Excel

Whether you know it or not, you already have a group of add-in programs waiting for you to install and load. The following add-in programs are included with Excel 2007:

✦ **Analysis ToolPak:** Adds extra financial, statistical, and engineering functions to Excel's pool of built-in functions.

✦ **Analysis ToolPak - VBA:** Enables VBA programmers to publish their own financial, statistical, and engineering functions for Excel.

✦ **Conditional Sum Wizard:** Helps you set up formulas that sum data only when the data meets the criteria you specify.

✦ **Euro Currency Tools:** Enables you to format worksheet values as euro currency and adds a EUROCONVERT function for converting other currencies into euros.

✦ **Internet Assistant VBA:** Enables VBA programmers to publish Excel data to the Web.

✦ **Lookup Wizard:** Helps you set up formulas that return data from an Excel list by using known data in that list (see Book III, Chapter 6).

✦ **Solver Add-In:** Calculates solutions to what-if scenarios based on cells that both adjust and constrain the range of values (see Book VII, Chapter 1).

The first time you attempt to load any of these add-ins included with Excel, the program immediately displays an alert dialog box, telling you that the add-in is not currently installed and asking you if you want to install it. (All the included add-ins are marked for installation on first use so that they show up in the list box in the Add-Ins dialog box but do not actually take up disk space until you're ready to use them.) Click the Yes button in this alert dialog box to have the selected add-in (or add-ins) in this list installed. Keep in mind that Excel needs access to your Office 2007 DVD or its files on your network in order to install any of these included add-in programs.

After you install and load these add-in programs, Excel displays new command buttons for most of them on the Add-Ins tab of the Ribbon that you click when you want to use them. So, for example, you click the Conditional Sum button on the Add-Ins tab when you want to use the Conditional Sum

Wizard add-in, and the Euro Conversion button when you want to open the Euro Conversion dialog box to convert a range of values from some old European currency such as francs or deutsch marks to euros.

To use one of the additional statistical or financial functions added as part of the Analysis ToolPak add-in, you don't access the Add-Ins tab. Instead, click the Function Wizard button on the Formula bar, then click either Financial or Statistical in the Select a Category drop-down list, and then locate the function to use in the Select a Function list box below.

Purchasing third-party add-ins

The add-ins included with Excel are not the only Excel add-ins that you can lay your hands on. Many third-party vendors sell Excel add-ins that you can often purchase online and then immediately download onto your hard drive.

To find third-party vendors and get information on their add-ins, open your Web browser and do a search for

```
Excel add-ins
```

Even before you do a Web search, you may want to visit Macro Systems Web site at

```
www.add-ins.com
```

This online outfit offers a wide variety of useful Excel add-ins. One example is the Name Splitter that automatically splits full names that have been entered into single cells into individual first name, middle name or initial, and last name cells (so that the list can then be better sorted and filtered by parts of the names).

Note that you can expect to pay Macro Systems between $25.00 and $50.00 for add-in programs such as these (really reasonably priced if you consider how many man-hours it would take to split up names into separate cells in huge worksheets).

Book II
Worksheet Design

The 5th Wave   By Rich Tennant

"I've used several spreadsheet programs, but this is the best one for designing quilt patterns."

Contents at a Glance

Chapter 1: Building Worksheets

In This Chapter

✔ **Designing worksheets**

✔ **Understanding the different types of cell entries**

✔ **Different ways of entering data in the worksheet**

✔ **Using Data Validation to restrict the data entries in cells**

✔ **Saving worksheets**

*B*efore you can begin building a new spreadsheet in Excel, you must have the design in mind. As it turns out, the design aspect of the creative process is often the easiest part because you can borrow the design from other workbooks that you've already created or from special workbook files, called *templates,* which provide you with the new spreadsheet's form, along with some of the standard, or *boilerplate,* data entries.

After you've settled upon the design of your new spreadsheet, you're ready to begin entering its data. In doing the data entry in a new worksheet, you have several choices regarding the method to use. For this reason, this chapter not only covers all the methods for entering data — from the most basic to the most sophisticated — but also includes hints on when each is the most appropriate. Note, however, that this chapter doesn't include information on building formulas, which comprises a major part of the data entry task in creating a new spreadsheet. Because this task is so specialized and so extensive, you find the information on formula building covered in Book III, Chapter 1.

Designer Spreadsheets

Each and every time you start Excel without also opening an existing workbook file, the program presents you with a new workbook (with the generic filename, Book1), consisting of three totally blank worksheets. At this point, you can either launch into building your new spreadsheet by using the workbook's three blank worksheets, or you can open a spreadsheet template or existing workbook file and then adapt the template's or workbook file's design by entering the data for the new spreadsheet.

Take it from a template

Spreadsheet templates are the way to go if you can find one that fits the design of the spreadsheet that you're building. You can choose from a couple of good sources for ready-made spreadsheet templates. First, you can try using the spreadsheet templates automatically installed with the Excel program. Second, you can also download free spreadsheet templates from the Microsoft Office Web site.

Instead of using ready-made templates, you can create your own templates from your favorite Excel workbooks. After you save a copy of a workbook as a template file, Excel automatically generates a copy of the workbook whenever you open the template file. This way, you can safely customize the contents of the new workbook without any danger of inadvertently modifying the original template.

Using the installed templates

The following templates are automatically installed when you start using Excel 2007:

✦ Billing Statement

✦ Blood Pressure Tracker

✦ Expense Report

✦ Loan Amortization

✦ Personal Monthly Budget

✦ Sales Report

✦ Time Card

To create a new worksheet based on any of these templates, click Office Button | New or press Alt+FN to open the New Workbook dialog box. Then, click Installed Templates under Templates in the pane on the left to display a thumbnail for each of the installed templates in the middle pane and a preview of the selected thumbnail in a preview pane on the right (see Figure 1-1).

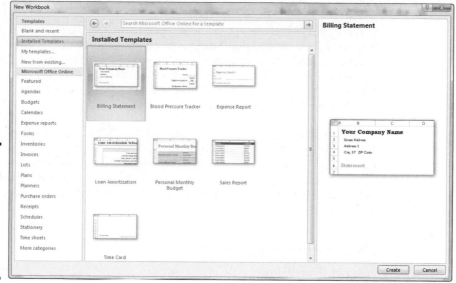

Book II
Chapter 1

Building Worksheets

Figure 1-1:
Selecting an
installed
template
from which
to generate
a new
workbook.

Figure 1-2 shows a copy of a blank billing statement generated from the Billing Statement template. As you can see on the Excel window title bar in this figure, when Excel generated this first workbook from the original template file, the program also gave it the temporary filename, BillingStatement1. If you were to then create a second copy of the sales invoice by once again opening the Billing Statement template, the program would name that copy BillingStatement2. This way, you don't have to worry about one copy overwriting another, and you never risk mistakenly saving changes to the original Billing Statement template file itself (which actually uses a completely different filename extension — .xltx for an Excel template as opposed to .xlsx for an Excel worksheet).

To fill in the blanks in a spreadsheet generated from one of the installed templates, you click the first blank cell that requires a data entry, type in the necessary data, and then press Tab or the Enter key to advance to the next blank cell (either over or down, depending on the template's design). If pressing Tab or Enter takes you past a blank cell in the worksheet that needs data, simply click the cell, type in the data, and then press Enter to complete the entry and advance to the next blank.

Note that when filling in a spreadsheet generated from an installed Solutions template, you have access to all the cells in the worksheet, those that contain standard headings as well as those that require personalized data entry.

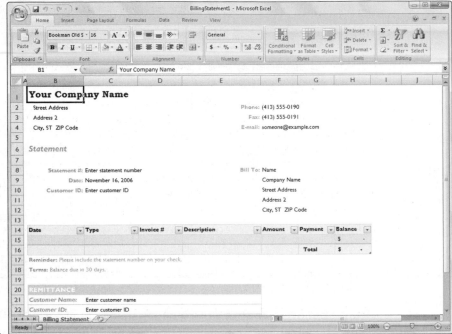

Figure 1-2:
A new billing statement worksheet generated from the Billing Statement template.

After you finish filling in the personalized data, save the workbook just as you would a workbook that you had created from scratch (see the "Saving the Data" section at the end of this chapter for details on saving workbook files).

You can customize the installed templates to make them easier to fill out and then save those modifications in a new template that you save on disk. For example, you can make your own custom billing template from one generated by the Billing Statement template by filling in your company name and address in the top section and your billing terms and a thank-you message in the bottom sections.

Saving changes to your customized templates

To save your changes as a new template file, follow these steps:

1. **Click the Save button on the Quick Access toolbar (the one with the disk icon), click Office Button | Save on the File pull-down menu, or press Ctrl+S.**

   Following any one of these methods opens the Save As dialog box, where the temporary filename (such as BillingStatement1) appears in the File Name text box.

2. **Edit the filename for your new template in the File Name text box.**

   Next, you need to change the file type from a regular Microsoft Excel Workbook to a Template in the Save as Type drop-down list box.

3. **Click the Save as Type drop-down button and then click Excel Template in the drop-down menu.**

   If you need your new template file to be compatible with earlier versions of Excel (versions 97 through 2003), click Excel 97-2003 Template rather than Excel Template on the Save as Type drop-down list. When you do this, Excel saves the new template file in the older binary file format (rather than the new XML file format) with the old .XLT filename extension instead of the new .XLTX filename extension. If your template contains macros that you want the user to be able to run when creating the worksheet, click Excel Macro-Enabled Template.

   Note that Excel automatically selects the Templates folder (indicated by the appearance of Templates in the address bar of the Save As dialog box on Windows Vista and in the Save In combo box on Windows XP) as the place to save your template. All spreadsheet template files that you save in this folder automatically appear.

4. **Click the Save button to close the Save As dialog box and save your customized template in the Templates folder.**

   After the Save As dialog box closes, you still need to close the customized template file in the Excel work area.

5. **Click Office Button | Close or press Alt+FC or Ctrl+W to close the customized template file.**

After saving the customized template file in the Templates folder, you can generate new workbooks from it by simply opening the New Workbook dialog box and then clicking the My Templates link in the pane on the left. Excel then opens the New dialog box with a My Templates tab showing all the template files you've saved in your Templates folder. The file icon for the customized template appears on this tab of the New dialog box. To generate a new workbook from the customized spreadsheet template, double-click this template file icon or, if you prefer, click the icon and then click OK.

Figure 1-3 shows a new Billing Statement worksheet file in Excel created from the original Billing Statement template after customizing a copy of it for my company, Mind Over Media, Inc.

To open this worksheet, all I had to do was double-click its template file icon on the My Templates tab of the New dialog box (opened by clicking the My Templates link in the Navigation pane of the New Workbook dialog box — Office Button | New or Alt+FN).

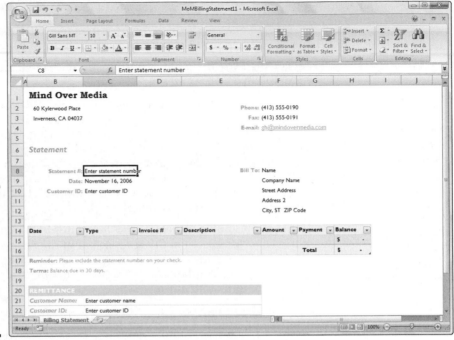

Figure 1-3:
A new
workbook
generated
from the
customized
MOM Billing
Statement
template.

Downloading Microsoft spreadsheet templates

If you have Internet access, you can easily check out and download any of
the spreadsheet templates offered by Microsoft directly from the New
Workbook dialog box.

Simply click the category of the template you want to download (featured
through More Categories) under Microsoft Office Online in the Navigation
pane on the left to search the Microsoft Online Web site for all templates in
the category. The thumbnails are displayed in the center pane of the New
Workbook dialog box, and the preview of the selected thumbnail is displayed
in the preview pane on the right. Figure 1-4 shows the New Workbook dialog
box after selecting Budgets in the Navigation pane and then previewing the
Expense Budget template by clicking its thumbnail in the center column listing the available Budget templates.

If you can't locate the type of template you want to use in any of the
categories listed in the Navigation pane, click the More Categories link.
Excel then displays a list of subcategories (Address Books through Other
Templates) in middle pane of the New Workbook dialog box. Then, if you
locate the kind of template you need in this list, click its subcategory name.
Excel then replaces the subcategory list in the middle pane with thumbnails
of the actual templates in that subcategory.

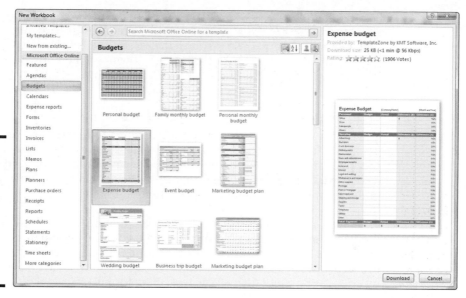

Figure 1-4:
Selecting
a Budget
template to
download
from
Microsoft
Office
Online.

Excel sorts the thumbnails of templates in the category you select in order
by their customer ratings. To sort them by name, click the Sort by Name
button (the one with the A above Z and an arrow pointing downward). To
display the preview for a particular template in the preview pane in the
right, click its thumbnail image in the middle pane.

When you find the template you want to download, click its thumbnail image
if it's not already selected and then click the Download button at the bottom
of the New Workbook dialog box to have Excel begin downloading it.

After Excel finishes downloading the template, the program automatically
opens the Excel Help dialog box, displaying information on the template
and how to use it. After you close the Excel Help dialog box, you return
to the Excel program window where a new workbook generated from the
downloaded template is automatically opened. You can then customize the
worksheet(s) in this workbook and save your changes (Ctrl+S) as you would
a spreadsheet that you created from scratch.

Keep in mind that after downloading a template from Microsoft Office
Online, you can use the template to generate new workbooks by opening it
from the My Templates tab of the New dialog box (open this dialog box by
clicking the My Templates link in the Navigation pane of the New Workbook
window — Office Button | New or Alt+FN).

If you know the type of template you want to find on the Microsoft Office
Online Web site, you can do a search for it from the New Workbook dialog
box. Simply click the Search text box at the top of the New Workbook dialog
box, then enter the type of templates to locate before you click the Start

Searching button on the right (the one with the arrow pointing to the right). Excel then searches the Microsoft Office Online Web site for all templates fitting your search terms and displays their thumbnails in the center column of the dialog box, where you can select and download them as you would any of the templates you find by selecting their category or subcategory.

Creating your own spreadsheet templates

You certainly don't have to rely on spreadsheet templates created by other people. Indeed, many times you simply can't do this because, even though other people may generate the type of spreadsheet that you need, their design doesn't incorporate and represent the data in the manner that you prefer or that your company or clients require.

When you can't find a ready-made template that fits the bill or that you can easily customize to suit your needs, create your own templates from sample workbooks that you've created or that your company has on hand. The easiest way to create your own template is to first create an actual workbook prototype, complete with all the text, data, formulas, graphics, and macros that it requires to function.

When readying the prototype workbook, make sure that you remove all headings, miscellaneous text, and numbers that are specific to the prototype and not generic enough to appear in the spreadsheet template. You may also want to protect all generic data, including the formulas that calculate the values that you or your users input into the worksheets generated from the template and headings that never require editing (see Book IV, Chapter 1 for information on how to protect certain parts of a worksheet from changes).

After making sure that both the layout and content of the boilerplate data are hunky-dory, save the workbook in the template file format (.xltx) in the Templates folder so that you can then generate new workbooks from it by opening it on the My Templates tab of the New dialog box (for details on how to do this, refer back to the steps in the previous section, "Saving changes to your customized templates").

As you may have noticed when looking through the Spreadsheet Solutions templates included in Excel (see Figure 1-2, for example) or browsing through the templates available on the Microsoft Office Online Web site, many spreadsheet templates abandon the familiar worksheet grid of cells, preferring a look very close to that of a paper form instead. When converting a sample workbook into a template, you can also remove the grid, use cell borders to underscore or outline key groups of cells, and color different cell groups to make them stand out (for information on how to do this kind of stuff, refer to Book II, Chapter 2).

Keep in mind that you can add online comments to parts of the template that instruct coworkers on how to properly fill in and save the data. These comments are helpful if your coworkers are unfamiliar with the template and may be less skilled in using Excel (see Book IV, Chapter 3, for details on adding comments to worksheets).

Designing a workbook from scratch

Not all worksheets come from templates. Many times, you need to create rather unique spreadsheets that aren't intended to function as standard models from which certain types of workbooks are generated. In fact, most of the spreadsheets that you create in Excel may be of this kind, especially if your business doesn't rely on the use of highly standardized financial statements and forms.

**Book II
Chapter 1**

**Building
Worksheets**

Planning your workbook

When creating a new workbook from scratch, you need to start by considering the layout and design of the data. When doing this mental planning, you may want to ask yourself some of the following questions:

✦ Does the layout of the spreadsheet require the use of data tables (with both column and row headings) or lists (with column headings only)?

✦ Do these data tables and lists need to be laid out on a single worksheet or can they be placed in the same relative position on multiple worksheets of the workbook (like pages of a book)?

✦ Do the data tables in the spreadsheet use the same type of formulas?

✦ Do some of the columns in the data lists in the spreadsheet get their input from formula calculation or do they get their input from other lists (called *lookup tables*) in the workbook?

✦ Will any of the data in the spreadsheet be graphed, and will these charts appear in the same worksheet (referred to as *embedded charts*), or will they appear on separate worksheets in the workbook (called *chart sheets*)?

✦ Does any of the data in the spreadsheet come from worksheets in separate workbook files?

✦ How often will the data in the spreadsheet be updated or added to?

✦ How much data will the spreadsheet ultimately hold?

✦ Will the data in the spreadsheet be shared primarily in printed or online form?

All these questions are an attempt to get you to consider the basic purpose and function of the new spreadsheet before you start building it, so that you can come up with a design that is both economical and fully functional.

Economy

Economy is an important consideration because when you open a workbook, all its data is loaded into your computer's dynamic memory (known simply as *memory*). This may not pose any problems if your computer is one of the latest generation of PCs with more memory than you can conceive of using at one time, but it can pose quite a problem if you share the workbook file with someone whose computer is not so well equipped. Also, depending on just how much data you cram into the workbook, you may even come to see Excel creep and crawl the more you work with it.

To help guard against this problem, make sure that you don't pad the data tables and lists in your workbook with extra empty "spacer" cells. Keep the tables as close together as possible on the same worksheet (with no more than a single blank column or row as a separator, which you can adjust to make as wide or high as you like), or — if the design allows — keep them in the same region of consecutive worksheets.

Functionality

Along with economy, you must pay attention to the functionality of the spreadsheet. This means that you need to allow for future growth when selecting the placement of its data tables, lists, and charts. This is especially important in the case of data lists because they have a tendency to grow longer and longer as you continue to add data, requiring more and more rows of the same few columns in the worksheet. This means that you should usually consider all the rows of the columns used in a data list as "off limits." In fact, always position charts and other supporting tables to the right of the list rather than somewhere below the last used row. This way, you can continue to add data to your list without ever having to stop and first move some unrelated element out of the way.

This spatial concern is not the same when placing a data table that will total the values both down the rows and across the columns table — for example, a sales table that sums your monthly sales by item with formulas that calculate monthly totals in the last row of the table and formulas that calculate item totals in the last column. In this table, you don't worry about having to move other elements, such as embedded charts or other supporting or unrelated data tables, because you use Excel's capability of expanding the rows and columns of the table from within so that as the table expands or contracts, surrounding elements move in relation to and with the table expansion and contraction. You do this kind of editing to the table because inserting new table rows and columns ahead of the formulas ensures that they can be included in the totaling calculations. In this way, the row and column of formulas in the data table acts as a boundary that floats with the expansion or contraction of its data but which keeps all other elements at bay.

Finalizing your workbook design

After you've more or less planned out where everything goes in your new spreadsheet, you're ready to start establishing the new tables and lists. Here are a few general pointers on how to set up a new data table that includes simple totaling calculations:

- ✦ Enter the title of the data table in the first cell, which forms the left and top edges of the table.

- ✦ Enter the row of column headings in the row below this cell, starting in the same column as the cell with the title of the table.

- ✦ Enter the row headings down the first column of the table, starting in the first row that will contain data (doing this leaves a blank cell where the column of row headings intersects the row of column headings).

- ✦ Construct the first formula that sums columns of (still empty) cell entries in the last row of the table, and then copy that formula across all the rest of the table columns.

- ✦ Construct the first formula that sums the rows of (still empty) cell entries in the last column of the table, and then copy that formula down the rest of the table rows.

- ✦ Format the cells to hold the table values, and then enter them in their cells or enter the values to be calculated and then format their cells (this is really your choice).

When setting up a new data list in a new worksheet, enter the list name in the first cell of the table, and then enter the row of column headings in the row below. Then, enter the first row of data beneath the appropriate column headings (see Book VI, Chapter 1, for details on designing a data list and inputting data into it).

Generating a new workbook from another workbook

The Templates area of the Navigation pane of the New Workbook dialog box contains a New from Existing link. You can click this link to open a copy of an existing workbook that you want to modify and then save as a new workbook. Use New from Existing when you have access to an existing workbook that contains a spreadsheet, which is very similar to the spreadsheet that you now need to build, and modifying the data in the original workbook would be faster than copying extensive sections of the original data into a blank workbook.

When you click the New from Existing link, Excel opens the New from Existing Workbook dialog box, where you select the original Excel workbook that you want to modify. After selecting its file icon and then clicking the Create New button, Excel opens a copy of the original file (indicated by adding a number to the original filename) that you can then safely modify to your heart's content without any danger of corrupting the original.

Please don't open the original workbook and start making modifications to its spreadsheet with the intention of then using the Office Button | Save As (Alt+FS) command to save your changes in a copy of the original file. It's just far too easy to select the Office Button | Save command by mistake and thereby save your changes in the original workbook. Always play it safe and use the New from Existing link in the New Workbook dialog box instead.

Opening new blank workbooks

Although Excel automatically opens a new workbook (called Book1 when you first start the program) that you can use in building a new spreadsheet from scratch, you will encounter occasions in using Excel when you need to open your own blank workbook. For example, if you launch Excel by opening an existing workbook that needs editing and then move on to building a new spreadsheet, you'll need to open a blank workbook (which you can do before or after closing the workbook with which you started Excel).

The easiest way to open a blank workbook is to press Ctrl+N. Excel responds by opening a new workbook, which is given a generic Book name with the next unused number (Book1, if you opened Excel with a blank Book1).

You can also open a blank workbook by choosing Office Button | New. Unlike when clicking the New button or pressing Ctrl+N, Excel responds to this action by opening the New Workbook dialog box where you then double-click the Blank Workbook option or click it and then click the Create button to open a new workbook.

As soon as you open a blank workbook, Excel makes its document window active. To then return to another workbook that you have open (which you would do if you wanted to copy and paste some of its data into one of the blank worksheets), click its button on the Windows taskbar or press Alt+Tab until its file icon is selected in the dialog box that appears in the middle of the screen.

If you ever open a blank workbook by mistake, you can just close it right away by pressing Ctrl+W, clicking Office Button | Close, or pressing Alt+FC. Excel then closes its document window and automatically returns you to the workbook window that was originally open at the time you mistakenly opened the blank workbook.

It Takes All Kinds (Of Cell Entries)

Before covering the many methods for getting data into the cells of your new spreadsheet, you need to understand which type of data that you're entering. To Excel, everything that you enter in any worksheet cell is either one of two types of data: *text* (also known as a *label*) or a *number* (also known as a *value* or *numeric entry*).

The reason that you should care about what type of data you're entering into the cells of your worksheet is that Excel treats your entry differently, depending on what type of data it thinks you've entered.

**Book II
Chapter 1**

✦ **Text** entries are automatically left-aligned in their cells, and if they consist of more characters than fit within the column's current width, the extra characters spill over and are displayed in blank cells in columns on the right (if these cells are not blank, Excel cuts off the display of any characters that don't fit within the cell borders until you widen its column).

✦ **Numbers** are automatically right-aligned in their cells, and if they consist of more characters (including numbers and any formatting characters that you add) than fit within the column's current width, Excel displays a string of number signs across the cell (######), telling you to widen the column (in some cases, such as decimal numbers, Excel will truncate the decimal places shown in the cell instead of displaying the number-sign overflow indicators).

So, now all you have to know is how Excel differentiates text data entries from numeric data entries.

What's in a label?

Here's the deal with text entries:

✦ All data entries beginning with a letter of the alphabet or a punctuation mark are considered text.

✦ All data entries that mix letters (A–Z) and numbers are considered text, even when the entry begins with a number.

✦ All numeric data entries that contain punctuation other than commas (,), periods (.), and forward slashes (/) are considered text, even when they begin with a number.

This means that in addition to regular text, such as *First Quarter Earnings* and *John Smith,* nonstandard data entries, including *C123, 666-45-0034,* and *123C,* are also considered text entries.

However, a problem exists with numbers that are separated by hyphens (also known as *dashes*): If the numbers that are separated by dashes correspond to a valid date, then Excel converts it into a date (which is most definitely a kind of numeric data entry — see the "Dates and times" section in this chapter for details). For example, if you enter *1-2-8* in a cell, Excel thinks that you want to enter the date January 2, 2008, in the cell, and the program automatically converts the entry into a date number (displayed as 1/2/2008 in the cell).

If you want to enter a number as text in a cell, you must preface its first digit with an apostrophe ('). For example, if you're entering a part number that consists of all numbers, such as 12-30-09, and you don't want Excel to convert it into the date December 30, 2009, you need to preface the entry with an apostrophe by entering into the cell:

'12-30-09

Likewise, if you want to enter 3/4 in a cell, meaning three out of four rather than the date March 4, you enter

'3/4

(Note that if you want to designate the fraction, three-fourths, you need to input =3/4, in which case Excel displays the value 0.75 in the cell display.)

When you complete an entry that starts with an apostrophe, the apostrophe is not displayed in the cell (it does appear, however, on the Formula bar). Instead, a tiny green triangle appears in the upper-left corner of the cell, and an alert symbol appears to the immediate left (as long as the cell cursor is in this cell). When you position the mouse pointer on this alert indicator, a drop-down button appears to its right (shown in the left margin). When you click this drop-down button, a drop-down menu similar to the one shown in Figure 1-5 appears. In this example, the first option indicates that the number is currently stored as text, and the second option enables you to convert it back into a number (by removing the apostrophe).

If you start a cell entry with the equal sign (=) or the at symbol (@) followed by other characters that aren't part of a formula, Excel displays an error dialog box as soon as you try to complete the data entry. Excel uses the equal sign to indicate the use of a formula, and what you have entered is not a valid formula. The program knows that Lotus 1-2-3 used the @ symbol to indicate the use of a built-in function, and what you have entered is not a valid built-in function. This means that you must preface any data entry beginning with the equal sign and at symbol that isn't a valid formula with an apostrophe in order to get it into the cell.

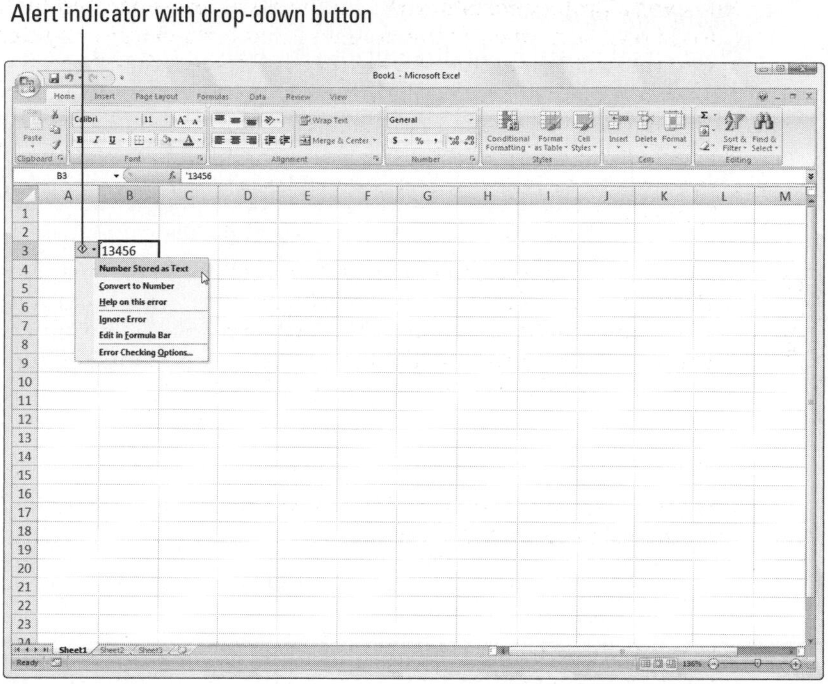

Alert indicator with drop-down button

Figure 1-5:
Opening the
drop-down
menu
attached to
the Number
Stored as
Text alert.

What's the value?

In a typical spreadsheet, numbers (or numeric data entries) can be as
prevalent as the text entries — if not more so. This is because traditionally,
spreadsheets were developed to keep financial records, which included
plenty of extended item totals, subtotals, averages, percentages, and grand
totals. Of course, you can create spreadsheets that are full of numbers that
have nothing to do with debits, credits, income statements, invoices, quarterly sales, and dollars and cents.

Number entries that you make in your spreadsheet can be divided into three
categories:

✦ **Numbers that you input** directly into a cell. (You can do this with the
keyboard, your voice if you use the Speech Recognition feature, or even
by handwriting if your keyboard is equipped with a writing tablet.)

✦ **Date and time numbers** that are also input directly into a cell but are
automatically displayed with the default Date and Time number formats
and are stored behind the scenes as special date serial and hour decimal
numbers.

✦ **Numbers calculated by formulas** that you build yourself by using simple
arithmetical operators and/or Excel's sophisticated built-in functions.

Inputting numbers

Numbers that you input directly into the cells of the worksheet — whether they are positive, negative, percentages, or decimal values representing dollars and cents, widgets in stock, workers in the Human Resources department, or potential clients — don't change unless you specifically change them, either by editing their values or replacing them with other values. This is quite unlike formulas with values that change whenever the worksheet is recalculated and Excel finds that the values upon which they depend have been modified.

When inputting numbers, you can mix the digits 0–9 with the following keyboard characters:

```
+ - ( ) $ . , %
```

You use these characters in the numbers you input as follows:

✦ Preface the digits of the number with a plus sign (+) when you want to explicitly designate the number as positive, as in +(53) to convert negative 53 into positive 53. Excel considers all numbers to be positive unless you designate them as negative.

✦ Preface the digits of the number with – or enclose them in a pair of parentheses to indicate that the number is a negative number, as in –53 or (53).

✦ Preface the digits of the number with a dollar sign ($), as in $500, to format the number with the Currency style format as you enter it (you can also apply this format after it's entered).

✦ Input a period (.) in the digits of the number to indicate the position of the decimal point in the number, as in 500.25. (Note that you don't have to bother entering trailing zeros after the decimal point because the General number format automatically drops them, even if you type them in.)

✦ Input commas (,) between the digits of a number to indicate the position of thousands, hundred thousands, millions, billions, and the like, and to assign the Comma style number format to the number, as in 642,153. (You can also have Excel add the commas by assigning the Comma format to the number after you input the number.)

✦ Append the percent sign (%) to the digits of a number to convert the number into a percentage and assign the Percent number style to it, as in 12%.

The most important thing to remember about the numbers that you input is that they inherit the type of number formatting currently assigned to the cells in which they're entered. When you first open a blank workbook, the number format appropriately called General (which some have called the equivalent of no number formatting because it doesn't add any special format characters, such as a constant number of decimal places or thousands separators) is applied to each cell of the worksheet. You can override the General format by adding your own formatting characters as you input the number in a cell or, later, by selecting the cell and then assigning a different number format to it (see Book II, Chapter 2 for details).

Dates and times

Excel stores dates and times that you input into a spreadsheet as special values. Dates are stored as serial numbers, and times are stored as decimal fractions. Excel supports two date systems: the 1900 date system used by Excel for Windows (also used by Lotus 1-2-3), which uses January 1, 1900, as serial number 1, and the 1904 system used by Excel for the Macintosh, which uses January 2, 1904, as serial number 1.

If you use Excel on the IBM-compatible PCs and Macintosh computers in your office, you can switch from the default 1900 date system to the 1904 date system for those worksheets that you create in the Windows version and then transfer to the Macintosh version. To switch to the 1904 date system, click the Advanced tab of the Excel Options dialog box (Office Button | Excel Options or Alt+FI) and then click the Use 1904 Date System check box in the When Calculating This Workbook section.

By storing dates as serial numbers representing the number of days that have elapsed from a particular date (January 1, 1900, or January 2, 1904), Excel can perform arithmetic between dates. For example, you can find out how many days there are between February 15, 1949, and February 15, 2009, by entering 2/15/09 in one cell and 2/15/49 in the cell below, and then creating a formula in the cell below that one that subtracts the cell with 2/15/49 from the one containing 2/15/09. Because Excel stores the date 2/15/09 as the serial number 39859 and the date 2/15/49 as the serial number 17944, it can calculate the difference and return the result of 21915 (days, which is equal to 60 years).

Although Excel has no problem calculating the number of days that have elapsed between two dates in a worksheet, this doesn't mean that it knows how to properly display the result. In the previous example referring to a formula that subtracts the date 2/15/49 entered in one cell from the date

2/15/09 entered in another, Excel displays the result in the cell with this subtraction formula as the date 12/31/59! This happens because the program mistakenly assumes that you want to see the calculated result in the same (date) number format as you used in the cells referred to in the formula. Fortunately, you can instantly rectify this mistake by clicking the drop-down button attached to the Number Format button in the Number group on the Home tab of the Ribbon and then clicking General on its drop-down list, or by clicking the Comma Style button and then clicking the Decrease Decimal button twice (in the same area of the Home tab) if you want to see the number of days as 21,915 — see Book II, Chapter 2 for all about formatting values in the spreadsheet.

When you use a date directly in a formula that performs date arithmetic, you must enclose the date in quotation marks. For example, if you want to enter a formula in a cell that calculates the number of days between February 15, 1949, and February 15, 2009, in the cell you have to enter the following formula:

```
="2/15/09"-"2/15/49"
```

Times of the day are stored as decimal numbers that represent the fraction of the 24-hour period starting with 0.0 for 12:00 midnight through 0.999 for 11:59:59 p.m. By storing times as decimal fractions, Excel enables you to perform time calculations such as those that return the elapsed time (in minutes) between any two times of the day.

Inputting dates and times using recognized formats

Although Excel stores dates as serial numbers and times as decimal fractions, luckily you don't have to use these numbers to enter dates or times of the day into cells of the worksheet. You simply enter dates by using any of the recognized Date number formats that are used by Excel, and you enter times by using any of the recognized Time number formats. Excel then assigns and stores the appropriate serial number or decimal fraction at the same time the program assigns the date or time format that you used for this value. Table 1-1 shows you typical date and time entries that you can use as examples when entering dates and times in the cells of a worksheet.

Table 1-1	Common Ways to Enter Dates and Times
What You Enter in the Cell	*Date or Time Recognized by Excel (As Displayed on the Formula Bar)*
1/6/2008	January 6, 2008
1/6/08	January 6, 2008
1-6-08	January 6, 2008
6-Jan-08	January 6, 2008
6-Jan	January 6
Jan-08	January, 2008

What You Enter in the Cell	Date or Time Recognized by Excel (As Displayed on the Formula Bar)
1/6/08 5:25	1/6/2008 5:25 a.m.
5:25	5:25:00 AM
5:25 P	5:25:00 PM
17:25	5:25:00 PM
17:25:33	5:25:33 PM

Understanding how Excel treats two-digit years

The only thing that's a tad bit tricky about inputting dates in a spreadsheet comes in knowing when you have to input all four digits of the year and when you can get away with entering only two. As Table 1-1 shows, if you input the date 1/6/08 in a cell, Excel recognizes the date as 1/6/2008 and not as 1/6/1908. In fact, if you enter the date January 6, 1908, in a spreadsheet, you must enter all four digits of the year (1908).

Here's how Excel decides whether a year for which you enter only the last two digits belongs to the 20th or 21st century:

✦ 00 through 29 belong to the 21st century, so Excels interprets 7/30/29 as July 30, 2029.

✦ 30 through 99 belong to the 20th century, so Excel interprets 7/30/30 as July 30, 1930.

This means that you don't have to enter the four digits of the year for dates in the years 2000 through 2029 or for dates in the years 1930 through 1999.

 Of course, if you can't remember these cutoffs and are just generally confused about when to enter two digits versus four digits, just go ahead and enter all four digits of the year. Excel never misunderstands which century the date belongs to when you spell out all four digits of the year.

Numeric formulas

Many numeric entries in a typical spreadsheet are not input directly but are returned as the result of a calculation by a formula. The numeric formulas that you build can do anything from simple arithmetic calculations to complex ANOVA statistical analyses (see Book III for complete coverage of all types of numeric formulas). Most spreadsheet formulas use numbers that are input into other cells of the worksheet in their calculations. Because these formulas refer to the address of the cell containing the input number rather than number itself, Excel is able to automatically recalculate the formula and return a new result anytime you change the values in the original cell.

The most important thing to remember about numeric formulas is that their calculated values are displayed in their cells in the worksheet while the contents of the formulas (that indicate how the calculation is done) are displayed on the Formula bar whenever its cell contains the cell cursor. All numbers returned by formulas inherit the nondescript General number format. The only way to get these calculated numbers to appear the way you want them in the worksheet is to select them and apply a new, more appropriate number format to them (see Book II, Chapter 2 for details).

Data Entry 101

I want to pass on to you a few basic rules of data entry:

+ You must select the cell where you want to make the data entry before you can make the entry in that cell.

+ Any entry that you make in a cell that already contains data replaces the original entry.

+ Every data entry that you make in any cell must be completed with some sort of action such as clicking the Enter button on the Formula bar (the button with the check mark that appears when you start entering data), pressing the Enter key, or clicking a new cell before the entry is officially entered in that cell.

I know that the first rule sounds so obvious that it should go without saying, but you'd be surprised how many times you look at the cell where you intend to add new data and then just start entering that data without realizing that you haven't yet moved the cell cursor to that cell. As a result, the data entry that you're making is not destined to go into the cell that you intended. In fact, you're in the process of making the entry in whatever cell currently contains the cell cursor, and if that cell is already occupied, you're in the process of replacing its entry with the one you meant to go somewhere else!

This is where the third rule is so important because even if you're in the process of messing up your spreadsheet by entering data in the wrong cell (and, if that cell is occupied, you're destroying a perfectly good entry), you haven't done it until you take the action that completes the entry (such as clicking the Enter button on the Formula bar or pressing the Enter key). This means that you can recover simply by clicking the Cancel button on the Formula bar or by pressing the Escape key on your keyboard. As soon as you do that, the errant data entry disappears from the Formula bar (and the original data entry — if it exists — returns), and you're then free to move the cell cursor to the desired cell and redo the entry there.

Data entry keyboard style

The only trick to entering data from the keyboard is to figure out the most efficient way to complete the entry in the current cell (and Excel gives you many choices in this regard). You can, of course, complete any data entry by clicking the Enter button on the Formula bar (presumably this is what Microsoft intended; otherwise, why have the button?), but clicking this button is not at all efficient when the mouse pointer isn't close to it.

You should know of another potential drawback to clicking the Enter button on the Formula bar to complete an entry: When you do this, Excel doesn't move the cell cursor but keeps it right in the cell with the new data entry. This means that you still have to move the cell cursor before you can safely make your next data entry. You're better off then pressing the Enter key because doing this not only completes the entry in the cell, but also moves the cell cursor down the cell in the next row.

Of course, pressing the Enter key is efficient only if you're doing the data entry for a table or list down each row across the succeeding columns. If you want to enter the data across each column of the table or list down succeeding rows, pressing Enter doesn't work to your advantage. Instead, you'd be better off pressing the → key or the Tab key to complete each entry (at least until you get to the cell in the last column of the table) because pressing these keys completes the entry and moves the cell cursor to the next cell on the right.

Take a look at Table 1-2 to get an idea of the keys that you commonly use to complete data entries. Keep in mind, however, that any key combination that moves the cell cursor (see Table 1-1 in Book I, Chapter 1, for a review of these keystrokes) also completes the data entry that you're making, as does clicking another cell in the worksheet.

Table 1-2	Keys Used in Completing Data Entry
Keys	*Cell Cursor Movement*
Enter	Down one row
↓	Down one row
Tab	Right one column
→	Right one column
Shift+Tab	Left one column
←	Left one column
↑	Up one row

TIP

If you have more than one cell selected (see Book II, Chapter 2 for more on this) and then press Ctrl+Enter to complete the data entry that you're making in the active cell of this selected range, Excel simultaneously enters that data entry into all the cells in the selection. You can use this technique to enter a single label or value in many places in a worksheet at one time.

If you have more than one worksheet selected (see Book II, Chapter 4) at the time that you make an entry in the current cell, Excel makes that entry in the corresponding cells of all the selected worksheets. For example, if you enter the heading *Cost Analysis* in cell C3 of Sheet1 when Sheet1 through Sheet3 are selected, Excel enters *Cost Analysis* in cell C3 of Sheet2 and Sheet3 as well.

You AutoComplete this for me

Excel automatically makes use of a feature called AutoComplete, which attempts to automate completely textual data entries (that is, entries that don't mix text and numbers). AutoComplete works this way: If you start a new text entry that begins with the same letter or letters as an entry that you've made recently in the same region of the worksheet, Excel completes the new text entry with the characters from the previous text entry that began with those letters.

For example, if you type the spreadsheet title *Sales Invoice* in cell A1 of a new worksheet and then, after completing the entry by pressing the ↓, start entering the table title *Summary* in cell A2, as soon as you type *S* in cell A2, Excel completes the new text entry so that it also states *Sales Invoice* by adding the letters *ales Invoice*.

When the AutoComplete feature completes the new text entry, the letters that it adds to the initial letter or letters that you type are automatically selected (indicated by highlighting). This way, if you don't want to repeat the original text entry in the new cell, you can replace the characters that Excel adds just by typing the next letter in the new (and different) entry. In the previous example, in which Sales Invoice was repeated in the cell where you want to input *Summary,* the *ales Invoice* text appended to the *S* that you type disappears the moment you type *u* in *Summary.*

Note that when you have two different entries that begin with the same first letter but have different second letters, typing the second letter of one entry causes Excel to complete the typing of that entry, leaving you free to insert its text in the cell by pressing the Enter key or using any of the other methods for completing a cell entry.

To make use of automatic text completion rather than override it as in the previous example, simply press a key (such as Enter or an arrow key), click the Enter button on the Formula bar, or click another cell to complete the completed input in that cell. For example, say you're building a sales table in which you're inputting sales for three different account representatives — George, Jean, and Alice. After entering each name manually in the appropriate row of the Account Representative column, you only need to type in their first initial (*G* to get George, *J* to get Jean, and *A* to get Alice) in subsequent cells and then press the ↓ or Enter key to move down to the next row of that column. Of course, in a case like this, AutoComplete is more like automatic typing, and it makes filling in the Account Representative names for this table extremely quick and easy.

If the AutoComplete feature starts to bug you when building a particular spreadsheet, you can temporarily turn it off; simply click the Enable AutoComplete for Cell Values check box, and remove the check mark on the Advanced tab of the Excel Options dialog box (Office Button | Excel Options or Alt+FI).

You AutoCorrect this right now!

Along with AutoComplete, Excel has an AutoCorrect feature that automatically fixes certain typos that you make in the text entries as soon as you complete them. For example, if you forget to capitalize a day of the week, AutoCorrect does this for you (turning *friday* into *Friday* in a cell as soon as you complete the entry). Likewise, if you mistakenly enter a word with two initial capital letters, AutoCorrect automatically lowercases the second capital letter (so that *QUarter* typed into a cell becomes *Quarter* upon completion of the cell entry).

In addition to these types of obvious capitalization errors, AutoCorrect also automatically takes care of common typos, such as changing *hsi* to *his* (an obvious transposition of two letters) or *inthe* to *in the* (an obvious case of a missing space between letters). In addition to the errors already recognized by AutoCorrect, you can add your own particular mistakes to the list of automatic replacements.

To do this, open the AutoCorrect dialog box and then add your own replacements in the Replace and With text boxes located on the AutoCorrect tab, shown in Figure 1-6. Here's how:

1. **Click Office Button | Excel Options or press Alt+FI, and then click the Proofing tab followed by the AutoCorrect Options button.**

The AutoCorrect dialog box opens for your language, such as English (United States).

2. **If the AutoCorrect options aren't already displayed in the dialog box, click the AutoCorrect tab to display them.**

3. **Click the Replace text box and then enter the typo exactly as you usually make it.**

4. **Click the With text box and enter the replacement that AutoCorrect should make (with no typos in it, please!).**

   Check the typo that you've entered in the Replace text box and the replacement that you've entered in the With text box. If everything checks out, go on to Step 5.

5. **Click the Add button to add your new AutoCorrect replacement to the list of automated replacements.**

6. **Click the OK button to close the AutoCorrect dialog box.**

Figure 1-6:
You can add your own automated replacements to the AutoCorrect tab.

You can use the AutoCorrect feature to automatically replace favorite abbreviations with full text, as well as to clean up all your personal typing mistakes. For example, if you have a client with the name Great Lakes Securities, and you enter this client's name in countless spreadsheets that you create, you can make an AutoCorrect entry so that Excel automatically replaces the abbreviation *gls* with *Great Lakes Securities*. Of course, after you use AutoCorrect to enter Great Lakes Securities in your first cell by typing *gls,* the AutoComplete feature kicks in, so the next time you type the *g* of *gls* to enter the client's name in another cell, it fills in the rest of the name, leaving you with nothing to do but complete the entry.

Keep in mind that AutoCorrect is not a replacement for Excel's spelling checker. You should still spell check your spreadsheet before sending it out because the spelling checker finds all those uncommon typos that haven't been automatically corrected for you (see Book II, Chapter 3 for details).

Constraining data entry to a cell range

One of the most efficient ways to enter data into a new table in your spreadsheet is to preselect the empty cells where the data entries need to be made and then enter the data into the selected range. Of course, this trick only works if you know ahead of time how many columns and rows the new table requires.

The reason that preselecting the cells works so well is that doing this constrains the cell cursor to that range, provided that you press *only* the keystrokes shown in Table 1-3. This means that if you're using the Enter key to move down the column as you enter data, Excel automatically positions the cell cursor at the beginning of the next column as soon as you complete the last entry in that column. Likewise, when using the Tab key to move the cell cursor across a row as you enter data, Excel automatically positions the cell cursor at the beginning of the next row in the table as soon as you complete the last entry in that row.

That way you don't have to concentrate on repositioning the cell cursor at all when entering the table data; you can keep your attention on the printed copy from which you're taking the data.

Table 1-3	Keystrokes for Moving Within a Selection
Keystrokes	*Movement*
Enter	Moves the cell cursor down one cell in the selection (moves one cell to the right when the selection consists of a single row)
Shift+Enter	Moves the cell cursor up one cell in the selection (moves one cell to the left when the selection consists of a single row)
Tab	Moves the cell cursor one cell to the right in the selection (moves one cell down when the selection consists of a single column)
Shift+Tab	Moves the cell cursor one cell to the left in the selection (moves one cell up when the selection consists of a single column)
Ctrl+period (.)	Moves the cell cursor from corner to corner of the cell selection

You can't very well use this preselection method on data lists because they're usually open-ended affairs to which you continually append new rows of data. The most efficient way to add new data to a new or existing data list is to format it as a table (see Book II, Chapter 2).

Getting Excel to put in the decimal point

Of course, if your keyboard has a ten-key entry pad, you'll want to use it rather than the numbers on the top row of the keyboard to make your numeric entries in the spreadsheet (make sure that the Num Lock key is engaged, or you'll end up moving the cell cursor rather than entering

numbers). If you have a lot of decimal numbers (suppose that you're building a financial spreadsheet with loads of dollars and cents entries), you may
also want to use Excel's Fixed Decimal Places feature so that Excel places a
decimal point in all the numbers that you enter in the worksheet.

To turn on this feature, click the Automatically Insert a Decimal Point check
box in the Editing Options section of the Advanced tab of the Excel Options
dialog box (Microsoft Office Button | Excel Options or Alt+FI) to put a check
mark in it. When you do this, the Places text box immediately below it determines the number of decimal places that the program is to add to each
number entry. You can then specify the number of places by changing its
value (2 is, of course, the default) either by entering a new value or selecting
one with its spinner buttons.

After turning on the Automatically Insert a Decimal Point option, Excel adds
a decimal point to the number of places that you specified to every numeric
data entry that you make at the time you complete its entry. For example, if
you type the digits 56789 in a cell, Excel changes this to 567.89 at the time
you complete the entry.

Note that when this feature is turned on and you want to enter a number
without a decimal point, you need to type a period at the end of the value.
For example, if you want to enter the number 56789 in a cell and *not* have
Excel change it to 567.89, you need to type

56789.

Ending the number in a period prevents Excel from adding its own decimal
point to the value when Fixed Decimal Places is turned on. Of course, you
need to turn this feature off after you finish making the group of entries
that require the same number of decimal places. To do this, click the
Automatically Insert a Decimal Point check box on the Advanced tab of the
Excel Options dialog box (Microsoft Office Button | Excel Options or Alt+FI)
to remove its check mark.

You AutoFill it in

Few Excel features are more helpful than the AutoFill feature, which enables
you to fill out a series of entries in a data table or list — all by entering only
the first item in the series in the spreadsheet. You can sometimes use the
AutoFill feature to quickly input row and column headings for a new data
table or to number the records in a data list. For example, when you need
a row of column headings that list the 12 months for a sales table, you can

enter *January* or *Jan.* in the first column and then have AutoFill input the other 11 months for you in the cells in columns to the right. Likewise, when you need to create a column of row headings at the start of a table with successive part numbers that start at L505-120 and proceed to L505-128, you enter L505-120 in the first row and then use AutoFill to copy the part numbers down to L505-128 in the cells below.

 The key to using AutoFill is the Fill handle, which is the small black square that appears in the lower-right corner of whatever cell contains the cell cursor. When you position the mouse pointer on the Fill handle, it changes from the normal thick, white-cross pointer to a thin, black-cross pointer (shown in the left margin). This change in shape is your signal that when you drag the Fill handle in a single direction, either down or to the right, Excel will either copy the current cell entry to all the cells that you select or use it as the first entry in a consecutive series, whose successive entries are then automatically entered in the selected cells.

**Book II
Chapter 1**

**Building
Worksheets**

Note that you can immediately tell whether Excel will simply copy the cell entry or use it as the first in a series to fill out by the ScreenTips that appear to the right of the mouse pointer. As you drag through subsequent cells, the ScreenTip indicates which entry will be made if you release the mouse button at that point. If the ScreenTip shows the same entry as you drag, you know Excel didn't recognize the entry as part of a consecutive series and is copying the entry verbatim. If, instead, the ScreenTips continue to change as you drag through cells showing you successive entries for the series, you know that Excel has recognized the original entry as part of a consecutive series.

Figures 1-7 and 1-8 illustrate how AutoFill works. In Figure 1-7, I entered January as the first column heading in cell B2 (using the Enter button on the Formula bar so as to keep the cell cursor in B2, ready for AutoFill). Next, I positioned the mouse pointer on the AutoFill handle in the lower-right corner of B2 before dragging the Fill handle to the right until I reached cell G2 (and the ScreenTip stated June).

Figure 1-8 shows the series that was entered in the cell range B2:G2 when I released the mouse button with cell G2 selected. For this figure, I also clicked the drop-down button attached to the Auto Fill Options button that automatically appears whenever you use the Fill handle to copy entries or fill in a series to show you the items on this pop-up menu. This menu contains a Copy Cells option button that enables you to override Excel's decision to fill in the series and have it copy the original entry (January, in this case) to all the selected cells.

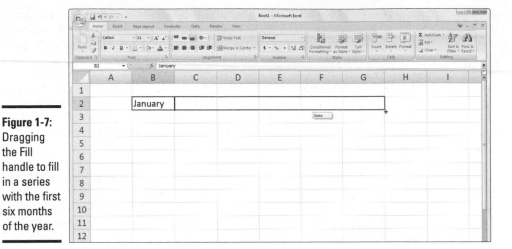

Figure 1-7:
Dragging
the Fill
handle to fill
in a series
with the first
six months
of the year.

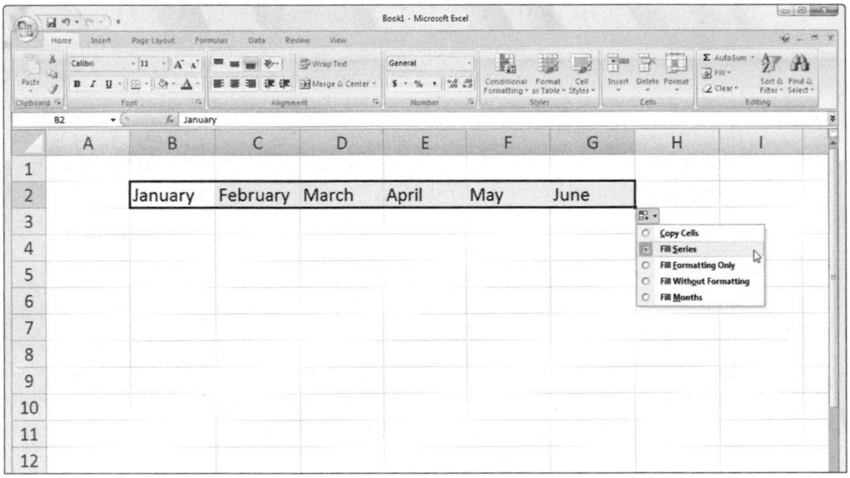

Figure 1-8:
The series
of monthly
column
headings
with the
Auto Fill
Options
drop-down
menu.

Note that you can also override Excel's natural decision to fill in a series or copy an entry before you drag the Fill handle. To do so, simply hold down the Ctrl key (which adds a tiny plus sign to the upper-right corner of the Fill handle). Continue to depress the Ctrl key as you drag the Fill handle and notice that the ScreenTip now shows that Excel is no longer filling in the series or copying the entry as expected.

When you need to consecutively number the cells in a range, use the Ctrl key to override Excel's natural tendency to copy the number to all the cells you select. For example, if you want to number rows of a list, enter the starting number (1 or 100, it doesn't matter) in the first row, then press Ctrl to have Excel fill in the rest of the numbers for successive rows in the list (2, 3, 4, and the like, or 102, 103, 104, and so on). If you forget to hold down the Ctrl key and end up with a whole range of cells with the same starting number, click the Auto Fill Options drop-down button and then click the Fill Series option button to rectify the mistake by converting the copied numbers to a consecutively numbered series.

When using AutoFill to fill in a data series, you don't have to start with the first entry in that particular series. For example, if you want to enter a row of column headings with the last six months of the year (June through December), you enter *June* first and then drag down or to the right until the mouse pointer selects the cell where you enter *December* (indicated by the December ScreenTip). Note also that you can reverse-enter a data series by dragging the Fill handle up or left. In the June-to-December column headings example, if you drag up or left, Excel enters June to January in reverse order.

Keep in mind that you can also use AutoFill to copy an original formula across rows and down columns of data tables and lists. When you drag the Fill handle in a cell that contains a formula, Excel automatically adjusts its cell references to suit the new row or column position of each copy (see Book III, Chapter 1 for details on copying formulas with AutoFill).

Filling series with increments other than one

Normally, when you drag the Fill handle to fill in a series of data entries, Excel increases or decreases each entry in the series by a single unit (a day, month, hour, or whatever). You can, however, get AutoFill to fill out a series of data entries that uses some other increment, such as every other day, every third month, or every hour-and-a-half.

Figure 1-9 illustrates a number of series all created with AutoFill that use increments other than one unit. The first example in row 3 shows a series of different times all 45 minutes apart, starting with 8:00 a.m. in cell A3 and extending to 2:45 p.m. in cell J3. The second example in row 6 shows a series of days of the week that uses every other day of the week starting with Monday in cell A6 and extending to Saturday in cell G6. The third example in row 9 shows a series of numbers, each of which increases by 15, that starts with 35 in cell A9 and increases to 170 in cell J9. The last example in row 13 shows a series with every other month, starting with Jan. in cell A13 and extending to Nov. in cell F13.

To create a series that uses an increment other than one unit, follow these four general steps:

1. **Enter the first two entries in the series in consecutive cells above one another in a column or side by side in a row.**

   Enter the entries one above the other when you intend to drag the Fill handle down the column to extend the series. Enter them side by side when you intend to drag the Fill handle to the right across the row.

2. **Position the cell cursor in the cell with the first entry in the series, and drag through the second entry.**

   Both entries must be selected (indicated by being enclosed within the expanded cell cursor) before you use the Fill handle to extend the series. Excel analyzes the difference between the two entries and uses its increment in filling out the data series.

3. **Drag the Fill handle down the column or across the row to extend the series by using the increment other than one unit.**

   Check the ScreenTips to make sure that Excel is using the correct increment in filling out your data series.

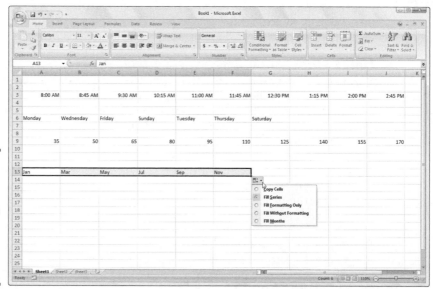

Figure 1-9: Various series created with AutoFill by using different increments.

4. **Release the mouse button when you reach the desired end of the series (indicated by the entry shown in thc ScreenTip appearing next to the black-cross mouse pointer).**

Creating custom AutoFill lists

Just as you can use AutoFill to fill out a series with increments different from one unit, you can also get it to fill out custom lists of your own design. For example, suppose that you often have to enter a standard series of city locations as the column or row headings in new spreadsheets that you build. Instead of copying the list of cities from one workbook to another, you can create a custom list containing all the cities in the order in which they normally appear in your spreadsheets. After you create a custom list in Excel, you can then enter all or part of the entries in the series simply by entering the first item in a cell and then using the Fill handle to extend out the series either down a column or across a row.

To create a custom series, you can either enter the list of entries in the custom series in successive cells of a worksheet before you open the Custom Lists dialog box, or you can type the sequence of entries for the custom series in the List Entries list box located on the right side of the Custom Lists tab in this dialog box, as shown in Figure 1-10.

**Book II
Chapter 1**

**Building
Worksheets**

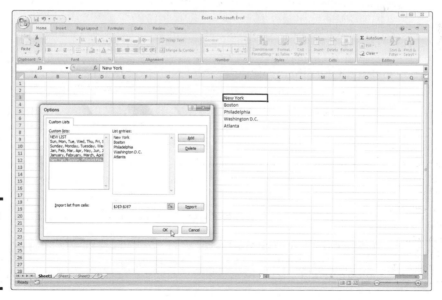

Figure 1-10:
Creating a
custom list
of cities for
AutoFill.

If you already have the data series for your custom list entered in a range of cells somewhere in a worksheet, follow these steps to create the custom list:

1. **Click the cell with the first entry in the custom series and then drag the mouse pointer through the range until all the cells with entries are selected.**

   The expanded cell cursor should now include all the cells with entries for the custom list.

2. **Click Office Button | Excel Options or press Alt+FI and then click the Edit Custom Lists button on the Popular tab.**

   The Custom Lists dialog box opens with its Custom Lists tab where you now should check the accuracy of the cell range listed in the Import List from Cells text box (the range in this box lists the first cell and last cell in the current selected range separated by a colon — you can ignore the dollar signs following each part of the cell address). To check that the cell range listed in the Import List from Cells text box includes all the entries for the custom list, click the Collapse Dialog Box button, located to the right of the Import List from Cells text box (shown in the left margin). When you click this button, Excel collapses the Custom Lists dialog box down to the Import List from Cells text box and puts a marquee (the so-called marching ants) around the cell range.

   If this marquee includes all the entries for your custom list, you can expand the Custom Lists dialog box by clicking the Expand Dialog box button (which replaces the Collapse Dialog Box button and is shown in the left margin) and proceed to Step 3. If this marquee doesn't include all the entries, click the cell with the first entry and then drag through until all the other cells are enclosed in the marquee. Then, click the Expand Dialog box button and go to Step 3.

3. **Click the Import button to add the entries in the selected cell range to the List Entries box on the right and to the Custom Lists box on the left side of the Custom Lists tab.**

   As soon as you click the Import button, Excel adds the data entries in the selected cell range to both the List Entries and the Custom Lists boxes.

4. **Click the OK button to close the Custom Lists dialog box.**

If you don't have the entries for your custom list entered anywhere in the worksheet, you have to follow the second and third steps listed previously and then take these three additional steps instead:

1. **Click the List Entries box and then type each of the entries for the custom list in the order in which they are to be entered in successive cells of a worksheet.**

   Press the Enter key after typing each entry for the custom list so that each entry appears on its own line in the List Entries box, or separate each entry with a comma.

2. **Click the Add button to add the entries that you've typed into the List Entries box on the right to the Custom Lists box, located on the left side of the Custom Lists tab.**

   Note that when Excel adds the custom list that you just typed to the Custom Lists box, it automatically adds commas between each entry in the list — even if you pressed the Enter key after making each entry. It also automatically separates each entry on a separate line in the List Entries box — even if you separated them with commas instead of carriage returns.

3. **Click the OK button to close the Custom Lists dialog box.**

After you've created a custom list by using one of these two methods, you can fill in the entire data series by entering the first entry of the list in a cell and then dragging the Fill handle to fill in the rest of the entries. If you ever decide that you no longer need a custom list that you've created, you can delete it by clicking the list in the Custom Lists box in the Custom Lists dialog box and then clicking the Delete button. Excel then displays an alert box indicating that the list will be permanently deleted when you click OK. Note that you can't delete any of the built-in lists that appear in this list box when you first open the Custom Lists dialog box.

Keep in mind that you can also fill in any part of the series by simply entering any one of the entries in the custom list and then dragging the Fill handle in the appropriate direction (down and to the right to enter succeeding entries in the list or up and to the left to enter preceding entries).

Limiting data entry with Data Validation

The Data Validation feature in Excel can be a real timesaver when doing repetitive data entry and can also go a long way in preventing incorrect entries in your spreadsheets. When you use Data Validation in a cell, you indicate what type of data entry is allowed in the cell. As part of restricting a data entry to a number (which can be a whole number, decimal, date, or time), you also specify the permissible values for that type of number (a whole number between 10 and 100 or a date between January 1, 2008, and December 31, 2008, for example).

When you restrict the data entry to text, you can specify the range of the minimum and maximum text length (in characters), or even better, a list of permissible text entries that you can select from a pop-up menu (opened by clicking a pop-up button that appears to the right of the cell whenever it contains the cell cursor).

When using Data Validation to restrict the type of data entry and its range of acceptable values in a cell, you can also specify an input message that is automatically displayed next to the cell when you select it and/or an error alert message that is displayed if you try to input the wrong type of entry or a number outside the permissible range.

To use the Data Validation feature, put the cell cursor in the cell where you want to restrict the type of data entry that you can make there, and then click the Data Validation button on the Data tab of the Ribbon (or press Alt+AVV). The Data Validation dialog box opens with the Settings tab selected (similar to the one shown in Figure 1-11).

You then click the drop-down button attached to the Allow drop-down list box and select among the following items:

+ **Any Value** to remove any previous restrictions thereby canceling data validation and once again enabling the user to enter anything he wishes into the cell.

+ **Whole Number** to restrict the entry to a whole number that falls within a certain range or adheres to particular parameters that you specify

+ **Decimal** to restrict the entry to a decimal number that falls within a certain range or adheres to particular parameters that you specify

+ **List** to restrict the entry to one of several text entries that you specify, which you can select from a pop-up menu that's displayed by clicking a pop-up button that appears to the right of the cell whenever it contains the cell cursor

+ **Date** to restrict the entry to a date that falls within a certain range or on or before a particular date

+ **Time** to restrict the entry to a time that falls within a certain range or on or before a particular time of the day

+ **Text Length** to restrict a text entry so that its length in characters doesn't fall below or go above a certain number or falls within a range that you specify

+ **Custom** to restrict the entry to the parameters specified by a particular formula entered in another cell of the worksheet

To specify an input message after selecting all the items on the Settings tab, click the Input Message tab of the Data Validation dialog box where you enter a short title for the input message (such as *How to Proceed*) in the Title text box, and then enter the text of your message in the Input Message list box below.

To specify an alert message, click the Error Alert tab of the Data Validation dialog box, where you can choose the kind of warning in the Style drop-down list: Stop (the default, which uses a red button with a cross in it), Warning (which uses a yellow triangle with an exclamation point in it), and Information (which uses a balloon with a blue *I* in it). After selecting the type of alert, you then enter the title for its dialog box in its Title text box, and enter the text of the alert message in the Error Message list box.

To apply the restriction you're defining in the Data Validation dialog box to all the other cells that are formatted the same way as in a cell range formatted as a table (see Book II, Chapter 2 for details), click the Apply These Changes to All Other Cells with the Same Settings check box before you click OK. To copy the restriction to a range that is not formatted as a table, use the Data Validation feature to set up the type of entry and permitted range in the first cell and then use the Fill handle to copy that cell's Data Validation settings to subsequent cells in the same column or row.

By far, the most popular use of the Data Validation feature is to create a drop-down menu from which you or someone who uses your spreadsheet can select the appropriate data entry. Figures 1-11 and 1-12 illustrate this type of usage.

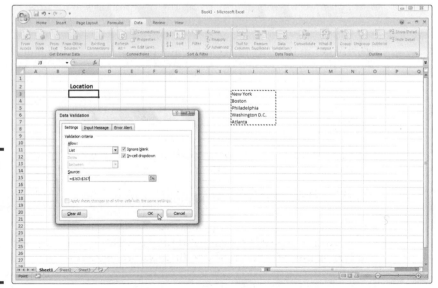

Figure 1-11: Creating a custom drop-down list in the Data Validation dialog box.

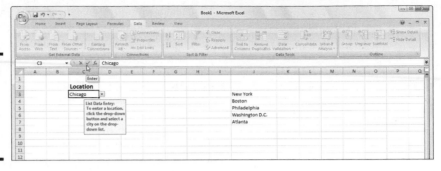

Figure 1-12:
Selecting
a city from
the custom
drop-down
list.

As Figure 1-11 shows, on the Settings tab of the Data Validation dialog box, I chose List from the Allow drop-down list box and then in the Source text box, I designated the cell range J3:J7, which just happens to contain the list of allowable entries (you can type them in the Source text box separated by commas if the list doesn't already exist someplace on the worksheet). Notice in this figure that, as soon as you select List in the Allow combo box, a check box appears. Keep this check box selected because it tells Excel to create a drop-down list (or pop-up menu, as it's also called) containing only the entries specified in the Source text box.

Figure 1-12 shows you what happens in the spreadsheet after you close the Data Validation dialog box. Here, you see the pop-up menu (with a list of cities taken from the cell range J3:J7) as it appears when you click the cell's new pop-up button. In this figure, you can also see the input message box that I created for this cell by using the options on the Input Message tab of the Data Validation dialog box. Note that you can reposition this message box (officially known as a *comment box*) so that it's close to the cell, but doesn't get in the way of selecting an entry, simply by dragging it with the mouse pointer.

Figure 1-13 demonstrates what happens if you try to input an entry that isn't on the drop-down list. For this figure, I deliberately disregarded the input instructions and typed *Chicago* as the location. As soon as I clicked the Enter button on the Formula bar, the custom alert dialog box (which I named *Entry Not on the List!*) appears. I created this alert dialog box by using the options located on the Error Alert tab of the Data Validation dialog box.

To find cells to which Data Validation has been applied, open the Go To dialog box (Ctrl+G or F5), and then click the Special button and click the Data Validation option button in the Go To Special dialog box. Click the Same option button under Data Validation to have Excel go to the next cell that uses the same Data Validation settings as the active cell. Leave the All option button under Data Validation selected to go to the next cell that uses any kind of Data Validation setting.

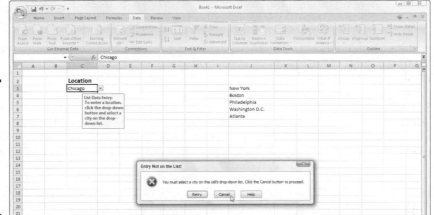

Figure 1-13:
Getting an error message after trying to input a city that's not on the list.

To get rid of Data Validation settings assigned to a particular cell or cell range, select the cell or range, then open the Data Validation dialog box (Alt+AVV), and then click the Clear All button before you click OK.

Although Data Validation is most often used to restrict new data entries in a spreadsheet, you can also use it to quickly identify values that are outside desired parameters in ranges of existing numeric data entries — see Book II, Chapter 3 for details.

Saving the Data

One of the most important tasks you ever perform when building your spreadsheet is *saving your work!* Excel offers three different ways to invoke the Save command:

✦ Click the Save button on the Quick Access toolbar (the one with the disk icon).

✦ Press Ctrl+S or F12.

✦ Click Office Button | Save.

To encourage frequent saving on your part, Excel provides you with a Save button on the Quick Access toolbar (the one with the picture of a floppy disk, the very first on the toolbar). You don't even have to take the time and trouble to choose the Save command from the File pull-down menu (opened by clicking the Office Button) or even press Ctrl+S; you can simply click this tool whenever you want to save new work on disk.

When you click the Save button, press Ctrl+S, or click Office Button | Save for the first time, Excel displays the Save As dialog box. Use this dialog box to replace the temporary document name (Book1, Book2, and so forth) with a more descriptive filename in the File Name text box, to select a new file format in the Save As Type drop-down list box, and to select a new drive and folder before you save the workbook as a disk file.

When you finish making changes in the Save As dialog box, click the Save button or press Enter to have Excel 2007 save your work. When Excel saves your workbook file, the program saves all the information in every worksheet in your workbook (including the last position of the cell cursor) in the designated folder and drive.

You don't have to fool with the Save As dialog box again unless you want to rename the workbook or save a copy of it in a different folder. If you want to do either of these things, you must click Office Button | Save As or press Alt+FA to choose the Save As command rather than click the Save button on the Quick Access toolbar or press Ctrl+S.

The Save As dialog box in Windows Vista

Figure 1-14 shows you the Save As dialog box as it appears in Excel 2007 when running the program under Windows Vista. Here, you can replace the temporary filename (Book1, Book2, and so on) with a more descriptive name by clicking the File Name text box and typing in the new name (up to 255 characters total including spaces).

Figure 1-14:
The Save As dialog box in Windows Vista enables you to select the filename and folder for the new workbook file as well as add tags to it.

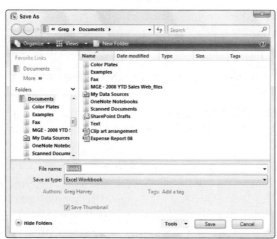

To select a new folder in which to save the new workbook file, follow these steps:

1. **Click the Browse Folders button (with the triangle pointing downward) to expand the Save As dialog box.**

When you expand the Save As dialog box, the dialog box displays the Navigation pane. You can select folders listed in the Favorite Links or Folders section.

2. **In the Navigation pane, click the name of the Favorites link containing the folder in which you want to save the file or click the Folders button (with the upward-pointing triangle) and then click the name of the folder.**

3. **(Optional) If you want to save the workbook file inside a new sub-folder within the folder currently open in the Save As dialog box, click the New Folder button on the toolbar and then replace the suggested New Folder name by typing the actual name of the folder and pressing Enter.**

4. **Click the Save button to save the file in the selected folder.**

Book II
Chapter 1

Building
Worksheets

When the Save As dialog box is expanded, you can add a title, subject, and tags to the new workbook file by clicking the Add a Title, Specify the Subject, or Add a Tag link. You can then use any or all of these pieces of information you add to the file when later searching for the workbook.

The Save As submenu options

When you click the Office Button and then highlight Save As option (rather than clicking it) or press Alt+FF, Excel opens a submenu containing the following save options:

✦ **Excel Workbook:** Click this option to save the workbook in the default .xlsx file format.

✦ **Excel Macro-Enabled Workbook:** Click this option to save the workbook in the default .xlsm file format with all macros (see Chapter 12) it contains enabled.

✦ **Excel Binary Workbook:** Click this option to save the workbook in the binary file format optimized that enables faster loading of really large workbooks with tons of data.

✦ **Excel 97-2003 Workbook:** Click this option to save the workbook in the .xls file format used by earlier versions of Excel 97 through Excel 2003 — note that an alert dialog box appears if Excel finds any features used in the workbook that aren't supported in this file format.

✦ **Other Formats:** Click this option to open the Save As dialog box where you can select other file formats such as Excel templates and add-ins by selecting its option on the Save as Type drop-down list before clicking the Save button.

The Save As dialog box in Windows XP

Figure 1-15 shows you the Save As dialog box as it appears in Excel 2007 when running the program under Windows XP.

Figure 1-15: The Save As dialog box in Windows XP makes it easy to select the filename and folder location for your new workbook file.

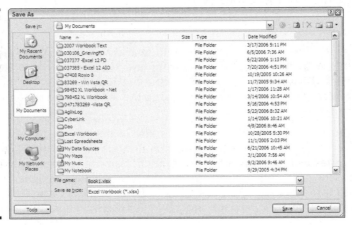

The Windows XP version of the Save As dialog box contains a bunch of large buttons that appear on the left side of the dialog box: My Recent Documents, Desktop, My Documents, My Computer, and My Network Places. Use these buttons to select the following folders in which to save your new workbook file:

✦ Click the My Recent Documents button to save your workbook in the Recent folder. The Recent folder resides in this hierarchy: Windows folder (on your hard drive)\Application Data folder\Microsoft folder\ Office folder\Recent folder.

✦ Click the Desktop button to save your workbook on your computer's desktop.

✦ Click the My Documents button to save your workbook in the My Documents folder.

✦ Click the My Computer button to save your workbook on one of the disks on your computer or in your own or a shared documents folder on your hard drive.

✦ Click the My Network Places button to save your workbook in one of the folders on your company's network.

To save your workbook in a new subfolder within the folder open in the Save As dialog box, click the Create New Folder button on the toolbar (or press Alt+4) and then type the name for the folder in the New Folder dialog box before you click OK.

Changing the default file location

Whenever you open the Save As dialog box to save a new workbook file, Excel 2007 automatically selects the folder listed in the Default File Location text box on the Save tab of the Excel Options dialog box (Office Button | Excel Options | Save or Alt+FIS).

When you first start using Excel, the default folder is either the My Documents (Windows XP) or the Documents folder (Windows Vista) under your user name on your hard drive. So, for example, the directory path of the default folder where Excel 2007 automatically saves new workbook files on my computer running Windows XP is

```
C:\Documents and Settings\Greg\My Documents
```

However, the directory path of the default folder where Excel 2007 automatically saves new workbook files on my other computer running Windows Vista is

```
C:\Users\Greg\Documents
```

The very generic My Documents or Documents folder may not be the place on your hard drive where you want all the new workbooks you create automatically saved. To change the default file location to another folder on your computer, follow these steps:

1. **Click Office Button | Excel Options | Save or press Alt+FIS to open the Save tab of the Excel Options dialog box.**

 The Default File Location text box displays the directory path to the current default folder.

2. **Click the Default File Location text box to select the current directory path.**

 To edit part of the path (such as the My Documents or Documents folder name after your user name), click the mouse pointer at that place in the path to set the Insertion point.

3. **Edit the existing path or replace it with the path to another existing folder in which you want all future workbooks to automatically be saved.**

4. **Click OK to close the Excel Options dialog box.**

**Book II
Chapter 1**

**Building
Worksheets**

Saving a new workbook in the old file format

Excel 2007 automatically saves each new workbook file in the new XML-based file format (see the Appendix for details) which carries the filename extension .xlsx. The problem with this XML file format is that it's not one that earlier versions of Excel can open. This means that if everybody who needs to work with the workbook you've just created hasn't yet upgraded to Excel 2007, you need to save the new workbook in the earlier file format used in versions 97 through 2003 with the old .xls filename extension.

To save a new workbook in the old binary Excel file format for back compatibility, be sure to click the Save as Type drop-down button and then click Excel 97-2003 Workbook on the drop-down menu.

Excel automatically displays the Excel Compatibility Checker dialog box whenever you try to save a workbook file containing Excel 2007 features that aren't supported in earlier versions of the program from Excel 97 through 2003. This dialog box lists each incompatible feature in the workbook and gives you details on what will happen to the feature if you go ahead and save the workbook file in the older file format. To ignore these warnings and go ahead and save your workbook in the 97-2003 binary format, click the Continue button in the Excel Compatibility Checker dialog box.

If you still want to have access to all the features in the Excel 2007 workbook but you still need to create a backwardly compatible version of the workbook file (even if it has less fidelity), first save the workbook in the XML file format with the .xlsx file extension. Then, save a copy in old 97-2003 binary file format with the .xls file extension by opening the Save As dialog box (Office Button | Save As or Alt+FA) and then selecting Excel 97-2003 on the Save as Type drop-down list before clicking the Save button.

Keep in mind that filename extensions such as .xlsx and .xls do not appear as part of the filename (even though they are appended) in the File Name text box in the Save As dialog box unless you've removed the check mark from the Hide Extensions for Known File Types check box found on the View tab of the Folder Options dialog box (Tools⇨Options) in any Windows Explorer window such as My Documents in Windows XP or Documents in Windows Vista.

Document Recovery to the Rescue

Excel 2007 offers a document recovery feature that can help you in the event of a computer crash because of a power failure or some sort of operating system freeze or shutdown. The AutoRecover feature saves your workbooks at regular intervals. In the event of a computer crash, Excel displays a Document Recovery Task pane the next time you start Excel after rebooting the computer.

When you first start using Excel 2007, the AutoRecover feature is set to automatically save changes to your workbook (provided that the file has already been saved) every ten minutes. You can shorten or lengthen this interval as you see fit. Click Office Button | Excel Options | Save or press Alt+FIS to open the Excel Options dialog box with the Save tab selected. Use the spinner buttons or enter a new automatic save interval into the text box marked Save AutoRecover Information Every 10 Minutes before clicking OK.

The Document Recovery Task pane shows the available versions of the workbook files that were open at the time of the computer crash. It identifies the original version of the workbook file and when it was saved along with the recovered version of the file and when it was saved. To open the recovered version of a workbook (to see how much of the work it contains that was unsaved at the time of the crash), position the mouse pointer over the AutoRecover version. Then click its drop-down menu button and click Open on its pop-up menu. After you open the recovered version, you can (if you choose) then save its changes by clicking the Save button on the Quick Access toolbar or by clicking Office Button | Save.

You then have these choices:

✦ To save the recovered version of a workbook without bothering to first open it, place your mouse over the recovered version, click its drop-down button, and choose the Save As option on the pop-up menu.

✦ To permanently abandon the recovered version (leaving you with *only* the data in the original version), click the Close button at the bottom of the Document Recovery Task pane. When you click the Close button, an alert dialog box appears, giving you the chance to retain the recovered versions of the file for later viewing.

✦ To retain the files for later viewing, select the Yes (I want to view these files later) option button before clicking OK.

✦ To retain only the original versions of the files shown in the Task pane, select the No (remove these files. I have saved the files I need) option button instead.

The AutoRecover feature only works on Excel workbooks that have been saved at least one time (as explained in the earlier section "Saving the Data"). In other words, if you build a new workbook and don't bother to save and rename it prior to experiencing a computer crash, the AutoRecover feature will not bring back any part of it. For this reason, it's really important that you get into the habit of saving new workbooks with the Save button on the Quick Access toolbar very shortly after beginning to work on a worksheet. Or you can use the trusty keyboard shortcut Ctrl+S.

Chapter 2: Formatting Worksheets

In This Chapter

✔ Selecting cell ranges and adjusting column widths and row heights

✔ Formatting cell ranges as tables

✔ Assigning number formats

✔ Making alignment, font, border, and pattern changes

✔ Using the Format Painter to quickly copy formatting

✔ Formatting cell ranges with Cell Styles

✔ Applying conditional formatting

*F*ormatting — the subject of this chapter — is the process by which you determine the final appearance of the worksheet and the data that it contains. Excel's formatting features give you a great deal of control over the way the data appears in your worksheet.

To all types of cell entries, you can assign a new font, font size, font style (such as bold, italics, underlining, or strikethrough), or color. You can also change the alignment of entries in the cells in a variety of ways, including the horizontal alignment, the vertical alignment, or the orientation; you can also wrap text entries in the cell or center them across the selection. To numerical values, dates, and times, you can assign one of the many built-in number formats or apply a custom format that you design. To the cells that hold your entries, you can apply different kinds of borders, patterns, and colors. And to the worksheet grid itself, you can assign the most suitable column widths and row heights so that the data in the formatted worksheet are displayed at their best.

Excel 2007 has a new Live Preview feature. And with the Table Styles and Cell Styles galleries and the command buttons in the Font, Alignment, and Number groups on the Home tab of the Ribbon, formatting the spreadsheet is quicker and easier than ever. Thanks to Live Preview, you can see how a new font, font size, or table or cell style would look on your selected data before you actually apply it (saving you tons of time otherwise wasted applying format after format until you finally select the right one). Thanks to having buttons for all the most commonly used formatting commands right up front on the Home tab, you can now readily fine-tune the formatting of cell in a worksheet by making almost all needed changes right from the Ribbon.

Making Cell Selections

Although you have to select the cells of the worksheet that you want to work with before you can accomplish many tasks used in building and editing a typical spreadsheet, perhaps no task requires cell selection like that of formatting. With the exception of the special Format as Table feature (which automatically selects the table to which its multiple formats are applied), selecting the cells whose appearance you want to enhance or modify is always your first step in their formatting.

In Excel, you can select a single cell, a block of cells (known as a *cell range*), or various discontinuous cell ranges (also known as a *nonadjacent selection*). Figure 2-1 shows a nonadjacent selection that consists of four different cell ranges (the smallest range is the single cell I9).

Note that a simple cell selection consisting of a single cell range is denoted in the worksheet both by highlighting the selected cells in a light blue color as well as by extending the border of the cell cursor so that it encompasses all the highlighted cells. In a nonadjacent cell selection, however, all selected cells are highlighted but only the active cell (the one whose address is displayed in the Name Box on the Formula bar) contains the cell cursor (whose borders are quite thin when compared to the regular cell cursor).

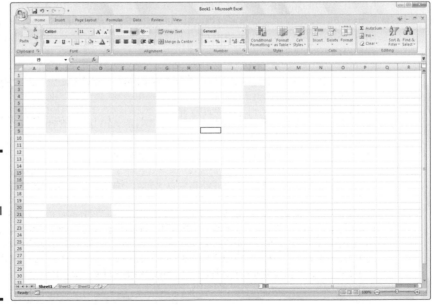

Figure 2-1:
Worksheet with a non-adjacent cell selection made up of several different sized ranges.

A range by any other name

Cell ranges are always noted in formulas by the first and last cell that you select, separated by a colon (:); therefore, if you select cell A1 as the first cell and cell H10 as the last cell, and then use the range in a formula, the cell range appears as A1:H10. This same block of cells can just as well be noted as H10:A1 if you selected cell H10 before cell A1. Likewise, the same range can be equally noted as H1:A10 or A10:H1, depending upon which corner cell you select first and which opposite corner you select last. Keep in mind that despite the various range notations that you can use (A1:H10, H10:A1, H1:A10, and A10:H1), you are working with the same block of cells, the main difference being that each has a different active cell whose address appears in the Name box on the Formula bar (A1, H10, H1, and A10, respectively).

Selecting cells with the mouse

Excel offers several methods for selecting cells with the mouse. With each method, you start by selecting one of the cells that occupies the corner of the range that you want to select. The first corner cell that you click becomes the *active cell* (indicated by its cell reference in the Formula bar), and the cell range that you then select becomes anchored on this cell.

After you select the active cell in the range, drag the pointer to extend the selection until you have highlighted all the cells that you want to include. Here are some tips:

✦ To extend a range in a block that spans several columns, drag left or right from the active cell.

✦ To extend a range in a block that spans several rows, drag up or down from the active cell.

✦ To extend a range in a block that spans several columns and rows, drag diagonally from the active cell in the most logical directions (up and to the right, down and to the right, up and to the left, or down and to the left).

If you ever extend the range too far in one direction, you can always reduce it by dragging in the other direction. If you've already released the mouse button and you find that the range is incorrect, click the active cell again (clicking any cell in the worksheet deselects a selected range and activates the cell that you click). Then select the range of cells again.

TIP

You can always tell which cell is the active cell forming the anchor point of a cell range because it is the only cell within the range that you've selected that isn't highlighted and is the only cell reference listed in the Name box on the Formula bar. As you extend the range by dragging the thick white-cross mouse pointer, Excel indicates the current size of the range in columns and rows in the Name box (as in 5R x 2C when you've highlighted a range of five rows long and two columns wide). However, as soon as you release the mouse button, Excel replaces this row and column notation with the address of the active cell.

You can also use the following shortcuts when selecting cells with the mouse:

✦ To select a single-cell range, click the thick white-cross mouse pointer somewhere inside the cell.

✦ To select all cells in an entire column, position the mouse pointer on the column letter in the column header and then click the mouse button. To select several adjacent columns, drag through their column letters in the column header.

✦ To select all cells in an entire row, position the mouse pointer on the row number in the row header and then click the mouse button. To select several adjacent rows, drag through the row numbers in the row header.

✦ To select all the cells in the worksheet, click the box in the upper-left of the worksheet at the intersection of row and column headers with the triangle in the lower-right corner. (You can also do this from the keyboard by pressing Ctrl+A.)

✦ To select a cell range composed of partial columns and rows without dragging, click the cell where you want to anchor the range, hold down the Shift key, and then click the last cell in the range and release the Shift key (Excel selects all the cells in between the first and the last cell that you click). If the range that you want to mark is a block that spans several columns and rows, the last cell is the one diagonally opposite the active cell. When using this Shift+click technique to mark a range that extends beyond the screen, use the scroll bars to display the last cell in the range (just make sure that you don't release the Shift key until after you've clicked this last cell).

✦ To select a nonadjacent selection comprised of several discontinuous cell ranges, drag through the first cell range, and then hold down the Ctrl key as you drag through the other ranges. After you have marked all the cell ranges to be included in the nonadjacent selection, you can release the Ctrl key.

Selecting cells with the keyboard

Excel also makes it easy for you to select cell ranges with the keyboard by using a technique known as *extending a selection*. To use this technique, you move the cell cursor to the active cell of the range; then press F8 to turn on Extend Selection mode (indicated by Extend Selection on the Status bar) and use the direction keys to move the pointer to the last cell in the range. Excel selects all the cells that the cell cursor moves through until you turn off Extend Selection mode (by pressing F8 again).

You can use the mouse as well as the keyboard to extend a selection when Excel is in Extend Selection mode. All you do is click the active cell, press F8, and then click the last cell to mark the range.

Book II
Chapter 2

You can also select a cell range with the keyboard without turning on Extend Selection mode. Here, you use a variation of the Shift+click method by moving the cell cursor to the active cell in the range, holding down the Shift key, and then using the direction keys to extend the range. After you've highlighted all the cells that you want to include, release the Shift key.

**Formatting
Worksheets**

To mark a nonadjacent selection of cells with the keyboard, you need to combine the use of Extend Selection mode with that of Add to Selection mode. To turn on Add to Selection mode (indicated by Add to Selection on the Status bar), you press Shift+F8. To mark a nonadjacent selection by using Extend Selection and Add to Selection modes, follow these steps:

1. **Move the cell cursor to the first cell of the first range you want to select.**

2. **Press F8 to turn on Extend Selection mode.**

3. **Use the arrow keys to extend the cell range until you've highlighted all its cells.**

4. **Press Shift+F8 to turn off Extend Selection mode and turn on Add to Selection mode instead.**

5. **Move the cell cursor to the first cell of the next cell range you want to add to the selection.**

6. **Press F8 to turn off Add to Selection mode and turn Extend Selection mode back on.**

7. **Use the arrow keys to extend the range until all cells are highlighted.**

8. **Repeat Steps 4 through 7 until you've selected all the ranges that you want included in the nonadjacent selection.**

9. **Press F8 to turn off Extend Selection mode.**

You AutoSelect that range!

Excel's AutoSelect feature provides a particularly efficient way to select all
or part of the cells in a large table of data. AutoSelect automatically extends
a selection in a single direction from the active cell to the first nonblank cell
that Excel encounters in that direction.

You can use the AutoSelect feature with the mouse or keyboard. The general
steps for using AutoSelect to select a table of data with the mouse are as
follows:

1. **Click the first cell to which you want to anchor the range that you are
    about to select.**

    In a typical data table, this cell may be the blank cell at the intersection
    of the row of column headings and the column of row headings.

2. **Position the mouse pointer on the edge of the cell in the direction that
    you want the range extended.**

    To extend the range up to the first blank cell to the right, position the
    pointer on the right edge of the cell. To extend the range left to the first
    blank cell, position the pointer on the left edge of the cell. To extend the
    range down to the first blank cell, position the pointer on the bottom
    edge of the cell. And to extend the range up to the first blank cell, posi-
    tion the pointer on the top edge of the cell.

3. **When the pointer changes shape from a cross to an arrowhead, hold
    down the Shift key and then double-click the mouse.**

    As soon as you double-click the mouse, Excel extends the selection to
    the first occupied cell that is adjacent to a blank cell in the direction of
    the edge that you double-clicked.

To get an idea of how AutoSelect works, consider how you use it to select
the data table (in the cell range A2:J7) shown in Figures 2-2 and 2-3. With the
cell cursor in cell A3 at the intersection of the row with the Date column
headings and the column with the Part row headings, you can use the
AutoSelect feature to select all the cells in the table in two operations:

✦ In the first operation, hold down the Shift key and then double-click the
  bottom edge of cell A2 to highlight the cells down to A7, selecting the
  range A2:A7 (see Figure 2-2).

✦ In the second operation, hold down the Shift key and then double-click
  the right edge of cell range A2:A7 to extend the selection to the last
  column in the table (selecting the entire table with the cell range A2:J7,
  as shown in Figure 2-3).

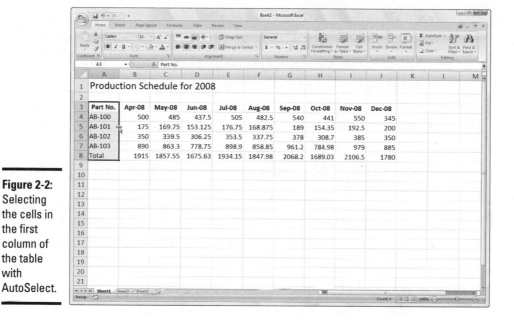

Figure 2-2:
Selecting the cells in the first column of the table with AutoSelect.

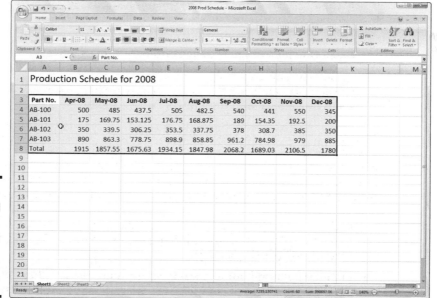

Figure 2-3:
Selecting all the remaining columns of the table with AutoSelect.

If you select the cells in the first row of the table (range A2:J2) in the first operation, you can then extend this range down the remaining rows of the table by double-clicking the bottom edge of one of the selected cells (it doesn't matter which one).

To use the AutoSelect feature with the keyboard, press the End key and one of the four arrow keys as you hold down the Shift key. When you hold down Shift and press End and an arrow key, Excel extends the selection in the direction of the arrow key to the first cell containing a value that is bordered by a blank cell.

In terms of selecting the table of data shown in Figures 2-2 and 2-3, this means that you would have to complete four separate operations to select all of its cells:

1. **With A2 as the active cell, hold down Shift and press End+↓ to select the range A2:A3.**

   Excel stops at A3 because this is the first cell containing a value bordered by a blank cell.

2. **Hold down Shift and press End+↓ again, extending the range down to cell A7.**

   Excel stops at A7 because this is the last occupied cell in that column. At this point, the cell range A2:A7 is selected.

3. **Hold down Shift and then, this time, press End+→.**

   Excel extends the range only to column B (because B2 is the first cell to the right of the active cell that contains a value and is bordered by the blank cell, A2). At this point, the cell range A2:B7 is selected.

4. **Hold down Shift and then press End+→ again.**

   This time, Excel extends the range all the way to column J (because cell J3 contains an entry and is bordered by a blank cell). Now all the cells in the table (the cell range A2:J7) are selected.

Selecting cells with Go To

Although you usually use the Go To feature to move the cell cursor to a new cell in the worksheet, you can also use this feature to select a range of cells. When you click the Go To option on the Find & Select button's drop-down menu on the Home tab of the Ribbon (or press Ctrl+G or F5), Excel displays a Go To dialog box similar to the one shown in Figure 2-4. To move the cell cursor to a particular cell, enter the cell address in the Reference text box and click OK. (Excel automatically lists the addresses of the last four cells or cell ranges that you specified in the Go To list box.)

Figure 2-4:
Selecting
the cell
range with
the Go To
dialog box.

Instead of just moving to a new section of the worksheet with the Go To feature, you can select a range of cells by taking these steps:

1. **Select the first cell of the range.**

   This becomes the active cell to which the cell range is anchored.

2. **On the Ribbon, click the Find & Select command button in the Editing group on the Home tab and then click Go To on its drop-down menu bar or press Ctrl+G or F5.**

   The Go To dialog box opens.

3. **Type the cell address of the last cell in the range in the Reference text box.**

   If this address is already listed in the Go To list box, you can enter this address in the text box by clicking it in the list box.

4. **Hold down the Shift key as you click OK or press Enter to close the Go To dialog box.**

   By holding down Shift as you click OK or press Enter, you select the range between the active cell and the cell whose address you specified in the Reference text box.

Instead of selecting the anchor cell and then specifying the last cell of a range in the Reference text box of the Go To dialog box, you can also select a range simply by typing in the address of the cell range in the Reference text box. Remember that when you type a range address, you enter the cell reference of the first (active) cell and the last cell in the range separated by a colon. For example, to select the cell range that extends from cell B2 to G10 in the worksheet, you would type the range address **b2:g10** in the Reference text box before clicking OK or pressing Enter.

Name that range!

One of the easiest ways to select a range of data is to assign a name to it and then choose that name on the pop-up menu attached to the Name box on the Formula bar or in the Go To list box in the Go To dialog box. Of course, you reserve this technique for cell ranges that you work with on a somewhat regular basis; for example, ranges with data that you print regularly, consult often, or have to refer to in formula calculations. It's probably not worth your while to name a range of data that doesn't carry any special importance in the spreadsheet.

To name a cell range, follow three simple steps:

1. **Select all the cells in the range that you intend to name.**

You can use any of the cell selection techniques that you prefer. When selecting the cells for the named range, be sure to include all the cells that you want selected each time you select its range name.

2. **Click the Name box on the Formula bar.**

Excel automatically highlights the address of the active cell in the selected range.

3. **Type the range name in the Name box and then press Enter.**

As soon as you start typing, Excel replaces the address of the active cell with the range name that you're assigning. As soon as you press the Enter key, the name appears in the Name box instead of the cell address of the active cell in the range.

When naming a cell range, however, you *must* observe the following naming conventions:

✦ Begin the range name with a letter of the alphabet rather than a number or punctuation mark.

✦ Don't use spaces in the range name; instead, use an underscore between words in a range name (as in Qtr_1).

✦ Make sure that the range name doesn't duplicate any cell reference in the worksheet by using either the standard A1 or R1C1 notation system.

✦ Make sure that the range name is unique in the worksheet.

After you've assigned a name to a cell range, you can select all its cells simply by clicking the name on the pop-up menu attached to the Name box on the Formula bar. The beauty of this method is that you can use it from anywhere in the same sheet or a different worksheet in the workbook because as soon as you click its name on the Name box pop-up menu, Excel takes you directly to the range, while at the same time automatically selecting all its cells.

Range names are also very useful when building formulas in your spreadsheet. For more on creating and using range names, see Book III, Chapter 1.

Adjusting Columns and Rows

Along with knowing how to select cells for formatting, you really also have to know how to adjust the width of your columns and the heights of your rows. Why? Because often in the course of assigning different formatting to certain cell ranges (such as new font and font size in boldface type), you may find that data entries that previously fit within the original widths of their column no longer do and that the rows that they occupy seem to have changed height all on their own.

In a blank worksheet, all the columns and rows are the same standard width and height. All columns start out 8.43 characters wide (or 64 pixels) and all rows start out 15 points high (or 20 pixels). As you build your spreadsheet, you end up with all sorts of data entries that can't fit within these default settings. This is especially true as you start adding formatting to their cells to enhance and clarify their contents.

Most of the time, you don't need to be concerned with the heights of the rows in your worksheet because Excel automatically adjusts them up or down to accommodate the largest font size used in a cell in the row and the number of text lines (in some cells, you may wrap their text on several lines). Instead, you'll spend a lot more time adjusting the column widths to suit the entries for the formatting that you assign to them.

Remember what happens when you put a text entry in a cell whose current width isn't long enough to accommodate all its characters. If the cells in columns to the right are empty, Excel lets the display of the extra characters spill over into the empty cells. If these cells are already occupied, however, Excel cuts off the display of the extra characters until you widen the column sufficiently. Likewise, remember that if you add formatting to a number so that its value and formatting can't both be displayed in the cell, those nasty overflow indicators appear in the cell as a string of pound signs (#####) until you widen the column adequately.

You AutoFit the column to its contents

The easiest way to adjust the width of a column to suit its longest entry is to use the AutoFit feature. AutoFit determines the best fit for the column or columns selected at that time, given their longest entries.

✦ **To use AutoFit on a single column:** Position the mouse pointer on the right edge of that column in the column header and then, when the pointer changes to a double-headed arrow, double-click the mouse.

✦ **To use AutoFit on multiple columns at one time:** Select the columns by dragging through them in the column header or by Ctrl+clicking the column letters, and then double-click the right edge of one of the selected columns when the pointer changes to a double-headed arrow.

These AutoFit techniques work well for adjusting all columns except for those that contain really long headings (such as the spreadsheet title that often spills over several blank columns in row 1), in which case, AutoFit makes the columns far too wide for the bulk of the cell entries.

For those situations, use the AutoFit Selection command, which adjusts the column width to suit only the entries in the cells of the column that you have selected. This way, you can select all the cells except for any really long ones in the column that purposely spill over to empty cells on the right, and then have Excel adjust the width to suit. After you've selected the cells in the column that you want the new width to fit, click the Format button in the Cells group on the Home tab and then click AutoFit Selection on the drop-down menu.

Adjusting columns the old fashioned way

AutoFit is nothing if not quick and easy. If you need more precision in adjusting your column widths, you have to do this manually either by dragging its border with the mouse or by entering new values in the Column Width dialog box.

✦ **To manually adjust a column width with the mouse:** Drag the right edge of that column onto the Column header to the left (to narrow) or to the right (to widen) as required. As you drag the column border, a ScreenTip appears above the mouse pointer indicating the current width in both characters and pixels. When you have the column adjusted to the desired width, release the mouse button to set it.

✦ **To adjust a column width in the Column Width dialog box:** Position the cell cursor in any one of the cells in the column that you want to adjust, click the Format button in the Cells group on the Home tab of the

Ribbon and then click Column Width on the drop-down list to open the Column Width dialog box, shown in Figure 2-5. Here, you enter the new width (in the number of characters between 0 and 255) in the Column Width text box before clicking OK.

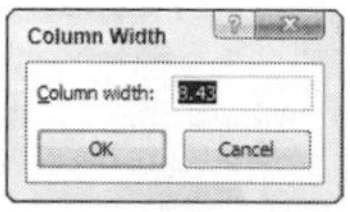

Figure 2-5:
Adjusting the column width in the Column Width dialog box.

You can apply a new column width that you set in the Column Width dialog box to more than a single column by selecting the columns (either by dragging through their letters on the Column header or holding down Ctrl as you click them) before you open the Column Width dialog box.

Setting a new standard width

You can use the Default Standard Width command to set all the columns in a worksheet to a new uniform width (other than the default 8.43 characters). To do so, simply click the Format button in the Cells group on the Home tab of the Ribbon and then click Standard Width on the drop-down menu. Doing this opens the Standard Width dialog box where you can replace the default 8.43 in the Standard Column Width text box with your new width (in characters), and then click OK or press Enter.

Note that when you set a new standard width for the columns of your worksheet, this new width doesn't affect any columns whose width you've previously adjusted either with AutoFit or in the Column Width dialog box.

Hiding out a column or two

You can use the Hide command to temporarily remove columns of data from the worksheet display. When you hide a column, you're essentially setting the column width to 0 (and thus, making it so narrow that for all intents and purposes, the sucker's gone). Hiding columns enables you to remove the display of sensitive or supporting data that needs to be in the spreadsheet but may not be appropriate in printouts that you distribute (keeping in mind that only columns and rows that are displayed in the worksheet get printed).

To hide a column, put the cell cursor in a cell in that column, click the Format button in the Cells group on the Home tab, and then click Hide & Unhide on the drop-down menu and Hide Columns on the continuation menu (or you can just press Alt+HOHC).

To hide more than one column at a time, select the columns either by dragging through their letters on the Column header or by holding down Ctrl as you click them before you choose this command sequence.

Excel lets you know that certain columns are missing from the worksheet by removing their column letters from the Column header so that if, for example, you hide columns D and E in the worksheet, column C is followed by column F on the Column header.

To restore hidden columns to view, select the visible columns on either side of the hidden one(s) — indicated by the missing letter(s) on the column headings — and then click the Format button in the Cells group on the Home tab before you click Hide & Unhide on the drop-down menu and Unhide Columns on the continuation menu (or you can just press Alt+HOHL).

Because Excel also automatically selects all the redisplayed columns, you need to deselect the selected columns before you select any more formatting or editing commands that will affect all their cells. You can do this by clicking a single cell anywhere in the worksheet or by dragging through a particular cell range that you want to work with.

Keep in mind that when you hide a column, the data in the cells in all its rows (1 through 1,048,576) are hidden (not just the ones you can see on your computer screen). This means that if you have some data in rows of a column that need printing and some in other rows of that same column that need concealing, you can't use the Hide command to remove their display until you've moved the cells with the data to be printed into a different column (see Book II, Chapter 5 for details).

Rambling rows

The controls for adjusting the height of the rows in your worksheet parallel those that you use to adjust its columns. The big difference is that Excel always applies AutoFit to the height of each row so that even though you find an AutoFit Row Height menu item under Cell size on the Format button's drop-down menu, you won't find much use for it (personally, I've never had any reason to use it).

Instead, you'll probably end up manually adjusting the heights of rows with the mouse or by entering new height values in the Row Height dialog box (opened by clicking Row Height on the Format button's drop-down menu on the Home tab) and occasionally hiding rows with sensitive or potentially confusing data. Follow these instructions for each type of action:

✦ **To adjust the height of a row with the mouse:** Position the mouse pointer on the lower edge of the row's border in the Row header and then drag up or down when the mouse pointer changes to a double-headed, vertical arrow. As you drag, a ScreenTip appears to the side of the pointer, keeping you informed of the height in characters and also pixels (remember that 15 points or 20 pixels is the default height of all rows in a new worksheet).

✦ **To change the height of a row in the Row Height dialog box:** Click Row Height on the Format button's drop-down menu in the Cells group of the Ribbon's Home tab and then enter the value for the new row height in the Row Height text box before you click OK or press Enter.

✦ **To hide a row:** Position the cell cursor in any one of the cells in that row and then click the Format button in the Cells group on the Home tab before you click Hide & Unhide on the drop-down menu and Hide Rows on the continuation menu (or press Alt+HOHR). To then restore the rows that you currently have hidden in the worksheet, click the Format button and then click Hide & Unhide | Unhide Rows on the drop-down and continuation menus (or just press Alt+HOHO) instead.

As with adjusting columns, you can change the height of more than one row and hide multiple rows at the same time by selecting the rows before you drag one of their lower borders, open the Row Height dialog box, or click Format | Hide & Unhide | Hide Rows on the Home tab, or press Alt+HOHR.

Formatting Ranges as Tables with Table Styles

Excel's new Format as Table feature enables you to both define an entire range of data as a table and format all its data all in one operation. After you define a cell range as a table, you can completely modify its formatting simply by clicking a new style thumbnail in the Table Styles gallery. Excel also automatically extends this table definition — and consequently its table formatting — to all the new rows you insert within the table and add at the bottom as well as any new columns you insert within the table or add to either the table's left or right end.

The Format as Table feature is so automatic that to use it, you only need to position the cell cursor somewhere within the table of data prior to clicking the Format as Table command button on the Ribbon's Home tab. Clicking the Format as Table command button opens its rather extensive Table Styles gallery with the formatting thumbnails divided into three sections — Light, Medium, and Dark — each of which describes the intensity of the colors used by its various formats (see Color Plate 11).

As soon as you click one of the table formatting thumbnails in this Table Styles gallery, Excel makes its best guess as to the cell range of the data table to apply it to (indicated by the marquee around its perimeter), and the Format As Table dialog box similar to the one shown in Figure 2-6 appears.

Figure 2-6:
Selecting a format from the Table gallery and indicating its range in the Format As Table dialog box.

This dialog box contains a Where Is the Data for Your Table text box that shows the address of the cell range currently selected by the marquee and a My Table Has Headers check box (selected by default).

If Excel does not correctly guess the range of the data table you want to format, drag through the cell range to adjust the marquee and the range address in the Where Is the Data for Your Table text box. If your data table doesn't use column headers, click the My Table Has Headers check box before you click the OK button — Excel will then add its own column headings (Column1, Column2, Column3, and so forth) as the top row of the new table.

Keep in mind that the table formats in the Table Styles gallery are not available if you select multiple nonadjacent cells before you click the Format as Table command button on the Home tab. You can only convert one range of cell data into a table at a time.

After you click the OK button in the Format As Table dialog box, Excel applies the format of the thumbnail you clicked in the gallery to the data table, and the command buttons on the Design tab of the Table Tools contextual tab appear on the Ribbon.

Figure 2-7 shows the Design tab and its command buttons after defining the cell range A3:J8 (with the scheduled production of various parts for 2008 as a table) by applying Table Style Light 1 to this cell range.

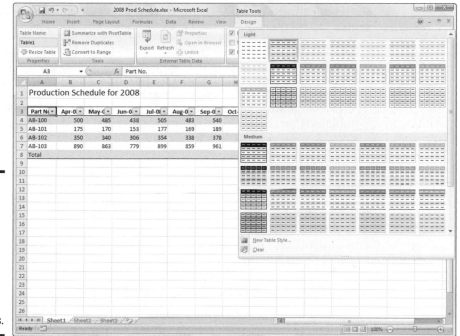

Figure 2-7:
After you select an initial table format, the Design tab under the Table Tools contextual tab appears.

As you can see in Figure 2-7, when Excel defines a range as a table, it automatically adds AutoFilter drop-down buttons to each of the column headings. To hide these AutoFilter buttons, click the Filter button on the Data tab or press Alt+AFF (you can always redisplay them by clicking the Filter button on the Data tab or by pressing Alt+AFF a second time).

The Design contextual tab enables you to use the Live Preview feature to see how your table data would appear in other table styles. Simply position the mouse pointer over any of the format thumbnails in the Table Style group to see the data in your table appear in that table format. Click the More button (the one with the horizontal bar above the downward pointing triangle) to redisplay the Table gallery and then mouse over the thumbnails in the Light, Medium, and Dark sections to have Live Preview apply them to the table.

Click the button with the triangle pointing downward to scroll up new rows of table formats in the Table Styles group and the button with the triangle pointing upward to scroll down rows without opening the Table gallery and possibly obscuring the actual data table in the Worksheet area.

In addition to enabling you to select a new format from the Table gallery in the Table Styles group, the Design tab contains a Table Styles Options group you can use to further customize the look of the selected format. The Table Style Options group contains the following check boxes:

✦ **Header Row:** Add Filter buttons to each of the column headings in the first row of the table.

✦ **Total Row:** Add a Total row to the bottom of the table that displays the sum of the last column of the table (assuming that it contains values). To apply another Statistical function to the values in a particular column, click the cell in that column's Total row to display a drop-down list button, and then the function to use the drop-down menu of functions, Average, Count, Count Numbers, Max, Min, Sum, StdDev (Standard Deviation), or Var (Variation), that appears when you click its drop-down button.

✦ **First Column:** Display the row headings in the first row of the table in bold.

✦ **Last Column:** Display the row headings in the last row of the table in bold.

✦ **Banded Rows:** Apply shading to every other row in the table.

✦ **Banded Columns:** Apply shading to every other column in the table.

Keep in mind that whenever you assign a format in the Table Styles gallery to one of the data tables in your workbook, Excel automatically assigns that table a generic range name (Table1, Table2, and so on). You can use the Table Name text box in the Properties group on the Design tab to rename the data table by giving it a more descriptive range name.

When you finish selecting and/or customizing the formatting of your data table, click a cell outside of the table to remove the Design contextual tab from the Ribbon. If you later decide that you want to further experiment with the table's formatting, click any of the table's cells to redisplay the Design contextual tab at the end of the Ribbon.

Formatting Cells from the Home Tab

Some spreadsheet tables require a lighter touch than the Format as Table command button offers. For example, you may have a data table where the only emphasis you want to add is to make the column headings bold at the top of the table and to underline the row of totals at the bottom (done by drawing a borderline along the bottom of the cells).

The formatting buttons that appear in the Font, Alignment, and Number groups on the Home tab enable you to accomplish just this kind of targeted cell formatting. Figure 2-8 shows you the Home tab with all the buttons in these three groups identified. See Table 2-1 for a complete rundown on the use of each of these formatting buttons.

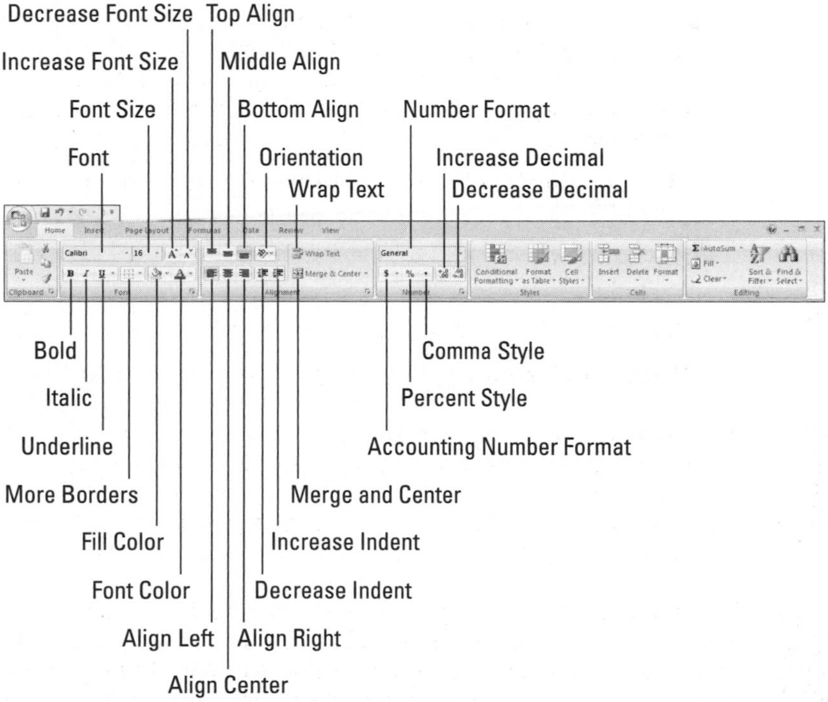

Book II
Chapter 2

Formatting
Worksheets

Figure 2-8:
The Font, Alignment, and Number groups on the Home tab contain almost all the formatting tools you ever need.

Table 2-1   **The Formatting Command Buttons in the Font, Alignment, and Number Groups on the Home Tab**

Group	Button Name	Function	Hot Keys
Font			
	Font	Displays a Font drop-down menu from which you can select a new font for your cell selection	Alt+HFF
	Font Size	Displays a Font Size drop-down menu from which you can select a new font size for your cell selection — click the Font Size text box and enter the desired point size if it doesn't appear on the drop-down menu	Alt+HFS
	Increase Font Size	Increases the size of the font in the cell selection by one point	Alt+HFG
	Decrease Font Size	Decreases the size of the font in the cell selection by one point	Alt+HFK
	Bold	Applies boldface to the entries in the cell selection	Alt+H1
	Italic	Italicizes the entries in the cell selection	Alt+H2
	Underline	Underlines the entries in the cell selection	Alt+H3U
	Borders	Displays a Borders drop-down menu from which you can select a border style for the cell selection	Alt+HB
	Fill Color	Displays a Color drop-down palette from which you can select a new background color for the cell selection	Alt+HH
	Font Color	Displays a Color drop-down palette from which you can select a new font color for the cell selection	Alt+HFC
Alignment			
	Align Left	Aligns all the entries in the cell selection with the left edge of their cells	Alt+HAL
	Center	Centers all the entries in the cell selection within their cells	Alt+HAC
	Align Right	Aligns all the entries in the cell selection with the right edge of their cells	Alt+HAR
	Decrease Indent	Decreases the margin between entries in the cell selection and their left cell borders by one tab stop	Alt+H5
	Increase Indent	Increases the margin between the entries in the cell selection and their left cell borders by one tab stop	Alt+H6
	Top Align	Aligns the entries in the cell selection with the top border of their cells	Alt+HAT
	Middle Align	Vertically centers the entries in the cell selection between the top and bottom borders of their cells	Alt+HAM

Group	Button Name	Function	Hot Keys
	Bottom Align	Aligns the entries in the cell selection with the bottom border of their cells	Alt+HAB
	Orientation	Displays a drop-down menu with options for changing the angle and direction of the entries inthe cell selection	Alt+HFQ
	Wrap Text	Wraps the entries in the cell selection that spill over their right borders onto multiple lines within the current column width	Alt+HW
	Merge and Center	Merges the cell selection into a single cell and then centers the entry in the first cell between its new left and right borders — click the Merge and Center drop-down button to display a menu of options that enable you to merge the cell selection into a single cell without centering the entries as well as to split up a merged cell back into its original individual cells	Alt+HMC
Numbers			
	Number Format	Displays the number format applied to the active cell in the cell selection — click its drop-down button to display a menu showing the active cell in the cell selection formatted with all of Excel's major Number formats	Alt+HN
	Accounting Number Format	Formats the cell selection using Accounting Number format, which adds a dollar sign, uses commas to separate thousands, displays two decimal places, and encloses negative values in a closed pair of parentheses — click the Accounting Number Format drop-down button to display a menu of other major currency number formats from which you can choose	Alt+HAN
	Percent Style	Formats the cell selection using the Percent Style Number format, which multiplies the values by 100 and adds a percent sign with no decimal places	Alt+HP
	Comma Style	Formats the cell selection with the Comma Style Number format, which uses commas to separate thousands, displays two decimal places, and encloses negative values in a closed pair of parentheses	Alt+HK
	Increase Decimal	Adds a decimal place to the values in the cell selection	Alt+H0
	Decrease Decimal	Removes a decimal place from the values in the cell selection	Alt+H9

Book II Chapter 2

Formatting Worksheets

Don't forget about the shortcut keys: Ctrl+B for toggling on and off bold in the cell selection, Ctrl+I for toggling on and off italics, and Ctrl+U for toggling on and off underlining for quickly adding or removing these attributes from the entries in the cell selection.

Formatting the Cell Selection with the Mini Toolbar

Excel 2007 makes it easy to apply common formatting changes to a cell selection right within the Worksheet area thanks to its new mini toolbar feature — nicknamed the mini-bar, which makes me thirsty just thinking about it!

To display the mini-bar, select the cells that need formatting and then right-click somewhere in the cell selection. The mini-bar then appears immediately above the cell selection's shortcut menu (see Figure 2-9).

As you can see in this figure, the mini-bar contains most of the buttons from the Font group of the Home tab (with the exception of the Underline button). It also contains the Center and Merge and Center buttons from the Alignment group (see "Altering the alignment" later in this chapter) and the Accounting Number Format, Percent Style, Comma Style, Increase Decimal, and Decrease Decimal buttons from the Number group. Simply click these buttons to apply their formatting to the current cell selection.

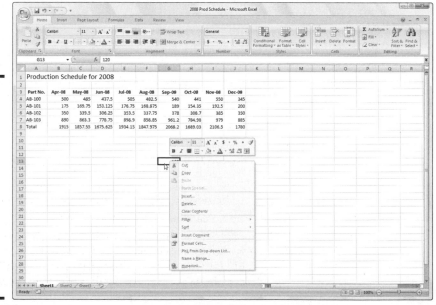

Figure 2-9:
Use the buttons on the mini toolbar to apply common formatting changes to the cell selection within the Worksheet area.

In addition, the mini-bar contains the Format Painter button from the Clipboard group of the Home tab, which you can use to copy the formatting in the active cell to a cell selection you make (see "Hiring Out the Format Painter" later in this chapter for details).

Using the Format Cells Dialog Box

Although the command buttons in the Font, Alignment, and Number groups on the Home tab give you immediate access to the most commonly used formatting commands, they do not represent all of Excel's formatting commands by any stretch of the imagination.

Book II
Chapter 2

To have access to all the formatting commands, you need to open the Format Cells dialog box either by clicking the Dialog Box Launcher in the Number group on the Ribbon's Home tab, clicking the More Number Formats option at the bottom of the Number Format button's drop-down menu in the same Number group, or by simply pressing Ctrl+1.

The Format Cells dialog box contains six tabs: Number, Alignment, Font, Border, Fill, and Protection. (In this chapter, I show you how to use them all except the Protection tab; for information on that tab, see Book IV, Chapter 1.)

*Formatting
Worksheets*

The keystroke shortcut that opens the Format Cells dialog box — Ctrl+1 — is one worth knowing. Just keep in mind that the keyboard shortcut is pressing the Ctrl key plus the *number* 1 key, and not the *function key* F1.

Assigning number formats

When you enter numbers in a cell or a formula that returns a number, Excel automatically applies the General number format to your entry. The General format displays numeric entries more or less as you enter them. However, the General format does make the following changes to your numeric entries:

+ Drops any trailing zeros from decimal fractions so that **4.5** appears when you enter **4.500** in a cell.

+ Drops any leading zeros in whole numbers so that **4567** appears when you enter **04567** in a cell.

+ Inserts a zero before the decimal point in any decimal fraction without a whole number so that **0.123** appears when you enter **.123** in a cell.

+ Truncates decimal places in a number to display the whole numbers in a cell when the number contains too many digits to be displayed in the current column width. It also converts the number to scientific notation when the column width is too narrow to display all integers in the whole number.

Remember that you can always override the General number format when you enter a number by entering the characters used in recognized number formats. For example, to enter the value 2500 and assign it the Currency number format that displays two decimal places, you enter **$2,500.00** in the cell.

Note that although you can override the General number format and assign one of the others to any numeric value that you enter into a cell, you can't do this when you enter a formula into a cell. To apply another format to a calculated result, select its cell and then assign the Currency number format that displays two decimal places by clicking Accounting Number Format in the Number group on the Ribbon's Home tab or by selecting Currency or Accounting on the Number tab of the Format Cells dialog box (Ctrl+1).

Using one of the predefined number formats

Any time you apply a number format to a cell selection (even if you do so with a command button in the Number group on the Ribbon's Home tab instead of selecting the format from the Number tab of the Format Cells dialog box), you're telling Excel to apply a particular group of format codes to those cells.

Figure 2-10 shows the Number tab of the Format Cells dialog box as it appears when you first open the dialog box. As you can see in this figure, when the Number tab is initially selected, the General category of number formats is highlighted in the Category list box with the words "General format cells have no specific number format" showing in the area to the right. Directly above this cryptic message (which is Excel-speak for "We don't care what you've put in your cell; we're not changing it!") is the Sample area. This area shows how the number in the active cell appears in whatever format you choose (this is blank if the active cell is blank or if it contains text instead of a number).

What you see is *not* always what you get

The number format that you assign to cells with numeric entries in the worksheet affects *only* the way they are displayed in their cells, and not their underlying values. For example, if a formula returns the value **3.456789** in a cell and you apply a number format that displays only two decimal places, Excel will display the value **3.46** in the cell. If you then refer to the cell in a formula that multiplies its value by **2**, Excel returns the result **6.913578** instead of the result **6.92** which would be the result if Excel was actually multiplying **3.46** by **2**. If you want to modify the underlying value in a cell, you use the ROUND function (see Book III, Chapter 5 for details).

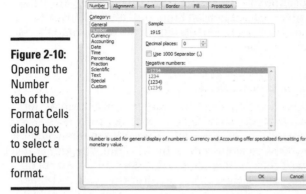

Figure 2-10:
Opening the
Number
tab of the
Format Cells
dialog box
to select a
number
format.

When you click the Number, Currency, Accounting, or Percentage category
in the Category list box, more options appear in the area just to the right of
the Category list box in the form of different check boxes, list boxes, and
spinner buttons. (Figure 2-11 shows the Format Cells dialog box when
Currency is selected in the Category list box.) These options determine how
you want items such as decimal places, dollar signs, comma separators, and
negative numbers to be used in the format category that you've chosen.

When you choose the Date, Time, Fraction, Special, or Custom category, a
large Type list box appears that contains handfuls of predefined category
types, which you can apply to your value to change its appearance. Just like
when you're selecting different formatting categories, the Sample area of the
Format Cells dialog box shows you how the various category *types* will affect
your selection.

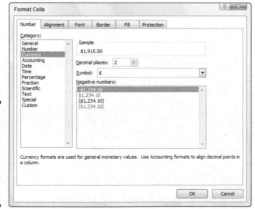

Figure 2-11:
Selecting
Currency in
the Category
list box of the
Number tab.

I should note here that Excel always tries to choose an appropriate format category in the Category list box based on the way you entered your value in the selected cell. If you enter 3:00 in a cell and then open the Number tab of the Format Cells dialog box (Ctrl+1), Excel highlights the h:mm time format in the Custom category in the Type list box.

Deciphering the Custom number formats

You probably noticed while clicking around the Category list box that, for the most part, the different categories and their types are pretty easy — if not a breeze — to comprehend. For most people, that self-assured feeling goes right out the window as soon as they click the Custom category and get a load of its accompanying Type list box, shown in Figure 2-12. It starts off with the nice word *General,* then 0, then 0.00, and after that, all hell breaks loose! Codes with 0s and #s (and other junk) start to appear, and it only goes downhill from there.

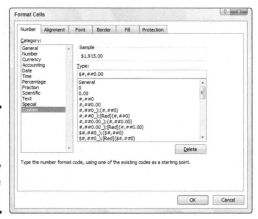

Figure 2-12: Selecting Custom in the Category list box of the Number tab.

As you move down the list, the longer codes are divided into sections separated by semicolons and enclosed within square brackets. Although at first glance these codes appear as so much gibberish, you'll actually find that they're quite understandable (well, would you believe *useful,* then?).

And these codes *can* be useful, especially after you understand them. You can use them to create number formats of your own design. The basic keys to understanding number format codes are as follows:

✦ Excel number formats use a combination of 0, ?, and # symbols with such punctuation as dollar signs, percent signs, and commas to stand for the formatted digits in the numbers that you format.

✦ The 0 is used to indicate how many decimal places (if any) are allowed in the format. The format code 0.00 indicates that two decimal places are used in the number. The format code 0 alone indicates that no decimal places appear (the display of all values is rounded up to whole numbers).

✦ The ? is used like the 0, except that it inserts spaces at the end as needed to make sure that values line up on the decimal point. For example, by entering the number format 0.??, such values as 10.5 and 24.71 line up with each other in their cells because Excel adds an extra space after the 5 to push it over to the left so that it's in line with the 7 of 71. If you used the number format 0.00 instead, these two values would not line up on the decimal point when they are right-aligned in their cells.

✦ The # symbol is used with a comma to indicate that you want thousands, hundred thousands, millions, zillions, and so on in your numbers, with each group of three digits to be separated with a comma.

✦ The $ (dollar sign) symbol is added to the beginning of a number format if you want dollar signs to appear at the beginning of every formatted number.

✦ The % (percent sign) symbol is added to the end of the number format if you want Excel to actually transform the value into a percentage (multiplying it by 100 and adding a percent sign).

Number formats can specify one format for positive values, another for negative values, a third for zero values, and even a fourth format for text in the cells. In such complex formats, the format codes for positive values come first, followed by the codes for negative values, and a semicolon separates each group of codes. Any format codes for how to handle zeros and text in a cell come third and fourth, respectively, in the number format, again separated by semicolons. If the number format doesn't specify special formatting for negative or zero values, these values are automatically formatted like positive values. If the number format doesn't specify what to do with text, text is formatted according to Excel's default values. For example, look at the following number format:

```
#,##0_);(#,##0)
```

This particular number format specifies how to format positive values (the codes in front of the semicolon) and negative values (the codes after the semicolon). Because no further groups of codes exist, zeros are formatted like positive values, and no special formatting is applied to text.

If a number format puts negative values inside parentheses, the positive number format portion often pads the positive values with a space that is the same width as a right parenthesis. To indicate this, you add an underscore (by pressing Shift and the hyphen key) followed immediately by a closed parenthesis symbol. By padding positive numbers with a space equivalent to a right parenthesis, you ensure that digits of both positive and negative values line up in a column of cells.

You can assign different colors to a number format. For example, you can create a format that displays the values in green (the color of money!) by adding the code [GREEN] at the beginning of the format. A more common use of color is to display just the negative numbers in red (ergo the saying "in the red") by inserting the code [RED] right after the semicolon separating the format for positive numbers from the one for negative numbers. Color codes include [BLACK], [BLUE], [CYAN], [GREEN], [MAGENTA], [RED], [WHITE], and [YELLOW].

Date number formats use a series of abbreviations for month, day, and year that are separated by characters, such as a dash (—) or a slash (/). The code m inserts the month as a number: mmm inserts the month as a three-letter abbreviation, such as Apr or Oct, and mmmm spells out the entire month, such as April or October. The code d inserts the date as a number: dd inserts the date as a number with a leading zero, such as 04 or 07; ddd inserts the date as a three-letter abbreviation of the day of the week, such as Mon or Tue; and dddd inserts the full name of the day of the week, such as Monday or Tuesday. The code yy inserts the last two digits of the year, such as 05 or 07; yyyy inserts all four digits of the year, such as 2005, 2007, and so on.

Time number formats use a series of abbreviations for the hour, minutes, and seconds. The code h inserts the number of the hour; hh inserts the number of the hour with leading zeros, such as 02 or 06. The code m inserts the minutes; the code mm inserts the minutes with leading zeros, such as 01 or 09. The code s inserts the number of seconds; ss inserts the seconds with leading zeros, such as 03 or 08. Add AM/PM or am/pm to have Excel tell time on a 12-hour clock, and add either AM (or am) or PM (or pm) to the time number depending on whether the date is before or after noon. Without these AM/PM codes, Excel displays the time number on a 24-hour clock, just like the military does. (For example, 2:00 PM on a 12-hour clock is expressed as 1400 on a 24-hour clock.)

So that's all you really need to know about making some sense of all those strange format codes that you see when you select the Custom category on the Number tab of the Format Cells dialog box.

Designing your own number formats

Armed with a little knowledge on the whys and wherefores of interpreting Excel number format codes, you are ready to see how to use these codes to create your own custom number formats. The reason for going through all that code business is that, in order to create a custom number format, you have to type in your own codes.

To create a custom format, follow this series of steps:

1. **Open a worksheet and enter a sample of the values or text to which you will be applying the custom format.**

   If possible, apply the closest existing format to the sample value as you enter it in its cell (for example, if you're creating a derivative of a Currency format, enter it with the dollar sign, commas, and decimal points that you know you'll want in the custom format).

2. **Open the Format Cells dialog box and use its categories to apply the closest existing number format to the sample cell.**

3. **Select Custom in the Category list box and then edit the codes applied by the existing number format that you chose in the Type list box until the value in the Sample section appears exactly as you want it.**

What could be simpler? Ah, but Step 3, there's the rub: editing weird format codes and getting them just right so that they produce exactly the kind of number formatting that you're looking for!

Actually, creating your own number format isn't as bad as it first sounds, because you "cheat" by selecting a number format that uses as many of the codes as possible that you need in the new custom number that you're creating. Then you use the Sample area to keep a careful eye on the results as you edit the codes in the existing number format. For example, suppose that you want to create a custom date format to use on the current date that you enter with Excel's built-in NOW function (see Book III, Chapter 3 for details). You want this date format to display the full name of the current month (January, February, and so on), followed by two digits for the date and four digits for the year, such as November 06, 2008.

To do this, use the Function Wizard to insert the current date into a worksheet cell; then with this cell selected, open the Format Cells dialog box and scroll down through the Custom category Type list box on the Number tab until you see the date codes `m/d/yyyy h:mm`. Highlight these codes and then edit them as follows in the Type text box directly above:

```
mmmm dd, yyyy
```

The mmmm format code inserts the full name of the month in the custom format; dd inserts two digits for the day (including a leading zero, like 02 and 03); the yyyy code inserts the year. The other elements in this custom format are the space between the mmmm and dd codes and a comma and a space between the dd and yyyy codes (these being purely "punctuational" considerations in the custom format).

What if you want to do something even fancier and create a custom format that tells you something like "Today is Saturday, January 11, 2008" when you format a cell containing the NOW function? Well, you select your first custom format and add a little bit to the front of it, as follows:

```
"Today is" dddd, mmmm dd, yyyy
```

In this custom format, you've added two more elements: Today is and dddd. The Today is code tells Excel to enter the text between the quotation marks verbatim; the dddd code tells the program to insert the whole name of the day of the week. And you thought this was going to be a hard section!

Next, suppose that you want to create a really colorful number format — one that displays positive values in blue, negative values in red (what else?), zero values in green, and text in cyan. Further suppose that you want commas to separate groups of thousands in the values, no decimal places to appear (whole numbers only, please), and negative values to appear inside parentheses (instead of using that tiny little minus sign at the start). Sound complex? Hah, this is a piece of cake.

Take four blanks cells in a new worksheet and enter **1200** in the first cell, **-8000** in the second cell, **0** in the third cell, and the text **Hello There!** in the fourth cell. Then select all four cells as a range (starting with the one containing 1200 as the first cell of the range). Open the Format Cells dialog box and select the Number tab and Number in the Category list. Then select the #,##0_);[Red](#,##0) code in the Custom category Type list box (it's the seventh set down from the top of the list box) and edit it as follows:

```
[Blue]#,##0_);[Red](#,##0);[Green];[Cyan]
```

Click OK. That's all there is to that. When you return to the worksheet, the cell with 1200 appears in blue as 1,200, the -8000 appears in red as (8,000), the 0 appears in green, and the text "Hello There!" appears in a lovely cyan.

Before you move on, you should know about a particular custom format because it can come in really handy from time to time. I'm referring to the custom format that hides whatever has been entered in the cells. You can use this custom format to temporarily mask the display of confidential information used in calculating the worksheet before you print and distribute the worksheet. This custom format provides an easy way to avoid distributing confidential and sensitive information while protecting the integrity of the worksheet calculations at the same time.

To create a custom format that masks the display of the data in a cell selection, you simply create an "empty" format that contains just the semicolon separators in a row:

;;;

This is one custom format that you can probably type by yourself!

After creating this format, you can blank out a range of cells simply by selecting them and then selecting this three-semicolon custom format in the Format Cells dialog box. To bring back a cell range that's been blanked out with this custom format, simply select what now looks like blank cells and then select one of the other (visible) formats that are available. If the cell range contains text and values that normally should use a variety of different formats, first use General to make them visible. After the contents are back on display, format the cells in smaller groups or individually, as required.

Altering the alignment

You can use Excel's Alignment options by using command buttons in the Alignment group of the Ribbon's Home tab and by using options on the Alignment tab of the Format Cells dialog box to change the way cell entries are displayed within their cells.

Alignment refers to both the horizontal and vertical placement of the characters in an entry with regard to its cell boundaries as well as the orientation of the characters and how they are read. Horizontally, Excel automatically right-aligns all numeric entries and left-aligns all text entries in their cells (referred to as General alignment). Vertically, Excel aligns all types of cell entries with the bottom of their cells.

In the Horizontal drop-down list on the Alignment tab of the Format Cells dialog box, Excel offers you the following horizontal text alignment choices:

✦ **General** (the default) right-aligns a numeric entry and left-align a text entry in its cell.

✦ **Left (Indent)** left-aligns the entry in its cell and indent the characters from the left edge of the cell by the number of characters entered in the Indent combo box (which is 0 by default).

✦ **Center** centers any type of cell entry in its cell.

✦ **Right (Indent)** right-aligns the entry in its cell and indent the characters from the right edge of the cell by the number of characters entered in the Indent combo box (which is 0 by default).

✦ **Fill** repeats the entry until its characters fill the entire cell display. When you use this option, Excel automatically increases or decreases the repetitions of the characters in the cell as you adjust the width of its column.

✦ **Justify** spreads out a text entry with spaces so that the text is aligned with the left and right edges of its cell. If necessary to justify the text, Excel automatically wraps the text onto more than one line in the cell and increases the height of its row. If you use the Justify option on numbers, Excel left-aligns the values in their cells just as if you had selected the Left align option.

✦ **Center Across Selection** centers a text entry over selected blank cells in columns to the right of the cell entry.

✦ **Distributed (Indent)** indents the text in from the left and right cell margins by the amount you enter in the Indent text box or select with its spinner buttons (which appear when you select this option on the Horizontal drop-down list) and then distribute the text evenly in the space in between.

For text entries in the worksheet, you can also add the Wrap Text check box option to any of the horizontal alignment choices (note that you can also access this option by clicking the Wrap Text button in the Alignment group of the Home tab on the Ribbon). When you select the Wrap Text option, Excel automatically wraps the text entry to multiple lines within its cells while maintaining the type of alignment that you've selected (something that automatically happens when you select the Justify alignment option).

Instead of wrapping text that naturally increases the row height to accommodate the additional lines, you can use the Shrink to Fit check box option on the Alignment tab of the Format Cells dialog box to have Excel reduce the size of the text in the cell sufficiently, so that all its characters fit within their current column widths.

In addition, Excel offers the following vertical text alignment options from the Vertical drop-down list:

✦ **Top** (the default) aligns any type of cell entry with the top edge of its cell.

✦ **Center** centers any type of cell entry between the top and bottom edges of its cell.

✦ **Bottom** aligns any type of cell entry with the bottom edge of its cell.

✦ **Justify** wraps the text of a cell entry on different lines spread out with blank space so that they are vertically aligned between the top and bottom edges of the cell.

✦ **Distributed** wraps the text of the cell entry on different lines distributed evenly between the top and bottom edges of its cell.

Finally, as part of its alignment options, Excel lets you alter the *orientation* (the angle of the characters in an entry in its cell) and *text direction* (the way the characters are read). The direction is left-to-right for European languages and right-to-left for some languages, such as Hebrew and Arabic (Chinese characters can also sometimes be read from right-to-left, as well).

Wrapping text entries to new lines in their cells

You can use the Wrap Text button on the Ribbon's Home tab or the Wrap Text check box in the Text Control section of the Alignment tab to have Excel create a multi-line entry from a long text entry that would otherwise spill over to blank cells to the right. In creating a multi-line entry in a cell, the program also automatically increases the height of its row if that is required to display all the text.

To get an idea of how text wrap works in cells, compare Figures 2-13 and 2-14. Figure 2-13 shows you two long text entries that spill over to succeeding blank cells to the right. Figure 2-14 shows you these same entries after they have been formatted with the Wrap Text option. The first long text entry is in cell A9 and the second is in cell A11. They both use General alignment (same as Left for text) with the Wrap Text option.

Book II
Chapter 2

Formatting
Worksheets

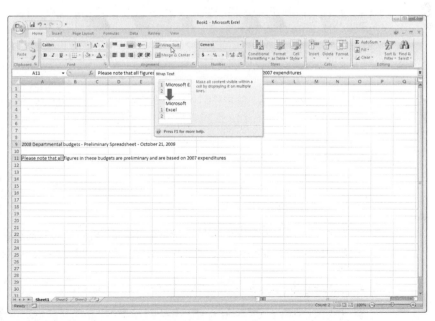

Figure 2-13: Spreadsheet with long text entries that spill over into blank cells on the right.

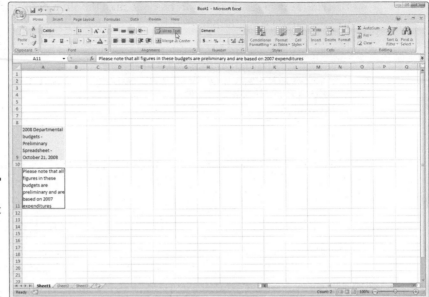

Figure 2-14:
Spreadsheet after wrapping long text entries in their cells.

When you create multi-line text entries with the Wrap Text option, you can decide where each line breaks by inserting a new paragraph. To do this, you put Excel in Edit mode by clicking the insertion point in the Formula bar at the place where a new line should start and pressing Alt+Enter. When you press the Enter key to return to Ready mode, Excel inserts an invisible paragraph marker at the insertion point that starts a new line both on the Formula bar and within the cell with the wrapped text.

If you ever want to remove the paragraph marker and rejoin text split on different lines, click the insertion point at the beginning of the line that you want to join on the Formula bar and press the Backspace key.

Reorienting your entries

Excel makes it easy to change the *orientation* (that is, the angle of the baseline on which the characters rest) of the characters in a cell entry by rotating up or down the baseline of the characters.

The Orientation command button in the Alignment group on the Ribbon's Home tab contains the following options on its drop-down menu:

✦ **Angle Counterclockwise** rotates the text in the cell selection up 45 degrees from the baseline.

✦ **Angle Clockwise** rotates the text in the cell selection down 45 degrees from the baseline.

✦ **Vertical Text** aligns the text in the cell selection in a column where one letter appears over the other.

✦ **Rotate Text Up** rotates the text in the cell selection up 90 degrees from the baseline.

✦ **Rotate Text Down** rotates the text in the cell selection down 90 degrees from the baseline.

✦ **Format Cell Alignment** opens the Alignment tab on the Format Cells dialog box.

You can also alter the orientation of text in the cell selection on the Alignment tab of the Format Cells dialog box (Ctrl+1) using the following options in its Orientation area:

✦ Enter the value of the angle of rotation for the new orientation in the Degrees text box or click the spinner buttons to select this angle. Enter a positive value (such as 45) to have the characters angled above the normal 90-degree line of orientation and a negative value (such as –45) to have them angled above this line.

✦ Click the point on the sample Text box on the right side of the Orientation area that corresponds to the angle of rotation that you want for the characters in the selected cells.

✦ Click the sample Text box on the left side of the Orientation area to have the characters stacked one on top of the other (as shown in the orientation of the word "Text" in this sample box).

After changing the orientation of entries in a selection, Excel automatically adjusts the height of the rows in the cell selection to accommodate the rotation up or down of the cell entries. Figure 2-15 shows a spreadsheet after rotating the column headings of the data table up 45 degrees. Note how Excel increased the height of row 3 to accommodate this change.

**Book II
Chapter 2**

Formatting Worksheets

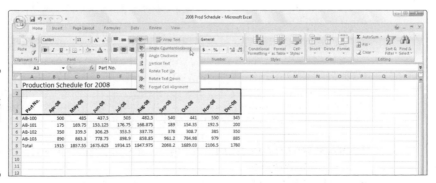

Figure 2-15:
Spreadsheet after rotating the column headings up 45 degrees.

Fancy fonts and colors

You can assign any of the fonts that you've installed for your printer to cells in a worksheet. Along with selecting a new *font* (also known as a *typeface*), you can choose a new font size (in points), assign a font style (such as bold, italic, underline, or strikethrough), as well as change the color of the font.

Note that you can always tell the font and font size of the cell entry in the active cell by looking at the font name displayed in the Font combo box and the point size displayed in the Font Size combo box in the Font group on the Home tab of the Ribbon. You can also tell which, if any, text attributes are assigned to the entry by looking at the Bold, Italic, and Underline buttons in this group. Excel indicates which of these attributes have been assigned to the cell by highlighting the **B**, *I*, or U button in the standard beige highlight color.

Selecting fonts and colors from the Ribbon

You can change the font, font size, font style, and font color using the command buttons in the Font group on the Home tab of the Ribbon. The only aspects you can't change or assign are the type of the underlining (besides single or double) and special font styles including strikethrough, superscript, and subscript.

To change the font with the command buttons in the Font group on the Ribbon's Home tab, select the cell, cell range, or nonadjacent selection to which you want to assign the new font, size, style, or color, and then do one of the following:

✦ To assign a new font to the selection, click the Font drop-down button and then click the font in the drop-down menu.

✦ To assign a new point size to the selection, click the Font Size pop-up button and then click the size on the pop-up menu (you can also do this by clicking the Font text box, typing the point size, and pressing Enter).

✦ To increase the font size a single point at a time, click the Increase Font Size button.

✦ To decrease the font size a single point at a time, click the Decrease Font Size button.

✦ To assign a new font style to a selection, click the appropriate tool in the Formatting toolbar: Click the Bold button (the one with **B**) to bold the selection, the Italic button (the one with *I*) to italicize the selection, and the Underline button (the one with the U) to underline the selection — to assign double underlining to the cell selection, click the drop-down button attached to the Underline button and then click Double Underline on its drop-down menu.

✦ To assign a new font color, click the Font Color pop-up button and then click the new color in the drop-down palette.

Live Preview enables you to see how the cell selection looks in a font or font size that you highlight on the Font or Font-Size drop-down menu — provided, of course, that the selection is not in the columns and rows obscured when these drop-down menus are displayed.

Note that you can immediately remove any font change that you make by clicking the Undo button on the Standard toolbar (or by pressing Ctrl+Z). You can also remove boldface, italics, and underlining assigned to a cell selection by clicking the appropriate button (Bold, Italic, and Underline) on the Formatting toolbar. This action removes the golden box that outlines the button's **B**, *I*, or U̲ icon.

Selecting fonts and colors in the Format Cells dialog box

You can also select a new font, font size, font style, and font color for your selection in the Font tab of the Format Cells dialog box (Ctrl+1). Figure 2-16 shows the Font tab of the Format Cells dialog box that appears when an empty cell that uses the Normal style is active in Excel 2007 on a computer running Windows Vista. In this figure, the current Font is Calibri (Body), the Font Style is Regular, the Font Size is 11 (points), the Underline is None, and the Color is Automatic (in Excel 2007 running on Windows XP, the font is Arial and the font size is 10 points).

Book II
Chapter 2

Formatting
Worksheets

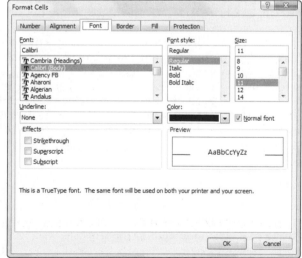

Figure 2-16:
You can change fonts, font sizes, attributes, and colors on the Font tab.

To select a new font color from the Font Color drop-down palette in the Font group on the Ribbon's Home tab or from the Color drop-down palette on the Font tab of the Format Cells dialog box, click its drop-down button. Both drop-down palettes contain color swatches arranged in two groups: Theme colors to select one of the colors used in Excel's themes (see Book V, Chapter 2) and Standard colors to select one of the primary Windows colors. To select a font color from either of these two groups, click its color swatch.

Changing the Automatic color

The Automatic color in Excel always refers to the Window Font color that is currently selected in the Advanced Appearance dialog box in Windows Vista or Windows XP. This color is black unless you change it in the Advanced Appearance dialog box.

To open the Advanced Appearance dialog box in Windows Vista, right-click the desktop and then click Personalize on the shortcut menu; click Window Color and Appearance in the Personalization Control Panel window; click the Open Classic Appearance Properties for More Color Options link in the Window Color and Appearance Control Panel window; and finally click the Advanced button in the Appearance

Settings dialog box and click Window in the Item drop-down list box.

To open the Advanced Appearance dialog box in Windows XP, right-click the desktop and then click Properties on the shortcut menu; click the Appearance tab in the Properties dialog box; and finally click the Advanced button on the Appearance tab.

In the Advanced Appearance dialog box, click Window on the Item drop-down menu and then click a new color on the Color drop-down palette in the last row (opposite Font) immediately above the OK and Cancel buttons and then click OK.

If none of the preset colors will do, click the More Colors option at the bottom of the drop-down palette to open the Colors dialog box. This dialog box contains a Standard tab where you can select a new color by clicking its hexagram swatch in the color honeycomb or shade of gray hexagram below. The Custom tab enables you to select a custom color by changing the RGB (Red, Green, and Blue) or HSL (Hue, Saturation, and Luminosity) values. You can do this either by dragging through the color grid and tint slider at the top of the Custom tab or by entering new values in the Red, Green, and Blue (when the RGB Color Model is selected) or the Hue, Sat, and Lum (when the HSL Color Model is selected) text boxes below or by selecting them with their spinner buttons.

Note that Excel adds a swatch for each custom color you select or define to a Recent Colors section that then appears on both the Font Color and Fill Color buttons' drop-down palettes, making it easy to apply these custom colors to the text and fills of other cells in the worksheet.

Basic borders, fills, and patterns

Excel makes it easy to add borders as well as to assign new background fill colors, gradients, and shading patterns to cells in the worksheet. You can use the borders to outline tables of data — particularly important cells — or to underscore rows of key data. You can also apply various color gradients and shading patterns to cells to draw attention to significant aspects of the spreadsheet.

When adding borders and shading, you can make your job a great deal easier by removing the light blue gridlines used in the Worksheet area to indicate the borders of the cells in the worksheet. To remove these gridlines, click the Gridlines check box on the View tab of the Ribbon (or press Alt+WVG) or click the View check box in the Gridlines column of the Sheet Options group on the Page Layout tab (or press Alt+PVG) to remove the check mark from its check box. After you've dispensed with a worksheet's gridlines, you can immediately tell whether you've added the kind of borders that you want and better judge the effect of the color and shading changes that you make.

Note that removing the display of the gridlines in the Workbook window has no effect whatsoever on the appearance of gridlines in a printed copy of the spreadsheet. If you turn on gridlines for a printout by clicking the Print check box in the Gridlines column of the Sheet Options group on the Page Layout tab (or press Alt+PPG) to add a check mark to this check box, Excel prints these lines on the printed version of the worksheet even when they do not appear on-screen.

Right on the borderline

When applying borderlines to a cell selection, you have a choice between using the options on the drop-down menu that's attached to the Borders button in the Font group on the Home tab and using the options on the Border tab of the Format Cells dialog box. You can compare the options offered by each in Figures 2-17 and 2-18. Figure 2-17 shows the border options on the drop-down menu and Figure 2-18 shows the options on the Border tab of the Format Cells dialog box.

**Book II
Chapter 2**

**Formatting
Worksheets**

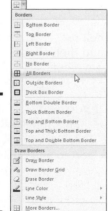

Figure 2-17:
The border options on the Borders button's drop-down menu.

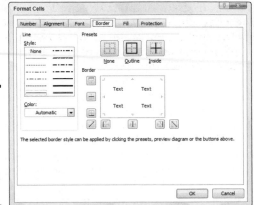

Figure 2-18:
The border
options on
the Border
tab of the
Format Cells
dialog box.

To apply borders to the cell selection by using the options on the Borders button's drop-down menu, click the option on the menu with the type of border you want drawn. To remove a borderline that you select in error, simply click the No Border option at the top of this drop-down menu.

While defining the borderlines to apply in the Border tab, you can select a new style for the borderlines by clicking the Line style in the Style sample area. To select a new color (besides boring old black) for the borderlines that you're about to apply, click the swatch of the new color you want to use in the Color drop-down palette.

When using the Borders palettes to assign borderlines to a cell selection, your options are limited to just the Border buttons displayed on the palette. This means that you don't have as much choice in terms of line style and type of borderlines (in other words, you can't be applying any dashed diagonal borderlines from this palette). You also can't change the color of the borderlines from the Borders palette.

To get rid of borderlines that you've added to a cell range, no matter which method you used to add them, select the range and then click the No Border option at the top of the Border button's drop-down menu.

Fun fills, great-looking gradients, and pretty patterns

In Excel 2007, you can not only select new background colors (referred to as fill colors) for the cell selection but you can also assign gradients (fills that gradually go from one color to another) and new dotted and crosshatched patterns to them.

When simply assigning a new fill color to the current cell selection, you can do this either by clicking a new color swatch on the Fill Color button's drop-down palette (located in the Font group on the Ribbon's Home tab) or by clicking the swatch in the Background Color area of the Fill tab in the Format Cells dialog box (Ctrl+1) shown in Figure 2-19.

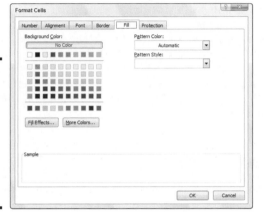

Figure 2-19: Using the options on the Fill tab to select a fill color, gradient, or shading pattern.

✦ To assign a gradient to the cell selection, click the Fill Effects button to open the Fill Effects dialog box (see Figure 2-20) and then select the beginning gradient color by clicking its swatch on the Color 1 drop-down color palette and the ending gradient color by clicking its swatch on the Color 2 drop-down palette. Note that you can then further refine the gradient by selecting a new shading style option button that determines the direction of the gradient pattern before you click OK. Try the following:

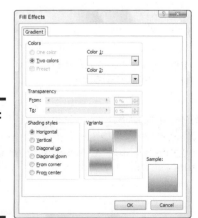

Figure 2-20: Selecting a new gradient to use in the Fill Effects dialog box.

✦ To add a dotted or crosshatched shading pattern to the cell selection (instead of a gradient — they don't go together), click the pattern square on the Pattern Style's drop-down palette. To change the color of the shading pattern (which is by default the black Automatic color), click a color swatch on the Pattern Color's drop-down palette.

Check the Sample area at the bottom of the Fill tab of the Format Cells dialog box to check out the shading pattern and make sure that it's the one you want to use before you click OK to apply it to the cell selection. If you don't like the effect once you've applied it to the cell selection, click the Undo button on the Quick Access toolbar or press Ctrl+Z immediately to remove it.

To get rid of all fill colors, gradients, and shading patterns used in a cell selection, click the No Fill option at the bottom of the Fill Color button's drop-down palette on the Home tab.

Hiring Out the Format Painter

The Format Painter button (with paintbrush icon) in the Clipboard group of the Home tab takes formatting from the current cell and applies it to cells that you "paint" by dragging its special thick-white-cross-plus-paintbrush mouse pointer through them. This tool, therefore, provides a quick-and-easy way to take a bunch of different formats (such as a new font, font size, bold, and italics) that you applied individually to a cell in the spreadsheet and then turn around and use them as the guide for formatting a new range of cells.

To use the Format Painter, follow these steps:

1. **Position the cell cursor in a cell that contains the formatting that you want copied to another range of cells in the spreadsheet.**

This cell becomes the sample cell whose formatting is taken up by Format Painter and copied in the cells that "paint" with its special mouse pointer.

2. **Click the Format Painter button (with the paintbrush icon) in the Clipboard group on the Home tab of the Ribbon.**

As soon as you click this button, Excel adds a paintbrush icon to the standard thick white-cross mouse pointer, indicating that the Format Painter is ready to copy the formatting from the sample cell.

3. **Drag the mouse pointer through the range of cells that you want formatted identically to the sample cell.**

The moment that you release the mouse button, the cells in the range that you just selected with the Format Painter become formatted the same way as the sample cell.

Normally, using the Format Painter is a one-shot deal because as soon as you release the mouse button after selecting a range of cells with the Format Painter, it turns off, and the mouse pointer reverts back to its normal function of just selecting cells in the worksheet (indicated by the return of the regular thick white-cross icon). If you ever want to keep the Format Painter turned on so that you can use it to format more than one range of cells in the worksheet, you need to double-click the Format Painter button on the Home tab instead of just single-clicking it. When you do this, the Format Painter button remains depressed (indicated by the orange highlight) on the Home tab until you click its command button again. During this time, you can "paint" as many different cell ranges in the worksheet as you desire.

Using Cell Styles

Cell styles combine a number of different formatting aspects that can include number format, text alignment, font and font size, borders, fills, and protection status (see Book IV, Chapter 1).

In Excel 2007, cell styles really come alive in the form of the new Cell Styles gallery (see Color Plate 12) that you open by clicking the Cell Styles button in the Styles group on the Ribbon's Home tab.

The Cell Styles gallery contains loads of readymade styles you can immediately apply to the current cell selection. These predefined cell styles are arranged into various sections: Good, Bad, and Neutral; Data and Model; Titles and Headings; Themed Cell Styles; and Number Format.

To apply one of the styles on the Cell Styles gallery, simply click the thumbnail of the desired style in the gallery after using the Live Preview feature to determine which style looks best on the data in your cell selection.

Using the Number Format cell styles

The Number Format section near the bottom of the Cell Styles gallery (see Figure 2-21) contains the following five predefined styles that you can use to format the values entered into the cell selection as follows:

✦ **Comma** sets the number format to the Comma Style (same as clicking the Comma Style command button in the Number group of the Home tab).

✦ **Comma (0)** sets the number format to the Comma Style format without any decimal places.

✦ **Currency** sets the number format to the Currency style format (same as clicking the Accounting Number Format command button in the Number group of the Home tab).

✦ **Currency (0)** sets the number format to the Currency style format without any decimal places (making your financial figures all dollars and no cents).

✦ **Percent** sets the number format to Percent style (same as clicking the Percent Style command button in the Number group of the Home tab).

You can combine the number formatting assigned from one of the Number Format cell styles with the other cell formatting assigned by the cell styles in the other three cell style groups: the Good, Bad, and Neutral (except for Normal which applies the General number format); Data and Model; and Themed Cell Styles. To do this, however, assign the number formatting by clicking its style in the Number Format section of the Cell Styles gallery before you assign the other formatting by clicking its style in one of the other three sections of the Cell Styles gallery.

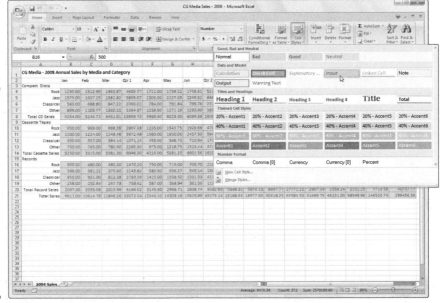

Figure 2-21: Cell selection in a worksheet after assigning the Currency (0) Number Format style and then the Input Data and Model style.

Click Normal, the first style in the Good, Bad, and Neutral section, in the Cell Styles gallery to return the formatting in the cell selection to its original state: General number format, left or right (depending on the contents), horizontal and bottom vertical alignment, Calibri (body) or Arial font, 11- or 10-point font size (depending on the operating system, Vista or XP), no borders, no fill, and locked protection status.

Defining a custom cell style by example

You don't have to live with just the predefined styles that Excel gives you on the Cell Styles gallery because you can readily create custom cell styles of your own.

By far the easiest way to create a new custom cell style is by example. When you create a cell style by example, you choose a cell that already displays all the formatting attributes (applied separately using the techniques discussed previously in this chapter) that you want included in the new cell style. Then, you follow these simple steps to create the new style by using the formatting in the sample cell:

Book II
Chapter 2

Formatting
Worksheets

1. **Position the cell cursor in the cell with the formatting that you want in the new style.**

2. **Click the New Cell Style option at the bottom of the Cell Styles drop-down gallery (opened by clicking the Cell Styles button in the Styles group on the Ribbon's Home tab).**

   This action opens the Style dialog box with a generic style name (Style 1, Style 2, and so on), and the formatting attributes applied to the cell are listed in the Style Includes (By Example) section of the dialog box.

3. **Type the name for the new style in the Style Name text box (replacing the Style 1, Style 2, generic style name).**

4. **Click OK to close the Style dialog box.**

When defining a style by example, select only one cell that you know contains all the formatting characteristics that you want in the new style. This way, you avoid the potential problem of selecting cells that don't share the same formatting. If you select cells that use different formatting when defining a style by example, the new style will contain only the formatting that all cells share in common.

After you close the Style dialog box, Excel adds a thumbnail for the new style to a Custom section at the top of the Cell Styles gallery. To apply this new custom cell style to other cell selections in the worksheet, all you have to do is click its thumbnail in the Custom section of the gallery.

Creating a new cell style from scratch

You can also create a custom cell style from scratch by defining each of its formatting characteristics in the Style dialog box as follows:

1. **Position the cell cursor in a cell that doesn't have any formatting applied to it and then click the New Cell Style option at the bottom of the Cell Styles drop-down gallery (opened by clicking the Cell Styles button in the Styles group on the Ribbon's Home tab).**

   This action opens the Style dialog box with a generic style name (Style 1, Style 2, and so on), and with the attributes for the Normal style listed in the Style Includes (By Example) section of the dialog box.

2. **Type a name for the new style that you are defining in the Style Name text box (replacing Style 1, Style 2 generic name).**

   Now you need to select the formatting settings for the new style.

3. **(Optional) Click the check box for any attribute (Number, Alignment, Font, Border, Fill, or Protection) that you don't want included in the new style.**

4. **Click the Format button in the Style dialog box.**

   This action opens the standard Format Cells dialog box, where you can use the options on its six tabs (Number, Alignment, Font, Border, Fill, and Protection) to select all the formatting attributes that you do want used when you apply the new style to a cell selection.

5. **After you finish assigning the formatting attributes that you want in the new style in the Format Cells dialog box, click OK to return to the Style dialog box.**

   The Style Includes (By Example) section now lists all the attributes that you assigned in the Format Cells dialog box.

6. **Click OK to close the Style dialog box.**

As soon as you click OK, Excel applies the formatting in your newly defined custom style to the current cell and adds the new style to the Custom section of the Cell Styles gallery. To apply this new custom cell style to other cell selections in the worksheet, all you have to do is click its thumbnail in the Custom section of the gallery.

To remove a custom style from the Cell Styles gallery that you've defined by example or from scratch, you have to right-click its thumbnail in the gallery and then click Delete on its shortcut menu.

Merging styles into other workbooks

All custom cell styles that you create are saved, along with the data and formatting in the worksheet, when you save the file. The only styles, however, that are available when you begin a new worksheet are those predefined styles provided by Excel.

If you've created custom styles in another workbook that you want to use in a new workbook or in an existing one that you've opened for editing, you have to merge them into that workbook as follows:

1. **Open the workbook file containing the custom styles that you want to copy and use.**

   You must have the workbook containing the custom styles to merge open, along with the workbook into which these custom styles will be copied.

2. **Click the button on the Windows Vista or XP taskbar for the workbook into which the custom styles will be merged.**

   This action makes the workbook into which the custom styles are to be copied the active one.

3. **Click the Merge Styles option at the bottom of the Cell Styles drop-down gallery (opened by clicking the Cell Styles button in the Styles group on the Ribbon's Home tab).**

   This action opens the Merge Styles dialog box with a list box that displays the filenames of the all the workbooks that are currently open in Excel.

4. **Click the name of the workbook that contains the custom styles you want merged into the active workbook and then click OK.**

   This action closes the Merge Styles dialog box. If the worksheet file that you selected contains custom styles with the same names as the custom styles defined in the active worksheet, Excel displays an alert box that asks if you want to merge the styles that have the same names. Click Yes to replace all styles in the active workbook with those that have the same name in the workbook file that you're copying from. Click No if you don't want the styles in the active workbook to be overwritten, in which case Excel merges the styles with unique names from the other worksheet.

After merging styles from another open workbook, you can close that workbook by clicking its button on the Windows taskbar and then clicking its Close Window. You can then begin applying the merged custom styles, which now appear in the Custom section at the top of the Cell Styles gallery, to cell selections by clicking their thumbnails in the gallery.

Conditional Formatting

Excel 2007's greatly expanded Conditional Formatting feature enables you to format a range of values so that unusual or unwanted values, or values outside certain limits, are automatically formatted in such a way as to call attention to them.

When you click the Conditional Formatting button in the Styles group on the Ribbon's Home tab, a drop-down menu appears with the following options:

✦ **Highlight Cells Rules** opens a continuation menu with various options for defining formatting rules that highlight the cells in the cell selection that contain certain values, text, or dates, or that have values greater or less than a particular value, or that fall within a certain ranges of values.

✦ **Top/Bottom Rules** opens a continuation menu with various options for defining formatting rules that highlight the top and bottom values, percentages, and above and below average values in the cell selection.

✦ **Data Bars** opens a palette with different color data bars that you can apply to the cell selection to indicate their values relative to each other by clicking the data bar thumbnail.

✦ **Color Scales** opens a palette with different three- and two-colored scales that you can apply to the cell selection to indicate their values relative to each other by clicking the color scale thumbnail.

✦ **Icon Sets** opens a palette with different sets of icons that you can apply to the cell selection to indicate their values relative to each other by clicking the icon set.

✦ **New Rule** opens the New Formatting Rule dialog box where you define a custom conditional formatting rule to apply to the cell selection.

✦ **Clear Rules** opens a continuation menu where you can remove conditional formatting rules for the cell selection by clicking the Selected Cells option, for the entire worksheet by clicking the Entire Sheet option, or for just the current data table by clicking the This Table option.

✦ **Manage Rules** opens the Conditional Formatting Rules Manager dialog box where you edit and delete particular rules as well as adjust their rule precedence by moving them up or down in the Rules list box.

Graphical conditional formatting

Perhaps the coolest (and certainly easiest) conditional formatting that you can apply to a cell range is with the sets of graphical markers pop-up palettes attached to the Data Bars, Color Scales, and Icon Sets options on the Conditional Formatting button's drop-down menu:

- **Data Bars** represents the relative values in the cell selection by the length of the color bar in each cell — data bars are great for helping you quickly spot the lower and higher values within a large range of data.

- **Color Scales** classify the relative values in a cell selection with a color gradation using a one-, two-, or three-color scale — color scales are great for identifying the distribution of values across a large range of data.

- **Icon Sets** classify the values in the cell selection into three to five categories and each icon within the set represents a range of values that go from high to low — icon sets are great for quickly identifying the different ranges of values in a range of data.

Figure 2-22 shows how the Data Bars option appears when applied to a cell selection in the cell range C2:C29 that contains a simple series of whole numbers, ranging from 0 to 27. As you can see, the Data Bars increase in length as the numbers increase, creating, in effect, a data bar chart in column C.

Identifying particular values or text entries in a cell range

The options attached to the Highlight Cell Rules and Top/Bottom Rules items on the Conditional Formatting button's drop-down menu enable you to specify a particular type of formatting when certain conditions are met.

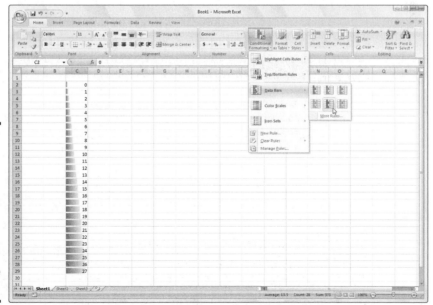

Figure 2-22: Selecting a Data Bar color to apply to the cell selection to indicate graphically their relative values.

The rules that you set up for meeting these formatting conditions can vary widely. You can set up a rule whereby a particular type of formatting is applied when a cell in the range contains a certain text entry (such as Fixed or Variable). You set up a rule whereby a particular type of formatting is applied when a cell in the range is exactly a particular value or exceeds or falls below a particular value. So too, you can set up a rule whereby a particular type of formatting is applied when the value is one of the top ten in the range, is below the average value in the range, or falls into the lower ten percent.

For example, to set up the rule that Excel formats any cell within a range with a light red fill color and dark red font color whenever it contains the word "Fixed," you follow these steps:

1. **Select the range of cells in the worksheet to which this conditional formatting rule is to be applied.**

2. **Click the Conditional Formatting button on the Ribbon's Home tab and then choose Highlight Cell Rules on the drop-down menu and click Text That Contains on the continuation menu.**

    Excel opens the Text That Contains dialog box with a text box on the left where you enter or select in the worksheet the text that tells Excel when to apply the conditional formatting and a drop-down list box on the right where you select or define the conditional formatting the program is to apply.

3. **Type** Fixed **in the Format Cells That Contain the Text box.**

    In this case, you don't have to change the formatting in the drop-down list box as Red Fill with Dark Red Text is the default formatting.

4. **Click OK to apply the conditional formatting rule to the selected cell range.**

Let's say you wanted to apply three different types of conditional formatting to the cells in a single range of the worksheet: one type of formatting whenever a cell in the range contains a target value, another when it exceeds this target value, and third when it falls below the target value.

Here are the steps for setting up the rules to apply a yellow fill with a dark yellow font to cells in a range when they contain 100,000, a green fill with dark green text when they're greater than 100,000, and a red fill with dark red text when they're less than 100,000:

1. **Select the range of cells in the worksheet to which the three conditional formatting rules are to be applied.**

    Start by defining the rule that applies yellow fill with dark yellow font to all values in the range that are equal to 100,000.

2. **Click the Conditional Formatting button on the Home tab and then highlight Highlight Cell Rules on the drop-down menu and click Equal To on the continuation menu.**

Excel opens the Equal To dialog box (shown in Figure 2-23) where you define the formatting rule when a cell contains 100,000.

3. **Type** 100,000 **in the Format Cells That Are EQUAL TO text box and then click Yellow Fill with Dark Yellow Text in the drop-down list box to the right before you click OK.**

Next, you define the rule that applies green fill with dark green font to all values that are greater than 100,000.

4. **Click the Conditional Formatting button on the Home tab and then choose Highlight Cell Rules on the drop-down menu and click Greater Than on the continuation menu.**

Excel opens the Greater Than dialog box where you define the formatting rule when a cell contains a value higher than 100,000.

5. **Type** 100,000 **in the Format Cells That Are GREATER THAN text box and then click Green Fill with Dark Green Text in the drop-down list box to the right before you click OK.**

Finally, you define the rule that applies red fill with dark red font to all values that are less than 100,000.

6. **Click the Conditional Formatting button on the Home tab and then choose Highlight Cell Rules on the drop-down menu and click Less Than on the continuation menu.**

Excel opens the Less Than dialog box where you define the formatting rule when a cell contains a value below 100,000.

7. **Type** 100,000 **in the Format Cells That Are LESS THAN text box and then leave the default Red Fill with Dark Red Text selected in the drop-down list box to the right when you click OK.**

As you define the three rules, Excel applies them to the range selected in the worksheet. If the cell range is blank at the time you set up these three rules, all the blank cells in the range are given a red fill. As you enter values into the cells, their text takes on the color assigned to their values: dark red font for values below 100,000, dark yellow for all values of 100,000, and dark green for all values above 100,000. In addition, when the values are equal to 100,000, Excel fills the cell with a light yellow background color and when values are above 100,000, a light green background color.

**Book II
Chapter 2**

**Formatting
Worksheets**

Figure 2-23:
Defining the rule that formats values equal to 100,000 in the cell range.

Finally, here are the steps you'd follow to create a rule that formats all values in a cell range that are below the average value in the range with a custom conditional format that applies bold italic to the font and a bright yellow fill color:

1. **Select the range of cells in the worksheet to which this conditional formatting rule is to be applied.**

2. **Click the Conditional Formatting button on the Home tab and then highlight Top/Bottom Rules on the drop-down menu and click Below Average on the continuation menu.**

   Excel opens the Below Average dialog box that contains a single drop-down list box where you define the formatting to be used when a value is below the calculated average for the cell range.

3. **Click Custom Format at the bottom of the Format Cells That Are BELOW AVERAGE drop-down list box.**

   Excel opens the Format Cells dialog box where you define all the attributes to be part of the custom conditional formatting.

4. **Click the Font tab in the Format Cells dialog box and then click Bold Italic in the Font Style list box.**

5. **Click the Fill tab in the Format Cells dialog box and then click the bright yellow swatch in the Background Color section before you click OK.**

   Excel closes the Format Cells dialog box, returning you to the Below Average dialog box which now displays Custom Format in the Format Cells That Are BELOW AVERAGE drop-down list box.

6. **Click OK to close the Below Average dialog box.**

Excel then applies the custom formatting of bold italic text with bright yellow fill color to all values in the cell selection that are below the calculated average (displayed after the Average heading on the Status bar at the bottom of the Excel program window).

Comparing columns in a table

The Compare Columns option on the Highlight Cells Rules continuation menu enables you to compare the values in two different columns within a cell range that you've formatted as a table (see "Formatting Ranges as Tables with Table Styles" earlier in this chapter for details).

When comparing columns of a table, you can set up a rule whereby Excel compares the values in the current column of the table to another column that you select and then formats the values in a particular way depending upon whether or not the values in the same rows of the table are greater than, less than, or equal to one another.

To compare values in two columns of a table, follow these steps:

1. **Select the column in the table with the values you want to compare to those in another column.**

For example to compare the values in the Estimated column to those in the Actual column in a table of expenses, you'd select the cells in the Estimated column.

2. **Click the Conditional Formatting button in the Styles group of the Home tab of the Ribbon; then highlight the Highlight Cells Rules option on the drop-down menu and click Compare Columns on the continuation menu.**

Excel opens the Compare Columns dialog box containing three drop-down list boxes: the first where you indicate the comparison operator (Greater Than, Less Than, or Equal To) to use, the second where you indicate the other column containing the values you want compared to those in the selected column, and the third where you indicate the type of formatting to apply when the comparison between values in the same row of the two columns is true.

**Book II
Chapter 2**

Formatting
Worksheets

3. **Click the Greater Than, Less Than, or Equal To option in the first drop-down list box to designate the comparison operator to use in comparing the columns.**

4. **Click the name of the column in the second drop-down list box that holds the values that are to be compared to those in the column currently selected in the table.**

5. **Click the type of preset formatting (Red Fill with Dark Red Text, Yellow Fill with Dark Yellow Text, Green Fill with Dark Green Text, and so forth) or click the Custom Format option and select the custom formatting in the Format Cells dialog box.**

If you define a custom format rather than select one of the preset formats, use the options on the Number, Font, Border, and Fill tabs of the Format Cells dialog box to designate all the formatting to be applied, and then click OK to close the Format Cells dialog box and return to the Compare Columns dialog box (where Custom Format appears in the third drop-down list box).

6. **(Optional) Click the Format Entire Row check box to put a check mark in it so that Excel applies the type of conditional formatting you defined in Step 5 to all the entries in the entire row of the table when the values in the current column and the one you selected in Step 4 fit the rule you set up in Step 3.**

This Format Entire Row check box option is quite useful when you want Excel to mark the entire rows of a table with the conditional formatting when the values in the two compared columns don't add up in a particular way (either by equaling each other or by being higher or lower than one another).

7. **Click OK to close the Compare Columns dialog box.**

Excel then formats all the cells in the current column of the table whose values fit the selected rule when they're compared to those in the other designated column.

If you selected the Format Entire Row check box, Excel formats all the entries in each row of the table where values in the two compared columns fit the selected rule.

Creating your own conditional formatting rules

Although Excel 2007 gives you a ton of readymade Highlight Cells Rules and Top/Bottom Rules to define, you may still find that you need to create your own rules for conditional formatting. To do this, you click the New Rule option near the bottom of the Conditional Formatting button's drop-down menu or you click the New Rule button in the Conditional Formatting Rules Manager dialog box (see the "Managing conditional formatting rules" section that immediately follows).

Figure 2-24 shows you the New Formatting Rule dialog box as it first appears after clicking the New Rule option or button. To create a new conditional formatting rule, you first click the type of rule to create in the Select a Rule Type list box and then specify the criteria and define the formatting using the various options that appear in the Edit the Rule Description section below — note that these options vary greatly depending on the type of rule you click in the Select a Rule list box above.

Figure 2-24: You define a new conditional formatting rule with the options in the New Formatting Rule dialog box.

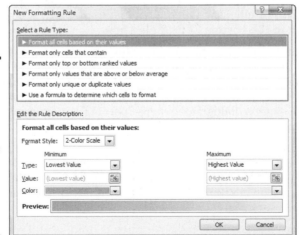

Select the Use a Formula to Determine Which Cells to Format rule type when you want to build a formula as the rule that determines when a particular type of conditional formatting is applied. Note that this formula can refer to cells outside the current cell selection to which the conditional formatting is applied, but it must be a logical formula, meaning that it uses comparison operators (see Book III, Chapter 1) and/or Logical functions (see Book III, Chapter 2) that when calculated return either a logical TRUE or FALSE value.

Managing conditional formatting rules

The Conditional Formatting Rules Manager dialog box (see Figure 2-25), which is opened by clicking the Manage Rules option at the very bottom of the Conditional Formatting button's drop-down menu, enables you to do all of the following:

✦ Create new rules by clicking the New Rule button to open the New Formatting Rule dialog box (see the "Creating your own conditional formatting rules" section immediately preceding).

✦ Edit existing rules by selecting the rule in the Rule list box and clicking the Edit Rule button in the Editing Formatting Rule dialog box (which looks just like the New Formatting Rule dialog box except it contains the rule type, criteria, and formatting for the particular rule you selected).

✦ Delete rules by clicking the rule in the Rule list box and then clicking the Delete Rule button — click the Apply button to remove formatting from the worksheet that was applied to the rule you just deleted.

✦ Change the order of precedence in which multiple conditional formatting rules assigned to the same cell selection or table are applied by promoting or demoting individual rules in the Rule list box by clicking the rules and then clicking either the Move Up button (with the thick arrow pointing upward) or Move Down button (with the thick arrow pointing downward) until the rules appear in the desired order of precedence.

Figure 2-25:
You create, edit, delete, and change the precedence of rules in the Conditional Formatting Rules Manager dialog box.

By default, the Conditional Formatting Rules Manager dialog box shows all the rules assigned only to the current cell selection. To see all the conditional formatting rules in a particular worksheet or table, click its name on the Show Formatting Rules For drop-down list at the top of the dialog box.

A rule that appears higher in the Rule list box of the Conditional Formatting Rules Manager dialog box has a higher precedence and is therefore applied before one lower in the list. When more than one rule is true, what happens depends on whether or not the formatting applied by those rules conflict. When they don't conflict (as when one rule formats the cells in bold italic and the other formats the cells with a light red fill), both formats are applied. However, when the formats conflict (as when one rule formats the cells with black fill and bright yellow text and the other formats the cells with yellow fill and black text), the rule with the higher precedence wins and only its conditional formatting is applied.

Chapter 3: Editing and Proofing Worksheets

In This Chapter

✓ Opening workbooks for editing

✓ Using basic cell-editing techniques

✓ Zooming in and out on the worksheet

✓ Freezing columns and rows on the screen

✓ Copying and moving data entries

✓ Finding and replacing data entries

✓ Proofing the worksheet

✓ Using Data Validation to circle invalid data entries in the worksheet

✓ Finding and eliminating errors with the Text to Speech feature

Creating a spreadsheet is almost never a one-time experience. Some of the spreadsheets that you'll create with Excel will require routine changes on a regular basis, while others will require more radical changes only once in a while. Regardless of the extent of the changes and their frequency, you can be sure that sooner or later, most of the spreadsheets you create in Excel will require editing.

In this chapter, you find out how to make simple editing changes in a worksheet by modifying the contents of a cell as well as how to do more complex editing in your worksheets. These techniques include how to use the Undo and Redo feature, zoom in and out on data, move and copy data, delete data entries and insert new ones, search and replace data entries, and proof the contents of the final worksheet.

However, before you can use any of these fine editing techniques, you have to open the workbook whose contents require editing. So, with that in mind, this chapter starts out by giving you the lowdown on finding and opening workbooks in Excel.

Opening a Workbook

One of the simplest ways to open a workbook for editing in Excel is to open its folder in Windows and then double-click the workbook file icon. If you haven't yet started Excel at the time you open the workbook, Windows automatically launches Excel at the same time that it opens the file. Remember that you can use the Documents or Computer Start menu options (when running Excel 2007 on Windows Vista) and the My Documents or My Computer Start menu or desktop shortcuts (when running Excel 2007 on Windows XP) to locate and then open your workbook files.

Keep in mind that Excel automatically saves workbook files in your Documents folder (when running the program on Windows Vista) and the My Documents folder (when running the program on Windows XP) unless you specifically select another folder.

If Excel is already running and you want to open a workbook file for editing from within Excel, you can click Microsoft Office Button | Open or press Alt+FO to launch the Open dialog box and locate and open the file.

If you can't remember where you saved the workbook that you need to edit (a common occurrence) and you're running Excel 2007 on Windows Vista, you can use the Search text box in the Open dialog box to locate the file, so you can open it right from within the dialog box. See the "Searching for workbooks when running Excel on Windows Vista" section later in this chapter for details. (If you're running Excel 2007 on Windows XP, you need to use the Windows Search feature on the Start menu to find the workbook file and then open it from the Search Results window outside of Excel — see "Searching for workbooks when running Excel on Windows XP" later in this chapter for details.)

The Open dialog box in Excel 2007 running on Windows Vista

If you're running Excel 2007 on Windows Vista, an Open dialog box very much like the one in Figure 3-1 appears. This dialog box is divided into two panes: the Navigation pane on the left where you can select a new folder to open and the main pane on the right showing the icons for all the subfolders in the current folder as well as the documents that Excel can open.

This current folder, whose contents are displayed in the Open dialog box, is either the one designated as the Default File Location on the Save tab of the Excel Options dialog box or the folder you last opened during your current Excel work session.

Figure 3-1:
Use the
Open dialog
box to find
and open a
workbook
for editing.

To open a workbook in another folder, click its link in the Favorite Links section of the Navigation pane or click the Expand Folders button (the one with the triangle pointing upward) and click its folder in this list.

If you open a new folder and it appears empty of all files (and you know that it's not an empty folder), this just means the folder doesn't contain any of the types of files that Excel can open directly, such as workbooks, template files, and macro sheets. To display all the files whether or not Excel can open them directly (meaning without some sort of conversion), click the drop-down button that appears next to the drop-down list box that currently contains Microsoft Office Excel Files and click All Files on its drop-down menu.

When the icon for the workbook file you want to work with appears in the Open dialog box, you can then open it either by clicking its file icon and then clicking the Open button or, if you're handy with the mouse, by just double-clicking the file icon.

Keep in mind that you can use the slider attached to the Views drop-down list button in the Open dialog box to change the way folder and file icons appear in the dialog box. When you select Large Icons or Extra Large Icons on this slider (or anywhere in between), the Excel workbook icons actually show data in the upper-left corner of the first worksheet for all Excel 2007 workbooks saved with the Save Thumbnail check box selected and Excel 97 through 2003 workbooks saved with the Save Preview Picture check box on the Summary tab of the workbook's Properties dialog box selected. This preview of part of the first sheet helps you quickly identify the workbook you want to open for editing or printing.

The Open dialog box in Excel 2007 running on Windows XP

Figure 3-2 shows you the Open dialog box that appears when running Excel 2007 under Windows XP. This dialog box is divided into two sections: a My Places panel on the left and a folder and file list box on the right.

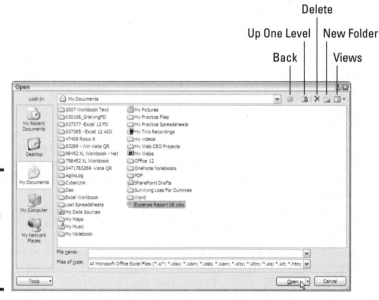

Figure 3-2: Use the Open dialog box to find and open a workbook for editing.

When you can't find the filename you're looking for in the list box, check to make sure that you're looking in the right folder — because if you're not, you're never going to find the missing file. To tell which folder is currently open, check the Look In drop-down list box at the top of the Open dialog box (refer to Figure 3-2).

If the folder that is currently open is not the one that has the workbook file you need to use, you then need to open the folder that does contain the file. In Excel, you can use the Up One Level button (refer to Figure 3-2) in the Open dialog box to change levels until you see the folder you want to open in the list box. To open the new folder, click its icon in the list box and then click the Open button or press Enter (or you can just double-click its icon).

If the workbook file you want is on another drive, click the Up One Level button until the C: drive icon appears in the Look In drop-down list box. You can then switch drives by clicking the drive icon in the list box and then choosing the Open button or pressing Enter (or you can just double-click the drive icon).

When you locate the file you want to use in the list box in the Open dialog box, open it by clicking its file icon and then clicking the Open button or pressing Enter (or by double-clicking the file icon).

Use the buttons displayed in the My Places panel on the left side of the Open dialog box (My Recent Documents, Desktop, My Documents, My Computer, and My Network Places) to easily open any folders associated with these buttons that contain workbook files:

✦ **My Recent Documents:** Click this button to open workbook files you save in the Recent folder (located inside the Office folder within the Microsoft folder).

✦ **Desktop:** Click this folder to open workbook files you save directly on the desktop of your computer.

✦ **My Documents:** Click this button to open workbook files you save in the Personal folder inside the Windows folder. (In fact, on some computers, the My Documents button in the Excel 2007 Open dialog box appears as the Personal button.)

✦ **My Computer:** Click this button to open workbook files you save in folders on the local disks on your computer.

✦ **My Network Places:** Click this button to open workbook files you save in folders on the disks attached to your company's network.

Keep in mind that you can select Preview on the Views button's drop-down menu. Doing so displays a preview pane on the right side of the Open dialog box. This dialog box shows data in the upper-left corner of the first worksheet for all Excel 2007 workbooks saved with the Save Thumbnail check box selected and all Excel 97 through 2003 workbooks saved with the Save Preview Picture check box on the Summary tab of the workbook's Properties dialog box selected. This preview of the first part of the initial worksheet can really help you quickly identify the workbook you want to open for editing or printing.

Opening more than one workbook at a time

If you know that you're going to edit more than one of the workbook files' sheets shown in the list box of the Open dialog box, you can select multiple files in the list box and Excel will then open all of them (in the order they're listed) when you click the Open button or press Enter.

Remember that in order to select multiple files that appear sequentially in the Open dialog box, you click the first filename and then hold down the Shift key while you click the last filename. To select files that are not listed sequentially, you need to hold down the Ctrl key while you click the various filenames.

After the workbook files are open in Excel, you can then switch documents by selecting their filename buttons on the Windows taskbar or by using the Flip feature (Alt+Tab) to select the workbook's thumbnail. (See Book II, Chapter 4 for more information on working on more than one worksheet at a time.)

Opening recently edited workbooks

If you know that the workbook you now need to edit is one that you had opened recently, you don't even have to fool around with the Open dialog box. Just click Microsoft Office Button to open the File pull-down menu and then click the link to the workbook file in the Recent Documents list displayed in the column on the right side.

Excel 2007 keeps a running list of the last nine files you opened in the Recent Documents list on the File pull-down menu. If the workbook you want to work with is one of those shown on this list, you can open its file by clicking its filename in the list or by typing its number (1, 2, 3, and so on).

If you want, you can have Excel list more or fewer files in the Recent Documents list on the File pull-down menu. To change the number of recently opened files listed, follow these simple steps:

1. **Click Office Button | Excel Options | Advanced or press Alt+FIA to open the Advanced tab of the Excel Options dialog box.**

2. **Type a new entry (between 1 and 50) in the Show This Number of Recent Documents in Recent Documents List or use the spinner buttons to increase or decrease this number.**

3. **Click OK or press Enter to close the Options dialog box.**

Note that if you don't want any files displayed in the Recent Documents list on the File pull-down menu, enter 0 in the Number of Documents in Recent Documents List text box or select it with the spinner buttons.

Finding misplaced workbooks

The only problem you can encounter in opening a document from the Open dialog box is locating the filename. Everything's hunky-dory as long as you can see the workbook filename listed in the Open dialog box or know which folder to open in order to display it. But what about those times when a file seems to have mysteriously migrated and is now nowhere to be found on your computer?

Searching for workbooks when running Excel on Windows Vista

When you run Excel 2007 under Windows Vista, the new operating system adds a Search text box to the Open dialog box (see Figure 3-3) that enables you to search for missing notebooks right from within the dialog box.

Figure 3-3:
Use the
Search text
box in the
Open dialog
box to
quickly
search for
any Excel
workbook
on your
computer.

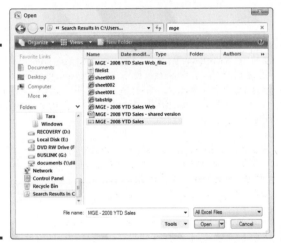

To use Vista's aptly-named Quick Search feature to find a workbook, click the Search text box in the upper-right corner of the Open dialog box and then begin typing search characters used in the workbook's filename or contained in the workbook itself.

As Vista finds any matches for the characters you type, the names of the workbook files (and other Excel files such as templates and macro sheets as well) appear in the Open dialog box. As soon as the workbook you want to open is listed, you can open it by clicking its icon and filename followed by the Open button or by double-clicking it.

Searching for workbooks when running Excel on Windows XP

Unfortunately, the Open dialog box in Excel 2007 when running the program under Windows XP does not have a search feature built into it. This means that to search for missing workbooks, you have to do it outside of Excel by using the Windows XP search feature.

To use the Windows search feature to find an Excel workbook, follow these steps:

1. **Click the Start button on the Windows XP taskbar and then click Search in the right column of the Search menu.**

Windows opens a Search Results dialog box similar to the one shown in Figure 3-4.

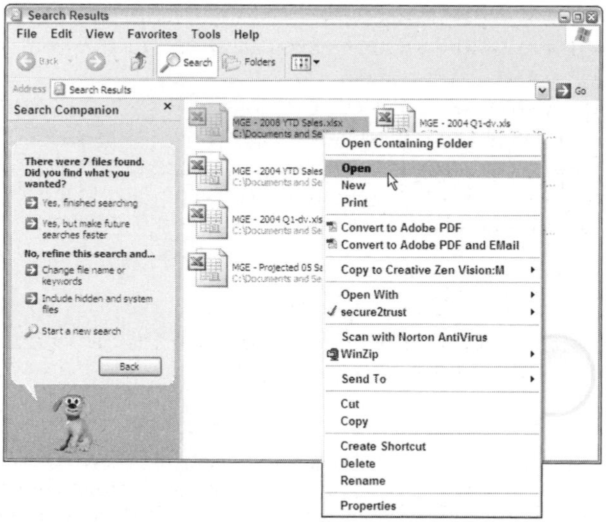

Figure 3-4:
Use the Windows XP Search Results dialog box to search for a missing Excel workbook you want to open.

2. **Click the Documents (Word Processing, Spreadsheet, and so on) link in the left panel of the Search Results dialog box.**

3. **(Optional) If you know the last time the workbook file was modified, click the appropriate option button (Within the Last Week, Past Month, or Within the Past Year).**

If you haven't the slightest idea the last time the workbook was edited, leave the Don't Remember option button selected.

4. **Click the All or Part of the Document Name text box and then type the filename or the part of the name that you're sure of.**

Type an asterisk (*) for multiple missing characters and a question mark (?) for single missing characters that you can't supply in the workbook filename such as **Budget*.xls?**, for which Budget 1-2005.xlsx and Budget 2-2005.xls are both matches.

5. **(Optional) To search for the workbook on a particular hard drive or folder or by a phrase or name entered in the spreadsheets in the file, click the Use Advanced Search Options link and then enter contents** to search for in the workbook in the A Word or Phrase in the Document text box.

Change the location to search as well as any other of the advanced options that help narrow the search.

Note that if you don't know the workbook filename but you do know the size, a key phrase, or a name it contains, just enter the appropriate advanced search criteria, leaving the All or Part of the Document Name text box blank.

6. **After you finish specifying all your search criteria, click the Search button to have Windows XP begin searching for the workbook file.**

After you click Search, Windows displays all the workbook files that match your search criteria in the list box on the right side of the Search Results dialog box. When you locate the workbook file you want to edit in Excel, right-click its file icon and filename and then click Open on the shortcut menu or simply double-click it.

Using the other Open options

The drop-down menu attached to the Open button in the Open dialog box enables you to open the selected workbook file(s) in special ways. These ways include

✦ **Open Read-Only:** This command opens the files you select in the Open dialog box's list box in a read-only state, which means that you can look but you can't touch. (Actually, you can touch; you just can't save your changes.) To save changes in a read-only file, you must use the File⇨Save As command from the Excel menu bar and give the workbook file a new filename.

✦ **Open as Copy:** This command opens a copy of the files you select in the Open dialog box. Use this method of file opening as a safety net: If you mess up the copies, you always have the originals to fall back on.

✦ **Open in Browser:** This command opens workbook files you save as Web pages in your favorite Web browser (which would normally be Microsoft Internet Explorer). Note that this command is not available unless the program identifies that the selected file or files were saved as Web pages rather than plain old Excel worksheet files.

✦ **Open and Repair:** This command attempts to repair corrupted workbook files before opening them in Excel. When you select this command, a dialog box appears giving you a choice between attempting to repair the corrupted file, or opening the recovered version, extracting the data out of the corrupted file, and placing it in a new workbook (which you can save with the File⇨Save command). Click the Repair button to attempt to recover and open the file. Click the Extract Data button if you previously tried unsuccessfully to have Excel repair the file.

Cell Editing 101

The biggest thing to remember about basic cell editing is that you have to put the cell cursor in the cell whose contents you want to modify. When modifying a cell's contents, you can replace the entry entirely, delete characters from the entry, and/or insert new characters into the entry:

✦ To replace a cell's contents, position the cell cursor in the cell and just start inputting your new entry over it. (Remember you can do this by typing from the keyboard, speaking the new entry with the Dictation function of the Speech Recognition feature, or writing it by hand with the Handwriting Recognition feature.) The moment you start inputting the new entry, the first characters that are input entirely replace the existing data entry. To finish replacing the original entry, complete the new cell entry by using whatever technique you like (such as pressing an arrow key or Enter, or clicking the Enter button on the Formula bar). To abort the replacement and restore the original cell entry, click the Cancel button on the Formula bar or press the Escape key on your keyboard.

✦ To delete characters in a cell entry, click the insertion point in the entry on the Formula bar, press F2, or double-click the mouse pointer in the cell to get Excel into Edit mode (indicated by Edit on the Status bar). Then, use the Home, End, or ← and → keys to move the insertion point to a proper place in the entry and the Backspace and Delete keys to remove unnecessary or incorrect characters. (Backspace deletes characters to the left of the insertion point, and Delete removes characters to the right of the insertion point.)

✦ To insert new characters in a cell entry, click the insertion point in the entry on the Formula bar, press F2, or double-click the mouse pointer in the cell to get Excel into Edit mode (indicated by Edit on the Status bar). Then, use the Home, End, or ← and → keys to move the insertion point to the place in the entry where the new characters are needed and start inputting the new characters. Excel automatically inserts the new characters at the insertion point, thus pushing existing text to the right. If Excel replaces existing characters instead, you need to press the Insert key to get out of overtype mode (in which the new characters you input eat up the existing ones on the right) before you start inputting.

When you edit the contents of a cell by inserting and/or deleting characters in it, you need to remember to click the Enter button on the Formula bar or press the Enter key to complete the editing change and switch the program from Edit back to Ready mode (indicated by the reappearance of Ready on the Status bar). If you're editing a cell with a simple text or number entry, you can also do this by clicking the mouse pointer in another cell to make it current (this doesn't work, however, when editing a formula because Excel will just include the address of the cell that you click as part of the edited formula). Also, you can't use any of the keystrokes that normally complete a new cell entry except for the Tab and Shift+Tab keystrokes for moving to the next and previous columns in the worksheet (all the rest, including the arrow keys, Home, and End, just move the insertion point within the cell entry).

Undo and Redo

Excel supports multiple levels of undo that you can use to recover from potentially costly editing mistakes that would require data re-entry or extensive repair operations. The most important thing to remember about the Undo command is that it is cumulative, meaning that you don't use it right away after making a boo-boo. In fact, you may have to select it multiple times to reverse several actions that you've taken before you get to the one that sets your spreadsheet right again.

You can select the Undo command either by clicking the Undo button on the Quick Access toolbar or by pressing Alt+Backspace or Ctrl+Z. Excel will then reverse the effect of the last edit you made in the worksheet. For example, if you edit a cell entry and erase some of its text in error, selecting Undo will restore the characters that you just erased to the entry. Likewise, if you delete a group of cells by mistake, selecting Undo will restore both their contents and formatting to the worksheet.

Book II
Chapter 3

Editing and Proofing
Worksheets

TIP

Editing in the cell versus on the Formula bar

When doing simple editing to a cell's contents, the question arises as to whether it's better to edit the contents in the cell directly or edit the contents on the Formula bar. When editing short entries that fit entirely within the current column width, it really is a matter of personal choice. Some people prefer editing on the Formula bar because it's out of the way of other cells in the same region of the worksheet. Other people prefer editing on the Formula bar because they find it easier to click the insertion point with the I-beam mouse pointer at precisely the place in the entry that needs editing. (When you press F2 to edit in the cell, Excel always positions the insertion point at the very end of the entry, and when you double-click the thick white mouse pointer in the cell, you really can't tell exactly where you're putting the insertion point until you finish double-clicking, at which time you see the flashing insertion point.)

When it comes to editing longer cell entries (that is, text entries that spill over into empty neighboring cells, and numbers that, if their digits weren't truncated by the number format assigned, wouldn't fit within the current cell width), you probably will want to edit their contents on the Formula bar. You can click the Expand Formula bar button (the one with two greater than symbols turned downward on top of the other) to display the entire contents of the cell without obscuring any of the cells of the worksheet, or you can click the Next Row (the one with the triangle pointing down) and the Previous Row buttons (the one with the triangle pointing up) to display the contents a row a time.

On the Quick Access toolbar, you can click the drop-down button attached to the Undo command button to display a pop-up menu that shows a brief menu of the actions that you've recently taken in the spreadsheet. Instead of undoing one action at a time, you undo multiple actions by dragging through them in the pop-up menu. As soon as you release the mouse button, Excel then restores the spreadsheet to the state that it was in before you took all the actions that you selected on this pop-up menu.

When you make an editing change in a spreadsheet, the Undo item on the Undo button's drop-down menu actually changes to reflect the action that you just took. For example, if you delete a group of cells by pressing the Delete key and then open the Undo button's drop-down menu, the first item on the Undo menu appears as follows:

```
Clear
```

If you then apply new formatting to a cell selection, such as assigning a new center alignment, and then open the Undo drop-down menu, the first item on the Undo menu now appears as follows:

```
Center Alignment
```

The Undo feature works by storing a "snapshot" of the worksheet in the memory of your computer at each stage in its editing. Sometimes, if you attempt a large-scale edit in a worksheet, Excel will determine that sufficient free memory doesn't exist to hold a snapshot of the worksheet in its current state and complete the planned editing change as well. For example, this can happen if you try to cut and paste a really large range in a big worksheet. In such a case, Excel displays an Alert dialog box that indicates a lack of enough memory and asks if you want to continue without Undo. If you then select the Yes option, Excel completes the planned edit but without the possibility of you being able to reverse its effects with Undo. Before you take such an action, consider how much time and effort would be required to manually restore the worksheet to its previous state if you make a mistake in carrying out your editing change.

After you use the Undo feature to reverse an editing change, the Redo button on the Quick Access toolbar becomes active. The Redo command item on the Redo button's drop-down menu has the name of the latest type of editing that you just reversed with the Undo button, such as Redo Clear when the last action you took was to restore a cell entry that you just deleted.

You use the Redo command to restore the worksheet to the condition that it was in before you last selected the Undo command. As with using the Undo button on the Quick Access toolbar, when you click the drop-down button attached to the Redo button, you can drag through a series of actions that you want repeated (assuming that you used the Undo command multiple times). You can also restore edits that you've undone one at a time by pressing Ctrl+Y.

You can use Undo and Redo to toggle between a Before and After view of your spreadsheet. For example, suppose that you update an entry in a cell that was used in formulas throughout a data table. As soon as you enter the new number in this cell, Excel recalculates the table and displays the new results. To once again view the original version of the table before you make this latest change, you use Undo (Ctrl+Z). After checking some values in the original table, you then restore the latest change to its numbers by selecting the Redo command (Ctrl+Y). You can then continue in this manner as long as you want, switching between Before and After versions by holding down the Ctrl key as you type Z and then type Y, alternating between Undo and then Redo.

Get that out of here!

Sometimes you need to delete an entry that you made in a cell of the spreadsheet without replacing it with any other contents. Excel refers to this kind of deletion as *clearing* the cell. This is actually more correct than referring to it as "emptying" the cell because although the cell may appear empty when you delete its contents, it may still retain the formatting assigned to it, and therefore not truly be empty.

For this reason, clicking the Clear button (the one with the eraser icon) in the Editing group on the far right of the Home tab (or pressing Alt+HE) opens a drop-down menu with these options:

✦ **Clear All:** Use this to get rid of both the contents and the formatting assigned to the current cell selection.

✦ **Clear Formats:** Use this to get rid of just the formatting assigned to the current cell selection without getting rid of the contents.

✦ **Clear Contents:** Use this to get rid of just the contents in the current cell selection without getting rid of the formatting assigned to it (this is the equivalent of pressing the Delete key).

✦ **Clear Comments:** Use this to get rid of just the comments assigned to the cells in the selection without touching either the contents or the formatting.

The Clear All option is great when you need to truly empty a cell of all formatting and contents while at the same time retaining that empty cell in the worksheet. However, what about the times when you need to get rid of the cell as well as all its contents? For example, suppose that you entered a column of numbers that you've totaled with a summing formula only to discover that midway in the list, you entered the same number twice, in one cell above the other. You don't want to just delete the duplicate number in one of the two cells, thus leaving a single empty cell in the middle of your list of values (although having an empty cell in the middle of the list won't skew the total, it just won't look professional!).

In this case, you want to delete both the duplicate entry and remove the newly emptied cell while at the same time pulling up the cells with the rest of the numbers in the list below along with the cell at the end that contains the formula that sums the values together. Excel offers just such a command on the Home tab in the form of the Delete button and its drop-down menu. When you click Delete Cells on the Delete button's drop-down menu (or press Alt+HDD), a Delete dialog box appears, similar to the one shown in Figure 3-5. This dialog box lets you choose how you want the remaining cells to be shifted when the selected cell (or cells) is removed from the worksheet.

Keep in mind that when you use the Delete Cells option, Excel zaps everything, including the contents, formatting, and any and all attached comments. Don't forget about the Undo button on the Quick Access toolbar or Ctrl+Z in case you ever zap something you shouldn't have!

Figures 3-5 and 3-6 illustrate how Delete works in the example where a duplicate entry has been mistakenly entered in a column of numbers that is totaled by a summing formula. In Figure 3-8, I selected cell B5 containing the duplicate $175,000 entry before clicking the Delete button's drop-down button and then clicking Delete Cells on its drop-down menu to display the Delete dialog box.

As this figure shows, when the Delete dialog box opens, the Shift Cells Up option button is automatically selected. Figure 3-6 shows the same worksheet after clicking the OK button in the Delete dialog box. Notice how Excel pulled up the entries in the cells below when it deleted the duplicate in cell B5, while at the same time automatically recalculating the summing formula to reflect the total of the remaining entries.

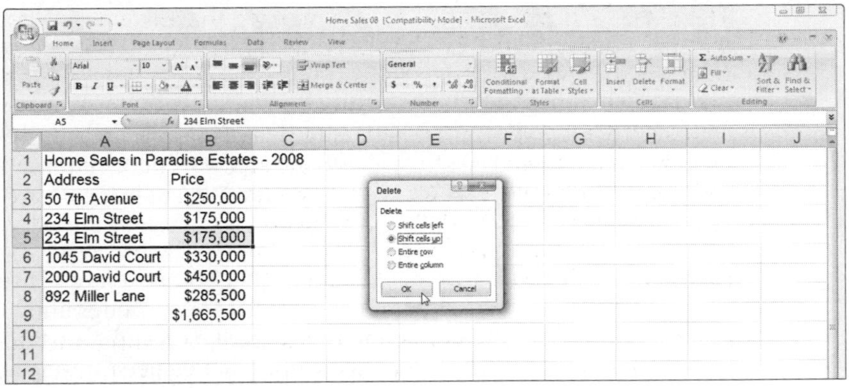

Figure 3-5:
Deleting a cell with a duplicate entry.

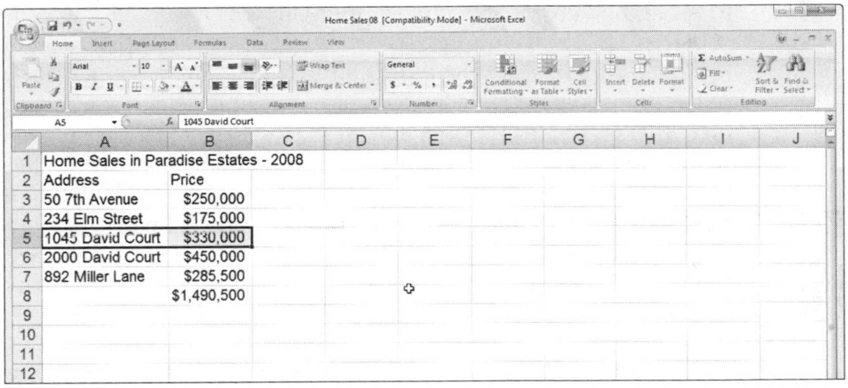

Figure 3-6:
Worksheet after deleting the cell with the duplicate entry.

Don't confuse the use of the Delete key and the Delete Cells command. When you press the Delete key, Excel automatically deletes just the contents of the cells that are selected (keeping whatever formatting is used intact), leaving seemingly blank cells in the worksheet. When you choose Delete Cells on the Delete button's drop-down menu, Excel displays the Delete dialog box, which deletes the selected cells and then shifts the remaining cells in the direction that you designate (up or to the left) to fill in what would otherwise be blank cells.

If you know that you want to use the Shift Cells Up option when deleting the current cell selection, you don't have to bother with opening the Delete dialog box at all: simply click the Delete button (rather than its drop-down button) and Excel will instantly delete the selection and pull all remaining cells up.

Can I just squeeze this in here?

The Insert command button in the Editing group of the Ribbon's Home tab is set very much like the Delete button immediately below it. You click the Insert button's drop-down button and then its Insert Cells option (or press Alt+HII) to open an Insert dialog box (see Figure 3-7) where you indicate how Excel is to deal with existing cell entries in order to accommodate the blank cells you need to squeeze in.

For example, suppose that you discover that you've left out three numbers from a column of summed numbers and that these values should have appeared in the middle of the column. To make this edit, position the cell cursor in the first cell of those cells whose values need to be shifted down to make room for the three missing entries and then drag the cell cursor down two rows so that you have selected the three cells with entries that you want to retain but also need to have moved down.

Figures 3-7 and 3-8 illustrate this situation. In Figure 3-7, I selected the cell range B5:B7, where cells for the three missing entries are to be inserted. I then clicked the drop-down button on the Insert button followed by Insert Cells on its drop-down menu. This action opened the Insert dialog box with the Shift Cells Down option button selected. Because I needed to have the cells in the selected range moved down to make room for the missing entries, I then simply clicked OK.

Figure 3-7:
Inserting three blank cells for missing entries in a column of summed numbers.

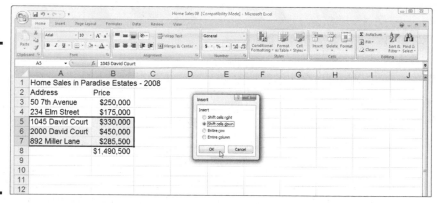

Figure 3-8 shows the spreadsheet after clicking OK in the Insert dialog box to insert three new blank cells in the cell range B5:B7; move down the existing $125,000, $350,000, and $285,000 entries to the cell range B8:B10; and then enter the missing entries in the newly inserted and blank range B5:B7.

As you can see, the sum formula in the last cell in this column (now shifted down to cell B11 from cell B8) has automatically been recalculated so that the total reflects the addition of the missing values that I entered in the newly inserted cells.

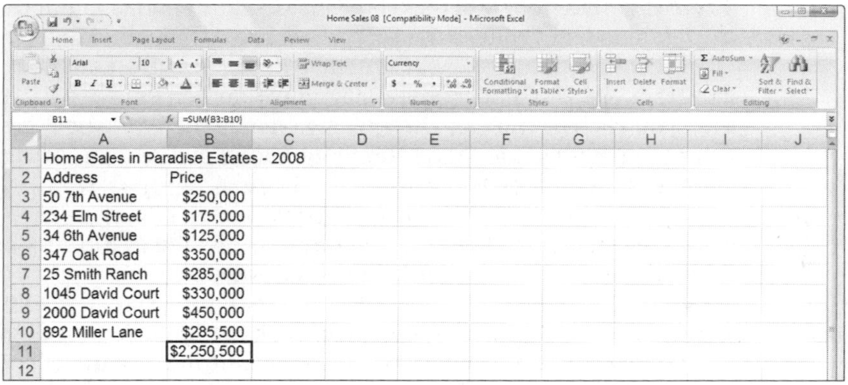

Figure 3-8:
Worksheet
after
entering the
missing
values in
the newly
inserted
cells.

If you know that you want to move existing cells down with the Shift Cells Down option when inserting new cells in the current cell selection, you don't have to bother with opening the Insert dialog box at all: Simply click the Insert button (rather than its drop-down button) and Excel will instantly insert new cells while moving the existing ones down.

A Spreadsheet with a View

The biggest problem with editing is finding and getting to the place in the worksheet that needs modification and then keeping your place in the worksheet as you make the changes. This problem is exacerbated by the fact that you probably often work with really large spreadsheets of which only a small portion can be displayed at any one time on your screen.

Excel provides a number of features that can help you find your way and keep your place in the spreadsheet that needs editing. Among these are its Zoom feature that enables you to increase or decrease the magnification of the worksheet window, thus making it possible to switch from a really up-close view to a really far-away view in seconds, and its Freeze Panes feature that enables you to keep pertinent information, such as column and row headings, on the worksheet window as you scroll other columns and rows of data into view.

"Zoom, zoom, zoom"

Excel 2007 makes it easier than ever before to see more data in the active worksheet window with its Zoom slider feature on the Status bar in the lower-right corner of the window (see Figure 3-9).

The Zoom slider contains two buttons on either end: a Zoom Out button on the left side that reduces the Worksheet area's magnification percentage by 10 percent each time you click it and a Zoom In button on the right side that increases the Worksheet area's magnification percentage by 10 percent each time you click it. You can also quickly change the Worksheet area's magnification percentage (and thus zoom out and in on the data) by dragging the slider's button to the left or right.

Note that the Zoom slider button is always located in the very center of the Zoom slider, putting the Worksheet area magnification at 100% (the normal screen, depending upon your computer monitor's screen resolution) when you first open the worksheet. As you click the Zoom Out or Zoom In button or drag the slider button, Excel keeps you informed of the current magnification percentage by displaying it to the immediate left of the Zoom Out button on the Status bar. Note too, that 10% is the lowest percentage you can select by dragging the button all the way to the left on the slider and 400% is the highest percentage you can select by dragging the button all the way to the right.

Although the Zoom slider is always available on the Status bar in any worksheet you have open, you can change the Worksheet area's magnification percentage by clicking the Zoom button on the Ribbon's View tab or by pressing Alt+WO. Doing this opens the Zoom dialog box where you can select preset magnification percentages 200%, 100%, 75%, 50%, and 25% by clicking its option button before you click OK. In addition, you enter any magnification percentage between a minimum of 10% and a maximum of 400% by clicking its Custom options button and entering the percentage in its text box before you click OK.

You can also have Excel change the magnification to suit the cell range that you've selected. To do this, select your cell range, click the Zoom to Selection button on the View tab, or press Alt+WY1. Note that you can also do this same thing by clicking the Fit Selection option button when the Zoom dialog box is open before you click OK.

If you own a version of Microsoft's IntelliMouse (that is, a mouse with a wheel in between the two mouse buttons), you can set it up in Excel so that rolling the wheel back and forth zooms out and in on the current worksheet. To do this, click the Zoom on Roll with IntelliMouse check box in the Editing Options section of the Advanced tab of the Excel Options dialog box (Office Button | Excel Options or Alt+FI). After you select this check box, instead of scrolling up the rows of the worksheet, rolling the wheel forward increases the magnification (by 15% until you reach the maximum 400%), and instead of scrolling down the rows of the sheet, rolling the wheel backward decreases the magnification (by 15% until you reach the minimum 10% value).

Figures 3-9 and 3-10 illustrate how you can use the Zoom feature to first zoom out to locate a region in a large spreadsheet that needs editing and then zoom in on the region to do the editing. In Figure 3-9, I zoomed out on the Income Analysis to display all its data by selecting a 53% magnification setting (I actually did this by dragging the Zoom slider button to the left until 53% appeared on the Status bar to the left of the Zoom Out button.). At the 53% setting, I could just barely make out the headings and read the numbers in the cells. I then located the cells that needed editing and selected their cell range (J20:L25) in the worksheet.

After selecting the range of cells to be edited, I then clicked the Zoom to Selection button on the View tab. You can see the result in Figure 3-10. As you can see on the Status bar, Excel boosted the magnification from 53% up to 273% the moment I clicked the Zoom to Selection button: a comfortable size for editing these cells on even one of the smaller computer monitors.

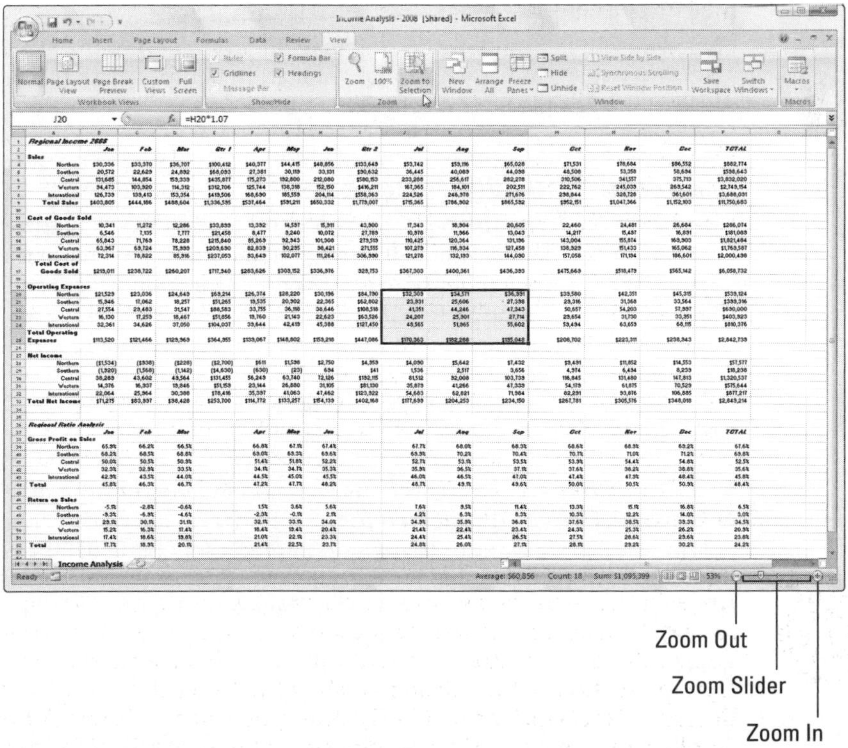

Figure 3-9:
Income
Analysis
spreadsheet
after
zooming out
to a 53%
magnifica-
tion setting.

Zoom Out

Zoom Slider

Zoom In

Income Analysis - 2008 [Shared] - Microsoft Excel
J20
=H20*1.07
J
K
L
18
19
20 $32,309 $34,571 $36,991
21 23,931 25,606 27,398
22 41,351 44,246 47,343
23 24,207 25,901 27,714
24 48,565 51,965 55,602
25 $170,363 $182,288 $195,048
26
Income Analysis

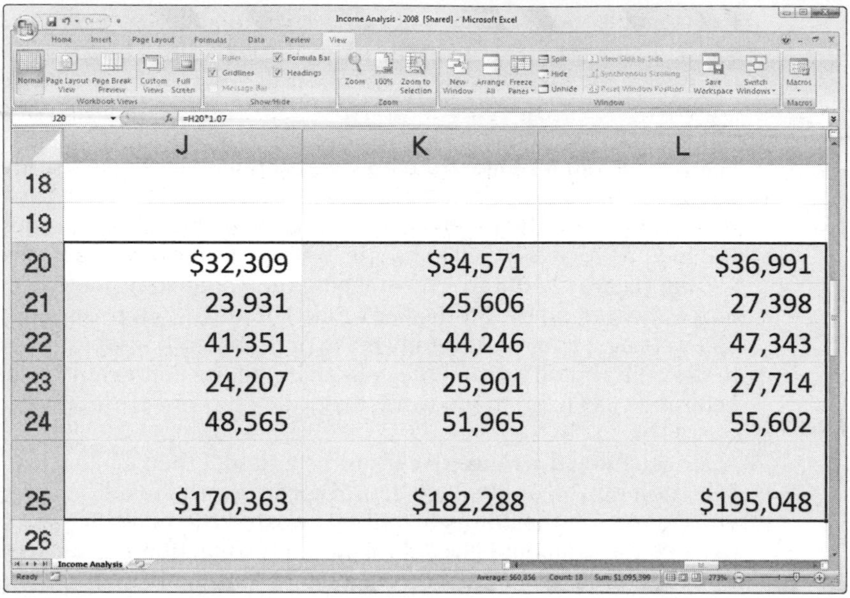

Figure 3-10: Spreadsheet after zooming in on a cell selection.

Because Excel immediately puts the slider button at whatever point you click, you can instantly return the magnification percentage to the normal 100% after selecting any other magnification. Simply click the line at the midpoint in the Zoom slider on the Status bar.

Freezing window panes

Figure 3-10 could be the poster-boy for the Freeze Panes feature. Although zooming in on the range of cells that needs editing has made their data entries easy to read, it has also removed all the column and row headings that give you any clue as to what kind of data you're looking at. If I had used the Freeze Panes command to freeze column A with the row headings and row 2 with the column headings, they would remain displayed on the screen — regardless of the magnification settings you select or how you scroll through the cells.

To use the Freeze Panes feature in this manner, you first position the cell cursor in the cell that's located to the immediate left of the column or columns that you want to freeze and immediately beneath the row or rows that you want to freeze before you click the Freeze Panes button on the Ribbon's View tab followed by Freeze Panes on the button's drop-down menu (you can also do this by pressing Alt+WF and pressing the Enter key to select the Freeze Pane option on the drop-down menu).

TIP

To freeze the top row of the worksheet (assuming that it contains column headings) from anywhere in the worksheet (it doesn't matter where the cell cursor is), click the Freeze Top Row option on the Freeze Panes button's drop-down menu. If you want to freeze the first column (assuming that it contains row headings) from anywhere in the worksheet, click the Freeze First Column option on the Freeze Panes button's drop-down menu instead.

Figures 3-11 and 3-12 illustrate how this works. Figure 3-11 shows the Income Analysis spreadsheet after freezing column A and rows 1 and 2. To do this, I positioned the cell cursor in cell B3 before clicking Freeze Panes on the Freeze Panes button's drop-down menu. Notice the thin black line that runs down column A and across row 2, marking which column and rows of the worksheet are frozen on the display and that will now remain in view — regardless of how far you scroll to the right to new columns or scroll down to new rows.

As Figure 3-12 shows, frozen panes stay on the screen even when you zoom in and out on the worksheet. For Figure 3-12, I repeated the steps I took in changing the magnification for Figures 3-9 and 3-10 (only this time with the frozen panes in place). First, I zoomed out on the Income Analysis spreadsheet by dialing the 35% magnification setting on the Zoom slider; second, I selected the range J20:L25 and then clicked the Zoom to Selection button on the View tab.

Book II
Chapter 3

Editing and Proofing Worksheets

Figure 3-11: Income Analysis spreadsheet after freezing column A and rows 1:2 on-screen.

	A	B	C	D	E	F	G	H	I
1	**Regional Income 2008**								
2		*Jan*	*Feb*	*Mar*	*Qtr 1*	*Apr*	*May*	*Jun*	*Qtr 2*
3	**Sales**								
4	Northern	$30,336	$33,370	$36,707	$100,412	$40,377	$44,415	$48,856	$133,649
5	Southern	20,572	22,629	24,892	$68,093	27,381	30,119	33,131	$90,632
6	Central	131,685	144,854	159,339	$435,877	175,273	192,800	212,080	$580,153
7	Western	94,473	103,920	114,312	$312,706	125,744	138,318	152,150	$416,211
8	International	126,739	139,413	153,354	$419,506	168,690	185,559	204,114	$558,363
9	**Total Sales**	$403,805	$444,186	$488,604	$1,336,595	$537,464	$591,211	$650,332	$1,779,007
10									
11	**Cost of Goods Sold**								
12	Northern	10,341	11,272	12,286	$33,899	13,392	14,597	15,911	43,900
13	Southern	6,546	7,135	7,777	$21,458	8,477	9,240	10,072	27,789
14	Central	65,843	71,769	78,228	$215,840	85,269	92,943	101,308	279,519
15	Western	63,967	69,724	75,999	$209,690	82,839	90,295	98,421	271,555
16	International	72,314	78,822	85,916	$237,053	93,649	102,077	111,264	306,990
17	**Total Cost of Goods Sold**	$219,011	$238,722	$260,207	$717,940	$283,626	$309,152	$336,976	929,753
18									
19	**Operating Expenses**								
20	Northern	$21,529	$23,036	$24,649	$69,214	$26,374	$28,220	$30,196	$84,790
21	Southern	15,946	17,062	18,257	$51,265	19,535	20,902	22,365	$62,802
22	Central	27,554	29,483	31,547	$88,583	33,755	36,118	38,646	$108,518
23	Western	16,130	17,259	18,467	$51,856	19,760	21,143	22,623	$63,526
24	International	32,361	34,626	37,050	$104,037	39,644	42,419	45,388	$127,450

Figure 3-12 shows the result. Note that with the frozen panes in place, this time Excel only selected a 129% magnification setting instead of the original 177% setting. This lower magnification setting is worth it because of all the important information that has been added to the cell range.

When you press the Ctrl+Home shortcut key when you've frozen panes in a worksheet, instead of positioning the cell cursor in cell A1 as normal, Excel positions the cell cursor in the first unfrozen cell. In the example illustrated in Figure 3-11, pressing Ctrl+Home from anywhere in the worksheet puts the cell cursor in B3. From there, you can position the cell cursor in A1 either by clicking the cell or by pressing the arrow keys.

To unfreeze the panes after you've finished editing, click the Unfreeze Panes option on the Freeze Panes button's drop-down menu (this option replaces Freeze Panes at the top of the menu).

Frozen Panes in the worksheet display have a parallel feature when printing a spreadsheet called Print Titles. When you use Print Titles in a report, the columns and rows that you define as the titles are printed at the top and to the left of all data on each page of the report (see Book II, Chapter 5 for details).

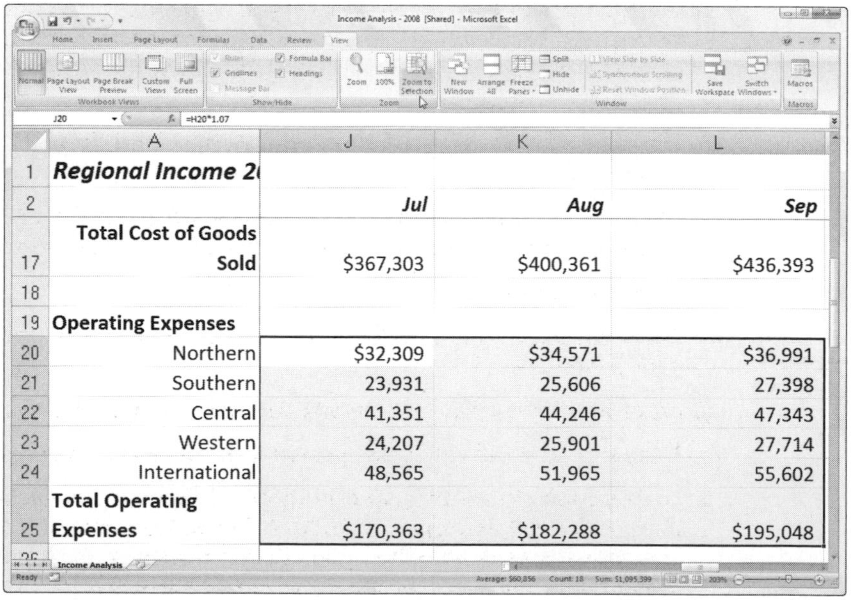

Figure 3-12: Spreadsheet after zooming in on a cell selection after freezing panes.

	A	J	K	L
1	**Regional Income 2**			
2		*Jul*	*Aug*	*Sep*
	Total Cost of Goods			
17	**Sold**	$367,303	$400,361	$436,393
18				
19	**Operating Expenses**			
20	Northern	$32,309	$34,571	$36,991
21	Southern	23,931	25,606	27,398
22	Central	41,351	44,246	47,343
23	Western	24,207	25,901	27,714
24	International	48,565	51,965	55,602
	Total Operating			
25	**Expenses**	$170,363	$182,288	$195,048

Saving custom views

In the course of creating and editing a worksheet, you may find that you need to modify the worksheet display many times as you work with the document. For example, you may find at some point that you need to reduce the magnification of the worksheet display to 75% magnification. At another point, you may need to return to 100% magnification and hide different columns in the worksheet. At some later point, you may have to redisplay the hidden columns and then freeze panes in the worksheet.

Excel's Custom Views feature enables you to save any of these types of changes to the worksheet display. This way, instead of taking the time to manually set up the worksheet display that you want, you can have Excel re-create it for you simply by selecting the view. When you create a view, Excel can save any of the following settings: the current cell selection, print settings (including different page setups), column widths and row heights (including hidden columns), display settings on the Advanced tab of the Excel Options dialog box, as well as the current position and size of the document window and the window pane arrangement (including frozen panes).

Book II Chapter 3

Editing and Proofing Worksheets

To create a custom view of your worksheet, follow these steps:

1. **Make all the necessary changes to the worksheet display so that the worksheet window appears exactly as you want it to appear each time you select the view. Also select all the print settings on the Page Layout tab that you want used in printing the view (see Book II, Chapter 5 for details).**

2. **Click the Custom Views command button on the View tab or press Alt+WCV.**

   This action opens the Custom Views dialog box, shown in Figure 3-13, where you add the view that you've just set up in the worksheet.

3. **Click the Add button.**

   This action opens the Add View dialog box, where you type a name for your new view.

4. **Enter a unique descriptive name for your view in the Name text box.**

   Make sure that the name you give the view reflects all its pertinent settings.

5. **To include print settings and hidden columns and rows in your view, leave the Print Settings and Hidden Rows, Columns and Filter Settings check boxes selected when you click the OK button. If you don't want to include these settings, clear the check mark from either one or both of these check boxes before you click OK.**

   When you click OK, Excel closes the Custom Views dialog box. When you next open this dialog box, the name of your new view will appear in the Views list box.

6. **Click the Close button to close the Custom Views dialog box.**

Custom views are saved as part of the workbook file. To be able to use them whenever you open the spreadsheet for editing, you need to save the workbook with the new view.

7. **Click the Save button on the Quick Access toolbar or press Ctrl+S to save the new view as part of the workbook file.**

Figure 3-13: Adding a new view in the Custom Views dialog box.

After you create your views, you can display the worksheet in that view at any time while working with the spreadsheet. To display a view, follow these steps:

1. **Click the Custom Views command button on the View tab or press Alt+WCV.**

2. **Double-click the name of the view that you want to use in displaying your worksheet in the Views list box or click the name and then click the Show button.**

Always start by defining a Normal 100% view in the Custom Views dialog box that represents the standard view of the worksheet before you go about defining custom views that hide columns, freeze panes, and mess with the worksheet's magnification. This way, you can recover from a special view (especially one that you only use in printing part of the spreadsheet but never use when editing it) simply by double-clicking Normal 100% in the Views list box of the Custom Views dialog box.

Copying and Moving Stuff Around

Moving and copying worksheet data are among the most common editing tasks that you perform when editing a typical spreadsheet. Excel offers two basic methods for moving and copying a cell selection in a worksheet: First, you can use drag-and-drop to drag the cells to a new location, or second, you can cut or copy the contents to the Clipboard and then paste them into the desired area. Moving and copying data to new areas in a spreadsheet are basically very straightforward procedures. You need to keep a few things in mind, however, when rearranging cell entries in a worksheet:

✦ When you move or copy a cell, Excel moves everything in the cell, including the contents, formatting, and any comment assigned to the cell (see Book IV, Chapter 3, for information on adding comments to cells).

✦ If you move or copy a cell so that it overlays an existing entry, Excel replaces the existing entry with the contents and formatting of the cell that you're moving or copying. This means that you can replace existing data in a range without having to clear the range before moving or copying the replacement entries. It also means that you must be careful not to overlay any part of an existing range that you don't want replaced with the relocated or copied cell entries.

✦ When you move cells referred to in formulas in a worksheet, Excel automatically adjusts the cell references in the formulas to reflect their new locations in the worksheet.

✦ When you copy formulas that contain cell references, Excel automatically adjusts the cell references in the copies relative to the change in their position in the worksheet (see Book III, Chapter 1, for details on copying formulas in a spreadsheet).

**Book II
Chapter 3**

Editing and Proofing
Worksheets

For situations in which you only need to copy a single data entry to cells in a single row or to cells in a single column of the worksheet, keep in mind that you can use AutoFill to extend the selection left or right or up or down by dragging the Fill handle (see Book II, Chapter 1, for information about using AutoFill to extend and copy a cell entry).

Doing it with drag-and-drop

Drag-and-drop provides the newest and quickest way to move or copy a range of cells in a single worksheet. To move a range, simply select the cells, position the pointer on any one of the edges of the range, and then drag the range to its new position in the worksheet and release the mouse button.

Note that you can't use drag-and-drop to copy or move a cell selection unless the first cell of the range into which the cells are being copied or moved is visible in the Excel work area. This means that you can't use drag-and-drop to copy or move cells between different worksheets in the same workbook or between different workbook files *unless* you first set up windows in the Excel work area that display both the cells that you're moving or copying and the cells into which they're being moved or copied (see Book II, Chapter 4, for information on setting up windows that enable this). Use the cut-and-paste method (as described in the following section) to move and copy cell selections beyond the current worksheet when you don't have such windows set up.

Moving cells with drag-and-drop

The only thing that you need to be mindful of when using drag-and-drop is that you must position the pointer on one of the edges of the cell range and *wait* until the pointer changes shape from a thick white cross to an outlined arrowhead pointing to the center of a black cross, (shown in the margin) before you begin dragging the range to its new position in the worksheet. Also, when positioning the pointer on an edge of the range, avoid the lower-right corner because locating the pointer there transforms it into the Fill handle (a simple black cross) used by the AutoFill feature to extend the cell range rather than move the range.

As you drag a cell range using drag-and-drop, Excel displays only the outline of the range with a ScreenTip that keeps you informed of its new cell or range address. When you have positioned the outline of the range so that it surrounds the appropriate cells in a new area of the worksheet, simply release the mouse button. Excel moves the selected cells (including the entries, formatting, and comments) to this area.

If the outline of the cell selection that you're dropping encloses any cells with existing data entries, Excel displays an Alert dialog box asking if you want to replace the contents of the destination cells. If you click OK in this dialog box, the overlaid data entries will be completely zapped when they're replaced by the incoming entries.

Copying cells with drag-and-drop

You can use drag-and-drop to copy cell ranges as well as to move them. To modify drag-and-drop so that the feature copies the selected cells rather than relocating them, hold down the Ctrl key when you position the pointer on one of the edges of the selected range (remember to avoid that lower-right corner!). Excel indicates that drag-and-drop is ready to copy rather than move the cell selection by changing the mouse pointer to an outline pointer with a small plus sign in the upper-right (shown in the margin). When the pointer assumes this shape, you simply drag the outline of the selected cell range to the desired position and release both the Ctrl key and mouse button.

Carried away with cut-and-paste

Given the convenience of using drag-and-drop, you may still prefer to use the more traditional cut-and-paste method when moving or copying cells in a worksheet. Cut-and-paste uses the Clipboard (a special area of memory shared by all Windows programs), which provides a temporary storage area for the data in your cell selection until you paste the selection into its new position in the worksheet.

To move a cell selection, click the Cut command button (the one with the scissors icon) in the Clipboard group at the beginning of the Ribbon's Home tab (or press the shortcuts, Alt+HX, Ctrl+X, or Shift+Delete). To copy the selection, click the Copy command button (with the two sheets of paper side by side immediately beneath the Cut button) on the Home tab (or press the shortcuts, Alt+HC, Ctrl+C, or Ctrl+Insert).

When you cut or copy a selection to the Clipboard, Excel displays a marquee around the cell selection (sometimes called *marching ants*), and the following message appears on the Status bar:

```
Select destination and press ENTER or choose Paste
```

To complete the move or copy operation, simply select the first cell in the range where you want the relocated or copied selection to appear and then press the Enter key, click the Paste button on the Home tab (or press the shortcuts Alt+HV, Ctrl+V, or Shift+Insert). Excel then completes the move or copy operation, pasting the range as required, starting with the active cell. When selecting the first cell of a paste range, be sure that you have sufficient blank cells below and to the right of the active cell so that the range you're pasting doesn't overlay any existing data that you don't want Excel to replace.

Unlike when moving and copying a cell selection with drag-and-drop, the cut-and-paste method doesn't warn you when it's about to replace existing cell entries in cells that are overlaid by the incoming cell range — it just goes ahead and replaces them with nary a beep or an alert! If you find that you moved the selection to the wrong area or replaced cells in error, immediately click the Undo button on the Quick Access toolbar or press Ctrl+Z to restore the range to its previous position in the worksheet.

"Paste it again, Sam"

When you complete a copy operation with cut-and-paste by clicking the Paste button in the Clipboard group at the beginning of the Ribbon's Home tab instead of pressing the Enter key, Excel copies the selected cell range to the paste area in the worksheet without removing the marquee from the original range. You can continue to paste the selection to other areas in the worksheet without having to open the Clipboard Task pane to recopy the cell range to the Clipboard. If you don't need to paste the cell range in any other place in the worksheet, you can press Enter to complete the copy operation. If you don't need to make further copies after using the Paste command, you can remove the marquee from the original selection simply by pressing the Escape or the Enter key.

Also, when you paste a cell selection that you've copied to the Clipboard (this doesn't apply when pasting cells that you've cut to the Clipboard), Excel displays the Paste Options button in the lower-right corner of the cell selection (shown in the margin). When you position the mouse pointer over this Paste Options button on a selection that contains only numbers and/or text with no formulas, a pop-up button appears that, when clicked, displays a pop-up menu with the following options:

- ✦ **Use Destination Theme:** Uses the colors, fonts, and graphics effects of the theme (see Book V, Chapter 2) you've assigned to the worksheet where you're pasting the cells that have been copied from another worksheet that uses a different theme.

- ✦ **Match Destination Formatting:** Uses the formatting applied to the cells where the selection is being copied.

- ✦ **Keep Source Formatting:** Uses the formatting applied to the cell selection that you're copying.

- ✦ **Values and Number Formatting:** Copies only the number formatting applied to the cell selection that you copied to the Clipboard.

- ✦ **Keep Source Column Widths:** Adjusts the columns in the cells where the selection is being copied to match the widths of the columns in the cell selection that you copied to the Clipboard.

- ✦ **Formatting Only:** Copies all the formatting (and only the formatting) applied to the cell selection that you copied to the Clipboard.

- ✦ **Link Cells:** Creates linking formulas that bring the data entries in the copied cell selection forward to the destination cells (rather than actually copying the contents to these cells). When you link cells, any changes that you make to the original cell entries are automatically applied to the linked copies.

When you're dealing with a selection that contains formulas as well as numbers and/or text, Excel adds two additional items to the Options pop-up menu:

- ✦ **Values Only:** Copies just the calculated values in the formulas in the cell selection without the formulas themselves.

- ✦ **Values and Source Formatting:** Copies only the calculated values in the formulas within the cell selection along with the formatting assigned to its original cells.

By default, Excel selects the Use Destination Theme item to copy the theme used in the original selection. To switch to one of the other options, click its item on the Paste Options drop-down menu.

Taking it out of the Clipboard Task pane

Excel puts the contents of all cell selections that you copy and paste (using the Copy and Paste command buttons or their keyboard equivalents) into the Office Clipboard. In fact, as you edit your spreadsheet in this manner, the Clipboard stores the contents of up to the last 24 copied-and-pasted cell selections (before replacing them with new copied-and-pasted selections). Up to that time, you can examine the contents of the Clipboard and even paste your cell selections in other places in your spreadsheet or even in documents open in other programs that you're running (see Book IV, Chapter 4 for information about pasting Excel data from the Clipboard into other applications).

To open the Clipboard Task pane on the left side of the Excel program window, click the Dialog Box Launcher in the Clipboard group on the Ribbon's Home tab (the button in the lower-right corner of the Clipboard group with an arrow pointing downward at a diagonal forty-five degree angle).

When the Clipboard Task pane is displayed, it shows all the individual copied-and-pasted items that have been placed there (up to a maximum of 24). While this pane is open, Excel also places there all selections that you cut or copy in the worksheet, even those that you paste by pressing the Enter key as well as those you don't paste elsewhere.

If you want Excel to place all selections that you cut and copy in the worksheet into the Office Clipboard even when the pane is not open, click the Collect Without Showing the Office Clipboard item on the Options button's drop-down menu at the bottom of the Clipboard pane.

To paste an item on the Clipboard into a cell of one of your worksheets, click the cell, and then position the mouse pointer over the item in the Clipboard Task pane. When the item's pop-up button appears, click this button and then click Paste on the pop-up menu, shown in Figure 3-14.

If you're doing a lot of cut-and-paste work in a spreadsheet using the Clipboard, you can have Excel automatically display the Clipboard Task pane as you do the editing. Simply open the Clipboard Task pane, click the Options button at the very bottom, and then click the Show Office Clipboard Automatically option on its pop-up menu to select this setting. When this setting is selected, Excel automatically opens the Clipboard Task pane if you put more than two items in the Clipboard during your work session. To have Excel display the Clipboard Task pane when you press Ctrl+CC, click the Show Clipboard When Ctrl+C Pressed Twice option on this menu.

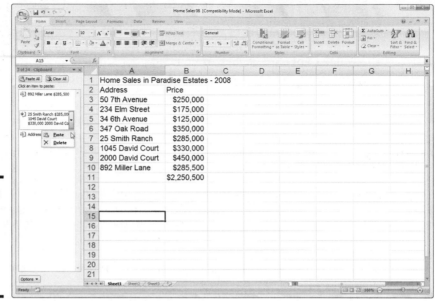

Figure 3-14:
Pasting an
entry into a
new cell
from the
Clipboard
Task pane.

Inserting rather than replacing copied cells

When you use cut-and-paste to move or copy a cell selection, you can have
Excel paste the data into the worksheet without replacing existing entries in
overlaid cells by clicking the Insert Cut Cells or Insert Copied Cells on the
Insert button's drop-down menu (depending on whether you cut or copied
the cells to the Clipboard) on the Ribbon's Home tab instead of clicking the
normal Paste command button. Excel then displays the Insert Paste dialog
box, where you can choose between a Shift Cells Right or a Shift Cells Down
option button. Select Shift Cells Right to have existing cells moved to
columns on the right to make room for the moved or copied cells. Select
Shift Cells Down to have the existing cells moved to lower rows to make
room for them.

If you want to shift existing cells down to make room for the ones you've cut
or copied to the Clipboard, you can simply click the Insert button on the
Home tab rather than bothering to click the Insert Cut Cells or Insert Copied
Cells option on the button's drop-down menu.

Pasting just the good parts with Paste Special

Normally, when you paste worksheet data from the Clipboard, Excel pastes
all the information (entries, formatting, and comments) from the cell selection into the designated paste area, thus replacing any existing entries in
the cells that are overlaid. You can, however, use the options on the Paste
button's drop-down menu or use the options in the Paste Special dialog box

(by clicking Paste Special on this drop-down menu or pressing Alt+HVS) to control what information is pasted into the paste range. If you open the Paste Special dialog box (see Figure 3-15), you also have access to options that perform simple mathematical computations (Add, Subtract, Multiply, and Divide) between the number of cell entries that overlay each other. (See Table 3-1.)

Figure 3-15:
The options in the Paste Special dialog box give you lots of control over how the selection in the Clipboard is pasted into the worksheet.

The options on the Paste button's drop-down menu include the following (the last three options appear on the As Picture pop-up menu):

✦ **Formulas:** Use this option to paste the actual formulas (and not just the calculated results) in the cell selection placed on the Clipboard into the new area of the worksheet.

✦ **Paste Values:** Use this option to paste only the calculated values from the formulas in the cell selection placed on the Clipboard into the new area of the worksheet.

✦ **No Borders:** Use this option to paste everything in the cell selection placed on the Clipboard into the new area of the worksheet except the borders assigned to it.

✦ **Transpose:** Use this option to switch the orientation of the entries in the cell selection placed on the Clipboard so that data that originally ran across the rows now runs down the columns in the new area of the worksheet and the data that ran down columns now runs across rows.

✦ **Paste Link:** Use this to paste links to the original cell selection placed on the Clipboard in the new areas of the worksheet, which are then immediately updated whenever you make changes to the original cell entries.

✦ **Paste Special:** Use this option to open the Paste Special dialog box. (Refer to Figure 3-15.)

✦ **Paste as Hyperlink:** Use this option to paste the cell selection placed on the Clipboard as a hyperlink in the new area of the worksheet (see Book IV, Chapter 2 for details).

✦ **Paste Picture Link:** Use this option to paste the cell selection placed on the Clipboard as a linked graphic object in the worksheet whose contents is updated whenever you make changes to the original cell entries (see Book V, Chapter 2 for details).

✦ **Paste As Picture:** Use this option to paste the cell selection placed on the Clipboard as a graphic object in the worksheet (see Book V, Chapter 2 for details).

✦ **Copy As Picture:** Use this option to open the Copy Picture dialog box where you can specify whether the cell selection is to be copied to the Clipboard as it appears on-screen (the default) or will print as a Microsoft Office graphic object (the default) or a Bitmap graphic — after copying.

The Paste Special dialog box, opened by clicking the Paste Special option on the Paste button's drop-down menu (Alt+HVS) and shown in Figure 3-15, contains two areas: Paste and Operation. The Paste option buttons (some of which duplicate the options on the drop-down menu) enable you to specify which components of the copied cell selection you want copied; see Table 3-1 for a list of options. The Operation option buttons in the Paste Special dialog box enable you to specify which mathematical operation, if any, should be performed between the overlaying values in copy and paste ranges. Select the Skip Blanks check box when you don't want Excel to replace existing entries in the paste range with overlaying blank cells in the copy range.

Table 3-1	The Paste Special Dialog Box Options
Option	*What It Does*
All	Pastes all types of entries (numbers, formulas, and text), their formats, and comments from the selection in the paste area
Formulas	Pastes only the entries (numbers, formulas, and text) from the selection in the paste area
Values	Pastes only numbers and text from the selection in the paste area, converting all formulas to their current calculated values so they're pasted into the worksheet as numbers
Formats	Pastes only the formats from the selection into the paste area
Comments	Pastes only the comments from the selection into the paste area
Validation	Pastes only the entries in cells that use Data Validation in the paste area (see Book II, Chapter 1 for info on Data Validation)
All Using Source Theme	Pastes all types of entries (numbers, formulas, and text), their formats, and comments from the selection in the paste area and uses the colors, fonts, and graphic effects in the theme assigned to their source worksheet (see Book V, Chapter 2)

Option	What It Does
All Except Borders	Pastes everything but the borders assigned to the cell selection into the paste area
Column Widths	Pastes everything into the paste area and adjusts the column widths in this area to match those of the original cell selection
Formulas and Number Formats	Pastes only the formulas and number formatting (omitting all text and numeric entries) from the cell selection into the paste area
Values and Number Formats	Pastes only the numbers and number formatting (omitting all text and converting all formulas to their calculated values) from the cell selection into the paste area
None	Performs no mathematical operation between the values in the cell selection placed on the Clipboard and those in the destination range in the worksheet (the default)
Add	Adds the values in the cell selection placed on the Clipboard to those in the destination range in the worksheet
Subtract	Subtracts the values in the cell selection placed on the Clipboard from those in the destination range in the worksheet
Multiply	Multiplies the values in the cell selection placed on the Clipboard with those in the destination range in the worksheet
Divide	Divides the values in the cell selection placed on the Clipboard by those in the destination range in the worksheet
Skip Blanks	Does not replace existing entries in the worksheet with any overlaying blank cells placed on the Clipboard as part of the cut or copied cell selection
Transpose	Switches the orientation of the entries in the cell selection placed on the Clipboard so that data that originally ran across the rows now runs down the columns in the new area of the worksheet and the data that ran down columns now runs across rows
Paste Link	Pastes links to the original cell selection placed on the Clipboard

The Transpose option on the Paste button's drop-down menu (duplicated by the Transpose check box in the Paste Special dialog box) is particularly helpful when you have a row of column headings that you want to convert into a column of row headings or when you have a column of row headings that you want to convert into a row of column headings. You can also use this option to pivot an entire table of data so that the data that runs across the rows now runs down the columns and vice versa.

Figure 3-16 illustrates just such a situation. Here, I selected the data and headings in the cell range A2:J7, clicked the Copy button on the Home tab of the Ribbon, and then moved the cell cursor to cell A12. After that, I clicked the Transpose option on the Paste button's drop-down menu.

The results of this transposition appear in the cell range A12:F21 in Figure 3-16. As you can see, in the transposed table, the original row headings are now the column headings just as the original column headings are now the row headings. Note, too, that in transposing the table, Excel retained the formulas that total the units produced each month, although now they appear in the last column of the table instead of the last row.

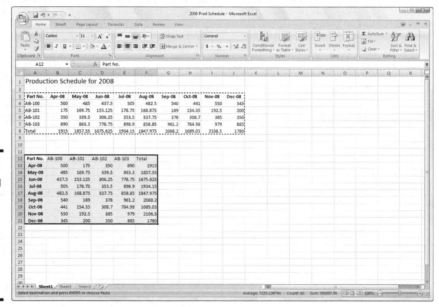

Figure 3-16:
Transposing a row of column headings into a column of row headings.

To convert a cell range that contains formulas to its calculated values (as though you had input them as numbers), select the cell range, click the Copy button on the Home tab, and then click the Paste Values option on the Paste button's drop-down menu *without* moving the cell cursor. This causes Excel to paste the calculated values on top of the formulas that created them, thus zapping the overlaid formulas and leaving you with only the computed values!

Find and Replace This Disgrace!

No discussion of spreadsheet editing would be complete without including the Find and Replace features in Excel. You can use the Find feature to quickly locate each and every occurrence of a specific *string* (a series of characters) in a worksheet. You can use the Replace feature to have Excel actually update the cells that it finds with new text or numbers.

Both the Find and the Replace features share the same dialog box (aptly called the Find and Replace dialog box). If you only want to find a cell's particular contents, you just use the options on the Find tab (which is automatically selected when you open the Find and Replace dialog box by clicking the Find option on the Find & Select button's drop-down menu on the Home tab of the Ribbon, or when you press Alt+HFDF or simply Ctrl+F). If you want to update the contents of some or all of the cells that you find, use the options on the Replace tab (which is automatically selected when you open the Find and Replace dialog box by clicking the Replace option on the Find & Select button's drop-down menu, or when you press Alt+HFDR or simply Ctrl+H).

The Find and Replace tabs in the Find and Replace dialog box contain a bunch of search options that you can use in finding and replacing stuff in your spreadsheet. The only problem is that these options are hidden when you first open the Find and Replace dialog box. To expand the Find and Replace dialog box to display the extra search options on the Find and Replace tab, click the Options button.

**Book II
Chapter 3**

Editing and Proofing
Worksheets

Finding stuff

To use the Find command to locate information in your worksheet, follow these steps:

1. **To search the entire worksheet, select a single cell. To restrict the search to a specific cell range or nonadjacent selection, select all the cells to be searched.**

2. **Click the Find option on the Find & Select button's drop-down menu on the Ribbon's Home tab or press Ctrl+F.**

   Excel opens the Find and Replace dialog box with the Find tab selected.

3. **Type the search string that you want to locate in the Find What combo box.**

   When entering the search string, you can use the question mark (?) or asterisk (*) wildcards to stand in for any characters that you're unsure of. Use the question mark to stand for a single character as in *Sm?th,* which will match either *Smith* or *Smyth.* Use the asterisk to stand for multiple characters as in *9*1,* which will locate *91, 94901,* or even *9553 1st Street.* To search for a wildcard character, precede the character with a tilde (~), as in *~*2.5,* to locate formulas that are multiplied by the number 2.5 (the asterisk is the multiplication operator in Excel).

   If the cell holding the search string that you're looking for is formatted in a particular way, you can narrow the search by specifying what formatting to search for.

4. **Click the Options>> button and then click the Format drop-down button to specify the formatting to search for in addition to your search string, and then click the Format item to select the formatting from the Find Format dialog box or click Choose Format from Cell to select the formatting directly from a cell in the worksheet.**

When you click the Format item, Excel opens a Find Format dialog box with the same tabs and options as the standard Format Cells dialog box. You then select the formatting that you want to search for in this dialog box and click OK.

When you click the Choose Format from Cell item on the Format button pop-up menu, the Find and Replace dialog box temporarily disappears until you click the cell in the worksheet that contains the formatting that you want to search for with the thick, white-cross mouse pointer with eyedropper icon.

Note that when using the Find feature to locate a search string, by default, Excel searches only the current worksheet for your search string. If you want Excel to search all the cells of all worksheets in the workbook, you need to follow Step 5.

5. **Click the Workbook option on the Within drop-down menu to have Excel search all worksheets in the workbook.**

If the Within drop-down list box doesn't appear at the bottom of your Find and Replace dialog box, click the Options>> button to expand it and add the Within, Search, and Look In drop-down list boxes along with the Match Case and Match Entire Cell Contents check boxes shown in Figure 3-17.

By default, Excel searches across the rows in the worksheet or current selection (that is, to the right and then down from the active cell). If you want to have the program search down the columns and then across the rows, you need to follow Step 6.

6. **Click the By Columns option on the Search drop-down menu to have Excel search down the columns (that is, down and then to the right from the active cell).**

By default, Excel locates the search string in the contents of each cell as entered on the Formula bar. This means that if you're looking for a cell that contains 1,250 and the spreadsheet contains the formula =750+500, whose calculated value as displayed in the cell is 1,250, Excel won't consider this cell to be a match because in searching the Formula bar, it finds =750+500 instead of 1,250.

To have Excel search the contents of each cell (and thus, consider a cell that displays your value to be a match even when its contents on the Formula bar don't contain the search string), you need to change the Look In setting from Formulas to Values. If you want Excel to search for the search string in the comments you've added to cells, you need to change the Look In setting to Comments.

7. **Click Values on the Look In drop-down menu to have Excel locate the search string in the contents of each cell as it's displayed in the worksheet. Click Comments on this pop-up menu instead to have Excel locate the search string in the comments that you've added to cells.**

   Note that when you select Comments to search the comments you've added to the spreadsheet, you can't specify any formatting to search for because the Format button in the Find and Replace dialog box becomes grayed out.

   By default, Excel ignores case differences between the search string and the content of the cells being searched so that *Assets, ASSETS,* and *assets* all match the search string, *Assets.* To find only exact matches, follow Step 8.

8. **Click the Match Case check box to find occurrences of the search string when it matches the case that you entered.**

   By default, Excel considers any occurrence of the search string to be a match — even when it occurs as part of another part of the cell entry. So when the search string is 25, cells containing 25, 15.25, 25 Main Street, and 250,000 are all considered matches. To find only complete occurrences of your search string in a cell, follow Step 9.

9. **Click the Match Entire Cell Contents check box to find occurrences of the search string only when it's the entire cell entry.**

   After you've entered the search string and search options as you want them, you're ready to start searching the spreadsheet.

10. **Click the Find All button to find all occurrences of the search string. Click the Find Next button to find just the first occurrence of the search string.**

    When you click Find All, Excel lists all the cells containing the search string in a list box at the bottom of the Find and Replace dialog box, as shown in Figure 3-17. You can then have Excel select the cell with a particular occurrence by clicking its link in this list box. You may have to drag the Find and Replace dialog box out of the way to see the selected cell.

    When you click Find Next, Excel selects the next cell in the spreadsheet (using the designated search direction). To find subsequent occurrences of the search string, you need to continue to click Find Next until you reach the cell that you're looking for. Again, you may have to drag the Find and Replace dialog box out of the way to see the cell that Excel has located and selected in the worksheet.

11. **After you finish searching the spreadsheet for the search string, click the Close button.**

Book II
Chapter 3

Editing and Proofing
Worksheets

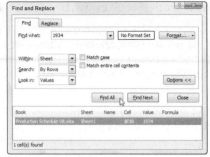

Figure 3-17:
Finding a
value in a
spreadsheet
by using the
options on
the Find tab.

Note that Excel retains your search string and search option conditions even after closing the Find and Replace dialog box. To repeat a search, just press Ctrl+F and then click Find All or Find Next. You can also reinstate a search string that you used earlier in your work session by clicking it on the Find What drop-down menu.

Finding and replacing stuff

The Find feature is sufficient if all you want to do is locate an occurrence of a search string in your worksheet. Many times, however, you will also want to change some or all of the cells that match the search string. For those situations, you use the Replace feature to locate the search string and replace it with some other string.

To search and replace information in your worksheet, follow these steps:

1. **To search and replace the entire worksheet, select a single cell. To restrict the search and replace operation to a specific cell, range, or nonadjacent selection, select all the cells to be edited.**

2. **Click the Replace option on the Find & Select button's drop-down menu on the Ribbon's Home tab or press Ctrl+H.**

   Excel opens the Find and Replace dialog box with the Replace tab selected (similar to the one shown in Figure 3-18). Note that if the Find and Replace dialog box is already open from clicking the Find option on the Find & Select button's drop-down menu or pressing Ctrl+F, all you have to do is click the Replace tab.

3. **Type the search string that you want to locate in the Find What combo box and specify any formatting to be searched by using its Format button.**

   Refer back to the previous steps on finding a search string for details on specifying the search string in the Find What combo box and specifying the formatting to be searched for.

4. **Type the replacement string in the Replace With combo box.**

   Enter this string *exactly* as you want it to appear in the cells of the worksheet. Use uppercase letters where uppercase is to appear, lowercase letters where lowercase is to appear, and the question mark and asterisk only where they are to appear (they don't act as wildcard characters in a replacement string).

5. **Click the Options>> button and then click the Format drop-down button and select Format to select the formatting to be added to your replacement string from the Find Format dialog box. Or click Choose Format from Cell and select the formatting directly from a cell in the worksheet.**

   When you click the Format item, Excel opens a Find Format dialog box with the same tabs and options as the standard Format Cells dialog box. You may then select the formatting that you want the replacement string to have in this dialog box and then click OK.

   When you click the Choose Format from Cell item on the Format button pop-up menu, the Find and Replace dialog box temporarily disappears until you click the cell in the worksheet that contains the formatting that you want the replacement string to have with the thick, white-cross mouse pointer with eyedropper icon.

6. **Make any necessary changes to the Within, Search, Look In, Match Case, and Match Entire Cell Contents options for the search string.**

   These options work just as they do on the Find tab. If these options aren't displayed on the Replace tab of your Find and Replace dialog box, click its Options button to expand the dialog box.

7. **Click the Find Next button to locate the first occurrence of the search string. Then, click the Replace button to replace the first occurrence with the replacement string or click the Find Next button again to skip this occurrence.**

   Using the Find Next and Replace buttons to search and replace on a case-by-case basis is by far the safest way to use the Find and Replace feature. If you're certain (really certain) that you won't mess up anything by replacing all occurrences throughout the spreadsheet, you can click the Replace All button to have Excel make the replacements globally without stopping to show you which cells are updated.

8. **When you finish replacing entries on a case-by-case basis, click the Close button.**

   This action abandons the Find and Replace operation and closes the Find and Replace dialog box. When you globally replace the search string, Excel automatically closes the Find and Replace dialog box after replacing the last search string match.

Book II
Chapter 3

Editing and Proofing
Worksheets

Remember that you can click the Undo button on the Quick Access toolbar or press Ctrl+Z to restore any replacements that you made in error.

Figure 3-18: Replacing dates in a spreadsheet by using the options on the Replace tab.

Spell Checking Heaven

You can use Excel's Spell Check feature to catch all the spelling mistakes that AutoCorrect lets slip through. To spell check your spreadsheet, click the Spelling button at the beginning of the Ribbon's Review tab or press Alt+RS or, simply, F7.

When you spell check a spreadsheet, Excel looks up each word in the Excel Dictionary. If the word is not found (as is often the case with less-common last names, abbreviations, acronyms, and technical terms), Excel selects the cell with the unknown spelling and then displays a Spelling dialog box showing the unknown word in the Not in Dictionary text box with suggested correct spellings shown in a Suggestions list box below, which is similar to the one shown in Figure 3-19.

Figure 3-19: Spell checking the spreadsheet with the Spelling dialog box.

You can then take any of the following actions to take care of the unknown word:

✦ Click one of the words in the Suggestions list box and then click the Change button to have Excel replace the unknown word with the selected suggestion and continue spell checking the rest of the spreadsheet.

✦ Click one of the words in the Suggestions list box and then click the Change All button to have Excel replace all occurrences of the unknown word with the selected suggestion throughout the entire spreadsheet and then continue spell checking.

✦ Click the Ignore Once button to let the misspelling slide just this once and continue spell checking the rest of the spreadsheet.

✦ Click the Ignore All button to ignore all occurrences of the unknown word in the spreadsheet and continue spell checking.

✦ Click the Add to Dictionary button to add the unknown word to a custom dictionary so that Excel will know the word the next time you spell check the worksheet.

✦ Click the AutoCorrect button to have Excel add the unknown word to the AutoCorrect list with the selected suggestion as its automatic replacement.

Keep in mind that Excel checks the spelling of the cells only in the current worksheet (and not all the sheets in the workbook). If you want Excel to spell check another worksheet, you need to click its sheet tab to make it active and then click the Spelling button on the Review tab (or press F7). If you want to spell check just a portion of the worksheet, select the range or nonadjacent cell selection before you start the spell check.

When Excel finishes checking the current worksheet or cell selection, the program displays an alert dialog box that indicates that the spell checking has been completed.

Changing the spelling options

When you use Spell Check feature, you can change certain spelling options to better suit the spreadsheet that you're checking. To change the spelling options, click the Options button at the bottom of the Spelling dialog box. This action opens the Proofing tab of the Excel Options dialog box with the following options in the When Correcting Spelling in Microsoft Office Programs section:

✦ **Ignore Words in UPPERCASE:** Remove the check mark from the check box so that Excel marks acronyms and other words entered in all upper-case letters as misspellings.

✦ **Ignore Words That Contain Numbers:** Remove the check mark from the check box so that Excel marks words such as B52 that contain letters and numbers as misspellings.

✦ **Ignore Internet and File Addresses**: Remove the check mark from the check box so that Excel marks Web URL addresses such as www. dummies.com and file pathnames such as c:\documents\finance as misspellings.

✦ **Flag Repeated Words:** Remove the check mark so that Excel no longer marks repeated words such as Bora Bora as misspellings.

✦ **Enforce Accented Uppercase in French**: Add a check mark so that Excel marks uppercase French words that don't have the proper accent marks as misspellings.

✦ **Suggest From Main Dictionary Only**: Have Excel use only the main dictionary when doing a spell check (thus, ignoring all words that you've added to a custom dictionary).

✦ **Custom Dictionaries:** Open the Custom Dictionaries dialog box where you can edit the words in a custom dictionary or add a new custom dictionary to be used in spell checking (see "Adding words to a custom dictionary" that follows).

✦ **French Modes:** Choose between the traditional or more modern spellings of French words.

Adding words to the custom dictionary

You use the Add to Dictionary button in the Spelling dialog box to add unknown words to a custom dictionary. By default, Excel adds words to a custom dictionary file named CUSTOM.DIC. This file is located in the UProof folder, which is located within the Microsoft folder inside the Application Data folder. The Application Data folder is either inside the Windows folder on your C: drive or, if you're on a network, this file may be located in your user name folder inside the Profiles folder that lies within the Windows folder on your C: drive.

If you want, you can create other custom dictionaries to use when spell checking your worksheets. To create a new custom dictionary, follow these steps:

1. **Click the Custom Dictionaries button in the When Correcting Spelling in Microsoft Office Programs section of the Proofing tab.**

Excel opens the Custom Dictionaries dialog box where you can create a new custom dictionary to use.

2. **Click the New button in the Custom Dictionaries dialog box.**

Excel opens the Create Custom Dictionary dialog box.

3. **Type the name for your new custom dictionary and then click the Save button.**

After the Create Custom Dictionary dialog box closes, the name of the custom dictionary you created appears underneath CUSTOM.DIC (Default) in the Dictionary List box.

4. **(Optional) To restrict the language of a custom dictionary, click the language in the Dictionary Language drop-down list after clicking the dictionary's name in the Dictionary List box to select it.**

5. **To make the new custom dictionary the default dictionary into which new words are saved, click the dictionary's name in the Dictionary list box to select it and then click the Change Default button.**

6. **Click OK to close the Custom Dictionaries dialog box and then click OK again to close the Excel Options dialog box.**

   Excel returns you to the Spelling dialog box.

7. **Click the Add to Dictionary button to add the unknown word to the new default custom dictionary and then continue spell checking your spreadsheet.**

Note that Excel continues to add all unknown words to your new custom dictionary until you change the default back to the original custom dictionary (or to another custom one that you've created). To change back and start adding unknown words to the original custom dictionary, select the CUSTOM. DIC file in the Custom Dictionaries dialog box and then click the Change Default button.

You can directly edit the words that you add to your custom dictionary. Click the Custom Dictionaries button on the Proofing tab of the Excel Options dialog box (Office Button | Excel Options | Proofing or Alt+FIP) and then click the Edit Word List button. Excel then opens a dialog box with the default dictionary's name that contains a Word(s) text box where you can enter new words to add to the custom dictionary and a Dictionary list box below that lists all the words added to the dictionary in alphabetical order. To add a new word to the dictionary, type it in the Word(s) text box (carefully, you don't want to add a misspelling to the dictionary) and then click the Add button. To remove a word, click it in the Dictionary list box and then click the Delete button.

Looking Up and Translating Stuff

In addition to the very useful Spelling button (discussed in the previous section), the Proofing group on the Review tab contains three other command buttons that can come in handy from time to time:

+ **Research** opens the Research pane with the All Reference Books option selected where you can look up text that you enter in the Search For text box or the contents of the current cell automatically entered into this text box.

+ **Thesaurus** opens the Research pane with the Thesaurus option selected where you can look up synonyms for a particular term that you enter into the Search For text box or for the contents of the current cell automatically entered into this text box.

+ **Translate** opens the Research pane with the Translation option selected where you can look up a translation for a particular term that you enter into the Search For text box or for the contents of the current cell automatically entered into this text box in the language listed in the To drop-down list box.

When the Research Task pane is open, you can change the online resource to use when looking up the term in the Search For text box by selecting it on the Show Results From drop-down list box immediately beneath. These online resources include the Encarta World Dictionary, Thesaurus (available for a variety of European languages), Translation (for translating to and from English and a variety of languages), Factiva iWorks, HighBeam Research, MSN Search (for Web searches), MSN Money Stock Quotes, and Thomson Gale Company Profiles (for the latest stock info and business information).

After you click the Start Searching button (the arrow pointing to the right in the green square to the immediate right of the Search For text box) or you select a new online resource, Excel searches for your search text online in the selected resources, and the program displays these results in the lower part of the Research Task pane (beneath the Show Results From drop-down list box and the Back button). Depending on the resource used, these results may appear in the form of links to specific Web pages that you can pursue by clicking them or in the form of listed information that you can read in the Research Task pane.

When you click a Web link in the research results, Excel opens your Web browser (usually Microsoft Internet Explorer 7.0, which ships with Microsoft Office 2007) where it displays the targeted linked page. After you finish reading its information and/or following the links on its page, you can return to Excel by clicking the Close button in the upper-right corner of the Web browser window.

To change which online resources appear on the Show Results From drop-down menu, click the Research Options link that appears at the very bottom of the Research Task pane. When you click this link, Excel opens a Research Options dialog box that enables you to add or remove particular reference books and sites by either removing or adding check marks to their check box items. To widen or narrow the Research Task pane, position the mouse pointer on the border between the right edge of the Excel program window and the Task pane and then when the pointer becomes a two-headed arrow, drag to the left (to widen) or right (to narrow).

Circling Invalid Data

In addition to using the Data Validation feature to restrict what kind of data can be entered into cell ranges of a worksheet, you can use it to mark all the data (by circling their cells) that are outside of expected or allowable parameters.

To use the Data Validation feature in this way, you follow this general procedure:

✦ Select the cell range(s) in the worksheet that need to be validated and marked.

✦ Open the Data Validation dialog box by clicking the Data Validation button on the Data tab of the Ribbon or by pressing Alt+AVV, and then use its options to set up the validation criteria that determine which values in the selected cell range are out of bounds (see Book II, Chapter 1 for details).

✦ Click the Circle Invalid Data option on the Data Validation button's drop-down list on the Data tab of the Ribbon.

Figure 3-20 shows an example of how you might use Data Validation to mark entries that are below a certain threshold. In this case, I set it up for Excel to mark all the monthly sales cells entries in this Sales worksheet that are above $50,000 by drawing a red circle around their cells.

To set this up in the 2008 Sales worksheet, I followed these three steps:

✦ Selected all the cell ranges (B3:D11, F3:H11, J3:L11, and N3:P11) with monthly sales data for all four quarters of the year as nonadjacent cell selections.

✦ Opened the Data Validation dialog box (Alt+AVV) and then on the Settings tab selected Decimal in the Allow drop-down list and Greater Than in the Data drop-down list, and entered 50000 in the Minimum text box before clicking OK.

✦ Clicked the Circle Invalid Data option on the Data Validation button's drop-down menu on the Data tab (you can also press Alt+AVI).

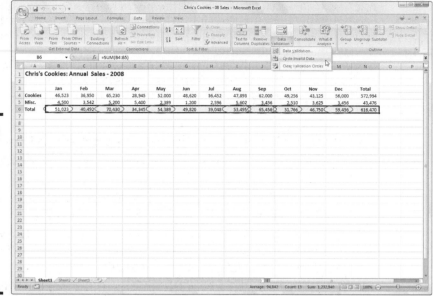

Figure 3-20:
Circling
invalid
entries in a
worksheet
where the
monthly
sales
entries are
above
$50,000.

To remove the circles from the cells marked as invalid, click the Clear
Validation Circles option on the Data Validation button's drop-down menu or
press Alt+AVR. To clear the validation settings from the cells, select the range,
then open the Data Validation dialog box and click its Clear All button before
you click OK.

Eliminating Errors with Text to Speech

Find and Replace is a great tool for eliminating errors that you've flagged in
the worksheet. Likewise, the Spell Check feature is great for eliminating input
errors that result from typos. Unfortunately, neither of these features can
help you to identify data input errors that result from actions, such as
mistyping the entry (without misspelling it) or transposing one entry with
another. The only way that you can flag and then correct these errors is by
checking and verifying the accuracy of each and every data entry in the
worksheet. Usually, you do this by checking the columns and rows of data in
a spreadsheet against the original documents from which you generated the
spreadsheet.

The Text to Speech translation feature requires no prior training or special microphones: All that's required is a pair of speakers or headphones connected to your computer.

Now for the bad news: Text to Speech is not available from any of the tabs on the Ribbon. The only way to access Text to Speech is by adding its various Speak Cells command buttons as custom buttons on the Quick Access toolbar as follows:

1. **Click Office Button | Excel Options | Customize or press Alt+FIC.**

   Doing this opens the Customize the Quick Access Toolbar tab of the Excel Options dialog box.

2. **Click Commands Not in the Ribbon on the Choose Commands From drop-down menu.**

   The Text to Speech command buttons include Speak Cells, Speak Cells – Stop Speaking Cells, Speak Cells by Column, Speak Cells by Row, and Speak Cells on Enter.

3. **Click the Speak Cells button in the Choose Commands From list box on the left and then click the Add button to add it to the bottom of the Customize Quick Access Toolbar list box on the right.**

4. **Repeat the process outlined in Step 3 until you've added the remaining Text to Speech buttons to the Quick Access toolbar: Speak Cells – Stop Speaking Cells, Speak Cells by Columns, Speak Cells by Rows, and Speak Cells on Enter.**

   If you want to reposition the Text to Speech buttons on the Quick Access toolbar, select each button in the Customize Quick Access Toolbar list box and then move it left on the bar by clicking the Move Up button or right by clicking Move Down. If you want to set off the Text to Speech buttons as a separate group on the Quick Access toolbar, add a <Separator> icon ahead of the Speak Cells command button (and following the Speak Cells on Enter button if you have buttons not related to the Text to Speech function that follow on the Quick Access toolbar).

5. **Click the OK button to close the Excel Options dialog box.**

Figure 3-21 shows the Quick Access toolbar in my Excel 2007 program window after adding all the Speak Cells command buttons to it and grouping them together with a <Separator> icon.

Book II
Chapter 3

Editing and Proofing Worksheets

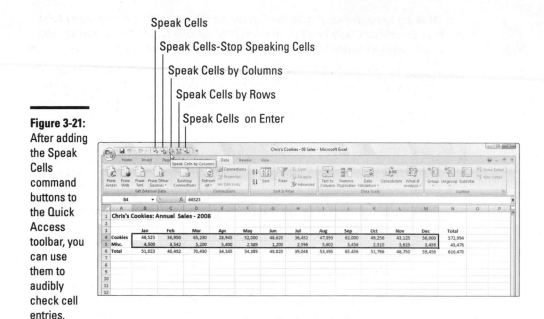

Speak Cells

Speak Cells-Stop Speaking Cells

Speak Cells by Columns

Speak Cells by Rows

Speak Cells on Enter

Figure 3-21:
After adding
the Speak
Cells
command
buttons to
the Quick
Access
toolbar, you
can use
them to
audibly
check cell
entries.

After adding the Text to Speech commands as custom Speak Cells buttons on the Quick Access toolbar, you can use them to corroborate spreadsheet entries and catch those hard-to-spot errors as follows:

1. **Select the cells in the worksheet whose contents you want read aloud by Text to Speech.**

2. **Click the Speak Cells custom button on the Quick Access toolbar to have the computer begin reading back the entries in the selected cells.**

   By default, the Text to Speech feature reads the contents of each cell in the cell selection by first reading down each column and then across the rows. If you want Text to Speech to read across the rows and then down the columns, click the Speak Cells by Rows button on the Quick Access toolbar (the button with the two opposing horizontal arrows).

3. **To have the Text to Speech feature read back each cell entry as you press the Enter key (at which point the cell cursor moves down to the next cell in the selection), click the Speak Cells on Enter custom button (the button with the curved arrow Enter symbol) on the Quick Access toolbar.**

As soon as you click the Speak Cells on Enter button, the computer tells you, "Cells will now be spoken on Enter." After selecting this option, you need to press Enter each time you want to hear an entry read back to you.

4. **To pause the Text to Speech feature when you're not using the Speak Cells on Enter option (Step 3) and you locate a discrepancy between what you're reading and what you're hearing, click the Speak Cells - Stop Speaking Cells button (the Speak Cells button with the x).**

Keep in mind that after you click the Speak Cells on Enter button on the Quick Access toolbar, the computer *only* speaks each new cell entry that you complete by pressing the Enter key (which moves the cell cursor down one row) and not by some other method, such as clicking the Enter button on the Formula bar or pressing the ↓ key.

Chapter 4: Managing Worksheets

In This Chapter

✓ Inserting and deleting columns and rows in a worksheet

✓ Splitting the worksheet into separate panes

✓ Outlining data in a worksheet

✓ Inserting, deleting, and reordering worksheets in a workbook

✓ Opening windows on different worksheets in a workbook

✓ Working with multiple workbooks

✓ Opening windows on different workbooks

✓ Creating and using custom workspaces

✓ Consolidating worksheet data

*B*eing able to manage and reorganize the information in your spreadsheet is almost as important as being able to input data and edit it. As part of these skills, you need to know how to manipulate the columns and rows of a single worksheet, the various worksheets within a single workbook, and, at times, other workbooks that contain supporting or relevant data.

This chapter examines how to reorganize information in a single worksheet by inserting and deleting columns and rows, as well as how to apply outlining to data tables that enables you to expand and collapse details by showing and hiding columns and rows. It also covers how to reorganize and manipulate the actual worksheets in a workbook and discusses strategies for visually comparing and transferring data between the different workbooks that you have open for editing.

Reorganizing the Worksheet

Every Excel 2007 worksheet that you work with has 16,384 columns and 1,048,576 rows — no more, no less, regardless of how many or how few of its cells you use. As your spreadsheet grows, you may find it beneficial to rearrange the data so that it doesn't creep. Many times, this involves deleting unnecessary columns and rows to bring the various data tables and lists in closer proximity to each other. At other times, you may need to insert new columns and rows in the worksheet so as to put a minimum of space between the groups of data.

Within the confines of this humongous worksheet space, your main challenge is often keeping tabs on all the information spread out throughout the sheet. At times, you may find that you need to split the worksheet window into panes so that you can view two disparate regions of the spreadsheet together in the same window and compare their data. For large data tables and lists, you may want to outline the worksheet data so that you can immediately collapse the information down to the summary or essential data and then just as quickly expand the information to show some or all of the supporting data.

Inserting and deleting columns and rows

The first thing to keep in mind when inserting or deleting columns and rows in a worksheet is that these operations affect all 1,048,576 rows in those columns and all 16,384 columns in those rows. As a result, you have to be sure that you're not about to adversely affect data in unseen rows and columns of the sheet before you undertake these operations. Note that, in this regard, inserting columns or rows can be almost as detrimental as deleting them if, by inserting them, you split apart existing data tables or lists whose data should always remain together.

One way to guard against inadvertently deleting existing data or splitting apart a single range is to use the Zoom slider on the Status bar to zoom out on the sheet and then check visually for intersecting groups of data in the hinterlands of the worksheet. You can do this quickly by dragging the Zoom slider button to the left to the 25% setting. Of course, even at the smallest zoom setting of 10%, you can see neither all the columns nor all the rows in the worksheet, and because everything's so tiny at that setting, you can't always tell whether or not the column or row you intend to fiddle with intersects those data ranges that you can identify.

Another way to check is to press End+→ or End+↓ to move the cell pointer from data range to data range across the column or row affected by your column or row deletion. Remember that pressing End plus an arrow key when the cell pointer is in a blank cell jumps the cell pointer to the next occupied cell in its row or column. That means if you press End+→ when the cell pointer is in row 52 and the pointer jumps to cell XFD52 (the end of the worksheet in that row), you know that there isn't any data in that row that would be eliminated by your deleting that row or shifted up or down by your inserting a new row. So too, if you press End+↓ when the cell pointer is in column D and the cell pointer jumps down to cell D1048576, you're assured that no data is about to be purged or shifted left or right by that column's deletion or a new column's insertion at that point.

When you're sure that you aren't about to make any problems for yourself in other, unseen parts of the worksheet by deleting or inserting columns, you're ready to make these structural changes to the worksheet.

Eradicating columns and rows

To delete columns or rows of the worksheet, select them by clicking their column letters or row numbers in the column or row header and then click the Delete button in the Cells group on the Ribbon's Home tab. Remember that you can select groups of columns and rows by dragging through their letters and numbers in the column or row header. You can also select nonadjacent columns and rows by holding down the Ctrl key as you click them.

When you delete a column, all the data entries within the cells of that column are immediately zapped. At the same time, all remaining data entries in succeeding columns to the right move left to fill the blank left by the now-missing column. When you delete a row, all the data entries within the cells of that row are immediately eliminated, and the remaining data entries in rows below move up to fill in the gap left by the missing row.

You can also delete rows and columns of the worksheet corresponding to those that are a part of the current cell selection in the worksheet by clicking the drop-down button attached to the Delete command button on the Home tab of the Ribbon and then clicking the Delete Sheet Rows or Delete Sheet Columns option, respectively, on its drop-down menu. If you find you can't safely delete an entire column or row, delete the cells you need to get rid of in the particular region of the worksheet instead by selecting them and then clicking the Delete Cells option on the Delete command button's drop-down list (see Book II, Chapter 3 for details).

Remember that pressing the Delete key is *not* the same as clicking the Delete button on the Home tab of the Ribbon. When you press the Delete key after selecting columns or rows in the worksheet, Excel simply clears the data entries in their cells without adjusting any of the existing data entries in neighboring columns and rows. Click the Delete command button on the Home tab when your purpose is *both* to delete the data in the selected columns or rows *and* to fill in the gap by adjusting the position of entries to the right and below the ones you eliminate.

Should your row or column deletions remove data entries referenced in formulas, the #REF! error value replaces the calculated values in the cells of the formulas affected by the elimination of the original cell references. You must then either restore the deleted rows or columns or re-create the original formula and then recopy it to get rid of these nasty formula errors. (See Book III, Chapter 2 for more on error values in formulas.)

Adding new columns and rows

To insert a new column or row into the worksheet, you select the column or row where you want the new blank column or row to appear (again by clicking its column letter or row number in the column or row header) and then click the Insert command button in the Cells group of the Ribbon's Home tab.

In inserting a blank column, Excel moves the existing data in the selected column to the column to the immediate right, while simultaneously moving any other columns of data on the right over one. In inserting the blank row, Excel moves the existing data in the selected row down to the row immediately underneath, while simultaneously adjusting any other rows of existing data that fall below it, down by one.

To insert multiple columns or rows at one time in the worksheet, select the columns or rows where you want the new blank columns or rows to appear (by dragging through their column letters and row numbers in the column and row header) before you click the Insert command button on the Home tab of the Ribbon.

You can also new insert rows and columns of the worksheet corresponding to those that are a part of the current cell selection in the worksheet by clicking the drop-down button attached to the Insert command button on the Home tab and then clicking the Insert Sheet Rows or Insert Sheet Columns option, respectively, on its drop-down menu. If you find that you can't safely insert an entire column or row, insert the blank cells you need in the particular region of the worksheet instead by selecting their cells and then clicking the Insert Cells option on the Insert command button's drop-down list (see Book II, Chapter 3 for details).

Whenever your column or row insertions reposition data entries that are referenced in other formulas in the worksheet, Excel automatically adjusts the cell references in the formulas affected to reflect the movement of their columns left or right, or rows up or down.

Splitting the worksheet into panes

Excel enables you to split the active worksheet window into two or four panes, each of which is equipped with its own scroll bars. After splitting up the window into panes, you can then use the pane's scroll bars to bring different parts of the same worksheet into view. This is great for comparing the data in different sections of a table that would otherwise not be legible if you zoomed out far enough to have both sections displayed in the worksheet window.

To split the worksheet window into panes, you can use any of the following methods:

✦ To split the window horizontally into two panes (upper and lower), drag the horizontal split bar (the thin bar located above the up scroll arrow on the vertical scroll bar) down until you reach the row border in the worksheet where you want the window divided.

✦ To split the window vertically into two panes (left and right), drag the vertical split bar (the thin bar located behind the right scroll arrow on the horizontal scroll bar) to the left until you reach the column border in the worksheet where you want the window divided.

✦ To split the window both horizontally and vertically into four panes (upper-left, upper-right, lower-left, and lower-right), drag the horizontal split bar down to the desired row and then the vertical split bar left to the desired column (or vice versa).

Book II
Chapter 4

Managing
Worksheets

Note that you can also split the window by positioning the cell pointer position in the worksheet in the cell whose top border marks the place where you want the horizontal division to take place and whose left border marks the place where you want the vertical division to take place before clicking the Split button on the View tab of the Ribbon (or pressing Alt+WS).

Excel displays the borders of the window panes you create in the document window with a bar that ends with the vertical or horizontal split bar. To modify the size of a pane, you position the white-cross pointer on the appropriate dividing bar. Then as soon as the pointer changes to a double-headed arrow, drag the bar until the pane is the correct size and release the mouse button.

When you split a window into panes, Excel automatically synchronizes the scrolling, depending on how you split the worksheet. When you split a window into two horizontal panes, as shown in Figure 4-1, the worksheet window contains a single horizontal scroll bar and two separate vertical scroll bars. This means that all horizontal scrolling of the two panes is synchronized, while the vertical scrolling of each pane remains independent.

When you split a window into two vertical panes, as shown in Figure 4-2, the situation is reversed. The worksheet window contains a single vertical scroll bar and two separate horizontal scroll bars. This means that all vertical scrolling of the two panes is synchronized, while horizontal scrolling of each pane remains independent.

Figure 4-1:
Dragging
the split bar
to divide the
worksheet
window
into two
horizontal
panes.

[Screenshot of Microsoft Excel — Income Analysis - 2008 [Shared] showing the Regional Income 2008 worksheet split into two horizontal panes.]

	Jan	Feb	Mar	Qtr 1	Apr	May	Jun	Qtr 2	Jul
1 Regional Income 2008									
3 Sales									
4 Northern	$30,336	$33,370	$36,707	$100,412	$40,377	$44,415	$48,856	$133,649	$53,742
5 Southern	20,572	22,629	24,892	$68,093	27,381	30,119	33,131	$90,632	36,445
6 Central	131,685	144,854	159,339	$435,877	175,273	192,800	212,080	$580,153	233,288
7 Western	94,473	103,920	114,312	$312,706	125,744	138,318	152,150	$416,211	167,365
8 International	126,739	139,413	153,354	$419,506	168,690	185,559	204,114	$558,363	224,526
9 **Total Sales**	$403,805	$444,186	$488,604	$1,336,595	$537,464	$591,211	$650,332	$1,779,007	$715,365
11 Cost of Goods Sold									
12 Northern	10,341	11,272	12,286	$33,899	13,392	14,597	15,911	43,900	17,343
13 Southern	6,546	7,135	7,777	$21,458	8,477	9,240	10,072	27,789	10,978
14 Central	65,843	71,769	78,228	$215,840	85,269	92,943	101,308	279,519	110,425
15 Western	63,967	69,724	75,999	$209,690	82,839	90,295	98,421	271,555	107,279
16 International	72,314	78,822	85,916	$237,053	93,649	102,077	111,264	306,990	121,278
17 **Total Cost of Goods Sold**	$219,011	$238,722	$260,207	$717,940	$283,626	$309,152	$336,976	929,753	$367,303
19 Operating Expenses									
20 Northern	$21,529	$23,036	$24,649	$69,214	$26,374	$28,220	$30,196	$84,790	$32,309
21 Southern	15,946	17,062	18,257	$51,265	19,535	20,902	22,365	$62,802	23,931
22 Central	27,554	29,483	31,547	$88,583	33,755	36,118	38,646	$108,518	41,351
23 Western	16,130	17,259	18,467	$51,856	19,760	21,143	22,623	$63,526	24,207
24 International	32,361	34,626	37,050	$104,037	39,644	42,419	45,388	$127,450	48,565
25 **Total Operating Expenses**	$113,520	$121,466	$129,969	$364,955	$139,067	$148,802	$159,218	$447,086	$170,363

When you split a window into two horizontal and two vertical panes, as shown in Figure 4-3, the worksheet window contains two horizontal scroll bars and two separate vertical scroll bars. This means that vertical scrolling is synchronized in the top two window panes when you use the top vertical scroll bar and synchronized for the bottom two window panes when you use the bottom vertical scroll bar. Likewise, horizontal scrolling is synchronized for the left two window panes when you use the horizontal scroll bar on the left, and synchronized for the right two window panes when you use the horizontal scroll bar on the right.

To remove all panes from a window when you no longer need them, you simply click the Split button on the View tab of the Ribbon, press Alt+WS, or drag the dividing bar either for the horizontal or vertical pane until you reach one of the edges of the worksheet window. You can also remove a pane by positioning the mouse pointer on a pane-dividing bar and then, when it changes to a double-header arrow, double-clicking it.

Keep in mind that you can freeze panes in the window so that information in the upper pane and/or in the leftmost pane remains in the worksheet window at all times, no matter what other columns and rows you scroll to or how much you zoom in and out on the data. (See Book II, Chapter 3 for more on freezing panes.)

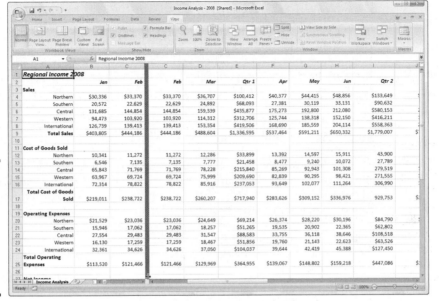

Figure 4-2:
Dragging
the split bar
to divide the
worksheet
window into
two vertical
panes.

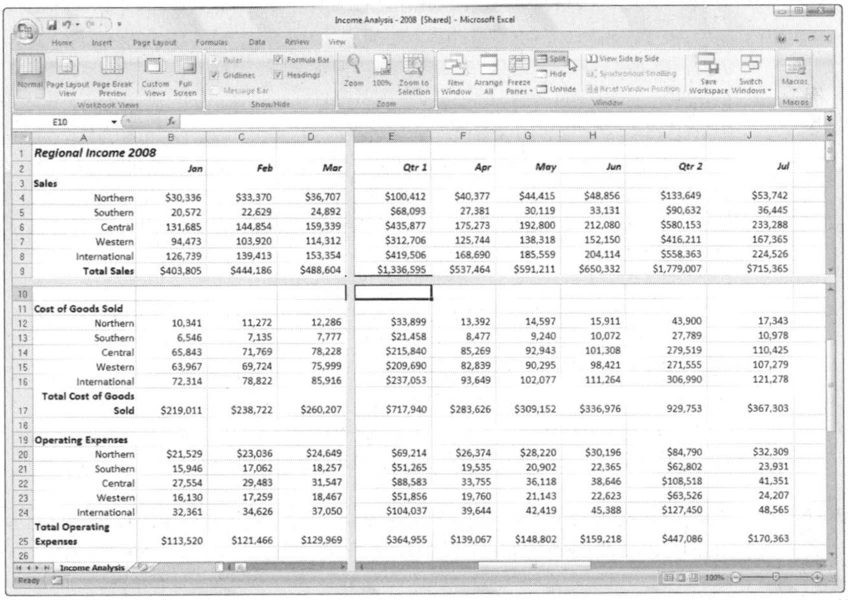

Figure 4-3:
Splitting the
worksheet
window into
four panes:
two hori-
zontal and
two vertical.

Outlining worksheets

The Outline feature enables you to control the level of detail displayed in a data table or list in a worksheet. After outlining a table or list, you can condense the table's display when you want to use only certain levels of summary information, and you can just as easily expand the outlined table or list to display various levels of detail data as needed. Being able to control which outline level is displayed in the worksheet makes it easy to print summary reports with various levels of data (see Book II, Chapter 5) as well as to chart just the summary data (see Book V, Chapter 1).

Spreadsheet outlines are a little different from the outlines you created in high school and college. In those outlines, you placed the headings at the highest level (I.) at the top of the outline with the intermediate headings indented below. Most worksheet outlines, however, seem backward in the sense that the highest level summary row and column are located at the bottom and far right of the table or list of data, with the columns and rows of intermediate supporting data located above and to the left of the summary row and column.

The reason that worksheet outlines often seem "backwards" when compared to word processing outlines is that, most often, to calculate your summary totals in the worksheet, you naturally place the detail levels of data above the summary rows and to the left of the summary columns that total them. When creating a word processing outline, however, you place the major headings above subordinate headings, while at the same time indenting each subordinate level, reflecting the way we read words from left to right and down the page.

Outlines for data tables (as opposed to data lists) are also different from regular word processed outlines because they outline the data in not one, but two hierarchies: a vertical hierarchy that summarizes the row data, and a horizontal hierarchy that summarizes the column data. (You don't get much of that in your regular term paper!)

Creating the outline

To create an outline from a table of data, position the cell cursor in the table or list containing the data to be outlined, and then click the Auto Outline option on the Group command button's drop-down menu on the Data tab on the Ribbon (or press Alt+AGA).

By default, Excel assumes that summary rows in the selected data table are below their detail data, and summary columns are to the right of their detail data, which is normally the case. If, however, the summary rows are above the detail data, and summary columns are to the left of the detail data, Excel can still build the outline.

Simply start by clicking the Dialog Box Launcher button in the lower-right corner of the Outline group on the Data tab of the Ribbon to open the Settings dialog box. In the Settings dialog box, clear the check marks from the Summary Rows below Detail and/or Summary Columns to Right of Detail check boxes in the Direction section. Also, you can have Excel automatically apply styles to different levels of the outline by selecting the Automatic Styles check box. (For more information on these styles, see the "Applying outline styles" section, later in this chapter.) To have Excel create the outline, click the Create button — if you click the OK button, the program simply closes the dialog box without outlining the selected worksheet data.

Figure 4-4 shows you the first part of the outline created by Excel for the CG Media Sales worksheet. Note the various outline symbols that Excel added to the worksheet when it created the outline. Figure 4-4 identifies most of these outline symbols (the Show Detail button with the plus sign is not displayed in this figure), and Table 4-1 explains their functions.

Table 4-1	Outline Symbols
Symbol	*Function*
Row and column level symbol	Displays a desired level of detail throughout the outline (1, 2, 3, and so on up to 8). When you click a row or column level symbol, Excel displays the level and all levels above it in the worksheet display.
Row and column level bar	Hides the display of the detail rows or columns the level bar includes, which is the same as clicking the collapse symbol (see below).
Expand (+) symbol	Expands the display to show the detail rows or columns that have been collapsed.
Collapse (–) symbol	Condenses the display to hide the detail rows or columns that are included in its row or column level bar.

If you don't see any of the outline symbols identified in Figure 4-4 and Table 4-1, this means that the Show Outline Symbols If an Outline Is Applied check box on the Advanced tab in the Excel Options dialog box (Alt+FIA) is not checked. All you have to do is open the Advanced tab of the Excel Options dialog box and click the Show Outline Symbols If an Outline Is Applied check box before you click OK to have Excel display the various outline symbols specific to your worksheet outline.

You can have only one outline per worksheet. If you've already outlined one table and then try to outline another table on the same worksheet, Excel will display the Modify Existing Outline alert box when you choose the Outline command. If you click OK, Excel adds the outlining for the new table to the existing outline for the first table (even though the tables are nonadjacent). To create separate outlines for different data tables, you need to place each table on a different worksheet of the workbook.

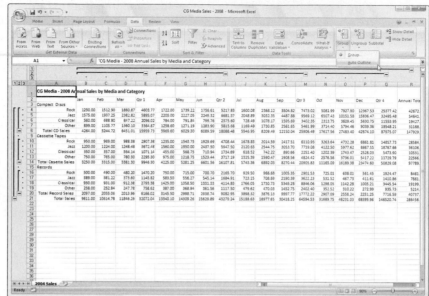

Figure 4-4:
Outlining the
2008 CG
Media
Sales table
arranged by
category
and date.

Applying outline styles

You can apply predefined row and column outline styles to the table or list
data. To apply these styles when creating the outline, be sure to select the
Automatic Styles check box in the Settings dialog box before you click its
Create button, opened by clicking the Dialog Box Launcher button in the
Outline group on the Data tab of the Ribbon. If you didn't select this
check box in the Settings dialog box before you created the outline, you can
do so afterwards by selecting all the cells in the outlined table of data, opening the Settings dialog box, clicking the Automatic Styles check box to put
a check mark in it, and then clicking the Apply Styles button before you
click OK.

Figure 4-5 shows you the sample CG Media Sales table after applying the
automatic row and column styles to the outlined table data. In this example,
Excel applied two row styles (RowLevel_1 and RowLevel_2) and two column
styles (ColLevel_1 and ColLevel_2) to the worksheet table.

The RowLevel_1 style is applied to the entries in the first-level summary row
(row 15) and makes the font appear in bold. The ColLevel_1 style is applied
to the data in the first-level summary column (column R, which isn't shown
in the figure), and it, too, simply makes the font bold. The RowLevel_2 style
is applied to the data in the second-level rows (rows 8 and 14), and this style
adds italics to the font. The ColLevel_2 style is applied to all second-level
summary columns (columns E, I, M, and Q), and it also italicizes the font.

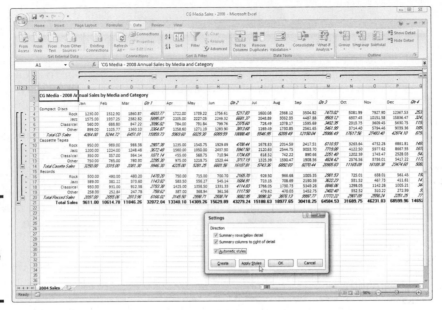

Book II
Chapter 4

Managing Worksheets

Figure 4-5:
Applying outline styles to the outlined data table.

Displaying and hiding different outline levels

The real effectiveness of outlining worksheet data becomes apparent only when you start using the various outline symbols to change the way the table data are displayed in the worksheet. By clicking the appropriate row or column level symbol, you can immediately hide detail rows and columns to display just the summary information in the table. For example, Figure 4-6 shows you the CG Media Sales table after clicking the number 2 row level button and number 2 column level button. Here, you see only the first- and second-level summary information, that is, the totals for the quarterly and annual totals for the two types of media.

You can also hide and display levels of the outlined data by positioning the cell cursor in the column or row and then clicking the Hide Detail (the one with the red minus sign) or the Show Detail button (the one with the green minus sign) in the Outline group of the Data tab of the Ribbon. Or you can press the hot keys, Alt+AH, to hide an outline level, and Alt+AJ to redisplay the level. The great thing about using these command buttons or their hot key equivalents is that they work even when the outline symbols are not displayed in the worksheet.

Figure 4-7 shows you the same table, this time after clicking the number 1 row level button and number 1 column level button. Here, you see only the first-level summary for the column and the row, that is, the grand total of the annual CG Media sales. To expand this view horizontally to see the total sales for each quarter, you would simply click the number 2 column level button. To expand this view even further horizontally to display each monthly total in the worksheet, you would click the number 3 column level button. So too, to expand the outline vertically to see totals for each type of media, you would click the number 2 row level button. To expand the outline one more level vertically so that you can see the sales for each type of music as well as each type of media, you would click the number 3 row level button.

When displaying different levels of detail in a worksheet outline, you can use the collapse or expand symbols along with the row level and column level buttons. For example, Figure 4-8 shows you another view of the CG Media outlined sales table. Here, in the horizontal dimension, you see all three column levels have been expanded, including the monthly detail columns for each quarter. In the vertical dimension, however, only the detail rows for the CD sales have been expanded. The detail rows for cassette tape sales are still collapsed. To create this view of the outline, you simply click the number 2 row level button, and then click the expand symbol (+) located to the left of the Total CD Sales row heading. When you want to view only the summary-level rows for each media type, you can click the collapse symbol (–) to the left of the Total CD Sales heading, or you can click its level bar (drawn from the collapse symbol up to the first music type to indicate all the details rows included in that level).

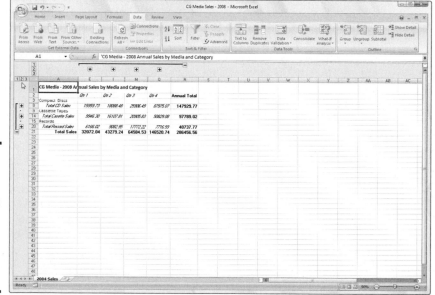

Figure 4-6:
Collapsed
outline with
the first- and
secondary-
level
summary
information
displayed.

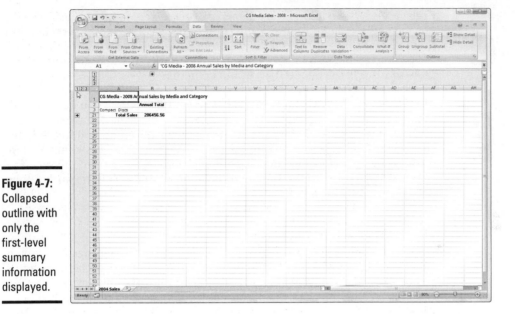

Figure 4-7:
Collapsed
outline with
only the
first-level
summary
information
displayed.

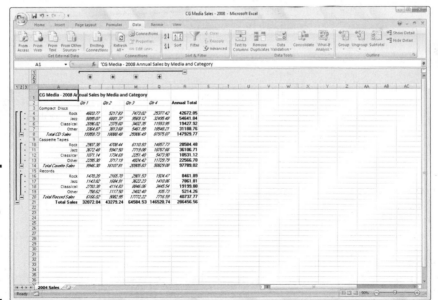

Figure 4-8:
Outline
expanded to
show only
CD sales
details for
all four
quarters.

Excel adjusts the outline levels displayed on the screen by hiding and redisplaying entire columns and rows in the worksheet. Therefore, keep in mind that changes that you make that reduce the number of levels displayed in the outlined table also hide the display of all data outside of the outlined table that are in the affected rows and columns.

After selecting the rows and columns you want displayed, you can then remove the outline symbols from the worksheet display to maximize the amount of data displayed on-screen. To do this without having to open the Options dialog box and fool around with the Outline Symbols check box on the View tab, press Ctrl+8 (the number eight on the top row of the standard keyboard). Ctrl+8 switches between showing and hiding all the outline symbols in a worksheet.

Manually adjusting the outline levels

Most of the time, Excel's Auto Outline feature correctly outlines the data in your table. Every once in a while, however, you will have to manually adjust one or more of the outline levels so that the outline's summary rows and columns include the right detail rows and columns. To adjust levels of a worksheet outline, you must select the rows or columns that you want to promote to a higher level (that is, one with a lower level number) in the outline and then click the Group button on the far right side of the Data tab of the Ribbon. If you want to demote selected rows or columns to a lower level in the outline, select the rows or columns with a higher level number and then click the Ungroup button on the Data tab.

Before you use the Group and Ungroup buttons to change an outline level, you must select the rows or columns that you want to promote or demote. To select a particular outline level and all the rows and columns included in that level, you need to display the outline symbols (Ctrl+8), and then hold down the Shift key as you click its collapse or expand symbol. Note that when you click an expand symbol, Excel selects not only the rows or columns visible at that level, but all the hidden rows and columns included in that level as well. If you want to select only a particular detail or summary row or column in the outline, you can click that row number or column letter in the worksheet window, or you can hold down the Shift key and click the dot (period) to the left of the row number or above the column letter in the outline symbols area.

If you select only a range of cells in the rows or columns (as opposed to entire rows and columns) before you click the Group and Ungroup command buttons, Excel displays the Group or Ungroup dialog box which contains a

Rows and Columns option button (with the Rows button selected by default). To promote or demote columns instead of rows, click the Columns option button before you select OK. To close the dialog box without promoting or demoting any part of the outline, click Cancel.

To see how you can use the Group and Ungroup command buttons on the Data tab of the Ribbon to adjust outline levels, consider once again the CG Media Sales table outline. When Excel created this outline, the program did not include row 3 (which contains only the row heading, Compact Discs) in the outline. As a result, when you collapse the rows by selecting the number 1 row level button to display only the first-level Total Sales summary row (refer to Figure 4-7), this row heading remains visible in the table, even though it should have been included and thereby hidden along with the other summary and detail rows.

You can use the Group command button to move this row (3) down a level so that it is included in the first level of the outline. You simply click the row number 3 to select the row and then click the Group command button on the Data tab (or press Alt+AGG). Figure 4-9 shows you the result of doing this. Notice how the outside level bar (for level 1) now includes this row. Now, when you collapse the outline by clicking the number 1 row level button, the heading in row 3 is hidden as well (see Figure 4-10).

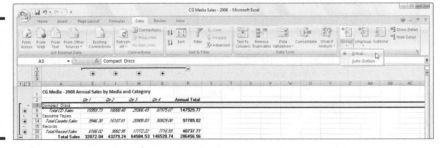

Figure 4-9: Manually adjusting the level 1 rows in the outlined sales table.

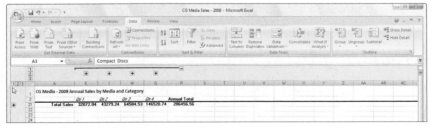

Figure 4-10: Collapsing the adjusted outline down to row level 1.

Removing an outline

To delete an outline from your worksheet, you click the drop-down button attached to the Ungroup button on the Data tab of the Ribbon, and then click the Clear Outline option on its drop-down menu (or you press Alt+AUC). Note that removing the outline does not affect the data in any way — Excel merely removes the outline structure. Also note that it doesn't matter what state the outline is in at the time you select this command. If the outline is partially or totally collapsed, deleting the outline automatically displays all the hidden rows and columns in the data table or list.

Keep in mind that restoring an outline that you've deleted is not one of the commands that you can undo (Ctrl+Z). If you delete an outline by mistake, you must re-create it all over again. For this reason, most often you'll want to expand all the outline levels (by clicking the lowest number column and row level button) and then hide all the outline symbols by pressing Ctrl+8 rather than permanently remove the outline. Note that if you press Ctrl+8 when your spreadsheet table isn't yet outlined, Excel displays an alert dialog box indicating that it can't show the outline symbols because no outline exists. This alert also asks you if you want to create an outline. To go ahead and outline the spreadsheet, click OK or press Enter. To remove the alert dialog box without creating an outline, click Cancel.

Creating different custom views of the outline

After you've created an outline for your worksheet table, you can create custom views that display the table in various levels of detail. Then, instead of having to display the outline symbols and manually click the Show Detail and Hide Detail buttons or the appropriate row level buttons and/or column level buttons to view a particular level of detail, you simply select the appropriate outline view in the Custom Views dialog box (View | Custom Views or Alt+WCV).

When creating custom views of outlined worksheet data, be sure that you leave the Hidden Rows, Columns, and Filter Settings check box selected in the Include in View section of the Add View dialog box. (See Book II, Chapter 3 for details on creating and using custom views in a worksheet.)

Reorganizing the Workbook

Any new workbook that you open comes already equipped with three blank worksheets. Although most of the spreadsheets you create and work with may never wander beyond the confines of the first of these three sheets, you do need to know how to organize your spreadsheet information three-dimensionally for those rare occasions when spreading all the information out in one humongous worksheet is not practical. However, the normal everyday problems related to keeping on top of the information in a single worksheet can easily go off the scale when you begin to use multiple worksheets in a workbook. For this reason, you need to be sure that you are fully versed in the basics of using more than one worksheet in a workbook.

To move between the sheets in a workbook, you can click the sheet tab for that worksheet or press Ctrl+PgDn (next sheet) or Ctrl+PgUp (preceding sheet) until the sheet is selected. If the sheet tab for the worksheet you want is not displayed on the scroll bar at the bottom of the document window, use the tab scrolling buttons (the buttons with the left- and right-pointing triangles) to bring it into view.

**Book II
Chapter 4**

**Managing
Worksheets**

To use the tab scrolling buttons, click the one with the right-pointing triangle to bring the next sheet into view, and click the one with the left-pointing triangle to bring the preceding sheet into view. The tab scrolling buttons with the directional triangles pointing to vertical lines display the very first or very last group of sheet tabs in a workbook. The button with the triangle pointing left to a vertical line brings the first group of sheet tabs into view; the button with the triangle pointing right to a vertical line brings the last group of sheet tabs into view. When you scroll sheet tabs to find the one you're looking for, for heaven's sake, don't forget to click the desired sheet tab to make the worksheet current.

Renaming sheets

The sheet tabs shown at the bottom of each workbook are the keys to keeping your place in a workbook. To tell which sheet is current, you have only to look at which sheet tab appears on the top, matches the background of the other cells in the worksheet, and has its name displayed in bold type. Typically, this means that the active sheet tab's background appears in white in contrast to the nonactive sheet tabs, which sport a light gray background.

When you start a new workbook, the sheet tabs are all the same width because they all have the default sheet names (Sheet1, Sheet2, and so on). As you assign your own names to the sheets, the tabs appear either longer or shorter, depending on the length of the sheet tab name. Just keep in mind that the longer the sheet tabs, the fewer you can see at one time, and the more sheet tab scrolling you'll have to do to find the worksheet you want.

To rename a worksheet, you take these steps:

1. **Press Ctrl+PgDn until the sheet you want to rename is active, or click its sheet tab if it's displayed at the bottom of the workbook window.**

   Don't forget that you have to select and activate the sheet you want to rename, or you end up renaming whatever sheet happens to be current at the time you perform the next step.

2. **Click Rename Sheet on the Format button's drop-down menu on the Home tab, press Alt+HOR, or right-click the sheet tab and then click Rename on its shortcut menu.**

   When you choose this command, Excel selects the current name of the tab and positions the insertion point at the end of the name.

3. **Replace or edit the name on the sheet tab and then press the Enter key.**

When you rename a worksheet in this manner, keep in mind that Excel then uses that sheet name in any formulas that refer to cells in that worksheet. So, for instance, if you rename Sheet2 to 2008 Sales and then create a formula in cell A10 of Sheet1 that adds its cell B10 to cell C34 in Sheet2, the formula in cell A10 becomes:

```
=B10+'2008 Sales'!C34
```

This is in place of the more obscure `=B10+Sheet2!C34`. For this reason, keep your sheet names short and to the point so that you can easily and quickly identify the sheet and its data without creating excessively long formula references.

Designer sheets

Excel 2007 enables you to color-code the worksheets in your workbook. This makes it possible to create a color scheme that helps either identify or prioritize the sheets and the information they contain (as you might with different colored folder tabs in a filing cabinet).

When you color a sheet tab, note that the tab appears in that color only when it's not the active sheet. The moment you select a color-coded sheet tab, it becomes white with just a bar of the assigned color appearing under the sheet name. Note, too, that when you assign darker colors to a sheet tab, Excel automatically reverses out the sheet name text to white when the worksheet is not active.

Color coding sheet tabs

To assign a new color to a sheet tab, follow these three steps:

1. **Press Ctrl+PgDn until the sheet whose tab you want to color is active, or click its sheet tab if it's displayed at the bottom of the workbook window.**

   Don't forget that you have to select and activate the sheet whose tab you want to color, or you end up coloring the tab of whatever sheet happens to be current at the time you perform the next step.

2. **Click the Format button on the Home tab and then highlight Tab Color, press Alt+HOT, or right-click the tab and then highlight Tab Color on the shortcut menu to display its pop-up color palette.**

3. **Click the color swatch in the color palette with the color and shade you want to assign to the current sheet tab.**

To remove color-coding from a sheet tab, click the No Color option at the bottom of the pop-up color palette (Alt+HOT) after selecting it to make the worksheet active.

Assigning graphic sheet backgrounds

If coloring the sheet tabs isn't enough for you, you can also assign a graphic image to be used as the background for all the cells in the entire worksheet. Just be aware that the background image must either be very light in color or use a greatly reduced opacity in order for your worksheet data to be read over the image. This probably makes most graphics that you have readily available unusable as worksheet background images. It can, however, be quite effective if you have a special corporate watermark graphic (as with the company's logo at extremely low opacity) that adds just a hint of a background without obscuring the data being presented in its cells.

To add a graphic file as the background for your worksheet, take these steps:

1. **Press Ctrl+PgDn until the sheet to which you want to assign the graphic as the background is active, or click its sheet tab if it's displayed at the bottom of the workbook window.**

   Don't forget that you have to select and activate the sheet to which the graphic file will act as the background, or you end up assigning the file to whatever sheet happens to be current at the time you perform the following steps.

2. **Click the Background command button in the Page Setup group of the Page Layout tab or press Alt+PSB.**

   Doing this opens the Sheet Background dialog box where you select the graphics file whose image is to become the worksheet background.

3. **Open the folder that contains the image you want to use and then click its graphic file icon before you click the Insert button.**

   As soon as you click the Insert button, Excel closes the Sheet Background dialog box, and the image in the selected file becomes the background image for all cells in the current worksheet. (Usually, the program does this by stretching the graphic so that it takes up all the cells that are visible in the Workbook window. In the case of some smaller images, the program does this by tiling the image so that it's duplicated across and down the viewing area.)

Keep in mind that a graphic image that you assign as the worksheet background doesn't appear in the printout, unlike the pattern and background colors that you assign to ranges of cells in the sheet.

To remove a background image, you simply click the Delete Background command button on the Page Layout tab of the Ribbon (which replaces the Background button the moment you assign a background image to a worksheet) or press Alt+PSB again, and Excel immediately clears the image from the entire worksheet.

Adding and deleting sheets

Although you only start out with three worksheets, you can have as many worksheets as you need in building and remodeling your spreadsheet. To add a new worksheet, click the Insert Worksheet button which always appears on its own tab immediately after the last sheet tab in the workbook.

Excel then inserts a new sheet at the back of the existing sheets in the workbook (and immediately in front of the tab with the Insert Worksheet button), and the program assigns it the next available sheet number (as in Sheet4, Sheet5, Sheet6, and so on).

You can also insert a new sheet (and not necessarily a blank worksheet) into the workbook by right-clicking a sheet tab and then clicking Insert at the top of the tab's shortcut menu. Excel opens the Insert dialog box containing different file icons that you can select — Chart, MS Excel 4.0 Macro, and MS Excel 5.0 Dialog, along with a variety of different worksheet templates — to insert a specialized chart sheet (see Book V, Chapter 1), macro sheet

(Book VIII, Chapter 1), or worksheet following a template design (see Book II, Chapter 1). Note that when you insert a new sheet using the Insert dialog box, Excel inserts the new worksheet, chart sheet, or macro sheet *in front* of the sheet that's active (and not at the end of the workbook as when you insert a worksheet by clicking the Insert Worksheet button).

If you find that three worksheets just never seem to be enough for the kind of spreadsheets you normally create, you can change the default number of sheets that are automatically available in all new workbook files that you open. To do this, open the Popular tab of the Excel Options dialog box (Office Button | Excel Options or Alt+FI), and then enter a number in the Include This Many Sheets text box or select the number with the spinner buttons (up to a maximum of 255 — that's a lotta sheets!). Of course, if you find that three sheets are always too much (because you only use one), you can reduce the default number from three by entering 1 or 2 in this text box (remember you can't go lower than 1 because a workbook with no worksheet is no workbook at all).

To remove a worksheet, make the sheet active and then click the drop-down button attached to the Delete button on the Home tab of the Ribbon and click Delete Sheet on its drop-down menu — you can press Alt+HDS or right-click its tab and then click Delete on its shortcut menu. If Excel detects that the worksheet contains some data, the program then displays an alert dialog box cautioning you that data may exist in the worksheet you're just about to zap. To go ahead and delete the sheet (data and all), you click the Delete button. To preserve the worksheet, click Cancel or press the Escape key.

Deleting a sheet is one of those actions that you can't undo with the Undo button on the Quick Access toolbar. This means that after you click the Delete button, you've kissed your worksheet goodbye, so please don't do this unless you're *certain* that you aren't dumping needed data. Also, keep in mind that you can't delete a worksheet if that sheet is the only one in the workbook until you've inserted another blank worksheet: Excel won't allow a workbook file to be completely sheetless.

Changing the sheets

Excel makes it easy to rearrange the order of the sheets in your workbook. To move a sheet, click its sheet tab and drag it to the new position in the row of tabs. As you drag, the pointer changes shape to an arrowhead on a dog-eared piece of paper, and you see a black triangle pointing downward above the sheet tabs. When this triangle is positioned over the tab of the sheet that is to follow the one you're moving, release the mouse button.

If you need to copy a worksheet to another position in the workbook, hold down the Ctrl key as you click and drag the sheet tab. When you release the mouse button, Excel creates a copy with a new sheet tab name based on the number of the copy and the original sheet name. For example, if you copy Sheet1 to a new place in the workbook, the copy is renamed Sheet1 (2). You can then rename the worksheet whatever you want.

Group editing

One of the nice things about a workbook is that it enables you to edit more than one worksheet at a time. Of course, you should be concerned with group editing only when you're working on a bunch of worksheets that share essentially the same layout and require the same type of formatting.

For example, suppose that you have a workbook that contains annual sales worksheets (named YTD04, YTD05, and YTD06) for three consecutive years. The worksheets share the same layout (with months across the columns and quarterly and annual totals, locations, and types of sales down the rows) but lack standard formatting.

To format any part of these three worksheets in a single operation, you simply resort to group editing, which requires selecting the three sales worksheets. Simply click the YTD04, YTD05, and YTD06 sheet tabs as you hold down the Ctrl key, or you can click the YTD04 tab and then hold down the Shift key as you click the YTD06 tab.

After you select the last sheet, the message [Group] appears in the title bar of the active document window (with the YTD04 worksheet, in this case).

The [Group] indicator lets you know that any editing change you make to the current worksheet will affect all the sheets that are currently selected. For example, if you select a row of column headings and add bold and italics to the headings in the current worksheet, the same formatting is applied to the same cell selection in all three sales sheets. All headings in the same cell range in the other worksheets are now in bold and italics. Keep in mind that you can apply not only formatting changes to a cell range, but also editing changes, such as replacing a cell entry, deleting a cell's contents, or moving a cell selection to a new place in the worksheet. These changes also affect all the worksheets you have selected as long as they're grouped together.

After you are finished making editing changes that affect all the grouped worksheets, you can break up the group by right-clicking one of the sheet tabs and then clicking Ungroup Sheets at the top of the shortcut menu.

As soon as you break up the group, the [Group] indicator disappears from the title bar, and thereafter, any editing changes that you make affect only the cells in the active worksheet.

To select all the worksheets in the workbook for group editing in one operation, right-click the tab of the sheet where you want to make the editing changes that affect all the other sheets, and then click Select All Sheets on its shortcut menu.

"Now you see them; now you don't"

Another technique that comes in handy when working with multiple worksheets is hiding particular worksheets in the workbook. Just as you can hide particular columns, rows, and cell ranges in a worksheet, you can also hide particular worksheets in the workbook. For example, you may want to hide a worksheet that contains sensitive (for-your-eyes-only) material, such as the one with all the employee salaries in the company or the one that contains all the macros used in the workbook.

As with hiding columns and rows, hiding worksheets enables you to print the contents of the workbook without the data in worksheets that you consider either unnecessary in the report or too classified for widespread distribution, but which, nonetheless, are required in the workbook. Then after the report is printed, you can redisplay the worksheets by unhiding them.

To hide a worksheet, make it active by selecting its sheet tab, then click the Format command button on the Home tab of the Ribbon and highlight the Hide & Unhide option on its drop-down menu, and then click Hide Sheet on its continuation menu (or press Alt+HOHS). Excel removes this sheet's tab from the row of sheet tabs, making it impossible for anyone to select and display the worksheet in the document window.

To redisplay any of the sheets you've hidden, click the Format command button on the Home tab and highlight the Hide & Unhide option on its drop-down menu and then click Unhide Sheet on its continuation menu (or press Alt+HOHH) to display the Unhide dialog box.

In the Unhide Sheet list box, click the name of the sheet that you want to display once again in the workbook. As soon as you click OK, Excel redisplays the sheet tab of the previously hidden worksheet — as simple as that! Unfortunately, although you can hide multiple worksheets in one hide operation, you can select only one sheet at a time to redisplay with the Unhide command.

Opening windows on different sheets

The biggest problem with keeping your spreadsheet data on different worksheets rather than keeping it all together on the same sheet is being able to compare the information on the different sheets. When you use a single worksheet, you can split the workbook window into horizontal or vertical panes and then scroll different sections of the sheet into view. The only way to do this when the spreadsheet data are located on different worksheets is to open a second window on a second worksheet and then arrange the windows with the different worksheets so that data from both desired regions are displayed on the screen. The easiest way to do this is to use Excel's View Side by Side command to tile the windows one above the other and automatically synchronize the scrolling between them.

Comparing windows side by side

Figure 4-11 helps illustrate how the View Side by Side feature works. This figure contains two windows showing parts of two different worksheets in the same workbook (CG Media Sales - 03-05.xls). These windows are arranged horizontally so that they fit one above the other. The top window shows the upper-left portion of the first worksheet with the 2003 sales data, while the lower window shows the upper-left portion of the second worksheet with the 2004 sales data. Note that both windows contain the same sheet tabs (although different tabs are active in the different windows) but that only the top, active window is equipped with a set of horizontal and vertical scroll bars. However, because Excel automatically synchronizes the scrolling between the windows, you can use the single set of scroll bars to bring different sections of the two sheets into view.

Here is the procedure I followed to create and arrange these windows in the CG Media Sales 03-05 workbook:

1. **Open the workbook file for editing and then create a new window by clicking the New Window command button on the View tab of the Ribbon — you can also do this by pressing Alt+WN.**

2. **Arrange the windows one on top of the other by clicking the View Side by Side command button (the one with the pages side by side to the immediate right of the Split button) in the Window group of the View tab or by pressing Alt+WB.**

3. **Click the lower window (indicated by the ":1" after the filename on its title bar) to activate the window and then click the 2008 Sales sheet tab to activate it.**

4. **Click the upper window (indicated by the ":2" following the filename on its title bar) to activate the window.**

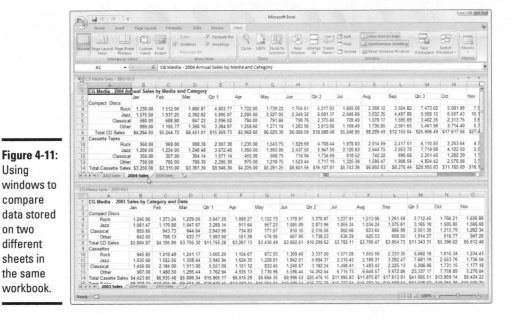

Figure 4-11:
Using windows to compare data stored on two different sheets in the same workbook.

Book II
Chapter 4

Managing
Worksheets

Immediately below the View Side by Side command button in the Windows group on the View tab of the Ribbon, you find these two command buttons:

✦ **Synchronous Scrolling:** When this button is selected, any scrolling that you do in the worksheet in the active window is mirrored and synchronized in the worksheet in the inactive window beneath it. To be able to scroll the worksheet in the active window independently of the inactive window, click the Synchronous Scrolling button to deactivate it.

✦ **Reset Window Position:** Click this button if you manually resize the active window (by dragging its size box) and then want to restore the two windows to their previous side-by-side arrangement.

To remove the side-by-side windows, click the View Side by Side command button again or press Alt+WB. Excel returns the windows to the display arrangement selected (see "Window arrangements" that follows for details) before clicking the View Side by Side command button the first time. If you haven't previously selected a display option in the Arrange Windows dialog box, Excel displays the active window full size.

Note that you can use the View Side by Side feature when you have more than two windows open on a single workbook. When three or more windows are open at the time you click the View Side by Side command button, Excel opens the Compare Side by Side dialog box. This dialog box displays a list of all the other open windows with which you can compare the active one. Once you click the name of this window and click OK in the Compare Side by Side dialog box, Excel places the active window above the one you just selected (using the arrangement shown in Figure 4-11).

Note, too, that you can use Excel's View Side by Side feature to compare worksheets in different workbooks just as well as different sheets in the same workbook (see "Comparing windows on different workbooks" later in this chapter).

Window arrangements

After creating one or more additional windows for a workbook (by clicking the New Window command button on the View tab), you can then vary their arrangement by selecting different arrangement options in the Arrange Windows dialog box, opened by clicking the Arrange All button on the View tab (or by pressing Alt+WA). The Arrange Windows dialog box contains the following four Arrange options:

- ✦ **Tiled:** Select this option button to have Excel arrange and size the windows so that they all fit side by side on the screen in the order in which you open them (when only two windows are open, selecting the Tiled or Vertical option results in the same side-by-side arrangement).

- ✦ **Horizontal:** Select this option button to have Excel size the windows equally and then place them one above the other (this is the default arrangement option that Excel uses when you click the View Side by Side command button).

- ✦ **Vertical:** Select this option button to have Excel size the windows equally and then place them next to one other, vertically from left to right.

- ✦ **Cascade:** Select this option button to have Excel arrange and size the windows so that they overlap one another with only their title bars visible.

After arranging your windows, you can then select different sheets to display in either window by clicking their sheet tabs, and you can select different parts of the sheet to display by using the window's scroll bars.

 To activate different windows on the workbook so that you can activate a different worksheet by selecting its sheet tab and/or use the scroll bars to bring new data into view, click the window's title bar or press Ctrl+F6 until its title bar is selected.

When you want to resume normal, full-screen viewing in the workbook window, click the Maximize button in one of the windows. To get rid of a second window, click its button on the taskbar and then click its Close

Window button on the far right side of the menu bar (the one with the X). (Be sure that you don't click the Close button on the far-right of the Excel title bar, because doing this closes your workbook file and exits you from Excel!)

Working with Multiple Workbooks

Working with more than one worksheet in a single workbook is bad enough, but working with worksheets in different workbooks can be really wicked. The key to doing this successfully is just keeping track of "who's on first"; you do this by opening and using windows on the individual workbook files you have open.

With the different workbook windows in place, you can then compare the data in different workbooks, use the drag-and-drop method to copy or move data between workbooks, or even copy or move entire worksheets.

Comparing windows on different workbooks

To work with sheets from different workbook files you have open, you manually arrange their workbook windows in the Excel Work area, or you click the View Side by Side command button on the View tab of the Ribbon or press Alt+WB. If you have only two workbooks open when you do this, Excel places the active workbook that you last opened above the one that opened earlier (with their active worksheets displayed). If you have more than two workbooks open, Excel displays the Compare Side by Side dialog box where you click the name of the workbook that you want to compare with the active one.

If you need to compare more than two workbooks on the same screen, instead of clicking the View Side by Side button on the View tab, you click the Arrange All button and then select the desired Arrange option (Tiled, Horizontal, Vertical, or Cascading) in the Arrange Windows dialog box. Just make sure when selecting this option that the Windows of Active Workbook check box is *not* selected (in other words, is empty of its check mark) in the Arrange Windows dialog box.

Transferring data between open windows

After the windows on your different workbooks are arranged on-screen the way you want them, you can compare or transfer information between them. To compare data in different workbooks, you switch between the different windows, activating and bringing the regions of the different worksheets you want to compare into view.

To move data between workbook windows, arrange the worksheets in these windows so that both the cells with the data entries you want to move and the cell range into which you want to move them are both displayed in their respective windows. Then, select the cell selection to be moved, drag it to the other worksheet window, to first cell of the range where it is to be moved to, and release the mouse button. To copy data between workbooks, you follow the exact same procedure, except that you hold down the Ctrl key as you drag the selected range from one window to another. (See Book II, Chapter 3 for information on using drag-and-drop to copy and move data entries.)

When you're finished working with workbook windows arranged in some manner in the Excel Work area, you can return to the normal full-screen view by clicking the Maximize button on one of the windows. As soon as you maximize one workbook window, all the rest of the arranged workbook windows are made full size as well. If you used the View Side by Side feature to set up the windows, you can do this by clicking the View Side by Side command button on the View tab again or by pressing Alt+WB.

Transferring sheets from one workbook to another

Instead of copying cell ranges from one workbook to another, you can move (or copy) entire worksheets between workbooks. You can do this with drag-and-drop or by using the Move or Copy Sheet option on the Format command button's drop-down menu on the Ribbon's Home tab.

To use drag-and-drop to move a sheet between open windows, you simply drag its sheet tab from its window to the place on the sheet tabs in the other window where the sheet is to be moved to. As soon as you release the mouse button, the entire worksheet is moved from one file to the other, and its sheet tab now appears among the others in that workbook. To copy a sheet rather than move it, you perform the same procedure, except that you hold down the Ctrl key as you drag the sheet tab from one window to the next.

To use the Move or Copy Sheet option on the Format command button's drop-down menu to move or copy entire worksheets, you follow these steps:

1. **Open both the workbook containing the sheets to be moved or copied and the workbook where the sheets will be moved or copied to.**

   Both the source and destination workbooks must be open in order to copy or move sheets between them.

2. **Click the workbook window with sheets to be moved or copied.**

   Doing this activates the source workbook so that you can select the sheet or sheets you want to move or copy.

3. **Select the sheet tab of the worksheet or worksheets to be moved or copied.**

To select more than one worksheet, hold down the Ctrl key as you click the individual sheet tabs.

4. **Click the Format button on the Home tab and then click Move or Copy Sheet on the drop-down menu or press Alt+HOM.**

Doing this opens the Move or Copy dialog box, as shown in Figure 4-12.

**Book II
Chapter 4**

Managing
Worksheets

Figure 4-12:
Copying a
worksheet
to another
workbook
in the Move
or Copy
dialog box.

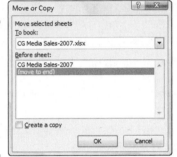

5. **Click the filename of the workbook into which the selected sheets are to be moved or copied in the To Book drop-down menu.**

If you want to move or copy the selected worksheets into a new workbook file, click the (New Book) item at the very top of this drop-down menu.

6. **Click the name of the sheet that should immediately follow the sheet(s) that you're about to move or copy into this workbook in the Before Sheet list box.**

If you want to move or copy the selected sheet(s) to the very end of the destination workbook, click (Move to End) at the bottom of this list box.

7. **If you want to copy the selected sheet(s) rather than move them, click the Create a Copy check box.**

If you don't select this check box, Excel automatically moves the selected sheet(s) from one workbook to the other instead of copying them.

8. **Click OK to close the Move or Copy dialog box and complete the move or copy operation.**

Saving a workspace

Excel's Workspace feature enables you to save the window arrangement that you've set up in a special workspace file (given the filename extension .xlw, which stands for *Excel workspace*). In a workspace file, Excel saves all the information about the open workbooks, including the window arrangement, magnification settings, and display settings. (The workspace file also saves the print areas defined in the open workbooks — see Book II, Chapter 5, for information on printing.)

Workspace files contain only such information about the open workbooks, not the actual workbook files. Therefore, you can't send a workspace file to a coworker and expect him or her to be able to successfully open the file without also sending the associated workbook files.

To save a workspace, you take the following steps:

1. **Open all the workbooks you want opened when you open the workspace file.**

2. **Arrange the windows for these workbooks as you want them to appear when you first open the workspace file.**

   To arrange the windows, click the Arrange All button on the View tab and then select the type of arrangement in the Arrange Windows dialog box (be sure that the Windows of Active Workbook check box is not selected).

3. **Select any display settings and magnification settings that you want used in the individual workbook windows when you first open the workspace file.**

   To change the display settings for a workbook, activate its window and then change the settings on the Advanced tab of the Excel Options dialog box (Alt+FIA). To change the magnification, use the Zoom slider on the Status bar.

4. **Click the Save Workspace command button on the View tab of the Ribbon or press Alt+WK.**

   Doing this opens the Save Workspace dialog box, which is just like the Save As dialog box, except that Workspaces (*.xlw) is selected as the default file type in the Save as Type combo box.

5. **Select the folder in which you want the workspace file saved in the Save In drop-down list box and then edit the desired filename in the File Name combo box.**

If you want the workspace file to open automatically each time you start Excel, save the file in the XLStart folder in your Office 2007 folder. This folder is located within the Microsoft Office folder, inside the Programs Folder on your hard drive (usually the C: drive).

6. **Click the Save button to save the workspace and to close the Save Workspace dialog box.**

After saving your workspace file, you can then open it as you would any other Excel workbook or template file: Choose File⇨Open, open the folder with the .xlw file you want to use, click its file icon, and then click the Open button. (See Book II, Chapter 3 for details on opening Excel files.)

Consolidating Worksheets

Excel allows you to consolidate data from different worksheets into a single worksheet. Using the program's Consolidate command button on the Data tab of the Ribbon, you can easily combine data from multiple spreadsheets. For example, you can use the Consolidate command to total all budget spreadsheets prepared by each department in the company or to create summary totals for income statements for a period of several years. If you used a template to create each worksheet you're consolidating, or an identical layout, Excel can quickly consolidate the values by virtue of their common position in their respective worksheets. However, even when the data entries are laid out differently in each spreadsheet, Excel can still consolidate them provided that you've used the same labels to describe the data entries in their respective worksheets.

Most of the time, you want to total the data that you're consolidating from the various worksheets. By default, Excel uses the SUM function to total all the cells in the worksheets that share the same cell references (when you consolidate by position) or that use the same labels (when you consolidate by category). You can, however, have Excel use any of other following statistical functions when doing a consolidation: AVERAGE, COUNT, COUNTA, MAX, MIN, PRODUCT, STDEV, STDEVP, VAR, or VARP (see Book III, Chapter 5 for more information on these functions).

To begin consolidating the sheets in the same workbook, you select a new worksheet to hold the consolidated data (if need be, insert a new sheet in the workbook by clicking the Insert Worksheet button). To begin consolidating sheets in different workbooks, open a new workbook. If the sheets in the various workbooks are generated from a template, open the new workbook for the consolidated data from that template.

Before you begin the consolidation process on the new worksheet, you choose the cell or cell range in this worksheet where the consolidated data is to appear (this range is called the *destination area*). If you select a single cell, Excel expands the destination area to columns to the right and rows below as needed to accommodate the consolidated data. If you select a single row, the program expands the destination area down subsequent rows of the worksheet, if required to accommodate the data. If you select a single column, Excel expands the destination area across columns to the right, if required to accommodate the data. If, however, you select a multi-cell range as the destination area, the program does not expand the destination area and restricts the consolidated data just to the cell selection.

If you want Excel to use a particular range in the worksheet for all consolidations you perform in a worksheet, assign the range name Consolidate_Area to this cell range. Excel then consolidates data into this range whenever you use the Consolidate command.

When consolidating data, you can select data in sheets in workbooks that you've opened in Excel or in sheets in unopened workbooks stored on disk. The cells that you specify for consolidation are referred to as the *source area,* and the worksheets that contain the source areas are known as the *source worksheets.*

If the source worksheets are open in Excel, you can specify the references of the source areas by pointing to the cell references (even when the Consolidate dialog box is open, Excel will allow you to activate different worksheets and scroll through them as you select the cell references for the source area). If the source worksheets are not open in Excel, you must type in the cell references as external references, following the same guidelines you use when typing a linking formula with an external reference (except that you don't type =). For example, to specify the data in range B4:R21 on Sheet1 in a workbook named CG Media - 2000 Sales.xls as a source area, you enter the following external reference:

```
'[CG Media - 2000 Sales.xls]Sheet1'!$b$4:$r$21
```

Note that if you want to consolidate the same data range in all the worksheets that use a similar filename (for example, CG Media - 2000 Sales, CG Media - 2001 Sales, CG Media - 2002 Sales, and so on), you can use the asterisk (*) or the question mark (?) as wildcard characters to stand for missing characters as in

```
'[CG Media - 20?? Sales.xls]Sheet1'!$b$4:$r$21
```

In this example, Excel consolidates the range A2:R21 in Sheet1 of all versions of the workbooks that use "CG - Media - 20" in the main file when this name is followed by another two characters (be they 00, 01, 02, 03, and so on).

When you consolidate data, Excel uses only the cells in the source areas that contain values. If the cells contain formulas, Excel uses their calculated values, but if the cells contain text, Excel ignores them and treats them as though they were blank (except in the case of category labels when you're consolidating your data by category as described later in this chapter).

Consolidating by position

You consolidate worksheets by position when they use the same layout (such as those created from a template). When you consolidate data by position, Excel does not copy the labels from the source areas to the destination area, only values. To consolidate worksheets by position, you follow these steps:

**Book II
Chapter 4**

**Managing
Worksheets**

1. **Open all the workbooks with the worksheets you want to consolidate. If the sheets are all in one workbook, open it in Excel.**

   Now you need to activate a new worksheet to hold the consolidated data. If you're consolidating the data in a new workbook, you need to open it (Office Button | New or Alt+FN). If you're consolidating worksheets generated from a template, use the template to create the new workbook in which you are to consolidate the spreadsheet data.

2. **Open a new worksheet to hold the consolidated data.**

   Next, you need to select the destination area in the new worksheet that is to hold the consolidated data.

3. **Click the cell at the beginning of the destination area in the consolidation worksheet, or select the cell range if you want to limit the destination area to a particular region.**

   If you want Excel to expand the size of the destination area as needed to accommodate the source areas, just select the first cell of this range.

4. **Click the Consolidate command button on the Data tab of the Ribbon or press Alt+AN.**

   Doing this opens the Consolidate dialog box similar to the one shown in Figure 4-13. By default, Excel uses the SUM function to total the values in the source areas. If you want to use another statistical function such as AVERAGE or COUNT, select the desired function in the Function drop-down list box.

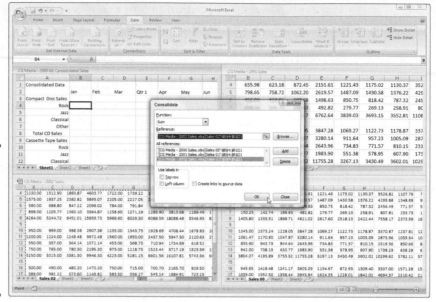

5. **(Optional) Click the function you want to use in the Function drop-down list box if you don't want the values in the source areas summed together.**

   Now, you need to specify the various source ranges to be consolidated and add them to the All References list box in the Consolidate dialog box. To do this, you specify each range to be used as the source data in the Reference text box and then click the Add button to add it to the All References list box.

6. **Select the cell range or type the cell references for the first source area in the Reference text box.**

   When you select the cell range by pointing, Excel minimizes the Consolidate dialog box to the Reference text box so that you can see what you're selecting. If the workbook window is not visible, choose it from the Switch Windows button on the View tab or the Windows taskbar and then select the cell selection as you normally would (remember that you can move the Consolidate dialog box minimized to the Reference text box by dragging it by the title bar).

   If the source worksheets are not open, you can click the Browse command button to select the filename in the Browse dialog box to enter it (plus an exclamation point) into Reference text box, and then you can type in the range name or cell references you want to use. If you prefer, you can type in the entire cell reference including the filename. Remember that you can use the asterisk (*) and question mark (?) wildcard characters when typing in the references for the source area.

7. Click the Add command button to add this reference to the first source area to the All References list box.

8. Repeat Steps 6 and 7 until you have added all the references for all the source areas that you want to consolidate.

9. Click the OK button in the Consolidate dialog box.

Excel closes the Consolidate dialog box and then consolidates all the values in the source areas in the place in the active worksheet designated as the destination area. Note that you can click the Undo button on the Quick Access toolbar or press Ctrl+Z to undo the effects of a consolidation if you find that you defined the destination and/or the source areas incorrectly.

Figure 4-14 shows you the first part of a consolidation for three years (2000, 2001, and 2002) of record store sales in the CG Media – 2000-02 Consolidated Sales.xlsx file in the workbook window in the upper-left corner. The Consolidated worksheet in this file totals the source area B4:R21 from the Sales worksheets in the CG Media – 2000 Sales.xlsx workbook with the 2000 annual sales, the CG Media – 2001 Sales.xlsx workbook with the 2001 annual sales, and the CG Media – 2002 Sales.xlsx workbook with the 2002 annual sales. These sales figures are consolidated in the destination area, B4:R21, in the Consolidated sheet in the CG Media – 2000-02 Consolidated Sales.xls workbook (however, because all these worksheets use the same layout, only cell B4, the first cell in this range, was designated at the destination area).

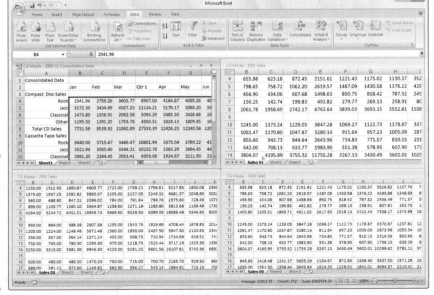

Figure 4-14:
Consolidated worksheet after having Excel total the sales data from three years.

Excel allows only one consolidation per worksheet at one time. You can, however, add to or remove source areas and repeat a consolidation. To add new source areas, open the Consolidate dialog box, then specify the cell references in the Reference text box and click the Add button. To remove a source area, click its references in the All References list box and then click the Delete button. To perform the consolidation with the new source areas, click OK. To perform a second consolidation in the same worksheet, choose a new destination area, open the Consolidate dialog box, clear all the source areas you don't want to use in the All References list box with the Delete button, and then redefine all the new source areas in the Reference text box with the Add button before you perform the consolidation by clicking the OK button.

Consolidating by category

You consolidate worksheets by category when their source areas do not share the same cell coordinates in their respective worksheets, but their data entries do use common column and/or row labels. When you consolidate by category, you include these identifying labels as part of the source areas. Unlike when consolidating by position, Excel copies the row labels and/or column labels when you specify that they should be used in the consolidation.

When consolidating spreadsheet data by category, you must specify whether to use the top row of column labels and/or the left column of row labels in determining which data to consolidate. To use the top row of column labels, you click the Top Row check box in the Use Labels In section of the Consolidate dialog box. To use the left column of row labels, you click the Left Column check box in this area. Then, after you've specified all the source areas (including the cells that contain these column and row labels), you perform the consolidation in the destination area by clicking the Consolidate dialog box's OK button.

Linking consolidated data

Excel allows you to link the data in the source areas to the destination area during a consolidation. That way, any changes that you make to the values in the source area are automatically updated in the destination area of the consolidation worksheet. To create links between the source worksheets and the destination worksheet, you simply click the Create Links to Source Data check box in the Consolidate dialog box to put a check mark in it when defining the settings for the upcoming consolidation.

When you perform a consolidation with linking, Excel creates the links between the source areas and the destination area by outlining the destination area (see "Outlining worksheets" earlier in this chapter for details). Each outline level created in the destination area holds rows or columns that contain the linking formulas to the consolidated data.

Figure 4-15 shows an outline created during consolidation after expanding only the level of the outline showing the consolidation of the Rock music CD sales. Here, you can see that during consolidation, Excel created three detail rows for each of the three years of sales (2000, 2001, and 2002) used in the linked consolidation. These rows contain the external reference formulas that link to the source data. For example, the formula in cell B4 contains the following formula:

```
='[CG Media - 2000 Sales.xls]Sales00'!$B$4
```

This formula links the value in cell B4 in the Sales 00 sheet of the CG Media – 2000 Sales.xls workbook. If you change this value in that worksheet, the new value is automatically updated in cell B4 in the CG Media – 2000-02 Consolidated Sales.xls workbook, which, in turn, changes the subtotal for the January Rock music CD sales in cell B7.

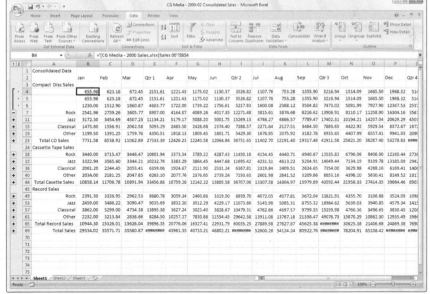

Figure 4-15: Consolidated worksheet with links to the sales data from three years.

Chapter 5: Printing Worksheets

In This Chapter

✔ Previewing pages in Page Layout View and Print Preview

✔ Quick Printing from the Quick Access toolbar

✔ Printing all the worksheets in a workbook

✔ Printing just some of the cells in a worksheet

✔ Changing page orientation

✔ Printing the whole worksheet on a single page

✔ Changing margins for a report

✔ Adding a header and footer to a report

✔ Printing column and row headings as print titles on every page

✔ Inserting page breaks in a report

✔ Printing the formulas in your worksheet

*P*rinting the spreadsheet is one of the most important tasks that you do in Excel (second only to saving your spreadsheet in the first place). Fortunately, Excel makes it easy to produce professional-looking reports from your worksheets. This chapter covers how to select the printer that you want to use; print all or just selected parts of the worksheet; change your page layout and print settings, including the orientation, paper size, print quality, number of copies, and range of pages; set up reports using the correct margin settings, headers and footers, titles, and page breaks; and use the Page Layout, Print Preview, and Page Break Preview features to make sure that the pages of your report are the way you want them to appear before you print them.

The printing techniques covered in this chapter focus primarily on printing the data in your spreadsheets. Of course in Excel, you can also print your charts in chart sheets. Not surprisingly, you will find that most of the printing techniques that you learn for printing worksheet data in this chapter also apply to printing charts in their respective sheets. (For specific information on printing charts, see Book V, Chapter 1.)

Selecting the Printer to Use

Windows Vista and XP allow you to install more than one printer for use with your applications. If you've installed multiple printers, the first one installed becomes the default printer, which is used by all Windows applications, including Excel 2007. If you get a new printer, you must first install it from the Windows Vista or XP Control Panel before you can select and use the printer in Excel.

To select a new printer to use in printing the current worksheet, follow these steps:

1. **Open the workbook with the worksheet that you want to print, activate that worksheet, and then click Office Button | Print or press Alt+FP or Ctrl+P.**

The Print dialog box opens (similar to the one shown in Figure 5-1).

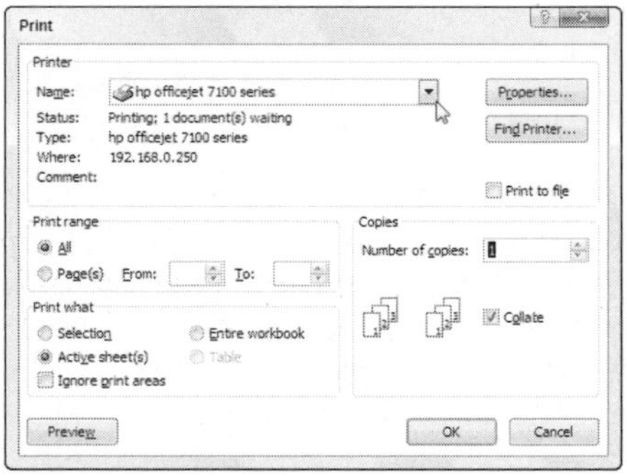

Figure 5-1:
Selecting a
new printer
to use in
the Print
dialog box.

2. **Click the name of the new printer that you want to use in the Name drop-down list box.**

If the printer that you want to use isn't listed on the drop-down list, you can try to find the printer with the Find Printer button. When you click this button, Excel opens the Find Printers dialog box, where you specify the location for the program to search for the printer that you want to use. Note that if you don't have a printer connected to your computer, clicking the Find Printer button and opening the Find Printers dialog box results in opening a Find in the Directory alert dialog box with the message, "The Active Directory Domain Service is Currently Unavailable." When you click OK in this alert dialog box, Excel closes it as well as the Find Printers dialog box.

3. **To change any of the default settings for the printer that you've selected, click the Properties button to the right of the Name drop-down list box and then select the new settings in the Properties dialog box for the printer that you selected.**

4. **Make any other required changes to the Print Range, Copies, or Collate settings in the Print dialog box.**

5. **Click OK to print the worksheet using the newly selected printer.**

Keep in mind that the printer you select and use in printing the current worksheet remains the selected printer in Excel until you change back to the original printer (or some other printer).

Previewing the Printout

Excel 2007 gives you two ways to check the page layout before you send the report to the printer. You can use the brand-new Page Layout view that shows all the pages plus the margins along with the worksheet and row headings and rulers. Or you can use the old standby Print Preview window that shows you the pages of the report more or less as they appear on the printed page.

Checking the paging in Page Layout view

The Page Layout view — activated by clicking the Page Layout View button (the center one) to the immediate left of the Zoom slider on the Status bar or the Page Layout View command button on the View tab of the Ribbon — gives you instant access to the paging of the active worksheet.

As you can see in Figure 5-2, when you switch to Page Layout view, Excel adds horizontal and vertical rulers to the column letter and row number headings. In the Worksheet area, this view shows the margins for each printed page with any headers and footers defined for the report along with the breaks between each (often you have to use the Zoom slider to reduce the screen magnification to display the page breaks on the screen).

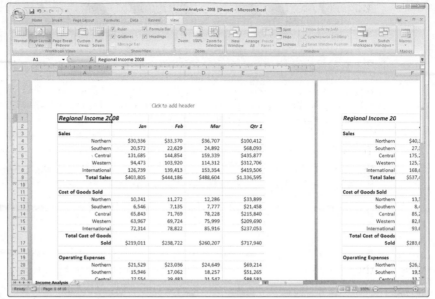

Figure 5-2:
Viewing a
spreadsheet
in Page
Layout view.

To see all the pages required to print the active worksheet, drag the slider button in the Zoom slider on the Status bar to the left until you decrease the screen magnification sufficiently to display all the pages of data.

Excel displays rulers using the default units for your computer (inches on a U.S. computer and centimeters on a European machine). To change the units, open the Advanced tab of the Excel Options dialog box (Office Button | Excel Options | Advanced or Alt+FIA) and then select the appropriate unit on the Ruler Units drop-down menu (Inches, Centimeters, or Millimeters) in the Display section.

To be able to turn off and on the Rulers in Page Layout view, add the Ruler command button (a custom button) to the Quick Access toolbar by opening the Customization tab of the Excel Options dialog box (Office Button | Excel Options | Customization or Alt+FIC). To do this, click View tab in the Choose Commands From drop-down list, then click Ruler in the list box below, followed by the Add button and OK.

Note that the Ruler command button acts as a toggle switch so that the first time you click this button, Excel removes the rulers from the Page Layout view, and the second time, the program adds them back again.

Previewing the pages with Print Preview

Save wasted paper and your sanity by using the Print Preview feature before you print any worksheet, section of worksheet, or entire workbook. Because of the peculiarities in paging worksheet data, check the page breaks for any report that requires more than one page. You can use Print Preview to see exactly how the worksheet data will be paged when printed and to make last minute changes to the page settings before sending the report on to the printer when everything looks okay.

To switch to Print Preview, click the Office Button, click the Print option's continuation button, and then click Print Preview (or press Ctrl+F2). Excel displays the first page of the report in a separate window with its own Print Preview contextual tab. When positioned over the spreadsheet, the mouse pointer becomes a magnifying glass. Look at Figure 5-3 to see the first page of a ten-page report in Print Preview.

Book II
Chapter 5

Printing
Worksheets

If you use Print Preview frequently, you can add a Print Preview button to the Quick Access toolbar and then open the window by clicking this button. To add a Print Preview button, click the Customize Quick Access Toolbar button and then click Print Preview on its drop-down menu (to remove the button, you simply click the Print Preview option on this drop-down menu a second time).

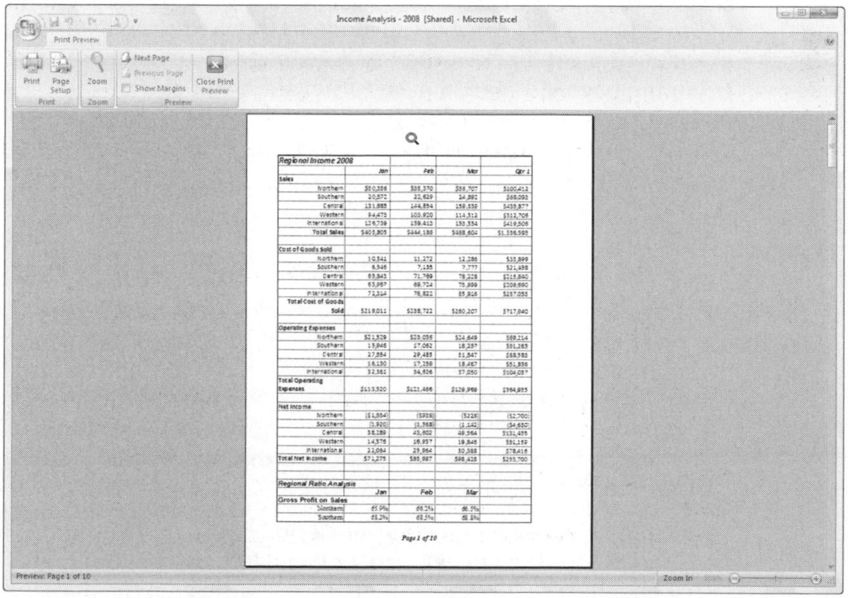

Figure 5-3:
Page 1 of a
10-page
report in
Print
Preview.

When Excel displays a full page in the Print Preview window, you can barely read its contents; increase the view to actual size if you need to verify some of the information. Zoom up to 100 percent by clicking the previewed page with the magnifying-glass mouse pointer or by clicking the Zoom button in the Print Preview tab. Check out the difference in Figure 5-4 — here you can see what the first page of the ten-page report looks like after I zoom in by clicking the Zoom pointer (with the magnifying-glass icon) on the top-central portion of the page.

After you enlarge a page to actual size, use the scroll bars to bring new parts of the page into view in the Print Preview window. If you prefer to use the keyboard, press the ↑ and ↓ keys or PgUp and PgDn to scroll up or down the page, respectively; press ← and → or Ctrl+PgUp and Ctrl+PgDn to scroll left and right, respectively.

To return to the full-page view, click the mouse pointer (in its arrowhead form) anywhere on the page or click the Zoom command button on the Print Preview tab.

Excel indicates the number of pages in a report on the Status bar of the Print Preview window (at the far-left bottom of your Excel screen). If your report has more than one page, view pages that follow by clicking the Next Page button in the Preview group of the Print Preview tab. To review a page you've already seen, back up a page by clicking the Previous Page button immediately below it. (The Previous Page button is grayed out if you're on the first page.) You can also advance to the next page by pressing the PgDn or ↓ key or move back to the previous page by pressing the PgUp or ↑ key when the page view is full page rather than actual size.

When you finish previewing the report, the Print Preview tab offers you following options:

✦ **Print:** Click this command button in the Print group to display the Print dialog box and print the report from the normal worksheet view.

✦ **Page Setup:** Click this command button in the Print group to open the Page Setup dialog box where you can take care of paging problems by choosing a new paper size, page order, orientation, or margins, or if you notice a problem with the header or footer (the text you enter in the top or bottom margin of the pages). For more on what printing parameters you can set here, see the section "Working with the Page Setup Options" later in this chapter.

✦ **Show Margins:** Select this check box in the Preview group to display markers for the current top, bottom, left, and right margins that you can then adjust by dragging them. (See "Massaging the margins," later in this chapter, for details.)

✦ **Close Print Preview:** Click this command button in the Preview group to close the Print Preview window and return to the previous worksheet view.

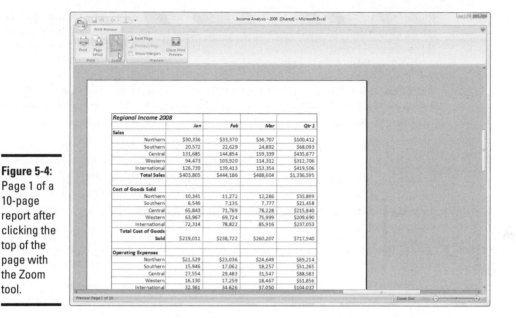

Figure 5-4:
Page 1 of a
10-page
report after
clicking the
top of the
page with
the Zoom
tool.

Quick Printing the Worksheet

As long as you want to use Excel's default print settings to print all the cells in the current worksheet, printing in Excel 2007 is a breeze. Simply add the Quick Print button to the Quick Access toolbar and then click this button to print the current worksheet. To add the Quick Print button to the Quick Access toolbar, click the Customize Quick Access Toolbar button and then click Quick Print on its drop-down menu. Excel then adds a button with an icon showing a printer with a check mark.

When you click the Quick Print button, Excel prints one copy of all the information in the current worksheet, including any charts and graphics — but not including comments you add to cells. (See Book IV, Chapter 3 for details about adding comments to your worksheet and Part V for details about charts and graphics.)

After you click the Quick Print button, Excel routes the print job to the Windows print queue, which acts like a middleman to send the job to the printer. While Excel sends the print job to the print queue, Excel displays a Printing dialog box to inform you of its progress (displaying such updates as *Printing Page 2 of 3*). After this dialog box disappears, you are free to go back to work in Excel. To stop a print job that is in the process of being sent to the print queue, click the Cancel button in the Printing dialog box.

If you don't realize that you want to cancel the print job until after Excel finishes shipping it to the print queue (that is, while the Printing dialog box appears on-screen), you must open the dialog box for your printer and cancel printing from there:

1. **Click the printer icon in the Notification area at the far right of the Windows Vista or XP taskbar (to the immediate left of the current time) with the secondary mouse button to open its shortcut menu.**

   This printer icon displays the ScreenTip 1 document(s) pending for *so-and-so*. For example, when I'm printing, this message reads 1 document(s) pending for Greg when I position the mouse pointer over the printer icon.

2. **Right-click the printer icon and then select the Open Active Printers command from its shortcut menu.**

   This opens the dialog box for the printer with the Excel print job in its queue (as described under the Document heading in the list box).

3. **Select the Excel print job that you want to cancel in the list box of your printer's dialog box.**

4. **Choose Document➪Cancel Printing from the menu bar.**

5. **Wait for the print job to disappear from the queue in the printer's dialog box and then click the Close button to get rid of it and return to Excel.**

Printing the Worksheet from the Print Dialog Box

Printing with the Quick Print button on the Quick Access toolbar is fine provided that all you want is a single copy of all the information in the current worksheet. If you want more copies, or more or less data (such as all the worksheets in the workbook or just a cell selection within a particular worksheet), then you need to print from the Print dialog box (shown in Figure 5-1).

Excel provides a number of ways to open the Print dialog box:

✦ Press Ctrl+P.

✦ Click Microsoft Office Button | Print.

✦ Press Alt+FP.

✦ Press Ctrl+Shift+F12.

Printing particular parts of the workbook

Within the Print dialog box are the Print Range and Print What sections (from which you can select how much of the information is printed), and the Copies section, from which you can change the number of copies printed. Here's what's in these areas and how you use their options:

✦ **All:** When the All option button is selected, all the pages in your document will print. Because this is the default choice, you would only need to select it if you previously printed a portion of the document by selecting the Page(s) option button.

✦ **Page(s):** Normally, Excel prints all the pages required to produce the information in the areas of the workbook that you want printed. Sometimes, however, you may need to reprint only a page or range of pages that you've modified within this section. To reprint a single page, enter its page number in both the From and To text boxes here or select these page numbers with the spinner buttons. To reprint a range of pages, put the first page number in the From text box and the last page number in the To text box. Excel automatically deselects the All option button and selects the Page(s) option button in the Page Range section as soon as you start typing in the From or To text box.

✦ **Selection:** Select this option button to have Excel print just the cells that are currently selected in your workbook. (Yes, you must remember to select these cells before opening the Print dialog box and choosing this printing option.)

✦ **Active Sheet(s):** Excel automatically displays and selects this option button and prints all the information in whatever worksheets are active in your workbook. Normally, this means printing just the data in the current worksheet. To print other worksheets in the workbook when this option button is selected, hold down Ctrl while you click the sheet's tab. To include all the sheets between two sheet tabs, click the first one and then hold Shift while you click the second tab (Excel selects all the tabs in between).

✦ **Entire Workbook:** Select this option button to have Excel print all the data in each of the worksheets in your workbook.

✦ **Table:** Select this option button to have Excel print only the data range that you formatted as a table. Note this option button remains grayed out and unavailable if your worksheet doesn't contain any tables.

✦ **Ignore Print Areas:** Click this check box to put a check mark in it when you want one of the other Print What options (Selection, Active Sheet(s), Entire Workbook, or Table) that you selected to be used in the printing rather than the Print Area you defined (see the "Setting and clearing the Print Area" section later in this chapter for details).

✦ **Number of Copies:** To print more than one copy of the report, enter the number of copies you want to print in the Number of Copies text box in the Copies section — or use the spinner buttons to select the required number.

✦ **Collate:** When you collate pages, you simply make separate stacks of each complete report, rather than print all copies of page one, and then all copies of page two, and so on. To have Excel collate each copy of the report for you, select the Collate check box in the Copies section to put a check mark in it.

After you finish choosing new print options, you can send the job to the printer by clicking OK or pressing Enter. To use another printer that's been installed for Windows (Excel lists the current printer in the Name text box and all printers installed for Windows on the Name pop-up list), select the new printer on the Name drop-down menu in the Printer section at the top of the dialog box before you start printing.

To open the report in the Print Preview window for last-minute checking before sending it to the printer, click the Preview button (see "Previewing the pages with Print Preview" earlier in this chapter).

Setting and clearing the Print Area

Excel includes a special printing feature called the *Print Area*. You click Print Area | Set Print Area on the Ribbon's Page Layout tab or press Alt+PRS to define any cell selection on a worksheet as the Print Area. After you define the Print Area, Excel then prints this cell selection anytime you print the worksheet (either with the Quick Print button on the Quick Access toolbar or by using the Office Button| Print command or one of its shortcuts).

Whenever you fool with the Print Area, you need to keep in mind that once you define it, its cell range is the only one you can print (regardless of what other Print What options you select in the Print dialog box unless you click the Ignore Print Areas check box and until you clear the Print Area.

To clear the Print Area (and therefore go back to the printing defaults Excel establishes in the Print dialog box — see the preceding section, "Printing particular parts of the workbook" for details — you just have to click Print Area | Clear Print Area on the Page Layout tab or simply press Alt+PRC.

Keep in mind that you can also define and clear the Print Area from the Sheet tab of the Page Setup dialog box opened by clicking the Page Setup button in the Print Preview tab of the Print Preview window (see "Checking the Printout with Print Preview" earlier in this chapter). To define the Print Area from this dialog box, click the Print Area text box on the Sheet tab, insert the cursor, and then select the cell range or ranges in the worksheet. Remember that you can reduce the Page Setup dialog box to just this text box by clicking its minimize box. To clear the Print Area from this dialog box, select the cell addresses in the Print Area text box and press the Delete key.

Working with the Page Setup Options

About the only thing the slightest bit complex in printing a worksheet is figuring out how to get the pages right. Fortunately, the command buttons in the Page Setup group on the Ribbon's Page Layout tab give you a great deal of control over what goes on which page.

There are three groups of buttons on the Page Layout tab that are helpful in getting your page settings exactly as you want them: the Page Setup group, the Scale to Fit group, and the Sheet Options group, all described in the following sections.

To see the effect of changes you make to the page setup settings in the Worksheet area, put the worksheet into Page Layout view by clicking the Page Layout button on the Status bar as you work with the command buttons in Page Setup, Scale to Fit, and Sheet Options groups on the Page Layout tab.

Using the buttons in the Page Setup group

The Page Setup group of the Page Layout tab contains the following important command buttons:

✦ **Margins:** Select one of three preset margins for the report or to set custom margins on the Margins tab of the Page Setup dialog box. (See "Massaging the margins" in this chapter.)

✦ **Orientation:** Choose between Portrait and Landscape mode for the printing (see "Getting the lay of the landscape" later in this chapter).

✦ **Size:** Select one of the preset paper sizes, or use it to set a custom size, change the printing resolution, or add a page number on the Page tab of the Page Layout dialog box.

✦ **Print Area:** Set and clear the Print Area. (See "Setting and clearing the Print Area" earlier in this chapter.)

✦ **Breaks:** Insert or remove page breaks. (See "Solving Page Break Problems" later in this chapter.)

Book II
Chapter 5

Printing
Worksheets

✦ **Background:** Open the Sheet Background dialog box where you can select a new graphic image or photo to be used as a background for all the worksheets in the workbook. (Note that this button changes to Delete Background as soon as you select a background image.)

✦ **Print Titles:** Open the Sheet tab of the Page Setup dialog box where you can define rows of the worksheet to repeat at the top and columns at the left as print titles for the report. (See "Putting out the print titles" later in this chapter.)

Massaging the margins

The Normal margin settings that Excel applies to a new report use standard top and bottom margins of 0.75 inch (¾ inch) and left and right margins of 0.7 inch with just over a ¼ inch separating the header and footer from the top and bottom margins, respectively.

In addition to the Normal margin settings, the program enables you to select two other standard margins from the Margins button's drop-down menu:

✦ **Wide** margins with 1-inch top, bottom, left, and right margins and ½ inch separating the header and footer from the top and bottom margins, respectively.

✦ **Narrow** margins with top and bottom margins of ¾ inch, and left and right margins of ¼ inch with slightly over ¼ inch separating the header and footer from the top and bottom margins, respectively.

Frequently, you find yourself with a report that takes up a full printed page and then just enough to spill over onto a second, mostly empty, page. To squeeze the last column or the last few rows of the worksheet data onto Page 1, try selecting Narrow on the Margins button's drop-down menu.

If that doesn't do it, you can try manually adjusting the margins for the report either from the Margins tab of the Page Setup dialog box or by dragging the margin markers in the Print Preview window. To get more columns on a page, try reducing the left and right margins. To get more rows on a page, try reducing the top and bottom margins.

To open the Margins tab of the Page Setup dialog box (shown in Figure 5-5), click Custom Margins on the Margins button's drop-down menu. There, enter the new settings in the Top, Bottom, Left, and Right text boxes — or select the new margin settings with their respective spinner buttons.

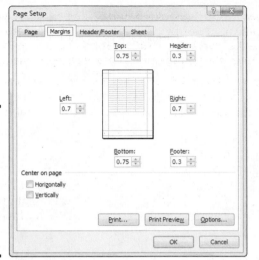

Figure 5-5:
Adjust your
report
margins
from the
Margins
tab in the
Page Setup
dialog box.

Select one or both Center on Page options in the Margins tab of the Page
Setup dialog box (refer to Figure 5-5) to center a selection of data (that takes
up less than a full page) between the current margin settings. In the Center
on Page section, select the Horizontally check box to center the data
between the left and right margins. Select the Vertically check box to center
the data between the top and bottom margins.

If you select the Show Margins check box on the Print Preview tab in the
Print Preview window (Alt+FWV) to change the margin settings, you can
modify the column widths as well as the margins. (See Figure 5-6.) To change
one of the margins, position the mouse pointer on the desired margin
marker (the pointer shape changes to a double-headed arrow) and drag the
marker with your mouse in the appropriate direction. When you release the
mouse button, Excel redraws the page, using the new margin setting. You
may gain or lose columns or rows, depending on what kind of adjustment
you make. Changing the column width is the same story: Drag the column
marker to the left or right to decrease or increase the width of a particular
column.

Getting the lay of the landscape

The drop-down menu attached to the Orientation button in the Page Setup
group of the Page Layout tab of the Ribbon contains two options:

✦ **Portrait** (the default), where the printing runs parallel to the short edge
of the paper.

✦ **Landscape,** where the printing runs parallel to the long edge of the paper.

Top margin   Header margin

Left margin   Column markers   Right margin

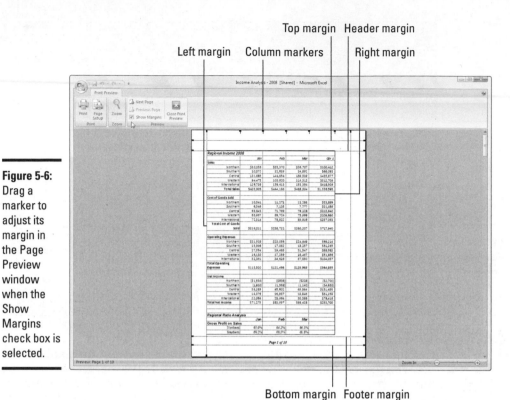

Figure 5-6: Drag a marker to adjust its margin in the Page Preview window when the Show Margins check box is selected.

Bottom margin   Footer margin

Because many worksheets are far wider than they are tall (such as budgets or sales tables that track expenditures over all 12 months), you may find that their worksheets page better if you switch the orientation from the normal portrait mode (which accommodates fewer columns on a page because the printing runs parallel to the short edge of the page) to landscape mode.

In Figure 5-7, you can see the Print Preview window with the first page of a report in landscape mode in the Page Layout view. For this report, Excel can fit three more columns of information on this page in landscape mode than it can in portrait mode. Therefore, the total page count for this report decreases from ten pages in portrait mode to six pages in landscape mode.

Putting out the print titles

Excel's Print Titles enable you to print particular row and column headings on each page of the report. Print titles are important in multi-page reports where the columns and rows of related data spill over to other pages that no longer show the row and column headings on the first page.

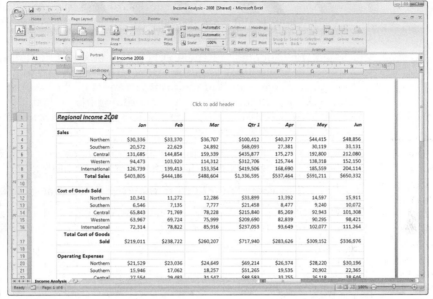

Figure 5-7:
A landscape
mode report
in Page
Layout view.

Don't confuse print titles with the header of a report. Even though both are printed on each page, header information prints in the top margin of the report; print titles always appear in the body of the report — at the top, in the case of rows used as print titles, and on the left, in the case of columns.

To designate rows and/or columns as the print titles for a report, follow these steps:

1. **Click the Print Titles button on the Ribbon's Page Layout tab or press Alt+PI.**

The Page Setup dialog box appears with the Sheet tab selected (refer to Figure 5-8).

To designate worksheet rows as print titles, go to Step 2a. To designate worksheet columns as print titles, go to Step 2b.

2a. **Select the Rows to Repeat at Top text box and then drag through the rows with information you want to appear at the top of each page in the worksheet below. If necessary, reduce the Page Setup dialog box to just the Rows to Repeat at Top text box by clicking the text box's Collapse/Expand button.**

In the example I show you in Figure 5-8, I click the minimize button associated with the Rows to Repeat at Top text box and then drag through rows 1 and 2 in column A of the Bo Peep Pet Detectives – Client List worksheet, and the program enters the row range $1:$2 in the Rows to Repeat at Top text box.

Note that Excel indicates the print-title rows in the worksheet by placing a dotted line (that moves like a marquee) on the border between the titles and the information in the body of the report.

2b. Select the Columns to Repeat at Left text box and then drag through the range of columns with the information you want to appear at the left edge of each page of the printed report in the worksheet below. If necessary, reduce the Page Setup dialog box to just the Columns to Repeat at Left text box by clicking its Collapse/Expand button.

Note that Excel indicates the print-title columns in the worksheet by placing a dotted line (that moves like a marquee) on the border between the titles and the information in the body of the report.

3. Click OK or press Enter to close the Page Setup dialog box.

After you close the Page Setup dialog box, the dotted line showing the border of the row and/or column titles disappears from the worksheet.

Figure 5-8:
Specify the rows and columns to use as print titles on the Sheet tab of the Page Setup dialog box.

In Figure 5-8, rows 1 and 2 containing the worksheet title and column headings for the Bo Peep Pet Detectives clients database are designated as the print titles for the report. In Figure 5-9, you can see the Print Preview window with the second page of the report. Note how these print titles appear on all pages of the report.

To clear print titles from a report if you no longer need them, open the Sheet tab of the Page Setup dialog box and then delete the row and column ranges from the Rows to Repeat at Top and the Columns to Repeat at Left text boxes before you click OK or press Enter.

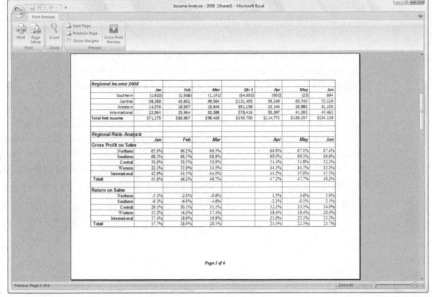

Figure 5-9:
Page 2 of a
sample
report in
Print
Preview
with defined
print titles.

Using the buttons in the Scale to Fit group

If your printer supports scaling options, you're in luck. You can always get a worksheet to fit on a single page simply by selecting the 1 Page option on the Width and Height drop-down menus attached to their command buttons in the Scale to Fit group on the Layout Page tab of the Ribbon. When you select these options, Excel figures out how much to reduce the size of the information you're printing to fit it all on one page.

If you preview this one page in the Print Preview window (Alt+FWV) and find that the printing is just too small to read comfortably, click the Page Setup button on the Print Preview tab, reopen the Page tab of the Page Setup dialog box, and try changing the number of pages in the Page(s) Wide and Tall text boxes (to the immediate right of the Fit To option button).

Instead of trying to stuff everything on one page, check out how your worksheet looks if you fit it on two pages across. Try this: Select 2 Pages on the Width button's drop-down menu on the Page Layout tab and leave 1 Page selected in the Height drop-down list. Alternately, see how the worksheet looks on two pages down: Select 1 Page on the Width button's drop-down menu and 2 Pages on the Height button's drop-down menu.

After using the Width and Height Scale to Fit options, you may find that you don't want to scale the printing. Cancel scaling by selecting Automatic on both the Width and Height drop-down menus and then entering **100** in the Scale text (or select 100 with its spinner buttons).

Using the Print buttons in the Sheet Options group

The Sheet Options group on the Ribbon's Page Layout tab contains two very useful Print check boxes (neither of which is automatically selected), the first in the Gridlines column and the second in the Headings column:

✦ Select the Print check box in the Gridlines column to print the column and row gridlines on each page of the report.

✦ Select the Print check box in the Headings column to print the row headings with the row numbers, and the column headings with the column letters on each page of the report.

 Select both check boxes (by clicking them to put check marks in them) when you want the printed version of your spreadsheet data to match as closely as their on-screen appearance. This is useful when you need to use the cell references on the printout to help you later locate the cells in the actual worksheet that need editing.

Headers and Footers

Headers and footers are simply standard text that appears on every page of the report. A header is printed in the top margin of the page, and a footer is printed — you guessed it — in the bottom margin. Both are centered vertically in the margins. Unless you specify otherwise, Excel does not automatically add either a header or footer to a new workbook.

 Use headers and footers in a report to identify the document used to produce the report and display the page numbers and the date and time of printing.

The easiest way to add a header or footer to a report is to add it after putting the worksheet in Page Layout view by clicking the Page Layout View button on the Status bar (or by clicking the Page Layout View button on the Ribbon's View tab or by just pressing Alt+WP).

When the worksheet's displayed in Page Layout view, position the mouse pointer over the section in the top margin of the first page marked Click to Add Header or in the bottom margin of the first page marked Click to Add Footer.

To create a centered header or footer, highlight the center section of this header/footer area and then click the mouse pointer to set the insertion point in the middle of the section. To add a left-aligned header or footer, highlight and then click to set the insertion point flush with the left edge of the left-hand section, or to add a right-aligned header or footer, highlight and click to set the insertion point flush with the right edge of the right-hand section.

Immediately after setting the insertion point in the left, center, or right section of the header/footer area, Excel adds a Header & Footer Tools contextual tab with its own Design tab (see Figure 5-10). The Design tab is divided into Header & Footer, Header & Footer Elements, Navigation, and Options groups.

Book II
Chapter 5

Printing Worksheets

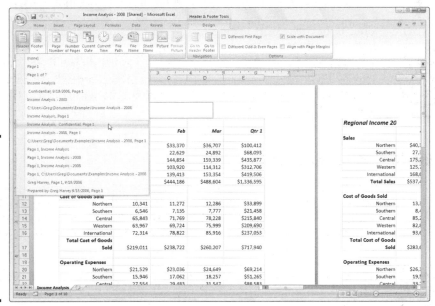

Figure 5-10: Defining a new header using the buttons on the Design tab of the Header & Footer contextual tab.

Adding a Header or Footer

The Header and Footer buttons on the Design tab of the Header & Footer Tools contextual tab enable you to add stock headers and footers in an instant. Simply clicking their examples from the drop-down menus that appear when you click them.

To create the centered header and footer for the report shown in Figure 5-11, I first selected

```
Income Analysis, Confidential, Page 1
```

on the Header button's drop-down menu. (Income Analysis is the name of the worksheet.)

To set up the footer, I chose

```
Page 1 of ?
```

in the Footer button's drop-down menu (which puts the current page number, along with the total number of pages, in the report). You can select this paging option in either the Header or Footer drop-down list box.

Check out the results in Figure 5-11, which is the first page of the report in Page Layout view. Here you can see the header and footer as they will print. You can also see how choosing Page 1 of ? works in the footer: On the first page, you see the centered footer: Page 1 of 6; on the second page, you would see the centered footer Page 2 of 6.

Figure 5-11: The first page of a report in Page Layout view shows you how the header and footer will print.

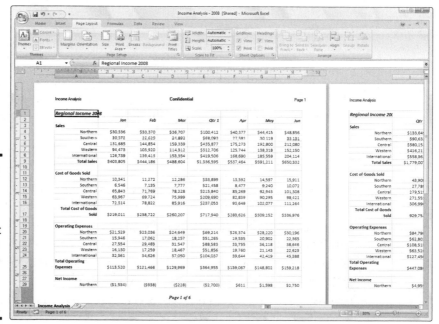

If, after selecting some stock header or footer info, you decide that you no longer need either the header or footer printed in your report, click the header or footer in Page Layout view and then click the (none) option at the top of the Header button's or Footer button's drop-down menu (the Design tab on the Header & Footer Tools contextual tab automatically appears and is selected on the Ribbon the moment you click the header or footer in Page Layout view).

Creating a custom header or footer

Most of the time, the stock headers and footers available on the Header button's and Footer button's drop-down menus are sufficient for your report printing needs. Every once in a while, however, you may want to insert information not available in these list boxes or in an arrangement Excel doesn't offer in the readymade headers and footers.

For those times, you need to use the command buttons that appear in the Header & Footer Elements group of the Design tab on the Header & Footer Tools contextual tab. These command buttons enable you to blend your own information with that generated by Excel into different sections of the custom header or footer you're creating.

The command buttons in the Header & Footer Elements group include the following:

✦ **Page Number:** Click this button to insert the &[Page] code that puts in the current page number.

✦ **Number of Pages:** Click this button to insert the &[Pages] code that puts in the total number of pages.

✦ **Current Date:** Click this button to insert the &[Date] code that puts in the current date.

✦ **Current Time:** Click this button to insert the &[Time] code that puts in the current time.

✦ **File Path:** Click this button to insert the &[Path]&[File] code that puts in the directory path along with the name of the workbook file.

✦ **File Name:** Click this button to insert the &[File] code that puts in the name of the workbook file.

✦ **Sheet Name:** Click this button to insert the &[Tab] code that puts in the name of the worksheet as shown on the sheet tab.

✦ **Picture:** Click this button to insert the &[Picture] code that inserts the image that you select from the Insert Picture dialog box (that shows the contents of the My Pictures folder on your computer by default).

✦ **Format Picture:** Click this button to apply the formatting that you choose from the Format Picture dialog box to the &[Picture] code that you enter with the Insert Picture button without adding any code of its own.

Book II
Chapter 5

Printing
Worksheets

To use these command buttons in the Header & Footer Elements group to create a custom header or footer, follow these steps:

1. **Put your worksheet into Page Layout view by clicking the Page Layout View button on the Status bar or by clicking View | Page Layout View on the Ribbon or pressing Alt+WP.**

   In Page Layout view, the text, Click to Add Header, appears centered in the top margin of the first page, and the text, Click to Add Footer, appears centered in the bottom margin.

2. **Position the mouse pointer in the top margin to create a custom header or in the bottom margin to create a custom footer, and then click the pointer in the left, center, or right section of the header or footer to set the insertion point and left-align, center, or right-align the text.**

   When Excel sets the insertion point, the text, Click to Add Header and Click to Add Footer, disappears and the Design tab on the Header & Footer Tools contextual tab becomes active on the Ribbon.

3. **To add program-generated information to your custom header or footer such as the filename, worksheet name, current date, and so forth, click its command button in the Header & Footer Elements group.**

   Excel inserts the appropriate header/footer code preceded by an ampersand (&) in the header or footer. These codes are replaced by the actual information (filename, worksheet name, graphic image, and the like) as soon as you click another section of the header or footer or finish the header or footer by clicking the mouse pointer outside of it.

4. **(Optional) To add your own text to the custom header or footer, type it at the insertion point.**

   When joining program-generated information indicated by a header/footer code with your own text, be sure to insert the appropriate spaces and punctuation. For example, to have Excel display `Page 1 of 4` in a custom header or footer, you do the following:

   a. **Type the word** Page **and press the spacebar.**

   b. **Click the Page Number command button and press the spacebar again.**

   c. **Type the word** of **and press the spacebar a third time.**

   d. **Click the Number of Pages command button.**

   This inserts `Page &[Page] of &[Pages]` in the custom header (or footer).

5. **(Optional) To modify the font, font size, or some other font attribute of your custom header or footer, drag through its codes and text, click the Home tab, and then click the appropriate command button in the Font group.**

In addition to selecting a new font and font size for the custom header or footer, you can add bold, italics, underlining, and a new font color to its text with the Bold, Italic, Underline, and Font Color command buttons on the Home tab.

6. **After you finish defining and formatting the codes and text in your custom header or footer, click a cell in the Worksheet area to deselect the header or footer area.**

Excel replaces the header/footer codes in the custom header or footer with the actual information, while at the same time removing the Header & Footer Tools contextual tab from the Ribbon.

Figure 5-12 shows you a custom footer I added to a spreadsheet in Page Layout view. This custom footer blends my own text, Preliminary, with program-generated page, date, and time information, and uses all three sections: left-aligned page information, a centered Preliminary warning, and right-aligned current date and time. Note the different font and bold formatting for the Preliminary warning in the center section.

Book II Chapter 5

Printing Worksheets

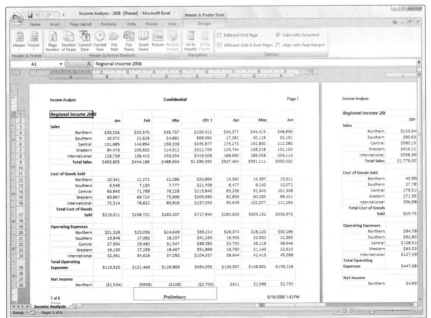

Figure 5-12: Spreadsheet in Page Layout view showing the custom footer.

Creating unique first-page headers and footers

Excel 2007 enables you to define a header or footer for the first page that's different from all the rest of the pages. Simply click the Different First Page check box to put a check mark in it. (This check box is part of the Options group of the Design tab on the Header & Footer Tools contextual tab that appears when you're defining or editing a header or footer in Page Layout view.)

After selecting the Different First Page check box, go ahead and define the unique header and/or footer for just the first page (now marked First Page Header or First Page Footer), and then, on the second page of the report, define the header and/or footer (marked simply Header or Footer) for the remaining pages of the report (see "Adding a Header or Footer" and "Creating a custom header or footer" earlier in the chapter for details).

Use this feature when your spreadsheet report has a cover page that needs no header or footer. For example, say you have a report that needs the current page number and total pages centered at the bottom of all pages but the first, cover page. To do this, select the Different First Page check box on the Design tab of the Header & Footer Tools contextual tab on the Ribbon and then define a centered Footer that displays the current page number and total pages (Page 1 of ?) on the second page of the report, leaving the Click to Add Footer text intact on the first page.

Excel will correctly number both the total number of pages in the report and the current page number without printing this information on the first page. So if your report has a total of six pages (including the cover page), the second page footer will read Page 2 of 6; the third page, Page 3 of 6; and so on, even if the first printed page has no footer at all.

Creating different even and odd page headers and footers

If you plan to do two-sided printing or copying of your spreadsheet report, you may want to define one header or footer for the even pages and another for the odd pages of the report. That way, the header or footer information (such as the report name or current page) alternates from being right-aligned on the odd pages (printed on the front side of the page) to being left-aligned on the even pages (printed on the back side of the page).

To create an alternating header or footer for a report, you click the Different Odd & Even Pages check box to put a check mark in it. (This check box is found in the Options group of the Design tab on the Header & Footer Tools contextual tab that appears when you're defining or editing a header or footer in Page Layout view.)

After that, create a header or footer on the first page of the report (now marked Odd Page Header or Odd Page Footer) in the third, right-aligned section header or footer area, and then re-create this header or footer on the second page (now marked Even Page Header or Even Page Footer), this time in the first, left-aligned section.

Solving Page Break Problems

The Page Break Preview feature in Excel enables you to spot page break problems in an instant as well as fix them, such as when the program want to split onto different pages information that you know should always appear on the same page.

Figure 5-13 shows a worksheet in Page Break Preview with an example of a bad vertical page break that you can remedy by adjusting the location of the page break on Pages 1 and 3. Given the page size, orientation, and margin settings for this report, Excel breaks the page between columns H and I.

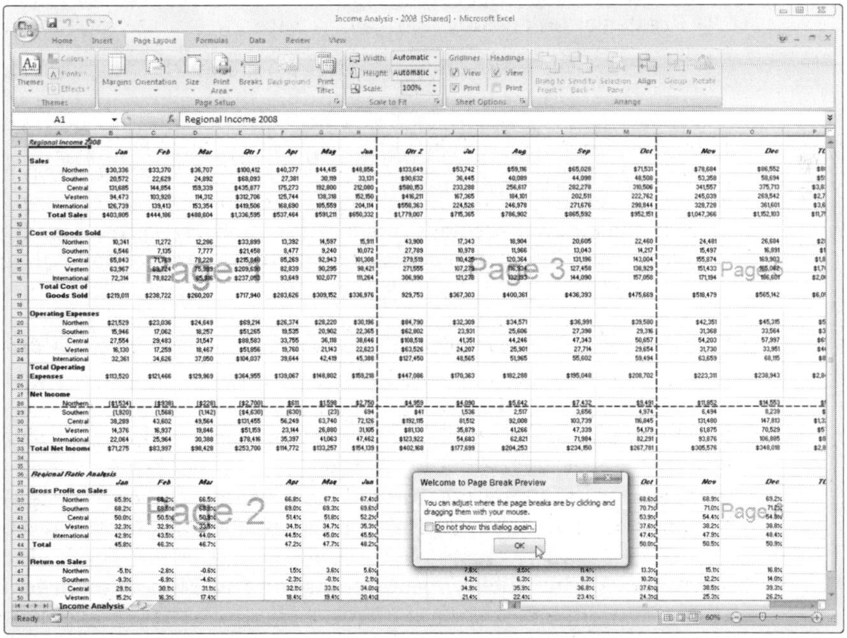

Figure 5-13:
Preview page breaks in a report in Page Break Preview.

To prevent the data in the Qtr2 column from being printed alone on its own pages, you need to move the page break to a column on the right. In this case, I chose to move the page break back between columns I (with Qtr2 data) and J (containing the July Information).

1. **Click the Page Break Preview button (the third one in the cluster of three to the left of the Zoom slider) on the Status bar or click View | Page Break Preview on the Ribbon or press Alt+WI.**

   This takes you into a Page Break Preview mode that shows your worksheet data at a reduced magnification (60 percent of normal in Figure 5-13) with the page numbers displayed in large light type and the page breaks shown by heavy lines between the columns and rows of the worksheet.

   The first time you choose this command, Excel displays a Welcome to Page Break Preview dialog box (shown in Figure 5-13). To prevent this dialog box from reappearing each time you use Page Break Preview, click the Do Not Show This Dialog Again check box before you close the Welcome to Page Break Preview alert dialog box.

2. **Click OK or press Enter to get rid of the Welcome to Page Break Preview alert dialog box.**

3. **Position the mouse pointer somewhere on the page break indicator (one of the heavy lines surrounding the representation of the page) that you need to adjust; when the pointer changes to a double-headed arrow, drag the page indicator to the desired column or row and release the mouse button.**

   For the example shown in Figure 5-13, I dragged the page break indicator between Pages 1 and 3 to the right so that it's between columns I and J. Excel then moved the page break back to this point, which puts all the Qtr1 and Qtr2 information together on Pages 1 and 2. This new page break then causes all the other columns of data to print together on the remaining pages.

   In Figure 5-14, you can see Page 1 of the report as it then appears in the · Print Preview window.

4. **After you finish adjusting the page breaks in Page Break Preview (and, presumably, printing the report), click the Normal button (the first one in the cluster of three to the left of the Zoom slider) on the Status bar or click View | Normal on the Ribbon or press Alt+WL to return the worksheet to its regular view of the data.**

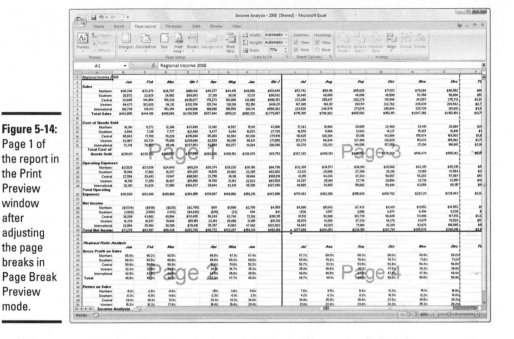

Figure 5-14:
Page 1 of the report in the Print Preview window after adjusting the page breaks in Page Break Preview mode.

You can also insert your own manual page breaks at the cell cursor's position by clicking Insert Page Break on the Breaks button's drop-down menu on the Page Layout tab (Alt+PBI), and remove them by clicking Remove Page Break on this menu (Alt+PBR). To remove all manual page breaks that you've inserted into a report, click Reset All Page Breaks on the Breaks button's drop-down menu (Alt+PBA).

Printing the Formulas in a Report

There's one more printing technique you may need every once in a while and that's how to print the formulas in a worksheet in a report instead of printing the calculated results of the formulas. You can check over a printout of the formulas in your worksheet to make sure that you haven't done anything stupid (like replace a formula with a number or use the wrong cell references in a formula) before you distribute the worksheet company-wide.

Before you can print a worksheet's formulas, you have to display the formulas, rather than their results, in the cells by clicking the Show Formulas button (the one that kind of looks like a page of a calendar with a tiny 15 above an *fx*) in the Formula Auditing group on the Formulas tab of the Ribbon (Alt+MH).

Excel then displays the contents of each cell in the worksheet as they normally appear only in the Formula bar or when you're editing them in the cell. Notice that value entries lose their number formatting, formulas appear in their cells (Excel widens the columns with best-fit so that the formulas appear in their entirety), and long text entries no longer spill over into neighboring blank cells.

Excel allows you to toggle between the normal cell display and the formula cell display by pressing Ctrl+`. (That is, press Ctrl and the key with the tilde on top.) This key — usually found in the upper-left corner of your keyboard — does double-duty as a tilde and as a weird backward accent mark: ` (Don't confuse that backward accent mark with the apostrophe that appears on the same key as the quotation mark!)

After Excel displays the formulas in the worksheet, you are ready to print it as you would any other report. You can include the worksheet column letters and row numbers as headings in the printout so that if you do spot an error, you can pinpoint the cell reference right away.

To include the row and column headings in the printout, put a check mark in the Print check box in the Headings column on the Sheet Options group of the Page Layout tab of the Ribbon before you send the report to the printer.

After you print the worksheet with the formulas, return the worksheet to normal by clicking the Show Formulas button on the Formulas tab of the Ribbon or by pressing Ctrl+`.

Book III
Formulas and Functions

The 5th Wave   By Rich Tennant

At FEMA, employees often use Excel's custom format function to create formulas for disaster.

Contents at a Glance

Chapter 1: Building Basic Formulas

In This Chapter

✔ Summing data ranges with AutoSum

✔ Creating simple formulas with operators

✔ Understanding the operators and their precedence in the formula

✔ Using the Insert Function button on the Formula bar

✔ Copying formulas and changing the type of cell references

✔ Building array formulas

✔ Using range names in formulas

✔ Creating linking formulas that bring values forward

✔ Controlling formula recalculation

✔ Dealing with circular references in formulas

Formulas, to put it mildly, are the very "bread and butter" of the worksheet. Without formulas, the electronic spreadsheet would be little better than its green-sheet paper equivalent. Fortunately, Excel gives you the ability to do all your calculations right within the cells of the worksheet without any need for a separate calculator.

The formulas that you build in a spreadsheet can run the gamut from very simple to extremely complex. Formulas can rely totally upon the use of simple *operators* or the use of built-in *functions,* both of which describe the type of operation or calculation to perform and the order in which to perform it. Or they can blend the use of operators and functions together. When you use Excel functions in your formulas, you need to learn what particular type of information that particular function uses in performing its calculations. The information that you supply a function and that it uses in its computation is referred to as the *argument(s)* of the function.

Formulas 101

From the simple addition formula to the most complex ANOVA statistical variation, all formulas in Excel have one thing in common: They all begin with the equal sign (=). This doesn't mean that you always have to type in the equal sign — although if you do, Excel expects that a formula of some type is to follow. When building a formula that uses a built-in function, often-times you use the Insert Function button on the Formula bar to select and insert the function, in which case, Excel adds the opening equal sign for you.

If you're an old Lotus 1-2-3 user and you type @@ to start a function, Excel automatically converts the @@ sign into the equal sign the moment that you complete the formula entry. It does mean, however, that each and every completed formula that appears on the Formula bar starts with the equal sign.

When building your formulas, you can use *constants* that actually contain the number that you want used in the calculation (such as "4.5%," "$25.00," or "–78.35"), or you can use cell addresses between the operators or as the arguments of functions. When you create a formula that uses cell addresses, Excel then uses the values that you've input in those cells in calculating the formula. Unlike when using constants in formulas, when you use cell addresses, Excel automatically updates the results calculated by a formula whenever you edit the values in the cells to which it refers.

Formula building methods

When building formulas manually, you can either type in the cell addresses or you can point to them in the worksheet. Using the Pointing method to supply the cell addresses for formulas is often easier and is always a much more foolproof method of formula building; when you type in a cell address, you are less apt to notice that you've just designated the wrong cell than when pointing directly to it. For this reason, stick to pointing when building original formulas and restrict typing cell addresses to the odd occasion when you need to edit a cell address in a formula and pointing to it is either not practical or just too much trouble.

When you use the Pointing method to build a simple formula that defines a sequence of operations, you stop and click the cell or drag through the cell range after typing each operator in the formula. When using the method to build a formula that uses a built-in function, you click the cell or drag through the cell range that you want used when defining the function's arguments in the Function Arguments dialog box.

Formulas and formatting

When defining a formula that uses operators or functions, Excel picks up the number formatting of the cells that are referenced in the formula. For example, if you add cell A2 to B3, as in =A2+B3, and cell B3 is formatted with the Currency Style format, the result will inherit this format and be displayed in its cell using the Currency Style.

As with the other types of cell entries, you must take some action to complete a formula and enter it into the current cell (such as clicking the Enter button on the Formula bar, pressing the Enter key, or pressing an arrow key). Unlike when entering numeric or text entries, however, you will want to stay clear of clicking another cell to complete the data entry. This is because, when you click a cell when building or editing a formula on the Formula bar, more often than not, you end up not only selecting the new cell, but also adding its address to the otherwise complete formula.

As soon as you complete a formula entry, Excel calculates the result, which is then displayed inside the cell within the worksheet (the contents of the formula, however, continue to be visible on the Formula bar anytime the cell is active). If you make an error in the formula that prevents Excel from being able to calculate the formula at all, Excel displays an Alert dialog box suggesting how to fix the problem. If, however, you make an error that prevents Excel from being able to display a proper result when it calculates the formula, the program displays an Error value rather than the expected computed value (see Book III, Chapter 2 for details on dealing with both of these types of errors in formulas).

Editing formulas

As with numeric and text entries, you can edit the contents of formulas either in their cells or on the Formula bar. To edit a formula in its cell, double-click the cell or press F2 to position the pointer in that cell (double-clicking the cell positions the insertion pointer in the middle of the formula, whereas pressing F2 positions it at the end of the formula — you can also double-click at the beginning or end of the cell to position the pointer there). To edit a formula on the Formula bar, use the I-beam pointer to position the insertion point at the place in the formula that needs editing first.

TIP

Using Excel like a handheld calculator

Sometimes, you may need to actually calculate the number that you need to input in a cell as a constant. Instead of reaching for your pocket calculator to compute the needed value and then manually entering it into a cell of your spreadsheet, you can set up a formula in the cell that returns the number that you need to input and then convert the formula into a constant

value. You convert the formula into a constant by pressing F2 to edit the cell, then immediately pressing F9 to recalculate the formula and display the result on the Formula bar, and then clicking the Enter button on the Formula bar or pressing the Enter key to input the calculated result into the cell (as though you had manually input the result in the cell).

As soon as you put the Excel program into Edit mode, Excel displays each of the cell references in the formula within the cell in a different color and uses this color to outline the cell or cell range in the worksheet itself. This enables you to quickly identify the cells and their values that are referred to in your formula and, if necessary, modify them as well. You can use any of the four sizing handles that appear around the cell or cell range to modify the cell selection in the worksheet and consequently update the cell references in the formula.

When you AutoSum numbers in a spreadsheet

The easiest and often the most used formula that you will create is the one that totals rows and columns of numbers in your spreadsheet. Usually, to total a row or column of numbers, you can click the Sum command button in the Editing group of the Home tab of the Ribbon (the one with the Σ on it). When you click this button, Excel inserts the built-in SUM function into the active cell and simultaneously selects what the program thinks is the most likely range of numbers that you want summed.

Figure 1-1 demonstrates how this works. For this figure, I positioned the cell cursor in cell B8, which is the first cell where I need to build a formula that totals the various parts produced in April. I then clicked the Sum button on the Home tab of the Ribbon.

As Figure 1-1 shows, Excel then inserted an equal sign followed by the SUM function and correctly suggested the cell range B4:B7 as the argument to this function (that is, the range to be summed). Because Excel correctly selected the range to be summed (leaving out the date value in cell B3), all I have to do is click the Enter button on the Formula bar to have the April total calculated.

Figure 1-2 shows another example of AutoSum to instantly build a SUM formula, this time to total the monthly production numbers for the part AB-100 in cell K4. Again, all I did to create the formula shown in Figure 1-2 was to select cell K4 and then click the Sum button on the Home tab. Again, Excel correctly selected B4:J4 as the range to be summed (rightly ignoring cell A4 with the row title) and input this range as the argument of the SUM function. All that remains to be done is to click the Enter button on the Formula bar to compute the monthly totals for part AB-100.

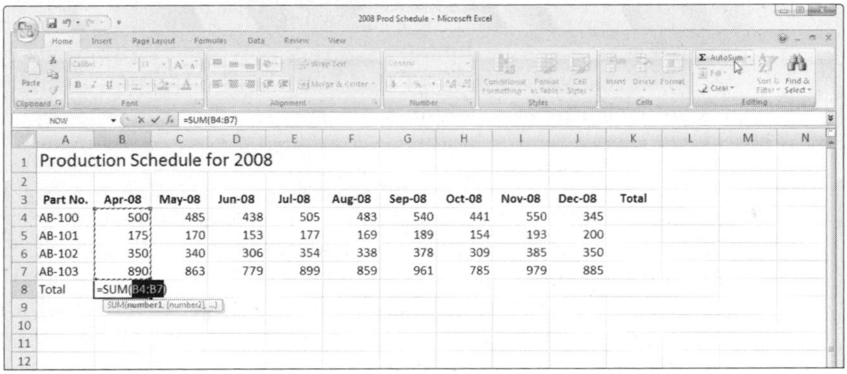

Figure 1-1: Using the AutoSum feature to create a SUM formula that totals a column of numbers.

If for some reason AutoSum doesn't select the entire or correct range that you want summed, you can adjust the range by dragging the cell cursor through the cell range or by clicking the marquee around the cell range, which turns the marching ants into a solid colored outline. Then position the mouse pointer on one of the sizing handles at the four corners. When it turns into a pair of black double-crossed arrows, drag the outline until it includes all the cells you want included in the total.

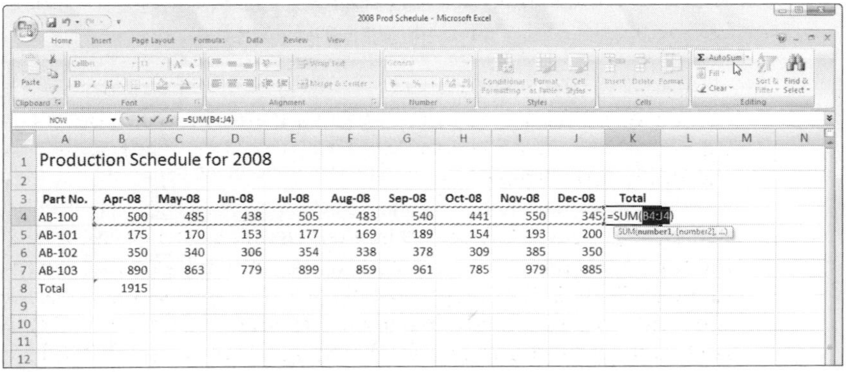

Figure 1-2: Using the AutoSum feature to create a SUM formula that totals a row of numbers.

Keep in mind that all Excel functions enclose their argument(s) in a closed pair of parentheses as shown in the examples with the SUM function. Even those rare functions that don't require any arguments at all still require the use of a closed pair of parentheses (even when you don't put anything inside of them).

Building formulas with operators

Many of the simpler formulas that you build require the sole use of Excel's operators, which are the symbols that indicate the type of computation that is to take place between the cells and/or constants interspersed between them. Excel uses four different types of operators: arithmetic, comparison, text, and reference. Table 1-1 shows all these operators arranged by type and accompanied by an example.

Table 1-1		The Different Types of Operators in Excel	
Type	*Character*	*Operation*	*Example*
Arithmetic	+ (plus sign)	Addition	=A2+B3
	– (minus sign)	Subtraction or negation	=A3–A2 or –C4
	* (asterisk)	Multiplication	=A2*B3
	/	Division	=B3/A2
Type	*Character*	*Operation*	*Example*
	%	Percent (dividing by 100)	=B3%
	^	Exponentiation	=A2^3
Comparison	=	Equal to	=A2=B3
	>	Greater than	=B3>A2
	<	Less than	=A2<B3
	>=	Greater than or equal to	=B3>=A2
	<=	Less than or equal to	=A2<=B3
	<>	Not equal to	=A2<>B3
Text	&	Concatenates (connects) entries to produce one continuous entry	=A2&" "&B3
Reference	: (colon)	Range operator that includes	=SUM(C4:D17)
	, (comma)	Union operator that combines multiple references into one reference	=SUM(A2,C4:D17,B3)
	(space)	Intersection operator that produces one reference to cells in common with two references	=SUM(C3:C6 C3:E6)

"Smooth operator"

Most of the time, you'll rely on the arithmetic operators when building formulas in your spreadsheets that don't require functions because these operators actually perform computations between the numbers in the various cell references and produce new mathematical results.

The comparison operators, on the other hand, produce only the logical value TRUE or the logical value FALSE, depending on whether the comparison is accurate. For example, if you enter the following formula in cell A10:

```
=B10<>C10
```

If B10 contains the number 15 and C10 contains the number 20, the formula in A10 returns the logical value TRUE. If, however, both cell B10 and C10 contain the value 12, the formula returns the logical value FALSE.

The single text operator (the so-called ampersand) is used in formulas to join together two or more text entries (an operation with the highfalutin' name *concatenation*). For example, suppose that you enter the following formula in cell C2:

```
=A2&B2
```

If cell A2 contains John and cell B2 contains Smith, the formula returns the new (squashed together) text entry, JohnSmith. To have the formula insert a space between the first and last names, you have to include the space as part of the concatenation as follows:

```
=A2&" "&B2
```

TIP

When AutoSum doesn't sum

Although the Sum button's primary function is to build formulas with the SUM function that totals ranges of numbers, that's not its only function (pun intended). Indeed, you can have the AutoSum feature build formulas that compute the average value, count the number of values, or return the highest or lowest value in a range — all you have to do is click the drop-down button that's attached to the Sum command button on the Home tab and then click Average, Count Numbers, Max, or Min on its drop-down menu.

Also, don't forget about the Average, Count, and Sum indicator on the Status bar. This indicator automatically shows you the average value, the count of the numbers, and the total of all numbers in the current cell selection. You can use this feature to preview the total that's to be returned by the SUM formula that you create with the AutoSum button by selecting the cell range that contains the numbers to be summed.

You most often use the comparison operators with the IF function when building more complex formulas that perform one type of operation when the IF condition is TRUE and another when it is FALSE. You use the concatenating operator (&) when you need to join text entries that come to you entered in separate cells but that need to be entered in single cells (like the first and last names in separate columns). See Book III, Chapter 2 for more on logical formulas, and Book III, Chapter 6 for more on text formulas.

Order of operator precedence

When you build a formula that combines different operators, Excel follows the set order of operator precedence, as shown in Table 1-2. When you use operators that share the same level of precedence, Excel evaluates each element in the equation by using a strictly left-to-right order.

Table 1-2	Natural Order of Operator Precedence in Formulas	
Precedence	*Operator*	*Type/Function*
1	–	Negation
2	%	Percent
3	^	Exponentiation
4	* and /	Multiplication and Division
5	+ and –	Addition and Subtraction
6	&	Concatenation
7	=, <, >, <=, >=, <>	All Comparison Operators

Suppose that you enter the following formula in cell A4:

`=B4+C4/D4`

Because multiplication has a higher level of precedence than addition (4 versus 5), Excel evaluates the division between cells C4 and D4 and then adds that result to the value in cell B4. If, for example, cell B4 contains 2, C4 contains 9, and D4 contains 3, Excel would essentially be evaluating this equation in cell A4:

`=2+9/3`

In this example, the calculated result displayed in cell A4 is 5 because the program first performs the division (9/3) that returns the result 3 and then adds it to the 2 to get the final result of 5.

If you had wanted Excel to evaluate this formula in a strictly left-to-right manner, you could get it to do so by enclosing the leftmost operation (the addition between B4 and C4) in a closed pair of parentheses. Parentheses alter the natural order of precedence so that any operation enclosed within a pair is performed before the other operations in the formula, regardless of level in the order (after that, the natural order is once again used).

To have Excel perform the addition between the first two terms (B4 and C4) and then divide the result by the third term (cell D4), you modify the original formula by enclosing the addition operation in parentheses as follows:

=(B4+C4)/D4

Assuming that cells B4, C4, and D4 still contain the same numbers (2, 9, and 3, respectively), the formula now calculates the result as 3.666667 and returns it to cell A4 (2+9=11 and 11÷3=3.66667).

If necessary, you can *nest* parentheses in your formulas by putting one set of parentheses within another (within another, within another, and so on). When you nest parentheses, Excel performs the calculation in the innermost pair of parentheses first before anything else and then starts performing the operations in the outer parentheses.

Consider the following sample formula:

=B5+(C5–D5)/E5

In this formula, the parentheses around the subtraction (C5–D5) ensure that it is the first operation performed. After that, however, the natural order of precedence takes over. So the result of the subtraction is then divided by the value in E5, and that result is then added to the value in B5. If you want the addition to be performed before the division, you need to nest the first set of parentheses within another set as follows:

=(B5+(C5–D5))/E5

In this revised formula, Excel performs the subtraction between the values in C5 and D5, adds the result to the value in cell B5, and then divides that result by the value in cell E5.

WARNING!

Of course, the biggest problem with parentheses is that you have to remember to enter them in pairs. If you forget to balance each set of nested parentheses by having a right parenthesis for every left parenthesis, Excel displays an Alert dialog box, informing you that it has located an error in the formula.

It will also suggest a correction that would balance the parentheses used in the formula. Although the suggested correction corrects the imbalance in the formula, it unfortunately doesn't give you the calculation order that you wanted — and if accepted, the suggested correction would give you what you consider an incorrect result. For this reason, be very careful before you click the Yes button in this kind of Alert dialog box. Do so only when you're certain that the corrected parentheses give you the calculation order that you want. Otherwise, click No and balance the parentheses in the formula by adding the missing parenthesis or parentheses yourself.

Using the Insert Function button

Excel supports a wide variety of built-in functions that you can use when building formulas. Of course, the most popular built-in function is by far the SUM function, which is automatically inserted when you click the Sum command button on the Home tab of the Ribbon (keep in mind that you can also use this drop-down button attached to the Sum button to insert the AVERAGE, COUNT, MAX, and MIN functions — see the "When you AutoSum numbers in a spreadsheet" section previously in this chapter for details). To use other Excel functions, you can use the Insert Function button on the Formula bar (the one with the *fx* shown in the left margin).

When you click the Insert Function button, Excel displays the Insert Function dialog box, similar to the one shown in Figure 1-3. You can then use its options to find and select the function that you want to use and to define the argument or arguments that the function requires in order to perform its calculation.

To select the function that you want to use, you can use any of the following methods:

✦ Click the function name if it's one that you've used lately and is therefore already listed in the Select a Function list box.

✦ Click the name of the category of the function that you want to use in the Or Select a Category drop-down list box (Most Recently Used is the default category), and then select the function that you want to use in that category in the Select a Function list box.

✦ Replace the text "Type a brief description of what you want to do and then click Go" in the Search for a Function text box with keywords or a phrase about the type of calculation that you want to do (such as "return on investment"), and then click the Go button or press Enter and click the function that you want to use in the Recommended category displayed in the Select a Function list box.

Figure 1-3:
Selecting a
function to
use in the
Insert
Function
dialog box.

When selecting the function to use in the Select a Function list box, click the function name to have Excel give you a short description of what the function does, displayed underneath the name of the function with its argument(s) shown in parentheses (referred to as the function's *syntax*). To get help on using the function, click the Help on This Function link displayed in the lower-left corner of the Insert Function dialog box to open the Help window in its own pane on the right. When you finish reading and/or printing this help topic, click the Close button to close the Help window and return to the Insert Function dialog box.

You can select the most commonly used types of Excel functions and enter them simply by clicking their names on the drop-down menus attached to their command buttons in the Function Library group of the Formulas tab of the Ribbon. These command buttons include Financial, Logical, Text, Date & Time, Lookup & Reference, and Math & Trig. In addition, you can select functions in the Statistical, Engineering, Cube, and Information categories from continuation menus that appear when you click the More Functions command button on the Formulas tab. And if you find you need to insert a function in the worksheet that you recently entered into the worksheet, chances are good that when you click the Recently Used command button, that function will be listed on its drop-down menu for you to select.

When you click OK after selecting the function that you want to use in the current cell, Excel inserts the function name followed by a closed set of parentheses on the Formula bar. At the same time, the program closes the Insert Function dialog box and then opens the Function Arguments dialog box, similar to the one shown in Figure 1-4. You then use the argument text box or boxes displayed in the Function Arguments dialog box to specify what numbers and other information are to be used when the function calculates its result.

TIP

All functions — even those that don't take any arguments, such as the TODAY function — follow the function name by a closed set of parentheses, as in =TODAY(). If the function requires arguments (and almost all require at least one), these arguments must appear within the parentheses following the function name. When a function requires multiple arguments, such as the DATE function, the various arguments are entered in the required order (as in *year, month, day* for the DATE function) within the parentheses separated by commas, as in DATE(33,7,23).

Figure 1-4:
Selecting
the argu-
ments for a
function in
the Function
Arguments
dialog box.

When you use the text boxes in the Function Arguments dialog box to input the arguments for a function, you can select the cell or cell range in the worksheet that contains the entries that you want used. Click the text box for the argument that you want to define, and then either start dragging the cell cursor through the cells or, if the Function Arguments dialog box is obscuring the first cell in the range that you want to select, click the Collapse Dialog Box button located to the immediate right of the text box (shown in the left margin). Dragging or clicking this button reduces the Function Arguments dialog box to just the currently selected argument text box, thus enabling you to drag through the rest of the cells in the range.

If you started dragging without first clicking the Collapse Dialog Box button, Excel automatically expands the Function Arguments dialog box as soon as you release the mouse button. If you clicked the Collapse Dialog Box button, you have to click the Expand Dialog Box button (which replaces the Collapse Dialog Box button located to the right of the argument text box — shown in the left margin) in order to restore the Function Arguments dialog box to its original size.

As you define arguments for a function in the Function Arguments dialog box, Excel shows you the calculated result following the heading, "Formula result =" near the bottom of the Function Arguments dialog box. When you finish entering the required argument(s) for your function (and any optional arguments that may pertain to your particular calculation), click OK to have Excel close the Function Arguments dialog box and replace the formula in the current cell display with the calculated result.

You can also type the name of the function instead of selecting it from the Insert Function dialog box. When you begin typing a function name after typing an equal sign (=), Excel's AutoComplete feature kicks in by displaying a drop-down menu with the names of all the functions that begin with the character(s) you type. You can then enter the name of the function you want to use by double-clicking its name in this drop-down menu. Excel then enters the function name along with the open parenthesis as in =DATE(so that you can then begin selecting the cell range(s) for the first argument.

For details on how to use different types of built-in functions for your spreadsheets, refer to the following chapters in Book III that discuss the use of various categories: Refer to Chapter 2 for information on Logical functions, Chapter 3 for Date and Time functions, Chapter 4 for Financial functions, Chapter 5 for Math and Statistical functions, and Chapter 6 for Lookup, Information, and Text functions.

Copying Formulas

Copying formulas is one of the most common tasks that you do in a typical spreadsheet that relies primarily on formulas. When a formula uses cell references rather than constant values (as most should), Excel makes the task of copying an original formula to every place that requires a similar location a piece of cake. The program does this by automatically adjusting the cell references in the original formula to suit the position of the copies that you make. It does this through a system known as *relative cell addresses,* whereby the column references in the cell address in the formula change to suit their new column position and the row references change to suit their new row position.

Figures 1-5 and 1-6 illustrate how this works. For Figure 1-5, I used the AutoSum button in cell B8 to build the original formula that uses the SUM function that totals the April 2003 sales. The formula in cell B7 reads:

```
=SUM(B4:B7)
```

I then used the AutoFill feature to copy this formula by dragging the Fill handle to include the cell range B8:K8 (copying the formula with the cut-and-paste method would work just as well, although it's a little more work). Note in the cell range C8:K8 that Excel did not copy the original formula to the other cells verbatim (otherwise each of the copied formulas would return the same result, 1,915, as the original in cell B8). If you look at the Formula bar in Figure 1-5, you see that the copy of the original formula in cell C8 reads:

```
=SUM(C4:C7)
```

In this copy, Excel adjusted the column reference of the range being summed from B to C to suit the new position of the copy. Figure 1-6 shows how this works when copying an original formula in the other direction, this time down a column. For this figure, I used the AutoSum button to create a SUM formula that totals all the monthly sales for part AB-100 in row 4. The formula in cell K4 reads:

```
=SUM(B4:J4)
```

I then used the Fill handle to copy this formula down the last column of the table to include the cell range K4:K7. You can see on the Formula bar in this figure that when Excel copied the original formula in cell K4 down to cell K5, it automatically adjusted the row reference to suit its new position so that the formula in cell K5 reads:

```
=SUM(B5:J5)
```

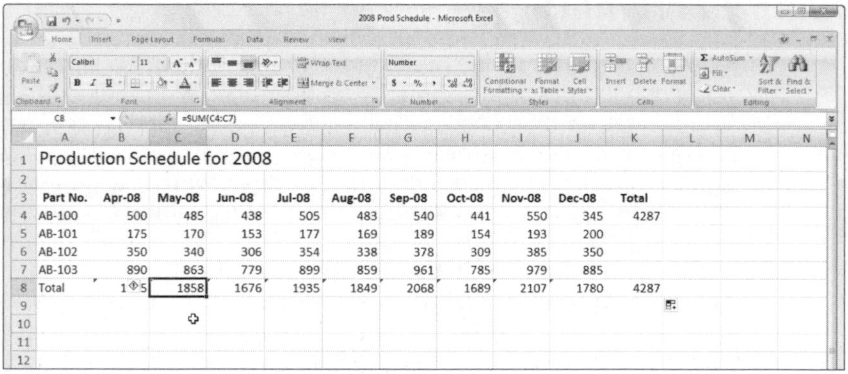

Figure 1-5:
Copying an original formula with the Fill handle across the last row of the data table.

Although at first glance it appears that Excel isn't making exact copies of the original formula when it uses the relative cell addressing, that isn't technically true. Although the cell column references in the first example in Figure 1-5 and the row references in the second example in Figure 1-6 appear to be adjusted to suit the new column and row position when you view the worksheet by using the R1C1 cell notation system, you'd actually see that, in R1C1 notation (unlike the default A1 system), each and every copy of the original formula is *exactly* the same.

For example, the original formula that I input into cell B8 (known as cell R8C2 in the R1C1 system) to sum the April 2003 sales for all the different part numbers reads as follows when you switch to R1C1 notation:

```
=SUM(R[-4]C:R[-1]C)
```

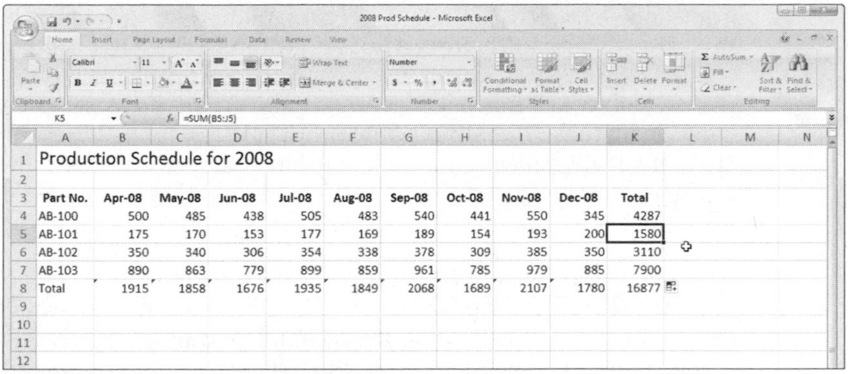

Figure 1-6:
Copying an original formula with the Fill handle down the last column of the data table.

In this notation, the SUM formula is more difficult to decipher, so I will explain and then translate it for you. In R1C1 notation, the cell range in the SUM argument is expressed in terms completely relative to the position of the cell containing the formula. The row portion of the cell range expresses how many rows above or below the one with the formula the rows are (negative integers indicate rows above, while positive integers indicate rows below). The column portion of the cell range in the SUM argument expresses how many columns to the left or right of the one with the formula the columns are (positive integers indicate columns to the right and negative integers columns to the left). When a column or row in the cell range is not followed by an integer in square brackets, this means that there is no change in the column or row.

Armed with this information, my translation R1C1 form of this formula may just make sense; it says, "sum the values in the range of the cells that is four rows (R[–4]) above the current cell in the same column (C) down through the cell that is just one row (R[–1]) above the current cell in the same column (C)." When this original formula is copied over to the columns in the rest of the table, it doesn't need to be changed because each copy of the formula performs this exact calculation (when expressed in such relative terms).

The original formula in cell K4 (R4C11 in R1C1-speak) appears as follows when you switch over to the R1C1 notation:

```
=SUM(RC[-9]:RC[-1])
```

It says, "sum the range of values in the cell nine columns to the left (C[–9]) in the same row through the cell that is one column to the left (C[–1]) in the same row." This is exactly what all the copies of this formula in the three rows below it do, so that when Excel copies this formula it doesn't change.

TIP

You can use the R1C1 notation to check that you've copied all the formulas in a spreadsheet table correctly. Just switch to the R1C1 system by selecting the R1C1 Reference Style check box on the Formulas tab of the Excel Options dialog box (Office Button | Excel Options). Then move the cell cursor through all the cells with copied formulas in the table. When R1C1 notation is in effect, all copies of an original formula across an entire row or down an entire column of the table should be identical when displayed on the Formula bar as you make their cells current.

Absolute references

Most of the time, relative cell references are exactly what you need in the formulas that you build, thus allowing Excel to adjust the row and/or column references as required in the copies that you make. You will encounter some circumstances, however, where Excel should not adjust one or more parts of the cell reference in the copied formula. This occurs, for example, whenever you want to use a cell value as a constant in all the copies that you make of a formula.

Figure 1-7 illustrates just such a situation. In this situation, you want to build a formula in cell B10 that calculates what percentage April's part production total (B8) is of the total nine-month production (cell K8). Normally, you would create the following formula in cell B10 with all its relative cell references:

```
=B8/K8
```

However, because you want to copy this formula across to the range C10:J10 to calculate the percentages for the eight months (May through December), you need to alter the relative cell references in the last part of the formula in cell K8 so that this cell reference with the nine-month production total remains unchanged in all your copies.

Figure 1-7: Using an absolute address in the formula to calculate monthly percentage of the total.

	A	B	C	D	E	F	G	H	I	J	K
1	Production Schedule for 2008										
2											
3	Part No.	Apr-08	May-08	Jun-08	Jul-08	Aug-08	Sep-08	Oct-08	Nov-08	Dec-08	Total
4	AB-100	500	485	438	505	483	540	441	550	345	4287
5	AB-101	175	170	153	177	169	189	154	193	200	1580
6	AB-102	350	340	306	354	338	378	309	385	350	3110
7	AB-103	890	863	779	899	859	961	785	979	885	7900
8	Total	1915	1858	1676	1935	1849	2068	1689	2107	1780	16877
9											
10	% Total	11.35%	11.01%	9.93%	11.47%	10.96%	12.25%	10.01%	12.48%	10.55%	
11											
12											

B10 = =B8/$K$8

You can start to understand the problem caused by adjusting a relative cell reference that should remain unchanged by just thinking about copying the original formula from cell B10 to C10 to calculate the percentage for May. In this cell, you want the following formula that divides the May production total in cell C8 by the nine-month total in cell K8:

=C8/K8

However, if you don't indicate otherwise, Excel adjusts both parts of the formula in the copies, so that C10 incorrectly contains the following formula:

=C8/L8

Because cell L8 is currently blank and blank cells have the equivalent of the value 0, this formula returns the #DIV/0 formula error as the result, thus indicating that Excel can't properly perform this arithmetic operation (see Book III, Chapter 2 for details on this error message).

To indicate that you don't want a particular cell reference (such as cell K8 in the example) to be adjusted in the copies that you make of a formula, you change the cell reference from a relative cell reference to an *absolute cell reference*. In the A1 system of cell references, an absolute cell reference contains dollar signs before the column letter and the row number, as in $K$8. In the R1C1 notation, you simply list the actual row and column number in the cell reference, as in R8C11, without placing the row and column numbers in square brackets.

If you realize that you need to convert a relative cell reference to an absolute reference as you're building the original formula, you can convert the relative reference to absolute by selecting the cell and then pressing F4. To get an idea of how this works, follow along with these steps for creating the correct formula =B7/$K$8 in cell B10:

1. **Click cell B10 to make it active.**

2. **Type = to start the formula; then click cell B8 and type / (the sign for division).**

   The Formula bar now reads =B8/.

3. **Click K8 to select this cell and add it to the formula.**

   The Formula bar now reads =B8/K8.

4. **Press F4 once to change the cell reference from relative (K8) to absolute ($K$8).**

   The Formula bar now reads =B8/$K$8. You're now ready to enter the formula and then make the copies.

5. **Click the Enter button on the Formula bar and then drag the Fill handle to cell J10 before you release the mouse button.**

Like it or not, you won't always anticipate the need for an absolute value until after you've built the formula and copied it to a range. When this happens, you have to edit the original formula, change the relative reference to absolute, and then make the copies again.

When editing the cell reference in the formula, you can change its reference by positioning the insertion point anywhere in its address and then pressing F4. You can also do this by inserting dollar signs in front of the column letter(s) and row number when editing the formula, although doing that isn't nearly as easy as pressing F4.

You can make an exact copy of a formula in another cell without using absolute references. To do this, make the cell with the formula that you want to copy the active one, use the I-beam pointer to select the entire formula in the Formula bar by dragging through it, and then click the Copy command button on the Home tab of the Ribbon (or press Ctrl+C). Next, click the Cancel button to deactivate the Formula bar, select the cell where you want the exact copy to appear, and then click the Paste command button on the Home tab (or press Ctrl+V). Excel then pastes an exact duplicate of the original formula into the active cell without adjusting any of its cell references (even if they are all relative cell references).

A mixed bag of references

Some formulas don't require you to change the entire cell reference from relative to absolute in order to copy them correctly. In some situations, you only need to indicate that the column letter or the row number remains unchanged in all copies of the original formula. A cell reference that is part relative and part absolute is called a *mixed cell reference*.

In the A1 notation, a mixed cell reference has a dollar sign just in front of the column letter or row number that should not be adjusted in the copies. For example, $C10 adjusts row 10 in copies down the rows but leaves column C unchanged in all copies across columns to its right. Another example is C$10, which adjusts column C in copies to columns to the right but leaves row 10 unchanged in all copies down the rows. (For an example of using mixed cell references in a master formula, refer to the information on using the PMT Function in Book III, Chapter 4.)

To change the cell reference that you select in a formula (by clicking the flashing insertion point somewhere in its column letter and row number) from relative to mixed, continue to press F4 until the type of mixed reference appears on the Formula bar. When the Formula bar is active and the insertion point is somewhere in the cell reference (either when building or editing the formula), pressing F4 cycles through each cell-reference possibility in the following order:

✦ The first time you press F4, Excel changes the relative cell reference to absolute (C10 to $C$10).

✦ The second time you press F4, Excel changes the absolute reference to a mixed reference where the column is relative and the row is absolute ($C$10 to C$10).

✦ The third time you select the Reference command, Excel changes the mixed reference where the column is relative and the row is absolute to a mixed reference where the row is relative and the column is absolute (C$10 to $C10).

✦ The fourth time you press F4, Excel changes the mixed reference where the row is relative and the column is absolute back to a relative reference ($C10 to C10).

If you bypass the type of cell reference that you want to use, you can return to it by continuing to press F4 until you cycle through the variations again to reach the one that you need.

Adding Array Formulas

As noted previously in this chapter, many spreadsheet tables use an original formula that you copy to adjacent cells by using relative cell references (sometimes referred to as a *one-to-many copy*). In some cases, you can build the original formula so that Excel performs the desired calculation not only in the active cell, but also in all the other cells to which you would normally copy the formula. You do this by creating an *array formula*. An array formula is a special formula that operates on a range of values. If a cell range supplies this range (as is often the case), it is referred to as an *array range*. If this range is supplied by a list of numerical values, they are known as an *array constant*.

Although the array concept may seem foreign at first, you are really quite familiar with arrays because the column-and-row structure of the Excel worksheet grid naturally organizes your data ranges into one-dimensional and two-dimensional arrays. (1-D arrays take up a single row or column while 2-D arrays take up multiple rows and columns.)

Figure 1-8 illustrates a couple of two-dimensional arrays with numerical entries of two different sizes. The first array is a 3 x 2 array in the cell range B2:C4. This array is a 3 x 2 array because it occupies three rows and two columns. The second array is a 2 x 3 array in the cell range F2:H3. This array is a 2 x 3 array because it uses two rows and three columns.

If you were to list the values in the first 3 x 2 array as an array constant in a formula, they would appear as follows:

`{1,4;2,5;3,6}`

Several things in this list are noteworthy. First, the array constant is enclosed in a pair of braces ({}). Second, columns within each row are separated by commas (,) and rows within the array are separated by semicolons (;). Third, the constants in the array are listed across each row and then down each column, and *not* down each column and across each row.

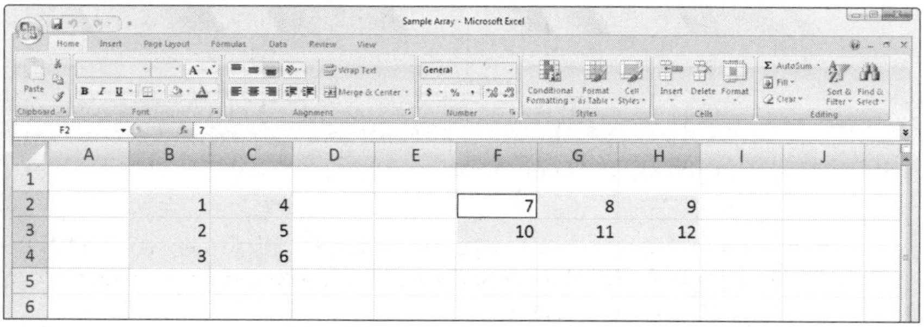

Figure 1-8:
Worksheet
with two
different
sizes of
arrays.

The second 2 x 3 array expressed as an array constant appears as follows:

`{7,8,9;10,11,12}`

Note again that you list the values across each row and then down each column, separating the values in different columns with commas and the values in different rows with a semicolon.

The use of array formulas can significantly reduce the amount of formula copying that you have to do in a worksheet by producing multiple results throughout the array range in a single operation. In addition, array formulas use less computer memory than standard formulas copied in a range. This can be important when creating a large worksheet with many tables because it may mean the difference between fitting all your calculations on one worksheet and having to split your model into several worksheet files.

Building an array formula

To get an idea of how you build and use array formulas in a worksheet, consider the sample worksheet shown in Figure 1-9. This worksheet is designed to compute the biweekly wages for each employee. It will do this by multiplying each employee's hourly rate by the number of hours worked in each pay period. Instead of creating the following formula in cell R10, you must copy down the cells R11 through R13:

`=A4*R4`

You can create the following array formula in the array range:

`={A4:A7*R4:R7}`

This array formula multiplies each of the hourly rates in the 4 x 1 array in the range A4:A7 with each of the hours worked in the 4 x 1 array in the range R4:R7. This same formula is entered into all cells of the array range (R10:R13) as soon as you complete the formula in the active cell R10. To see how this is done, follow along with the steps required to build this array formula:

1. **Make cell R10 the active cell, and then select the array range R10:R13 and type = (equal sign) to start the array formula.**

   You always start an array formula by selecting the cell or cell range where the results are to appear. Note that array formulas, like standard formulas, begin with the equal sign.

2. **Select the range A4:A7 that contains the hourly rate for each employee as shown, type an * (asterisk for multiplication), and then select the range R4:R7 that contains the total number of hours worked during the first pay period.**

3. **Press Ctrl+Shift+Enter to insert an array formula in the array range.**

   When you press Ctrl+Shift+Enter to complete the formula, Excel inserts braces around the formula and copies the array formula {=A4:A7*R4:R7} into each of the cells in the array range R10:R13.

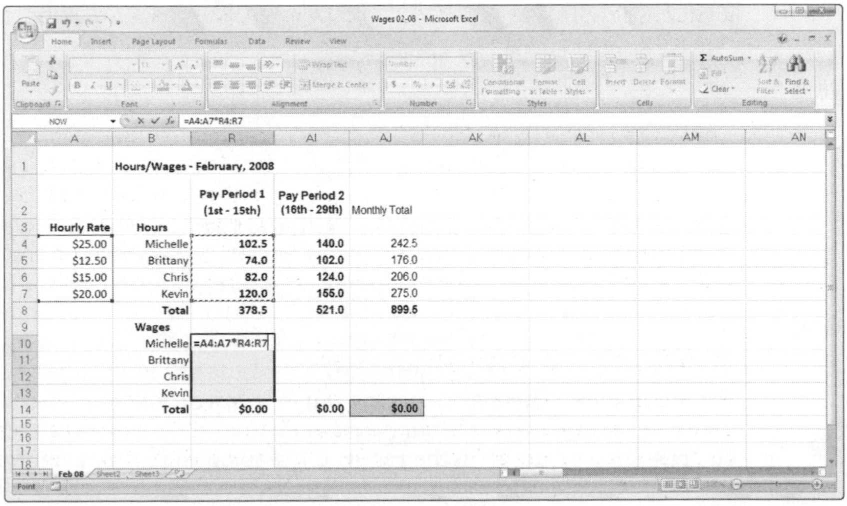

Figure 1-9:
Building an array formula to calculate hourly wages for the first pay period.

When entering an array formula, you must remember to press Ctrl+Shift+ Enter instead of just the Enter key because it is this special key combination that tells Excel that you are building an array formula, so that the program encloses the formula in braces and copies it to every cell in the array range. Also, don't try to create an array formula by editing it on the Formula bar and then inserting curly braces because this doesn't cut it. The only way to create an array formula is by pressing Ctrl+Shift+Enter to complete the formula entry.

Figure 1-10 shows you the February wage table after completing all the array formulas in three ranges: R10:R13, AI10:AI13, and AJ10:AJ13. In the second cell range, AI10:AI13, I entered the following array formula to calculate the hourly wages for the second pay period in February:

`{=A4:A7*AI4:AI7}`

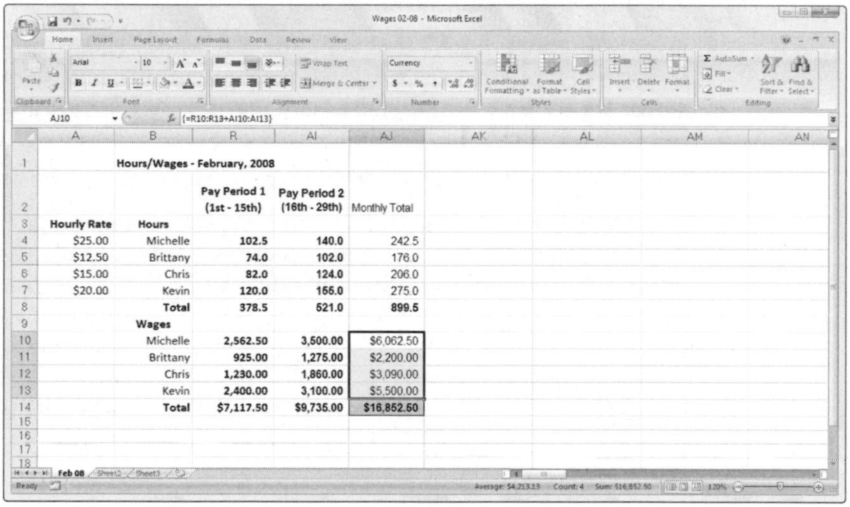

Figure 1-10:
Hourly wage spreadsheet after entering all three array formulas.

In the third cell range, AJ10:AJ13, I entered the following array formula to calculate the total wages paid to each employee in February 2003:

`{=R10:R13+AI10:AI13}`

When you enter an array formula, the formula should produce an array with the same dimensions as the array range that you selected. If the resulting array returned by the formula is smaller than the array range, Excel expands the resulting array to fill the range. If the resulting array is larger than the array range, Excel doesn't display all the results. When expanding the results in an array range, Excel considers the dimensions of all the arrays used in the arguments of the operation. Each argument must have the same number of rows as the array with the most rows and the same number of columns as the array with the most columns.

Editing an array formula

Editing array formulas differs somewhat from editing normal formulas. In editing an array range, you must treat the range as a single unit and edit it in one operation (corresponding to the way in which the array formula was entered). This means that you can't edit, clear, move, insert, or delete individual cells in the array range. If you try, Excel will display an Alert dialog box stating "You cannot change part of an array."

To edit the contents of an array formula, select a cell in the array range and then activate Edit mode by clicking the formula or the Formula bar or pressing F2. When you do this, Excel displays the contents of the array formula without the customary braces. The program also outlines the ranges referred to in the array formula in the cells of the worksheet in different colors that match those assigned to the range addresses in the edited formula on the Formula bar. After you make your changes to the formula contents, you must remember to press Ctrl+Shift+Enter to enter your changes and have Excel enclose the array formula in braces once again.

If you want to convert the results in an array range to their calculated values, select the array range and click the Copy button on the Ribbon's Home tab or press Ctrl+C. Then, without changing the selection, click the Paste Values option on the Paste button's drop-down menu (or press Alt+HVV). As soon as you convert an array range to its calculated values, Excel no longer treats the cell range as an array.

**Book III
Chapter 1**

**Building Basic
Formulas**

Ranges Names in Formulas

Thus far, all the example formulas in this chapter have used a combination of numerical constants and cell references (both relative and absolute and using the A1 and R1C1 notation). Although cell references provide a convenient method for pointing out the cell location in the worksheet grid, they are not at all descriptive of their function when used in formulas. Fortunately, Excel makes it easy to assign descriptive names to the cells, cell ranges, constants, and even formulas that make their function in the worksheet much more understandable.

To get an idea of how names can help to document the purpose of a formula, consider the following formula for computing the sale price of an item that uses standard cell references:

```
=B4*B2
```

Now consider the following formula that performs the same calculation but, this time, with the use of range names:

```
=Retail_Price*Discount_Rate
```

Obviously, the function of the second formula is much more comprehensible, not only to you as the creator of the worksheet but also to anyone else who has to use it.

Range names are extremely useful not only for documenting the function of the formulas in your worksheet, but also for finding and selecting cell ranges quickly and easily. This is especially helpful in a large worksheet that you aren't very familiar with or only use intermittently. After you assign a name to a cell range, you can locate and select all the cells in that range with the Go To dialog box. Simply click the Go To option on the Find & Select button's drop-down menu on the Home tab of the Ribbon (or press Ctrl+G or F5). Then double-click the range name in the Go To list box, or click the range name and click OK or press Enter. Excel then selects the entire range and, if necessary, shifts the worksheet display so that you can see the first cell in that range on the screen.

Defining range names

You can define a name for the selected cell range or nonadjacent selection by typing its range name into the Name box on the Formula bar and then pressing Enter. You can also name a cell, cell range, or nonadjacent selection by clicking the Define Name command button on the Ribbon's Formulas tab or by pressing Alt+MMD. Excel then opens the New Name dialog box, where you can input the selection's range name in the Name text box.

If Excel can identify a label in the cell immediately above or to the left of the active one, the program inserts this label as the suggested name in the Name text box. The program also displays the scope of the range name in the Scope drop-down list box and the cell reference of the active cell or the range address of the range or nonadjacent selection that is currently marked (by using absolute references) in the Refers To text box below. You can do the following:

✦ To change the scope from the entire workbook to a particular worksheet in the workbook so that range name is only recognized on that sheet, click the sheet's name on the Scope drop-down list.

✦ To change the cell range the name refers to, select the cells in the work-sheet (remember you can collapse the New Name dialog box to the Refers To text box by clicking its Collapse button).

✦ To accept the suggested or edited name, scope, and cell selection, click the OK button, shown in Figure 1-11.

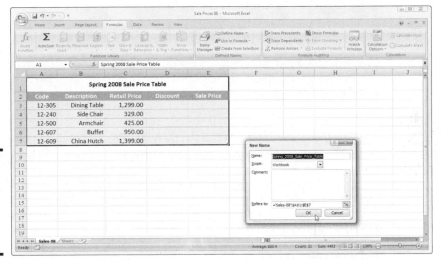

Figure 1-11:
Adding a new range name in the New Name dialog box.

**Book III
Chapter 1**

Building Basic Formulas

When naming a range in the Name text box of the New Name dialog box, you need to follow the same naming conventions as when defining a name in the Name box on the Formula bar. Basically, this means that the name must begin with a letter rather than a number, contain no spaces, and not dupli-cate any other name in the workbook (see Book II, Chapter 2 for more on naming ranges).

If you want to assign the same range name to similar ranges on different worksheets in the workbook, preface the range name with the sheet name followed by an exclamation point and then the descriptive name. For exam-ple, if you want to give the name Costs to the cell range A2:A10 on both Sheet1 and Sheet2, you name the range Sheet1!Costs on Sheet1 and Sheet2!Costs on Sheet2. If you have renamed the worksheet to something more descriptive than Sheet1, you need to enclose the name in single quotes if it contains a space when you enter the range. For example, if you rename Sheet1 to Inc. Statement 04, you enter the range name including the work-sheet reference for the Costs cell range as follows:

```
'Inc. Statement 04'!Costs
```

TIP

When you preface a range name with the sheet name as shown in this example, you don't have to use the sheet name part of the range name in the formulas that you create on the same worksheet. In other words, if you create a SUM formula that totals the values in the 'Inc. Statement 04'!Costs range somewhere on the Inc. Statement 04 worksheet, you can enter the formulas as follows:

```
=SUM(Costs)
```

However, if you were to create this formula on any other worksheet in the workbook, you would have to include the full range name in the formula, as in:

```
=SUM('Inc. Statement 04'!Costs)
```

Naming constants and formulas

In addition to naming cells in your worksheet, you can also assign range names to the constants and formulas that you use often. For example, if you are creating a spreadsheet table that calculates sales prices, you can assign the discount percentage rate to the range name discount_rate. Then, you can supply this range name as a constant in any formula that calculates the sale discount used in determining the sale price for merchandise.

Figure 1-12 illustrates how you would assign a constant value to the range name discount_rate. Here, you see the New Name dialog box after I entered discount_rate as the name in the Name text box and =15% as the discount rate in the Refers To text box. After assigning this constant percentage rate to the range name discount_rate in this manner, you can apply it to any formula by typing or pasting in the name (see the "Using names in building formulas" section that follows in this chapter for details).

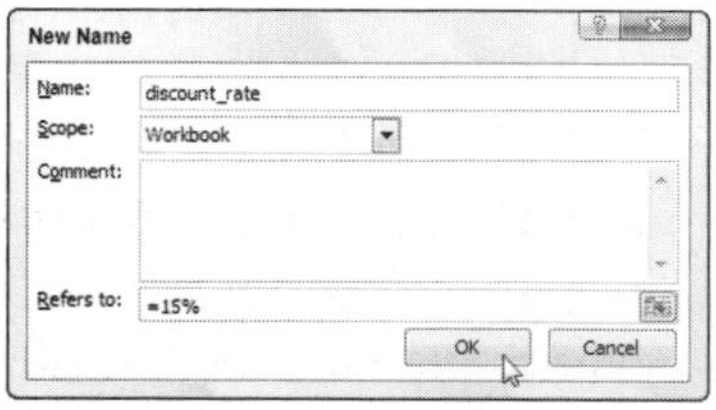

Figure 1-12: Defining the discount rate constant as a range name in the New Name dialog box.

New Name	
Name:	discount_rate
Scope:	Workbook
Comment:	
Refers to:	=15%
	OK Cancel

In addition to naming constants, you can also give a range name to a formula that you use repeatedly. When building a formula in the Refers To text box of the New Name dialog box (Alt+MGR), keep in mind that Excel automatically applies absolute references to any cells that you point to in the worksheet. If you want to create a formula with relative cell references that Excel adjusts when you enter or paste the range name in a new cell, you must press F4 to convert the current cell reference to relative or type in the cell address without dollar signs.

When creating the constant in the New Name dialog box, don't change the Scope setting from Workbook to a particular sheet in the workbook unless you're positive that you'll never need to use that constant in a formula on any other worksheet. If you limit the scope to a particular worksheet, Excel 2007 does not let you use the range name in a formula on any other worksheet (you'll get the #NAME? error), and Scope is the one aspect you can't change when editing a range name via the Name Manager. (I discuss managing range names later in this chapter).

Using names in building formulas

After you assign a name to a cell or cell range in your worksheet, you can then click the range name on the Use in Formula button's drop-down list on the Ribbon's Formulas tab to paste it into the formulas that you build (Alt+MS).

For example, in the sample Sales Price table shown in Figure 1-13, after assigning the discount rate of 15% to the range name, discount_rate, you can create the formulas that calculate the amount of the sale discount. To do this, you multiply the retail price of each item by the discount_rate constant using the Use in Formula command button by following these steps:

1. **Make cell D3 active.**

2. **Type = (equal sign) to start the formula.**

3. **Click cell C3 to select the retail price for the first item and then type * (asterisk).**

   The formula on the Formula bar now reads, =C3*.

4. **Click the Use in Formula button on the Formulas tab or press Alt+MS1.**

   This action opens the drop-down menu on the Use in Formula button on which you can select the discount_rate range name.

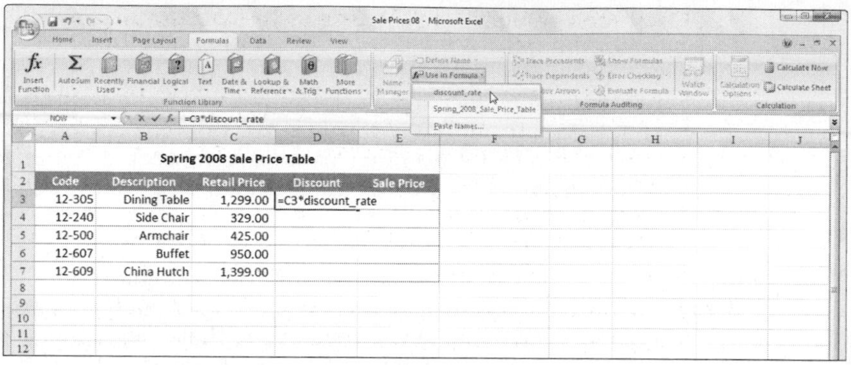

Figure 1-13:
Pasting the
range name
for the
discount_
rate con-
stant into a
formula.

5. **Click the name discount_rate in the Use in Formula button's drop-down menu.**

   The formula now reads =C3*discount_rate on the Formula bar.

6. **Click the Enter button on the Formula bar to input the formula in cell D3.**

   Now, all that remains is to copy the original formula down column D.

7. **Drag the Fill handle in cell D3 down to cell D7 and release the mouse button to copy the formula and calculate the discount for the entire table.**

Creating names from column and row headings

You can use the Create from Selection command button on the Formulas tab of the Ribbon to assign existing column and row headings in a table of data to the cells in that table. When using this command button, you can have Excel assign the labels used as column headings in the top or bottom row of the table, the labels used as row headings in the leftmost or rightmost column, or even a combination of these headings.

For example, the sample worksheet in Figure 1-14 illustrates a typical table layout that uses column headings in the top row of the table and row headings in the first column of the table. You can assign these labels to the cells in the table by using the Create from Selection command button as follows:

1. **Select the cells in the table, including those with the column and row labels that you want to use as range names.**

   For the example shown in Figure 1-14, you select the range B2:E7.

2. **Click the Create from Selection command button on the Formulas tab or press Alt+MC.**

   This action opens the Create Names from Selection dialog box that contains four check boxes: Top Row, Left Column, Bottom Row, and Right Column. The program selects the check box or boxes in this dialog box based on the arrangement of the labels in your table. In the example shown in Figure 1-14, Excel selects both the Top Row and Left Column check boxes because the table contains both column headings in the top row and row headings in the left column.

3. **After selecting (or deselecting) the appropriate Create Names From Values In The check boxes, click the OK button to assign the range names to your table.**

Note that when you select both the Top Row and Left Column check boxes in the Create Names dialog box, Excel assigns the label in the cell in the upper-left corner of the table to the entire range of values in the table (one row down and one column to the right).

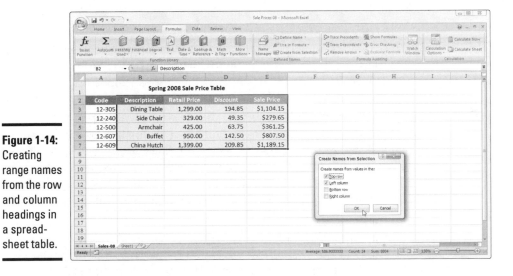

Figure 1-14: Creating range names from the row and column headings in a spreadsheet table.

Book III
Chapter 1

Building Basic Formulas

In the example illustrated in Figure 1-14, Excel assigns the name Description (the heading for column B) to the cell range C3:E7. Similarly, the program assigns the column headings to the appropriate data in the table in the rows below, and assigns the row headings to the data in the appropriate columns to the right so that the name Retail_Price is assigned to the cell range C3:C7 and the name China_Hutch is assigned to the cell range C7:E7.

Managing range names

As you assign range names in your workbook, their names appear in the Name Manager dialog box (see Figure 1-15). You open this dialog box by clicking the Name Manager command button on the Formulas tab of the Ribbon or by pressing Alt+MN.

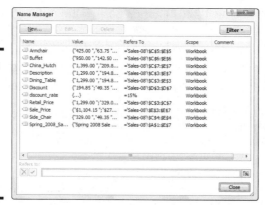

Figure 1-15: The Name Manager lists all range names defined in the work-book.

The Name Manager enables you to do any of the following:

✦ Create new range names for the worksheet or workbook in the New Name dialog box opened by clicking the New button (see "Defining range names" earlier in this chapter).

✦ Edit existing range names in the Edit Name dialog box by clicking the name in the list box and then clicking the Edit button — you can change both the name and cell selection when editing a range name.

✦ Delete existing range names by clicking the name and then clicking the Delete button followed by the OK button in the alert dialog box asking you to confirm its deletion.

✦ Filter the range names in the list box of the Name Manager by clicking the Filter button and then clicking a filter option (Names Scoped to Worksheet, Names Scoped to Workbook, Names with Errors, Names without Errors, Defined Names, or Table Names) on its drop-down menu.

Be careful that you don't delete a range name that is already used in formulas in the worksheet. If you do, Excel will return the #NAME! error value to any formula that refers to the name you deleted!

Applying names to existing formulas

Excel doesn't automatically replace cell references with the descriptive names that you assign to them in the New Name or Create Names from Selection dialog boxes. To replace cell references with their names, you need to click the Apply Names option on the Define Name button's drop-down menu or press Alt+MMA.

When you choose this command, Excel opens the Apply Names dialog box, where you select the range names that you want applied in formulas used in your worksheet by selecting the names in the Apply Names list box.

Note that when you first open this dialog box, it contains just two check boxes: Ignore Relative/Absolute and Use Row and Column Names (both of which are checked). You can click the Options>> button to expand the Apply Names dialog box and display other options that you can use when applying your range names, shown in Figure 1-16. The Apply Names options include the following:

✦ **Ignore Relative/Absolute check box:** The program replaces cell references with the names that you've selected in the Apply Names list box, regardless of the type of reference used in their formulas. If you want Excel to replace only those cell references that use the same type of references as are used in your names (absolute for absolute, mixed for mixed, and relative for relative), deselect this check box. Most of the time, you'll want to leave this check box selected because Excel automatically assigns absolute cell references to the names that you define and relative cell references to the formulas that you build.

✦ **Use Row and Column Names check box:** The names created from row and column headings with the Create Names command appear in your formulas. Deselect this option if you don't want these row and column names to appear in the formulas in your worksheet.

✦ **Omit Column Name If Same Column check box:** This prevents Excel from repeating the column name when the formula is in the same column. Deselect this check box when you want the program to display the column name even in formulas in the same column as the heading used to create the column name.

✦ **Omit Row Name If Same Row check box:** This prevents Excel from repeating the row name when the formula is in the same row. Deselect this check box when you want the program to display the row name even in formulas in the same row as the heading used to create the row name.

✦ **Name Order:** Choose the Row Column option button (the default) if you want the row name to precede the column name when both names are displayed in the formulas, or choose the Column Row option button if you want the column name to precede the row name.

After applying all the range names by using the default Apply Names options (that is, Ignore Relative/Absolute, Use Row and Column Names, Omit Column Name If Same Column, Omit Row Name If Same Row, and Name Order options selected), Excel replaces all the cell references in the formulas in the Sale Price table. In cell E3, for example, in place of the original formula, =C3–D3, the cell now contains the formula:

```
=Retail_Price-Discount
```

Cell D3, to the immediate left, instead of =C3*discount_rate now contains:

```
=Retail_Price*discount_rate
```

Only one problem occurs with applying names by using the default settings. This problem begins to shows up as soon as you select cell E4. Although this formula subtracts cell D4 from C4, its contents now also appear as

```
=Retail_Price-Discount
```

This is identical in appearance to the contents of cell E3 above (and, in fact, identical in appearance to cells E5, E6, and E7 in the cells below).

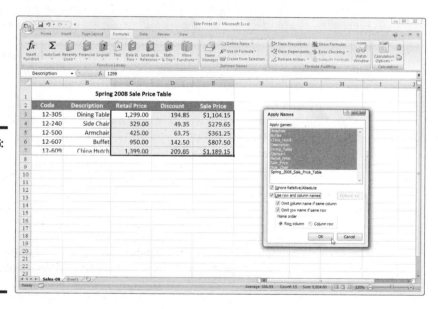

Figure 1-16: Using the options in the Apply Names dialog box to assign range names to formulas.

The reason that the formulas all appear identical (although they're really not) is because I selected the Omit Column Name If Same Column and Omit Row Name If Same Row check boxes. When you use these settings, Excel doesn't bother to repeat the row name when the formula is in the same row, and Excel repeats the column name when the formula is in the same column.

If you were to deselect the Omit Row Name if Same Row check box while still selecting the Use Row and Column Names check box in the Apply Names dialog box, the formula in cell E3 would appear as follows:

```
=Table  Retail_Price-Table  Discount
```

If you were then to select cell E4 below, the formula would now appear quite differently in this form:

```
=Side_Chair  Retail_Price-Side_Chair  Discount
```

Now Excel displays both the row and column names separated by a space for each cell reference in the formulas in this column. Remember that the space between the row name and column name is called the *intersection operator* (see Table 1-1). You can interpret the formula in E3 as saying, "Take the cell at the intersection of the Table row and Retail_Price column and subtract it from the cell at the intersection of the Table row and Discount column." The formula in E4 is similar, except that it says, "Take the cell at the intersection of the Side_chair row and Retail_Price column and subtract it from the cell at the intersection of the Side_chair row and Discount column."

Adding Linking Formulas

Linking formulas are formulas that transfer a constant or other formula to a new place in the same worksheet, same workbook, or even a different workbook without copying it to its new location. When you create a linking formula, it brings forward the constant or original formula to a new location so that the result in the linking formula remains dynamically tied to the original. If you change the original constant or any of the cells referred to in the original formula, the result in the cell containing the linking formula is updated at the same time as the cell containing the original constant or formula.

**Book III
Chapter 1**

**Building Basic
Formulas**

You can create a linking formula in one of two ways:

✦ Select the cell where you want the linking formula, type = (equal sign), and then click the cell with the constant (text or number) or the formula that you want to bring forward to that cell. Complete the cell entry by clicking the Enter button on the Formula bar or pressing the Enter key.

✦ Select the cell with the constant or formula that you want to bring forward to a new location, and click the Copy button in the Clipboard group on the Ribbon's Home tab or press Ctrl+C. Then click the cell where the linking formula is to appear before you click the Paste Link option on the Paste button's drop-down menu.

When you use the first simple formula method to create a link, Excel uses a relative cell reference to refer to the cell containing the original value or formula (as in =A10 when referring to an entry in cell A10). However, when you use the second copy-and-paste link method, Excel uses an absolute cell reference to refer to the original cell (as in =$A$10 when referring to an entry in cell A10).

When you create a linking formula to a cell on a different sheet of the same workbook, Excel inserts the worksheet name (followed by an exclamation point) in front of the cell address. So, if you copy and paste a link to a formula in cell A10 on a different worksheet called Income 05, Excel inserts the following linking formula:

```
='Income 05'!$A$10
```

When you create a linking formula to a cell in a different workbook, Excel inserts the workbook filename enclosed in square brackets before the name of the worksheet, which precedes the cell address. So, if you bring forward a formula in cell A10 on a worksheet called Cost Analysis in the Projected Income 06 workbook, Excel inserts this linking formula:

```
='[Projected Income 06.xls]Cost Analysis'!$A$10
```

If you ever need to sever a link between the cell containing the original value or formula and the cell to which it's been brought forward, you can do so by editing the linking formula. Press F2, then immediately recalculate the formula by pressing F9, and then click the Enter button on the Formula bar or press Enter. This replaces the linking formula with the currently calculated result. Because you've converted the dynamic formula into a constant, changes to the original cell no longer affect the one to which it was originally brought forward.

Controlling Formula Recalculation

Normally, Excel recalculates your worksheet automatically as soon you change any entries, formulas, or names on which your formulas depend. This system works fine as long as the worksheet is not too large or doesn't contain tables whose formulas depend on several values.

When Excel does calculate your worksheet, the program recalculates only those cells that are affected by the change that you've made. Nevertheless, in a complex worksheet that contains many formulas, recalculation may take several seconds (during which time, the pointer will change to an hourglass and the word "Recalculation" followed by the number of cells left to be recalculated will appear on the left side of the Formula bar).

Because Excel recalculates dependent formulas in the background, you can always interrupt this process and make a cell entry or choose a command even when the pointer assumes the hourglass shape during the recalculation process. As soon as you stop making entries or selecting commands, Excel resumes recalculating the worksheet.

To control when Excel calculates your worksheet, you click the Options button on the Formulas tab of the Ribbon and then click the Manual option button or press Alt+MXM. After switching to manual recalculation, when you make a change in a value, formula, or name that would usually cause Excel to recalculate the worksheet, the program displays the message "Calculate" on the Status bar.

When you're ready to have Excel recalculate the worksheet, you then click the Calculate Now (F9) command button (the one with a picture of the handheld calculator) on the Ribbon's Formulas tab or press F9 or Ctrl+=. This tells the program to recalculate all dependent formulas and open charts and makes the Calculate status indicator disappear from the Status bar.

After switching to manual recalculation, Excel still automatically recalculates the worksheet whenever you save the file. When you are working with a really large and complex worksheet, recalculating the worksheet each time you want to save your changes can make this process quite time-consuming. If you want to save the worksheet without first updating dependent formulas and charts, you need to deselect the Recalculate Workbook before Saving check box in the Calculation Options section of the Formulas tab of the Excel Options dialog box (Office Button | Excel Options | Formulas or Alt+FIF).

If your worksheet contains data tables used to perform what-if analyses, switch from Automatic to Automatic except Data Tables recalculation by clicking Automatic Except for Data Tables on the Calculation Options button's drop-down menu on the Formulas tab or pressing Alt+MXE. Doing so enables you to change a number of variables in the what-if formulas before having Excel recalculate the data table (see Book VII, Chapter 1 for more on performing what-if analyses).

Automatic, Automatic Except for Data Tables, and Manual are by no means the only calculation options available in Excel. Table 1-3 explains each of the options that appear in the Calculation Options section of the Formulas tab of the Excel Options dialog box.

Table 1-3	The Calculation Options in Excel 2007
Option	*Purpose*
Automatic	Calculates all dependent formulas and updates open or embedded charts every time you make a change to a value, formula, or name. This is the default setting for each new worksheet that you start.
Automatic Except for Data Tables	Calculates all dependent formulas and updates open or embedded charts. Does not calculate data tables created with the Data Table feature (see Book VII, Chapter 1, for information on creating data tables). To recalculate data tables when this option button is selected, click the Calculate Now (F9) command button on the Formulas tab of the Ribbon or press F9 in the worksheet.
Manual	Calculates open worksheets and updates open or embedded charts only when you click the Calculate Now (F9) command button on the Formulas tab of the Ribbon or press F9 or Ctrl+= in the worksheet.
Recalculate Workbook before Saving	When this check box is selected, Excel calculates open worksheets and updates open or embedded charts when you save them even when the Manually option button is selected.
Enable Iterative Calculation	When this check box is selected, Excel sets the iterations, that is, the number of times that a worksheet is recalculated, when performing goal seeking (see Book VII, Chapter 1) or resolving circular references to the number displayed in the Maximum Iterations text box.
Maximum Iterations	Sets the maximum number of iterations (100 by default) when the Iteration check box is selected.
Maximum Change	Sets the maximum amount of change to the values during each iteration (0.001 by default) when the Iteration check box is selected.

Circular References

A *circular reference* in a formula is one that depends, directly or indirectly, on its own value. The most common type of circular reference occurs when you mistakenly refer in the formula to the cell in which you're building the formula itself. For example, suppose that cell B10 is active when you build the formula

```
=A10+B10
```

As soon as you click the Enter button on the Formula bar or press Enter or an arrow key to insert this formula in cell B10 (assuming the program is in Automatic recalculation mode), Excel displays an Alert dialog box, stating that it cannot calculate the formula due to the circular reference.

If you then press Enter or click OK to close this Alert dialog box, an Excel Help window appears containing general information about circular references in two sections: Locate and Remove a Circular Reference and Make a Circular Reference Work by Changing the Number of Times Microsoft Excel Iterates Formulas.

When you close this Excel Help window by clicking its Close button, Excel inserts 0 in the cell with the circular reference, and the Circular Reference status indicator followed by the cell address with the circular reference appears on the Status bar.

Some circular references are solvable by increasing the number of times they are recalculated (each recalculation bringing you closer and closer to the desired result), whereas others are not (for no amount of recalculating brings them closer to any resolution) and need to be removed from the spreadsheet.

The formula in cell B10 is an example of a circular reference that Excel is unable to resolve because the formula's calculation depends directly on the formula's result. Each time the formula returns a new result, this result is fed into the formula, thus creating a new result to be fed back into the formula. Because this type of circular reference sets up an endless loop that continuously requires recalculating and can never be resolved, you need to fix the formula reference or remove the formula from the spreadsheet.

Figure 1-17 illustrates the classic example of a circular reference, which ultimately can be resolved. Here, you have an income statement that includes bonuses equal to 20 percent of the net earnings entered as an expense in cell B15 with the formula

```
=-B21*0.2
```

**Book III
Chapter 1**

**Building Basic
Formulas**

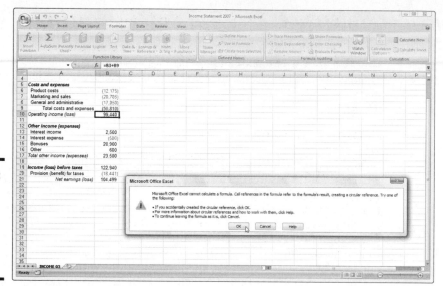

Figure 1-17:
Income
statement
with a
resolvable
circular
reference.

This formula contains a circular reference because it refers to the value in B21, which itself indirectly depends on the amount of bonuses (the bonuses being used an expense in the formulas that determine the amount of net earnings in cell B21).

To resolve the circular reference in cell B15 and calculate the bonuses based on net earnings in B21, you simply need to select the Enable Iterative Calculation check box in the Calculation Options section of the Formulas tab in the Excel Options dialog box (Microsoft Office Button I Excel Options I Formulas or Alt+FIF). However, if manual recalculation is selected, you must click the Calculate Now (F9) command button on the Formulas tab of the Ribbon or press F9 or Ctrl+= as well.

Chapter 2: Logical Functions and Error Trapping

In This Chapter

✔ Understanding formula error values

✔ Understanding the logical functions

✔ Creating IF formulas that trap errors

✔ Auditing formulas

✔ Changing the Error Checking options

✔ Masking Error Values in your printouts

Troubleshooting the formula errors in a worksheet is the main topic of this chapter. Here, you see how to locate the source of all those vexing formula errors so that you can shoot them down and set things right! The biggest problem with errors in your formulas — besides how ugly such values as #REF! and #DIV/0! are — is that they spread like wildfire through the workbook to other cells containing formulas that refer to their error-laden cells. If you're dealing with a large worksheet in a really big workbook, you may not be able to tell which cell actually contains the formula that's causing all the hubbub. And if you can't apprehend the cell that is the cause of all this unpleasantness, you really have no way of restoring law and order to your workbook.

Keeping in mind that the best defense is a good offense, you also find out in this chapter how to trap potential errors at their source and thereby keep them there. This technique, known affectionately as *error trapping* (just think of yourself as being on a spreadsheet safari), is easily accomplished by skillfully combining the IF function to combine with the workings of the original formula.

Understanding Error Values

If Excel can't properly calculate a formula that you enter in a cell, the program displays an *error value* in the cell as soon as you complete the formula entry. Excel uses several error values, all of which begin with the number sign

(#). Table 2-1 shows you the error values in Excel along with the meaning and the most probable cause for its display. To remove an error value from a cell, you must discover what caused the value to appear and then edit the formula so that Excel can complete the desired calculation.

Table 2-1		Error Values in Excel
Error Value	Meaning	Causes
#DIV/0	Division by zero	The division operation in your formula refers to a cell that contains the value 0 or is *blank*.
#N/A	No value available	Technically, this is not an error value but a special value that you can manually enter into a cell to indicate that you don't yet have a necessary value.
#NAME?	Excel doesn't recognize a name	This error value appears when you incorrectly type the range name, refer to a deleted range name, or forget to put quotation marks around a text string in a formula (causing Excel to think that you're referring to a range name).
#NULL!	You specified an intersection of two cell ranges whose cells don't actually intersect	Because the space is the intersection, this error will occur if you insert a space instead of a comma (the union operator) between ranges used in function arguments.
#NUM!	Problem with a number in the formula	This error can be caused by an invalid argument in an Excel function or a formula that produces a number too large or too small to be represented in the worksheet.
#REF!	Invalid cell reference	This error occurs when you delete a cell referred to in the formula or if you paste cells over the ones referred to in the formula.
#VALUE!	Wrong type of argument in a function or wrong type of operator	This error is most often the result of specifying a mathematical operation with one or more cells that contain text.

If a formula in your worksheet contains a reference to a cell that returns an error value, that formula returns that error value as well. This can cause error values to appear throughout the worksheet, thus making it very difficult for you to discover which cell contains the formula that caused the original error value so that you can fix the problem.

Using Logical Functions

Excel uses the following seven logical functions, which appear on the Logical command button's drop-down menu on the Formulas tab of the Ribbon (Alt+ML). All the logical functions (except IFERROR) return either the logical TRUE or logical FALSE to their cells when their functions are evaluated. Here are the names of the functions along with their argument syntax:

✦ AND(*logical1*,*logical2*,...) — tests whether the *logical* arguments are TRUE or FALSE. If they are all TRUE, the AND function returns TRUE to the cell. If any are FALSE, the AND function returns FALSE.

✦ FALSE() — takes no argument and simply enters logical FALSE in its cell.

✦ IF(*logical_test*,*value_if_true*,*value_if_false*) — tests whether the *logical_test* expression is TRUE or FALSE. If TRUE, the IF function uses the *value_if_true* argument and returns it to the cell. If FALSE, the IF function uses the *value_if_false* argument and returns it to the cell.

✦ IFERROR(*value*,*value_if_error*) — tests whether the value expression is an error. IFERROR returns *value_if_error* if the expression is an error, or *value* of the expression if it is not an error.

✦ NOT(*logical*) — tests whether the *logical* argument is TRUE or FALSE. If TRUE, the NOT function returns FALSE to the cell. IF FALSE, the NOT function returns TRUE to the cell.

✦ OR(*logical1*,*logical2*,...) — tests whether the *logical* arguments are TRUE or FALSE. If any are TRUE, the OR function returns TRUE. If all are FALSE, the OR function returns FALSE.

✦ TRUE() — takes no argument and simply enters logical TRUE in its cell.

The *logical_test* and *logical* arguments that you specify for these logical functions usually employ the comparison operators (=, <, >, <=, >=, or <>), which themselves return logical TRUE or logical FALSE values. For example, suppose that you enter the following formula in your worksheet:

```
=AND(B5=D10,C15>=500)
```

In this formula, Excel first evaluates the first *logical* argument to determine whether the contents in cell B5 and D10 are equal to each other. If they are, the first comparison returns TRUE. If they are not equal to each other, this comparison returns FALSE. The program then evaluates the second *logical* argument to determine whether the content of cell C15 is greater than or equal to 500. If it is, the second comparison returns TRUE. If it is not greater than or equal to 500, this comparison returns FALSE.

**Book III
Chapter 2**

**Logical Functions
and Error Trapping**

After evaluating the comparisons in the two *logical* arguments, the AND function compares the results: If *logical* argument 1 and *logical* argument 2 are both found to be TRUE, then the AND function returns logical TRUE to the cell. If, however, either argument is found to be FALSE, then the AND function returns false to the cell.

When you use the IF function, you specify what's called a *logical_test* argument whose outcome determines whether the *value_if_true* or *value_if_false* argument is evaluated and returned to the cell. The *logical_test* argument normally uses comparison operators, which return either the logical TRUE or logical FALSE value. When the argument returns TRUE, the entry or expression in the *value_if_true* argument is used and returned to the cell. When the argument returns FALSE, the entry or expression in the *value_if_false* argument is used.

Consider the following formula that uses the IF function to determine whether to charge tax on an item:

```
=IF(E5="Yes",D5+D5*7.5%,D5)
```

If cell E5 (the first cell in the column where you indicate whether the item being sold is taxable or not) contains "Yes," the IF function uses the *value_if_true* argument that tells Excel to add the extended price entered in cell D5, multiply it by a tax rate of 7.5%, and then add the computed tax to the extended price. If, however, cell D5 is blank or contains anything other than the text "Yes," then the IF function uses the *value_if_false* argument, which tells Excel to just return the extended price to cell D5 without adding any tax to it.

As you can see, the *value_if_true* and *value_if_false* arguments of the IF function can contain constants or expressions whose results are returned to the cell that holds the IF formula.

Error-Trapping Formulas

Sometimes, you know ahead of time that certain error values are unavoidable in a worksheet as long as it's missing certain data. The most common error value that gets you into this kind of trouble is our old friend, the #DIV/0! error value. Suppose, for example, that you're creating a new sales workbook from your sales template, and one of the rows in this template contains formulas that calculate the percentage that each monthly total is of the quarterly total. To work correctly, the formulas must divide the value in the cell that contains the monthly total by the value in the cell that contains the quarterly total. When you start a new sales workbook from its template, the cells that contain the formulas for determining the quarterly totals contain zeros, and these zeros put #DIV/0! errors in the cells with formulas that calculate the monthly/quarterly percentages.

These particular #DIV/0! error values in the new workbook don't really represent mistakes as such because they automatically disappear as soon as you enter some of the monthly sales for each quarter (so that the calculated quarterly totals are no longer 0). The problem that you may have is convincing your non–spreadsheet-savvy coworkers (especially the boss) that, despite the presence of all these error values in your worksheet, the formulas are hunky-dory. All that your coworkers see is a worksheet riddled with error values, and these error values undermine your coworkers' confidence in the correctness of your worksheet.

Well, I have the answer for just such "perception" problems. Rather than risk having your boss freak out over the display of a few little #DIV/0! errors here and there, you can set up these formulas so that, whenever they're tempted to return any type of error value (including #DIV/0!), they instead return zeros in their cells. Only when absolutely no danger exists of cooking up error values will Excel actually do the original calculations called for in the formulas.

This sleight of hand in an original formula not only effectively eliminates errors from the formula but also prevents their spread to any of its dependents. To create such a formula, you use the IF function, which operates one way when a certain condition exists and another when it doesn't.

To see how you can use the IF function in a formula that sometimes gives you a #DIV/0! error, consider the sample worksheet shown in Figure 2-1. This figure shows a blank Production Schedule worksheet for storing the 2008 production figures arranged by month and part number. Because you haven't yet had a chance to input any data into this table, the SUM formulas in the last row and column contain 0 values. Because cell K7 with the grand total currently also contains 0, all the percent-of-total formulas in the cell range B9:J9 contain #DIV/0! error values.

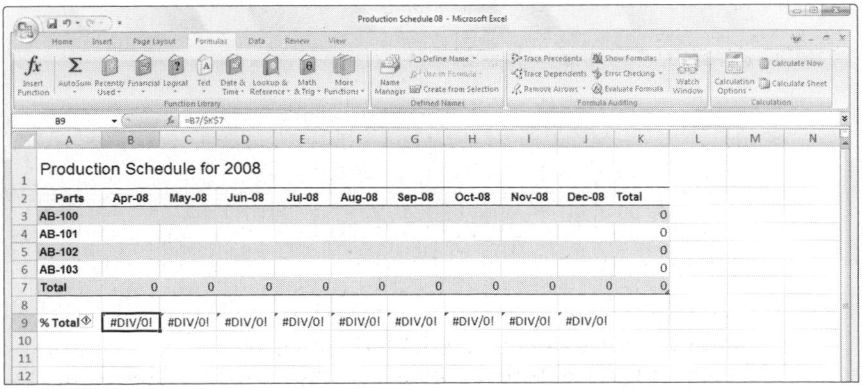

Book III
Chapter 2

Logical Functions
and Error Trapping

Figure 2-1:
Blank 2008
Production
Schedule
spreadsheet
that's full of
#DIV/0!
errors.

The first percent-of-total formula in cell B9 contains the following:

```
=B7/$K$7
```

Because cell K7 with the grand total contains 0, the formula returns the #DIV/0! error value. Now, I show you how to set a trap for the error in the *logical_test* argument inside an IF function. After the *logical_test* argument, you enter the *value_if_true* argument (which is 0 in this example) and the *value_if_false* argument (which is the B7/$K$7). With the addition of the IF function, the final formula looks like this:

```
=IF($K$7=0,0,B7/$K$7)
```

This formula then inputs 0 into cell B9, as shown in Figure 2-2, when the formula actually returns the #DIV/0! error value (because cell K7 is still empty or has a 0 in it), and returns the percentage of total production when the formula doesn't return the #DIV/0! error value (because cell K7 with the total production divisor is no longer empty or contains any other value besides 0). Next, all you have to do is copy this error-trapping formula in cell B9 over to J9 to remove all the #DIV/0! errors from this worksheet.

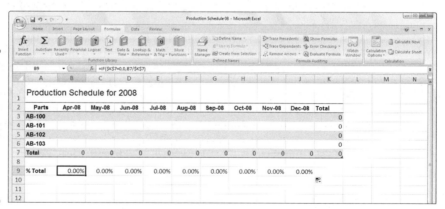

Figure 2-2: 2008 Production Schedule spreadsheet after trapping all the #DIV/0! errors.

The error-trapping formula created with the IF function in cell B9 works fine as long as you know that the grand total in cell K7 will contain either 0 or some other numerical value. It does not, however, trap any of the various error values, such as #REF! and #NAME?, nor does it account for the special #NA (Not Available) value. If, for some reason, one of the formulas feeding into the SUM formula in K7 returns one of these beauties, they will suddenly cascade throughout all the cells with the percent-of-total formulas (cell range B9:J9).

To trap all error values in the grand total cell K7 and prevent them from spreading to the percent-to-total formulas, you need to add the ISERROR function to the basic IF formula. The ISERROR function returns the logical value TRUE if the cell specified as its argument contains any type of error value, including the special #N/A value (if you use ISERR instead of ISERROR, it checks for all types of error values except for #N/A).

To add the ISERROR function, place it in the IF function as the *logical_test* argument. If, indeed, K7 does contain an error value or the #N/A value at the time the IF function is evaluated, you specify 0 as the *value_if_true* argument so that Excel inputs 0 in cell B9 rather than error value or #N/A. For the *value_if_false* argument, you specify the original IF function that inputs 0 if the cell K7 contains 0; otherwise, it performs the division that computes what percentage the January production figure is of the total production.

This amended formula with the ISERROR and two IF functions in cell B9 looks like this:

```
=IF(ISERROR($K$7),0,IF($K$7=0,0,B7/$K$7))
```

As soon as you copy this original formula to the cell range C9:J9, you've protected all the cells with the percent-of-total formulas from displaying and spreading any of those ugly error values.

 Some people prefer to remove the display of zero values from any template that contains error-trapping formulas so that no one interprets the zeros as the correct value for the formula. To remove the display of zeros from a worksheet, deselect the Show a Zero in Cells That Have Zero Values check box in the Display Options for this Worksheet section of the Advanced tab of the Excel Options dialog box (Office Button | Excel Options or Alt+FI). By this action, the cells with error-trapping formulas remain blank until you give them the data that they need to return the correct answers!

Formula Auditing

If you don't happen to trap those pesky error values before they get out into the spreadsheet, then you end up having to track down the original cell that caused all the commotion and set it right. Fortunately, Excel offers some very effective formula-auditing tools for tracking down the cell that's causing your error woes by tracing the relationships between the formulas in the cells of your worksheet. By tracing the relationships, you can test formulas to see which cells, called *direct precedents* in spreadsheet jargon, directly feed the formulas and which cells, called *dependents* (nondeductible, of course), depend on the results of the formulas. Excel even offers a way to visually backtrack the potential sources of an error value in the formula of a particular cell.

The formula-auditing tools are found in the command buttons located in the Formula Auditing group on the Formulas tab of the Ribbon. These command buttons include the following:

✦ **Trace Precedents:** When you click this button, Excel draws arrows to the cells (the so-called *direct precedents*) that are referred to in the formula inside the selected cell. When you click this button again, Excel adds "tracer" arrows that show the cells (the so-called indirect precedents) that are referred to in the formulas in the direct precedents.

✦ **Trace Dependents:** When you click this button, Excel draws arrows from the selected cell to the cells (the so-called *direct dependents*) that use, or depend on, the results of the formula in the selected cell. When you click this button again, Excel adds tracer arrows identifying the cells (the so-called *indirect dependents*) that refer to formulas found in the direct dependents.

✦ **Remove Arrows:** Clicking this button removes all the arrows drawn, no matter what button or pull-down command you used to put them there — click the drop-down button attached to this button to display a drop-down menu with three options: Remove Arrows to remove all arrows (just like clicking the Remove Arrows command button); Remove Precedent Arrows to get rid of the arrows that were drawn when you clicked the Trace Precedents button; and Remove Dependent Arrows to get rid of the arrows that were drawn when you clicked the Trace Dependents button.

✦ **Show Formulas:** To display all formulas in their cells in the worksheet instead of their calculated values (just like pressing Ctrl+`).

✦ **Error Checking:** When you click this button or click the Error Checking option on its drop-down menu, Excel displays the Error Checking dialog box, which describes the nature of the error in the current cell, gives you help on it, and enables you to trace its precedents. Click the Trace Error option on this button's drop-down menu to attempt to locate the cell that contains the original formula that has an error. Click the Circular References option on this button's drop-down menu to display a continuation menu with a list of all the cell addresses containing circular references in the active worksheet — click a cell address on this menu to select the cell with a circular reference formula in the worksheet (see Book III, Chapter 1 for more on circular references in formulas).

✦ **Evaluate Formula:** Clicking this button opens the Evaluate Formula dialog box, where you can have Excel evaluate each part of the formula in the current cell. The Evaluate Formula feature can be quite useful in formulas that nest many functions within them.

✦ **Watch Window:** Clicking this button opens the Watch Window dialog box, which displays the workbook, sheet, cell location, range name, current value, and formula in any cells that you add to the watch list. To add a cell to the watch list, click the cell in the worksheet, click the Add Watch button in the Watch Window dialog box, and then click Add in the Add Watch dialog box that appears.

Clicking the Trace Precedents and Trace Dependents buttons in the Formula Auditing group of the Formulas tab on the Ribbon lets you see the relationship between a formula and the cells that directly and indirectly feed it, as well as those cells that directly and indirectly depend on its calculation. Excel establishes this relationship by drawing arrows from the precedent cells to the active cell and from the active cell to its dependent cells.

If these cells are on the same worksheet, Excel draws solid red or blue arrows extending from each of the precedent cells to the active cell and from the active cell to the dependent cells. If the cells are not located locally on the same worksheet (they may be on another sheet in the same workbook or even on a sheet in a different workbook), Excel draws a black dotted arrow. This arrow comes from or goes to an icon picturing a miniature worksheet that sits to one side, with the direction of the arrowheads indicating whether the cells on the other sheet feed the active formula or are fed by it.

Tracing precedents

You can click the Trace Precedents command button on the Formulas tab of the Ribbon or press Alt+MP to trace all the generations of cells that contribute to the formula in the selected cell (kinda like tracing all the ancestors in your family tree). Figures 2-3 and 2-4 illustrate how you can use the Trace Precedents command button or its hot key equivalent to quickly locate the cells that contribute, directly and indirectly, to the simple addition formula in cell B9.

Figure 2-3 shows the worksheet after I clicked the Trace Precedents command button the first time. As you can see, Excel draws trace arrows from cells A5 and C5 to indicate that they are the direct precedents of the addition formula in cell B9. In Figure 2-4, you see what happened when I clicked this command button a second time to display the indirect precedents of this formula (think of them as being a generation earlier in the family tree). The new tracer arrows show that cells A2, A3, and A4 are the direct precedents of the formula in cell A5 — indicated by a border around the three cells. (Remember that cell A5 is the first direct precedent of the formula in cell B9.) Likewise, cells B2 and B3 as well as cell C4 are the direct precedents of the formula in cell C5. (Cell C5 is the second direct precedent of the formula in cell B9.)

**Book III
Chapter 2**

**Logical Functions
and Error Trapping**

Each time you click the Trace Precedents command button, Excel displays another (earlier) set of precedents (until no more generations exist). If you are in a hurry (as most of us are most of the time), you can speed up the process and display both the direct and indirect precedents in one operation by double-clicking the Trace Precedents command button. To clear the worksheet of tracer arrows, click the Remove Arrows command button on the Formulas tab.

Figure 2-5 shows what happened after I clicked the Trace Precedents command button (after clicking it twice before, as shown in Figures 2-4 and 2-5). Clicking the command button reveals both the indirect precedents for cell C5. The formulas in cells C2 and C3 are the direct precedents of the formula in cell C5. The direct precedent of the formula in cell C2 (and, consequently, the indirect precedent of the one in cell C5) is not located on this worksheet. This fact is indicated by the dotted tracer arrow coming from that cute miniature worksheet icon sitting on top of cell A3.

Figure 2-3: Clicking the Trace Precedents command button shows the direct precedents of the formula.

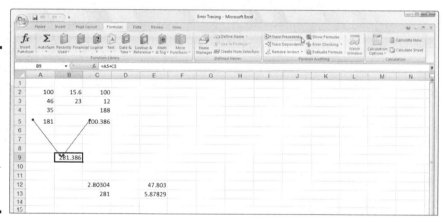

Figure 2-4: Clicking the Trace Precedents command button again shows the indirect precedents of the formula.

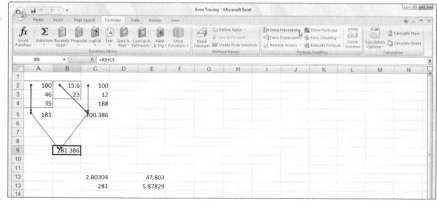

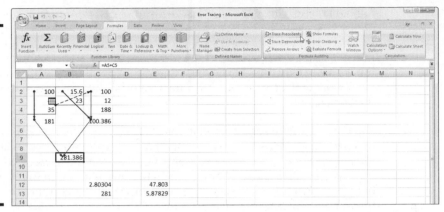

Figure 2-5:
Clicking the
Trace
Precedents
command
button a
third time
shows a
precedent
on another
worksheet.

To find out exactly which workbook, worksheet, and cell(s) hold the direct precedents of cell C2, I double-clicked somewhere on the dotted arrow (clicking the icon with the worksheet miniature doesn't do a thing). Double-clicking the dotted tracer arrow opens the Go To dialog box, which shows a list of all the precedents (including the workbook, worksheet, and cell references). To go to a precedent on another worksheet, double-click the reference in the Go To list box, or select it and click OK. (If the worksheet is in another workbook, this workbook file must already be open before you can go to it.)

The Go To dialog box, shown in Figure 2-6, displays the following direct precedent of cell C2, which is cell B4 on Sheet2 of the same workbook:

```
'[Error Tracer.xls]Sheet2'!$B$4
```

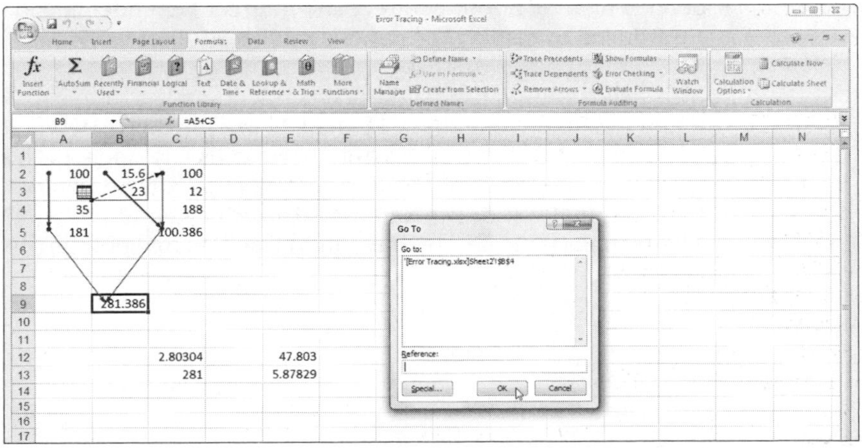

Figure 2-6:
Double-
clicking the
dotted
tracer arrow
opens the
Go To dialog
box showing
the location.

To jump directly to this cell, double-click the cell reference in the Go To dialog box.

You can also select precedent cells that are on the same worksheet as the active cell by double-clicking somewhere on the cell's tracer arrow. Excel selects the precedent cell without bothering to open up the Go To dialog box.

You can use the Special button in the Go To dialog box (refer to Figure 2-6) to select all the direct or indirect precedents or the direct or indirect dependents that are on the same sheet as the formula in the selected cell. After opening the Go To dialog box (Ctrl+G or F5) and clicking the Special button, you simply click the Precedents or Dependents option button and then choose between the Direct Only or All Levels option button before you click OK.

Tracing dependents

You can click the Trace Dependents command button in the Formula Auditing group of the Formulas tab on the Ribbon or press Alt+MD to trace all the generations of cells that either directly or indirectly utilize the formula in the selected cell (kind of like tracing the genealogy of all your progeny). Tracing dependents with the Trace Dependents command button is much like tracing precedents with the Trace Precedents command button. Each time you click this button, Excel draws another set of arrows that show a generation of dependents further removed. To display both the direct and indirect dependents of a cell in one fell swoop, double-click the Trace Dependents command button.

Figure 2-7 shows what happened after I selected cell B9 and then double-clicked the Trace Dependents command button on the Formulas tab of the Ribbon to display both the direct and indirect dependents and then clicked it a third time to display the dependents on another worksheet.

As this figure shows, Excel first draws tracer arrows from cell B9 to cells C12 and C13, indicating that C12 and C13 are the direct dependents of cell B9. Then, it draws tracer arrows from cells C12 and C13 to E12 and E13, respectively, the direct dependents of C12 and C13 and the indirect dependents of B9. Finally, it draws a tracer arrow from cell E12 to another sheet in the workbook (indicated by the dotted tracer arrow pointing to the worksheet icon).

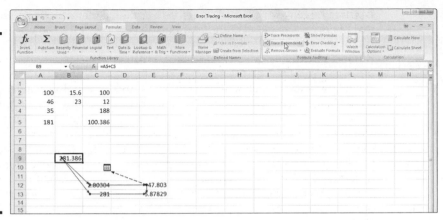

Figure 2-7:
Clicking the
Trace
Dependents
command
button
shows all
the depend-
ents of the
formula in
cell B9.

Error checking

Whenever a formula yields an error value other than #N/A (refer to Table 2-1 for a list of all the error values) in a cell, Excel displays a tiny error indicator (in the form of the triangle) in the upper-left corner of the cell and an alert options button appears to the left of that cell when you make it active. If you position the mouse pointer on that options button, a drop-down button appears to its right that you can click to display a drop-down menu, and a ScreenTip appears below describing the nature of the error value.

When you click the drop-down button, a menu appears, containing an item with the name of the error value followed by the following items:

✦ **Help on This Error:** Opens an Excel Help window with information on the type of error value in the active cell and how to correct it.

✦ **Show Calculation Steps:** Opens the Evaluate Formula dialog box where you can walk through each step in the calculation to see the result of each computation.

✦ **Ignore Error:** Bypasses error checking for this cell and removes the error alert and Error options button from it.

✦ **Edit in Formula Bar:** Activates Edit mode and puts the insertion point at the end of the formula on the Formula bar.

✦ **Error Checking Options:** Opens the Formulas tab of the Excel Options dialog box where you can modify the options used in checking the work-sheet for formula errors (see "Changing the Error Checking options" sec-tion that immediately follows for details).

If you're dealing with a worksheet that contains many error values, you can use the Error Checking command button (the one with the check mark on top of a red alert exclamation mark) in the Formula Auditing group on the Ribbon's Formulas tab to locate each error.

When you click the Error Checking command button, Excel selects the cell with the first error value and opens the Error Checking dialog box (see Figure 2-8) that identifies the nature of the error value in the current cell.

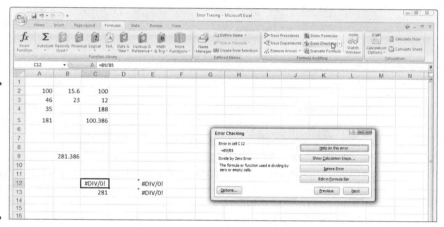

Figure 2-8: Flagging an error value in a worksheet in the Error Checking dialog box.

The command buttons in the Error Checking dialog box directly correspond to the menu options that appear when you click the cell's alert options button (except that Error Checking Options on this drop-down menu is simply called the Options button in this dialog box).

In addition, the Error Checking dialog box contains Next and Previous buttons that you can click to have Excel select the cell with the next error value or return to the cell with the previously displayed error value.

REMEMBER

Note that when you click the Next or Previous button when Excel has flagged the very first or last error value in the worksheet, the program displays an alert dialog box letting you know that the error check for the worksheet is complete. When you click the OK button, Excel closes both the alert dialog box and the Error Checking dialog box. Also note that clicking the Ignore Error button is the equivalent of clicking the Next button.

Changing the Error Checking options

When you select Error Checking Options on the alert options drop-down menu attached to a cell with an error value or click the Options button in the Error Checking dialog box, Excel opens the Formulas tab of the Excel Options dialog box. This tab displays the Error Checking and Error Checking Rules options that are currently in effect in Excel. You can use these options on this Formulas tab to control when the worksheet is checked for errors and what cells are flagged:

✦ **Enable Background Error Checking check box:** Has Excel check your worksheets for errors when the computer is idle. When this check box is selected, you can change the color of the error indicator that appears as a tiny triangle in the upper-left corner of the cell (normally this indicator is green) by clicking a new color on the Indicate Errors Using This Color's drop-down palette.

✦ **Reset Ignored Errors button:** Restores the error indicator and alert options button to all cells that you previously told Excel to ignore by choosing the Ignore Error item on the alert options drop-down menu attached to the cell.

✦ **Cells Containing Formulas That Result in an Error check box:** Has Excel insert the error indicator and adds the alert options button to all cells that return error values.

✦ **Inconsistent Calculated Column Formula in Tables check box:** Has Excel flag formulas in particular columns of cell ranges formatted as tables that vary in their computations from the other formulas in the column.

✦ **Cells Containing Years Represented as 2 Digits check box:** Has Excel flag all dates entered as text with just the last two digits of the year as errors by adding an error indicator and alert options button to their cells.

✦ **Numbers Formatted as Text or Preceded by an Apostrophe check box:** Has Excel flag all numbers entered as text as errors by adding an error indicator and alert options button to their cells.

✦ **Formulas Inconsistent with Other Formulas in Region check box:** Has Excel flag any formula that differs from the others in the same area of the worksheet as an error by adding an error indicator and alert options button to its cell.

✦ **Formulas Which Omit Cells in a Region check box:** Has Excel flag any formula that omits cells from the range that it refers to as an error by adding an error indicator and alert options button to its cell.

✦ **Unlocked Cells Containing Formulas check box:** Has Excel flag any formula whose cell is unlocked when the worksheet is protected as an error by adding an error indicator and alert options button to its cell (see Book IV, Chapter 1 for information on protecting worksheets).

✦ **Formulas Referring to Empty Cells check box:** Has Excel flag any formula that refers to blank cells as an error by adding an error indicator and alert options button to its cell.

✦ **Data Entered in a Table Is Invalid check box:** Has Excel flag any formulas for which you've set up Data Validation (see Book II, Chapter 1 for details) and that contain values outside of those defined as valid.

Error tracing

Tracing a formula's family tree, so to speak, with the Trace Precedents and Trace Dependents command buttons on the Ribbon's Formulas tab is fine, as far as it goes. However, when it comes to a formula that returns a hideous error value, such as #VALUE! or #NAME!, you need to turn to Excel's trusty Trace Error option.

Excel gives you a real choice when it comes to accessing the Trace Error Option. To select this option in the current cell containing an untraced error value, you can do either of the following:

✦ Click the Trace Error option on the cell's alert options drop-down menu.

✦ Click the Trace Error option on the Error Checking command button's drop-down menu or press Alt+MKE.

When Trace Error loses the trail

The Trace Error option finds errors along the path of a formula's precedents and dependents until it finds either the source of the error or one of the following problems:

✔ It encounters a branch point with more than one error source. In this case, Excel doesn't make a determination on its own as to which path to pursue.

✔ It encounters existing tracer arrows. Therefore, *always* click the Remove Arrows command button to get rid of trace arrows before you click the Trace Error option on the Error Checking button's drop-down menu.

✔ It encounters a formula with a circular reference (see Book III, Chapter 1 for more on circular references).

Selecting the Trace Error option is a lot like using both the Trace Precedents and the Trace Dependents command button options, except that the Trace Error option works only when the active cell contains some sort of error value returned by either a bogus formula or a reference to a bogus formula. In tracking down the actual cause of the error value in the active cell (remember that these error values spread to all direct and indirect dependents of a formula), Excel draws blue tracer arrows from the precedents for the original bogus formula and then draws red tracer arrows to all the dependents that contain error values as a result.

Figure 2-9 shows the sample worksheet after I made some damaging changes that left three cells — C12, E12, and E13 — with #DIV/0! errors (meaning that somewhere, somehow, I ended up creating a formula that is trying to divide by zero, which is a real no-no in the wonderful world of math). To find the origin of these error values and identify its cause, I clicked the Trace Error option on the Error Checking command button's drop-down menu while cell E12 was the active cell to engage the use of Excel's faithful old Trace Error feature.

You can see the results in Figure 2-9 (unfortunately without color, so you can't tell which trace arrows were drawn in blue or red). Note that Excel has selected cell C12, although cell E12 was active when I selected the Trace Error option. To cell C12, Excel has drawn two blue tracer arrows (you'll have to take my word for it) that identify cells B5 and B9 as its direct precedents. From cell C12, the program has drawn a single red tracer arrow from cell C12 to cell E12 that identifies its direct dependent.

As it turns out, Excel's Trace Error option is right on the money because the formula in cell C12 contains the bad apple rotting the whole barrel. I revised the formula in cell C12 so that it divided the value in cell B9 by the value in cell B5 without making sure that cell B5 first contained the SUM formula that totaled the values in the cell range B2:B4. The #DIV/0! error value showed up — remember that an empty cell contains a zero value as if you had actually entered 0 in the cell — and immediately spread to cells E12 and E13, which, in turn, use the value returned in C12 in their own calculations. Thus, these cells were infected with #DIV/0! error values as well.

As soon as you correct the problem in the original formula and thus get rid of all the error values in the other cells, Excel automatically converts the red tracer arrows (showing the proliferation trail of the original error) to regular blue tracer arrows, indicating merely that these restored cells are dependents of the formula that once contained the original sin. You can then remove all the tracer arrows from the sheet by clicking the Remove Arrows command button in the Formula Auditing group of the Ribbon's Formulas tab (or by pressing Alt+MAA).

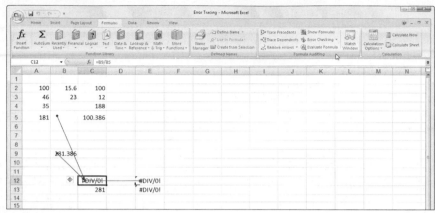

Figure 2-9:
Using the
Trace Error
option to
show the
precedents
and depend-
ents of the
formula.

Evaluating a formula

The Evaluate Formula command button in the Formula Auditing group of the Ribbon's Formulas tab (the one with *fx* inside a magnifying glass) opens the Evaluate Formula dialog box, where you can step through the calculation of a complicated formula to see the current value returned by each part of the calculation. This is often helpful in locating problems that prevent the formula from returning the hoped for or expected results.

To evaluate a formula step-by-step, position the cell pointer in that cell and then click the Evaluate Formula command button on the Formulas tab (or press Alt+MV). This action opens the Evaluate Formula dialog box with an Evaluation list box that displays the contents of the entire formula that's in the current cell.

To have Excel evaluate the first expression or term in the formula (shown underlined in the Evaluation list box) and replace it with the currently calculated value, click the Evaluate button. If this expression uses an argument or term that is itself a result of another calculation, you can display its expression or formula by clicking the Step In button (see Figure 2-10) and then calculate its result by clicking the Evaluate button. After that, you can return to the evaluation of the expression in the original formula by clicking the Step Out button.

After you evaluate the first expression in the formula, Excel underlines the next expression or term in the formula (by using the natural order of precedence and a strict left-to-right order unless you have used parentheses to override this order), which you can then replace with its calculated value by clicking the Evaluate button. When you finish evaluating all the expressions and terms of the current formula, you can close the Evaluate Formula window by clicking its Close button in the upper-right corner of the window.

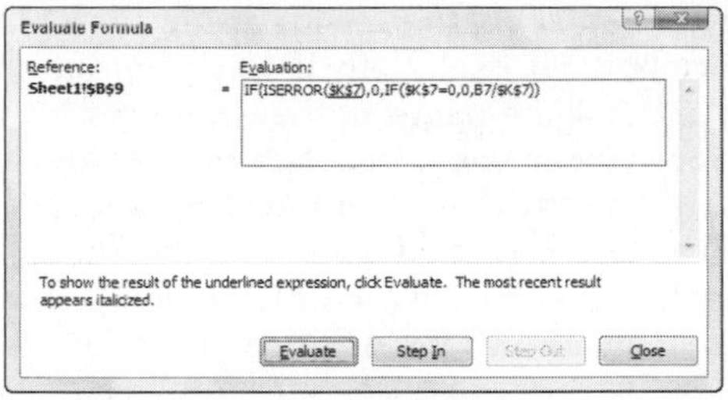

Figure 2-10:
Calculating
each part of
a formula in
the Evaluate
Formula
dialog box.

Evaluate Formula
Reference: Evaluation:
Sheet1!$B$9   •   IF(ISERROR($K$7),0,IF($K$7=0,0,B7/$K$7))
To show the result of the underlined expression, click Evaluate. The most recent result appears italicized.
[Evaluate]   [Step In]   [Step Out]   [Close]

Instead of the Evaluate Formula dialog box, open the Watch Window dialog box by clicking the Watch Window button on the Formulas tab (Alt+MW) and add formulas to it when all you need to do is to keep an eye on the current value returned by a mixture of related formulas in the workbook. This enables you to see the effect that changing various input values has on their calculations (even when they're located on different sheets of the workbook).

Removing Errors from the Printout

What if you don't have the time to trap all the potential formula errors or track them down and eliminate them before you have to print out and distribute the spreadsheet? In that case, you may just have to remove the display of all the error values before you print the report.

To do this, click the Sheet tab in the Page Setup dialog box opened by clicking the Page Setup button in the Print Preview window (Ctrl+F2 or Alt+FWV).

Click the Sheet tab in the Page Setup dialog box and then click the drop-down button attached to the Cell Errors As drop-down list box. The default value for this drop-down list box is "Displayed," meaning that all error values are displayed in the printout exactly as they currently appear in the work-sheet. This drop-down menu also contains the following items that you can click to remove the display of error values from the printed report:

✦ Click the <blank> option to replace all error values with blank cells.

✦ Click the — option to replace all error values with two dashes.

✦ Click the #N/A option to replace all error values (except for #N/A entries, of course) with the special #N/A value (which is considered an error value when you select the <blank> or — options).

**Book III
Chapter 2**

**Logical Functions
and Error Trapping**

Blanking out error values or replacing them with dashes or #N/A values has no effect on them in the worksheet itself, only in any printout you make of the worksheet. You need to view the pages in the Print Preview window (Ctrl+F2 or Alt+FWV) before you can see the effect of selecting an option besides the Displayed option in the Cell Errors As drop-down list box. Also, remember to reset the Cell Errors As option on the Sheet tab of the Page Setup dialog box back to the Displayed option when you want to print a version of the worksheet that shows the error values in all their cells in the worksheet printout.

Chapter 3: Date and Time Formulas

In This Chapter

✔ Understanding dates and times in Excel

✔ Creating formulas that calculate elapsed dates and times

✔ Using the Date functions

✔ Using the Time functions

C reating formulas that use dates and times can be a little confusing if you don't have a good understanding of how Excel treats these types of values. After you're equipped with this understanding, you can begin to make good use of the many date and time functions that the program offers.

This chapter begins with a quick overview of date and time numbers in Excel and how you can use them to build simple formulas that calculate differences between elapsed dates and times. The chapter goes on to survey Excel built-in date and time functions, including the date functions that are available after you've installed and activated the Analysis ToolPak add-in.

Understanding Dates and Times

Excel doesn't treat the dates and times that you enter in the cells of your worksheet as simple text entries (for more information on inputting numbers in a spreadsheet, see Book II, Chapter 1). Any entry with a format that resembles one of the date and time number formats utilized by Excel is automatically converted, behind the scenes, into a serial number. In the case of dates, this serial number represents the number of days that have elapsed since the beginning of the twentieth century so that January 1, 1900, is serial number 1; January 2, 1900, is serial number 2; and so forth. In the case of times, this serial number is a fraction that represents the number of hours, minutes, and seconds that have elapsed since midnight, which is serial number 0.00000000, so that 12:00:00 p.m. (noon) is serial number 0.50000000; 11:00:00 p.m. is 0.95833333; and so forth.

As long as you format a numeric entry so that it conforms to a recognized date or time format, Excel enters it as a date or time serial number. Only when you enter a formatted date or time as a text entry (by prefacing it with an apostrophe) or import dates and times as text entries into a worksheet do you have to worry about converting them into date and time serial numbers, which enables you to build spreadsheet formulas that perform calculations on them.

Changing the Regional date settings

Excel isn't set up to automatically recognize European date formats in which the number of the day precedes the number of the month and year. For example, you may want 6/11/1969 to represent November 6, 1969, rather than June 11, 1969. If you're working with a spreadsheet that uses this type of European date system, you have to customize Windows' Regional settings for the United States so that the Short Date format in Windows programs, such as Excel and Word 2007, use the D/m/yyyy (day, month, year) format rather than the default M/d/yyyy (month, day, year) format.

You can do this by following these steps:

1. **Click the Start button on the Windows taskbar and then click Control Panel.**

   The Control Panel window normally opens in Category view. If it is in Classic view, switch to Category view by clicking the Control Panel Home link in Windows Vista or the Switch to Category View link in Windows XP in the Navigation pane on the left side of the Control Panel dialog box.

2. **Click the Clock, Language, and Region link in the Windows Vista Control Panel or click the Date, Time, Language, and Regional Options link in the Windows XP Control Panel.**

3. **Click the Regional and Language Options link in the Windows Vista Control Panel or the Change the Format of Numbers, Dates, and Times link in the Windows XP Control Panel.**

   The Regional and Language Options dialog box opens with the Formats tab selected in Windows Vista and the Regional Options tab selected in Windows XP.

4. **In Windows Vista, click the Customize This Format button at the bottom of the Regional and Language Options dialog box. In Windows XP, click the Customize button located to the right of your current format setting in the Regional and Language Options dialog box.**

   The Customize Regional Options dialog box opens.

5. **Click the Date tab in the Customize Regional Options dialog box.**

6. **Click the Short Date format and then type** D/m/yyyy, **the new date format.**

   You have to type this European date format because the United States regional settings don't automatically include this format in the Short Date Style drop-down list. After manually entering this format, the European date format becomes part of the list that you can then select from in the future.

7. **Click OK twice, once to close the Customize Regional Options dialog box and then a second time to close the Regional and Language Options dialog box.**

8. **Click the Close button in the upper-right corner of the Control Panel window or press Alt+F4 to close this window.**

After changing the Short Date format in the Windows Vista or XP Control Panel, the next time you open Excel, it automatically interprets short dates using the D/m/yyyy format; so that, for example, 3/5/04 is May 3, 2004, rather than March 5, 2004.

Don't forget to change the Short Date format back to its original M/d/yyyy format in the Customize Regional Options dialog box when working with spreadsheets that follow the "month-day-year" Short Date format preferred in the United States. Also, don't forget that you have to restart Excel to get it to pick up on the changes that you make to the Regional settings in the Windows Vista or XP Control Panel.

Book III
Chapter 3

Date and
Time Formulas

Building formulas that calculate elapsed dates

Most of the date formulas that you build are designed to calculate the number of days or years that have elapsed between two dates. To do this, you build a simple formula that subtracts the later date from the earlier date.

For example, if you input the date 4/25/75 in cell B11 and 6/3/04 in cell C11 and you want to calculate the number of days that have elapsed between April 25, 1975, and June 3, 2004, in cell D11, you would enter the following subtraction formula in that cell:

=C11-B11

Excel then inputs the number of days between these dates in cell D5. The only problem is that the program will also apply the Date format used by these two dates so that the result in cell D5 appears as the date:

2/8/1929

To display this result as a whole number, as you'd expect, you still have to format the result with another number format. If, for example, you apply the General number format to the cell D5 (you can do this quickly by pressing Ctrl+Shift+` or Ctrl+~), the calculated result in this cell becomes the much more sensible number of days:

10632

TIP

If you want the result between two dates expressed in the number of years rather than the number of days, divide the result of your subtraction by the number of days in a year. In this example, you can enter the formula =D11/365 in cell E11 to return the result 29.12877, which you can then round off to 29 by clicking the Decrease Decimal button in the Number group on the Home tab of the Ribbon or by pressing Alt+H9 until only 29 remains displayed in the cell.

Building formulas that calculate elapsed times

Some spreadsheets require that formulas calculate the amount of elapsed time between a starting and ending time. For example, suppose that you keep a worksheet that records the starting and stopping times for your hourly employees, and you need to calculate the number of hours and minutes that elapse between these two times in order to figure their daily and monthly wages.

To build a formula that calculates how much time has elapsed between two different times of the day, subtract the ending time of day from the starting time of day. For example, suppose that you enter a person's starting time in cell B14 and ending time in C14. In cell D14, you would enter the following subtraction formula:

=C14-B14

Excel then returns the difference in cell D14 as a decimal value representing what fraction that difference represents of an entire day (that is, a 24-hour period). If, for example, cell B14 contains a starting time of 9:15 a.m. and cell C14 contains an ending time of 3:45 p.m., Excel returns the following decimal value to cell D14:

6:30 AM

To convert this time of day into its equivalent decimal number, you convert the time format automatically given to it to the General format (Ctrl+Shift+` or Ctrl+~), which displays the following result in cell D14:

0.270833

To convert this decimal number representing the fraction of an entire day into the number of hours that have elapsed, you simply multiply this result by 24 as in =D14*24, which gives you a result of 6.5 hours when you apply the General format (Ctrl+Shift+` or Ctrl+~) to it.

Using Date Functions

Excel contains a number of built-in date functions that you can use in your spreadsheets. When you install and activate the Analysis ToolPak add-in (see Book I, Chapter 3 for details), you have access to a number of additional Date functions — many of which are specially designed to deal with the normal Monday through Friday, five-day workweek (excluding, of course, your precious weekend days from the calculations).

TODAY

The easiest date function has to be TODAY. This function takes no arguments and is always entered as follows:

=TODAY()

When you enter the TODAY function in a cell by clicking it on the Date & Time command button's drop-down list on the Ribbon's Formulas tab or by typing it, Excel returns the current date by using the following Date format:

7/23/2008

Keep in mind that the date inserted into a cell with the TODAY function is not static. Whenever you open a worksheet that contains this function, Excel recalculates the function and updates its contents to the current date. This means that you don't usually use TODAY to input the current date when you're doing it for historical purposes (an invoice, for example) and never want it to change.

If you do use TODAY and then want to make the current date static in the spreadsheet, you need to convert the function into its serial number. You can do this for individual cells: First, select the cell, press F2 to activate Edit mode, press F9 to replace =TODAY() with today's serial number on the Formula bar, and click the Enter button to insert this serial number into the cell. You can do this conversion on a range of cells by selecting the range, copying it to the Clipboard by clicking the Copy button on the Home tab of the Ribbon (or pressing Ctrl+C), and then immediately pasting the calculated values into the same range by clicking the Paste Values option on the Paste command button's drop-down menu (or pressing Alt+HVV).

DATE and DATEVALUE

The DATE function on the Date & Time command button's drop-down menu returns a date serial number for the date specified by the *year, month,* and *day* argument. This function uses the following syntax:

```
DATE(year,month,day)
```

This function comes in handy when you have a worksheet that contains the different parts of the date in separate columns, similar to the one shown in Figure 3-1. You can use it to combine the three columns of date information into a single date cell that you can use in sorting and filtering (see Book VI, Chapters 1 and 2 to find out how to sort and filter data).

The DATEVALUE function on the Date & Time button's drop-down menu returns the date serial number for a date that's been entered into the spreadsheet as text so that you can use it in date calculations. This function takes a single argument:

```
DATEVALUE(date_text)
```

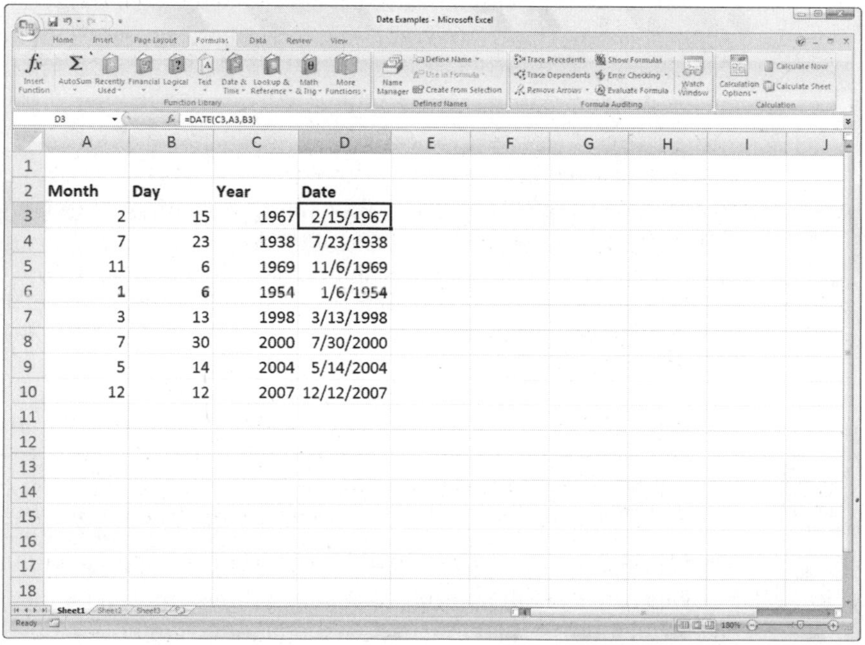

Figure 3-1: Using the DATE function to combine separate date information into a single entry.

Suppose, for example, that you've made the following text entry in cell B12:

`'5/21/2004`

(Remember that when you preface an entry with an apostrophe, Excel inserts that entry as text even if the program would otherwise put it in as a value.) You can then convert this text entry into a date serial number by entering the following formula in cell C12 next door:

`=DATEVALUE(B12)`

Excel then returns the date serial number, 38128 to cell C12, which you can convert into a more intelligible date by formatting it with one of Excel's Date number formats (Ctrl+1).

You must convert the DATE and DATEVALUE functions into their calculated date serial numbers in order to sort and filter them. To convert these functions individually, select a cell, press F2 to activate Edit mode, and then press F9 to replace the function with the calculated date serial number; finally, click the Enter button on the Formula bar to insert this serial number into the cell. To do this conversion on a range of cells, select the range, copy it to the Clipboard by pressing Ctrl+C, and then immediately paste the calculated serial numbers into the same range by clicking the Paste Values option on the Paste command button's drop-down menu (or press Alt+HVV).

DAY, WEEKDAY, MONTH, and YEAR

The DAY, WEEKDAY, MONTH, and YEAR date functions on the Date & Time command button's drop-down menu all return just parts of the date serial number that you specify as their argument:

✦ DAY(*serial_number*) to return the day of the month in the date (as a number between 1 and 31).

✦ WEEKDAY(*serial_number*,[*return_type*]) to return the day of the week (as a number between 1 and 7 or 0 and 6). The optional *return_type* argument is a number between 1 and 3; 1 (or no *return_type* argument) specifies the first type where 1 equals Sunday and 7 equals Saturday; 2 specifies the second type where 1 equals Monday and 7 equals Sunday; and 3 specifies the third type where 0 equals Monday and 6 equals Sunday.

✦ MONTH(*serial_number*) to return the number of the month in the date serial number (from 1 to 12).

✦ YEAR(*serial_number*) to return the number of the year (as an integer between 1900 and 9999) in the date serial number.

**Book III
Chapter 3**

**Date and
Time Formulas**

For example, if you enter the following DAY function in a cell as follows:

```
DAY(DATE(08,4,15))
```

Excel returns the value 15 to that cell. If, instead, you use the WEEKDAY function as follows:

```
WEEKDAY(DATE(08,4,15))
```

Excel returns the value 4, which represents Wednesday (using the first *return_type* where Sunday is 1 and Saturday is 7) because the optional *return_type* argument isn't specified. If you use the MONTH function on this date as in the following:

```
MONTH(DATE(08,4,15))
```

Excel returns 4 to the cell. If, however, you use the YEAR function on this date as in the following:

```
YEAR(DATE(08,4,15))
```

Excel returns 1908 to the cell (instead of 2008).

This means that if you want to enter a year in the twenty-first century as the *year* argument of the DATE function, you need to enter all four digits of the date, as in the following:

```
DATE(2008,4,15)
```

Note that you can use the YEAR function to calculate the difference in years between two dates. For example, if cell B12 contains 7/23/1978 and cell C12 contains 7/23/2008, you can enter the following formula using the YEAR function to determine the difference in years:

```
=YEAR(C12)-YEAR(B12)
```

Excel then returns 2/9/1900 to the cell containing this formula, which becomes 40 as soon as you apply the General number format to it (by pressing Ctrl+ Shift+` or Ctrl+~).

Don't use these functions on dates entered as text entries. Always use the DATEVALUE function to convert these text dates and then use the DAY, WEEKDAY, MONTH, or YEAR functions on the serial numbers returned by the DATEVALUE function to ensure accurate results.

The Ribbon in Excel 2007

The Excel 2007 user interface, as demonstrated by the color plates in this section, is highly graphical and fairly colorful. The centerpiece of this graphical user interface is the Ribbon, which appears as a wide band at the top of the Excel program. The Ribbon provides you with quick access to almost all Excel commands in the form of command buttons arranged in related groups.

The Excel Ribbon contains seven standard tabs: Home, Insert, Page Layout, Formulas, Data, Review, and View. When you first launch Excel, the Home tab on the Ribbon is automatically displayed. To select another tab and display its command buttons, click the tab or press and release the Alt key and then type the hot key letter assigned to the tab (shown underlined in the tab names at the beginning of this paragraph).

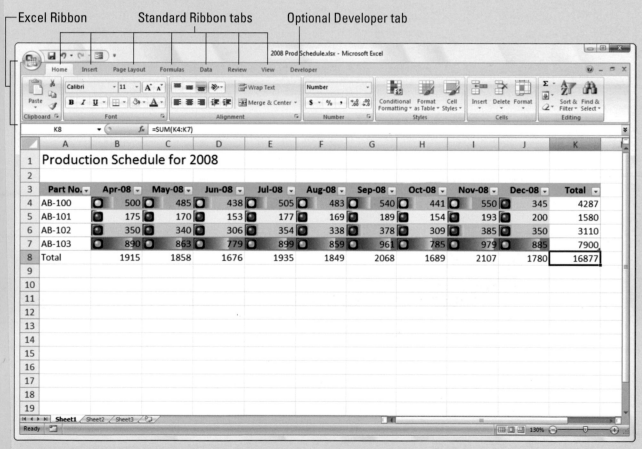

Color Plate 1: Excel 2007 worksheet showing the Ribbon's Home tab

To minimize the Ribbon so that only the standard tab buttons are displayed as you work in Excel, double-click one of the tab buttons or press Ctrl+F1. After that, Excel expands the Ribbon to display the command buttons on a tab only when you select it by clicking its button or pressing Alt and its hot key letter. After you select a command on any of the Ribbon's tabs, Excel once again collapses the Ribbon down to its buttons (until you double-click a tab or press Ctrl+F1 again).

Color Plate 2: The Ribbon's Insert tab

The Insert tab contains command buttons for adding various kinds of extra elements to your worksheets, including pivot tables, all types of graphic objects and art, charts, hyperlinks, digital signatures, and special symbols.

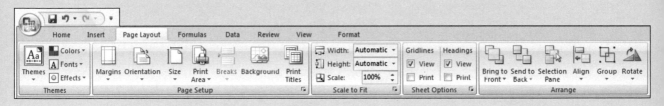

Color Plate 3: The Ribbon's Page Layout tab

The Page Layout tab contains the command buttons for changing the page settings for a printed version of your spreadsheet. It also contains buttons for changing the underlying theme in the current worksheet, as well as those for changing the alignment and stacking of graphic objects added to the worksheet using command buttons on the Insert tab.

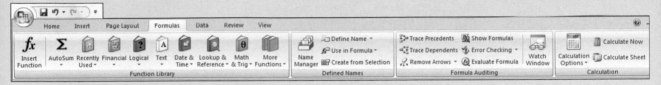

Color Plate 4: The Ribbon's Formulas tab

The Formulas tab contains command buttons for building and auditing spreadsheet formulas. Here you find buttons for selecting particular functions arranged according to category, summoning up the Function wizard, and summing ranges with AutoSum. In addition, the Formulas tab contains command buttons for naming and managing ranges, as well as applying them to formulas. Finally, this tab contains buttons for finding and eliminating errors in your formulas, as well as determining when worksheet formulas are recalculated and even manually recalculating them.

Color Plate 5: The Ribbon's Data tab

The Data tab contains command buttons primarily designed for dealing with data lists in the worksheet. This tab includes buttons for setting up connections for importing data from external database tables into the worksheet, as well as buttons for maintaining and reusing these connections. In addition, this tab contains buttons for sorting, filtering, consolidating, outlining, and subtotaling data in these lists. Finally, this tab includes command buttons for doing all types of what-if data analysis.

Color Plate 6: The Ribbon's Review tab

The Review tab contains command buttons for proofing your spreadsheet and annotating it with comments. The proofing tools include spell checking, looking up terms in various online resources, finding synonyms in the Thesaurus, as well as translating terms from English into another language or another language into English. This tab also contains command buttons for turning on and off worksheet protection, as well as sharing workbooks with coworkers on the same network.

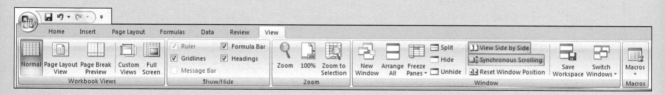

Color Plate 7: The Ribbon's View tab

The View tab contains command buttons for modifying and controlling the worksheet display. This tab includes buttons for selecting a new worksheet view, showing and hiding various screen elements, zooming in and out on the worksheet, dividing the worksheet into different windows, and arranging these windows on-screen.

Excel Contextual Tabs

In addition to the standard tabs, at certain times as you work in the program Excel adds special Contextual tabs to the end of the Ribbon. As the name implies, a Contextual tab is designed to give you access to command buttons that you may need only when performing a special task, such as defining a header and footer for a spreadsheet report, formatting a table of data, or creating a new embedded chart or pivot table.

Contextual tabs always appear at the end of the Ribbon. Their tab names, however, do not appear on the same bar containing the standard tabs, but rather on the bar immediately above it that displays the name of the active workbook along with the Microsoft Excel program name. This is done because many Contextual tabs divvy up their specialized commands on several of their own (sub) tabs whose names and tags appear on the same level as the standard tabs (all huddled beneath the name of the Contextual tab on the bar above).

Color Plate 8: The Drawing Tools Contextual tab

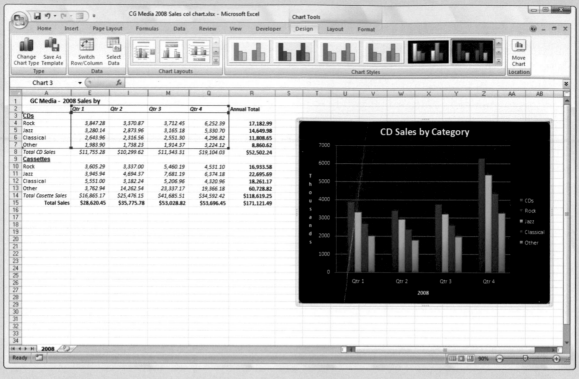

Color Plate 9: The Chart Tools Contextual tab

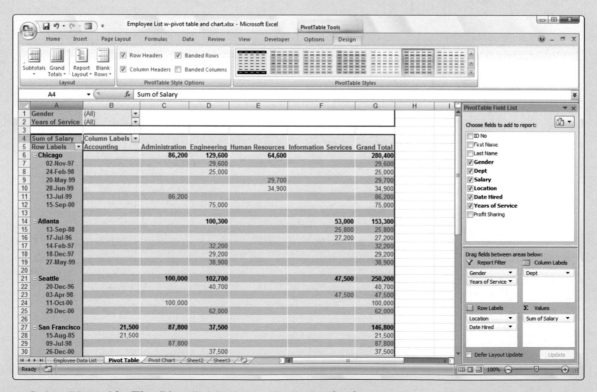

Color Plate 10: The PivotTable Tools Contextual tab

Excel Galleries with Live Preview

Some of the command buttons on the tabs of the Excel Ribbon are attached to drop-down galleries that appear when you click them. These galleries contain thumbnails showing a variety of styles and formatting that you can apply to selected text or graphic elements in the worksheet. Thanks to the Live Preview feature in Excel 2007, you can see how your selected data or graphics appear in any of a gallery's styles simply by positioning the mouse pointer on the style's thumbnail. This enables you to see exactly how your worksheet data or graphics look in the prospective style before you actually select that style by clicking its thumbnail in the gallery.

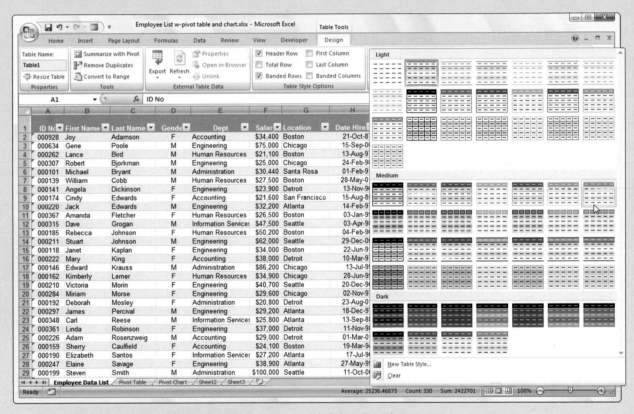

Color Plate 11: The Table Styles Gallery with Live Preview

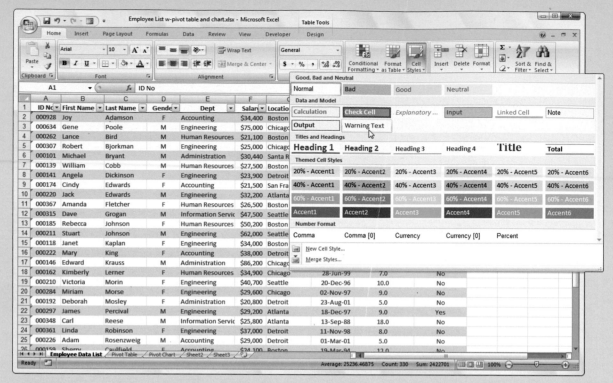

Color Plate 12: The Cell Styles Gallery with Live Preview

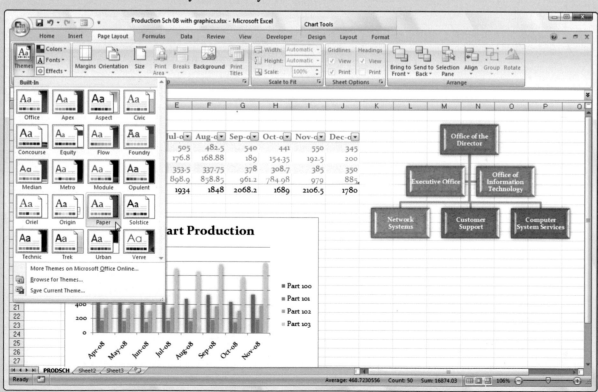

Color Plate 13: The Themes Gallery with Live Preview

DAYS360

The DAYS360 function on the Date & Time command button's drop-down menu returns the number of days between two dates based on a 360-day year (that is, one in which there are 12 equal months of 30 days each). The DAYS360 function takes the following arguments:

```
DAYS360(start_date,end_date,[method])
```

The *start_date* and *end_date* arguments are date serial numbers or references to cells that contain such serial numbers. The optional *method* argument is either TRUE or FALSE, where FALSE specifies the use of the U.S. calculation method and TRUE specifies the use of the European calculation method:

✦ **U.S. (NASD) method (FALSE or *method* argument omitted):** In this method, if the starting date is equal to the 31st of the month, it becomes equal to the 30th of the same month; if the ending date is the 31st of a month and the starting date is earlier than the 30th of the month, the ending date becomes the 1st of the next month; otherwise, the ending date becomes equal to the 30th of the same month.

✦ **European method (TRUE):** In this method, starting and ending dates that occur on the 31st of a month become equal to the 30th of the same month.

Analysis ToolPak Date Functions

When you activate the Analysis ToolPak add-in, Excel adds six new Date functions to the Date and Time category in the Insert Function dialog box (see Book I, Chapter 3 for details on installing and activating the Analysis ToolPak add-ins). These Date functions expand your abilities to do date calculations in the worksheet — especially those that work only with normal, Monday through Friday, workdays.

After you activate the Analysis Tookpak add-in, Excel automatically adds the extra date functions to the Date & Time button's drop-down menu on the Formulas tab of the Ribbon (Alt+ME).

EDATE

The EDATE (for Elapsed Date) function calculates a future or past date that is so many months ahead or behind the date that you specify as its *start_date* argument. You can use the EDATE function to quickly determine the particular date at a particular interval in the future or past (for example, three months ahead or one month ago).

The EDATE function takes two arguments:

```
EDATE(start_date,months)
```

The *start_date* argument is the date serial number that you want used as the base date. The *months* argument is a positive (for future dates) or negative (for past dates) integer that represents the number of months ahead or months past to calculate.

For example, suppose that you enter the following EDATE function in a cell:

```
=EDATE(DATE(2004,1, 31),1)
```

Excel returns the date serial number, 38046, which becomes 2/29/2004 when you apply the first Date format to its cell.

EOMONTH

The EOMONTH (for End of Month) function calculates the last day of the month that is so many months ahead or behind the date that you specify as its *start_date* argument. You can use the EOMONTH function to quickly determine the end of the month at a set interval in the future or past.

For example, suppose that you enter the following EOMONTH function in a cell:

```
=EOMONTH(DATE(2008,1,1),1)
```

Excel returns the date serial number, 39507, which becomes 2/29/2008 when you apply the first Date format to its cell.

NETWORKDAYS

The NETWORKDAYS function returns the number of workdays that exist between a starting date and ending date that you specify as arguments:

```
NETWORKDAYS(start_date,end_date,[holidays])
```

When using this function, you can also specify a cell range in the worksheet or array constant to use as an optional *holidays* argument that lists the state, federal, and floating holidays observed by your company. Excel then excludes any dates listed in the *holidays* argument when they occur in between *start_date* and *end_date* arguments.

Figure 3-2 illustrates how this function works. In this worksheet, I created a list in the cell range B3:B13 with all the observed holidays in the calendar year 2003. I then entered the following NETWORKDAYS function in cell E4:

```
NETWORKDAYS(DATE(2007,12,31),DATE(2008,12,31),B3:B13)
```

The preceding function calculates the number of workdays between December 31, 2007, and December 31, 2008 (2632 total work days), and then subtracts the dates listed in the cell range B3:B13 if they fall on a weekday. As all 11 holidays in the range B3:B13 happen to fall on a weekday in the year 2008, the number of workdays between December 31, 2007, and December 31, 2008, is calculated as 252 in cell E14 (263–11=252).

WEEKNUM

The WEEKNUM function returns a number indicating where the week in a particular date falls within the year. This function takes the following arguments:

```
WEEKNUM(serial_number,[return_type])
```

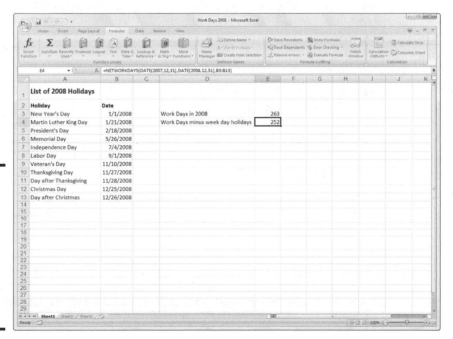

Figure 3-2:
Using the NETWORK DAYS function to find the number of workdays between two dates.

Book III
Chapter 3

Date and
Time Formulas

In this function, the *serial_number* argument is the date whose week in the year you want to determine. The optional *return_type* argument is number 1 or 2, where number 1 (or omitted) indicates that the new week begins on Sunday and weekdays are numbered from 1 to 7. Number 2 indicates that the new week begins on Monday and that weekdays are also numbered from 1 to 7.

For example, if you enter the following WEEKNUM function in a cell:

```
=WEEKNUM(DATE(2003,1,19))
```

Excel returns the number 4, indicating that the week containing the date January 19, 2003, is the fourth week in the year when the Sunday is considered to be the first day of the week (January 19, 2003, is a Sunday). Note that if I had added 2 as the optional *return-type* argument, Excel would return 3 as the result because January 19, 2003, is deemed to fall on the last day of the third week of the year when Monday is considered the first day of the week.

WORKDAY

You can use the WORKDAY function to find out the date that is so many workdays before or after a particular date. This function takes the following arguments:

```
WORKDAY(start_date,days,[holidays])
```

The *start_date* argument is the initial date that you want used in calculating the date of the workday that falls so many days before or after it. The *days* argument is the number of workdays ahead (positive integer) or behind (negative integer) the *start_date*. The optional *holidays* argument is an array constant or cell range that contains the dates of the holidays that should be excluded (when they fall on a weekday) in calculating the new date.

For example, suppose that you want to determine a due date for a report that is 30 workdays after February 1, 2008, by using the same holiday schedule entered in the cell range B3:B11 in the Work Days 2008 workbook, shown in Figure 3-2. To do this, you enter the following formula:

```
=WORKDAY(DATE(2008,2,1),30,B3:B11)
```

Excel then returns the serial number 39524 to the cell, which then appears as March 17, 2008 (St. Patrick's Day), when you format it with the first Date format.

YEARFRAC

The YEARFRAC (for Year Fraction) function enables you to calculate the fraction of the year, which is computed from the number of days between two dates. You can use the YEARFRAC function to determine the proportion of a whole year's benefits or obligations to assign to a specific period.

The YEARFRAC function uses the following arguments:

```
YEARFRAC(start_date,end_date,[basis])
```

The optional *basis* argument in the YEARFRAC function is a number between 0 and 4 that determines the day count basis to use in determining the fractional part of the year:

✦ 0 (or omitted) to base it on the U.S. (NASD) method of 30/360 (see DAYS360 earlier in the chapter for details on the U.S. method)

✦ 1 to base the fraction on actual days/actual days

✦ 2 to base the fraction on actual days/360

✦ 3 to base the fraction on actual days/365

✦ 4 to base the fraction on the European method of 30/360 (see DAYS360 earlier in the chapter for details on the European method)

For example, if you enter the following YEARFRAC formula in a cell to find what percentage of the year remains as of October 15, 2008:

```
=YEARFRAC(DATE(2008,10,15),DATE(2008,12,31),2)
```

Excel returns the decimal value 0.213889 to the cell, indicating that just over 21 percent of the year remains.

Using Time Functions

Excel offers much fewer time functions when compared to the wide array of date functions. Like the date functions, however, the time functions enable you to convert text entries representing times of day into time serial numbers so that you can use them in calculations. The time functions also include functions for combining different parts of a time into a single serial time number, as well as those for extracting the hours, minutes, and seconds from a single time serial number.

Book III
Chapter 3

Date and Time Formulas

NOW

The NOW function on the Date & Time command button's drop-down menu gives you the current time and date based on your computer's internal clock. You can use the NOW function to date- and time-stamp the worksheet. Like the TODAY function, NOW takes no arguments and is automatically recalculated every time you open the spreadsheet:

```
=NOW()
```

When you enter the NOW function in a cell, Excel puts the date before the current time. It also formats the date with the first Date format and the time with the 24-hour Time format. So, if the current date was July 23, 2008, and the current time was 1:44 p.m. at the moment when Excel calculates the NOW function, your cell would contain the following entry:

```
7/23/2008 13:44
```

Note that the combination date/time format that the NOW function uses is a custom number format. If you want to assign a different date/time to the date and time serial numbers returned by this function, you have to create your own custom number format and then assign it to the cell that contains the NOW function (see Book II, Chapter 2 for information on creating custom number formats).

TIME and TIMEVALUE

The TIME function on the Date & Time command button's drop-down menu enables you to create a decimal number representing a time serial number, ranging from 0 (zero) to 0.99999999, representing time 0:00:00 (12:00:00 AM) to 23:59:59 (11:59:59 PM). You can use the TIME function to combine the hours, minutes, and seconds of a time into a single time serial number when these parts are stored in separate cells.

The TIME function takes the following arguments:

```
TIME(hour,minute,second)
```

When specifying the *hour* argument, you use a number between 0 and 23 (any number greater than 23 is divided by 24 and the remainder is used as the hour value). When specifying the *minute* and *second* arguments, you use a number between 0 and 59 (any *minute* argument greater than 59 is converted into hours and minutes, just as any *second* argument greater than 59 is converted into hours, minutes, and seconds).

For example, if cell A3 contains 4, cell B3 contains 37, and cell C3 contains 0, and you enter the following TIME function in cell D3:

```
=TIME(A3,B3,C3)
```

Excel enters 4:37 a.m. in cell D3. If you then assign the General number format to this cell (Ctrl+Shift+` or Ctrl+~), it would then contain the time serial number, 0.192361.

The TIMEVALUE function converts a time entered or imported into the spreadsheet as a text entry into its equivalent time serial number so that you can use it in time calculations. The TIMEVALUE function uses a single *time_text* argument as follows:

```
TIMEVALUE(time_text)
```

So, for example, if you put the following TIMEVALUE function in a cell to determine the time serial number for 10:35:25:

```
=TIMEVALUE("10:35:25")
```

Excel returns the time serial number 0.441262 to the cell. If you then assign the first Time number format to this cell, the decimal number appears as 10:35:25 a.m. in the cell.

HOUR, MINUTE, and SECOND

The HOUR, MINUTE, and SECOND functions on the Date & Time command button's drop-down menu enable you to extract specific parts of a time value in the spreadsheet. Each of these three time functions takes a single *serial_number* argument that contains the hour, minute, or second that you want to extract.

So, for example, if cell B5 contains the time 1:30:10 p.m. (otherwise known as serial number 0.5626157) and you enter the following HOUR function in cell C5:

```
=HOUR(B5)
```

Excel returns 13 as the hour to cell C5 (hours are always returned in 24-hour time). If you then enter the following MINUTE function in cell D5:

```
=MINUTE(B5)
```

Excel returns 30 as the number of minutes to cell D5. Finally, if you enter the following SECOND function in cell E5:

```
=SECOND(B5)
```

Excel returns 10 as the number of seconds to cell E5.

Chapter 4: Financial Formulas

In This Chapter

✔ Understanding how Excel rounds up values

✔ Using basic investment functions

✔ Using basic depreciation functions

✔ Using basic currency conversion functions

Money! There's nothing quite like it. You can't live with it, and you certainly can't live without it. Many of the spreadsheets that you work with exist only to let you know how much of it you can expect to come in or to pay out. Excel contains a fair number of sophisticated financial functions for determining such things as the present, future, or net present value of an investment; the payment, number of periods, or the principal or interest part of a payment on an amortized loan; the rate of return on an investment; or the depreciation of your favorite assets.

By activating the Analysis ToolPak add-in, you add over 30 specialized financial functions that run the gamut from those that calculate the accrued interest for a security paying interest periodically and only at maturity, all the way to those that calculate the internal rate of return and the net present value for a schedule of nonperiodic cash flows.

Financial Functions 101

The key to using any of Excel's financial functions is to understand the terminology used by their arguments. Many of the most common financial functions, such as PV (Present Value), NPV (Net Present Value), FV (Future Value), and PMT (Payment), take similar arguments:

✦ **PV** is the present value that is the principal amount of the annuity.

✦ **FV** is the future value that represents the principal plus interest on the annuity.

✦ **PMT** is the payment made each period in the annuity. Normally, the payment is set over the life of the annuity and includes principal plus interest without any other fees.

✦ **RATE** is the interest rate per period. Normally, the rate is expressed as an annual percentage.

✦ **NPER** is the total number of payment periods in the life of the annuity. You calculate this number by taking the Term (the amount of time that interest is paid) and multiplying it by the Period (the point in time when interest is paid or earned) so that a loan with a three-year term with 12 monthly interest payments has 3 x 12, or 36 payment periods.

When using financial functions, keep in mind that the *fv, pv,* and *pmt* arguments can be positive or negative, depending on whether you're receiving the money (as in the case of an investment) or paying out the money (as in the case of a loan). Also keep in mind that you want to express the *rate* argument in the same units as the *nper* argument, so that if you make monthly payments on a loan and you express the *nper* as the total number of monthly payments, as in 360 (30 x 12) for a 30-year mortgage, you need to express the annual interest rate in monthly terms as well. For example, if you pay an annual interest rate of 7.5 percent on the loan, you express the *rate* argument as 0.075/12 so that it is monthly as well.

The PV, NPV, and FV functions

The PV (Present Value), NPV (Net Present Value), and FV (Future Value) functions all found on the Financial button's drop-down menu on the Ribbon's Formulas tab (Alt+MI) enable you to determine the profitability of an investment.

Calculating the Present Value

The PV, or Present Value, function returns the present value of an investment, which is the total amount that a series of future payments is worth presently. The syntax of the PV function is as follows:

```
=PV(rate,nper,pmt,[fv],[type])
```

The *fv* and *type* arguments are optional arguments in the function (indicated by the square brackets). The *fv* argument is the future value or cash balance that you want to have after making your last payment. If you omit the *fv* argument, Excel assumes a future value of zero (0). The *type* argument indicates whether the payment is made at the beginning or end of the period: Enter 0 (or omit the *type* argument) when the payment is made at the end of the period and use 1 when it is made at the beginning of the period.

Figure 4-1 contains several examples using the PV function. All three PV functions use the same annual percentage rate of 7.25 percent and term of 10 years. Because payments are made monthly, each function converts these annual figures into monthly ones. For example, in the PV function in cell E3, the annual interest rate in cell A3 is converted into a monthly rate by dividing by 12 (A3/12) and the annual term in cell B3 is converted into equivalent monthly periods by multiplying by 12 (B3 x 12).

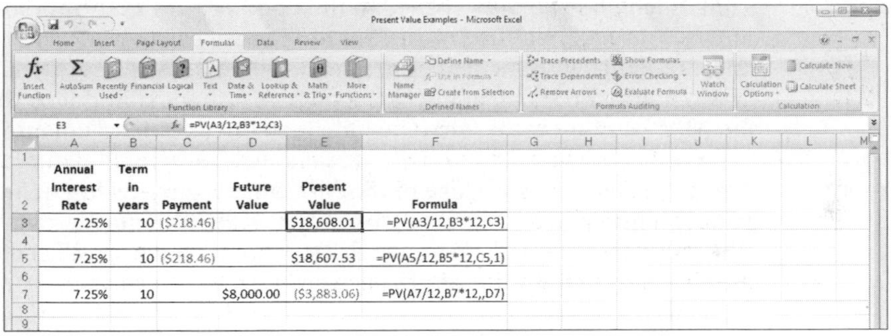

Figure 4-1:
Using the
PV function
to calculate
the present
value of
various
investments.

Note that although the PV functions in cells E3 and E5 use the *rate, nper,* and *pmt* ($218.46) arguments, their results are slightly different. This is caused by the difference in the *type* argument in the two functions: the PV function in cell E3 assumes that each payment is made at the end of the period (the *type* argument is 0 whenever it is omitted), while the PV function in cell E5 assumes that each payment is made at the beginning of the period (indicated by a *type* argument of 1). When the payment is made at the beginning of the period, the present value of this investment is $0.49 higher than when the payment is made at the end of the period, reflecting the interest accrued during the last period.

The third example in cell E7 (shown in Figure 4-1) uses the PV function with an *fv* argument instead of the *pmt* argument. In this example, the PV function states that you would have to make monthly payments of $3,883.06 for a 10-year period to realize a cash balance of $8,000, assuming that the investment returned a constant annual interest rate of 7 1/4 percent. Note that when you use the PV function with the *fv* argument instead of the *pmt* argument, you must still indicate the position of the *pmt* argument in the function with a comma (thus the two commas in a row in the function) so that Excel doesn't mistake your *fv* argument for the *pmt* argument.

Calculating the Net Present Value

The NPV function calculates the net present value based on a series of cash flows. The syntax of this function is

=NPV(*rate*,*value1*,[*value2*],[...])

where *value1, value2,* and so on are between 1 and 13 value arguments representing a series of payments (negative values) and income (positive values), each of which is equally spaced in time and occurs at the end of the period. The NPV investment begins one period before the period of the *value1* cash flow and ends with the last cash flow in the argument list. If your first cash flow occurs at the beginning of the period, you must add it to the result of the NPV function rather than include it as one of the arguments.

Figure 4-2 illustrates the use of the NPV function to evaluate the attractiveness of a five-year investment that requires an initial investment of $30,000 (the value in cell G3). The first year, you expect a loss of $22,000 (cell B3); the second year, a profit of $15,000 (cell C3); the third year, a profit of $25,000 (cell D3); the fourth year, a profit of $32,000 (cell E3); and the fifth year, a profit of $38,000 (cell F3). Note that these cell references are used as the *value* arguments of the NPV function.

Unlike when using the PV function, the NPV function doesn't require an even stream of cash flows. The *rate* argument in the function is set at 8 percent. In this example, this represents the discount rate of the investment; that is, the interest rate that you may expect to get during the five-year period if you put your money into some other type of investment, such as a high-yield money-market account. This NPV function in cell A3 returns a net present value of $31,718.63, indicating that you can expect to realize about $1,719 more from investing your $30,000 in this investment than you would from investing the money in a money-market account at an interest rate of 8 percent.

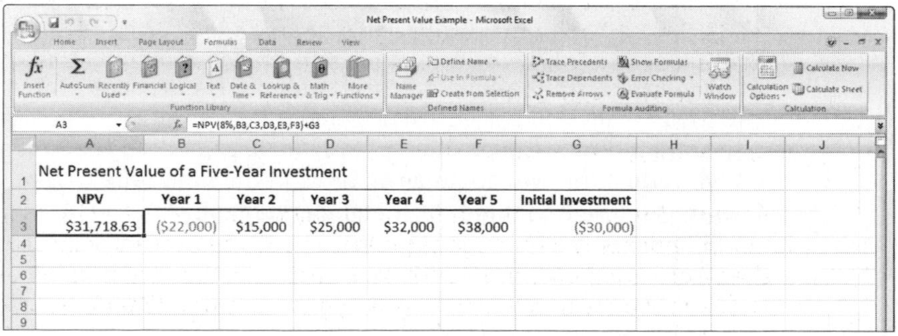

Figure 4-2:
Using the NPV function to calculate the net present value of an investment.

Calculating the Future Value

The FV function calculates the future value of an investment. The syntax of this function is

```
=FV(rate,nper,pmt,[pv],[type])
```

The *rate, nper, pmt,* and *type* arguments are the same as those used by the PV function. The *pv* argument is the present value or lump-sum amount for which you want to calculate the future value. As with the *fv* and *type* arguments in the PV function, both the *pv* and *type* arguments are optional in the FV function. If you omit these arguments, Excel assumes their values to be zero (0) in the function.

You can use the FV function to calculate the future value of an investment, such as an IRA (Individual Retirement Account). For example, suppose that you establish an IRA at age 43 and will retire 22 years hence at age 65 and that you plan to make annual payments into the IRA at the beginning of each year. If you assume a rate of return of 8.5 percent a year, you would enter the following FV function in your worksheet:

```
=FV(8.5%,22,-1000,,1)
```

Excel then indicates that you can expect a future value of $64,053.66 for your IRA when you retire at age 65. If you had established the IRA a year prior and the account already has a present value of $1,085, you would amend the FV function as follows:

```
=FV(8.5%,22,-1000,-1085,1)
```

In this case, Excel indicates that you can expect a future value of $70,583.22 for your IRA at retirement.

The PMT function

The PMT function on the Financial button's drop-down menu on the Formulas tab of the Ribbon calculates the periodic payment for an annuity, assuming a stream of equal payments and a constant rate of interest. The PMT function uses the following syntax:

```
=PMT(rate,nper,pv,[fv],[type])
```

As with the other common financial functions, *rate* is the interest rate per period, *nper* is the number of periods, *pv* is the present value or the amount the future payments are worth presently, *fv* is the future value or cash balance that you want after the last payment is made (Excel assumes a future value of zero when you omit this optional argument as you would when calculating loan payments), and *type* is the value 0 for payments made at the end of the period or the value 1 for payments made at the beginning of the period (if you omit the optional *type* argument, Excel assumes that the payment is made at the end of the period).

The PMT function is often used to calculate the payment for mortgage loans that have a fixed rate of interest. Figure 4-3 shows you a sample worksheet that contains a table using the PMT function to calculate loan payments for a range of interest rates (from 5 percent to 6 ƒ 1/4 percent) and principals ($350,000 to $359,000). The table uses the initial principal that you enter in cell B2, copies it to cell A7, and then increases it by $1,000 in the range A8:A16. The table uses the initial interest rate that you enter in cell B3, copies to cell B6, and then increases this initial rate by 1/4 of a percent in the range C6:G6. The term in years in cell B4 is a constant factor that is used in the entire loan payment table.

To get an idea of how easy it is to build this type of loan payment table with the PMT function, follow these steps for creating it in a new worksheet:

1. **Enter the titles** Loan Payments **in cell A1,** Principal **in cell A2,** Interest Rate **in cell A3, and** Term (in years) **in cell A4.**

2. **Enter** $350,000 **in cell B2, enter** 5% **in cell B3, and enter** 30 **in cell B4.**

These are the starting values with which you build the Loan Payments table.

3. **Position the cell pointer in B6 and then build the formula =B3.**

By creating a linking formula that brings forward the value in B3 with the formula, you ensure that the value in B6 will immediately reflect any change that you make in cell B3.

4. **Position the cell pointer in cell C6 and then build the formula =B6+.25%.**

By adding 1/4 of a percent to the interest rate to the value in B6 with the formula =B6+.25% in C6 rather than creating a series with the AutoFill handle, you ensure that the value in cell C6 will always be 1/4 of a percent larger than any value entered in cell B6.

5. **Drag the Fill handle in cell C6 to extend the selection to the right to cell G6 and then release the mouse button.**

6. **Position the cell pointer in cell A7 and then build the formula =B2.**

Again, by using the formula =B2 to bring the initial principal forward to cell A7, you ensure that cell A7 always has the same value as cell B2.

7. **Position the cell pointer in A8 active and then build the formula =A7+1000.**

   Here too, you use the formula =A7+1000 rather than create a series with the AutoFill feature so that the value in A8 will always be 1000 greater than any value placed in cell A7.

8. **Drag the Fill handle in cell A8 down until you extend the selection to cell A16 and then release the mouse button.**

9. **In cell B7, click the Insert Function button on the Formula bar, click Financial in the Or Select a Category drop-down list, and then double-click the PMT function in the Select a Function list box.**

   The Function Arguments dialog box opens, where you specify the *rate, nper,* and *pv* arguments. Be sure to move the Function Arguments dialog box to the right so that no part of it obscures the data in columns A and B of your worksheet before proceeding with the following steps for filling in the arguments.

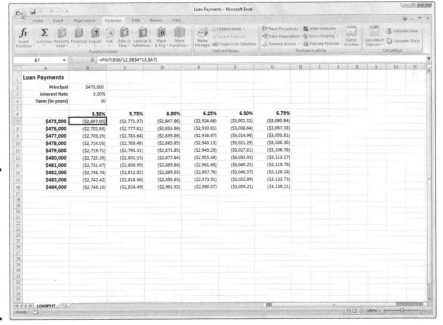

Figure 4-3:
Loan
Payments
table using
the PMT
function to
calculate
various loan
payments.

10. **Click cell B6 to insert B6 in the Rate text box and then press F4 twice to convert the relative reference B6 to the mixed reference B$6 (column relative, row absolute) before you type /12.**

You convert the relative cell reference B6 to the mixed reference B$6 so that Excel does *not* adjust the row number when you copy the PMT formula down each row of the table, but *does* adjust the column letter when you copy the formula across its columns. Because the initial interest rate entered in B3 (and then brought forward to cell B6) is an *annual* interest rate, but you want to know the *monthly* loan payment, you need to convert the annual rate to a monthly rate by dividing the value in cell B6 by 12.

11. **Click the Nper text box, click cell B4 to insert this cell reference in this text box, and then press F4 once to convert the relative reference B4 to the absolute reference $B$4 before you type *12.**

You need to convert the relative cell reference B4 to the absolute reference $B$4 so that Excel adjusts neither the row number nor the column letter when you copy the PMT formula down the rows and across the columns of the table. Because the term in B3 (which is then brought forward to cell B6) is an *annual* period, but you want to know the *monthly* loan payment, you need to convert the yearly periods to monthly periods by multiplying the value in cell B4 by 12.

12. **Click the Pv text box, then click A7 to insert this cell reference in this text box, and then press F4 three times to convert the relative reference A7 to the mixed reference $A7 (column absolute, row relative).**

You need to convert the relative cell reference A7 to the mixed reference $A7 so that Excel won't adjust the column letter when you copy the PMT formula across each column of the table, but will adjust the row number when you copy the formula down across its rows.

13. **Click OK to insert the formula =PMT(B$6/12,$B$4*12,$A7) in cell B7.**

Now you're ready to copy this original PMT formula down and then over to fill in the entire Loan Payments table.

14. **Drag the Fill handle on cell B7 down until you extend the fill range to cell B16 and then release the mouse button.**

After you've copied the original PMT formula down to cell B16, you're ready to copy it to the right to G16.

15. **Drag the Fill handle to the right until you extend the fill range B7:B16 to cell G16 and then release the mouse button.**

After copying the original formula with the Fill handle, be sure to widen columns B through G sufficiently to display their results (you can do this in one step by dragging through the headers of these columns and then double-clicking the right border of column G).

After you've created a loan table like this, you can then change the beginning principal or interest rate, as well as the term to see what the payments would be under various other scenarios. You can also turn on the Manual Recalculation so that you can control when the Loan Payments table is recalculated.

For information on how to switch to manual recalculation and use this mode to control when formulas are recalculated, see Book III, Chapter 1. For information on how to protect the worksheet so that users can input new values only into the three input cells (B2, B3, and B4) to change the starting loan amount, interest rate, and the term of the loan, see Book IV, Chapter 1.

Depreciation functions

Excel lets you choose from four different Depreciation functions, each of which uses a slightly different method for depreciating an asset over time. These built-in Depreciation functions found on the Financial button's drop-down menu on the Formulas tab of the Ribbon include the following:

✦ SLN(*cost,salvage,life*) to calculate straight-line depreciation

✦ SYD(*cost,salvage,life,per*) to calculate sum-of-years-digits depreciation

✦ DB(*cost,salvage,life,period,*[*month*]) to calculate declining balance depreciation

✦ DDB(*cost,salvage,life,period,*[*factor*]) to calculate double-declining balance depreciation

As you can see, with the exception of the optional *month* argument in the DB function and the optional *factor* argument in the DDB function, all the Depreciation functions require the *cost, salvage,* and *life* arguments, and all but the SLN function require a *period* argument as well:

✦ *Cost* is the initial cost of the asset that you're depreciating.

✦ *Salvage* is the value of the asset at the end of the depreciation (also known as the salvage value of the asset).

✦ *Life* is the number of periods over which the asset is depreciating (also known as the useful life of the asset).

✦ *Per or Period* is the period over which the asset is being depreciated. The units that you use in the period argument must be the same as those used in the life argument of the Depreciation function so that if you express the life argument in years, you must also express the period argument in years.

Book III Chapter 4

Financial Formulas

Note that the DB function accepts an optional *month* argument. This argument is the number of months that the asset is in use in the first year. If you omit the *month* argument from your DB function, Excel assumes the number of months of service to be 12.

When using the DDB function to calculate the double-declining balance method of depreciation, you can add an optional *factor* argument. This argument is the rate at which the balance declines in the depreciation schedule. If you omit this optional *factor* argument, Excel assumes the rate to be 2 (thus, the name *double-declining balance*).

Figure 4-4 contains a Depreciation table that uses all four depreciation methods to calculate the depreciation of office furniture originally costing $50,000 to be depreciated over a 10-year period, assuming a salvage value of $1,000 at the end of this depreciation period.

The Formula bar shown in Figure 4-4 shows the SLN formula that I entered into cell B9:

```
=B8-SLN($B$3,$B$5,$B$4)
```

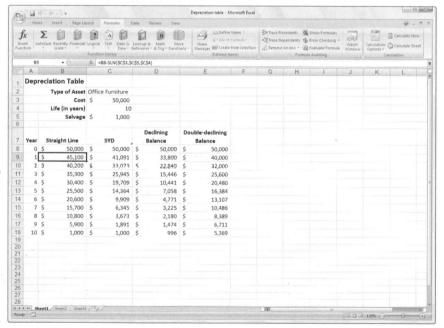

Figure 4-4:
Depreciation
Table show-
ing 10-year
depreciation
of an asset
using
various
methods.

This formula subtracts the amount of straight-line depreciation to be taken in the first year of service from the original cost of $50,000 (this value is brought forward from cell B3 by the formula =B3). After creating this original formula in cell B9, I then used the Fill handle to copy it down to cell B18, which contains the final salvage value of the asset in the 10th year of service.

Cell C9 contains a similar formula for calculating the sum-of-years-digits depreciation for the office furniture. This cell contains the following formula:

```
=C8-SYD($B$3,$B$5,$B$4,$A9)
```

This formula subtracts the amount of sum-of-years-digits depreciation to be taken at the end of the first year from the original cost of $50,000 in cell C8 (also brought forward from cell B3 by the formula =B3). After creating this original formula in cell C9, I again used the Fill handle to copy it down to cell C18, which also contains the final salvage value of the asset in the 10th year of service.

I used the same basic procedure to create the formulas using the DB and DDB depreciation methods in the cell ranges D8:D18 and E8:E18, respectively. Cell D9 contains the following DB formula:

```
=D8-DB($B$3,$B$5,$B$4,$A9)
```

Cell E9 contains the following DDB formula:

```
=E8-DDB($B$3,$B$5,$B$4,$A9)
```

Note that, like the SYD function, both of these depreciation functions require the use of a *period* argument, which is supplied by the list of years in the cell range A9:A18. Note also, that the values in cell B4, which supplies the *life* argument to the SYD, DB, and DDB functions, matches the year units used in this cell range.

Analysis ToolPak financial functions

By activating the Analysis ToolPak add-in (see Book I, Chapter 3), you add a whole bunch of powerful financial functions to the Financial button's drop-down menu on the Formulas tab of the Ribbon. Table 4-1 shows all the financial functions that are added to the Insert Function dialog box when the Analysis ToolPak is activated. As you can see from this table, the Analysis ToolPak financial functions are varied and quite sophisticated.

**Book III
Chapter 4**

Financial Formulas

Table 4-1   **Financial Functions in the Analysis ToolPak**

Function	What It Calculates
ACCRINT(*issue,first_interest,settlement, rate,*[*par*]*,frequency,*[*basis*]*,*[*calc_methd*])	Calculates the accrued interest for a security that pays periodic interest
ACCRINTM(*issue,maturity,rate,*[*par*]*,* [*basis*])	Calculates the accrued interest for a security that pays interest at maturity
AMORDEGRC(*cost,date_purchased,first_ period,salvage,period,rate,*[*basis*]) and AMORLINC(*cost, date_purchased,first_ period,salvage,period,rate,*[*basis*])	Used in French accounting systems for calculating depreciation. AMORDEGRC and AMORLINC return the depreciation for each accounting period. AMORDEGRC works like AMORLINC except that it applies a depreciation coefficient in the calculation that depends upon the life of the assets.
COUPDAYBS(*settlement,maturity, frequency,*[*basis*])	Calculates the number of days from the beginning of a coupon period to the settlement date
COUPDAYS(*settlement,maturity, frequency,*[*basis*])	Calculates the number of days in the coupon period
COUPDAYSNC(*settlement,maturity, frequency,*[*basis*])	Calculates the number of days from the settlement date to the next coupon date
COUPNCD(*settlement,maturity,frequency,* [*basis*])	Calculates a number that represents the next coupon date after a settlement date
COUPNUM(*settlement,maturity, frequency,*[*basis*])	Calculates the number of coupons payable between the settlement date and maturity date, rounded up to the nearest whole coupon
COUPPCD(*settlement,maturity,frequency,* [*basis*])	Calculates a number that represents the previous coupon date before the settlement date
CUMIPMT(*rate,nper,pv,start_period,end_ period,type*)	Calculates the cumulative interest paid on a loan between the start_period and end_period. The type argument is 0 when the payment is made at the end of the period and 1 when it's made at the beginning of the period.
CUMPRINC(*rate,nper,pv,start_period, end_period,type*)	Calculates the cumulative principal paid on a loan between the start_period and end_period. The type argument is 0 when the payment is made at the end of the period and 1 when it's made at the beginning of the period.
DISC(*settlement,maturity,pr,redemption,* [*basis*])	Calculates the discount rate for a security
DOLLARDE(*fractional_dollar,fraction*)	Converts a dollar price expressed as a fraction into a dollar price expressed as a decimal number

Function	What It Calculates
DOLLARFR(*decimal_dollar,fraction*)	Converts a dollar price expressed as a decimal number into a dollar price expressed as a fraction
DURATION(*settlement,maturity,coupon, yld,frequency,[basis]*)	Calculates the Macauley duration for an assumed par value of $100 (duration is defined as the weighted average of the present value of the cash flows and is used as a measure of the response of a bond price to changes in yield)
EFFECT(*nominal_rate,npery*)	Calculates the effective annual interest rate given the nominal interest rate and the number of compounding periods per year
INTRATE(*settlement,maturity,investment, redemption,[basis]*)	Calculates the interest rate for a fully invested security
MDURATION(*settlement,maturity,coupon, yld,frequency,[basis]*)	Calculates the modified Macauley duration for a security with an assumed part value of $100
NOMINAL(*effect_rate,npery*)	Calculates the nominal annual interest rate given the effect rate and the number of compounding periods per year
ODDFPRICE(*settlement,maturity,issue, first_coupon,rate,yld,redemption, frequency,[basis]*)	Calculates the price per $100 face value of a security having an odd (short or long) first period
ODDFYIELD(*settlement,maturity,issue, first_coupon,rate,pr,redemption, frequency,[basis]*)	Calculates the yield of a security that has an odd (short or long) first period
ODDLPRICE(*settlement,maturity, last_ interest,rate,yld,redemption,frequency, [basis]*)	Calculates the price per $100 face value of a security having an odd (short or long) last coupon period
ODDLYIELD(*settlement,maturity,last_ interest,rate,pr,redemption,frequency, [basis]*)	Calculates the yield of a security that has an odd (short or long) last period
PRICE(*settlement,maturity,rate,yld, redemption,frequency,[basis]*)	Calculates the price per $100 face value of a security that pays periodic interest
PRICEDISC(*settlement,maturity,discount, redemption,[basis]*)	Calculates the price per $100 face value of a discounted security
PRICEMAT(*settlement,maturity,issue,rate, yld,[basis]*)	Calculates the price per $100 face value of a security that pays interest at maturity
RECEIVED(*settlement,maturity,investment, discount,[basis]*)	Calculates the amount received at maturity for a fully invested security
TBILLEQ(*settlement,maturity,discount*)	Calculates the bond-equivalent yield for a Treasury bill

Book III Chapter 4

Financial Formulas

(continued)

Table 4-1 *(continued)*

TBILLPRICE(*settlement,maturity,discount*)	Calculates the price per $100 face value for a Treasury bill
TBILLYIELD(*settlement,maturity,pr*)	Calculates the yield for a Treasury bill
XIRR(*values,dates,[guess]*)	Calculates the internal rate of return for a schedule of cash flows that are not periodic
XNPV(*rate,values,dates*)	Calculates the net present value for a schedule of cash flows that are not periodic
YIELD(*settlement,maturity,rate,pr, redemption,frequency,[basis]*)	Calculates the yield on a security that pays periodic interest (used to calculate bond yield)
YIELDDISC(*settlement,maturity,pr, redemption,[basis]*)	Calculates the annual yield for a discounted security
YIELDMAT(*settlement,maturity,issue,rate, pr,[basis]*)	Calculates the annual yield of a security that pays interest at maturity

You may note in Table 4-1 that many of the Analysis ToolPak financial functions make use of an optional *basis* argument. This optional *basis* argument is a number between 0 and 4 that determines the day count basis to use in determining the fractional part of the year:

✦ 0 (or omitted) to base it on the U.S. (NASD) method of 30/360 (see the DAYS360 function in Book III, Chapter 3 for details on the U.S. method)

✦ 1 to base the fraction on actual days/actual days

✦ 2 to base the fraction on actual days/360

✦ 3 to base the fraction on actual days/365

✦ 4 to base the fraction on the European method of 30/360 (see the DAYS360 function in Book III, Chapter 3 for details on the European method)

For detailed information on the other required arguments in the Analysis ToolPak financial functions shown in this table, select the function on the Financial button's drop-down list and then click the Help on This Function link in the lower-left corner of its Function Arguments dialog box.

Chapter 5: Math and Statistical Formulas

In This Chapter

✔ **Rounding off numbers**

✔ **Raising numbers to powers and finding square roots**

✔ **Conditional summing**

✔ **Using basic statistical functions, such as AVERAGE, MIN, and MAX**

✔ **Building formulas that count**

✔ **Using specialized statistical functions**

This chapter examines two larger categories of Excel functions: Math & Trig and Statistical functions. The Math & Trig functions found on the Math & Trig command button's drop-down menu on the Ribbon's Formulas tab (the button with the (on the book cover) include all the specialized trigonometric functions (such as those that return the sine, cosine, or tangents of various angles) and logarithmic functions (for finding the base-10 and natural logarithms of a number), along with the more common math functions for summing numbers, rounding numbers up or down, raising a number to a certain power, and finding the square root of numbers.

The Statistical functions are found on a continuation menu accessed from the More Functions command button's drop-down menu on the Formulas tab (the button with the two books). Statistical functions include the more common functions that return the average, highest, and lowest values in a cell range all the way to the very sophisticated and specialized functions that calculate such things as the chi-squared distribution, binomial distribution probability, frequency, standard deviation, variance, and — my personal favorite — the skewness of a distribution in a particular population.

Math & Trig Functions

The mathematical functions are technically known as the Math & Trig category when you encounter them on the Math & Trig command button on the Ribbon's Formulas tab or in the Insert Function dialog box (opened by clicking the Insert Function Wizard button on the Formula bar).

This category groups together all the specialized trigonometric functions with the more common arithmetic functions. Although the trigonometric functions are primarily of use to engineers and scientists, the mathematical functions provide you with the ability to manipulate any type of values. This category of functions includes SUM, the most commonly used of all functions; functions such as INT, EVEN, ODD, ROUND, and TRUNC that round off the values in your worksheet; functions such as PRODUCT, SUMPRODUCT, and SUMSQ that you can use to calculate the products of various values in the worksheet; and the SQRT function that you can use to calculate the square root of a value.

Rounding off numbers

You use the ROUND function on the Math & Trig command button's drop-down menu to round up or down fractional values in the worksheet as you might when working with financial spreadsheets that only need to show monetary values to the nearest dollar. Unlike when applying a number format to a cell, which affects only the number's display, the ROUND function actually changes the way Excel stores the number in the cell that contains the function. ROUND uses the following syntax:

```
ROUND(number,num_digits)
```

In this function, the *number* argument is the value that you want to round off, and *num_digits* is the number of digits to which you want the number rounded. If you enter 0 (zero) as the *num_digits* argument, Excel rounds the number to the nearest integer. If you make the *num_digits* argument a positive value, Excel rounds the number to the specified number of decimal places. If you enter the *num_digits* argument as a negative number, Excel rounds the number to the left of the decimal point.

Instead of the ROUND function, you can use the ROUNDUP or ROUNDDOWN function. Both ROUNDUP and ROUNDDOWN take the same *number* and *num_digits* arguments as the ROUND function. The difference is that the ROUNDUP function always rounds up the value specified by the number argument, whereas the ROUNDDOWN function always rounds the value down.

Figure 5-1 illustrates the use of the ROUND, ROUNDUP, and ROUNDDOWN functions in rounding off the value of the mathematical constant pi (π). In cell A3, I entered the value of this constant (with just nine places of nonrepeating fraction displayed when the column is widened) into this cell, using Excel's PI function in the following formula:

```
=PI()
```

I then used the ROUND, ROUNDUP, and ROUNDDOWN functions in the cell range B3 through B10 to round this number up and down to various decimal places.

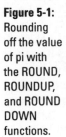

Figure 5-1: Rounding off the value of pi with the ROUND, ROUNDUP, and ROUND DOWN functions.

Cell B3, the first cell that uses one of the ROUND functions to round off the value of pi, rounds this value to 3 because I used 0 (zero) as the *num_digits* argument of its ROUND function (causing Excel to round the value to the nearest whole number).

In Figure 5-1, note the difference between using the ROUND and ROUNDUP functions both with 2 as their *num_digits* arguments in cells B5 and B7, respectively. In cell B5, Excel rounds the value of pi off to 3.14, whereas in cell B7, the program rounds its value up to 3.15. Note that using the ROUNDDOWN function with 2 as its *num_digits* argument yields the same result, 3.14, as does using the ROUND function with 2 as its second argument.

The whole number and nothing but the whole number

You can also use the INT (for Integer) and TRUNC (for Truncate) functions on the Math & Trig command button's drop-down menu to round off values in your spreadsheets. You use these functions only when you don't care about all or part of the fractional portion of the value. When you use the INT function, which requires only a single *number* argument, Excel rounds the value down to the nearest integer (whole number). For example, cell A3 contains the value of pi, as shown in Figure 5-1, and you enter the following INT function formula in the worksheet:

```
=INT(A3)
```

Excel returns the value 3 to the cell, the same as when you use 0 (zero) as the *num_digits* argument of the ROUND function in cell B3.

The TRUNC function uses the same number and *num_digits* arguments as the ROUND, ROUNDUP, and ROUNDDOWN functions, except that in the TRUNC function, the *num_digits* argument is purely optional. This argument is required in the ROUND, ROUNDUP, and ROUNDDOWN functions.

The TRUNC function doesn't round off the number in question; it simply truncates the number to the nearest integer by removing the fractional part of the number. However, if you specify a *num_digits* argument, Excel uses that value to determine the precision of the truncation. So, going back to the example illustrated in Figure 5-1, if you enter the following TRUNC function, omitting the optional *num_digits* argument as in:

```
=TRUNC($A$3)
```

Excel returns 3 to the cell just like the formula =ROUND($A$3,0) does in cell B3. However, if you modify this TRUNC function by using 2 as its *num_digits* argument, as in:

```
=TRUNC($A$3,2)
```

Excel then returns 3.14 (by cutting rest of the fraction) just as the formula =ROUND($A$3,2) does in cell B5.

The only time you notice a difference between the INT and TRUNC functions is when you use them with negative numbers. For example, if you use the TRUNC function to truncate the value –5.4 in the following formula:

```
=TRUNC(-5.4)
```

Excel returns–5 to the cell. If, however, you use the INT function with the same negative value as in:

```
=INT(-5.4)
```

Excel returns –6 to the cell. This is because the INT function rounds numbers down to the nearest integer using the fractional part of the number.

Let's call it even or odd

Excel's EVEN and ODD functions on the Math & Trig command button's drop-down menu also round off numbers. The EVEN function rounds the value specified as its *number* argument up to the nearest even integer. The ODD function, of course, does just the opposite: rounding the value up to the nearest odd integer. So, for example, if cell C18 in a worksheet contains the value 345.25 and you use the EVEN function in the following formula:

```
=EVEN(C18)
```

Excel rounds the value up to the next whole even number and returns 346 to the cell. If, however, you use the ODD function on this cell as in:

```
=ODD(C18)
```

Excel rounds the value up to the next odd whole number and returns 347 to the cell instead.

Building in a ceiling

The CEILING function on the Math & Trig command button's drop-down menu enables you to not only round up a number, but also set the multiple of significance to be used when doing the rounding. This function can be very useful when dealing with figures that need rounding to particular units.

For example, suppose that you're working on a spreadsheet that lists the retail prices for the various products that you sell, all based upon a particular markup over wholesale, and that many of these calculations result in many prices with cents below 50. If you don't want to have any prices in the list that aren't rounded to the nearest 50 cents or whole dollar, you can use the CEILING function to round up all these calculated retail prices to the nearest half dollar.

The CEILING function uses the following syntax:

```
CEILING(number,significance)
```

The *number* argument specifies the number you want to round up and the *significance* argument specifies the multiple to which you want to round. For the half-dollar example, suppose that you have the calculated number $12.35 in cell B3 and you enter the following formula in cell C3:

```
=CEILING(B3,0.5)
```

Excel then returns $12.50 to cell C3. Further, suppose that cell B4 contains the calculated value $13.67, and you copy this formula down to cell C4 so that it contains:

```
=CEILING(B4,0.5)
```

Excel then returns $14.00 to that cell.

POWER and SQRT

Although you can use the caret (^) operator to build a formula that raises a number to any power, you also need to be aware that Excel includes a math function called POWER found on the Math & Trig command button's drop-down menu that accomplishes the same thing. For example, to build a formula that raises 5.9 to the third power (that is, cubes the number), you can use the exponentiation operator as in:

=5.9^3

You can have Excel perform the same calculation with the POWER function by entering this formula:

=POWER(5.9,3)

In either case, Excel returns the same result, 205.379. The only difference between using the exponentiation operator and the POWER function occurs on that rare, rare occasion when you have to raise a number by a fractional power. In that case, you need to use the POWER function instead of the caret (^) operator to get the correct result. For example, suppose that you need to raise 20 by the fraction 3/4; to do this, you build the following formula with the POWER function:

=POWER(20,3/4)

To use the exponentiation operator to calculate the result of raising 20 by the fraction 3/4, you can convert the fraction into decimal form as in:

=20^0.75

The SQRT function on the Math & Trig command button's drop-down menu enables you to calculate the square root of any number that you specify as its sole *number* argument. For example, if you use the SQRT function to build the following formula in a cell:

=SQRT(144)

Excel returns 12 to that cell.

The SQRT function can't deal with negative numbers, so if you try to find the square root of a negative value, Excel returns a nice #NUM! error value to that cell. To avoid such a nuisance, you need to use the ABS (for absolute) math function, which returns the absolute value of a number (that is, the number without a sign). For example, suppose that cell A15 contains ($49.00), showing that it's something you owe, and you want to return the square root of this number in cell A16. To avoid the dreaded #NUM! error, you nest the ABS function inside the SQRT function. The ABS function returns the absolute value of the number you specify as its sole argument (that is, the value without its sign). To nest this function inside the SQRT function, you create the following formula:

```
=SQRT(ABS(A15))
```

Excel then returns 7 instead of #NUM! to cell A16 because the ABS function removes the negative sign from the 49.00 before the SQRT function calculates its square root (remember that Excel always performs the calculations in the innermost pair of parentheses first).

The SUM of the parts

No function in the entire galaxy of Excel functions comes anywhere close to the popularity of the SUM function in the spreadsheets that you build. So popular is this function, in fact, that Excel has its own AutoSum command button located on the Home tab of the Ribbon (the one with the Σ on it) that you most often use to build your SUM formulas. You should, however, be aware of the workings of the basic SUM function that the AutoSum button enables you to use so easily.

For the record, the syntax of the SUM function is as follows:

```
SUM(number1,[number2],[...])
```

When using the SUM function, only the *number1* argument is required; this is the range of numbers in a cell range or array constant that you want added together. Be aware that you can enter up to a total of 29 other optional *number* arguments in a single SUM formula, all of which are separated by a comma (,). For example, you can build a SUM formula that totals numbers in several different ranges as in:

```
=SUM(B3:B10,Sheet2!B3:B10,Sheet3!B3:B10)
```

In this example, Excel sums the values in the cell range B3:B10 on Sheet1, Sheet2, and Sheet3 of the workbook, giving you the grand total of all these values in whatever cell you build this SUM formula.

Conditional summing

The SUM function is perfect when you want to get the totals for all the numbers in a particular range or set of ranges. But what about those times when you only want the total of certain items within a cell range? For those situations, you can use the SUMIF function on the Math & Trig command button's

Book III
Chapter 5

Math and Statistical Formulas

drop-down menu. The SUMIF function enables you to tell Excel to add together the numbers in a particular range *only* when those numbers meet the criteria that you specify. The syntax of the SUMIF function is as follows:

```
SUMIF(range,criteria,[sum_range])
```

In the SUMIF function, the *range* argument specifies the range of cells that you want Excel to evaluate when doing the summing; the *criteria* argument specifies the criteria to be used in evaluating whether to include certain values in the range in the summing; and finally, the optional *sum_range* argument is the range of all the cells to be summed together. If you omit the *sum_range* argument, Excel sums only the cells specified in the *range* argument (and, of course, only if they meet the criteria specified in the *criteria* argument).

Summing only certain cells with SUMIF

Figure 5-2 illustrates how you can use the SUMIF function to total sales by the items sold. This figure shows a Sales data list sorted by the store location (there are three locations: Mission Street, Anderson Rd., and Curtis Way, of which only Mission Street and one sale on Anderson Rd. are visible) and then the item sold. To total the sales of Lemon tarts at all three locations, I created the following SUMIF formula in cell I3:

```
=SUMIF(item_sold,"=Lemon tarts",daily_sales)
```

In this example, item_sold is the range name given to the cell range C3:C62, which contains the list of each item that has been sold in the first five days of January, 2008 (Lemon tarts, Blueberry muffins, Lots of chips cookies, or Strawberry pie), and daily_sales is the range name assigned to the cell range G3:G62, which contains the extended sales made at each store for each item.

The SUMIF formula in cell I3 then looks for each occurrence of "Lemon tarts" in the item_sold range (the *criteria* argument for the SUMIF function) in the Item column of the Cookie Sales list and then adds its extended sales price from the daily_sales range in the Daily Sales column to the total.

The formulas in cells I4, I5, and I6 contain SUMIF functions very similar to the one in cell I3, except that they substitute the name of the dessert goodie in question in place of the =Lemon tarts *criteria* argument. The formula in cell I8, however, is slightly different: This formula sums the sales for all items except for Strawberry pies. It does this with the SUMIF function in the following formula:

```
=SUMIF(item_sold,"<>Strawberry pie",daily_sales)
```

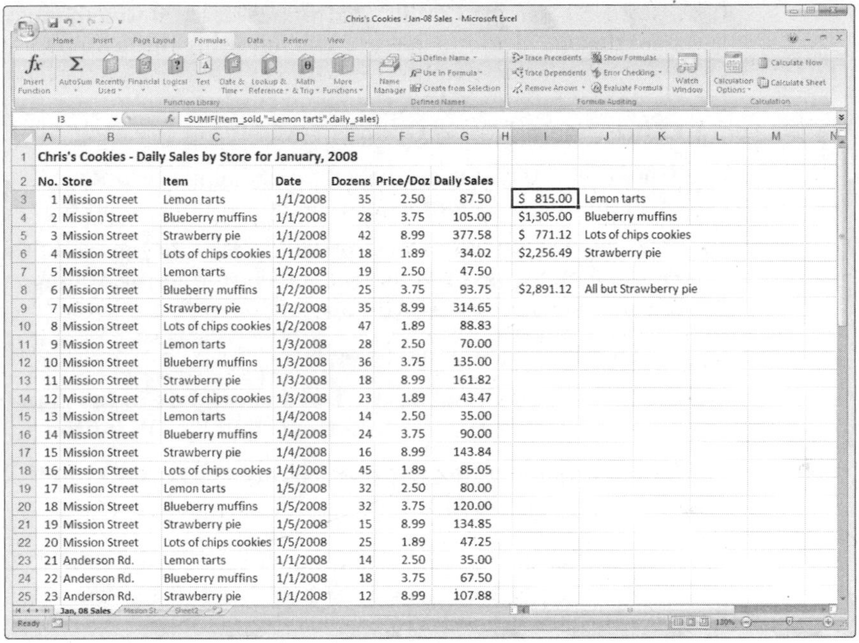

Figure 5-2:
Using
SUMIF to
total sales
by items
sold.

Because I prefaced the item Strawberry pie with the not (<>) operator (which can be placed before or after the open double quotation mark), Excel sums the daily sale for every item except for Strawberry pie.

Using the Conditional Sum Wizard

The SUMIF function is just great when you have only one criterion that you want to apply in doing the summing. It does not, however, work when you have multiple criteria that you need to use in determining which numbers get added to the total and which don't. For those situations, you can turn to the Conditional Sum Wizard, a nifty little Excel add-in tool that walks you through the steps of building more complex SUM formulas that utilize IF conditions that can include multiple criteria.

For example, harkening back to the Chris' Cookies Daily Sales spreadsheet shown in Figure 5-2, suppose that you need the sum of all the sales made in the Anderson Rd. store location for all items except for Strawberry pie but only for dates after January 1, 2008. You can use the Conditional Sum Wizard to create the SUM formula that calculates this special subtotal in no time flat.

**Book III
Chapter 5**

**Math and Statistical
Formulas**

Before you can use the Conditional Sum Wizard, however, you have to install and load this Excel add-in program by following these steps:

1. **Open the Add-Ins tab of the Excel Options dialog box by clicking Office Button | Excel Options | Add-Ins or pressing Alt+FIAA.**

   The Add-Ins tab of the Excel Options dialog box opens; it contains a list of all the add-in programs installed on your computer.

2. **Click the Go button at the bottom of the Add-Ins tab of the Excel Options dialog box after you make sure that the Manage drop-down list box contains Excel Add-Ins.**

   Excel opens the Add-Ins dialog box.

3. **Click the Conditional Sum Wizard check box in the Add-Ins dialog box to put a check mark in it and then click the OK button.**

4. **If an alert dialog box appears, asking you if you want to install the add-in, click its Yes button.**

After you install and load the Conditional Sum Wizard add-in, Excel adds the Conditional Sum command button to the Solutions group at the end of the Ribbon's Formula tab. When you click this command button, Excel opens the Conditional Sum Wizard — Step 1 of 4 dialog box (similar to the one shown in Figure 5-3). You then follow these steps to build a SUM formula by using multiple criteria:

1. **Enter the address or name of the cell range that contains the values to sum, including the column headings, or drag through the range in the current worksheet.**

   If you drag through the cells rather than type their range address or range name, Excel automatically reduces the Conditional Sum Wizard — Step 1 of 4 dialog box to the Where Is the Listtext box until you release the mouse button.

   For this example, you want to sum the daily sales for the store location on Anderson Rd., for the item that is anything but Strawberry pie, and for the date that is any date after January 1, 2008. So you select the entire range of data (including the column headings in row 2) except for column A, which tracks only the record number.

2. **Click the Next button.**

   The Conditional Sum Wizard — Step 2 of 4 dialog box displays (similar to the one shown in Figure 5-4). Here, you specify which column to sum and what criteria to apply when doing the summing.

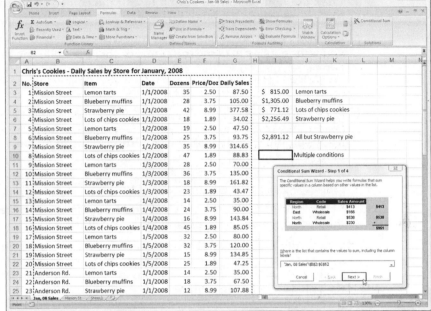

Figure 5-3:
Specifying
the values to
sum in the
Conditional
Sum
Wizard —
Step 1 of 4
dialog box.

3. **Click the name of the column that you want summed in the Column to Sum drop-down list box.**

   For this example, select the Daily Sales column as the column to sum.

   After you specify the column to sum, you're ready to build and then add the various conditions (criteria) to be applied when doing the summing.

4. **Click the name of the column to be included in the first condition in the Column drop-down list box.**

   For the first condition in this example, click Store in the Column drop-down list.

5. **In the Is drop-down list box, click the comparison operator that you want to use in the condition.**

   For this example, you want to leave the default equal to (=) operator selected in the Is drop-down list box.

6. **Click the name of the number or label that you want used as the value of the condition in the This Value drop-down list box.**

   For this example, click Anderson Rd. in the This Value drop-down list so that the condition reads Store = Anderson Rd.

7. **Click the Add Condition button to add the condition that you just built to the Conditions list box.**

You now repeat Steps 5 through 7 for all the additional conditions that you want applied in doing the sum. For this example, you build and add two more conditions: Item <> Strawberry pie and Date > 1/1/2008 (see Figure 5-4).

8. **Repeat Steps 5 through 7 to add any and all additional conditions to the Conditions list box.**

9. **After you finish adding all the conditions that you want applied in doing the summing, click the Next button.**

In the Conditional Sum Wizard — Step 3 of 4 dialog box that appears, you indicate whether to copy just the formula to a single cell (the default) or to copy the formula plus the values that you specified in the This Value drop-down list for each condition that you created.

10. **Leave the Copy Just the Formula to a Single Cell option button selected to just insert the new SUM formula in the worksheet. Click the Copy the Formula and Conditional Values option button to copy the values and formula in the worksheet.**

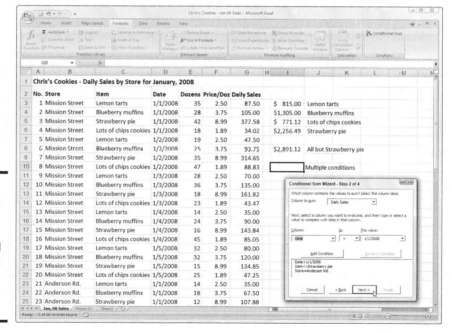

Figure 5-4: Adding the criteria to use in the Conditional Sum Wizard — Step 2 of 4 dialog box.

If you elect to copy only the formula to a cell, you have only one more step to complete in the Conditional Sum Wizard — Step 4 of 4 dialog box, and that is to designate the cell in the worksheet where the SUM formula is to go.

If you elect to copy the conditional values plus the formula, the Conditional Sum Wizard adds as many wizard dialog boxes as necessary to individually specify the cell location for each conditional value, as well as the one for the SUM formula.

For this example, the Conditional Sum Wizard would add three more dialog boxes if you were to click the Copy the Formula and Conditional Values option button, making a total of seven steps in the Conditional Sum Wizard. This is to accommodate specifying a cell for copying the conditional value, Anderson Rd. in Step 4 of 7, another for copying Strawberry pie in Step 5 of 7, another for copying 1/1/2008 in Step 6 of 7, and finally, a cell to hold the SUM formula in Step 7 of 7.

11. **Click the Next button to display the Conditional Sum Wizard — Step 4 of 4 dialog box.**

If you selected the Copy Just the Formula to a Single Cell option back in Step 10, you now designate the address of the cell to hold the formula in Step 12. If, however, you selected the Copy the Formula and Conditional Values option, you need to specify the cell address for each conditional value plus the conditional SUM formula in however many Conditional Sum Wizard dialog boxes remain.

12. **Click the cell in the worksheet where you want the conditional SUM formula or the first conditional value in the worksheet to appear.**

If you're designating conditional values, click the Next button and continue on in this manner until you reach the final wizard dialog box and have designated the location of the conditional SUM formula.

13. **Click the Finish button in the final wizard dialog box to close the Conditional Sum Wizard and calculate the total based on your condition(s).**

Figure 5-5 shows the resulting SUM formula in cell I10 created by the Conditional Sum Wizard, which calculates the total where the store location is Anderson Rd., the sales item is anything but Strawberry pie, and the date of the sale is after January 1, 2008. As you can see in this figure, in order to accomplish conditional summing, the Conditional Sum Wizard used no less than three IF functions nested within each other within a SUM function all entered as an array formula (indicated by the pair of curly braces surrounding the entire formula).

**Book III
Chapter 5**

Math and Statistical Formulas

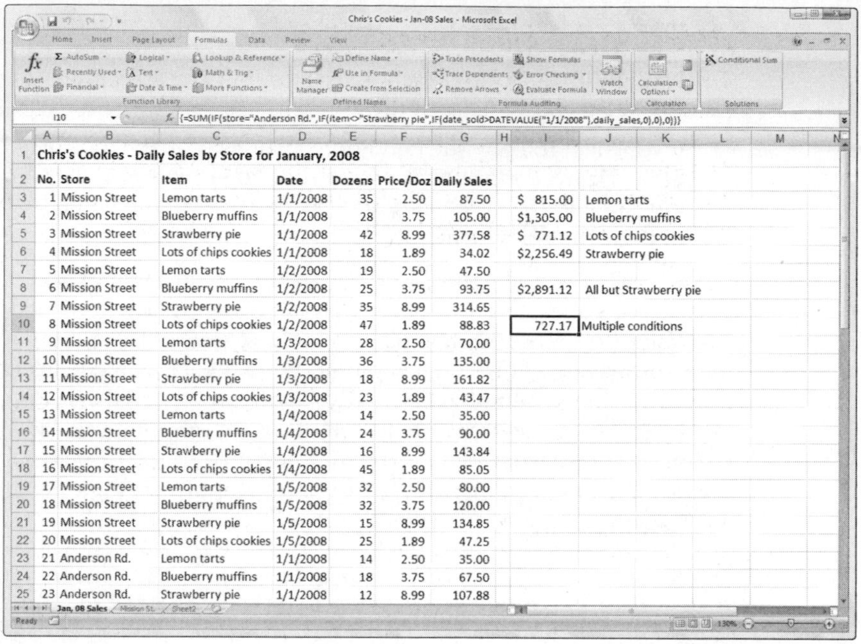

Figure 5-5:
Daily Sales spreadsheet with SUM formula that totals values based on multiple conditions.

Statistical Functions

Excel includes one of the most complete sets of statistical functions available outside a dedicated statistics software program. When you want to access these functions from the Ribbon's Formulas tab instead of the Insert Function dialog box, you need to click the More Functions command button and then highlight the Statistical option at the very top of the drop-down menu (or press Alt+MQS). Doing this displays a continuation menu listing all the Statistical functions in alphabetical order.

The statistical functions run the gamut from the more mundane AVERAGE, MAX, and MIN functions to the more exotic and much more specialized CHITEST, POISSON, and PERCENTILE statistical functions.

In addition to the more specialized statistical functions, Excel offers an assortment of counting functions that enable you to count the number of cells that contain values, are nonblank (and thus contain entries of any kind), or count only the cells in a given range that meet the criteria that you specify.

AVERAGE, MAX, and MIN

The AVERAGE, MAX (for maximum), and MIN (for minimum) functions are the most commonly used of the statistical functions because they are of use to both the average number cruncher as well as the dedicated statistician. All three functions follow the same syntax as the good old SUM function. For example, the syntax of the AVERAGE function uses the following arguments just as the SUM, MAX, and MIN functions do:

```
AVERAGE(number1,[number2],[...])
```

Just as in the SUM function, the *number* arguments are between 1 and 30 numeric arguments for which you want the average. Figure 5-6 illustrates how you can use the AVERAGE, MAX, MIN, and MEDIAN functions in a worksheet. This example uses these functions to compute a few statistics on the selling prices of homes in a particular neighborhood. These statistics include the average, highest, lowest, and median selling price for the homes sold in April and May of 2008. All the statistical functions in this worksheet use the same *number* argument; that is, the cell range C4:C8.

Book III
Chapter 5

Math and Statistical Formulas

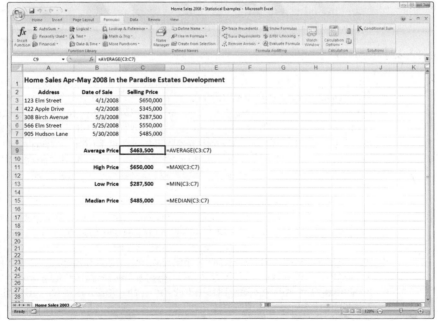

Figure 5-6: Home sales spreadsheet using common statistical functions.

The AVERAGE function computes the arithmetic mean of the values in this range by summing them and then dividing them by the number of values in the range. This AVERAGE function is equivalent to the following formula:

```
=SUM(C4:C8)/COUNT(C4:C8)
```

Note that this formula uses the SUM function to total the values and another statistical function called COUNT to determine the number of values in the list. The MAX and MIN functions simply compute the highest and lowest values in the cell range used as the *number* argument. The MEDIAN function computes the value that is in the middle of the range of values; that is, the one where half the values are greater and half are less. This is the reason that the median sales price (in cell C16) differs from the average sales price (in cell C10) in this worksheet.

Counting cells

Sometimes you need to know how many cells in a particular cell range, column or row, or even worksheet in your spreadsheet have cell entries and how many are still blank. Other times, you need to know just how many of the occupied cells have text entries and how many have numeric entries. Excel includes a number of counting functions that you can use in building formulas that calculate the number of cells in a particular region or worksheet that are occupied and can tell you what general type of entry they contain.

Building counting formulas

Figure 5-7 illustrates the different types of counting formulas that you can build to return such basic statistics as the total number of cells in a particular range, the number of occupied cells in that range, as well as the number of numeric and text entries in the occupied range. In this example spreadsheet, I gave the name sales_data to the cell range A1:C8 (shown selected in Figure 5-7).

I then used the sales_data range name in a number of formulas that count its different aspects. The most basic formula is the one that returns the total number of cells in the sales_data range. To build this formula in cell C10, I used the ROWS and COLUMNS information functions (see Book III, Chapter 6, for more on these types of functions) to return the number of rows and columns in the range, and then I created the following formula that multiplies these two values together:

```
=ROWS(sales_data)*COLUMNS(sales_data)
```

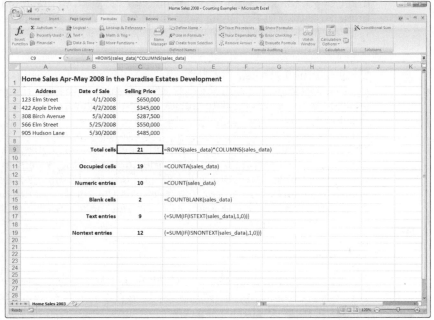

Figure 5-7:
Home sales spreadsheet with various counting formulas.

**Book III
Chapter 5**

Math and Statistical Formulas

This formula, of course, returns 24 to cell C10. In the next formula, I calculated the number of these 24 cells that contain data entries (of whatever type) using the COUNTA function. This function counts the number of cells that are not empty in the ranges that you specify. The COUNTA function uses the following syntax:

```
COUNTA(value1,[value2],[...])
```

The *value* arguments (all of which are optional except for value1) are up to 30 different values or cell ranges that you want counted. Note that the COUNTA function counts a cell as long it has some entry, even if the entry is empty text set off by a single apostrophe ('). In the example shown in Figure 5-7, cell C12 contains the following COUNTA function:

```
=COUNTA(sales_data)
```

This formula returns 19 to cell C12. The next formula in the sample spreadsheet calculates the number of numeric entries in the cell range called sales_data. To do this, you use the COUNT function. The COUNT function takes the same arguments as COUNTA, the only difference being that COUNT counts a value or cell specified in its *value* arguments only if it contains a numeric entry.

Cell C14 contains the following formula for calculating the number of numeric entries in the Home Sales table range called sales_data:

```
=COUNT(sales_data)
```

Excel returns 10 to cell C12. Note that in calculating this result, Excel counts the five date entries (with the date of each sale) in the cell range B4:B8 as well as the five numeric data entries (with the selling prices of each home) in the cell range C4:C8.

The next formula in the sample spreadsheet shown in Figure 5-7 uses the COUNTBLANK function to calculate the number of blank cells in the sales_data range. The COUNTBLANK function works just like the COUNTA and COUNT functions except that it returns the number of nonoccupied cells in the range. For this example, I entered the following COUNTBLANK function in cell C16:

```
=COUNTBLANK(sales_data)
```

Excel then returns 5 to cell C16 (which makes sense because you know that of the 24 total cells in this range, Excel already said that 19 of them have entries of some kind).

The last two counting formulas in the sample spreadsheet shown in Figure 5-7 return the number of text and nontext entries in the sales_data cell range. To do this, instead of counting functions, they use the ISTEXT and ISNONTEXT information functions as part of the IF conditions used with the good old SUM function.

The first formula for returning the number of text entries in the sales_data range in cell C18 is:

```
{=SUM(IF(ISTEXT(sales_data),1,0))}
```

The second formula for returning the number of nontext entries in the sales_data range in cell C20 is just like the one in cell C18 except that it uses the ISNONTEXT function instead of ISTEXT, as follows:

```
{=SUM(IF(ISNONTEXT(sales_data),1,0))}
```

The ISTEXT function in the formula in cell C18 returns logical TRUE when a cell in the sales_data range contains a text entry and FALSE when it does not. The ISNONTEXT function in the formula in cell C20 returns logical TRUE when a cell is blank or contains a numeric entry (in other words, anything but text) and FALSE when it contains text.

In both these formulas, the ISTEXT and ISNONTEXT functions are used as the *logical_test* arguments of an IF function with 1 as the *value_if_true* argument and 0 as the *value_if_false* argument (so that the cells are counted only when the ISTEXT or ISNONTEXT functions return the logical TRUE values). These IF functions are then nested within SUM functions, and these SUM functions, in turn, are entered as array formulas.

Note that you must enter these formulas in the worksheet as array formulas (by pressing Ctrl+Shift+Enter) so that Excel performs its counting calculations on each and every cell in the sales_data cell range. If you just enter the SUM formula with the nested IF and ISTEXT and ISNONTEXT functions as regular formulas, they would return 0 as the count for both text and nontext entries in the sales_data cell range (see Book III, Chapter 1 for details on building array formulas).

Counting occupied cells in entire rows, columns, and worksheets

You can use the COUNTA function to count the number of occupied cells in an entire row or column of a worksheet or even an entire worksheet in your workbook. For example, to count all the occupied cells in row 17 of a worksheet, you enter the following COUNTA formula:

```
=COUNTA(17:17)
```

If you want to find the number of nonblank cells in column B of the worksheet, you enter the following COUNTA formula:

```
=COUNTA(B:B)
```

To find out the number of occupied cells in the entire second worksheet of your workbook (assuming that it's still called Sheet2), you enter this COUNTA formula:

```
=COUNTA(Sheet2!1:1048576)
```

Note that you can also enter the argument for this COUNTA function by designating the entire range of column letters (rather than the range of row numbers) as in:

```
=COUNTA(Sheet2!A:XFD)
```

However, Excel automatically converts the argument that specifies the range of columns to rows, using absolute references ($1:$1048576) as soon as you enter the COUNTA function in its cell.

When entering COUNTA functions that return the number of occupied cells in an entire row, column, or worksheet, you must be sure that you do *not* enter the formula in a cell within that row, column, or worksheet. If you do, Excel displays a Circular Reference Alert dialog box when you try to enter the formula in the worksheet. This happens because you are asking Excel to use the cell with the formula that does the counting in the count itself (definitely the type of circular logic that the program doesn't allow).

Book III
Chapter 5

Math and Statistical Formulas

Conditional counting

Excel includes a COUNTIF function that you can use to count cells in a range only when they meet a certain condition. The COUNTIF function takes two arguments and uses the following syntax:

```
COUNTIF(range,criteria)
```

The *range* argument specifies the range of cells from which the conditional count is to be calculated. The *criteria* argument specifies the condition to use. You can express this argument as a number, expression, or text that indicates which cells to count. When specifying a number for the *criteria* argument, you don't have to enclose the number in quotes. For example, in a cell range named table_data, to count the number of entries that contain the number 5, you enter the following COUNTIF formula:

```
=COUNTIF(table_data,5)
```

However, when specifying an expression or text as the *criteria* argument, you must enclose the expression or text in closed quotes as in "=5", ">20", or "New York". So, if you want to use COUNTIF to find out how many cells in the table_data range have values greater than 5, you enter this version of the COUNTIF function:

```
=COUNTIF(table_data,">5")
```

When you want to use the COUNTIF function to find out the number of cells whose contents are equal to the contents of a particular cell in the worksheet, you just add the cell reference as the function's *criteria* argument. For example, if you want to count the number of cells in the table_data range that are equal to the contents of cell B3 in the worksheet, you enter this formula:

```
=COUNTIF(table_data,B3)
```

However, when you want to specify an expression other than equality that refers to the contents of a cell in the worksheet, you must enclose the operator in a pair of double quotation marks and then add the ampersand (&) concatenation operator before the cell reference. For example, if you want to count how many cells in the table_data range have a value greater than the contents of cell B3, you enter this form of the COUNTIF function:

```
=COUNTIF(table_data,">"&B3)
```

Note that when specifying text as the condition, you can use the two wildcard characters: the asterisk (*) to represent an unspecified amount of characters and the question mark (?) to represent single characters in the COUNTIF function's *criteria* argument. For example, to count all the cells in the table_data range whose text entries end with the word *Street,* you use the asterisk in the COUNTIF *criteria* argument as follows:

```
=COUNTIF(table_data,"*Street")
```

To count the cells in the table_data range whose text entries contain the word *discount* anywhere in the entry, you sandwich *discount* between two asterisks in the COUNTIF *criteria* argument as follows:

```
=COUNTIF(table_data,"*discount*")
```

To count the cells in the table_data range whose cell entries consist of any two characters followed by the letter *y* (as in *day, say, pay,* and so on), you use two question marks to stand in for the nonspecific characters followed by a *y* in the COUNTIF *criteria* argument as in:

```
=COUNTIF(table_data,"??y")
```

When using the COUNTIF function to find the number of cells, you can include other statistical functions as the *criteria* argument. For example, suppose that you want to know the number of cells in the table_data range whose values are less than the average value in the range. To do this, you insert the AVERAGE function in the COUNTIF *criteria* argument as follows:

```
=COUNTIF(table_data,"<"&AVERAGE(table_data))
```

Using specialized statistical functions

You can use the built-in statistical functions found on the Statistical continuation menu or located in the Statistical category in the Insert Function dialog box, both of which I discuss earlier in this chapter. Excel also offers a complete set of special analysis tools as part of the Analysis ToolPak add-in.

The tools included in the Analysis ToolPak enable you to analyze worksheet data by using such things as ANOVA, F-Test, rank and percentile, t-Test, and Fourier analysis. Before you can use the statistical functions added by the Analysis ToolPak, you must install and load it as follows:

1. **Open the Add-Ins tab of the Excel Options dialog box by clicking Office Button | Excel Options | Add-Ins or pressing Alt+FIAA.**

   The Add-Ins tab of the Excel Options dialog box opens; it contains a list of all the add-in programs installed on your computer.

2. **Click the Go button at the bottom of the Add-Ins tab of the Excel Options dialog box after you make sure that the Manage drop-down list box contains Excel Add-Ins.**

   Excel opens the Add-Ins dialog box.

3. **Click the Analysis ToolPak check box in the Add-Ins dialog box to put a check mark in it and then click the OK button.**

4. **If an alert dialog box asking you if you want to install the add-in appears, click its Yes button.**

After you load the Analysis ToolPak in this manner, you then access the statistical analysis tools by clicking the Data Analysis command button in the Analysis group added to the end of the Ribbon's Data tab. When you choose this command, Excel opens the Data Analysis dialog box, as shown in Figure 5-8.

Figure 5-8:
Selecting a statistical analysis tool added by the Analysis ToolPak.

The Data Analysis dialog box lists all the statistical analysis tools added by the Analysis ToolPak from ANOVA: Single Factor at the very top down to z-Test: Two Sample for Means at the bottom of the list. To use one of these tools in your spreadsheet, click its name in the Analysis Tools list box and then click OK. Excel then opens another dialog box specific to the tool that you selected, where you can specify the data and the options that you want used in the analysis.

For general help with the function and use of the various statistical analysis tools added by the Analysis ToolPak, click the Help button (the one with the question mark) in the Data Analysis dialog box. For specific help on a statistical analysis function you've selected, click the Help button in the particular function's dialog box.

Chapter 6: Lookup, Information, and Text Formulas

In This Chapter

✓ Looking up data in a table and adding it to a list

✓ Using the Lookup Wizard to perform two-way lookups

✓ Transposing vertical cell ranges to horizontal and vice versa

✓ Getting information about a cell's contents

✓ Evaluating a cell's type with the IS information functions

✓ Using text functions to manipulate text entries

✓ Creating formulas that combine text entries

This chapter covers three categories of Excel functions: the lookup and reference functions that return values and cell addresses from the spreadsheet, the information functions that return particular types of information about cells in the spreadsheet, and the text functions that enable you to manipulate strings of text in the spreadsheet.

In these three different categories of Excel functions, perhaps none are as handy as the lookup functions that enable you to have Excel look up certain data in a table and then return other related data from that same table based on the results of that lookup. In fact, this type of procedure is considered of such great importance that Excel includes a Lookup Wizard add-in that walks you through the steps for building lookup formulas that perform a special type of two-way table lookup.

Lookup and Reference

The lookup functions are located on the Lookup & Reference command button's drop-down list (Alt+MO) on the Ribbon's Formulas tab. Excel makes it easy to perform table lookups that either return information about entries in the table or actually return related data to other data lists in the spreadsheet. By using Lookup tables to input information into a data list, you not only reduce the amount of data input that you have to do, but also eliminate the possibility of data entry errors. Using Lookup tables also makes it a snap to update your data lists: All you have to do is make the edits to the entries in the original Lookup table or schedule to have all their data entries in the list updated as well.

The reference functions in Excel enable you to return specific information about particular cells or parts of the worksheet; create hyperlinks to different documents on your computer, network, or the Internet; and transpose ranges of vertical cells so that they run horizontally and vice versa.

Looking up a single value with VLOOKUP and HLOOKUP

The most popular of the lookup functions are HLOOKUP (for Horizontal Lookup) and VLOOKUP (for Vertical Lookup) functions. These functions are located in the Lookup & Reference category in the Insert Function dialog box. They are part of a powerful group of functions that can return values by looking them up in data tables.

The VLOOKUP function searches vertically (top to bottom) the leftmost column of a Lookup table until the program locates a value that matches or exceeds the one you are looking up. The HLOOKUP function searches horizontally (left to right) the topmost row of a Lookup table until it locates a value that matches or exceeds the one that you're looking up.

The VLOOKUP function uses the following syntax:

```
=VLOOKUP(lookup_value,table_array,col_index_num,[range_lookup])
```

The HLOOKUP function follows the nearly identical syntax:

```
=HLOOKUP(lookup_value,table_array,row_index_num,[range_lookup])
```

In both functions, the *lookup_value* argument is the value that you want to look up in the Lookup table, table_array is the cell range or name of the Lookup table that contains both the value to look up and the related value to return.

The *col_index_num* argument in the VLOOKUP function is the number of the column whose values are compared to the *lookup_value* argument in a vertical table. The *row_index_num* argument in the HLOOKUP function is the number of the row whose values are compared to the *lookup_value* in a horizontal table.

When entering the *col_index_num* or *row_index_num* arguments in the VLOOKUP and HLOOKUP functions, you must enter a value greater than zero that does not exceed the total number of columns or rows in the Lookup table.

The optional *range_lookup* argument in both the VLOOKUP and the HLOOKUP functions is the logical TRUE or FALSE that specifies whether you want Excel to find an exact or approximate match for the *lookup_value* in the table_array. When you specify TRUE or omit the *range_lookup* argument in the VLOOKUP or HLOOKUP function, Excel finds an approximate match. When you specify FALSE as the *range_lookup* argument, Excel finds only exact matches.

Finding approximate matches pertains only when you're looking up numeric entries (rather than text) in the first column or row of the vertical or horizontal Lookup table. When Excel doesn't find an exact match in this Lookup column or row, it locates the next highest value that doesn't exceed the *lookup_value* argument and then returns the value in the column or row designated by the *col_index_num* or *row_index_num* arguments.

When using the VLOOKUP and HLOOKUP functions, the text or numeric entries in the Lookup column or row (that is, the leftmost column of a vertical Lookup table or the top row of a horizontal Lookup table) must be unique. These entries must also be arranged or sorted in ascending order; that is, alphabetical order for text entries, and lowest-to-highest order for numeric entries (see Book VI, Chapter 1 for detailed information on sorting data in a spreadsheet).

Figure 6-1 shows an example of using the VLOOKUP function to return either a 15% or 20% tip from a tip table, depending on the pretax total of the check. Cell F5 contains the VLOOKUP function:

```
=VLOOKUP(Pretax_Total,Tip_Table,IF(Tip_Percentage=0.15,2,3))
```

This formula returns the amount of the tip based on the tip percentage in cell F3 and the pretax amount of the check in cell F4.

To use this tip table, enter the percentage of the tip (15% or 20%) in cell F2 (named Tip_Percentage) and the amount of the check before tax in cell F3 (named Pretax_Total). Excel then looks up the value that you enter in the Pretax_Total cell in the first column of the Lookup table, which includes the cell range A2:C101 and is named Tip_Table.

Excel then moves down the values in the first column of Tip_Table until it finds a match, whereupon the program uses the *col_index_num* argument in the VLOOKUP function to determine which tip amount from that row of the table to return to cell F4. If Excel finds that the value entered in the Pretax_Total cell ($16.50 in this example) doesn't exactly match one of the values in the first column of Tip_Table, the program continues to search down the comparison range until it encounters the first value that exceeds the pretax total (17.00 in cell A19 in this example). Excel then moves back up to the previous row in the table and returns the value in the column that matches the *col_index_num* argument of the VLOOKUP function (this is because the optional *range_lookup* argument has been omitted from the function).

Note that the tip table example in Figure 6-1 uses an IF function to determine the *col_index_num* argument for the VLOOKUP function in cell F4. The IF function determines the column number to be used in the tip table by matching the percentage entered in Tip_Percentage (cell F2) with 0.15. If they match, the function returns 2 as the *col_index_num* argument and the VLOOKUP function returns a value from the second column (the 15% column B) in the Tip_Table range. Otherwise, the IF function returns 3 as the *col_index_num* argument and the VLOOKUP function returns a value from the third column (the 20% column C) in the Tip_Table range.

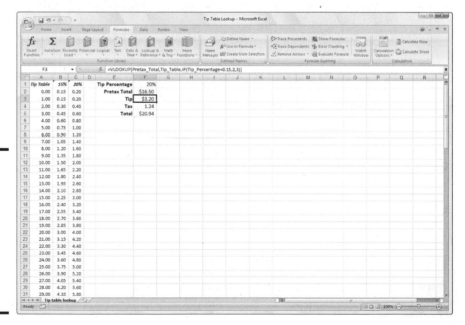

Figure 6-1:
Using the VLOOKUP function to return the amount of the tip to add from a Lookup table.

Figure 6-2 shows an example that uses the HLOOKUP function to look up the price of each bakery item stored in a separate price Lookup table and then to return that price to the Price/Doz column of the Daily Sales list. Cell F7 contains the original formula with the HLOOKUP function that is then copied down column F:

```
=HLOOKUP(item,prices,2,FALSE)
```

In this HLOOKUP function, the range name Item that's given to the Item column in the range C7:C66 is defined as the *lookup_value* argument and the cell range name Prices that's given to the cell range D3:G4 is the *table_array* argument. The *row_index_num* argument is 2 because you want Excel to return the prices in the second row of the Prices Lookup table, and the optional *range_lookup* argument is FALSE because the item name in the Daily Sales list must match exactly the item name in the Prices Lookup table.

By having the HLOOKUP function use the Prices Lookup table to input the price per dozen for each bakery goods item in the Daily Sales list, you make it a very simple matter to update any of the sales in the list. All you have to do is change its Price/Doz cost in the Prices Lookup table, and the HLOOKUP function immediately updates the new price in the Daily Sales list wherever the item is sold.

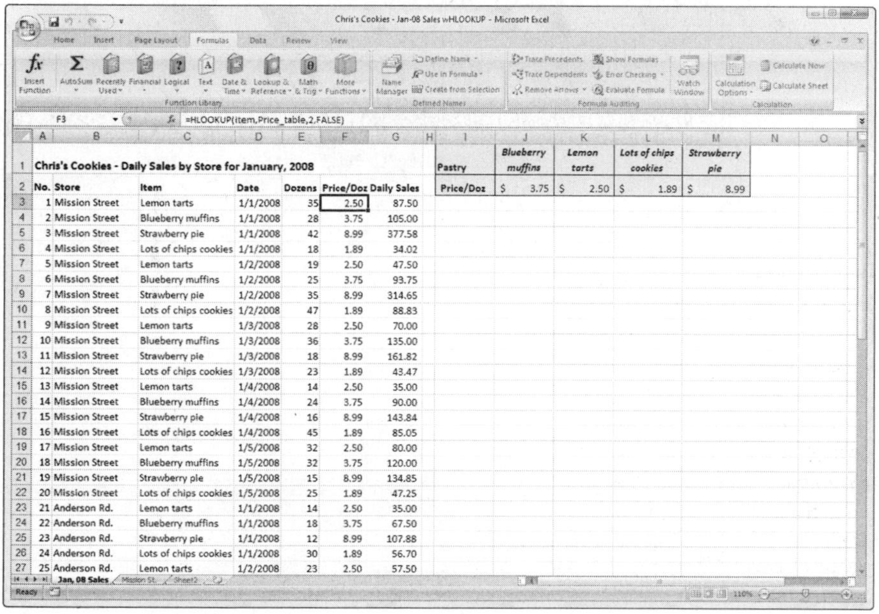

Figure 6-2: Using the HLOOKUP function to return the price of a bakery item from a Lookup table.

Performing a two-way lookup

In both the VLOOKUP and HLOOKUP examples, Excel only compares a single value in the data list to a single value in the vertical or horizontal Lookup table. Sometimes, however, you may have a table in which you need to perform a two-way lookup, whereby a piece of data is retrieved from the Lookup table based on looking up a value in the top row (with the table's column headings) and a value in the first column (with the table's row headings).

Figure 6-3 illustrates a situation in which you would use two values, the production date and the part number, to look up the expected production. In the 2008 Production Schedule table, the production dates for each part form the column headings in the first row of the table, and the part numbers form the row headings in its first column of the table.

To look up the number of parts to be produced for a particular month, you need to the use the MATCH function, which returns the relative position of a particular value in a cell range or array. The syntax of the MATCH function is as follows:

```
=MATCH(lookup_value,lookup_array,[match_type])
```

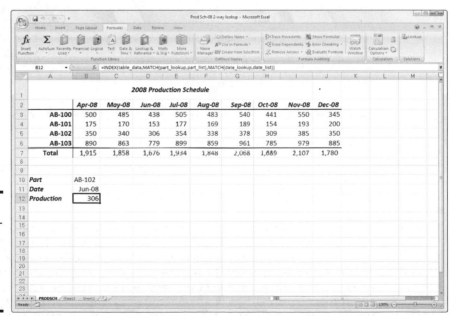

Figure 6-3: Doing a two-way lookup in the Production Schedule table.

The *lookup_value* argument is, of course, the value whose position you want returned when a match is found, and the *lookup_array* is the cell range or array containing the values that you want to match. The optional *match_type* argument is the number 1, 0, or –1, which specifies how Excel matches the value specified by the *lookup_value* argument in the range specified by the *lookup_array* argument:

✦ Use *match_type 1* to find the largest value that is less than or equal to the *lookup_value*. Note that the values in the *lookup_array* must be placed in ascending order when you use the 1 *match_type* argument (Excel uses this type of matching when the *match_type* argument is omitted from the MATCH function).

✦ Use *match_type 0* to find the first value that is exactly equal to the *lookup_value*. Note that the values in the *lookup_array* can be in an order when you use the 0 *match_type* argument.

✦ Use *match_type –1* to find the smallest value that is greater than or equal to the *lookup_value*. Note that the values in the *lookup_array* must be placed in descending order when you use the –1 *match_type* argument.

In addition to looking up the position of the production date and part number in the column and row headings in the Production Schedule table, you need to use an INDEX function, which uses the relative row and column number position to return the number to be produced from the table itself. The INDEX function follows two different syntax forms: array and reference. You use the array form when you want a value returned from the table (as you do in this example), and you use the reference form when you want a reference returned from the table.

The syntax of the array form of the INDEX function is as follows:

```
=INDEX(array,[row_num],[col_num])
```

The syntax of the reference form of the INDEX function is as follows:

```
=INDEX(reference,[row_num],[col_num],[area_num])
```

The *array* argument of the array form of the INDEX function is a range of cells or array constant that you want Excel to use in the lookup. If this range or constant contains only one row or column, the corresponding *row_num* or *col_num* arguments are optional. If the range or array constant has more than one row or more than one column, and you specify both the *row_num* and the *col_num* arguments, Excel returns the value in the *array* argument that is located at the intersection of the *row_num* argument and the *col_num* argument.

**Book III
Chapter 6**

**Lookup, Information,
and Text Formulas**

For the MATCH and INDEX functions in the example shown in Figure 6-3, I assigned the following range names to the following cell ranges:

✦ Table_data to the cell range A2:J6 with the production data plus column and row headings

✦ Part_list to the cell range A2:A6 with the row headings in the first column of the table

✦ Date_list to the cell range A2:J2 with the column headings in the first row of the table

✦ Part_lookup to cell B10 that contains the name of the part to look up in the table

✦ Date_lookup to cell B11 that contains the name of the production date to look up in the table

As Figure 6-3 shows, cell B12 contains a rather long and — at first glance — complex formula using the range names outlined previously and combining the INDEX and MATCH functions:

```
=INDEX(table_data,MATCH(part_lookup,part_list),MATCH(date_
     lookup,date_list))
```

So you can better understand how this formula works, I break the formula down into its three major components: the first MATCH function that returns the *row_num* argument for the INDEX function, the second MATCH function that returns the *col_num* argument for the INDEX function, and the INDEX function itself that uses the values returned by the two MATCH functions to return the number of parts produced.

The first MATCH function that returns the *row_num* argument for the INDEX function is:

```
=MATCH(part_lookup,part_list)
```

This MATCH function uses the value input into cell B10 (named part_lookup) and looks up its position in the cell range A2:A6 (named part_list). It then returns this row number to the INDEX function as its *row_num* argument. In the case of the example shown in Figure 6-3 where part AB-102 is entered in the part_lookup cell in B10, Excel returns 4 as the *row_num* argument to the INDEX function.

The second MATCH function that returns the *col_num* argument for the INDEX function is:

```
=MATCH(date_lookup,date_list)
```

This second MATCH function uses the value input into cell B11 (named date_lookup) and looks up its position in the cell range A2:J2 (named date_list). It then returns this column number to the INDEX function as its *col_num* argument. In the case of the example shown in Figure 6-3 where June 1, 2008 (formatted as Jun-08), is entered in the date_lookup cell in B11, Excel returns 4 as the *col_num* argument to the INDEX function.

This means that for all its supposed complexity, the INDEX function shown on the Formula bar in Figure 6-3 contains the equivalent of the following formula:

```
=INDEX(table_data,4,4)
```

As Figure 6-3 shows, Excel returns 306 as the planned production value for part AB-102 in June, 2008. You can verify that this is correct by manually counting the rows and the columns in the table_data range (cell range A2:J6). If you count down four rows (including row 2, the first row of this range), you come to Part 102 in column A. If you then count four columns over (including column A with AB-102), you come to cell D5 in the Jun-08 column with the value 306.

Using the Lookup Wizard

Instead of using the INDEX and MATCH lookup functions to do a two-way lookup, you can use the Lookup Wizard add-in to build the necessary formulas. Before you can use the Lookup Wizard, you must install and load it by following these steps:

1. **Open the Add-Ins tab of the Excel Options dialog box by clicking Office Button | Excel Options | Add-Ins or pressing Alt+FIAA.**

   The Add-Ins tab of the Excel Options dialog box opens; it contains a list of all the add-in programs installed on your computer.

2. **Click the Go button at the bottom of the Add-Ins tab of the Excel Options dialog box after you make sure that the Manage drop-down list box contains Excel Add-Ins.**

   Excel opens the Add-Ins dialog box.

3. **Click the Lookup Wizard check box in the Add-Ins dialog box to select it and then click the OK button.**

4. **Click the Yes button in the alert dialog box asking you if you want to install the add-in.**

After you install and load the Lookup Wizard add-in, Excel adds a Lookup command button to the Solutions group at the end of the Ribbon's Formulas tab that you can launch by clicking it.

To better understand how this works, follow these steps for using the Lookup Wizard to extract the number of items produced for a particular part number and date in the Production Schedule table shown in Figure 6-3:

1. **Click the Lookup command button in the Solutions group on the Ribbon's Formulas tab.**

   Excel opens the Lookup Wizard — Step 1 of 4 dialog box (similar to the one shown in Figure 6-4), where you select the range of cells that contains the values to be used in the lookup. In the example shown in Figure 6-4, I selected the cell range A2:J6 as the range on which to perform the lookup (and because this range is named table_data, I could have entered it in the Where Is the Range to Search, Including the Row and Column Labels combo box instead of selecting the cell range).

2. **Click the Next button in the Lookup Wizard — Step 1 of 4 dialog box.**

   After you click the Next button, the Lookup Wizard — Step 2 of 4 dialog box appears (similar to the one shown in Figure 6-5), where you select first the column and then the row that contains the value you want looked up in the cell range that you just designated in the Step 1 of 4 dialog box.

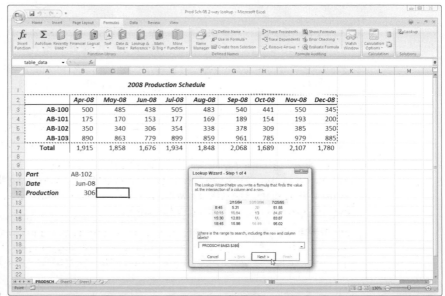

Figure 6-4: Selecting the cell range to search in the Step 1 of 4 dialog box.

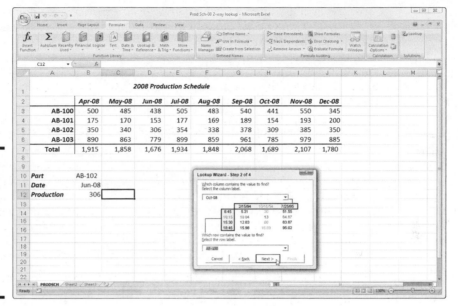

Figure 6-5:
Selecting
the column
and rows
with the
values to
find in the
Step 2 of 4
dialog box.

3. **Click the name of the column in the Which Column Contains the Value to Find drop-down list that you open by clicking its drop-down button.**

For this example, I designate Oct-08 as the column to use by clicking its name on this column drop-down list.

4. **Click the name of the row in the Which Row Contains the Value to Find drop-down list that you open by clicking its drop-down button.**

For this example, I designate part AB-100 as the row to use by clicking its name on this row drop-down list.

5. **Click the Next button in the Lookup Wizard — Step 2 of 4 dialog box.**

Excel displays the Lookup Wizard — Step 3 of 4 dialog box, where you choose between the Copy Just the Formula to a Single Cell option button and the Copy the Formula and Lookup Parameters option button.

6. **Leave the Copy Just the Formula to a Single Cell option button selected to have only the formula inserted in a cell. Click the Copy the Formula and Lookup Parameters option button to have column and row information copied along with the formula.**

For this example, I clicked the Copy the Formula and Lookup Parameters option button to have Excel copy both the date and the part number into the worksheet above the lookup formula that it creates (see Figure 6-6).

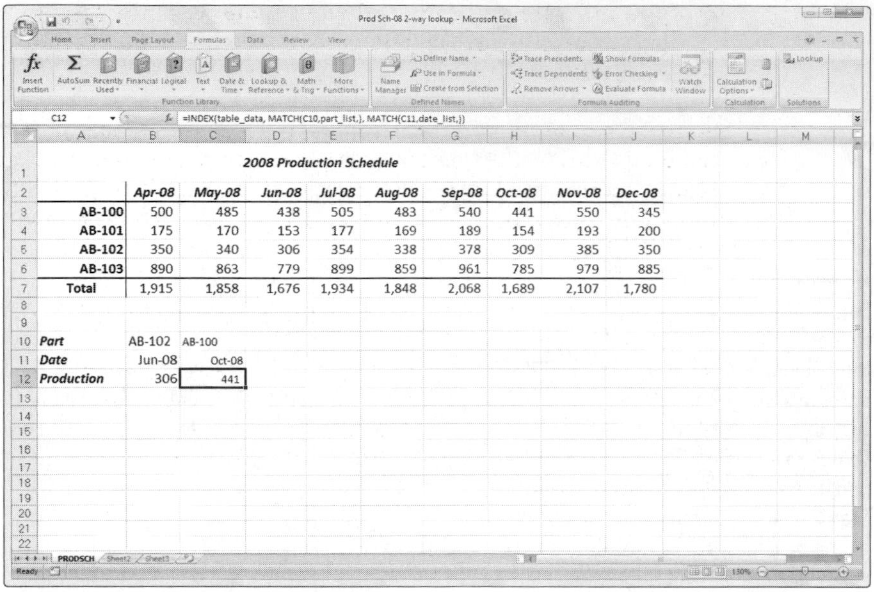

Figure 6-6: Spreadsheet after inserting the lookup formula with parameters in the cell range C10:C12.

7. **Click the Next button in the Lookup Wizard — Step 3 of 4 dialog box.**

When you leave the Copy Just the Formula to a Single Cell option button selected, Excel displays the Lookup Wizard — Step 4 of 4 dialog box where you indicate the cell where the formula is to be copied (see Step 10).

When you click the Copy the Formula and Lookup Parameters option button, the Lookup Wizard — Step 4 of 6 dialog box appears. In this dialog box, you designate the address of the cell into which to copy the column parameter (Oct-08 in this example).

8. **Type the address of the cell where you want the column parameter copied, or click the cell directly in the spreadsheet and then click the Next button.**

Excel displays the Lookup Wizard — Step 5 of 6 dialog box where you indicate the address of the cell into which to copy the row parameter (AB-100 in this example).

9. **Type the address of the cell where you want the row parameter copied, or click the cell directly in the spreadsheet and then click the Next button.**

Excel displays the Lookup Wizard — Step 6 of 6 dialog box, where you indicate the address of the cell into which to copy the formula that looks up the value at the intersection of the column and row parameter.

10. **Type the address of the cell where you want the lookup formula to appear, or click the cell directly in the spreadsheet and then click the Finish button.**

Figure 6-6 shows what happened when I clicked the Finish button in the Lookup Wizard — Step 6 of 6 dialog box. As you can see, the final formula created and inserted into cell C12 by the Lookup Wizard uses the INDEX function to look up the column and row numbers returned by the following two MATCH functions:

```
=INDEX(table_data,MATCH(C10,part_list),MATCH(C11,date_list))
```

So there you have it — a foolproof way to create a sophisticated two-way lookup formula without having to go through all the trouble of correctly nesting the MATCH functions within an INDEX function, not to mention entering all the necessary arguments and properly pairing parentheses yourself!

Reference functions

The reference functions on the Lookup & Reference command button's drop-down list on the Formulas tab of the Ribbon are designed to deal specifically with different aspects of cell references in the worksheet. This group of functions includes:

**Book III
Chapter 6**

Lookup, Information, and Text Formulas

✦ ADDRESS to return a cell reference as a text entry in a cell of the worksheet

✦ AREAS to return the number of areas in a list of values (*areas* are defined as a range of contiguous cells or a single cell in the cell reference)

✦ COLUMN to return the number representing the column position of a cell reference

✦ COLUMNS to return the number of columns in a reference

✦ HYPERLINK to create a link that opens another document stored on your computer, network, or the Internet (you can also do this with the Insert➪Hyperlink command — see Book IV, Chapter 2 for details)

✦ INDIRECT to return a cell reference specified by a text string and bring the contents in the cell to which it refers to that cell

✦ ROW to return the row number of a cell reference

✦ ROWS to return the number of rows in a cell range or array

✦ TRANSPOSE to return a vertical array as a horizontal array and vice versa

Get the skinny on columns and rows

The COLUMNS and ROWS functions return the number of columns and rows in a particular cell range or array. For example, if you have a cell range in the spreadsheet named product_mix, you can find out how many columns it contains by entering this formula:

```
=COLUMNS(product_mix)
```

If you want to know how many rows this range uses, you then enter this formula:

```
=ROWS(product_mix)
```

As indicated in the previous chapter, you can use the COLUMNS and ROWS functions together to calculate the total number of cells in a particular range. For example, if you want to know the exact number of cells used in the product_mix cell range, you create the following simple multiplication formula by using the COLUMNS and ROWS functions:

```
=COLUMNS(product_mix)*ROWS(product_mix)
```

Don't confuse the COLUMNS (plural) function with the COLUMN (singular) function and the ROWS (plural) function with the ROW (singular) function. The COLUMN function returns the number of the column (as though Excel were using the R1C1 reference system) for the cell reference that you specify as its sole argument. Likewise, the ROW function returns the number of the row for the cell reference that you specify as its argument.

Transposing cell ranges

The TRANSPOSE function enables you to change the orientation of a cell range (or array — see the section on entering array formulas in Book III, Chapter 1 for details). You can use this function to transpose a vertical cell range where the data runs down the rows of adjacent columns to one where the data runs across the columns of adjacent rows and vice versa. To successfully use the TRANSPOSE function, not only must you select a range that has an opposite number of columns and rows, but you must also enter it as an array formula.

For example, if you're using the TRANSPOSE function to transpose a 2 x 5 cell range (that is, a range that takes up two adjacent rows and five adjacent columns), you must select a blank 5 x 2 cell range (that is, a range that takes five adjacent rows and two adjacent columns) in the worksheet before you use the Insert Function button to insert the TRANSPOSE function in the first cell. Then, after selecting the 2 x 5 cell range that contains the data that you want to transpose in the Array text box of the Function Arguments dialog box, you need to press Ctrl+Shift+Enter to close this dialog box and enter the TRANSPOSE function into the entire selected cell range as an array formula (enclosed in curly braces).

Suppose that you want to transpose the data entered into the cell range A10:C11 (a 2 x 3 array) to the blank cell range E10:F12 (a 3 x 2 array) of the worksheet. When you press Ctrl+Shift+Enter to complete the array formula, after selecting the cell range A10:A11 as the *array* argument, Excel puts the following array formula in every cell of the range:

```
{=TRANSPOSE(A10:C11)}
```

Figure 6-7 illustrates the use of the TRANSPOSE function. The cell range B2:C4 contains the original 3 x 2 array that I showed earlier in Figure 1-8 in Book III, Chapter 1 when discussing how you add array formulas to your worksheet. To convert this 3 x 2 array in the cell range B2:C4 to a 2 x 3 array in the range B6:D7, I followed these steps:

1. **Select the blank cell range B6:D7 in the worksheet.**

2. **Click the Lookup & Reference command button on the Ribbon's Formulas tab and then click the TRANSPOSE option on the button's drop-down menu.**

   Excel inserts =TRANSPOSE() on the Formula bar and opens the Function Arguments dialog box where the Array argument text box is selected.

3. **Drag through the cell range B2:C4 in the worksheet so that the Array argument text box contains B2:C4 and the formula on the Formula bar now reads =TRANSPOSE(B2:C4).**

4. **Press Ctrl+Shift+Enter to close the Insert Arguments dialog box (don't click OK) and to insert the TRANSPOSE array formula into the cell range B6:D7, as shown in Figure 6-7.**

Clicking the OK button in the Function Arguments dialog box inserts the TRANSPOSE function into the active cell of the current cell selection. Doing this returns the #VALUE! error value to the cell. You must remember to press Ctrl+Shift+Enter to both close the dialog box and put the formula into the entire cell range.

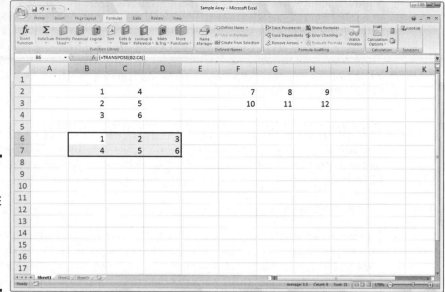

Figure 6-7:
Using the
TRANSPOSE
function to
change the
orientation
of a simple
array.

If all you want to do is transpose row and column headings or a simple table
of data, you don't have to go through the rigmarole of creating an array formula using the TRANSPOSE function. Simply copy the range of cells to be
transposed with the Copy command button on the Home tab of the Ribbon.
Position the cell cursor in the first empty cell where the transposed range is
to be pasted before you click the Transpose option on the Paste command
button's drop-down menu.

Information, Please . . .

The information functions on the continuation menu accessed by clicking
the More Functions command button on the Formulas tab of the Ribbon and
then highlighting the Information option (or by pressing Alt+MQI) consist of
a number of functions designed to test the contents of a cell or cell range
and give you information on its current contents.

These kinds of information functions are often combined with IF functions,
which determine what type of calculation, if any, to perform. The information function then becomes the *logical_test* argument of the IF function, and
the outcome of the test, expressed as the logical TRUE or logical FALSE
value, decides whether its *value_if_true* or its *value_if_false* argument is executed (see Book III, Chapter 2 for information on using information functions
that test for error values to trap errors in a spreadsheet).

In addition to the many information functions that test whether the contents of a cell are of a certain type, Excel offers a smaller set of functions that return coded information about a cell's contents or formatting and about the current operating environment in which the workbook is functioning. The program also offers an N (for Number) function that returns the value in a cell and an NA (for Not Available) function that inserts the #NA error value in the cell.

Getting specific information about a cell

The CELL function is the basic information function for getting all sorts of data about the current contents and formatting of a cell. The syntax of the CELL function is:

```
=CELL(info_type,[reference])
```

The *info_type* argument is a text value that specifies the type of cell information you want returned. The optional *reference* argument is the reference of the cell range for which you want information. When you omit this argument, Excel specifies the type of information specified by the *info_type* argument for the last cell that was changed in the worksheet. When you specify a cell range as the *reference* argument, Excel returns the type of information specified by the *info_type* argument for the first cell in the range (that is, the one in the upper-left corner, which may or may not be the active cell of the range).

Table 6-1 shows the various *info_type* arguments that you can specify when using the CELL function. Remember that you must enclose each *info_type* argument in the CELL function in double-quotes (to enter them as text values) to prevent Excel from returning the #NAME? error value to the cell containing the CELL function formula. So, for example, if you want to return the contents of the first cell in the range B10:E80, you enter the following formula:

```
=CELL("contents",B10:E80)
```

Book III Chapter 6

Lookup, Information, and Text Formulas

Table 6-1	The *info_type* Arguments of the CELL Function
info_type	*Returns*
"address"	Cell address of the first cell in the reference as text using absolute cell references
"col"	Column number of the first cell in the reference
"color"	1 when the cell is formatted in color for negative values; otherwise returns 0 (zero)

(continued)

Table 6-1 *(continued)*

info_type	*Returns*
"contents"	Value of the upper-left cell in the reference
"coord"	Absolute reference of the cell range as text
"filename"	Filename (including the full pathname) of the file containing the cell reference: returns empty text,"", when the workbook containing the reference has not yet been saved
"format"	Text value of the number format of the cell (see Table 6-2): returns "-" at the end of the text value when the cell is formatted in color for negative values and "()" when the value is formatted with parentheses for positive values or for all values
"parentheses"	1 when the cell is formatted with parentheses for positive values or for all values
"prefix"	Text value of the label prefix used in the cell: single quote (') when text is left-aligned; double quote (") when text is right-aligned; caret (^) when text is centered; backslash (\) when text is fill-aligned; and empty text ("") when cell contains any other type of entry
"protect"	0 when the cell is unlocked and 1 when the cell is locked (see Book IV, Chapter 1 for details on protecting cells in a worksheet)
"row"	Row number of the first cell in the reference
"type"	Text value of the type of data in the cell: "b" for blank when cell is empty; "l" for label when cell contains text constant; and "v" for value when cell contains any other entry
"width"	Column width of the cell rounded off to the next highest integer (each unit of column width is equal to the width of one character in Excel's default font size)

Table 6-2 shows the different text values along with their number formats (codes) that can be returned when you specify "format" as the *info_type* argument in a CELL function (refer to Book II, Chapter 3 for details on number formats and the meaning of the various number format codes).

Table 6-2	**Text Values Returned by the "format"** *info_type*
Text Value	*Number Formatting*
"G"	General
"F0"	0
",0"	#,##0
"F2"	0.00
",2"	#,##0.00

Text Value	Number Formatting
"C0"	$,##0_);($,##0)
"C0-"	$,##0_);[Red]($,##0)
"C2"	$,##0.00_);($,##0.00)
"C2-"	$,##0.00_);[Red]($,##0.00)
"P0"	0%
"P2"	0.00%
"S2"	0.00E+00
"G"	# ?/? or # ??/??
"D4"	m/d/yy or m/d/yy h:mm or mm/dd/yy
"D1"	d-mmm-yy or dd-mmm-yy
"D2"	d-mmm or dd-mmm
"D3"	mmm-yy
"D5"	mm/dd
"D7"	h:mm AM/PM
"D6"	h:mm:ss AM/PM
"D9"	h:mm
"D8"	h:mm:ss

For example, if you use the CELL function that specifies "format" as the *info_type* argument on cell range A10:C28 (which you've formatted with the Comma style button on the Formula bar), as in the following formula:

```
=CELL("format",A10:C28)
```

Excel returns the text value ",2-" (sans quotes) in the cell where you enter this formula signifying that the first cell uses the Comma style format with two decimal places and that negative values are displayed in color (red) and enclosed in parentheses.

Are you my type?

Excel provides another information function that returns the type of value in a cell. Aptly named, the TYPE function enables you to build formulas with the IF function that execute one type of behavior when the cell being tested contains a value and another when it contains text. The syntax of the TYPE function is:

```
=TYPE(value)
```

The *value* argument of the TYPE function can be any Excel entry: text, number, logical value, or even an Error value or a cell reference that contains such a value. The TYPE function returns the following values, indicating the type of contents:

✦ 1 for numbers

✦ 2 for text

✦ 3 for logical value (TRUE or FALSE)

✦ 4 for an array range or constant (see Book III, Chapter 1)

The following formula combines the CELL and TYPE functions nested within an IF function. This formula returns the type of the number formatting used in cell D11 only when the cell contains a value. Otherwise, it assumes that D11 contains a text entry, and it evaluates the type of alignment assigned to the text in that cell:

```
=IF(TYPE(D11)=1,CELL("format",D11),CELL("prefix",D11))
```

Using the IS functions

The IS information functions (as in ISBLANK, ISERR, and so on) are a large group of functions that perform essentially the same task. They evaluate a value or cell reference and return the logical TRUE or FALSE, depending on whether the value is or isn't the type for which the IS function tests. For example, if you use the ISBLANK function to test the contents of cell A1 as in:

```
=ISBLANK(A1)
```

Excel returns TRUE to the cell containing the formula when A1 is empty and FALSE when it's occupied by any type of entry.

Excel offers nine built-in IS information functions:

✦ ISBLANK(*value*) to evaluate whether the value or cell reference is empty

✦ ISERR(*value*) to evaluate whether the value or cell reference contains an Error value (except for #NA)

✦ ISERROR(*value*) to evaluate whether the value or cell reference contains an Error value (including #NA)

✦ ISLOGICAL(*value*) to evaluate whether the value or cell reference contains the logical TRUE or FALSE value

✦ ISNA(*value*) to evaluate whether the value or cell reference contains the special #NA Error value

✦ ISNONTEXT(*value*) to evaluate whether the value or cell reference contains any type of entry other than text

✦ ISNUMBER(*value*) to evaluate whether the value or cell reference contains a number

✦ ISREF(*value*) to evaluate whether the value or cell reference is itself a cell reference

✦ ISTEXT(*value*) to evaluate whether the value or cell reference contains a text entry

In addition to these nine IS functions, Excel adds two more, ISEVEN and ISODD, when you activate the Analysis ToolPak add-in. The ISEVEN function evaluates whether the number or reference to a cell containing a number is even, whereas the ISODD function evaluates whether it is odd. (For an example of how to use the ISERROR function, refer to the section on error trapping in Book III, Chapter 2.)

Much Ado about Text

Normally, when you think of doing calculations in a spreadsheet, you think of performing operations on its numeric entries. You can, however, use the text functions as well as the concatenation operator (&) to perform operations on its text entries as well (referred to collectively as *string operations*).

Using text functions

Text functions found on the Text command button's drop-down menu on the Ribbon's Formulas tab (Alt+MT) include two types of functions: functions such as VALUE, TEXT, and DOLLAR that convert numeric text entries into numbers and numeric entries into text, and functions such as UPPER, LOWER, and PROPER that manipulate the strings of text themselves.

Many times, you need to use the text functions when you work with data from other programs. For example, suppose that you purchase a target client list on disk, only to discover that all the information has been entered in all uppercase letters. In order to use this data with your word processor's Mail merge feature, you would use Excel's PROPER function to convert the entries so that only the initial letter of each word is in uppercase.

Text functions such as the UPPER, LOWER, and PROPER functions all take a single *text* argument that indicates the text that should be manipulated. The UPPER function converts all letters in the *text* argument to upper-case. The LOWER function converts all letters in the *text* argument to lowercase. The PROPER function capitalizes the first letter of each word as well as any other letters in the *text* argument that don't follow another letter, and changes all other letters in the *text* argument to lowercase.

Figure 6-8 illustrates a situation in which you would use the PROPER function. Here, both last and first name text entries have been made in all uppercase letters. Follow these steps for using the PROPER function to convert text entries to the proper capitalization:

1. **Position the cell cursor in cell C3 and then click the Text command button on the Ribbon's Formulas tab (or press Alt+MT) and then click PROPER on its drop-down menu.**

   The Function Arguments dialog box for the PROPER function opens with the Text box selected.

2. **Click cell A3 in the worksheet to insert A3 in the Text box of the Function Arguments dialog box and then click OK to insert the PROPER function into cell C3.**

   Excel closes the Insert Function dialog box and inserts the formula =PROPER(A3) in cell C3, which now contains the proper capitalization of the last name Aiken.

3. **Drag the Fill handle in the lower-right corner of cell C3 to the right to cell D3 and then release the mouse button to copy the formula with the PROPER function to this cell.**

   Excel now copies the formula =PROPER(B3) to cell D3, which now contains the proper capitalization of the first name, Christopher. Now you're ready to copy these formulas with the PROPER function down to row 17.

4. **Drag the fill handle in the lower-right corner of cell D3 down to cell D17, and then release the mouse button to copy the formulas with the PROPER function down.**

   The cell range C3:D17 now contains first and last name text entries with the proper capitalization (see Figure 6-8). Before replacing all the upper-case entries in A3:B17 with these proper entries, you convert them to their calculated values. This action replaces the formulas with the text as though you had typed each name in the worksheet.

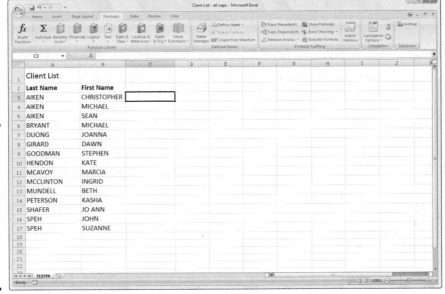

Figure 6-8:
Using the PROPER function to convert names in all uppercase letters to proper capitalization.

5. **With the cell range C3:D17 still selected, click the Copy command button on the Home tab of the Ribbon.**

6. **Immediately click the Paste Values option on the Paste command button's drop-down menu.**

   You've now replaced the formulas with the appropriate text. Now you're ready to move this range on top of the original range with the all-uppercase entries. This action will replace the uppercase entries with the ones using the proper capitalization.

7. **With the cell range C3:D17 still selected, position the white-cross pointer on the bottom of the range; when the pointer changes to an arrowhead, drag the cell range until its outline encloses the range A3:B17, and then release the mouse button.**

   Excel displays an alert box asking if you want the program to replace the contents of the destination's cells.

8. **Click OK in the Alert dialog box to replace the all-uppercase entries with the properly capitalized ones in the destination cells.**

Your worksheet now looks like the one shown in Figure 6-9. Everything is fine in the worksheet with the exception of the two last names, Mcavoy and Mcclinton. You have to manually edit cells A11 and A12 to capitalize the *A* in McAvoy and the second *C* in McClinton.

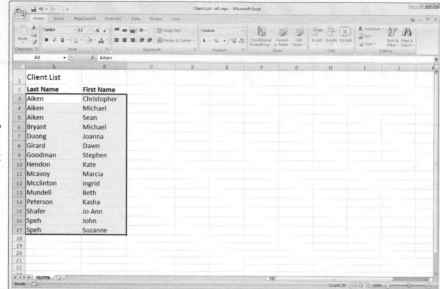

Figure 6-9:
Spreadsheet after replacing names in all uppercase letters with properly capitalized names.

Concatenating text

You can use the ampersand (&) operator to concatenate (or join) separate text strings together. For example, in the Client list spreadsheet shown in Figure 6-9, you can use this operator to join together the first and last names currently entered in two side-by-side cells into a single entry, as shown in Figure 6-10.

To join the first name entry in cell B3 with the last name entry in cell A3, I entered the following formula in cell C3:

=B3&" "&A3

Notice the use of the double quotes in this formula. They enclose a blank space that is placed between the first and last names joined to them with the two concatenation operators. If I don't include this space in the formula and just join the first and last names together with this formula:

=B3&A3

Excel would return ChristopherAiken to cell C3, all as one word.

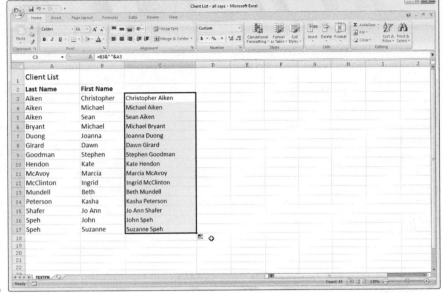

Figure 6-10:
Spreadsheet after con-catenating the first and last names in column C.

After entering the concatenation formula that joins the first and last names in cell C3 separated by a single space, I then drag the Fill handle in cell C3 down to C17 to join all the other client names in a single cell in column C.

After the original concatenation formula is copied down the rows of column C, I copy the selected cell range C3:C17 to the Clipboard by clicking the Copy button in the Clipboard group of the Home tab on the Ribbon, and then immediately click the Paste Values option on the Paste command button's drop-down menu. This pastes calculated text values over the concatenation formulas, thereby replacing the original formulas. The result is a list of first and last names together in the same cell in the range C3:C17, as though I had manually input each one.

Book IV
Worksheet Collaboration and Review

The 5th Wave   By Rich Tennant

"My girlfriend ran a spreadsheet of my life, and generated this chart. My best hope is that she'll change her major from 'Computer Sciences' to 'Rehabilitative Services'."

Contents at a Glance

Chapter 1: Protecting Workbooks and Worksheet Data

In This Chapter

✔ Assigning a password to open a workbook

✔ Assigning a password to make changes in a workbook

✔ Using the Locked and Hidden Protection formats

✔ Protecting a worksheet and selecting what actions are allowed

✔ Enabling cell range editing by particular users in protected sheet

✔ Protecting a workbook

✔ Protecting and sharing a workbook

*B*efore you start sending out your spreadsheets for review (especially out of house), you need to make them secure. Security in Excel exists on two levels. The first is protecting the workbook file so that only people entrusted with the password can open the file to view, print, or edit the data. The second is protecting the worksheets in a workbook from unwarranted changes so that only people entrusted with that password can make modifications to the contents and design of the spreadsheet.

When it comes to securing the integrity of your spreadsheets, you can decide which aspects of the sheets in the workbook your users can and cannot change. For example, you might prevent changes to all formulas and headings in a spreadsheet, while still enabling users to make entries in the cells referenced in the formulas themselves.

Password-Protecting the File

By password-protecting the workbook, you can prevent unauthorized users from opening the workbook and/or editing the workbook. You set a password for opening the workbook file when you're dealing with a spreadsheet whose data is of a sufficiently sensitive nature that only a certain group of people in the company should have access to it (such as spreadsheets dealing with personal information and salaries). Of course, after you set the password required in order to open the workbook, you must supply this password to those people who need access in order to make it possible for them to open the workbook file.

You set a password for modifying the workbook when you're dealing with a spreadsheet whose data needs to be viewed and printed by different users, none of whom are authorized to make changes to any of the entries. For example, you might assign a password for modifying a workbook before distributing it companywide, after the workbook's been through a complete editing and review cycle and all the suggested changes have been merged (see Book IV, Chapter 3 for details).

If you're dealing with a spreadsheet whose data is of a sensitive nature and should not be modified by anyone who's authorized to open it, you need to set both a password for opening and a password for modifying the workbook file. You assign either one or both of these types of passwords to a workbook file at the time you save it with the Office Button | Save As command (Alt+FA).

When you choose this command (or click the Save button on the Quick Access toolbar or press Ctrl+S for a new file that's never been saved before), Excel opens the Save As dialog box. You can then set the password to open and/or the password to modify the file by taking these steps:

1. **Click the Tools button in the Save As dialog box and then click General Options on its drop-down menu.**

Doing this opens the General Options dialog box, similar to the one shown in Figure 1-1, where you can enter a password to open and/or a password to modify in the File Sharing section. When entering a password, you can make it as long as 255 characters, consisting of a combination of letters and numbers with spaces. When adding letters to your passwords, keep in mind that these passwords are case-sensitive. This means that opensesame and OpenSesame are not the same password because of the different use of uppercase and lowercase letters.

When entering a password, make sure that you don't enter something that you can't easily reproduce or, for heaven's sake, that you can't remember. You must be able to immediately reproduce the password in order to assign it, and you must be able to reproduce it later if you want to be able to open or change the darned workbook ever again.

2. **(Optional) If you want to assign a password to open the file, type the password (up to 255 characters maximum) in the Password to Open text box.**

As you type the password, Excel masks the actual characters you type by rendering them as dots in the text box.

If you decide to assign a password for opening and modifying the workbook at the same time, proceed to Step 3. Otherwise, skip to Step 4.

When entering the password for modifying the workbook, you want to assign a password that's different from the one you just assigned for opening the file (if you did assign a password for opening the file in this step).

Figure 1-1:
Setting a
password to
open and
modify in
the Save
Options
dialog box.

3. **(Optional) If you want to assign a password for modifying the workbook, click the Password to Modify text box and then type the password for modifying the workbook there.**

   Before you can assign a password to open the file and/or to modify the file, you must confirm the password by reproducing it in a Confirm Password dialog box exactly as you originally entered it.

4. **Click the OK button.**

   Doing this closes the General Options dialog box and opens a Confirm Password dialog box, where you need to exactly reproduce the password. If you just entered a password in the Password to Open text box, you need to reenter this password in the Confirm Password dialog box. If you just entered a password in the Password to Modify text box, you need only to reproduce this password in the Confirm Password dialog box.

   However, if you entered a password in both the Password to Open text box and the Password to Modify text box, you must reproduce both passwords. In the first Confirm Password dialog box, enter the password you entered in the Password to Open text box. Immediately after you click OK in the first Confirm Password dialog box, the second Confirm Password dialog box appears, where you reproduce the password you entered in the Password to Modify text box.

5. **Type the password exactly as you entered it in the Password to Open text box (or Password to Modify text box, if you didn't use the Password to Open text box), and then click OK.**

   If your password does not match exactly (in both characters and case) the one you originally entered, Excel displays an alert dialog box, indicating that the confirmation password is not identical. When you click OK in this alert dialog box, Excel returns you to the original General Options dialog box where you can do one of two things:

   - Reenter the password in the original text box.

   - Click the OK button to redisplay the Confirm Password dialog box, where you can try again to reproduce the original. (Make sure that you've not engaged the Caps Lock key by accident.)

   If you assigned both a password to open the workbook and one to modify it, Excel displays a second Confirm Password dialog box as soon as you click OK in the first one and successfully reproduce the password to open the file. You then repeat Step 5, this time, exactly reproducing the password to modify the workbook before you click OK.

   When you finish confirming the original password(s), you are ready to save the workbook in the Save As dialog box.

6. **(Optional) If you want to save the password-protected version under a new filename or in a different folder, edit the name in the File Name text box and then select the new folder.**

7. **Click the Save button to save the workbook with the password to open and/or password to modify.**

   As soon as you do this, Excel saves the file if this is the first time you've saved it. If not, the program displays an alert dialog box indicating that the file you're saving already exists and asking you if you want to replace the existing file.

8. **Click the Yes button if the alert dialog box that asks if you want to replace the existing file appears.**

Entering the password to gain access

After you save a workbook file to which you've assigned a password for opening it, you must thereafter be able to faithfully reproduce the password in order to open the file (at least until you change or delete the password). When you next try to open the workbook, Excel opens a Password dialog box like the one shown in Figure 1-2, where you must enter the password exactly as it was assigned to the file.

If you mess up and type the wrong password, Excel displays an alert dialog box letting you know that the password you entered is incorrect. When you click OK to clear the alert, you are returned to the original Excel window where you must repeat the entire file opening procedure (hoping that this time you're able to enter the correct password). When you supply the correct password, Excel immediately opens the workbook for viewing and printing (and editing as well, unless you've also assigned a password for modifying the file). If you're unable to successfully reproduce the password, you are unable to open the file and put it to any use!

Figure 1-2:
Entering the password required to open a protected workbook file.

The last chance you have to chicken out of password-protecting the opening of the file is before you close the file during the work session in which you originally assign the password. If, for whatever reason, you decide that you don't want to go through the hassle of having to reproduce the password each and every time you open this file, you can get rid of it by clicking Office Button | Save As or pressing Alt+FA, clicking General Options on the Tools drop-down menu, and then deleting the password in the Password to Open text box before clicking OK in the General Options dialog box and the Save button in the Save As dialog box. Doing this re-saves the workbook file without a password to open it so that you don't have to worry about reproducing the password the next time you open the workbook for editing or printing.

A password-protected workbook file for which you can't reproduce the correct password is the ultimate nightmare (especially if you're talking about a really important spreadsheet with loads and loads of vital data). So for heaven's sake, don't forget your password, or you'll be stuck. Excel does not provide any sort of command for overriding the password and opening a protected workbook, nor does Microsoft offer any such utility. If you think that you might forget the workbook's password, be sure to write it down somewhere and then keep that piece of paper in a secure place, preferably under lock and key. It's always better to be safe than sorry when it comes to passwords for opening files.

Entering the password to make changes

If you've protected your workbook from modifications, as soon as you attempt to open the workbook (and have entered the password to open the file, if one has been assigned), Excel immediately displays the Password dialog box similar to the one shown in Figure 1-3, where you must accurately reproduce the password assigned for modifying the file.

Figure 1-3:
Entering the password required to modify a protected workbook file.

As when supplying the password to open a protected file, if you type the wrong password, Excel displays the alert dialog box letting you know that the password you entered is incorrect. When you click OK to clear the alert, you are returned to the Password dialog box where you can try reentering the password in the Password text box.

When you supply the correct password, Excel immediately closes the Password dialog box and you are free to edit the workbook in any way you wish (unless certain cell ranges or worksheets are protected). If you're unable to successfully reproduce the password, you can click the Read Only command button, which opens a copy of the workbook file into which you can't save your changes unless you use the Office Button | Save As command and then rename the workbook and/or locate the copy in a different folder.

When you click the Read Only button, Excel opens the file with a [Read-Only] indicator appended to the filename as it appears on the Excel title bar. If you then try to save changes with the Save button on the Quick Access toolbar or Office Button | Save command, the program displays an alert dialog box, indicating that the file is read-only and that you must save a copy by renaming the file in the Save As dialog box. As soon as you click OK to clear the alert dialog box, Excel displays the Save As dialog box where you can save the copy under a new filename and/or location. Note that the program automatically removes the password for modifying from the copy so that you can modify its contents anyway you like.

Because password-protecting a workbook against modification does not prevent you from opening the workbook and then saving an unprotected version under a new filename with the Save As command, you can assign passwords for modifying files without nearly as much trepidation as assigning them for opening files. Assigning a password for modifying the file assures you that you'll always have an intact original of the spreadsheet from which you can open and save a copy, even if you can never remember the password to modify the original itself.

Changing or deleting a password

Before you can change or delete a password for opening a workbook, you must first be able to supply the current password you want to change to get the darned thing open. Assuming you can do this, all you have to do to change or get rid of the password is open the Save As dialog box (Office Button | Save As or Alt+FA), and then click the General Options item on the Tools drop-down menu to open the General Options dialog box, which opens with the password in the Password to Open text box selected.

To delete the password, simply press the Delete key to remove all the asterisks from this text box. To reassign the password, replace the current password with the new one you want to assign by typing it over the original one. Then, when you click OK in the General Options dialog box, reenter the new password in the Confirm Password dialog box and then click its OK button.

Finally, after closing the General Options dialog box, you simply click the Save button in the Save As dialog box and then click Yes in the alert dialog box, which asks you if you want to replace the existing file.

To change or delete the password for modifying the workbook, you follow the same procedure, except that you have to be able to successfully reproduce the password for modifying the workbook after opening it, and then change or delete the password that's entered into the Password to Modify text box in the General Options dialog box.

Protecting the Spreadsheet

After you've got the spreadsheet the way you want it, you often need the help of Excel's Protection feature to keep it that way. Nothing's worse than having an inexperienced data entry operator doing major damage to the formulas and functions that you've worked so hard to build and validate. To keep the formulas and standard text in a spreadsheet safe from any unwarranted changes, you need to protect its worksheet.

Before you start using the Protect Sheet and Protect Workbook command buttons on the Review tab of the Ribbon, you need to understand how protection works in Excel. All cells in the workbook can have one of two different protection formats: locked or unlocked, and hidden or unhidden.

Whenever you begin a new spreadsheet, all the cells in the workbook have the locked and unhidden status. However, this status in and of itself means nothing until you turn on protection with the Protect Sheet and Protect Workbook command buttons on the Review tab. At that time, you are then prevented from making any editing changes to all locked cells and from viewing the contents of all hidden cells on the Formula bar when they contain the cell cursor.

What this means in practice is that, prior to turning on worksheet protection, you go through the spreadsheet removing the Locked protection format from all the cell ranges where you or your users need to be able to do data entry and editing even when the worksheet is protected. You also assign the Hidden protection format to all cell ranges in the spreadsheet where you don't want the contents of the cell to be displayed when protection is turned on in the worksheet. Then, when that formatting is done, you activate protection for all the remaining Locked cells and block the Formula bar display for all the Hidden cells in the sheet.

When setting up your own spreadsheet templates, you will want to unlock all the cells where users need to input new data and keep locked all the cells that contain headings and formulas that never change. You may also want to hide cells with formulas if you're concerned that their display might tempt the users to waste time trying to fiddle with or finesse them. Then, turn on worksheet protection prior to saving the file in the template file format (see Book II, Chapter 1, for details). You are then assured that all spreadsheets generated from that template automatically inherit the same level and type of protection as you assigned in the original spreadsheet.

Changing the Locked and Hidden cell formatting

To change the status of cells from locked to unlocked or from unhidden to hidden, you use the Locked and Hidden check boxes found on the Protection tab of the Format Cells dialog box (Ctrl+1).

To remove the Locked protection status from a cell range or nonadjacent selection, you follow these two steps:

1. **Select the range or ranges to be unlocked.**

   To select multiple ranges to create a nonadjacent cell selection, hold down the Ctrl key as you drag through each range.

2. **Click the Format command button on the Ribbon's Home tab and then click the Lock Cell option near the bottom of its drop-down menu or press Alt+HOL.**

Excel lets you know that the cells in the selected range are no longer locked by removing the highlighting from the lock icon in front of the Lock Cell option on the Format button's drop-down menu.

You can also change the protection status of a selected range of cells with the Locked check box on the Protection tab of the Format Cells dialog box. Simply open the Format Cells dialog box (Ctrl+1), click the Protection tab, and then click the Locked check box to remove the check mark before you click OK.

To hide the display of the contents of the cells in the current selection, you click the Hidden check box instead of the Locked check box on the Protection tab of the Format Cells dialog box before you click OK.

Remember that changing the protection formatting of cell ranges in the worksheet (as described above) does nothing in and of itself. It's not until you turn on the protection for your worksheet (as outlined in the next section) that your unlocked and hidden cells work or appear any differently from the locked and unhidden cells. At that time, only unlocked cells accept edits, and only unhidden cells display their contents on the Formula bar when they contain the cell cursor.

Protecting the worksheet

When you've gotten all cell ranges that you want unlocked and hidden correctly formatted in the worksheet, you're ready to turn on protection. To do this, you click the Protect Sheet command button on the Ribbon's Review tab or press Alt+RPS to open the Protect Sheet dialog box, shown in Figure 1-4.

When you first open this dialog box, only the Protect Worksheet and Contents of Locked Cells check box at the very top and the Select Locked Cells and Select Unlocked Cells check boxes in the Allow All Users of This Worksheet To list box are selected. All the other check box options (including a number that are not visible without scrolling up the Allow All Users of This Worksheet To list box) are unselected.

Figure 1-4:
Selecting the protection options in the Protect Sheet dialog box.

This means that if you click OK at this point, the *only* things that you'll be permitted to do in the worksheet are edit *unlocked* cells and select cell ranges (of any type: both locked and unlocked alike).

If you really want to keep other users out of all the locked cells in a worksheet, click the Select Locked Cells check box in the Allow All Users of This Worksheet To list box to remove its check mark. That way, your users are completely restricted to just those unlocked ranges where you permit data input and content editing.

Don't, however, deselect the Select Unlocked Cells check box as well as the Select Locked Cells check box, because doing this makes the cell cursor disappear from the worksheet, making the cell address in the Name Box on the Formula bar the sole way for you and your users to keep track of their position in the worksheet (which is, believe me, the quickest way to drive you and your users stark raving mad).

Selecting what actions are allowed in a protected sheet

In addition to enabling users to select locked and unlocked cells in the worksheet, you can enable the following actions in the protected worksheet by selecting their check boxes in the Allow All Users of This Worksheet To list box of the Protect Sheet dialog box:

- ✦ **Format Cells:** Enables the formatting of cells (with the exception of changing the locked and hidden status on the Protection tab of the Format Cells dialog box).

- ✦ **Format Columns:** Enables formatting so that users can modify the column widths and hide and unhide columns.

- ✦ **Format Rows:** Enables formatting so that users can modify the row heights and hide and unhide rows.

- ✦ **Insert Columns:** Enables the insertion of new columns in the worksheet.

- ✦ **Insert Rows:** Enables the insertion of new rows in the worksheet.

- ✦ **Insert Hyperlinks:** Enables the insertion of new hyperlinks to other documents, both local and on the Web. (See Book IV, Chapter 2, for details.)

- ✦ **Delete Columns:** Enables the deletion of columns in the worksheet.

- ✦ **Delete Rows:** Enables the deletion of rows in the worksheet.

- ✦ **Sort:** Enables the sorting of data in unlocked cells in the worksheet. (See Book VI, Chapter 1, for details.)

- ✦ **Use AutoFilter:** Enables the filtering of data in the worksheet. (See Book VI, Chapter 2, for more information.)

- ✦ **Use PivotTable Reports:** Enables the manipulation of pivot tables in the worksheet. (For more about pivot tables, see Book VII, Chapter 2.)

✦ **Edit Objects:** Enables the editing of graphic objects, such as text boxes, embedded images, and the like, in the worksheet. (See Book V, Chapter 2, for details.)

✦ **Edit Scenarios:** Enables the editing of what-if scenarios, including modifying and deleting them. (For details of what-if scenarios, see Book VII, Chapter 1.)

Assigning a password to unprotect the sheet

In addition to enabling particular actions in the protected worksheet, you can also assign a password that's required in order to remove the protections from the protected worksheet. When entering a password in the Password to Unprotect Sheet text box of the Protect Sheet dialog box, you observe the same guidelines as when assigning a password to open or to make changes in the workbook (255 characters maximum that can consist of a combination of letters, numbers, and spaces, with the letters being case sensitive).

As with assigning a password to open or make changes to a workbook, when you enter a password (whose characters are masked with asterisks) in the Password to Unprotect Sheet text box and then click OK, Excel displays the Confirm Password dialog box. Here, you must accurately reproduce the password you just entered (including uppercase and lowercase letters) before Excel turns on the sheet protection and assigns the password for removing protection.

If you don't successfully reproduce the password, when you click OK in the Confirm Password dialog box, Excel replaces it with an alert dialog box indicating that the confirmation password is not identical to the one you entered in the Protect Sheet dialog box. When you click OK to clear this alert dialog box, you are returned to the Protect Sheet dialog box where you may modify the password in the Password to Unprotect Sheet text box before you click OK and try confirming the password again.

As soon as you accurately reproduce the password in the Confirm Password dialog box, Excel closes the Protect Sheet dialog box and enables protection for that sheet, using whatever settings you designated in that dialog box.

If you don't assign a password to unprotect the sheet, any user with a modicum of Excel knowledge can lift the worksheet protection and make any manner of changes to its contents, including wreaking havoc on its computational abilities by corrupting its formulas. Keep in mind that it makes little sense to turn on the protection in a worksheet if you're going to permit anybody to turn it off by simply clicking the Unprotect Sheet command button on the Review tab (which automatically replaces the Protect Sheet command button as soon as you turn on protection in the worksheet).

Removing protection from a worksheet

When you assign protection to a sheet, your input and editing are restricted solely to unlocked cells in the worksheet, and you can perform only those additional actions that you enabled in the Allow Users of this Worksheet To list box. If you try to replace, delete, or otherwise modify a locked cell in the protected worksheet, Excel displays an alert dialog box with the following message:

```
The cell or chart you are trying to change is protected
and therefore read-only
```

The message then goes on to tell you that to modify a protected worksheet, you must first remove the protection by using the Unprotect Sheet command button in the Changes group on the Review tab.

If you've assigned a password to unprotect the sheet, when you click the Unprotect Sheet button, the program displays the Unprotect Sheet dialog box where you must enter the password exactly as you assigned it. As soon as you remove the protection by entering the correct password in this dialog box and clicking OK, Excel turns off the protection in the sheet, and you can once again make any kinds of modifications to its structure and contents in both the locked and unlocked cells.

Keep in mind that when you protect a worksheet, only the data and graphics on that particular worksheet are protected. This means that you can modify the data and graphics on other sheets of the same workbook without removing protection. If you have data or graphics on other sheets of the same workbook that also need protecting, you need to activate that sheet and then repeat the entire procedure for protecting it as well (including unlocking cells that need to be edited and selecting which other actions, if any, to enable in the worksheet, and whether or not to assign a password to unprotect the sheet) before distributing the workbook. When assigning passwords to unprotect the various sheets of the workbook, you may want to stick with a single password rather than have to worry about remembering a different password for each sheet, which is a bit much, don't you think?

Enabling cell range editing by certain users

You can use the Allow Users to Edit Ranges command button in the Changes group on the Review tab of the Ribbon to enable the editing of particular ranges in the protected worksheet by certain users. When you use this feature, you give certain users permission to edit particular cell ranges, if they can correctly provide the password you assign to that range.

To give access to particular ranges in a protected worksheet, you follow these steps:

1. **Click the Allow Users to Edit Ranges command button on the Ribbon's Review tab or press Alt+RU.**

Note that the Allow Users to Edit Ranges command button is grayed out and unavailable if the worksheet is currently protected. In that case, you must remove protection by clicking the Unprotect Sheet command button on the Review tab before you retry Step 1.

Excel opens the Allow Users to Edit Ranges dialog box where you can add the ranges you want to assign, as shown in Figure 1-5.

2. **Click the New button.**

Doing this opens the New Range dialog box where you give the range a title, define its cell selection, and provide the range password, as shown in Figure 1-6.

3. **If you wish, type a name for the range in the Title text box (otherwise, Excel assigns a name such as Range1, Range2, and so on).**

Next, you designate the cell range or nonadjacent cell selection to which access is restricted.

4. **Click the Refers to Cells text box and then type in the address of the cell range (without removing the = sign) or select the range or ranges in the worksheet.**

Next, you need to enter a password that's required to get access to the range. Like all other passwords in Excel, this one can be up to 255 characters long, mixing letters, numbers, and spaces. Pay attention to the use of upper- and lowercase letters, because the range password is case-sensitive.

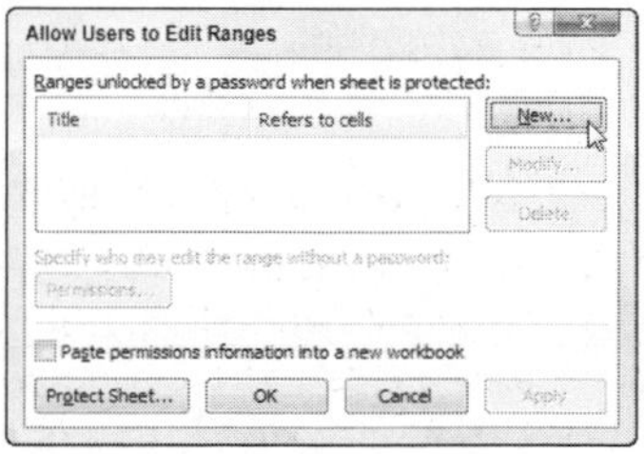

Figure 1-5: Designating the range to be unlocked by a password in a protected worksheet.

5. Type in the password for accessing the range in the Range Password text box.

You need to use the Permissions button in the New Range dialog box to open the Permissions dialog box for the range you're setting.

6. Click the Permissions button in the New Range dialog box.

Next, you need to add the users who are to have access to this range.

7. Click the Add button in the Permissions dialog box.

Doing this opens the Select Users or Groups dialog box where you designate the names of the users to have access to the range.

8. Click the name of the user in the Enter the Object Names to Select list box at the bottom of the Select Users or Groups dialog box. To select multiple users from this list, hold down the Ctrl key as you click each user name.

If this list box is empty, click the Advanced button to expand the Select Users or Groups dialog box and then click the Find Now button to locate all users for your location. You can then click the name or Ctrl+click the names you want to add from this list, and then when you click OK, Excel returns you to the original form of the Select Users or Groups dialog box and adds these names to its Enter the Object Names to Select list box.

9. Click OK in the Select Users or Groups dialog box.

Doing this returns you to the Permissions dialog box where the names you've selected are now listed in the Group or User Names list box. Now you need to set the permissions for each user. When you first add users, each one is permitted to edit the range without a password. To restrict the editing to only those who have the range password, you need to click each name and then click the Deny check box.

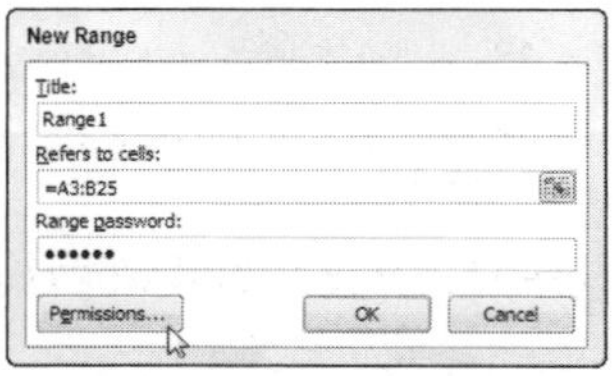

Figure 1-6:
Assigning the range title, address, and password in the New Range dialog box.

10. **Click the name of the first user who must know the password and then click the Deny check box in the Permissions For list box.**

You need to repeat Step 10 for each person in the Group or Users Names list box that you want to restrict in this manner (see Figure 1-7).

Figure 1-7: Setting the permissions for each user in the Permissions dialog box.

11. **Repeat Step 10 for each user who must know the password and then click OK in the Permissions dialog box.**

As soon as you click OK, Excel displays a warning alert dialog box, letting you know that you are setting a deny permission that takes precedence over any allowed entries, so that if the person is a member of two groups, one with an allow entry and the other with a deny entry, the deny entry permission rules (meaning that they have to know the range password).

12. **Click the Yes button in the Security alert dialog box.**

Doing this closes this dialog box and returns you to the New Range dialog box.

13. **Click OK in the New Range dialog box.**

Doing this opens the Confirm Password dialog box where you must accurately reproduce the range password.

14. **Type the range password in the Reenter Password to Proceed text box and then click the OK button.**

Doing this returns you to the Allow Users to Edit Ranges dialog box where the title and cell reference of the new range is displayed in the Ranges Unlocked by a Password When Sheet Is Protected list box, as shown in Figure 1-8.

**Book IV
Chapter 1**

**Protecting
Workbooks and
Worksheet Data**

Figure 1-8:
Getting
ready to
protect the
sheet in the
Allow Users
to Edit
Ranges
dialog box.

If you need to define other ranges available to other users in the work-sheet, you can do so by repeating Steps 2 through 14.

When you finish adding ranges to the Allow Users to Edit Ranges dialog box, you're ready to protect the worksheet. If you want to retain a record of the ranges you've defined, go to Step 15. Otherwise, skip to Step 16.

15. **(Optional) Click the Paste Permissions Information Into a New Workbook check box to put a check mark in it if you want to create a new workbook that contains all the permissions information.**

When you select this check box, Excel creates a new workbook whose first worksheet lists all the ranges you've assigned, along with the users who may gain access by providing the range password. You can then save this workbook for your records. Note that the range password is not listed on this worksheet — if you want to add it, be sure that you password-protect the workbook so that only you can open it.

Now, you're ready to protect the worksheet. If you want to do this from within the Allow Users to Edit Ranges dialog box, you click the Protect Sheet button to open the Protect Sheet dialog box. If you want to protect the worksheet later on, you click OK to close the Allow Users to Edit Ranges dialog box and then click the Protect Sheet command button on the Review tab of the Ribbon (or press Alt+RPS) when you're ready to activate the worksheet protection.

16. **Click the Protect Sheet button to protect the worksheet; otherwise, click the OK button to close the Allow Users to Edit Ranges dialog box.**

If you click the Protect Sheet button, Excel opens the Protect Sheet dialog box where you can set a password to unprotect the sheet. This dialog box is also where you select the actions that you permit all users to perform in the protected worksheet (as outlined earlier in this chapter).

After you turn on protection in the worksheet, only the users you've designated are able to edit the cell range or ranges you've defined. Of course, you need to supply the range password to all the users allowed to do editing in the range or ranges at the time you distribute the workbook to them.

Be sure to assign a password to unprotect the worksheet at the time you protect the worksheet if you want to prevent unauthorized users from being able to make changes to the designated editing ranges in the worksheet. If you don't, any user can make changes by turning off the worksheet protection and thereby gaining access to the Allow Users to Edit Ranges command by clicking the Unprotect Sheet command button on the Review tab of the Ribbon.

Doing data entry in the unlocked cells of a protected worksheet

The best part of protecting a worksheet is that you and your users can jump right to unlocked cells and avoid even dealing with the locked ones (that you can't change anyway) by using the Tab and Shift+Tab keys to navigate the worksheet. When you press the Tab key in a protected worksheet, Excel jumps the cell cursor to the next unlocked cell to the right of the current one in that same row. When you reach the last unlocked cell in that row, the program then jumps to the first unlocked cell in the rows below. To move back to a previous unlocked cell, you press Shift+Tab. When Excel reaches the last unlocked cell in the spreadsheet, it automatically jumps back to the very first unlocked cell on the sheet.

Of course, provided that you haven't changed the behavior of the Enter key in the Editing Options section on the Advanced tab of the Excel Options dialog box (Office Button | Excel Options or Alt+FI), you can also use the Enter key to move down the columns instead of across the rows. However, pressing the Enter key to progress down a column selects locked cells in that column as well as the unlocked ones, whereas pressing the Tab key skips all those cells with the Locked protection format.

Figure 1-9 illustrates how you can put the Tab key to good use in filling out and navigating a protected worksheet. This figure shows a new invoice for Spa Holiday Hot Tubs that's been generated from a template. Because the SPHT Invoice sheet in the original template is protected, this sheet is protected as well in the SPA Holiday Invoice1 workbook created from it. The only cells that are unlocked in this sheet are C3, C4, C5, C6, G4, G5, E6, and the cell range B8:C18. All the rest of the cells in this worksheet are locked and off limits.

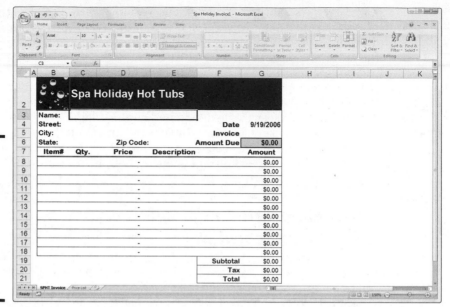

Figure 1-9:
Using the
Tab key to
move from
unlocked
cell to
unlocked
cell in a
protected
worksheet.

To fill in the data for this new invoice, you can press the Tab key to complete the data entry in each field such as Name, Street, Date, City, Invoice, and so on. By pressing Tab, you don't have to waste time moving through the locked cells that contain headings that you can't modify anyway. If you need to back up and return to the previous field in the invoice, you just press Shift+Tab to go back to the previous unlocked cell.

If you want to make it impossible for the user to select anything but the unlocked cells in the protected worksheet, you can do so by removing the check mark from the Select Locked Cells check box in the Allow All Users of This Worksheet To list box of the Protect Sheet dialog box.

Protecting the workbook

There is one last level of protection that you can apply to your spreadsheet files, and that is protecting the entire workbook. When you protect the workbook, you ensure that its users can't change the structure of the file by adding, deleting, or even moving and renaming any of its worksheets. To protect your workbook, you click the Protect Workbook command button on the Ribbon's Review tab followed by the Protect Structure and Windows option on its drop-down menu (press Alt+RPW).

Excel displays a Protect Structure and Windows dialog box like the one shown in Figure 1-10. This dialog box contains two check boxes: Structure (which is automatically checked) and Windows (which is not selected). This dialog box also contains a Password (Optional) text box where you can enter a password that must be supplied before you can unprotect the workbook. Like every other password in Excel, the password to unprotect the workbook can be up to 255 characters maximum, consisting of a combination of letters, numbers, and spaces, with all the letters being case-sensitive.

Figure 1-10:
Protecting a workbook in the Protect Structure and Windows dialog box.

When you protect a workbook with the Structure check box selected, Excel prevents you or your users from doing any of the following tasks to the file:

+ Inserting new worksheets

+ Deleting existing worksheets

+ Renaming worksheets

+ Hiding or viewing hidden worksheets

+ Moving or copying worksheets to another workbook

+ Displaying the source data for a cell in a pivot table or displaying a table's Report Filter fields on separate worksheets (see Book VII, Chapter 2, for details)

+ Creating a summary report with the Scenario Manager (see Book VII, Chapter 1, for details)

When you turn on protection for a workbook after checking the Windows check box in the Protect Structure and Windows dialog box, Excel prevents you from changing the size or position of the workbook's windows (not usually something you need to control).

After you've enabled protection in a workbook, you can then turn it off by clicking the Protect Structure and Windows option on the Unprotect Workbook command button's drop-down menu or by pressing Alt+RPW again. If you've assigned a password to unprotect the workbook, you must accurately reproduce it in the Password text box in the Unprotect Workbook dialog box that then appears.

Protecting a shared workbook

Many times you will want to protect a workbook that you intend to share on a network. That way, you can allow simultaneous editing of the contents of its worksheets (assuming that you don't also protect individual sheets), while at the same time preventing anybody but you from removing the Change tracking (and thus deleting the Change History log — see Book IV, Chapter 3).

If the workbook is not currently shared, you can both protect the workbook and share it by clicking the Protect and Share Workbook command button on the Ribbon's Review tab or by pressing Alt+RO. Note that if the workbook is already shared, you must stop sharing the file before you can use this command (see Book IV, Chapter 1, for details on how to do this).

When you click the Protect and Share Workbook command button, Excel opens the Protect Shared Workbook dialog box, similar to the one shown in Figure 1-11. In this dialog box, you click the Sharing with Track Changes check box to enable file sharing and to turn on the Change tracking. As soon as you click this check box to put a check mark in it, Excel makes available the Password (Optional) text box where you can enter a password that must be supplied before you can stop sharing the workbook.

If you enter a password in this text box (and you should — otherwise, there's little reason to use this option, because anyone can remove the protection from the shared workbook and thus stop the file sharing), Excel immediately displays the Confirm Password dialog box where you must accurately reproduce the password.

When you do this, Excel displays an alert dialog box that informs you that it will now save the workbook, and when you click the Yes button, the program saves the workbook as a shared file and protects it from being made exclusive without the password. The program also adds a [Shared] indicator to the filename at the top of the Excel program window to let you know that the workbook is being shared.

Figure 1-11:
Setting up
protection
for a shared
workbook in
the Protect
Shared
Workbook
dialog box.

To remove the protection from the shared workbook and, at the same time, stop sharing it, you choose the Unprotect Shared Workbook command button (that replaces the Protect and Share Workbook button) in the Changes group on the Review tab of the Ribbon. After you enter the password to unprotect the file in the Unprotect Sharing dialog box and click OK, Excel displays an alert dialog box, informing you that your action is about to remove the file from shared use and erase the Change History log file. If you click Yes, you'll prevent users who are currently editing the workbook from saving their changes. If you're sure that no one else is using the workbook, you can continue and remove the file sharing by clicking the Yes button.

Chapter 2: Linking Workbooks with Hyperlinks

In This Chapter

- Linking your spreadsheet to other Excel workbooks, Office documents, and Web pages
- Linking to e-mail addresses
- Following the links that you create in the worksheet
- Editing hyperlinks in a worksheet
- Creating formulas that use the HYPERLINK function

The subject of this chapter is linking your worksheet with other documents through the use of *hyperlinks*. Hyperlinks are the kinds of links used on the Web to take you immediately from one Web page to another or from one Web site to another. Such links can be attached to text (thus the term, *hypertext*) or to graphics such as buttons or pictures. The most important aspect of a hyperlink is that it immediately takes you to its destination whenever you click the text or button to which it is attached.

In an Excel worksheet, you can create hyperlinks that take you to a different part of the same worksheet, to another worksheet in the same workbook, to another workbook or other type of document on your hard drive, or to a Web page on your company's intranet or on the World Wide Web.

Hyperlinks 101

To add hyperlinks in an Excel worksheet, you must define two things:

- ✦ The object to which you want to anchor the link and then click to activate
- ✦ The destination to which the link takes you when activated

The objects to which you can attach hyperlinks include any text that you enter into a cell or any graphic object that you draw or import into the worksheet (see Book V, Chapter 2, for details on adding graphics to your worksheet). The destinations that you can specify for links can be a new cell or range, the same workbook file, or another file outside the workbook.

The destinations that you can specify for hyperlinks that take you to another place in the same workbook file include

✦ **The cell reference** of a cell on any of the worksheets in the workbook that you want to go to when you click the hyperlink.

✦ **The range name** of the group of cells that you want to select when you click the hyperlink. The range name must already exist at the time you create the link.

The destinations that you can specify for hyperlinks that take you outside the current workbook include

✦ **The filename** of an existing file that you want to open when you click the hyperlink. This file can be another workbook file or any other type of document that your computer can open.

✦ **The URL address** of a Web page that you want to visit when you click the hyperlink. This page can be on your company's intranet or on the World Wide Web and is opened in your Web browser.

✦ **A new document** that you want to create in Excel or some other program on your computer when you click the hyperlink. You must specify the filename and file extension (which indicates what type of document to create and what program to launch).

✦ **An e-mail address** for a new message that you want to create in your e-mail program when you click the hyperlink. You must specify the recipient's e-mail address and the subject of the new message when you create the link.

Adding hyperlinks

The steps for creating a new hyperlink in the worksheet are very straightforward. The only thing you need to do beforehand is to add the jump text in the cell where you want the link or to draw or import the graphic object to which the link is to be attached (as described in Book V, Chapter 2). Then, to add a hyperlink to the text in this cell or the graphic object, follow these steps:

1. **Position the cell cursor in the cell containing the text or click the graphic object to which you want to anchor the hyperlink.**

After you have selected the cell with the text or the graphic object, you're ready to open the Insert Hyperlink dialog box.

2. **Click the Hyperlink command button on the Ribbon's Insert tab or press Alt+NI or Ctrl+K.**

The Insert Hyperlink dialog box opens, which is similar to the one shown in Figure 2-1. If you selected a graphic object or a cell that contains some entry besides text before opening this dialog box, you notice that the Text to Display text box contains <<Selection in Document>> and that this box is grayed out (because there isn't any text to edit when anchoring a link to a graphic). If you selected a cell with a text entry, that entry appears in the Text to Display text box. You can edit this text in this box; however, be aware that any change that you make to it here is reflected in the current cell when you close the Insert Hyperlink dialog box.

The ScreenTip button located to the immediate right of the Text to Display text box enables you to add text describing the function of the link when you position the mouse pointer over the cell or graphic object to which the link is attached. To add a ScreenTip for your link, follow Step 3. Note that if you don't add your own ScreenTip, Excel automatically creates its own ScreenTip that lists the destination of the new link when you position the mouse pointer on its anchor.

3. **(Optional) Click the ScreenTip button and then type the text that you want to appear next to mouse pointer in the Set Hyperlink ScreenTip dialog box before you click OK.**

By default, Excel selects the Existing File or Web Page button in the Link To area on the left side of the Insert Hyperlink dialog box, thus enabling you to assign the link destination to a file on your hard disk or to a Web page. To link to a cell or cell range in the current workbook, click the Place in This Document button. To link to a new document, click the Create New Document button. To link to a new e-mail message, click the E-Mail Address button.

Book IV
Chapter 2

Linking Workbooks with Hyperlinks

4. **Select the type of destination for the new link by clicking its button in the Link To panel on the left side of the Insert Hyperlink dialog box.**

   Now all that you need to do is to specify the destination for your link. How you do this depends on which type of link you're adding; see the following instructions for details.

   - **Linking to a cell or named range in the current workbook:** After clicking the Place in This Document button in the Link To panel, enter the address of the cell to link to in the Type the Cell Reference text box and then click the name of the sheet that contains this cell listed under the Cell Reference range in the Or Select a Place in This Document list box. To link to a named range, simply click its name under Defined Names in the Or Select a Place in This Document list box.

   - **Linking to an existing file:** After clicking the Existing File or Web Page button in the Link To panel, open its folder in the Look In drop-down list box and then click its file icon in the list box that appears immediately below this box. If you're linking to a Web page, click the Address text box and enter the URL address (as in `http://` and so on) there. If the file or Web page that you select contains bookmarks (or range names, in the case of another Excel workbook) that name specific locations in the file to which you link, click the Bookmark button and then click the name of the location (bookmark) in the Select Place in Document dialog box before you click OK.

   - **Creating a new document:** After clicking the Create New Document button in the Link To panel, enter a filename for the new document in the Name of New Document text box. Include the three-letter file-name extension if this new document is not an Excel workbook, such as `.doc` to create a new Word document or `.txt` to create a new text file. To specify a different folder in which to create the new document, click the Change button to the right of the current path and then select the appropriate drive and folder in the Create New Document dialog box and click OK. If you want to edit the contents of the new document right away, leave the Edit the New Document Now option button selected. If you prefer to edit the new document at a later time, click the Edit the New Document Later option button.

   - **Creating a new e-mail message:** After clicking the E-Mail Address button in the Link To panel, enter the e-mail address (as in `gharvey@mindovermedia.com`) in the E-Mail Address text box and then click the Subject text box and enter the subject of the new e-mail message.

5. **Specify the destination for the new hyperlink by using the text boxes and list boxes that appear for the type of link destination that you selected.**

Now you're ready to create the link.

6. **Click the OK button in the Insert Hyperlink dialog box.**

As soon as you click OK, Excel closes the Insert Hyperlink dialog box and returns you to the worksheet with the new link (unless you specified that the new link is to create a new document *and* you left the Edit New Document Now option button selected, in which case, you're in a new document — possibly in another application program such as Microsoft Word). If you anchored your new hyperlink to a graphic object, that object is still selected in the worksheet (to deselect the object, click a cell outside its boundaries). If you anchored your hyperlink to text in the current cell, the text now appears in blue and is underlined (you may not be able to see the underlining until you move the cell cursor out of the cell).

Figure 2-1:
Creating a
new hyper-
link in the
Insert
Hyperlink
dialog box.

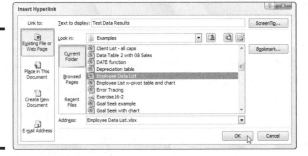

When you position the mouse pointer over the cell with the hypertext or the graphic object with the hyperlink, the mouse pointer changes from a thick, white cross to a hand with the index finger pointing upward. The ScreenTip that you assigned appears below and to the right of the hand mouse pointer.

If you didn't assign your own ScreenTip to the hyperlink when creating it, Excel adds its own message that shows the URL destination of the link. If the link is a hypertext link (that is, if it's anchored to a cell containing a text entry), the message in the ScreenTip also adds the following message:

```
Click once to follow. Click and hold to select this cell.
```

**Book IV
Chapter 2**

**Linking Workbooks
with Hyperlinks**

Follow that link!

To follow a hyperlink, click the link text or graphic object with the hand mouse pointer. Excel then takes you to the destination. If the destination is a cell in the workbook, Excel makes that cell current. If the destination is a cell range, Excel selects the range and makes the first cell of the range current. If this destination is a document created with another application program, Excel launches the application program (assuming that it's available on the current computer). If this destination is a Web page on the World Wide Web, Excel launches your Web browser, connects you to the Internet, and then opens the page in the browser.

After you follow a hypertext link to its destination, the color of its text changes from the traditional blue to a dark shade of purple (without affecting its underlining). This color change indicates that the hyperlink has been followed (note, however, that graphic hyperlinks don't show any change in color after you follow them). Followed hypertext links regain their original blue color when you reopen their workbooks in Excel.

Editing hyperlinks

Excel makes it easy to edit any hyperlink that you've added to your spreadsheet. The only trick to editing a link is that you have to be careful not to activate the link during the editing process. This means that you must always remember to right-click the link's hypertext or graphic to select the link that you want to edit, because clicking results only in activating the link.

When you right-click a link, Excel displays its shortcut menu. If you want to modify the link's destination or ScreenTip, click Edit Hyperlink on this shortcut menu. This action opens the Edit Hyperlink dialog box with the same options as the Insert Hyperlink dialog box (shown previously in Figure 2-1). You can then use the Link To buttons on the left side of the dialog box to modify the link's destination or the ScreenTip button to add or change the ScreenTip text.

Removing a hyperlink

If you want to remove the hyperlink from a cell entry or graphic object without getting rid of the text entry or the graphic, right-click the cell or graphic and then click the Remove Hyperlink item on the cell's or object's shortcut menu.

If you want to clear the cell of both its link and text entry, click the Delete item on the cell's shortcut menu. To get rid of a graphic object along with its hyperlink, right-click the object (this action opens its shortcut menu) and then immediately click the object to remove the shortcut menu without either deselecting the graphic or activating the hyperlink. At this point, you can press the Delete key to delete both the graphic and the associated link.

Copying and moving a hyperlink

When you need to copy or move a hyperlink to a new place in the worksheet, you can use either the drag-and-drop or the cut-and-paste method. Again, the main challenge to using either method is selecting the link without activating it because clicking the cell or graphic object containing the link only results in catapulting you over to the link's destination point.

To select a cell that contains hypertext, use the arrow keys to position the cell cursor in that cell or use the Go To feature (F5 or Ctrl+G) and enter the cell's address in the Go To dialog box to move the cell cursor there. To select a graphic object that contains a hyperlink, right-click the graphic to select it as well as to display its shortcut menu, and then immediately click the graphic (with the left mouse button) to remove the shortcut menu while keeping the object selected.

After you have selected the cell or graphic with the hyperlink, you can move the link by clicking the Cut command button on the Home tab of the Ribbon (Ctrl+X) or copy it by clicking the Copy command button (Ctrl+C) and then paste it into its new position by clicking the Paste command button (Ctrl+V). When moving or copying hypertext from one cell to another, you can just click the cell where the link is to be moved or copied and then press the Enter key.

To move the selected link by using the drag-and-drop method, drag the cell or object with the mouse pointer (in the shape of a white arrowhead pointing to a black double-cross) and then release the mouse button to drop the hypertext or graphic into its new position. To copy the link, be sure to hold down the Ctrl key (which changes the pointer to a white arrowhead with a plus sign to its right) as you drag the outline of the cell or object.

When attempting to move or copy a cell by using the drag-and-drop method, remember that you have to position the thick, white-cross mouse pointer on one of the borders of the cell before the pointer changes to a white arrow-head pointing to a black double-cross. If you position the pointer anywhere within the cell's borders, the mouse changes to the hand with the index finger pointing upward, indicating that the hyperlink is active.

Using the HYPERLINK Function

Instead of using the Hyperlink command button on the Insert tab of the Ribbon, you can use Excel's HYPERLINK function to create a hypertext link (you can't use this function to attach a hyperlink to a graphic object). The HYPERLINK function uses the following syntax:

```
=HYPERLINK(link_location,[friendly_name])
```

How to tell a UNC from a URL address and when to care

The address that you use to specify a remote hyperlink destination comes in two basic flavors: UNC (Universal Naming Convention) and the more familiar URL (Universal Resource Locator). The type of address that you use depends on whether the destination file resides on a server on a network (in which case, you use a UNC address) or on a corporate intranet or the Internet (in which case, you use a URL address). Note that URLs also appear in many flavors, the most popular being those that use the Hypertext Transfer Protocol (HTTP) and begin with `http://` and those that use the File Transfer Protocol (FTP) and start with `ftp://`.

The UNC address for destination files on network servers start with two backslash characters (\\), following this format:

```
\\server\share\path\filename
```

In this format, the name of the file server containing the file replaces *server*, the name of the shared folder replaces *share*, the directory path specifying any subfolders of the shared folder replaces *path*, and the file's complete filename (including any filename extension, such as `.xls` for Excel worksheet) replaces *filename*.

The URL address for files published on Web sites follows this format:

```
internet service//internet
    address/path/filename
```

In this format, *internet service* is replaced with the Internet protocol to be used (either HTTP or FTP in most cases), *internet address* is replaced with the domain name (such as `www.dummies.com`) or the number assigned to the internet server, *path* is the directory path of the file, and *filename* is the complete name (including filename extensions such as `.htm` or `.html` for Web pages).

The *link_location* argument specifies the name of the document to open on your local hard disk, on a network server (designated by a UNC address), or on the company's intranet or the World Wide Web (designated by the URL address — see the sidebar, "How to tell a UNC from a URL address and when to care," for details). The optional *friendly_name* argument is the hyperlink text that appears in the cell where you enter the HYPERLINK function. If you omit this argument, Excel displays the text specified as the *link_location* argument in the cell.

When specifying the arguments for a HYPERLINK function that you type on the Formula bar (as opposed to one that you create by using the Insert Function feature by filling in the text boxes in the Function Arguments dialog box), you must remember to enclose both the *link_location* and *friendly_name* arguments in closed double quotes. For example, to enter a HYPERLINK function in a cell that takes you to the home page of the *For Dummies* Web site and displays the text, "Dummies Home Page" in the cell, enter the following in the cell:

```
=HYPERLINK("http://www.dummies.com","Dummies Home Page")
```

Chapter 3: Sending Workbooks Out for Review

In This Chapter

✓ Finishing a workbook to get it ready to send out for review

✓ Digitally signing a finished workbook

✓ Tracking changes made to a shared workbook

✓ Adding and reviewing comments in a workbook

✓ Adding ink annotations to a workbook on a Tablet PC

✓ Sending a workbook out for review as an e-mail attachment

In this day and age of networked personal computers and high-speed Internet access, Excel offers you the capability of not only sharing your Excel spreadsheets with coworkers and clients, but also tracking and managing your collective editing changes, which in effect, enables you to create spreadsheets by committee.

In this chapter, you discover how to add the finishing touches to the workbook you're getting ready to distribute, and then track the changes made to that workbook after you share it so that your coworkers can simultaneously edit it. You also find out how to merge changes that different workers independently make to the contents of the workbook so that you end up with a single updated version.

As part of the review process, you may want to just comment on aspects of the spreadsheet and suggest possible changes rather than make these changes yourself or even mark up the spreadsheet with digital ink if your computer is equipped with a graphics tablet or is a Tablet PC. In this chapter, you find out how to get your two cents in by annotating a spreadsheet with text notes that indicate suggested improvements or corrections as well as highlight potential change areas with ink.

Preparing a Workbook

Excel 2007 includes a number of different Prepare commands that you can use to get a spreadsheet ready for distribution within the company or outside the organization. When you select the Prepare option on the File pull-down menu (Office Button | Prepare or Alt+FE), a submenu appears with these seven options:

✦ **Properties** to display the Document Information Panel at the top of the worksheet where you can examine or add various types of metadata (data about the document)

✦ **Inspect Document** to open the Document Inspector, which checks your documents for hidden content that you can redisplay and metadata (data about the document) that you can delete prior to distributing the file by clicking their Remove All buttons

✦ **Encrypt Document** to add encryption and increase the security of the workbook

✦ **Restrict Permission** to limit changes to the workbook by restricting particular users to whom you intend to distribute the file to read-only status

✦ **Add a Digital Signature** to sign the workbook file with a digital ID that you obtain from one of Microsoft's partners such as secure2trust or IntelliSafe Vault Desktop (or that you create yourself), certifying the source of the workbook prior to sending it out for review

✦ **Run Compatibility Checker** to check a 2007 workbook file saved with the Excel Workbook (*.xlsx) XML file format option for any loss in fidelity when it's saved in the older Excel 97-2003 Workbook (*.xls) binary file format for distribution to users still running previous versions of Microsoft Excel

✦ **Mark as Final** to mark the workbook file as final prior to sending it out for review (this becomes a property of the workbook for which you can search)

Adding properties to a workbook

You can add information about your workbook document (called metadata) in the Document Information Panel, an area at the top of the Worksheet area (see Figure 3-1) displayed by clicking Office Button | Prepare | Properties or pressing Alt+FEP. You can then use the metadata that you enter into the Author, Title, Subject, Keywords, Category, Status, and Comments fields in the Document Information Panel in all the quick searches (Windows Vista) or file searches (Windows XP) you perform. Doing so enables you to quickly locate the file for opening in Excel for further editing and printing or distributing to others to review.

When entering more than one piece of data into a particular field such as Subject or Keywords, separate each piece with a comma. Also, note that Excel automatically adds Final to the Status field in the Document Information Panel when you choose the Mark as Final option on the Prepare submenu opened by clicking the Office Button and then clicking the Prepare option or pressing Alt+FE. When you're done adding metadata information to the fields, close the Document Information Panel by clicking its Close button (with an X) in the upper-right corner.

Click the Advanced Properties option on the Document Properties drop-down button's menu (this button is located in the upper-left corner of the Document Information Panel) to open the Properties dialog box for the current workbook in Excel. This dialog box contains five tabs (General, Summary, Statistics, Contents, and Custom) that give you tons of information about the current workbook file including the file's location, size, and date last saved. In addition, you can review, edit, and add more metadata about the file using the fields on the Summary tab of this dialog box.

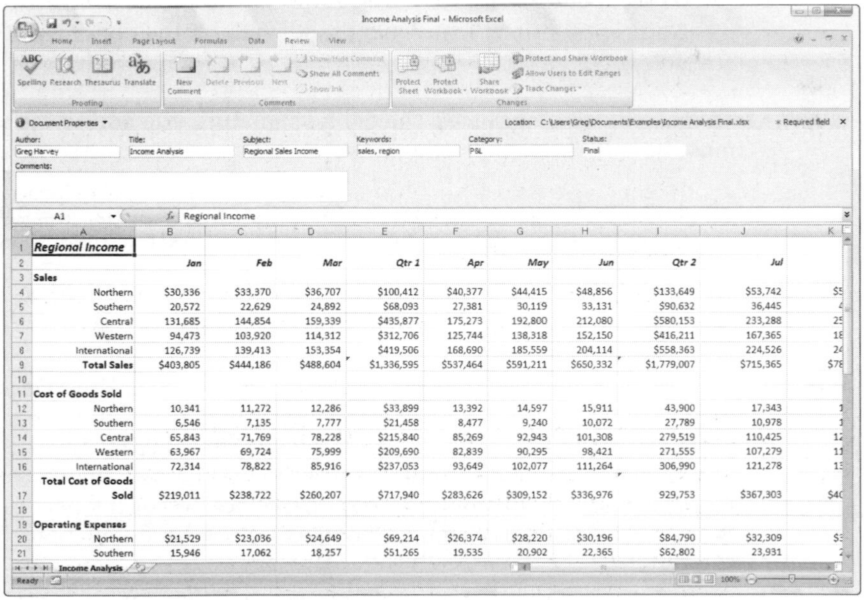

Figure 3-1: Adding metadata to a workbook in the Document Information Panel.

Digitally signing a document

Excel 2007 enables you to add digital signatures to the workbook files that you send out for review. After checking the spreadsheet and verifying its accuracy and readiness for distribution, you can (assuming that you have the authority within your company) digitally sign the workbook in one of two ways:

✦ Add a visible signature line as a graphic object in the workbook that contains your name, the date of the signing, your title, and, if you have a Tablet PC, your inked handwritten signature.

✦ Add an invisible signature to the workbook indicated by the Digital Signature icon on the Status bar and metadata added to the document that verifies the source of the workbook.

By adding a digital signature, you warranty the following three things about the Excel workbook you're about to distribute:

✦ **Authenticity:** The person who signs the Excel workbook is the person he says he is (and not somebody else posing as the signer).

✦ **Integrity:** The content of the file has not been modified in any way since the workbook was digitally signed.

✦ **Non-repudiation:** The signer stands behind the content of the workbook and vouches for its origin.

To make these assurances, the digital signature you add to the workbook must be valid in the following ways:

✦ The certificate that is associated with the digital signature must be issued to the signing publisher by a reputable certificate authority.

✦ The certificate must be current and valid.

✦ The signing publisher must be deemed trustworthy.

Microsoft partners such as secure2trust or IntelliSafe Vault Desktop offer digital ID services to which you can subscribe. As reputable certificate authorities, their protection services vouch for your trustworthiness as a signing publisher and the currency of the certificates associated with your digital signatures. In addition, they enable you to set the permissions for the workbook that determine who can open the document and how they can use it.

Adding a signature line to a workbook

If you want to add a physical signature to your finalized workbook, follow these steps:

1. **Inspect the worksheet data, save all final changes in the workbook file, and then position the cell cursor in a blank cell in the vicinity where you want the signature line graphic object to appear.**

Excel adds the signature line graphic object in the area containing the cell cursor. If you don't move the cell cursor to a blank area, you may have to move the signature line graphic so that graphic's box doesn't obscure existing worksheet data or other graphics or embedded charts.

2. **Click the Microsoft Office Signature Line option on the Signature Line button's drop-menu on the Ribbon's Insert tab or press Alt+NG and press Enter.**

Excel displays an alert dialog box with a rather longwinded spiel about digital signatures. This dialog box contains two buttons: Signature Services from the Office Marketplace and an OK button. If you want to get information about subscribing to a digital ID service, click the Signature Services from the Office Marketplace command button. Otherwise, proceed to Step 3.

3. **Click OK in the alert dialog box — to avoid ever seeing the dialog box again, click the Don't Show This Message Again check box before you click OK.**

Excel closes the alert dialog box and displays the Signature Setup dialog box similar to the one shown in Figure 3-2.

Figure 3-2:
Filling out
the signing
information
in the
Signature
Setup
dialog box.

4. **Type the signer's name into the Suggested Signer text box and then press Tab.**

5. **Type the signer's title into the Suggested Signer's Title text box and then press Tab.**

6. **Type the signer's e-mail address into the Suggested Signer's E-mail Address text box.**

7. **(Optional) Click the Allow the Signer to Add Comments in the Sign Dialog check box to add a check mark to it if you want to add your own comments as to the purpose for signing the document in the Sign dialog box.**

8. **(Optional) Click the Show Sign Date in Signature Line check box to remove its check mark, if you don't need the date displayed as part of the digital signature.**

9. **Click OK to close the Signature Setup dialog box.**

   Excel adds a signature line graphic object in the vicinity of the cell cursor with a big X that contains your name and title (shown in Figure 3-3).

Figure 3-3:
Filling in the signature in the Sign dialog box.

10. **Double-click this signature line graphic object or right-click the object and then click Sign on its shortcut menu.**

    Excel opens the Sign dialog box similar to the one shown in Figure 3-3.

11. **Add your signature to the list box containing the insertion point.**

    To add your signature, click the Select Image link on the right, select a graphic file that contains a picture of your handwritten signature in the Select Signature Image dialog box, and then click Select. If you're using a Tablet PC or your computer has a digital tablet connected to it, you add this signature by physically signing your signature with digital ink.

If you selected the Allow the Signer to Add Comments in the Sign Dialog check box in Step 7, the Sign dialog box contains a Purpose for Signing This Document text box that you fill out in Step 12.

12. **Click the Purpose for Signing This Document text box and then type in the reason for digitally signing the workbook.**

By default, Excel issues a digital certificate for the person whose name is entered in the Suggested Signer text box back in Step 4. If you want to use a certificate issued to someone else in the organization, follow Step 12. Otherwise, proceed to Step 13.

13. **(Optional) Click the Change command button to open the Select Certificate dialog box and then click the name of the person whose certificate you want to use in the list box and click OK.**

To view the certificate for the person you selected, click the View Certificate command button before you click OK. Excel opens the Certificate dialog box showing the Certificate information including whether or not the certificate is trusted.

14. **Click the Sign button to close the Sign dialog box.**

Excel displays a Signature Confirmation dialog box indicating that your signature has successfully been added to the workbook and warning you that the signature becomes invalid if you save any further changes to the document.

15. **Click OK to close the Signature Confirmation dialog box.**

Immediately after closing the Signature Confirmation dialog box, Excel adds your name to the digital signature graphic object, adds the Digital Signature icon to the Status bar (between the Ready status message and the Record Macro button), and opens the Signatures task pane that displays the signer's name and date, as shown in Figure 3-4.

To display all the information about the digital signature added to the workbook, right-click its graphic object and then click Signature Details on its shortcut menu. To delete a digital signature from a workbook (which you need to do should you discover the sheets in the book still require modification), right-click the signature graphic and then click Remove Signature on its shortcut menu and click OK in its confirmation alert dialog box.

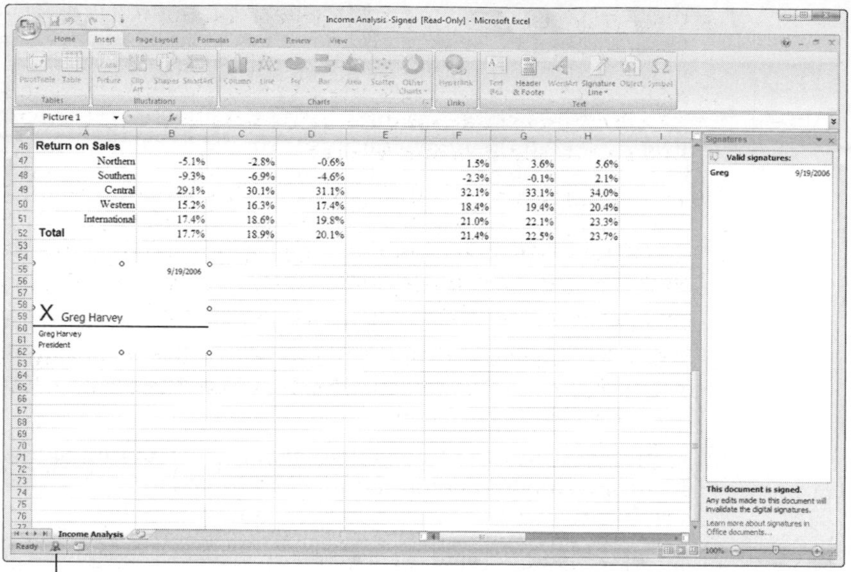

Figure 3-4:
Workbook
after adding
digital
signature
line graphic
with the
Signature
task pane
displayed.

Digital Signature icon

In place of a signature line, you can add a digital stamp (traditionally, in Asian countries such as China, Japan, and Korea, authorities sign a document not with a written signature but by affixing their official stamp to the document, usually in red ink). To literally add your stamp of approval, rather than your signature, to a workbook, click the Stamp Signature Line option on the Signature Line button's drop-down menu on the Insert tab of the Ribbon. You then follow steps very similar to those previously outlined for adding a digital signature line except that you must select a graphic file that contains the image you want stamped in the workbook in lieu of your signature.

Adding an invisible digital signature to a workbook

Sometimes your workbook may not need to have an actual signature line graphic, but those who receive your file still need to know that the workbook's content and publisher are trustworthy.

In such a case, you can digitally sign the workbook without adding a signature block by following these steps:

1. **Inspect the worksheet data and then save all final changes in the workbook file.**

2. **Highlight the Prepare option on the Office pull-down menu (opened by clicking the Office Button) and then click Add a Digital Signature on its submenu or press Alt+FES.**

Excel displays an alert dialog box with the lowdown on digital signatures, containing a Signature Services from the Office Marketplace button and an OK button. If you want to get information about subscribing to a digital ID service, click the Signature Services from the Office Marketplace command button. Otherwise, proceed to Step 3.

3. **Click OK in the alert dialog box — to avoid ever seeing the dialog box again, click the Don't Show This Message Again check box before you click OK.**

Excel opens the Sign dialog box containing a single Purpose for Signing This Document text box.

4. **Type in the reason for digitally signing the workbook in the Purpose for Signing This Document text box.**

By default, Excel issues a digital certificate for the creator of the workbook. If you want to use a certificate issued to someone else in the organization, follow Step 5. Otherwise, proceed to Step 6.

5. **(Optional) Click the Change command button to open the Select Certificate dialog box and then click the name of the person whose certificate you want to use in the list box and click OK.**

To view the certificate for the person you selected, click the View Certificate command button before you click OK. Excel opens the Certificate dialog box showing the certificate information including whether or not the certificate is trusted.

6. **Click the Sign button to close the Sign dialog box.**

Excel displays a Signature Confirmation dialog box indicating that your signature has successfully been added to the workbook and warning you that the signature becomes invalid if you save any further changes to the document.

7. **Click OK to close the Signature Confirmation dialog box.**

Immediately after closing the Signature Confirmation dialog box, Excel adds the Digital Signature icon to the Status bar (between the Ready status message and the Record Macro button) while at the same time opening the Signatures task pane that displays the signer's name and date.

To display all the information about the digital signature added to the workbook, position the mouse pointer over the signer's name in the Signatures task pane; then click its drop-down button before you click Signature Details on its drop-down menu. To delete a digital signature from a workbook (which you need to do should you discover the sheets in the book still require modification), you need to click Remove Signature on this drop-down menu and click OK.

Obtaining a Digital ID for signing a workbook

A digital ID, also known as a digital certificate, is necessary to digitally sign the documents you send out for review. If you try to digitally sign a document using one of the methods outlined in the previous two sections and you don't have a digital ID, at the time you try to open the Sign dialog box to sign the document or select a stamp, the program displays the Get a Digital ID dialog box. In this dialog box, you can choose between the following options:

✦ Purchasing a certificate from a trusted third-party vendor by clicking the Get a Digital ID from a Microsoft Partner option button

✦ Creating your own certificate by clicking the Create Your Own Digital ID option button prior to clicking OK

If you select the Create Your Own Digital ID option, the people to whom you send the workbook file on any other network computer or any computer outside of the company won't be able to verify the authenticity of your digital signature or stamp. Therefore, always select the Get a Digital ID from a Microsoft Partner option when the security concerns regarding the workbook's source and contents require this kind of third-party verification.

When you click the Get a Digital ID from a Microsoft Partner option button before you click OK in the Get a Digital ID dialog box (or you click the Add Signature Services option on the Signature Line button's drop-down menu on the Insert tab or press Alt+NGA), Excel launches your Web browser that opens a Microsoft Office Online Office Marketplace Web page with links to trusted third-party vendors of digital certificates. You can then explore these links and use them to sign up for digital certificates to use in digitally signing your workbook files.

When you click the Create Your Own Digital ID option button before clicking OK in the Get a Digital ID dialog box, Excel opens a Create a Digital ID dialog box where you enter the following information in the four text boxes:

+ **Name:** By default, this text box contains the name of the suggested signer of this workbook. Edit the name in this box only when you're creating a certificate for another person in the organization.

+ **E-mail Address:** Enter the e-mail address of the person whose name is listed as the signer of the certificate in this text box.

+ **Organization:** By default, this text box contains the name of the company to whom the computer is registered. Edit the text in this box only when you're creating a certificate for another organization.

+ **Location:** Enter your physical location or the name or ID of your personal computer in this text box.

After you enter all the information in these four text boxes in the Create a Digital ID dialog box and click the Create button, Excel opens the Sign dialog box where you enter or select your signature or stamp.

Workbook Sharing 101

If you use Excel on a computer that's connected to a network, you can share the spreadsheets that you create with others who have network access. Workbook sharing is perfect for spreadsheets that require frequent or regular data updates, especially for those whose data comes from several different departments, such as spreadsheets that track budgets or schedule projects that rely on input from many departments.

By sharing a workbook, you enable several people to edit its contents at the same time. Most often, you facilitate this process by saving the workbook file in a folder or network drive to which everyone who needs to edit the spreadsheet has access.

You can share an Excel workbook on a network in one of two ways:

+ Set up file sharing for the workbook by clicking the Share Workbook command button on the Ribbon's Review tab (Alt+RW).

+ Turn on Change tracking for the workbook by clicking the Highlight Changes option on the Track Changes command button's drop-down menu on the Ribbon's Review tab (Alt+RGH).

Whenever you share a workbook using either of these two methods, Excel automatically saves your workbook under the same filename with the shared information. The program then indicates that the workbook can now be shared by appending [Shared] to the workbook's filename as it appears on the title bar of the Excel program window. When a second person on another computer on the network opens the shared workbook file, Excel opens a copy of the workbook file and the [Shared] indicator also appears on the title bar of his or her Excel program window appended to its filename.

This is in stark contrast to what happens when you try to open an unshared workbook on your computer that's already open on another computer on the network. In that case, Excel displays a File in Use alert dialog box informing you that the workbook you want to open is already open. You can then choose between clicking the Read Only button to open the file in read-only mode (in which you can't save your changes under the original filename) and clicking the Notify button to have the program open the file in read-only mode and then notify you when the other person closes the workbook so you can save your changes.

If you click the Notify button, as soon as the other person who was editing the workbook closes the file, Excel then displays a File Now Available alert dialog box, letting you know that the file is now available to save your editing. You then click its Read-Write button to close this alert dialog box, and after that, you're free to save your editing changes to the original filename with the Save command (Ctrl+S).

Note that you don't have to be running Excel 2007 on your computer in order to open and edit a shared workbook. Workbook sharing is supported by the earlier versions of Excel (97 through 2003). You can't, however, save changes to a shared workbook if you're using an earlier version of Excel.

Also note that when you make changes to a shared workbook, Excel uses your user name to identify the modifications that you made. To modify your user name, you edit the contents of the User Name text box on the Popular tab of the Excel Options dialog box (Office Button | Excel Options or Alt+FI).

When you share a workbook, Excel disables some of the program's editing features so they can't be used in editing the shared spreadsheet. The following tasks are not enabled in a shared workbook:

✦ Deleting worksheets from the workbook

✦ Merging cells in the worksheets of a workbook

✦ Applying conditional formats to the cells of the worksheets (although all conditional formats in effect before you share the workbook remain in effect)

✦ Setting up or applying data validation to cells of the worksheets (although all data validation restrictions and messages remain in effect in the shared workbook)

✦ Inserting or deleting blocks of cells in a worksheet (although you can insert or delete entire columns and rows from the sheet)

✦ Drawing shapes and adding text boxes (see Book V, Chapter 2, for details)

✦ Assigning passwords for protecting individual worksheets or the entire workbook (although all protection and passwords defined prior to sharing the workbook remain in effect — see Book IV, Chapter 1, for details on protecting worksheets)

✦ Grouping or outlining data in a worksheet (see Book II, Chapter 4, for details)

✦ Inserting automatic subtotals in a worksheet (see Book VI, Chapter 1, for details)

✦ Creating data tables or pivot tables in a worksheet (see Book VII, Chapters 1 and 2, for details)

✦ Creating, revising, or assigning macros (although you can run macros that were created in the worksheet before it was shared, provided that they don't perform any operations that aren't supported by a shared workbook — see Book VIII, Chapter 1, for details)

Turning on file sharing

The first way to share a workbook is by turning on file sharing as follows:

1. **Open the workbook to be shared and then make any last-minute edits to the file, especially those that are not supported in a shared workbook.**

   Keep in mind when making these last-minute changes that when you share a workbook, some of Excel's editing features become unavailable to you and any others working in the file. (Refer to the list in the previous section for exactly which features are unavailable.)

   Before turning on file sharing, you may want to save the workbook in a special folder on a network drive to which everyone who is to edit the file has access.

2. **Click Office Button | Save As or press Alt+FA and then select the network drive and the folder in the Save As dialog box in which you want to the make the shared version of this file available before you click the Save button.**

3. **Click the Share Workbook command button on the Review tab of the Ribbon or press Alt+RW.**

Excel opens a Share Workbook dialog box (similar to the one shown in Figure 3-5). This dialog box contains two tabs: an Editing tab that enables you to turn on file sharing for all the users who have the file open, and an Advanced tab where you control how the amount of time that changes is tracked and how updates are handled.

Figure 3-5: Turning on file sharing on the Editing tab of the Share Workbook dialog box.

4. **Click the Allow Changes by More Than One User at the Same Time check box on the Editing tab.**

By default, Excel maintains a Change History log for 30 days. If you wish, you can use the Advanced tab settings to modify whether or not Excel maintains this Change History log (necessary if you want to reconcile and merge changes) or to change how long the program saves this log. You can also change when changes are updated, how conflicts are handled, and whether or not your print settings and data filtering settings are shared.

5. **(Optional) Click the Advanced tab and then change the options on this tab that affect how long a change log is maintained and how editing conflicts are handled.**

See the following section, "Modifying the Workbook Share options," for details on changing these settings.

6. Click the OK button to close the Share Workbook dialog box.

As soon as Excel closes the Share Workbook dialog box, an alert dialog box appears, telling you that Excel will now save the workbook and asking you if you want to continue.

7. Click the OK button in the Microsoft Excel alert dialog box to save the workbook with the file sharing settings.

Immediately after you click OK and close the alert dialog box, Excel saves the workbook and the [Shared] indicator appears at the end of the filename on the Excel program window's title bar.

Modifying the Workbook Share options

As soon as you turn on file sharing for a workbook, Excel also turns on a Change History log that records all the changes made by different individuals to the same workbook file. You can use the Change History log to view information about the various changes made to a shared workbook and to determine which of the changes to retain if conflicting changes are made by different people to the same cells of a workbook. You can also use the Change History log when merging changes from different copies of the same workbook into a single file.

By default, Excel maintains the Change History log for a period of 30 days from the date that you first share the workbook. If you wish, you can change the length of time that Excel maintains the Change History log or, even, in rare circumstances, elect to not keep the log.

To make changes to the length of time that Excel maintains the Change History log, you click the Advanced tab in the Share Workbook dialog box (Alt+RW), as shown in Figure 3-6. This tab contains the following sections with options for not only changing how long the Change History log is maintained, but also controlling when and how updates are handled:

◆ **Track Changes:** Enables you to modify how long Excel keeps the Change History log by entering a new value in the Keep Change History For text box or selecting a new value with the spinner buttons. Click the Don't Keep Change History option button should you ever decide that you don't need the Change History log.

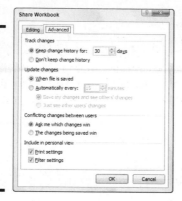

Figure 3-6:
Modifying
the sharing
options
on the
Advanced
tab of the
Share
Workbook
dialog box.

✦ **Update Changes:** Enables you to select when changes made by different users are saved. By default, Excel saves changes when the file is saved. To have the program save changes every so many minutes, click the Automatically Every option button and then enter the number of minutes for the save interval in the Minutes text box or select this interval value with its spinner buttons. When automatically saving changes every so many minutes, by default, Excel saves only your changes while showing you changes made to the workbook by others. To have the program just display the changes made to the file by others when the save interval is reached without saving your changes, click the Just See Other Users' Changes option button.

✦ **Conflicting Changes Between Users:** Enables you to select how changes made to the same cells of a shared workbook by different users are treated. By default, Excel is set to ask you which user's changes to accept and which to deny. If you want Excel to accept the changes made by any user at the time she or he saves the workbook, click the Changes Being Saved Win option button.

✦ **Include in Personal View:** Enables you to determine which of your personal settings are saved when you save the workbook. By default, Excel saves both your personal print settings (including such things as page breaks, changes to the print area, and changes to the printing settings — see Book II, Chapter 5, for details) and the filtering settings you select with the AutoFilter buttons (see Book VI, Chapter 2, for details). Deselect the Print Settings and/or Filter Settings check boxes at the bottom of the Advanced tab if you decide that you don't need these settings saved as part of the shared workbook.

Turning on Change tracking

The second way to share a workbook on a network is by turning on Change tracking. When you do this, Excel tracks all changes you make to the contents of the cells in the shared workbook by highlighting their cells and adding comments that summarize the type of change you make. When you turn on Change tracking, Excel automatically turns on file sharing along with the workbook's Change History log.

To turn on Change tracking in a workbook, you take these steps:

1. **Open the workbook for which you want to track changes and that you wish to share, and then make any last-minute edits to the file, especially those that are not supported in a shared workbook.**

When making these last-minute changes, keep in mind that, when you share a workbook, some of Excel's editing features become unavailable to you and any others working in the file. (Refer to the "Workbook Sharing 101" section, earlier in this chapter, for a list of exactly which features are unavailable.)

Before turning on file sharing, you may want to save the workbook in a special folder on a network drive to which everyone who is to edit the file has access.

2. **Click Office Button | Save As or press Alt+FA and then select the network drive and the folder in the Save As dialog box in which you want to the make the Change tracking version of this file available before you click Save.**

3. **Click the Highlight Changes option on the Track Changes command button's drop-down menu on the Review tab or press Alt+RGH.**

Doing this opens the Highlight Changes dialog box, shown in Figure 3-7, where you turn on Change tracking and indicate which changes to highlight.

**Book IV
Chapter 3**

Figure 3-7:
Turning on
Change
tracking in
the Highlight
Changes
dialog box.

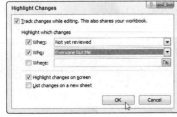

**Sending Workbooks
Out for Review**

4. Click the Track Changes While Editing check box.

Doing this turns on Change tracking and automatically turns on file sharing for the workbook.

By default, Excel selects the When combo box and chooses the All option from its drop-down menu to have all changes made to the workbook tracked. To track the changes only from the time you last saved the workbook, you click the Since I Last Saved item on the When drop-down menu. To track all changes that you've not yet reviewed (and decided whether or not to accept), you click the Not Yet Reviewed item on the When drop-down menu (most often, you want this option so that you can use the Accept/Reject Changes option on the Track Changes command button's drop-down menu to review each person's changes and decide whether or not to keep them). To track changes from a particular date, click Since Date on the When drop-down menu: Excel then inserts the current date into the When combo box, which you can then edit, if necessary.

5. (Optional) If you don't want to track all changes in the workbook, click the When drop-down button and then click the menu item on its drop-down menu (Since I Last Saved, Not Yet Reviewed, or Since Date).

By default, Excel tracks the changes made by anybody who opens and edits the workbook (including you). If you want to exempt yourself from Change tracking or restrict it to a particular user, you click the Who check box and then click Everyone But Me or the user's name on the Who drop-down menu.

6. (Optional) If you want to restrict Change tracking, click the name of the person to whom you want to restrict Change tracking in the Who drop-down list.

Note that selecting any option on the Who drop-down menu automatically selects the Who check box by putting a check mark in it.

By default, Change Tracking tracks changes made to any and all cells in every sheet in the workbook. To restrict the Change tracking to a particular range or nonadjacent cell selection, click the Where check box and then select the cells.

7. (Optional) If you want to restrict Change tracking to a particular cell range or cell selection in the workbook, click the Where combo box and then select the cell range or nonadjacent cell selection in the workbook.

Clicking the Where text box and selecting a cell range in the workbook automatically selects the Where check box by putting a check mark in it.

By default, Excel highlights all editing changes in the cells of the worksheet on the screen by selecting the Highlight Changes on Screen check box. If you don't want the changes marked in the cells, you need to deselect this check box.

8. **(Optional) If you don't want changes displayed in the cells on-screen, click the Highlight Changes on Screen check box to remove its check mark.**

Note that after you finish saving the workbook as a shared file, you can return to the Highlight Changes dialog box and then select its List Changes on a New Sheet check box to have all your changes listed on a new worksheet added to the workbook. Note too, that if you select this check box when the Highlight Changes on Screen check box is selected, Excel both marks the changes in their cells and lists them on a new sheet. If you deselect the Highlight Changes on Screen check box while the List Changes on a New Sheet check box is selected, Excel just lists the changes on a new worksheet without marking them in the cells of the worksheet.

9. **Click OK to close the Highlight Changes dialog box.**

As soon as Excel closes the Highlight Changes dialog box, an alert dialog box appears, telling you that Excel will now save the workbook and asking you if you want to continue.

10. **Click OK in the Microsoft Excel alert dialog box to save the workbook with the Change tracking and file sharing settings.**

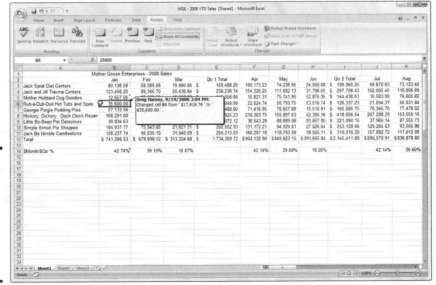

Figure 3-8: Displaying the comment added to a cell highlighted by Change tracking.

After you turn on Change tracking in a shared workbook, Excel highlights the following changes:

✦ Changes to the cell contents, including moving and copying the contents to new cells in the worksheet

✦ Deletion of the cell contents

✦ Insertion of new rows, columns, or cells in a worksheet

When Change tracking is turned on in a workbook, the program does *not,* however, highlight any of these changes:

✦ Formatting changes made to the cells

✦ Hidden or unhidden rows and columns in the worksheet

✦ Renamed sheet tabs in the workbook

✦ Insertion or deletion of a worksheet in the workbook

✦ Comments added to the cells

✦ Changes to cell values resulting from the recalculation of formulas or to cells whose values depend upon those formulas

In highlighting changes you make to the shared workbook, Excel draws a thin line (in another color — usually blue) around the borders of the cell, while at the same time placing a triangle of the same color in the cell's upper-left corner. When you position the thick white-cross mouse pointer on a highlighted cell, Excel displays a comment indicating the change made to the cell along with the date and time it was made and who made it, as shown in Figure 3-8.

When you turn on Change tracking, you also necessarily turn on file sharing, and when file sharing is in effect, you can't make certain kinds of editing changes. For a complete list of these changes, refer back to the section, "Workbook Sharing 101," earlier in this chapter.

Merging changes from different users

At some point after sharing a workbook, you'll want to update the workbook to incorporate the changes made by different users. When merging changes, you may also have to deal with conflicting changes made to the same cells and decide which changes to accept and which to reject. After you've merged all the input and decided how to deal with all the conflicting changes, you may even want to turn off file sharing to prevent users from doing any further editing.

Resolving conflicts

When you turn on file sharing for a workbook, Excel automatically updates the changes made to the shared workbook whenever anybody who's editing the file saves his or her changes. Should the program identify cells in the workbook that contain conflicting changes (that is, different values placed in the same cell by different users), it flags the cell in the workbook and then displays the conflict in the Resolve Conflicts dialog box, as shown in Figure 3-9. To accept your change to the cell in question, you click the Accept Mine button. To accept the change made by another user, you click the Accept Other button instead.

After you accept your change or the other user's change in the case of the first conflict, Excel flags the next case and displays a description of the conflicting values in the Resolve Conflicts dialog box. When you finish accepting or rejecting your change or the one made by another user for the last conflicting value, Excel automatically closes the Resolve Conflicts dialog box, and you can save your changes to the workbook by clicking Office Button | Save or by pressing Ctrl+S.

If you want Excel to accept only your changes in all cases of conflicting values, click the Accept All Mine button. To have Excel reject all your changes and accept all those made by others, click the Accept All Others button instead.

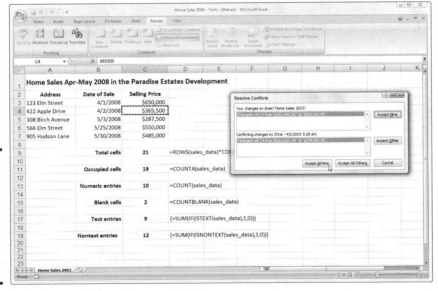

Figure 3-9: Deciding which change to accept in the Resolve Conflicts dialog box.

TIP

If you know that you always want all your changes to be accepted in the case of conflicting values, open the Share Workbook dialog box (Alt+RW) and then click the Changes Being Saved Win option button on the Advanced tab before you click OK. If you prefer to have your changes (including conflicting ones) automatically saved at set intervals, click the Automatically option button and set the number of minutes between saves in the Minutes text box before you click OK.

Accepting or rejecting highlighted changes

When you turn on Change tracking for a workbook, you can decide which changes to accept or reject by clicking the Accept/Reject Changes option on the Track Changes command button's drop-down menu on the Ribbon's Review tab (or pressing Alt+RGC). When you do this, Excel reviews all the highlighted changes made by you and others who've worked on the shared file, enabling you to accept or reject individual changes.

When you first choose the Accept/Reject Changes option, Excel displays the alert dialog box, informing you that Excel will save the workbook. When you click OK to close this alert dialog box, the program opens the Select Changes to Accept or Reject dialog box, which contains the same three check boxes and associated drop-down items (When, Who, and Where) as the Highlight Changes dialog box.

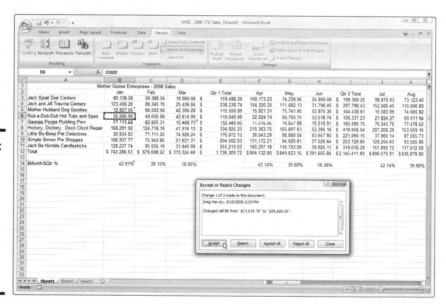

Figure 3-10: Deciding whether or not to accept a change in the Accept or Reject Changes dialog box.

By default, the When check box is selected along with the Not Yet Reviewed setting in the Select Changes to Accept or Reject dialog box. When this setting is selected, Excel displays all the changes in the workbook that you haven't yet reviewed for everyone who has modified the shared file. To review only those changes you made on the current date, click the Since Date item on the When drop-down list. To review changes made since a particular date, edit the current date in the Since Date drop-down list.

To review only changes that everyone has made except you, only those changes you've made, or only those changes a particular coworker has made, click the appropriate item (Everyone But Me, your name, or another user's name) on the Who drop-down list. If you want to restrict the review to a particular range or region of a worksheet, click the Where combo box and then select the range or nonadjacent cell ranges with the cells to review.

After you select which changes to review in the Select Changes to Accept or Reject dialog box, click the OK button. Excel then closes this dialog box, highlights the cell in the worksheet that contains the first change to review, and opens the Accept or Reject Changes dialog box (similar to the one shown in Figure 3-10), where you indicate whether or not to accept or reject the change. To accept the change, you click the Accept button. To reject the change and keep the original value, you click the Reject button instead. Excel then highlights the next cell in the worksheet that needs reviewing, while at the same time displaying a description of the change in the Accept or Reject Changes dialog box.

If you know ahead of time that you want to accept or reject all the changes that have been made since you last reviewed the workbook or the date you specified, click the Accept All button or the Reject All button, respectively. When you accept or reject the last change identified in the workbook, the Accept or Reject Changes dialog box automatically closes, and you can then save the workbook (Ctrl+S) with the editing changes made as a result of this review.

How to stop sharing a workbook

If you decide that you no longer want to share a particular workbook, you can turn off the file sharing. To do this, open the Share Workbook dialog box (Alt+RW) and remove the check mark from the Allow Changes by More Than One User at the Same Time check box on the Editing tab before you click OK.

**Book IV
Chapter 3**

**Sending Workbooks
Out for Review**

As soon as you click OK, Excel displays an Information alert dialog box indicating that your action is about to remove the workbook from shared use and, at the same time, erase the Change History log. It also informs you that users who are currently editing this workbook will be unable to save their changes even if you should later change your mind and turn the file sharing back on again.

Because users are prevented from saving their changes and the Change History log is erased as soon as you turn off file sharing and make the workbook once again exclusive, you don't *ever* want to turn off file sharing until *after* you're sure that you have everybody's comments and changes saved to the workbook and have reviewed and merged the changes you want to keep.

If you're sure that you've met these two conditions, you can click the Yes button in the Information alert dialog box to turn off file sharing and once again make the workbook your exclusive property. Click the No button, however, to abort this procedure if you have any doubt about having all your users' changes erased.

It's always a good idea to inform the users of your shared workbook of your intention to remove the file from shared use well in advance of the actual date. Your best bet is to e-mail each user and let him or her know exactly the date and time after which the workbook will no longer be shared and open to their edits. That way, each person on the team knows the exact time after which his or her changes and comments will no longer be accepted (which is often a good inducement for the procrastinators on the team to send you their last-minute suggestions and changes).

Removing a user from the shared workbook

Sometimes, rather than preventing everyone from sharing a particular workbook, you may only need to stop particular users from being able to edit it. To remove a specific user from sharing in the editing, you open the Share Workbook dialog box (Alt+RW), click the name of the person you want to remove in the Who Has This Workbook Open Now list box, and then click the Remove User button.

As soon as you click this button, Excel displays an alert dialog box informing you that if the user you selected is currently editing the workbook, your action will prevent him or her from saving the workbook so that all unsaved work is automatically lost. To proceed with removing the user, click the OK button in this alert dialog box. To abandon the removal until after you've verified that the user isn't currently editing the file, click the Cancel button instead.

Workbooks on Review

Even if you don't use Excel on a network, you still can add your comments to the cells of a workbook that ask for clarification or suggest changes, and then distribute copies of the workbook by e-mail to other people who need to review and, perhaps, respond to your remarks. Excel makes it easy to annotate the cells of a worksheet, and the command buttons on the Review tab of the Ribbon make it easy to review these notes prior to e-mailing the workbook to others who have to review the comments, and even reply to suggested changes.

And if you're running Excel 2007 on a Tablet PC, the Review tab of your Ribbon has a Start Inking command button (not included on this tab when running Excel on a regular PC). When you click the Start Inking command button, Excel adds an Ink Tools contextual tab to the Ribbon. You can then use the command buttons on its Pens tab to highlight and mark up various parts of the spreadsheet with digital ink.

Adding comments

You can add comments to the current cell by clicking the New Comment command button on the Ribbon's Review tab or by pressing Alt+RC. Excel responds by adding a comment box (similar to the one shown in Figure 3-11) with your name listed at the top (or the name of the person who shows up in the User Name text box on the Popular tab of the Excel Options dialog box). You can then type the text of your comment in this box. When you finish typing the text of the note, click the cell to which you're attaching the note or any other cell in the worksheet to close the Comment box.

Displaying and hiding comments

Excel indicates that you've attached a comment to a worksheet cell by adding a red triangle to the cell's upper-right corner. To display the comment box with its text, you position the thick, white-cross mouse pointer on this red triangle, or you can click the Show All Comments command button on the Review tab (Alt+RA) to display all comments in the worksheet.

When you display a comment by positioning the mouse pointer on the cell's red triangle, the comment disappears as soon as you move the pointer outside the cell. When you display all the comments on the worksheet by clicking the Show All Comments command button on the Review tab, you must click the Show All Comments button a second time before Excel closes their comment boxes (or press Alt+RA).

Book IV Chapter 3

Sending Workbooks Out for Review

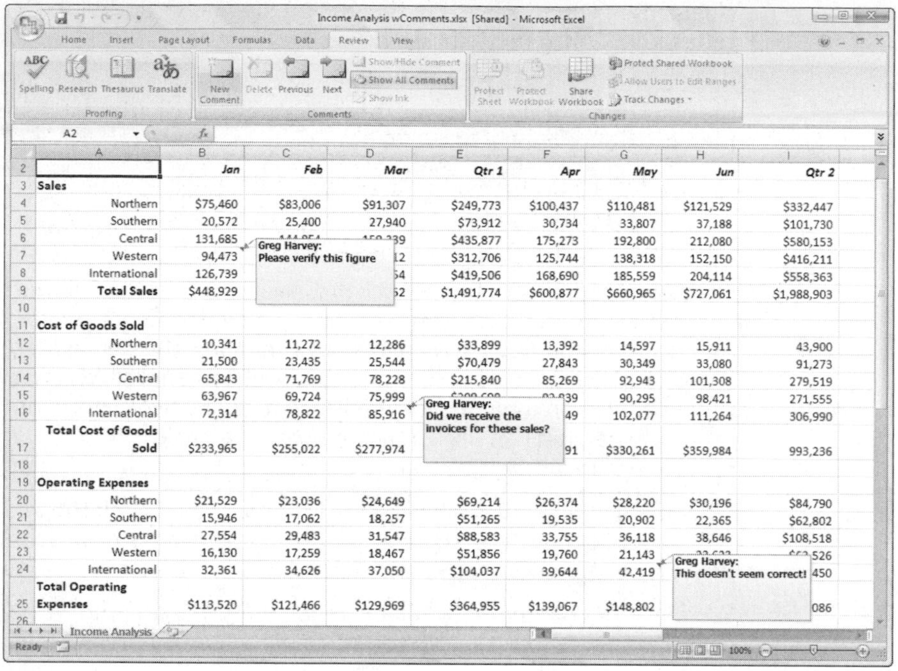

Figure 3-11:
Adding
comments
to the cells
of a spread-
sheet.

Editing and formatting comments

When you first add a comment to a cell, its Comment box appears to the right of the cell with an arrow pointing to the red triangle in the cell's upper-right corner. If you need to, you can reposition a cell's Comment box and/or resize it so that it doesn't obscure certain cells in the immediate region. You can also edit the text of a comment and change the formatting of the text font.

To reposition or resize a Comment box or edit the note text or its font, you make the cell current by putting the cell cursor in it, and then click the Edit Comment command button, which replaces the New Comment button as the first button in the Comments group on the Review tab of the Ribbon, or press Alt+RT. (You can also do this by right-clicking the cell and then clicking Edit Comment on the cell's shortcut menu.)

Whichever method you use, Excel then displays the cell's comment box and positions the insertion point at the end of the comment text. To reposition the comment box, position the mouse pointer on the edge of the box (indicated with cross-hatching and open circles around the perimeter). When the mouse pointer assumes the shape of a white arrowhead pointing to a black double-cross, you can then drag the outline of the comment box to a new position in the worksheet. After you release the mouse button, Excel draws a new line ending in an arrowhead from the repositioned Comment box to the red triangle in the cell's upper-right corner.

When editing and formatting the comments you've added to the worksheet, you can do any of the following:

✦ To resize the comment box, you position the mouse pointer on one of the open circles at the corners or in the middle of each edge on the box's perimeter. When the mouse pointer changes into a double-headed arrow, you drag the handle of the Comment box until its dotted outline is the size and shape you want. (Excel automatically reflows the comment text to suit the new size and shape of the box.)

✦ To edit the text of the comment (when the insertion point is positioned somewhere in it), drag the I-beam mouse pointer through text that needs to be replaced or press the Backspace key (to remove characters to the left of the insertion point) or Delete key (to remove characters to the right). You can insert new characters in the comment to the right of the insertion point by simply typing them.

✦ To change the formatting of the comment text, select the text by dragging the I-beam mouse pointer through it, then click the appropriate command button in the Font and Alignment groups on the Home tab of the Ribbon (you can use Live Preview to see how a new font or font size, on its respective drop-down menu, looks in the comment, provided that these drop-down menus don't cover the comment box in the worksheet).

You can also right-click the text and click Format Comment on the shortcut menu. Doing this opens the Format Comment dialog box (with the same options as the Font tab of the Format Cells dialog box) where you can change the font, font style, font size, font color, or add special effects including underlining, strikethrough, as well as super- and subscripting.

When you finish making your changes to the comment box and text, close the comment box by clicking its cell or any of the other cells in the worksheet.

Deleting comments

When you no longer need a comment, you can delete it by selecting its cell before you do any of the following:

✦ Click the Comments option on the Clear button's drop-down menu on the Home tab of the Ribbon or press Alt+HEM.

✦ Click the Delete command button in the Comments group on the Review tab of the Ribbon or press Alt+RD.

✦ Right-click the cell and then click Delete Comment on its shortcut menu.

**Book IV
Chapter 3**

**Sending Workbooks
Out for Review**

If you delete a comment in error, you can restore it to its cell by clicking the Undo command button on the Quick Access toolbar or pressing Ctrl+Z.

Marking up a worksheet with digital ink

If you're fortunate enough to be running Excel 2007 on a Tablet PC computer, you can mark up your worksheets with digital ink. Excel 2007 running on a Tablet PC contains a Start Inking command button located at the very end of the Ribbon's Review tab. When you click this command button (or press Alt+RK), Excel displays a Pens tab on the Ink Tools contextual tab.

By default, Excel chooses the felt tip pen as the pen type for annotating the worksheet with digital ink. If you'd prefer to use a ballpoint pen or highlighter in marking up the worksheet, click the Ballpoint Pen command button or Highlighter command button in the Pens group.

When using the highlighter or either of the two pen types (felt tip or ballpoint pen), you can select a new line weight for the ink by clicking the point size (running from f 3/4 all the way up to 6 points) on the Weight command button's drop-down menu. You can also select a new ink color (yellow being the default color for the highlighter, red for the felt tip pen, and black for ballpoint pen) by clicking its color swatch on the Color command button's drop-down palette.

After you select the pen type, color, and line weight, you can use the physical pen that comes with your Tablet PC to mark up the spreadsheet as follows:

✦ To highlight data in the spreadsheet with the highlighter, drag the highlight mouse pointer through the cells (just as though you had an actual yellow highlighter in your hand).

✦ To circle data in the spreadsheet with the felt tip pen, drag the pen tip mouse pointer around the cells in the worksheet.

✦ To add a comment with the ballpoint pen, drag the pen tip mouse pointer to write out your text in the worksheet.

If you make a mistake with ink, you need to remove it and start over again. To delete the ink, click the Eraser command button in the Pens group and then click somewhere on the highlighting, drawing, or handwriting you want to erase with the eraser mouse pointer (sometimes you have to drag through the ink to completely remove it). Then, reselect the highlighter or felt tip or ballpoint pen and reapply your ink annotation.

When you finish marking up the worksheet with ink, click the Close Ink Tools command button on the Pens tab of the Ink Tools contextual tab. Excel then closes the Ink Tools contextual tab, once again displaying only the normal Ribbon tabs.

Sending a workbook as an e-mail attachment

Excel makes it easy to send out workbooks that you've annotated for review to clients, coworkers, and managers. You can send the workbook as a simple attachment to an e-mail message by clicking the Office Button, highlighting the Send option, and then clicking the Email option on its submenu (or pressing Alt+FDE).

When you do this, Excel opens your e-mail program (such as Windows Mail, Outlook, or Outlook Express) and starts a new e-mail message. In the message, Excel automatically fills in the Subject line with the name of the active workbook and attaches a copy of the file to the new message. You can fill in the recipient's e-mail address in the To text box, type in the body of the message, and then click the Send button to send the message off to your recipient or recipients.

When the e-mail recipients open the e-mail message with an attached workbook file, they can save the file to disk and then open it as they would any other Excel workbook.

To save a workbook attached to an e-mail message, right-click the filename of the attached workbook that appears on the message's header and then click Save As on the shortcut menu. If you want to open the workbook directly in Excel, click Open on the attachment's shortcut menu instead. If your e-mail program is Windows Mail, Outlook, or Outlook Express, you may receive an Opening Mail Attachment alert dialog box warning that the file may contain potentially damaging viruses and suggesting that you first save the workbook to disk. If you're sure of the source of the e-mail and aren't worried about a virus, click the Open It option button in this alert dialog box and then click OK.

Chapter 4: Sharing Worksheets and Worksheet Data

In This Chapter

✔ **Understanding the basics of data sharing between Windows programs**

✔ **Getting Excel data and charts into a Word document**

✔ **Getting Excel data and charts into the slides of a PowerPoint presentation**

✔ **Exporting your Outlook Contacts into an Excel worksheet**

✔ **Using Smart Tags to share online information**

✔ **Saving workbooks as PDF, XPS, and HTML files**

✔ **Publishing workbooks to a document server or SharePoint site**

Sharing data between Excel and other Windows programs that you use is the topic of this chapter. In many cases, data sharing involves getting Excel data tables, data lists, and charts into other Office programs that you use, especially Microsoft Word documents and PowerPoint presentations. In other cases, data sharing involves getting data generated in other programs, such as in tables and lists created in Microsoft Word and contacts maintained in Microsoft Outlook, into an Excel worksheet.

In addition to data sharing that involves bringing data stored in different types of documents into Excel worksheets, the program continues to support data sharing in the form of *Smart Tags* that can bring information into the spreadsheet that's related to a particular type of data entry, such as a person's name, a company's stock symbol, or the name of a city. Information imported through the use of Smart Tags can come from local sources, such as your Outlook Contacts file, as well as from online sources, such as MSN MoneyCentral on the Web.

Also, you can share worksheet data by publishing the Excel workbook in a shared space such as a document workspace or document management server where users can access the data by opening up the workbook file in their own copies of Excel. Finally, you can give people access to worksheet data using programs other than Excel, including Acrobat Reader, the XML Paper Specification Viewer, and their own Web browsers by saving the workbook in a special PDF, XPS, or HTML file format or by publishing the workbook to SharePoint server running Excel Calculation Services.

Office 2007 Data Sharing Basics

You share information between Excel and other Windows programs in two ways: You either copy or move discrete objects or blocks of data from one program's file to another, or you open an entire file created with one program in the other program.

The key to sharing blocks of data or discrete objects in Excel is the Windows Clipboard. Remember that Excel always gives you access to contents of the Clipboard in the form of the Clipboard task pane, which you can open by clicking the Dialog Box Launcher button in the lower-right corner of the Clipboard group at the beginning of the Home tab on the Ribbon. When the Clipboard task pane is open, you can then copy its objects or blocks of text into cells of the open worksheet simply by clicking the item in this task pane.

Because very few people purchase Excel 2007 as a separate program outside the Microsoft Office 2007 suite, it should be no surprise that most of the file sharing happens between Excel and one of the other major applications included in Microsoft Office (such as Word, PowerPoint, and Access).

However, before you rush off and start wildly throwing Excel 2007 worksheets into Word 2007 documents and Excel 2007 charts into PowerPoint 2007 presentations, you need to realize that Microsoft offers you a choice in the way that you exchange data between your various Office programs. You can either embed the worksheet or chart in the other program or set up a link between the Excel-generated object in the other program and Excel itself.

✦ *Embedding* means that the Excel object (whether it's a worksheet or a chart) actually becomes part of the Word document or PowerPoint presentation. Any changes that you then need to make to the worksheet or chart must be made within the Word document or PowerPoint presentation. This presupposes, however, that you have Excel on the same computer as Word or PowerPoint and that your computer has enough memory to run them both.

✦ *Linking* means that the Excel object (worksheet or chart) is only referred to in the Word document or PowerPoint presentation. Any changes that you make to the worksheet or chart must be made in Excel itself and then updated when you open the Word document or PowerPoint presentation to which it is linked.

Use the embedding method when the Excel object (worksheet or chart) is not apt to change very often, if at all. Use the linking method when the Excel object (worksheet or chart) changes fairly often, when you always need the latest and greatest version of the object to appear in your Word document or PowerPoint presentation, or when you don't want to make the Word or PowerPoint document any bigger by adding the Excel data to it.

Be aware that when you link an Excel worksheet or chart to another Office document and you want to show that document or print it on a different computer, you must copy both the Excel workbook with the linked worksheet/chart and the Word or PowerPoint file to that computer. Also be aware that when you embed an Excel worksheet or chart in another Office document and then want to edit it on another computer, that computer must have both Excel and the other Microsoft Office program (Word or PowerPoint) installed on it.

Use the embedding or linking techniques only when you have a pretty good suspicion that the Excel stuff is far from final and that you want to be able to update the Excel data either manually (with embedding) or automatically (with linking). If your Excel stuff will remain unchanged, just use the old standby method of copying the Excel data to the Clipboard with the Copy command button on the Home tab (or pressing Ctrl+C) and then switching to the Word or PowerPoint document and pasting it in place with the Paste command button (or pressing Ctrl+V).

Excel maintains a very close relationship with Microsoft Access, thus making it easy to import data from any of the tables or queries set up for a database into your Excel worksheet. For details on how to bring in data from Access, see Book VI, Chapter 2.

Excel and Word 2007

Of all the Office programs (besides our beloved Excel), Microsoft Word 2007 is the one that you are most apt to use. You will probably find yourself using Word to type up any memos, letters, and reports that you need in the course of your daily work (even if you really don't understand how the program works). From time to time, you may need to bring some worksheet data or

**Book IV
Chapter 4**

**Sharing Worksheets
and Worksheet Data**

charts that you've created in your Excel workbooks into a Word document that you're creating. When those occasions arise, check out the information in the next section.

Although Word has a Table feature that supports calculations through a kind of mini-spreadsheet operation, you probably will be more productive if you create the data (formulas, formatting, and all) in an Excel workbook and then bring that data into your Word document by following the steps outlined in the next section. Likewise, although you can keep, create, and manage the data records that you use in mail merge operations within Word, you probably will find it more expedient to create and maintain them in Excel — considering that you are already familiar with how to create, sort, and filter database records in Excel.

Getting Excel data into a Word document

As with all the other Office programs, you have two choices when bringing Excel data (worksheet cell data or charts) into a Word document: You can embed the data in the Word document, or you can link the data that you bring into Word to its original Excel worksheet. Embed the data or charts when you want to be able to edit right within Word. Link the data or charts when you want to be able to edit in Excel and have the changes automatically updated when you open the Word document.

Happily embedded after

The easiest way to embed a table of worksheet data or a chart is to use the good old drag-and-drop method: Simply drag the selected cells or chart between the Excel and Word program windows instead of to a new place in a worksheet. The only trick to dragging and dropping between programs is the sizing and maneuvering of the Excel and Word program windows themselves. Figures 4-1 and 4-2 illustrate the procedure for dragging a table of worksheet data (with first January sales for the Mission Street store) from its worksheet (named Mission Street) into a memo started in Word.

Before I could drag the selected worksheet data, I had to size and position the Excel and Word program windows. To do this, I opened the Spring Sales spreadsheet in Excel and then launched Word and started a new document. To tile the windows one above the other, I simply right-clicked the Windows Vista taskbar and then clicked the Show Windows Stacked option on its shortcut menu (if you're running Excel on Windows XP, you click the Tile Windows Horizontally option to accomplish the same thing).

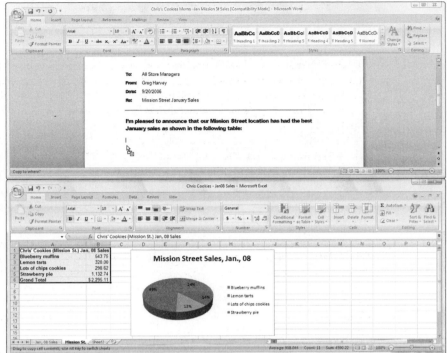

Figure 4-1:
Dragging the cell range A2:E9 formatted as a table from the Spring Sales workbook to the Word memo.

In Figure 4-1, you can see that the Excel window is positioned below the Word window after selecting the Show Windows Stacked option. At that point, I had only to select the worksheet data in the Excel worksheet and then hold down the Ctrl key (to copy) as I dragged the outline up to the Word window.

As I passed over the border between the Excel and Word program windows, the mouse pointer changed shape to the international "oh-no-you-don't" symbol. When I reached the safe havens of the Word document area, however, the pointer changed again, this time to the shape of an arrowhead sticking up from a box with a plus sign (how's that for a description?). To indicate where in the Word document to embed the selected data, I simply positioned the arrowhead-sticking-up-from-a-box-with-a-plus-sign pointer at the place in the document where the Excel stuff is to appear. Then I released the mouse button. Figure 4-2 shows you the embedded worksheet table that appeared after I released the mouse button.

**Book IV
Chapter 4**

**Sharing Worksheets
and Worksheet Data**

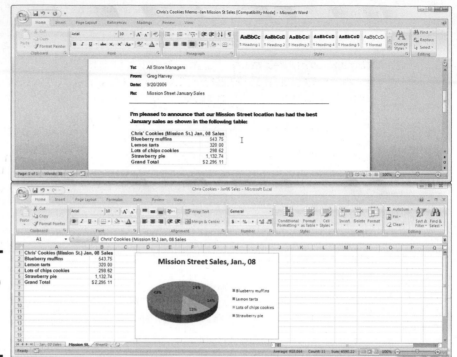

Figure 4-2:
Word memo
after copy-
ing the
worksheet
data.

You can also use the cut-and-paste method to embed worksheet data into a Word document. Simply select the cells in Excel and then copy them to the Clipboard by clicking the Copy button on the Home tab of the Ribbon (Ctrl+C). Then, open the Word document and position the cursor at the place where the spreadsheet table is to appear. Click the Paste Special option on the Paste button's drop-down menu on the Home tab of Word's Ribbon (or press Alt+HVS). Click Microsoft Office Excel Worksheet Object in Word's Paste Special dialog box and then click OK. Word then embeds the data in the body of the Word document just as though you had Ctrl+dragged the data from the Excel window over to the Word window.

If you don't want gridlines to appear in the worksheet data that you copy to a Word document (as shown in Figure 4-2), be sure to remove their display in Excel before you do the copying. To remove gridlines from a worksheet, you just click the Gridlines check box to remove the check mark in the Show/Hide group of the View tab on the Ribbon (or press Alt+WVG).

Editing embedded stuff

The great thing about embedding Excel stuff (as opposed to linking, which I get to in a later section) is that you can edit the data right from within Word. Figure 4-3 shows the table after I centered it with the Center button on Word's Formatting toolbar. Notice what happens when I double-click the embedded table (or click the table once and then choose Worksheet Object⇨Edit on the table's shortcut menu): A frame with columns and rows, scroll bars, and sheet tabs miraculously appears around the table. Notice, also, that the tabs on the Word Ribbon have changed to ones on the Excel Ribbon (it's like being at home when you're still on the road). At this point, you can edit any of the table's contents by using the Excel commands that you already know. In this case, I selected the Page Layout tab and then clicked the View check box under the Gridlines heading to remove the cell borders from the table.

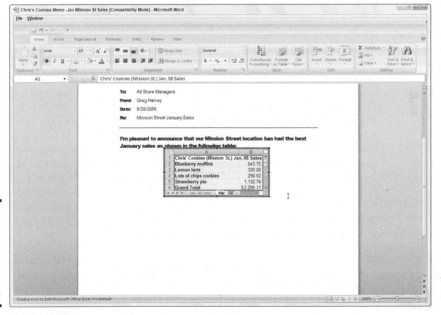

Figure 4-3: Editing the embedded worksheet data in the Sales memo.

The links that bind

Of course, as nice as embedding is, you will encounter occasions when linking the Excel data to the Word document is the preferred method (and, in fact, even easier to do). Figure 4-4 illustrates how easy this linking process is. First, I select a chart that I created in the worksheet by *single*-clicking it, not double-clicking it, as I would do to edit the chart in the worksheet.

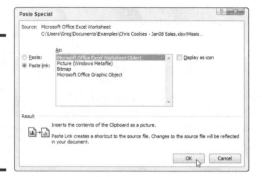

Figure 4-4: Selecting the Paste Link option in Word's Paste Special dialog box.

Then, after copying the chart (or selected data) to the Clipboard by clicking the Copy command on the Excel Ribbon's Home tab, I switched over to Word and my memo to all store managers. After positioning the insertion point at the beginning of the paragraph where the chart needs to be, I clicked the Paste Special option on the Paste button's drop-down menu on the Home tab of Word's Ribbon (you can also do this by pressing Alt+HVS). Figure 4-4 shows the Paste Special dialog box that appears. In this dialog box, the crucial thing is to select the Paste Link option button and Microsoft Office Excel Worksheet Object in the list box before clicking OK. Figure 4-5 shows the Word memo after I clicked OK and pasted the Excel chart into place.

Editing linked data

Editing data linked to Excel (as a chart or cells) is not quite as delightful as editing embedded worksheet data. For one thing, you first have to go back to Excel and make your changes — although you can easily open Excel and its workbook just by double-clicking the linked chart. The nice thing, however is that any changes that you make to the original data or chart are immediately reflected in the Word document the moment you open it.

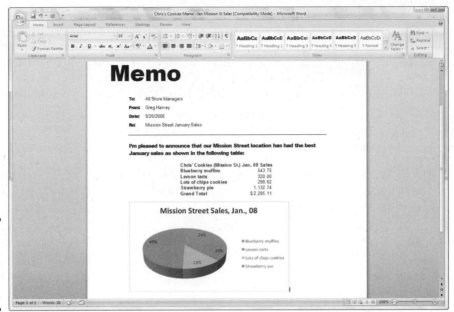

Figure 4-5:
Pasting the
linked chart
into the
Word memo.

Excel and PowerPoint 2007

The process of embedding and linking worksheet data and charts in the slides of your Microsoft PowerPoint presentations is very similar to the techniques outlined for Word. To embed a cell selection or chart, drag the data or chart object from the Excel worksheet to the PowerPoint slide. If you prefer using the cut-and-paste method, copy the data or chart to the Clipboard (Ctrl+C), switch to PowerPoint, and click the Paste Special option on the Paste button's drop-down menu on the Home tab of the PowerPoint Ribbon (or press Alt+HVS). Then, make sure that the Microsoft Office Excel Worksheet Object is selected in the As list box and the Paste option button is selected in PowerPoint's Paste Special dialog box before you click OK.

If you want to link Excel data or a chart that you pasted into a PowerPoint presentation slide to its source Excel workbook, the only thing you do differently is to click the Paste Link option button in the Paste Special dialog box before you click OK.

Sometimes, after making changes to the linked data or chart in Excel, you need to manually update the link in the PowerPoint presentation slide to ensure that your presentation has the latest and greatest version of the Excel data. To manually update a linked table of Excel spreadsheet data or a linked chart, go to the slide in question, right-click the table or chart, and then click Update Link on its shortcut menu.

Figure 4-6 illustrates how easy it is to edit a chart that you create in Excel and then copy to a PowerPoint 2007 slide. To edit the copied chart from in PowerPoint, all I have to do is click the chart area on the slide. The PowerPoint Ribbon then adds a Chart Tools contextual tab to its Ribbon. Here, you see the PowerPoint Ribbon after clicking the Design tab so that I can select a new style for the pie chart from the Chart Styles gallery.

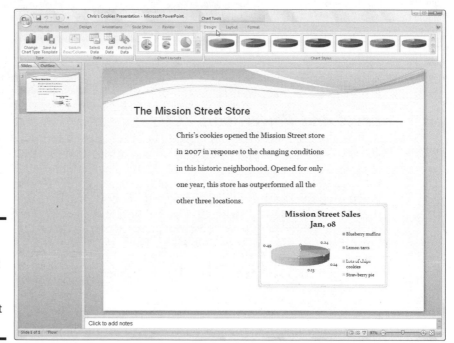

Figure 4-6:
Editing an
Excel chart
embedded
into a
PowerPoint
slide.

Excel and Outlook 2007

Microsoft Outlook 2007 gives you access to a group of powerful utilities for scheduling and managing personal information and doing e-mail rather than a standard application program, such as Word 2007 or Excel 2007. Among its useful utilities are

✦ The Contacts module, where you can store all sorts of information about the people that you deal with day in and day out

✦ The Calendar module, where you can schedule your appointments

✦ The Tasks module, where you can keep track of all the thousands of things that you need to get done

You can use Outlook's File⇨Import and Export command to exchange data between an Excel spreadsheet and any Outlook folder, such as Contacts, Calendar, or Tasks (heck, you can export your e-mail messages to an Excel workbook from the Inbox, Drafts, or Outbox folders).

When you choose the File⇨Import and Export command from the Outlook menu bar, the program starts the Import and Export Wizard. Figure 4-7 shows the first dialog box in this wizard where you choose the type of action to perform. To bring data from an Excel worksheet file into one of the Outlook modules or folders, click the Import from Another Program or File item in the Choose an Action to Perform list box. To export Outlook data from one of its modules or folders into an Excel workbook, click the Export to a File item at the very top of this list box.

Figure 4-7:
Using the Import and Export Wizard to transfer data between Excel and Outlook.

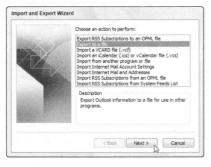

The following steps guide you through exporting the data in your Outlook 2007 Contacts folder into a new Excel workbook file. The steps for exporting other folders (such as the Inbox or Tasks folder) are almost the same. The steps for importing the data stored in an Excel worksheet into one of your Outlook folders are very similar, except that instead of specifying Excel as the type of file to create, you specify it as the type of file to import.

1. **Open Outlook and then choose File⇨Import and Export from the Outlook menu bar.**

   This action opens the first dialog box in the Import and Export Wizard (shown in Figure 4-7).

2. **Click Export to a File in the Choose an Action to Perform list box and then click the Next> button.**

   This action opens the second dialog box (now called Export to a File) in the Import and Export Wizard, where you indicate the type of file to create for the exported Outlook data.

3. **Click Microsoft Excel in the Create a File of Type list box and then click the Next> button.**

   This action opens the next dialog box in the Export to a File version of the Import and Export Wizard, where you select the Outlook folder whose information is to be copied into the Excel workbook.

4. **Click the Contacts folder icon in the Select Folder to Export From list box and then click the Next> button.**

   This action opens the next Export to a File dialog box in the Import and Export Wizard (shown in Figure 4-8), where you indicate the name and location of the new Excel workbook that is to contain the Outlook Contacts data.

Figure 4-8: Selecting the Outlook folder to export in the Export to a File dialog box.

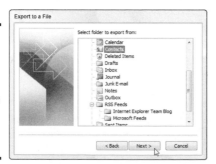

5. **Click the Browse button to the right of the Save Exported File As text box.**

This action opens the Browse dialog box (similar to the Save As dialog box), where you can select the folder and enter the filename for the workbook file where the Contacts data is to be stored. Enter a new filename in the File Name text box unless you specifically want to replace an existing workbook file with the exported Outlook data (at which time, you must confirm the replacement).

6. **Select the drive and folder in which to create the new file in the Favorites Links or Folders sections of the Navigation pane (Windows Vista) or on the Save In drop-down list (Windows XP) and then enter the new filename in the File Name text box before you click OK.**

This action closes the Browse dialog box and returns you to the Export to a File dialog box, where the complete path and filename of your new Excel workbook file appears.

7. **Click the Next> button.**

This action opens the next Export to a File dialog box in the Import and Export Wizard, which shows you what action the wizard will take as soon as you click the Finish button.

Before you click Finish to start exporting the data to your new Excel workbook, you may want to specify exactly which fields in the Contacts file to export. If you don't do this, the Import and Export Wizard copies all the fields to the new Excel workbook (and there are a lot of them, to say the least). If you don't need all the data, follow Steps 8 through 11. If you do want all the data exported, skip to Step 12.

8. **(Optional) Click the Map Custom Fields button to specify exactly which fields to export.**

This action opens the Map Custom Fields dialog box, where you specify exactly which fields to use (see Figure 4-9).

Figure 4-9:
Mapping the fields to be exported from the Contacts file into the new Excel workbook.

9. **Click the Clear Map button to completely clear the To list box.**

After the To list box is clear, you're ready to drag the fields that you want exported out of the From list box to drop them in the To list box. If you don't want all the fields within a particular category of the Contacts file, click the Expand button next to its name to display all its subfields and then drag only the fields in that section that you want to export. For example, if you don't want the Title field and Suffix field in the Name category, click its Expand button and then drag the First Name, Middle Name, and Last Name fields over.

10. **Drag the fields that you want exported from the outline in the From list box over to the To list box.**

Drag the fields over in the order in which you want them to appear in the resulting workbook file. If you drag a field and then discover that it's in the wrong order in the To list box, you reposition it by dragging it up or down in this list.

After you have all the fields that you want exported in the To list box in the order in which you want them in the Excel workbook, proceed to Step 11.

11. **Click OK in the Map Custom Fields dialog box.**

This action closes the Map Custom Fields dialog box and returns you to the final Export to a File dialog box; click the Finish button to begin the exporting of the Outlook Contacts data to your new workbook file.

12. **Click the Finish button in the Export to a File dialog box.**

After the Import and Export Wizard finishes exporting the Contacts data in the fields that you specified, it saves it to the new Excel workbook file. You can then open this file in Excel and work with this data as though you had entered it directly into an Excel worksheet.

Using Smart Tags

The Smart Tag feature provides another way to link certain types of information that you enter into your spreadsheet with other sources. A Smart Tag is automatically attached to a cell when Excel recognizes its contents as being of a certain type of data. For example, when you install Excel, it provides you with two basic types of Smart Tags:

✦ **Recent Outlook e-mail recipients** enable you to send e-mail, schedule a meeting, open the Contact information, add to the Contacts list, or insert the address for a person who is identified as someone from whom you've recently received an e-mail in Microsoft Outlook.

✦ **Smart Tag lists (MSN MoneyCentral Financial Symbols)** enable you to insert stock quote information for a stock symbol that you enter — you can also visit the MSN MoneyCentral Web site and get information about the company who issued the stock, the stock performance, or any related news about the company and its business.

Excel indicates that it has recognized the data that you've entered into a cell as a type of Smart Tag data by inserting a purple triangle in the lower-right corner of the cell. When you position the thick white-cross pointer on the cell, the Smart Tag indicator appears. When you then position the mouse pointer on the Smart Tag indicator, a drop-down button appears. When clicked, the button displays a drop-down menu with a list of items representing the different actions that you can perform with the Smart Tag (these vary with the type of Smart Tag information involved).

Before you can use the Recent Outlook e-mail recipients and the Smart Tag lists (MSN MoneyCentral Financial Symbols Smart Tags that are installed with Excel), you must activate the Smart Tag feature in the program. To do this, follow these simple steps:

1. **Click Office Button I Excel Options I Proofing or press Alt+FIP.**

Excel opens the Proofing tab of the Excel Options dialog box containing the AutoCorrect options.

2. **Click the AutoCorrect Options command button.**

Excel opens the AutoCorrect dialog box with the AutoCorrect, AutoFormat As You Type, and Smart Tags tabs.

3. **Click the Label Data with Smart Tags check box on the Smart Tags tab to put a check mark in it.**

Excel activates the options on the Smart Tags tab (indicated by the fact they're no longer grayed out and you can now select and de-select the Smart Tag recognizers you want to use).

4. **Click the check boxes for all the other recognizers you want active in Excel by clicking their check boxes to put a check mark in them.**

5. **Click OK to close the AutoCorrect dialog box and then click OK again to close the Excel Options dialog box. See Figure 4-10.**

**Book IV
Chapter 4**

**Sharing Worksheets
and Worksheet Data**

Figure 4-10:
Activating
the Smart
Tags in the
AutoCorrect
dialog box.

After you activate Smart Tags in Excel, they start popping in the cells of the worksheet as you enter your data, indicated by both the purple triangle in the lower-right cell corner and the Smart Tag indicator.

If you think that both the triangle and Smart Tag indicator are a bit much, you can change how Smart Tags appear in the worksheet. Simply open the Smart Tags tab in the AutoCorrect dialog box and then click the drop-down button attached to the Show Smart Tags As drop-down list box; you can then choose between the None and Button Only menu option. Of course, choosing None renders all your Smart Tags invisible (and thus, unusable). However, by choosing the Button Only option, you remove the purple triangles from the cells, while still retaining the ability to display the Smart Tag indicator by passing the mouse pointer over the cell and to open its action menu by clicking its drop-down button.

Excel doesn't save the Smart Tags that it identifies in your worksheets unless you embed them in the sheet before saving the workbook. To do this, click the Embed Smart Tags in This Workbook check box at the bottom of the Smart Tags tab of the AutoCorrect dialog box and then save the workbook.

Adding more Smart Tags

The eServices part of the Microsoft Office Web site has a bunch of different types of Smart Tags that you can download and add for use in Microsoft Office programs, such as Excel. These downloadable (and free) Smart Tags run the gamut from the Expedia Smart Tag — for getting travel-related information by entering destinations — all the way to the FedEx Smart Tag — for tracking your packages by its tracking number.

To get new Smart Tags for Excel, click the More Smart Tags button on the Smart Tags tab of the AutoCorrect dialog box. When you do this, Excel opens your Web browser, which then takes you to the Available Smart Tags page of the Office Marketplace Web site, where you can follow links for getting Smart Tags in three major categories: Communication Services, Reference, and News & Travel.

Using the Financial Symbols Smart Tag

If your work involves tracking stocks in your spreadsheets, you'll appreciate the power and convenience of the Smart Tag lists (MSN MoneyCentral Financial Symbols) Smart Tag. All you have to do is enter a bona fide stock symbol in the cell of a worksheet to have it recognized as being a member of this type of data.

Figures 4-11 and 4-12 illustrate how this works. In cell A1, I input the text entry, MSFT, in all caps (which just happens to be the stock indicator for our beloved Microsoft Corporation). No sooner had I pressed the Enter key than Excel inserted a purple triangle in the lower-right corner of the cell, signifying that the program recognized this cell entry as constituting a Smart Tag.

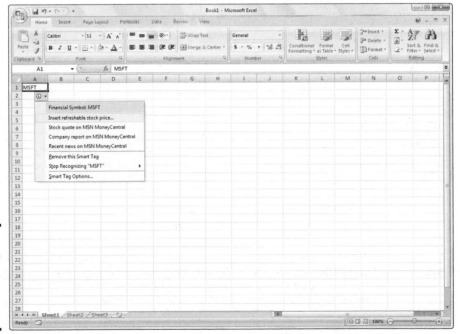

Figure 4-11: Selecting an action from the MSFT Smart Tag menu.

In Figure 4-11 you see the particular Smart Tag drop-down menu associated with the Financial Symbol Smart Tag. You open this menu by clicking the drop-down button attached to its Smart Tag indicator. For this particular example, I clicked the Insert Refreshable Stock Price option to import the Stock Quotes table provided by MSN Money, shown in Figure 4-12.

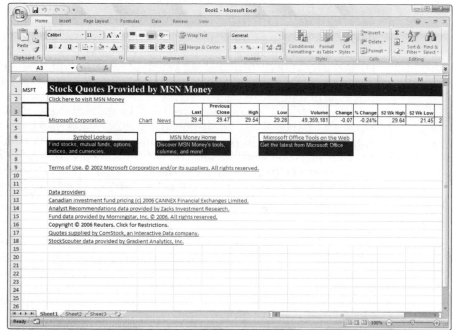

Figure 4-12: Worksheet after importing refreshable table with current stock information for the MSFT Smart Tag.

If you click the Stock Quote on MSN Money Central option on the MSFT Smart Tag's drop-down menu, Excel launches your Web browser and connects you to the Money page on the MSN Web site with the current quote on Microsoft's stock. This Web page gives you complete and current Microsoft stock quote information that you can then bring into Excel by doing a Web query (see Book VI, Chapter 2).

Saving Workbooks in Other Usable File Formats

Sometimes you may need to share worksheet data with co-workers and clients who do not have Excel installed on their computers. Therefore, they can't open up and print Excel workbook files saved either in the new default .xlsx XML file format favored by Excel 2007 or in the older .xls binary format used in versions 97 through 2003.

For those rare occasions (for it's just hard to imagine anybody getting by without Excel installed on their computers), you can convert your Excel workbook to one of three usable file formats for opening and printing with readily-available software programs that support them:

+ PDF files for opening with Adobe Reader or Adobe Acrobat

+ XPS files for opening with the XML Paper Specification Viewer or newer Web browser such as Internet Explorer 7

+ HTML files for opening with all types and versions of Web browsers

Before you can save files in the PDF file format, you must download and install the Excel Microsoft Save as PDF or XPS Add-in program from the Microsoft Web site. To do this, open the Excel Help window and then search for "PDF and XPS" in the Search text box. Then, click the Enable Support for Other File Formats, Such as PDF and XPS link in the Help window. Locate the Microsoft Save as PDF or XPS Add-in for 2007 Microsoft Office Programs link the help screen describing PDF and XPS file formats. Finally, follow the online instructions for downloading and installing this add-in program on the Microsoft Downloads Web site. After you install this add-in, Excel adds a PDF or XPS option to the Save As submenu on the Office menu.

Saving worksheets as PDF files

The PDF (Portable Document File) file format, developed by Adobe Systems Incorporated, enables people to open up and print documents without any access to the original programs with which the documents were created. All they then need installed in order to be able to open and print the worksheet-as-PDF file is a copy of Abode Reader (a free download from www.abode.com) or a copy of Adobe's Acrobat software.

For the first time ever, Excel enables you to save your workbook files directly in this special PDF file format (after you install the Save as PDF or XPS add-in). To save a workbook as a PDF file, click the Office Button and then position the mouse over the continuation button attached to the Save As option (the triangle pointing to the right) and click the PDF or XPS option on the submenu (or simply press Alt+FFP) to open the Publish as PDF or XPS dialog box. If you don't need to edit the file name (Excel automatically appends .pdf to the current file name) or the folder location, simply click the Publish button, and Excel will save the workbook in a PDF file and automatically open it up for your inspection in Adobe Reader.

If you create an Excel 2007 workbook that incorporates new features not supported in earlier versions of Excel, instead of saving the workbook as an .xls file, thereby losing all of its 2007 enhancements, consider saving it as a PDF file so that co-workers still using pre-2007 Excel versions can still have access to the data in all its glory via the Adobe Reader.

Saving worksheets as XPS files

The XPS (XML Paper Specification) file format also enables people to open up and print Excel worksheets without access to the Excel program. In fact, spreadsheets saved in the XPS file format can be opened by anyone who uses Internet Explorer 7 on Windows Vista or uses Internet Explorer 6 or higher after installing Win FX Runtime Components or, barring that, a special XML Paper Specification Viewer (that is a free download from the Microsoft Web site at www.microsoft.com).

To save a workbook as an XPS file, click the Office Button and then position the mouse over the continuation button attached to the Save As option (the triangle pointing to the right) and click the PDF or XPS option on the submenu (or simply press Alt+FFP) to open the Publish as PDF or XPS dialog box. Then, be sure and click the XPS Document (*.xps) option on the Save as Type drop-down list box.

If you don't need to edit the filename (Excel automatically appends .xps to the current filename) or the folder location, simply click the Publish button, and Excel will save the workbook in an XPS file.

If you want Excel to automatically open the new XPS file for your inspection in Internet Explorer 7 on Windows Vista, Internet Explorer 6 or higher with Win FX Runtime Components, or the XML Paper Specification Viewer, click the Open File After Publishing check box to put a check mark in it.

By default, the Standard (Publishing Online and Printing) option button is selected in the Optimize For section at the bottom of the Publish as PDF or XPS dialog box. If you want to make your XPS file version of the spreadsheet smaller for viewing online, click the Minimum Size (Publishing Online) option button before you click the Publish button.

Saving worksheets as HTML files

If converting your worksheets to PDF or XPS files is way too complex for your needs, you can save your worksheets as good old HTML files for viewing and printing in anybody's Web browser (as well as for publishing to your Web site). To save:

1. **Click Office Button | Save As or press Alt+FA to open the Save As dialog box and then click Web Page on the Save as Type drop-down list.**

Excel opens the Save As dialog box similar to the one shown in Figure 4-13.

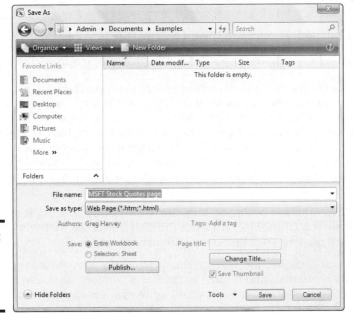

Figure 4-13: Saving a worksheet as an HTML file.

2. **Select the folder in which you want to save the HTML file with the Favorites or Folders in the Navigation pane on Windows Vista or in the Save In drop-down list box on Windows XP.**

Next, you need to give a new filename to your Web page in the File Name text box. Note that Excel automatically appends the filename extension .htm (for Hypertext Markup page) to whatever filename you enter here. When selecting a filename, keep in mind that some file servers (especially those running some flavor of UNIX) are sensitive to upper- and lowercase letters in the name.

3. **Enter the filename for the new HTML file in the File Name text box.**

By default, Excel selects the Entire Workbook option button, meaning that all the worksheets in the workbook that contain data will be included in the new HTML file. To save only the data on the current worksheet in the HTML file, you need to take Step 4.

4. **(Optional) If you want only the current worksheet saved in the new HTML file, click the Selection: Sheet option button.**

If you want, you can have Excel add a Page title to your new HTML file by taking Step 5. The page appears centered at the top of the page right above your worksheet data. Don't confuse the Page title with the Web page header that appears on the Web browser's title bar — the only way to set the Web page header is to edit this HTML tag after the HTML file is created.

5. **(Optional) If you want to add a Page title to your HTML file, click the Change Title button and then type the text in the Page Title text box in the Set Page Title dialog box before you click OK.**

You're now ready to save your spreadsheet as an HTML file by clicking the Save button. If you want to see how this file looks in your Web browser immediately upon saving it, click the Publish button to open the Publish as Web Page dialog box and save the file from there after selecting the Open Published Web Page in Browser check box. And if you want Excel to automatically save an HTML version of the worksheet each time you save the workbook, you click the AutoRepublish Every Time This Workbook Is Saved check box as well.

6. **Click the Save button to save the file without opening it in your Web browser. Otherwise, click the Publish button so that you can see the Web page in your browser right after saving it.**

If you click the Save button, Excel closes the Save As dialog box, saves the file to disk, and returns to the Excel window (that now contains the HTML version of your workbook or worksheet in place of the original .xls file).

If you click the Publish button to view the new HTML file in your browser, Excel opens the Publish as Web Page dialog box, where you click the Open Published Web Page in Browser check box to put a check mark in it before clicking the Publish button.

7. **Click the Open Published Web Page in Browser check box and then click the Publish button.**

When you click the Publish button, Excel closes the Publish As Web Page dialog box, saves the spreadsheet as an HTML file, and then immediately launches your default Web browsing program while at the same time opening the new HTML file in the browser. After you finish looking over the new HTML file in your Web browser, click its program window's Close button to close the browser and HTML file and to return to Excel and the original worksheet.

If you add the Web Page Preview and Web Options commands as custom buttons to the Quick Access toolbar, you can use them to preview how a worksheet will appear as a Web page locally in your Web browser as well as control a whole variety of Web page save options. To add these buttons, open the Customize tab of the Excel Options dialog box (Alt+FIC) and then add the Web Page Preview and Web Options from Commands Not in the Ribbon section (see Book I, Chapter 3 for details on adding custom buttons to the Quick Access toolbar).

Publishing Workbooks to Shared Spaces

If you work in a large enterprise, you may share some of your worksheets by publishing them on a centralized document management server or to a Microsoft SharePoint site. Once there, team members and selected clients can then access the worksheet data either by opening their workbook files in Excel 2007 for editing or in a Web browser, such as Internet Explorer 7, for reviewing and printing.

To help you share worksheet data in this way, the Publish submenu accessed from the Excel File pull-down menu (Office Button | Publish or Alt+FU) contains the following options:

✦ **Excel Services** to save the current workbook to a SharePoint site on a server running Excel Calculation Services (see *Microsoft SharePoint 2007 For Dummies* by Vanessa Williams, published by Wiley Publishing, for details)

✦ **Document Management Server** to save the current workbook to a document management server

✦ **Create Document Workspace** to open the Document Workspace task pane where you create a document workspace (by entering its name and URL address) where a copy of the current workbook is saved and synchronized to your original

Book V
Charts and Graphics

The 5th Wave   By Rich Tennant

"The top line represents our revenue, the middle
line is our inventory, and the bottom line shows
the rate of my hair loss over the same period."

Contents at a Glance

Chapter 1: Charting Worksheet Data

In This Chapter

✔ Understanding how to chart worksheet data

✔ Creating an embedded chart or one on its own chart sheet

✔ Editing an existing chart

✔ Formatting the elements in a chart

✔ Selecting the right type of chart

✔ Adding a custom chart type

✔ Printing a chart alone or with its supporting data

Charts present the data from your worksheet visually by representing the data in rows and columns as bars on a chart, for example, or as pieces of a pie in a pie chart. For a long time, charts and graphs have gone hand-in-hand with spreadsheets, because they allow you to see trends and patterns that you often can't readily visualize from the numbers alone. Which has more consistent sales, the Southeast region or the Northwest region? Monthly sales reports may contain the answer, but a bar chart based on the data shows it more clearly.

In this chapter, you first become familiar with the terminology that Excel uses as it refers to the parts of a chart — terms that may be new, such as *data marker* and *chart data series,* as well as terms that are probably familiar already, such as *axis.* After you get acquainted with the terms, you begin to put them to use going through the simple steps required to create the kind of chart that you want either as part of the worksheet or a separate chart sheet.

The art of preparing a chart (and much of the fun) is matching a chart type to your purposes. To help you with this, I guide you through a tour of all the chart types available in Excel 2007, from old standbys, such as bar and column charts, to ones that may be new, such as radar charts and surface charts. Finally, you discover how to print charts, either alone or as part of the worksheet.

Worksheet Charting 101

The typical Excel chart is comprised of several distinct parts. Figure 1-1 shows an Excel column chart in a separate document window with labels identifying the parts of this chart. Table 1-1 summarizes the parts of the typical chart.

Table 1-1	Parts of a Typical Chart
Part	*Description*
Chart Area	Everything inside the chart window, including all parts of the chart (labels, axes, data markers, tick marks, and other elements in this table).
Data marker	A symbol on the chart that represents a single value in the spreadsheet. A symbol may be a bar in a bar chart, a pie in a pie chart, or a line on a line chart. Data markers with the same shape or pattern represent a single data series in the chart.
Chart data series	A group of related values, such as all the values in a single row in the chart — all the production numbers for Part 100 in the sample chart, for example. A chart can have just one data series (shown in a single bar or line), but it usually has several.
Series formula	A formula describing a given data series. The formula includes a reference to the cell that contains the data series name (such as the name Jun-08), references to worksheet cells containing the categories and values plotted in the chart, and the plot order of the series. The series formula can also have the actual data used to plot the chart. You can edit a series formula and control the plot order.
Axis	A line that serves as a major reference for plotting data in a chart. In two-dimensional charts there are two axes — the x (horizontal/category) axis and the y (vertical/value) axis. In most two-dimensional charts (except, notably, column charts), Excel plots categories (labels) along the x-axis and values (numbers) along the y-axis. Bar charts reverse the scheme, plotting values along the y-axis. Pie charts have no axes. Three-dimensional charts have an x-axis, a y-axis, and a z-axis. The x- and y-axes delineate the horizontal surface of the chart. The z-axis is the vertical axis, showing the depth of the third dimension in the chart.
Tick mark	A small line intersecting an axis. A tick mark indicates a category, scale, or chart data series. A tick mark can have a label attached.
Plot area	The area where Excel plots your data, including the axes and all markers that represent data points.

Part	Description
Gridlines	Optional lines extending from the tick marks across the plot area, thus making it easier to view the data values represented by the tick marks.
Chart text	A label or title that you add to the chart. *Attached text* is a title or label linked to an axis such as the Chart Title, Vertical Axis Title, and Horizontal Axis Title that you can't move independently of the chart. *Unattached text* is text that you add such as a text box with the Text Box command button on the Insert tab of the Ribbon.
Legend	A key that identifies patterns, colors, or symbols associated with the markers of a chart data series. The legend shows the data series name corresponding to each data marker (such as the name of the red columns in a column chart).

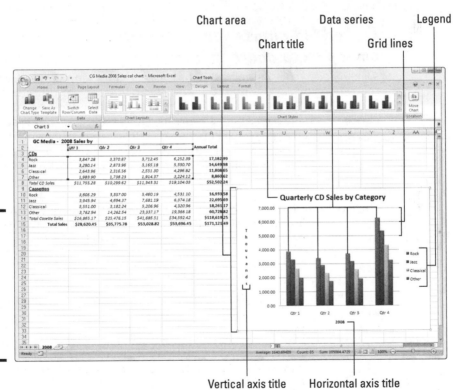

Figure 1-1: Typical column chart containing a variety of standard chart elements.

Moving an embedded chart onto its own Chart sheet

If it's really important that the chart remain a separate element in the workbook, you can move the embedded chart onto its own chart sheet. Simply click the embedded chart if it's not already selected in the worksheet and then click the Move Chart command button on the Design tab of the Chart Tools contextual tab on the Ribbon or press Alt+CCM. Excel then opens the Move Chart dialog box where you then click the New Sheet option button and click OK to switch the embedded chart to a chart on a separate chart sheet.

Embedded charts versus charts on separate chart sheets

An *embedded chart* is a chart that appears right within the worksheet so that when you save or print the worksheet, you save or print the chart along with it. Note that your charts don't have to be embedded. You can also choose to create a chart in its own chart sheet in the workbook at the time you create it. Embed a chart on the worksheet when you want to be able to print the chart along with its supporting worksheet data. Place a chart on its own sheet when you intend to print the charts of the worksheet data separately.

You can print any chart that you've embedded in a worksheet by itself without any worksheet data (as though it were created on its own chart sheet) by selecting it before you open the Print dialog box.

Creating a new embedded chart

Excel 2007 makes it super easy to create a new embedded chart in your worksheet. All you do is follow these three easy steps:

1. **Select the range of cells containing the data that you want to plot, including the column and row headings.**

The labels in the top row of selected data become category labels in the chart. In other words, they appear along the x-axis in most charts to describe the data being charted. The labels in the first selected column on the left are used to name the data series in the chart. Excel assigns values to appear along the y-axis based on the data in those data series.

To plot only the subtotals or totals in a data table, outline the data table (see Book II, Chapter 4, for details), and then collapse the outline down to the level that just shows the subtotals or totals, which you can then select as a range by dragging through their cells.

2. **Click the Ribbon's Insert tab and then click the command button for the type of chart you want to create (Column, Line, Pie, Bar, Area, XY (Scatter), or Other Charts (to create Stock, Surface, Doughnut, Bubble, or Radar chart).**

Excel then opens the drop-down gallery for the type of chart you selected. This gallery contains thumbnails for all the subtypes available under that chart type.

3. **Click the thumbnail of the subtype of the chart you want to create on the chart button's drop-down gallery.**

That's all there is to it! Figures 1-2 and 1-3 illustrate how fantastically easy this process really is. In Figure 1-2, I select the range of data (A3:J7) to be graphed as an XY (Scatter) chart, click the Scatter command button on the Insert tab of the Ribbon, and click the Scatter with Straight Lines and Markers chart subtype on its drop-down gallery.

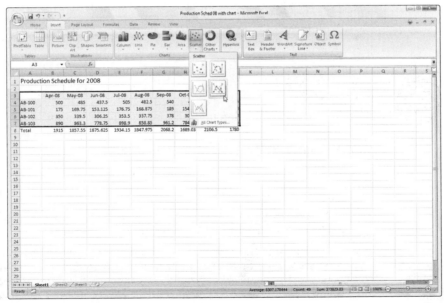

Figure 1-2:
Selecting the sub-chart type on the XY (Scatter) chart gallery.

Trying on your choices in the Chart Layouts and Chart Styles galleries

When selecting a new layout or style for your chart, you can display all the layout and style choices in its respective Chart Layouts and Chart Styles gallery by clicking that gallery's More button (the one with the horizontal bar directly over a triangle pointing downward). Although doing this displays the thumbnails of all your layout and styles choices for the new chart, the gallery can also obscure the chart in the worksheet so that Live Preview, which enables you to see how a layout or style looks in the chart before you select, is rendered useless.

To avoid this situation, click the Next Row button (the one immediately above the More button on each gallery with the triangle pointing downward) to bring up and display the next row of layout and style choices within the height of the Ribbon. That way, you can highlight the thumbnails displayed in the single row of the Chart Layouts and Chart Styles galleries to see how each looks on the chart with Live Preview, and if none of the choices seem right, you bring up the next row of the gallery by clicking the Next Row button again.

Figure 1-3 shows you the result. Here you see the brand-new XY (Scatter) chart with straight lines and markers immediately after Excel creates the chart in the worksheet. As you can see, when first created, the embedded chart partially obscures the data in the table (which now appears selected with bounding boxes).

Because the new embedded chart is still selected — indicated by the sizing handles in the corners and midsections on the perimeter of the chart (those three little dots), the bounding boxes in blue, green, and purple around the charted data in the worksheet table, and the selection of the Design tab under the Chart Tools contextual tab and the appearance of its command buttons on the Ribbon — you can move the embedded chart out of the way to a new location by positioning the mouse pointer on its border and then dragging its outline to a new position. To also resize it, position the mouse pointer over one of eight sizing handles and drag the side or sides as needed.

If you don't even have time to follow these three steps to chart your data, you can chart the selected cell range as a clustered column chart (with the data series in rows) on its own chart sheet (place in front of the worksheet with the selected data) simply by pressing F11. Figure 1-4 shows this chart using the same worksheet selected in Figure 1-2.

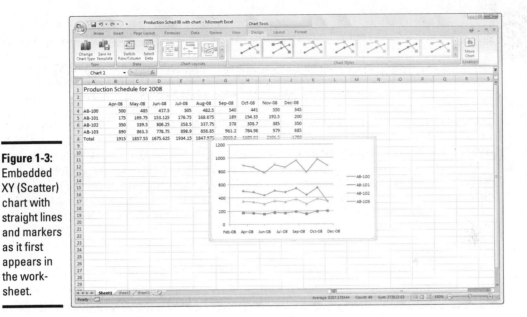

Figure 1-3:
Embedded
XY (Scatter)
chart with
straight lines
and markers
as it first
appears in
the work-
sheet.

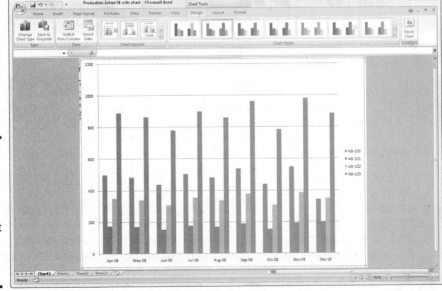

Figure 1-4:
Clustered
column
chart as it
appears on
its own chart
sheet right
after you
press F11.

Keep in mind that all charts that you create are dynamically linked to the worksheet that they represent. This means that if you modify any of the values that are plotted in the chart, Excel immediately redraws the chart to reflect the change, assuming that the worksheet still uses automatic recalculation. When Manual recalculation is turned on, you must remember to press F9 or click the Calculate Now (F9) command button on the Formulas tab of the Ribbon (Alt+MC2) in order to get Excel to redraw the chart to reflect any changes to the worksheet values it represents.

If after creating a new chart, you decide that you want to see how your data would appear in a different kind of chart, all you have to do is click the Change Chart Type command button and then click the type of chart you want to try in the Navigation pane on the left (Column through Radar) followed by the thumbnail of the subtype of chart in the gallery on the right before you click OK.

Refining the chart from the Design tab

You can use the command buttons on the Design tab of the Chart Tools contextual tab to make all kinds of changes to your new chart. The Design tab contains the following command buttons:

✦ **Change Chart Type:** Click this button to change the type of chart and then click the thumbnail of the new chart type in the Change Chart Type dialog box, which shows all the kinds of charts in Excel.

✦ **Switch Row/Column:** Click this button to immediately interchange the worksheet data used for the Legend Entries (series) with that used for the Axis Labels (Categories) in the selected chart.

✦ **Save As Template:** Click this button to open Save Chart Template dialog box where you save the current chart's formatting and layout (usually after thoroughly customizing) as a template to use in creating future charts.

✦ **Select Data:** Click this button to open the Select Data Source dialog box where you can not only interchange the Legend Entries (series) with the Axis Labels (Categories) but also edit out or add particular entries to either category.

✦ **Chart Layouts:** Click the More button (the last one with the horizontal bar and triangle pointing downward) in the Chart Layouts group to display all the thumbnails on the Chart Layouts drop-down gallery and then click the thumbnail of the new layout style you want applied to the selected chart.

✦ **Chart Styles:** Click the More button (the last one with the horizontal bar and triangle pointing downward) in the Chart Styles group to display all the thumbnails on the Chart Styles drop-down gallery and then click the thumbnail of the new chart style you want applied to the selected chart.

✦ **Move Chart:** Click this to open the Move Chart dialog box, where you move an embedded chart to its own chart or move a chart on its own sheet to one of the worksheets in the workbook as an embedded chart.

Modifying the chart layout and style

As soon as Excel draws a new chart in your worksheet, the program adds the Chart Tools contextual tab to the end of the Ribbon and selects its Design tab. You can then use the Chart Layouts and Chart Styles galleries to further refine the new chart.

Figure 1-5 shows the original XY (Scatter) chart (created in Figure 1-3) after repositioning the chart below the table of data and resizing it and then clicking the Layout 1 thumbnail on the Chart Layouts gallery and the Style 42 thumbnail on the Chart Styles drop-gallery. Selecting Style 42 gives the clustered column chart its high contrast, whereas selecting Layout 1 adds the generic chart and axis titles and positions them as shown in the figure.

Figure 1-5:
Embedded
XY (Scatter)
chart after
selecting a
new chart
layout
and style
from the
Design tab.

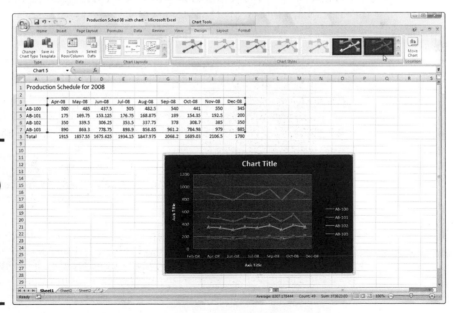

Switching the rows and columns in a chart

Normally when Excel creates a new chart, it automatically graphs the data by rows in the cell selection so that the column headings appear along the horizontal (category) axis at the bottom of the chart and the row headings appear in the legend (assuming that you're dealing with a chart type that utilizes an x- and y-axis).

You can click the Switch Row/Column command button on the Design tab of the Chart Tools contextual tab to switch the chart so that row headings appear on the horizontal (category) axis and the column headings appear in the legend (or you can press Alt+JCW).

Figures 1-6 and 1-7 demonstrate how this works. In Figure 1-6, you see an embedded clustered column chart that graphs the quarterly sales of CDs by CG Media in 2008 as it was originally created (after resizing and repositioning the chart and applying Layout 9 and Style 26 from the Chart Layouts and Chart Styles galleries, respectively, and after replacing the generic Chart Title with the actual Quarterly CD Sales by Category title and rotating the Vertical Title).

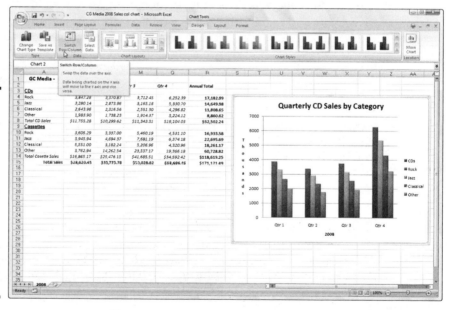

Figure 1-6: Original clustered column chart with column headings on the horizontal axis and row headings in the legend.

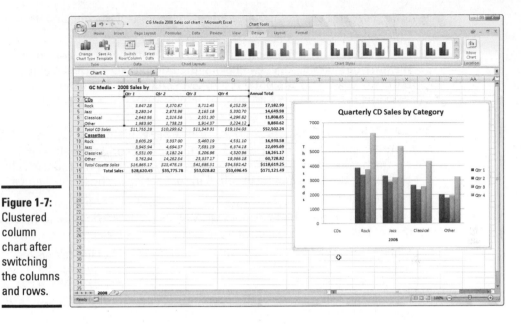

Figure 1-7:
Clustered
column
chart after
switching
the columns
and rows.

As you can see in Figure 1-6, when Excel created this clustered column chart, the program placed the column headings (Qtr 1, Qtr 2, Qtr 3, and Qtr 4) on the horizontal (category) axis at the bottom of the chart to identify the different clusters of columns, and used the row headings (CDs, Rock, Jazz, Classical, and Other) in the legend to identify by color each individual column's data bar in every cluster of columns.

Figure 1-7 shows the same clustered column chart after clicking the Switch Row/Column command button on the Design tab of the Chart Tools contextual tab. Now, column headings (Qtr 1, Qtr 2, Qtr 3, and Qtr 4) are used in the legend and the row headings (CDs, Rock, Jazz, Classical, and Other) appear along the horizontal (category) axis.

Editing the source of the data graphed in the chart

When you click the Select Data command button on the Design tab of the Chart Tools contextual tab (or press Alt+JCE), Excel opens a Select Data Source dialog box. The controls in this dialog box enable you to make the following changes to the source data:

✦ Modify the range of data being graphed in the chart by clicking the Chart Data Range text box and then making a new cell selection in the worksheet or typing in its range address.

✦ Switch the row and column headings back and forth by clicking its Switch Row/Column button.

✦ Edit the labels used to identify the data series in the legend or on the horizontal (category) by clicking the Edit button on the Legend Entries (Series) or Horizontal (Categories) Axis Labels side and then selecting the cell range with appropriate row or column headings in the worksheet.

✦ Add additional data series to the chart by clicking the Add button on the Legend Entries (Series) side and then selecting the cell containing the heading for that series in the Series Name text box and the cells containing the values to be graphed in that series in the Series Values text box.

✦ Delete a label from the legend by clicking its name in the Legend Entries (Series) list box and then clicking the Remove button.

✦ Modify the order of the data series in the chart by clicking the series name in the Legend Entries (Series) list box and then clicking the Move Up button (the one with the arrow pointing upward) or the Move Down button (the one with the arrow pointing downward) until the data series appears in the desired position in the chart.

✦ Indicate how to deal with empty cells in the data range being graphed by clicking the Hidden and Empty Cells button and then selecting the appropriate Show Empty Cells As option button (Gaps, the default; Zero and Connect Data Points with Line, for line charts) and click the Show Data in Hidden Rows and Columns check box to have Excel graph data in the hidden rows and columns within the selected chart data range.

The example clustered column chart in Figures 1-6 and 1-7 illustrates a common situation where you need to use the options in the Select Data Source dialog box. The worksheet data range for this chart, A2:Q7, includes the CDs row heading in cell A3 that is essentially a heading for an empty row (E3:Q3). As a result, Excel includes this empty row as the first data series in the clustered column chart. However, because this row has no values in it (the heading is intended only to differentiate the CD sales from the cassette sales in the data table), its cluster has no data bars (columns) in it — a fact that becomes quite apparent when you switch the column and row headings as in Figure 1-7.

To remove this empty data series from the clustered column chart, you follow these steps:

1. **Click the embedded chart to select it and then click the Select Data command button on the Design tab of the Chart Tools.**

Excel opens the Select Data Source dialog box similar to the one shown in Figure 1-8.

2. **Click the Switch Row/Column button in the Select Data Source dialog box to place the row headings (CDs, Rock, Jazz, Classical, and Other) in the Legend Entries (Series) list box.**

3. **Click CDs at the top of the Legend Entries (Series) list box and then click the Remove button.**

   Excel removes the empty CDs data series from the clustered column chart as well as removing the CDs label from the Legend Entries (Series) list box in the Select Data Source dialog box.

4. **Click the Switch Row/Column button in the Select Data Source dialog box again to exchange the row and column headings in the chart and then click the Close button to close the Select Data Source dialog box.**

After you close the Select Data Source dialog box, you will notice that the various colored outlines in the chart data range no longer include row 3 with the CDs row heading (A3) and its empty cells (E3:Q3).

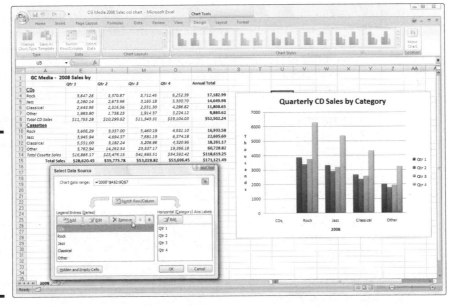

Figure 1-8:
Removing
the empty
CDs label
from the
legend of
the original
clustered
column
chart.

Customizing chart elements from the Layout tab

The command buttons on the Layout tab on the Chart Tools contextual tab make it easy to customize particular parts of your chart. Table 1-2 shows you the options that appear on the Layout tab. Note that depending on the type of chart that's selected at the time, some of these options may be unavailable.

Table 1-2		Layout Tab Options
Tab Group	*Option Name*	*Purpose*
Current Selection	Chart Elements	This combo box shows the name of the element currently selected in the chart (Chart Area, Chart Title, Legend, and so on) and enables you to select a new element in the current chart.
	Format Selection	Opens a Format dialog box for the currently selected chart element that you can use to modify formatting.
	Reset to Match Style	Resets any formatting changes made to the currently selected chart element to match the style selected for the chart.
Insert	Picture	This command button enables you to add a picture saved in a graphics file or one of Microsoft's clip art images to the chart (see Book V, Chapter 2 for details).
	Shapes	This command button's drop-down menu enables you to add any of a whole bunch of preset graphic shapes to the chart (see Book V, Chapter 2 for details).
	Text Box	This command button enables you to add a horizontal or vertical text box to the chart (see Book V, Chapter 2 for details).
Labels	Chart Title	This command button's drop-down menu enables you to add a chart title centered above the chart's plot area (Above Chart) or centered at the top of the chart's plot area (Centered Overlay Title), or to remove a chart title (None).
	Axis Titles	This command button's drop-down menu enables you to add, reposition, or remove the chart's horizontal (category) axis titles and vertical (value) axis titles.
	Legend	This command button's drop-down menu enables you to add, position, or remove the legend from the chart.
	Data Labels	This command button's drop-down menu enables you to add, position, and remove labels that identify each data series represented in the chart.

Tab Group	Option Name	Purpose
	Data Table	This command button's drop-down menu enables you to add, position, and remove a data table beneath the chart that displays the values graphed in the chart.
Axes	Axes	This command button's drop-down menu enables you to reposition, reformat, or remove the chart's horizontal (category) axis titles and vertical (value) axis.
	Gridlines	This command button's drop-down menu enables you to display or hide horizontal and vertical gridlines in the chart area.
Background	Plot Area	This command button's drop-down menu enables you to remove the plot area background or redisplay it.
	Chart Wall	This command button's drop-down menu enables you to clear or redisplay a 3-D chart's back walls.
	Chart Floor	This command button's drop-down menu enables you to clear or redisplay a 3-D chart's floor.
	3-D Rotation	This command button enables you to open the Format Chart Area dialog box for a 3-D chart where you can modify a whole number of aspects of the chart including its 3-D shadow and rotation.
Analysis	Trendline	This command button's drop-down menu enables you to display or hide linear, exponential, linear forecast, or two period moving average trend lines that display a trend implied by the charted data — trendlines are often added to XY (Scatter) charts that correlate two different sets of numerical data to graphically point out the correlation between the two sets.
	Lines	This command button's drop-down menu enables you to display or hide drop lines on a 2-D or 3-D line or area chart that connect related values as well as high-low lines on a 2-D line chart that emphasize the high and low values in the chart.
	Up/Down Bars	This command button's drop-down menu enables you to display or hide up/down bars in the chart that emphasize the high and low values in the chart.
	Error Bars	This command button's drop-down menu enables you to display or hide error bars with standard error, error bars with percentage, or error bars with deviation that show how much the data markers in the selected data series are above or below a particular value, percentage, or standard deviation in the chart.
Properties	Chart Name	This text box shows you the generic name (Chart 1, Chart 2, Chart 3, and so forth) of the selected chart and enables you to edit or replace it with a more descriptive chart name.

Adding hidden rows and columns of data to a chart

The sales data graphed in the sample clustered column chart shown in Figure 1-6 through 1-8 only includes the quarterly CD sales totals in each music category. To do this, I outlined the sales data in this entire table and then collapsed the outlined columns down to its second level so that only the quarterly subtotals and yearly grand totals were displayed (see Book I, Chapter 4 for details) before selecting the range A2:Q7 as the clustered column chart's data range. Because all the columns with the monthly sales data in each quarter were hidden at that time I originally created the chart (as a result of collapsing the outlined columns to the second level), Excel didn't include their data as part of it.

If I decide that I do want to see the monthly sales represented in the clustered column chart, to accomplish this all I have to do is click the Hidden and Empty Cell button in the Select Data Source dialog box and then click the Show Data in Hidden Rows and Columns check box to put a check mark in it in the Hidden and Empty Cell Settings dialog box. Excel then immediately redraws the chart adding columns representing the monthly sales to those for the quarterly subtotals in all four of its clusters.

To make a change to a particular chart element from the Layout tab, click its command button and then click the option you want to use on the drop-down menu (note that some options have continuation drop-down menus attached to them).

If none of the preset options on a drop-down or continuation menu fits your needs, click the More option at the bottom of the menu to open a format dialog box for the selected chart element normally containing Fill, Border Color, Border Styles, Shadow, 3-D Format, and Alignment tabs with oodles of options that you can use to customize the chart element.

The Properties group at the end of the Layout tab contains the sole Chart Name text box that you can use to modify the generic chart name (Chart 1, Chart 2, and so forth) to something more descriptive. If your worksheet contains more than one chart, you may find it advantageous to give it a more descriptive name so that it's easy to identify in the Selection Pane.

Adding data labels to the series in a chart

Data labels display values from the worksheet represented in the chart at each of its data points. To add data labels to your selected chart and position them, click the Data Labels button on the Layout tab and then click one of the following options on its drop-down menu:

+ **Center** to position the data labels in the middle of each data point

+ **Inside End** to position the data labels inside each data point near the end

+ **Inside Base** to position the data labels at the base of each data point

+ **Outside End** to position the data labels outside of the end of each data point

+ **More Data Label Options** to open the Format Data Labels dialog box where you can use the options on the Label Options, Number, Fill, Border Color, Border Styles, Shadow, 3-D Format, and Alignment tabs to customize the appearance and position of the data labels

To remove all data labels from the data points in a selected chart, click the None option at the top of the Data Labels button's drop-down menu on the Layout tab of the Chart Tools contextual tab (Alt+CAB).

Adding a data table to a chart

Sometimes, instead of data labels that can easily obscure the data points in the chart, you'll want Excel to draw a data table beneath the chart showing the worksheet data it represents in graphic form. To add the worksheet data to your selected chart, click the Data Table button on the Layout tab and then click one of these options:

+ **Show Data Table** to have Excel draw the table at the bottom of the chart

+ **Show Data Table with Legend Keys** to have Excel draw the table at the bottom of the chart, including the color keys used in the legend to differentiate the data series in the first column

+ **More Data Table Options** to open the Format Data Table dialog box where you can use the options on the Data Table Options, Fill, Border Color, Border Styles, Shadow, and 3-D Format tabs to customize the appearance and position of the data table

Figure 1-9 illustrates how the sample clustered column chart (introduced in Figure 1-6) looks with a data table added to it. This data table includes the legend keys as its first column.

If you decide that having the worksheet data displayed in a table at the bottom of the chart is no longer necessary, simply click the None option on the Data Table command button's drop-down menu on the Layout tab of the Chart Tools contextual tab (Alt+CAD).

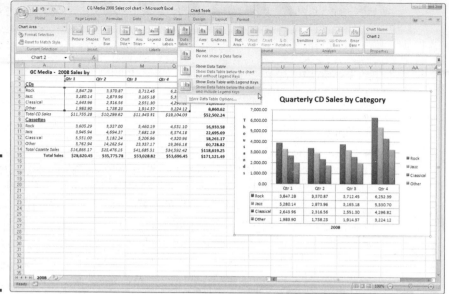

Figure 1-9:
Embedded
clustered
column
chart with
data table
with legend
keys.

Editing the chart titles

When Excel first adds titles to a new chart, it gives them generic names such as Chart Title and Axis Title (for both the x- and y-axis title). To replace these generic titles with the actual chart titles, click the title in the chart itself or click the name of the title on the Chart Elements drop-down list (Chart Elements is the very first command button in the Current Selection group on the Format tab under Chart Tools — its combo box displays the name of the element currently selected in the chart). Excel lets you know that a particular chart title is selected by placing selection handles around its perimeter.

After selecting a title, you can then click the insertion point in the text and then edit as you would any worksheet text, or you can triple-click to select the entire title and completely replace it with the text you type. To force part of the title onto a new line, click the insertion point at the place in the text where the line break is to occur. After the insertion point is positioned in the title, press Enter to start a new line.

After you finish editing the title, click somewhere else on the chart area to deselect it (or a worksheet cell, if you've finished formatting and editing the chart).

Formatting chart elements from the Format tab

The Format tab on the Chart Tools contextual tab contains options and command buttons that make it easy to format particular chart elements after you select them. Table 1-3 gives you the lowdown on all the options on the Format tab.

Table 1-3		Format Tab Options
Tab Group	**Option Name**	**Purpose**
Current Selection	Chart Elements	Click this command button to select a new chart element by clicking its name on the button's drop-down menu.
	Format Selection	Click this command button to open a Format dialog box for the currently selected chart element as displayed on the Chart Elements drop-down list button.
	Reset to Match Style	Click this command button to remove all custom formatting from the selected chart and to return it to the original formatting bestowed by the style selected for the chart.
Shape Styles	Shape Styles	Click the Shape Styles' More button to display a drop-down gallery in which you can preview and select new colors and shapes for the currently selected chart element as displayed on the Chart Elements drop-down list button.
	Shape Fill	Click this command button to display a drop-down color palette in which you can preview and select a new fill color for the currently selected chart element as displayed on the Chart Elements drop-down list button.
	Shape Outline	Click this command button to display a drop-down color palette in which you can preview and select an outline color for the currently selected chart element as displayed on the Chart Elements drop-down list button.
	Shape Effects	Click this command button to display a drop-down menu containing a variety of graphics effect options (including Shadow, Glow, Soft Edges, Bevel, and 3-D Rotation), many of which have their own pop-up palettes which allow you to preview their special effects, where you can select a new graphics effect for the currently selected chart element as displayed on the Chart Elements drop-down list button.
WordArt Styles	WordArt Styles	Click the WordArt Styles More button to display a drop-down WordArt gallery in which you can preview and select a new WordArt text style for the titles selected in the chart — if the Chart Area is the currently selected chart element as displayed on the Chart Elements drop-down list button, the program applies the WordArt style you preview or select to all titles in the chart.

(continued)

Table 1-3 *(continued)*

Tab Group	Option Name	Purpose
	Text Fill	Click this command button to display a drop-down color palette in which you can preview and select a new text fill color for the titles selected in the chart — if the Chart Area is the currently selected chart element as displayed on the Chart Elements drop-down list button, the program applies the WordArt style you preview or select to all titles in the chart.
	Text Outline	Click this command button to display a drop-down color palette in which you can preview and select a new text outline color for the titles selected in the chart — if the Chart Area is the currently selected chart element as displayed on the Chart Elements drop-down list button, the program applies the WordArt style you preview or select to all titles in the chart.
	Text Effects	Click this command button to display a drop-down menu with the Shadow, Reflection, and Glow graphics effect options active, each of which have their own pop-up palettes which you can use to preview and select special effects for the titles selected in the chart — if the Chart Area is the currently selected chart element as displayed on the Chart Elements drop-down list button, the program applies the WordArt style you preview or select to all titles in the chart.
Arrange	Bring to Front	Click this button to bring the selected embedded chart or other graphic object to the top of its stack or click the Bring Forward option on the button's drop-down menu to move the object to a higher layer in the stack (see Book V, Chapter 2 for details).
	Send to Back	Click this button to send the selected embedded chart or other graphic object to the bottom of its stack or click the Send Backward option on the button's drop-down to menu to move the object to a lower level in the stack (see Book V, Chapter 2 for details) — note that this command button and its options are available only when more than one embedded chart or other graphic object is selected in the worksheet.
	Selection Pane	Click this command button to display and hide the Selection and Visibility task pane which shows all the graphic objects in the worksheet and enables you to hide and redisplay them as well as promote or demote them to different layers (see Book V, Chapter 2 for details) — note that this command button and its options are available only when more than one embedded chart or other graphic object is selected in the worksheet.
	Align	Click this button to display a drop-menu that enables you to snap the selected chart to an invisible grid on another graphic object as well as to choose between a number of different alignment options when multiple graphic objects are selected (see Book V, Chapter 2 for details).

Tab Group	Option Name	Purpose
	Group	Click this button to display a drop-down menu that enables you to group the selected embedded chart with other graphic objects (such as text boxes or predefined shapes) for purposes of positioning and formatting (see Book V, Chapter 2 for details) — note that this command button and its options are available only when more than one embedded chart or other graphic object is selected in the worksheet.
	Rotate	Click this button to display a drop-down menu with options that enable you to rotate or flip a selected graphic object — note that this command button and its options are available only when graphic objects other than embedded charts are selected in the worksheet.
Size	Height	Use this text box to modify the height of the selected embedded chart by typing a new value in it or selecting one with the spinner buttons.
	Width	Use this text box to modify the width of the selected embedded chart by typing a new value in it or selecting one with the spinner buttons.

Selecting chart elements for formatting

Excel gives you a choice of methods for selecting individual chart elements:

✦ Click the element directly in the chart to select it — use the ScreenTip that appears at the mouse pointer to identify the chart object before you click to select it.

✦ Click the name of the chart element on the Chart Elements drop-down list in the Current Selection group on the Format tab on the Chart Tools contextual tab — Excel shows you which element is currently selected by displaying its name inside the Chart Elements combo box.

After you select an element in the chart by clicking it, you can cycle through and select the other elements in succession by pressing the ↑ and ↓ keys. Pressing the → key selects the next object; pressing the ← key selects the previous object.

You can tell when an element is selected in the chart itself because selection handles appear around it and its name appears in the Chart Elements combo box on the Format tab.

Once a chart element is selected, you can then make any of the following changes to it:

✦ Format the element by selecting the appropriate command button in the Shape Styles group or by clicking the Format Selection button in the Current Selection group to open the Format dialog box for that element and use its options to make the desired changes.

✦ Move the element within the chart by positioning the arrowhead pointer in their midst and then dragging their boundary — with some elements, you can use the selection handles to resize or reorient the object.

✦ Remove the element from the chart by pressing the Delete key.

All chart elements have shortcut menus attached to them. If you know that you want to choose a command from the shortcut menu as soon as you select a part of the chart, you can both select the object and open the shortcut menu by right-clicking the chart object. (You don't have to click the object with the left button to select it and then click again with the right to open the menu.)

Formatting the chart titles

When you select a Chart Layout on the Design tab that adds chart titles to your chart, or you add them manually using options on the Chart Title and Axis Title command buttons' drop-down menus on the Layout tab, Excel uses the Calibri (Body) font for the chart title (in 18-point size) and the x- and y-axes (in 10-point size). To change the font used in a title or any of its attributes, select the title and then use the appropriate command buttons in the Font group on the Home tab.

Use Live Preview to see how a particular font or font size for the selection looks in the chart before you select it (assuming that the drop-down menus don't obscure the chart titles. Simply click the Font or Font Size drop-down button and then highlight different font names or sizes to have the selected chart title appear in them.

If you need to change other formatting options for the titles in the chart, you can do so using the command buttons on the Format tab of the Chart Tools contextual tab. To format the entire text box that contains the title, click one of the following buttons in the Shape Styles group:

✦ **Shape Styles More** button to display its drop-down gallery where you click the thumbnail of a style that formats both the text and text box for the selected chart title

✦ **Shape Fill** button to select a new color for the text box containing the selected chart title from its drop-down palette

✦ **Shape Outline** button to select a new color for the outline of the text box for the selected chart text from its drop-down palette

✦ **Shape Effects** button to apply a new effect (shadow, reflection, glow, soft edges, and so on) to the text box containing the selected chart title from its drop-down list

To format just the text in chart titles, click one of the various buttons in the WordArt Styles group:

✦ **WordArt Styles More** button to display its drop-down gallery where you click a thumbnail to apply a new WordArt style to the text of the selected chart title (or the text of all chart titles when the Chart Area is selected)

✦ **Text Fill** button (the one with the A) to select a new fill color for the text in the selected chart title from its drop-down palette

✦ **Text Outline** button (immediately below the Text Fill button) to select a new outline color for the text in the selected chart title from it drop-down palette

✦ **Text Effects** button (immediately below the Text Outline button) to apply a text effect (Shadow, Reflection, Glow, Bevel, and so on) to the text of the selected chart title from its drop-down list

Figure 1-10 shows a clustered column chart after selecting the chart area and then applying Colored Fill – Accent 1 (with a medium blue background with white text) from the Shape Styles gallery and the From Center gradient in the Dark Gradients section of the Gradient option's pop-up palette on the Shape Fill button's drop-down list to the chart's background.

Formatting the chart axes

The axis is the scale used to plot the data for your chart. Most chart types will have axes. All 2-D and 3-D charts have an x-axis known as the horizontal axis and a y-axis known as the vertical axis with the exception of pie charts and radar charts. The horizontal, x-axis is also referred to as the category axis and the vertical, y-axis as the value axis except in the case of XY (Scatter) charts where the horizontal, x-axis is also a value axis just like the vertical y-axis because this type of chart plots two sets of values against each other.

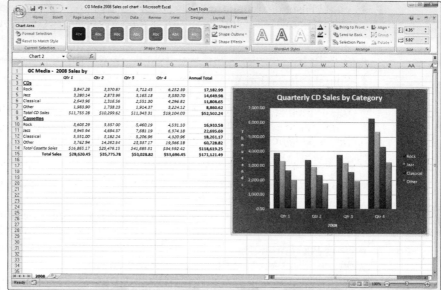

Figure 1-10: Clustered column chart after formatting its chart titles and chart area with options on the Format tab.

When you create a chart, Excel sets up the category and values axes for you automatically, based on the data you are plotting, which you can then adjust in various ways. The most common ways you will want to modify the category axis of a chart is to modify the interval between its tick marks and where it crosses the value axis in the chart. The most common ways you will want to modify a value axis of a chart is to change the scale that they use and assign a new number formatting to their units.

To make such changes to a chart axis, click the axis on the Chart Elements button's drop-down list on the Format tab (doing this is a whole lot easier than trying to click the actual axis in the chart to select it, although this is possible as well) and then click the tab's Format Selection button to open the Format Axis dialog box with the Axis Options tab selected.

Figure 1-11 shows you the options that you can modify for the category axis in a typical 2-D chart. The options for modifying the category axis include

✦ **Interval between Tick Marks** to modify the spacing between the major vertical tick marks (assuming they're displayed) by entering the whole number of units to place between the tick marks in the chart in its text box

✦ **Interval between Labels** to modify the spacing between the axis labels by clicking the Specify Interval Unit option button and then entering the whole number of units to place between the labels in its text box

✦ **Categories in Reverse Order** to reverse the order in which the data markers and their categories appear on the horizontal axis by clicking its check box to put a check mark in it

+ **Label Distance from Axis** to modify the distance between the axis labels and the horizontal axis by entering a new value between 0 and 1000 in its text box

+ **Axis Type** to indicate for formatting purposes that the axis labels are text entries by clicking the Text Axis option button, or indicate that they are dates by clicking the Date Axis option button

+ **Major Tick Mark Type** to change how the major vertical tick marks intersect the horizontal axis by clicking the Inside, Outside, or Cross option on its drop-down list

+ **Minor Tick Mark Type** to change how the minor vertical tick marks intersect the horizontal axis by clicking the Inside, Outside, or Cross option on its drop-down list

+ **Axis Labels** to reposition the axis labels from beneath the horizontal axis (the Low option) to above the chart's frame by clicking the High option or to completely remove their display in the chart by clicking the None option on its drop-down list

+ **Vertical Axis Crosses** to reposition the point at which the vertical axis crosses the horizontal axis by clicking the At Category Number option button and then entering the number of the category in the chart (with 1 indicating the leftmost category) after which it is to cross or by clicking the At Maximum option button to have the vertical axis cross after the very last category on the right edge of the chart's frame

+ **Position Axis** to reposition the horizontal axis so that its first category is located at the vertical axis on the left edge of the chart's frame and the last category is on the right edge of the chart's frame by clicking the On Tick Marks option button

Figure 1-11:
The options on the Axis Options tab of the Format Axis dialog box when Horizontal (Category) Axis is selected in a typical 2-D chart.

Figure 1-12 shows you the options that you can modify for the value axis in a typical 2-D chart. The options for modifying the value axis include

✦ **Minimum** to determine the point where the axis begins — perhaps $4,000 instead of the default of $0 — by clicking its Fixed option button and then entering a value higher than 0.0 in its text box

✦ **Maximum** to determine the highest point displayed on the vertical axis by clicking its Fixed option button and then entering the new maximum value in its text box — note that data values in the chart greater than the value you specify here simply aren't displayed in the chart.

✦ **Major Unit** to modify the distance between major horizontal tick marks (assuming they're displayed) in the chart by clicking its Fixed option button and then entering the number of the new distance in its text box

✦ **Minor Unit** to modify the distance between minor horizontal tick marks (assuming they're displayed) in the chart by clicking its Fixed option button and then entering the number of the new distance in its text box

✦ **Values in Reverse Order** to place the lowest value on the chart at the top of the scale and the highest value at the bottom (as you might want to do in a chart to emphasize the negative effect of the larger values) by clicking its check box to put a check mark in it

✦ **Logarithmic Scale** to base the value axis scale upon powers of ten and recalculate the Minimum, Maximum, Major Unit, and Minor Unit accordingly by clicking its check box to put a check mark in it — enter a new number in its text box if you want the logarithmic scale to use a base other than 10.

✦ **Display Units** to divide the values displayed on the value axis by the basic unit that you click on its drop-down list (Hundreds, Thousands, 10000, 100000, Millions, 10000000, 100000000, Billions, or Trillions) — click the Show Display Units Label on Chart check box to put a check mark in it when you also want a label designating the basic unit displayed along the value axis.

✦ **Major Tick Mark Type** to change how the major horizontal tick marks intersect the vertical axis by clicking the Inside, Outside, or Cross option on its drop-down list

✦ **Minor Tick Mark Type** to change how the minor horizontal tick marks intersect the vertical axis by clicking the Inside, Outside, or Cross option on its drop-down list

✦ **Axis Labels** to reposition the value axis labels from the left edge of the chart's frame (the Low option) to the right edge of the chart's frame by clicking the High option or remove their display from the chart by clicking the None option on its drop-down list

✦ **Horizontal Axis Crosses** to reposition the point at which the horizontal axis crosses the vertical axis by clicking the Axis Value option button and then entering the value in the chart at which it is to cross or by clicking the Maximum Axis Value option button to have the horizontal axis cross after at the highest value, putting the category axis labels at the top of the chart's frame

Figure 1-12:
The options on Axis Options tab of the Format Axis dialog box when the Vertical (Value) Axis is selected in a typical 2-D chart.

To assign a new number format to a value scale (General being the default), click the Number tab in the Format Axis dialog box and then click the number format category and specify the number of decimal places (where applicable) that you want displayed.

Selecting the Perfect Chart Type

When you display your data visually, choosing the right chart is probably just as important as deciding to use a chart at all. A chart displays the data visually, but different charts display the data in very different ways. Certain general guidelines may be familiar to you already. Line charts are useful for showing changes over time. Pie charts are useful for showing the relationship of parts to the whole.

As you continue to work with Excel 2007, you may find it beneficial to become more and more familiar with the chart types available and the formats available for those chart types. Using the best chart type and format will help you display your data visually in the most meaningful way. Following is a discussion of the major chart types available in Excel, with some simple guidelines on when to use each type.

Column charts

A column chart, unlike a bar chart to which it is often compared, emphasizes variation over a period of time. In a column chart, categories appear horizontally and values appear vertically, whereas in a bar chart, categories appear vertically.

Figure 1-13 shows the gallery that appears when you click the Column command button on the Insert tab of the Ribbon or press Alt+NC. This gallery contains a variety of subtypes within the five column chart categories: 2-D Column, 3-D Column, Cylinder, Cone, and Pyramid.

TIP

The cylinder, cone, and pyramid chart subtypes are really just variations on the three 3-D Column subtypes. Select one of these alternative column chart subtypes when you want to assign different shapes to the columns (cylindrical-, conical-, or pyramid-shaped) in your column chart.

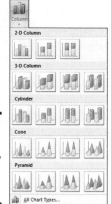

Figure 1-13:
The Column
Chart gallery
with its five
subtypes.

Line charts

A line chart shows the relationship of the changes in the data over a period of time. Although similar to an area chart, which shows the relative importance of values, the line chart emphasizes trends rather than the amount of change.

Figure 1-14 shows the gallery that appears when you click the Line command button on the Insert tab of the Ribbon or press Alt+NN. This gallery contains seven subtypes within the two line chart categories: 2-D Line and 3-D Line.

Figure 1-14:
The Line Chart gallery with its 2-D and 3-D subtypes.

Pie charts

Unlike the other charts discussed so far, which can show multiple data series, pie charts contain just one chart data series. A pie chart shows the relationship of the parts to the whole.

Figure 1-15 shows the gallery that appears when you click the Pie command button on the Insert tab of the Ribbon or press Alt+NE. This gallery contains six different subtypes within the two pie chart categories: 2-D Pie and 3-D Pie — note that both categories contain subtypes that explode the individual segments.

To emphasize the importance of one part, emphasize one "slice" by making it a bright color or broad pattern or by labeling it clearly. This is best done by choosing one of the various exploded 2-D or 3-D pie charts.

Figure 1-15:
The Pie Chart gallery with 2-D and 3-D subtypes.

Bar charts

Excel refers to charts with horizontal bars as "bar charts" and those with vertical bars as "column charts." A bar chart (horizontal) emphasizes the comparison between items at a fixed period of time.

Figure 1-16 shows the gallery that appears when you click the Bar command button on the Insert tab of the Ribbon or press Alt+NB. This gallery contains a variety of different subtypes within the five bar chart categories: 2-D Bar, 3-D Bar, Cylinder, Cone, and Pyramid.

Figure 1-16: The Bar Chart gallery with its five subtypes.

Area charts

An area chart shows the relative importance of values over time. For example, an area chart of the sales made by various account representatives over the first three months in the quarter might clearly reveal the relative importance of the sales from each person.

An area chart is similar to a line chart, but because the area between lines is filled in, the area chart puts greater emphasis on the magnitude of values and somewhat less emphasis on the flow of change over time than the line chart.

Figure 1-17 shows the gallery that appears when you click the Area command button on the Ribbon's Insert tab or press Alt+NA. This gallery contains six different subtypes within the two area chart categories: 2-D Area and 3-D Area.

Figure 1-17:
The Area
Chart gallery
with its 2-D
and 3-D
subtypes.

XY (Scatter) charts

Scatter charts are useful for showing a correlation among the data points
that may not be easy to see from data alone. You may want to answer
such questions as, "Does better nutrition mean that athletes have longer
careers?" or "Do people with better insurance coverage have fewer acci-
dents?" With an XY scatter chart, you can chart the two data series — for
example, ad expenditures and overall sales — and look for a correlation.

An XY (Scatter) chart uses numeric values along both axes instead of values
along the vertical axis and categories along the horizontal axis. You then use
a legend to show what the lines represent. If you wish, you can add axis
labels of your own.

Figure 1-18 shows the gallery that appears when you click the Scatter
command button on the Ribbon's Insert tab or press Alt+ND. This gallery
contains five different subtypes of the XY (Scatter) chart. Note that only the
first subtype for comparing pairs of values does not use lines to connect
the data points (creating, in effect, trendlines for each data series).

Figure 1-18:
The XY
(Scatter)
Chart gallery
with its five
types.

Other Charts

All the other types of charts — Stock, Surface, Doughnut, Bubble, and Radar —
are lumped together on the drop-down gallery that appears when you click
the Other Charts command button on the Ribbon's Insert tab or press Alt+NO.
Figure 1-19 shows you this gallery with these five remaining chart types and
their various subtypes.

Figure 1-19:
The Other Charts gallery with its Stock, Surface, Doughnut, Bubble, and Radar chart subtypes.

Stock charts

Stock charts, as their name implies, are used to plot stock quotes over a certain time period, such as a single business day or week. As Figure 1-19 illustrates, Excel offers you a choice of four different types of stock charts:

✦ **High-Low-Close** requires that you select three series of data in the high-low-close order. This means that the high values are in the leftmost column (or topmost row), the low values are in the next column to the right (or next row down), and the close values are in the rightmost column (or bottom-most row) of the data range used in the chart.

✦ **Open-High-Low-Close** requires the addition of the opening values to the high-close-low values in the order open-high-low-close (meaning that the open values must be in the leftmost column or topmost row of the data range with all the other values following suit).

✦ **Volume-High-Low-Close** plots the number of shares traded (the volume) along with the high-low-close of the stock. As with the other types of stock charts, the values in the data range specified for this subtype must be arranged in the order volume-high-low-close.

✦ **Volume-Open-High-Low-Close** combines the number of shares traded (the volume) with opening, high, low, and close values of the stock. As with the other types of stock charts, the values in the data range specified for this subtype must be arranged in the order volume-open-high-low-close.

Surface charts

Surface charts plot trends in values across two dimensions in a continuous curve. The trends in a surface chart imply the combined effects of two variables on a third. For that reason, all the different types of surface charts (see Figure 1-19) are 3-D charts that have an x-, y-, and z-axis (the last two subtypes are 3-D surface charts shown from above so that they appear to be two-dimensional). In order to use a surface, you need at least two data series, both of which are numeric as with an XY (Scatter) chart.

Doughnut Charts

A doughnut chart is similar to a pie chart except for its ability to display more than one data series (pie charts always graph just a single data series). Also, because the doughnut has a hole in the middle, you can use this space to display additional explanatory text.

Figure 1-19 shows the two types of doughnut charts. The only difference between the first and second type is that the second type explodes the various segments, which can often be more effective when you want to emphasize one data group over another.

Bubble charts

Bubble charts compare sets of three values as kind of a combination of an XY (Scatter) chart with an Area chart. When you build a bubble chart, the size of each bubble represented on the x-y grid represents the third set of values being charted. The downside to using a Bubble chart to plot data is that each bubble takes up so much room that they often overlap each other unless you are plotting just a very few data samples. As Figure 1-19 shows, Bubble charts are available in only two varieties: The first type draws the bubbles as 2-D circles, whereas the second type draws them with a 3-D visual effect.

Radar charts

A radar chart shows changes in data relative both to a center point and to each other. Each category in a radar chart has its own value axis radiating from the center point. Lines connect all the data markers in the same series. A radar chart is useful for making relative comparisons among items.

Figure 1-19 shows the three different radar chart types available. The second type places data markers at each data point, while the third type fills the area covered by each data series in the chart.

Saving a customized chart as a template

After going through extensive editing and formatting of one of Excel's basic chart types, you may want to save your work of art as a custom chart type that you can then use again with different data without having to go through all the painstaking steps to get the chart looking just the way you want it. Excel makes it easy to save any modified chart that you want to use again as a custom chart type.

To convert a chart on which you've done extensive editing and formatting into a custom chart type, you take these steps:

1. **Click the embedded chart to select it in the worksheet, or click its sheet tab if the chart's on a separate chart sheet.**

2. **Click the Save As Template command button on the Design tab of the Chart Tools contextual tab or press Alt+JCT.**

   Excel opens the Save Chart Template dialog box. The program automatically suggests Chart1.crtx as the filename, Chart Template Files (*.crtx) as the file type, and the Charts folder in the Microsoft Templates folder as the location.

3. **Edit the generic chart template filename in the File Name text box to give the chart template file a descriptive name without removing the .crtx filename extension.**

4. **Click the Save button to close the Save Chart Template dialog box.**

After creating a custom chart template in this manner, you can then use the template anytime you need to create a new chart that requires similar formatting by following these steps:

1. **Select the data in the worksheet to be graphed in a new chart using your chart template.**

2. **Click the Dialog Box Launcher button in the lower-right corner of the Charts group on the Insert tab of the Ribbon.**

   The Create Chart dialog box appears.

3. **Click the Templates option in the Navigation pane of the Create Chart dialog box.**

   Excel then displays thumbnails for all the chart templates you've saved in the main section of the Create Chart dialog box. To identify these thumbnails by filename, position the mouse pointer over the thumbnail image.

4. **Click the thumbnail for the chart template you want to use to select it and then click OK.**

As soon as you click OK, Excel applies the layout and all the formatting saved as part of the template file to the new embedded chart created with the data in the current cell selection.

Printing Charts

To print an embedded chart as part of the data on the worksheet, you simply print the worksheet (from the Print dialog box by pressing Ctrl+P). To print an embedded chart by itself without the supporting worksheet data, click the chart to select it before you press Ctrl+P to open the Print dialog box where the Selected Chart option button will be selected in the Print What section. To print a chart that's on a separate chart sheet, activate the chart sheet by clicking its sheet tab and then press Ctrl+P to open the Print dialog box where the Active Sheet(s) option button is selected in the Print What section.

When you want to print an embedded chart alone, that is, without its supporting data or in its own chart sheet, you may want to select the print quality options on the Chart tab of the Page Setup dialog box (which you can open by clicking the Preview button in the Print dialog box or by pressing Alt+FWV and then clicking the Page Setup command button on the Print Preview tab) before sending the chart to the printer. The Print Quality options on the Chart tab include the following:

✦ **Draft Quality:** Select this check box to print the chart using your printer's draft-quality setting.

✦ **Print in Black and White:** Select this check box to have your color printer print the chart in black and white.

Chapter 2: Adding Graphic Objects

In This Chapter

✓ Understanding what graphic objects are and how Excel treats them

✓ Managing graphic objects on the worksheet

✓ Adding clip art to the spreadsheet

✓ Adding text boxes with arrows

✓ Importing graphics files in the worksheet

✓ Inserting WordArt in the spreadsheet

✓ Applying graphic themes to the worksheet

✓ Creating organization charts and other diagrams with SmartArt

*J*ust as charts can really help to clarify trends and implications that aren't readily apparent in your worksheet data, graphics that you add to a worksheet can really spruce up your charts and make them read even better. Although you may often look to Excel graphic objects as chart enhancements, you can also use them to enhance regular spreadsheet data. Depending on the type of spreadsheet, you may even end up using graphic elements not simply as a way to embellish the data, but also as a superior way to actually present it in the worksheet, especially when the data require diagrammatic presentation.

Excel supports two types of graphic objects: those that you create yourself from the Shapes gallery or with the SmartArt, Text Box, and WordArt command buttons on the Insert tab of the Ribbon, and those created by others that you import with its Picture and Clip Art command buttons. This chapter covers how to create graphics with text and text as graphics as well as basic graphic shapes. It also covers how to import two different types of graphic images: Microsoft's clip art graphics along with pictures and digital photos stored in a variety of different graphics file formats that Excel can read.

Graphic Objects 101

It is important to understand that all graphic objects (including embedded charts as covered in Book V, Chapter 1), whether you create them or import them, are discrete objects in the worksheet that you can select and manipulate. To select a graphic object, you simply click it. Excel lets you know that the object is selected by placing white circular sizing handles around the perimeter. The program also adds a green circular rotation handle that appears directly above and connected to the sizing handle of the graphic's perimeter (the handle is on the top edge, in the middle) if the graphic can be rotated. On some drawn objects (especially 3D ones), yellow diamond shaping handles also appear at the places where you can manipulate some part of the object's shape, as shown in Figure 2-1.

To select multiple graphic objects in the worksheet, hold down the Shift or Ctrl key as you click each object. When you select more than one object, any manipulations that you perform affect all the selected objects.

To deselect a graphic object, just click the thick, white cross pointer in any cell in the worksheet that it doesn't cover. To deselect an object when you have several graphics selected at one time, click an unobstructed cell or another graphic.

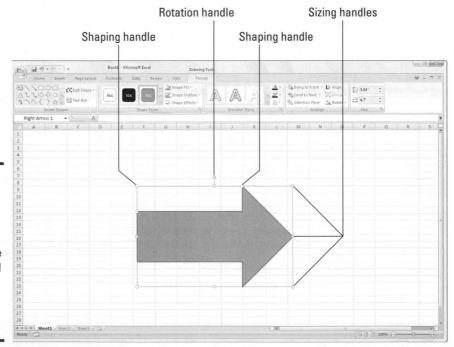

Figure 2-1: When you click a graphic object to select it, the rotation and circular sizing handles appear.

Manipulating graphics

When you position the mouse pointer on a graphic object's sizing handle, the pointer becomes a double-headed arrow that you can then drag to increase or decrease the overall size and shape of the object. To constrain a graphic while resizing it, click the sizing handle and then press and hold down the Shift key as you drag the mouse. Holding down the Shift key restricts your dragging so that the graphic retains its original proportions as you make it bigger or smaller. To constrain the proportions of an object in two dimensions, hold down the Shift key as you drag one of the corner sizing handles.

 When you position the mouse pointer on a graphic object's rotation handle, the pointer becomes a curved arrow pointing clockwise (shown in the left margin). When you click and hold down the mouse button to drag the rotation handle, the pointer becomes four curved arrows in a circle pointing in the clockwise direction. You can then rotate the graphic to any degree in a circle that pivots around the rotation handle.

 When you position the mouse pointer on a graphic's shaping handle (if it has one), the pointer becomes an arrowhead without any handle (shown in the left margin). You can then drag this pointer to reshape the side or section of the graphic. In the case of some 3-D graphic shapes, dragging the Shaping handle rotates a part of the graphic in such a way that it alters the object's perspective, thus changing the way it's viewed.

To move the selected graphic object, position the mouse pointer somewhere inside the object's perimeter. Then, when the pointer becomes an arrowhead with a double-cross at its point, drag the object to its new position within the worksheet. To copy the selected object, hold down the Ctrl key as you drag the graphic (when you press the Ctrl key, a plus sign, indicating that the object is being copied, appears above the arrowhead pointer).

 When moving graphics in a worksheet, you can make use of an invisible grid to help you position them. This is especially helpful when you're trying to align one graphic with another (for example, when aligning two charts side by side in a worksheet). To turn on the grid, you do one of the following, depending on the type of graphic object:

✦ Click the Snap to Grid option on the Align button's drop-down menu on the Format tab on the Drawing Tools contextual tab when the selected graphic object is a drawn graphic such as a predefined shape, text box, piece of clip art, or WordArt.

✦ Click the Snap to Grid option on the Align button's drop-down menu on the Format tab on the Picture Tools contextual tab when the selected graphic object is a picture or digital photo imported with the Picture command button on the Insert tab.

✦ Click the Arrange button on the Format tab on the SmartArt contextual tab followed by the Align button and then click the Snap to Grid option on its drop-down menu when the graphic object is a piece of SmartArt.

After the Snap to Grid feature is turned on, whenever you position an object very close to an invisible horizontal or vertical gridline, it snaps to this line as soon as you release the mouse button.

You can "nudge" a selected graphic object into its desired position by pressing the arrow keys. When you press an arrow key, Excel moves the object just a very little bit in that direction. Nudging is very useful when you have an object that's almost in place and requires very little handling to get it into just the right position.

If you no longer need a graphic object, you can get rid of it by clicking it to select the object and then pressing the Delete key to remove it.

Moving graphic objects to new layers

All graphic objects that you add to a worksheet lay on different invisible layers that reside on top of the worksheet and over the worksheet data in the cells below. This means that if you move a graphic object over a cell that contains an entry, the graphic hides the data beneath it. Likewise, if you draw a shape or add an image and then position it on top of another graphic object (such as an embedded chart or other shape or picture), it also covers up the graphic below.

Figure 2-2 illustrates this situation. In this figure, you see the clip art image of a globe with a map of the world partially covering some worksheet data and an embedded clustered column chart both on the same layer below. On top of the globe, I have drawn a crescent moon shape and have given it a glow, which now resides on the very top layer, obscuring part of the globe, part of the chart, and some of the worksheet data on the layers below it.

The three graphic objects — the globe, the crescent moon, and the clustered column chart — are identified in the Selection and Visibility task pane displayed on the right side of the program window as Moon 3, Picture 1, and Chart 1, respectively.

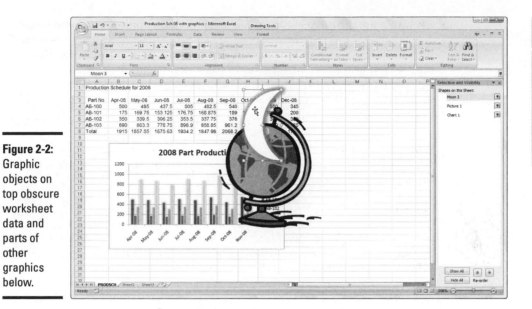

Figure 2-2:
Graphic objects on top obscure worksheet data and parts of other graphics below.

You display the Selection and Visibility task pane by clicking the Selection Pane command button on the Format tab on the Chart Tools, Drawing Tools, or Picture Tools contextual tab, depending on the type of graphic object selected. When a SmartArt graphic object is selected, you need to click the Arrange command button before you can click the Selection Pane button on the Format tab of the SmartArt Tools contextual tab.

Excel makes it easy to move the graphic objects on the same worksheet to other layers using the Selection and Visibility task pane. Simply click the name of the object in this task pane that you want to move and then click the Bring Forward button (the one with the arrow pointing upward at the bottom of the task pane in the Re-order section) or the Send Backward button (the one with the arrow pointing downward) to move it. Clicking the Bring Forward button moves the selected object up a level in the Selection and Visibility task pane just as clicking the Send Backward button moves the object down a level. (See Figure 2-3.)

Note that any graphic object that appears above others in the list in the Selection and Visibility task pane obscures all the objects below it, provided that the objects' check boxes in the task pane are not empty but contain eye icons (meaning that they're visible in the worksheet) *and* that the objects overlap each other in whole or part in their placement on the worksheet. Also keep in mind that you can't use the Bring Forward and Send Backward buttons to move an embedded chart to another layer because this is the one type of graphic object that always stays put on the same layer as the worksheet — you can, however, move other types of graphic objects that overlap the chart a layer beneath the chart by clicking its name followed by the Send Backward button.

Figure 2-3: Worksheet after moving the globe and crescent moon graphics backward so that no part of either one obscures the embedded chart.

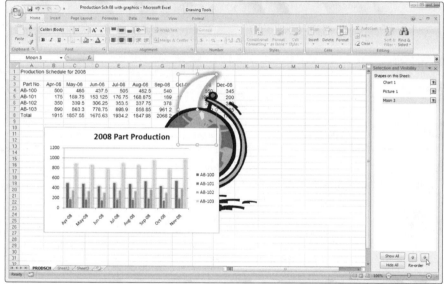

If the Selection and Visibility task pane is not open, you can use the Bring to Front and Send to Back command buttons on the Format tab of the Chart Tools, Drawing Tools, and Picture Tools contextual tabs to move them to new layers:

✦ Click the Bring to Front command button to bring the selected graphic object to the top of the stack.

✦ Click the Send to Back button to send the object to the bottom of the stack.

✦ Click the Bring Forward option on the Bring to Front button's drop-down menu to bring the selected object up to the next higher layer.

✦ Click the Send Backward option on the Send to Back button's drop-down menu to send the selected object down to the next layer.

Figure 2-3 illustrates how easy it is to move a graphic object to a different level in the Selection and Visibility task pane. For this figure, I clicked Picture 1 in the list and then clicked the Send Backward button at the bottom of the task pane in the Re-order area. I then clicked Moon 3 in the list and clicked the Send Backward button twice to move it to the bottom of the list in the Selection and Visibility task pane at the bottom of the graphics stack in the worksheet, just as they appear in the figure.

Aligning graphic objects

When you're dealing with two graphic objects, one on top of the other, and you want to align them with each other, you can use the options on the Align command button's drop-down menu on the Format tab of the Drawing Tools or Picture Tools contextual menu. The alignment options on this button's drop-down menu include

+ **Align Left** to left align the graphic on the top layer with the one underneath

+ **Align Center** to center the graphic on the top layer with the one underneath

+ **Align Right** to right align the graphic on the top layer with the one underneath

+ **Align Top** to top align the graphic on the top layer with the one underneath

+ **Align Middle** to center vertically the graphic on the top layer with the one underneath

+ **Align Bottom** to bottom align the graphic on the top layer with the one underneath

+ **Distribute Horizontally** to equally distribute the selected graphic objects (three or more) horizontally

+ **Distribute Vertically** to equally distribute the selected graphic objects (three or more) vertically

Grouping graphic objects

Sometimes you need to work with more than one graphic object (for example, the globe and the crescent moon graphic objects in Figures 2-2 and 2-3). If you find that you're constantly selecting two or more objects at the same time in order to move them or rotate them together, you can make life a lot simpler by grouping the graphics. When you group selected graphic objects, Excel then makes them into a single graphic object, which you can then manipulate.

To group a bunch of graphics together, select them all (either by Shift+clicking or Ctrl+clicking each one). After they are selected, right-click the object on the top layer and then choose Group⇨Group on the object's shortcut menu or click the Group option on the Group command button's drop-down menu on the Format tab of the Drawing Tools or Picture Tools contextual menu.

Excel indicates that the selected graphics are now grouped in the worksheet (and for all intents and purposes, a single graphic object) by placing a single set of sizing handles around the perimeter formed by all the former separate graphics and by giving them a group number in the Selection and Visibility task pane. You can then manipulate the grouped graphic as a single entity by moving it, sizing it, rotating it, and so forth as you would any other object.

The great thing about grouping a bunch of different objects is that Excel never forgets that they were once separate objects that you could independently manipulate. This means that you can always turn them back into separate graphics by ungrouping them. To do this, right-click the composite graphic object and then choose Group⇨Ungroup on its shortcut menu or click the Ungroup option on the Group command button's drop-down menu on the Format tab of the Drawing Tools or Picture Tools contextual menu.

Excel shows that the composite object is once again separated into many different objects by displaying sizing handles around each object's perimeter. You can then deselect them all and manipulate each one once again independently by selecting it alone before moving, resizing, or rotating it. If you decide that you want the now independent objects to be joined as a group once again, you can do this by right-clicking any one of the graphics in the erstwhile group and then choosing Group⇨Regroup on its shortcut menu or clicking the Regroup option on the Group command button's drop-down menu on the Format tab.

Figure 2-4 illustrates grouping in action. For this figure, I selected both the crescent moon and the globe graphic below. In this figure, I'm in the process of choosing the Group option on the Group command button's drop-down menu on the Format tab of the Drawing Tools contextual tab, which will turn them into a single composite graphic object. After choosing this option, not only will the moon move whenever I reposition the globe, but the moon will also resize when I modify the shape, and would rotate together with the globe if I were to turn the globe on its head.

Figure 2-4:
Grouping
the moon
and globe to
turn them
into a single
graphic
object.

Managing graphic objects in the Selection and Visibility task pane

As previously discussed in the "Moving graphic objects to new layers" section earlier in this chapter, the Selection and Visibility task pane that you display by clicking the Selection Pane button on the Format tab of the Chart Tools, Drawing Tools, or Picture Tools contextual tab on the Ribbon makes it easy to move graphic objects that overlap one another in some manner to different layers in the stack.

When dealing with a SmartArt graphic, you have to click the Arrange button on the Format tab of the SmartArt Tools contextual tab Ribbon to get access to the Selection Pane command button.

In addition to rearranging graphic objects on different layers, you can use this task pane to select particular graphic objects for editing or formatting as well as to temporarily hide their display in the worksheet:

✦ To select a graphic object in the worksheet, click its name in the list in the Selection and Visibility task pane — to select multiple graphics, press Ctrl as you click their names in the list.

✦ To hide a particular graphic object in the worksheet, click the check box that appears after its name in the list to remove the eye icon, and to redisplay it, click this check box a second time to restore the eye icon.

✦ To hide all the graphic objects (including embedded charts) on the worksheet, click the Hide All button at the bottom of the task pane, and to redisplay them, click the Show All button.

Click the graphic object's name in the Selection and Visibility task pane to select it for editing or formatting whenever the object is difficult to select directly in the worksheet by clicking its shape or image, which is often the case when the object's part of a stack of graphics.

Importing Graphics

Excel makes it easy for you to import two types of graphic objects into your spreadsheet:

✦ **Clip art:** Over 150,000 readymade illustrations are offered by Microsoft for use in its various Microsoft Office programs, including Excel 2007. Clip art drawings are now so numerous that the images are classified into a bunch of different categories ranging from Abstract to Web Elements.

✦ **Pictures:** Digital art and photos saved in various types of graphics file formats.

Adding clip art

To bring in a piece of clip art included with Office 2007, you click the Clip Art button on the Ribbon's Insert tab or press Alt+NF. When you do this, Excel 2007 displays the Clip Art Task pane (similar to the one shown in Figure 2-5 from which you search for the type of art you want to use. To locate the clip(s) you want to insert into the current worksheet in the Clip Art Task pane, you follow these steps:

1. **Click the Search For text box at the top, and then enter the keyword(s) for the type of clip art you want to find.**

When entering keywords for finding particular types of clip art, try entering general, descriptive terms such as trees, flowers, people, flying, and the like.

Figure 2-5:
Use the Clip
Art Task
pane to
search for
clip art.

2. **(Optional) Click the Search In drop-down button and remove (deselect) check marks from any clip art collections that you don't want to search.**

   By default, Excel searches all the collections of clip art (including the Media Gallery Online collection on the Web). To limit your search, you need to make sure that only the clip art collections you want to include in the search have check marks before their names.

3. **(Optional) To limit the search to clip art only, click the Results Should Be drop-down button and remove check marks from the All Media Types, Photographs, Movies, and Sounds categories.**

   You can further limit the types of clip art files included in the search by clicking the plus sign in front of Clip Art and then removing check marks from any and all types of clips (such as CorelDraw or Macintosh PICT) that you don't want or need to use.

4. **Click the Go button to the immediate right of the Search For text box to initiate the search.**

When you click the Go button, Excel searches all of the places you specify in the Search In list and displays the thumbnails of the search results in the Clip Art Task pane.

You cannot use the search feature in the Clip Art Task pane until after you index the clips with the Clip Organizer. To do this, click the Organize Clips link near the bottom of the Clip Art Task pane. When you click this link, Excel opens the Add Clips to Organizer window in which you click the Now button to have all your media files indexed by keywords. After the Clip Organizer finishes indexing your clip art, you are ready to search for clips as outlined in the preceding steps.

If you have difficulty finding a piece of clip art, try editing its keywords to make finding it the next time easier. To do this, click the image's drop-down button and then choose Edit Keywords on its drop-down menu. Doing this opens the Keywords dialog box that shows all the keywords assigned to the image. To add your own keyword to the list, enter it into the Keyword drop-down text box and click the Add button. Also, if you see an image that is close to, but not exactly, what you want, try finding like images by clicking the image's drop-down button, and then choosing Find Similar Style on its pop-up menu.

To insert one of the thumbnails displayed in the Clip Art task pane into the current worksheet (see Figure 2-6), click the thumbnail. You can also insert an image by positioning the mouse over it to display its drop-down button, and then clicking the drop-down button and choosing Insert at the top of its drop-down menu.

Figure 2-6:
Click the thumbnail in your search results in the Clip Art task pane to insert its image in the worksheet.

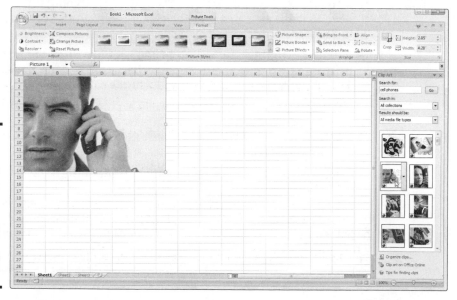

When you insert a clip art image into the worksheet, it is automatically selected (indicated by the selection handles around its perimeter and its rotation handle at the top). To deselect the clip art image and set it in the worksheet, click anywhere in the worksheet outside of the image.

Adding pictures from graphics files

If you want to bring in an image such as a digital photo or a scanned image saved in its own graphics file, click the Picture button on the Ribbon's Insert tab or press Alt+NP. This opens the Insert Picture dialog box (which works just like opening an Excel workbook file in the Open dialog box) where you select the graphics file and then import it into the worksheet by clicking its Insert button.

If you want to bring in a graphic image created in another graphics program that's not saved in its own file, you select the graphic in that program and then copy it to the Clipboard (press Ctrl+C). When you get back to your worksheet, place the cursor where you want the picture to go and then paste the image in place (press Ctrl+V or click the Paste command button at the very beginning of the Home tab).

When you insert a picture from a graphics file into the worksheet, it's automatically selected (indicated by the selection handles around its perimeter and its rotation handle at the top). To deselect the graphic image and set it in the worksheet, click anywhere in the worksheet outside of the image.

Editing clip art and imported pictures

While an imported clip art image or a picture is selected in your worksheet (indicated by the selection handles around its perimeter and a rotation handle at the top), you can make any of the following editing changes to it:

✦ Move the clip art image or imported picture to a new location in the chart by dragging it.

✦ Resize the clip art image box or imported picture by dragging the appropriate selection handle.

✦ Rotate the clip art image or imported picture by dragging its rotation handle (the green circle at the top) in a clockwise or counterclockwise direction.

✦ Delete the clip art image or imported picture by pressing the Delete key.

Formatting clip art and imported pictures

When an imported clip art image or picture is selected, Excel adds the Picture Tools contextual tab to the Ribbon and automatically selects its sole Format tab.

The Format tab is divided into four groups: Adjust, Picture Styles, Arrange, and Size. The Adjust group contains the following important command buttons:

✦ **Brightness** to increase or decrease the picture's brightness by selecting a new preset positive percentage (to increase) or negative percentage (to decrease) where 0% is normal or by clicking Picture Corrections Options to open the Format Picture dialog box where you can adjust it with the Brightness slider.

✦ **Contrast** to increase or decrease the picture's contrast by selecting a new preset positive percentage (to increase) or negative percentage (to decrease) where 0 percent is normal or by clicking Picture Corrections Options to open the Format Picture dialog box where you can adjust it with the Contrast slider.

✦ **Recolor** to open a drop-down menu where you can select a new color for the image or select a transparent color that drops out of the picture.

✦ **Compress Pictures** to open the Compress Pictures dialog box where you can compress all images in the worksheet or just the selected graphic image to make them more compact and thus make the Excel workbook somewhat smaller when you save the images as part of its file.

✦ **Change Pictures** to open the Insert Picture dialog box where you can select an image in a new graphics file to replace the picture — when replacing the currently selected picture with the new image, Excel automatically sizes and formats the new image with the settings applied to the old.

✦ **Reset Picture** button to remove all formatting changes made and return the picture to the state it was in when you originally inserted it into the worksheet.

You can also format a clip art image or imported picture by opening the Format Picture dialog box (right-click the image and then click Format Picture on its shortcut menu) and then selecting the appropriate options on its Fill, Line, Line Style, Shadow, 3-D Format, 3-D Rotation, Picture, and Text Box tabs.

In addition to the command buttons in the Adjust group, you can use the command buttons in the Picture Styles group. Click a thumbnail on the Picture Styles drop-down gallery to select a new orientation and style for the selected picture or select a new border shape on the Picture Shape button's drop-down palette, border color on the Picture Border button's drop-down color palette, or a new shadow or 3-D rotation effect on the Picture Effects button's drop-down menu.

Figure 2-7 shows the imported Mind over Media, Inc. logo as it's being formatted in Live Preview with Double Frame, Black on the Picture Styles drop-down gallery. Note that in this style, Excel places the image in an inner light black frame surrounded by a much heavier outer frame.

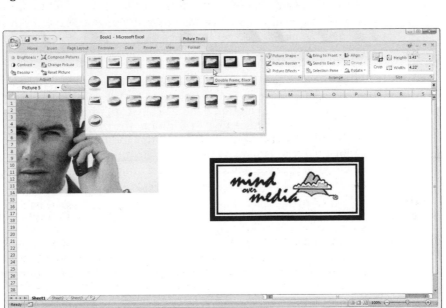

Figure 2-7:
Live Preview in the Picture Styles gallery enables you to see how a style affects your picture before you apply it.

Drawing Graphics

The Shapes gallery along with the SmartArt, Text Box, and WordArt command buttons found on the Insert tab of the Ribbon enable you to draw a wide variety of graphic objects. Some of these graphic objects, including the callout graphics on the Shapes gallery and all the SmartArt, Text Box, and WordArt graphics, enable you to combine text and graphics.

Drawing predefined shapes

The Shapes gallery, opened by clicking the Shapes command button in the Illustrations group on the Ribbon's Insert tab, contains a wide variety of predefined shapes that you can draw in your worksheet simply by dragging the mouse pointer.

When you open the Shapes gallery by clicking its command button (the one with the bar above the downward pointing triangle), you see that the gallery is divided into nine sections: Recently Used Shapes, Lines, Rectangles, Basic Shapes, Block Arrows, Equation Shapes, Flowchart, Stars and Banners, and Callouts.

After you click the thumbnail of one of the preset shapes in this drop-down gallery, the mouse pointer becomes a crosshair and you use it to draw the graphic by dragging it until it's approximately the size you want.

After you release the mouse button, the shape you've drawn in the worksheet is still selected. This is indicated by the selection handles around its perimeter and the rotation handle at the top, which you can use to reposition and resize it, if need be. In addition, the program activates the Format tab on the Drawing Tools contextual tab and you can use the Shape Styles gallery or other command buttons to further format the shape until it's exactly the way you want it. To set the shape and remove the selection and rotation handles, click anywhere in the worksheet outside of the shape.

When drawing a rectangle or an oval, you can constrain the tool to draw a square or circle by holding down the Shift key as you drag the mouse. Note that when drawing a two-dimensional shape, such as a rectangle, square, oval, or circle, Excel automatically draws the shape with a blue fill that obscures any data or graphic objects that are beneath the shape on layers below.

In addition to drawing your own basic shapes, lines, and arrows from the gallery, you can draw block arrows, equation symbols, flow chart symbols, banners, and callouts by selecting them from their respective areas on the Shapes gallery. Note that, when you draw one of the callouts, Excel positions the insertion point within the selected callout shape, thus enabling you to then enter the text of the callout. After you finish entering the text, click somewhere outside the shape to deselect the callout (see the "Adding text boxes" section that follows for information on how to edit and format the callout text).

Adding text boxes

Text boxes are special graphic objects that combine text with a rectangular graphic object. They're great for calling attention to significant trends or special features in the charts that you create (see Book V, Chapter 1, for details).

To create a text box, click the Text Box command button on the Insert tab of the Ribbon and then drag the mouse pointer to draw the outline of the box. As soon as you release the mouse button, Excel places the insertion point in the upper-left corner of the box.

You can then start typing the text that you want displayed in the text box. When the text that you type reaches the right edge of the text box, Excel automatically starts a new line. If you reach the end of the text box and keep typing, Excel then scrolls the text up, and you then have to resize the text box to display all the text that you've entered. If you want to break a line before it reaches the right edge of the text box, press the Enter key. When you finish entering the text, click anywhere on the screen outside the text box to deselect.

Keep in mind that although text boxes are similar to cell Comments in that they also display the text that you enter in a rectangular box, they do differ from Comments in that text boxes are *not* attached to particular cells and *are* always displayed in the worksheet (Comments only show when you position the mouse pointer over the cell or select the comment with the Reviewing toolbar — see Book IV, Chapter 3, for details).

Note that text boxes differ somewhat from other graphic objects that you add to the worksheet. Unlike other graphic objects in Excel, text boxes display two different border patterns when you select them: A dotted-line pattern is displayed when you click inside the text box, thus enabling you to format and edit the text, and a solid-line pattern is displayed when you click the border of the text box or start dragging the box to reposition it, thus indicating that you can format and edit the box itself.

Formatting a text box

After you've added a text box, you can format its text by changing the font, font size, font style, and alignment of the text (including its orientation); you can also format the text box by changing its background color and line style, object positioning properties, and — perhaps most important of all — its text margins.

To change the formatting of all the text entered in a text box, click its TextBox name in the Selection and Visibility task pane or click its graphic object in the worksheet until the solid outline appears around the box, and then click the appropriate command buttons in the Font and Alignment groups on the Ribbon's Home tab. Choose from the following options:

✦ **Font** or **Font Size** drop-down list buttons and the **Increase Font Size** and **Decrease Font Size** command buttons to change the font or font size of the text — use Live Preview to see how the new font and font size looks in the text box.

✦ **Bold, Italic,** or **Underline** command buttons to add these attributes to the text in the text box.

✦ **Font Color** drop-down list button to apply a new color to the text in the text box.

✦ **Align Text Left, Center,** or **Align Text Right** command buttons to change the horizontal alignment of the text in regards to the left and right edges of the text box.

✦ **Top Align, Middle Align,** or **Bottom Align** command buttons to change the vertical alignment of the text in regards to the top and bottom edges of the text box.

✦ **Increase Indent** or **Decrease Indent** command buttons to indent text within the box's borders or remove previous indenting.

✦ **Orientation** command button to modify the orientation of the text in the text box by selecting the Vertical Text, Rotate Text Up, or the Rotate Text Down option.

To change the formatting of some of the text in a text box, click the insertion point in the text box and select the text before you use one of these command buttons to modify its appearance.

To change the formatting of the text box itself, click its TextBox name in the Selection and Visibility task pane or click its graphic object in the worksheet until the solid outline appears around the box, then click the Format tab on the Drawing Tools contextual tab on the Ribbon, and then choose among the following formatting options:

✦ **Edit Shape** drop-down list button (the one with the dots around the graphic object in the Insert Shapes group) to change the text box to another shape or edit the wrap points

✦ **Text Box** drop-down list button to convert a horizontal text box to a vertical text box by clicking the Vertical Text Box option

✦ **Shape Styles** gallery to select a new outline, fill, and text color all at one time by clicking one of the gallery's thumbnails (after using Live Preview to see how the new color scheme looks)

✦ **Shape Fill** drop-down list button to select a new color, gradient, picture, or texture for the text box fill or to remove any existing fill (by clicking No Fill option)

✦ **Shape Outline** drop-down list button to select a new color, line weight, or line style for the outline of the text box or to remove its outline (by clicking the No Outline option)

✦ **Shape Effects** drop-down list button to select a new special effect such as a shadow, glow, or other 3-D effect using the options and palettes available from its drop-down menu

✦ **WordArt Styles** drop-down palette to apply a new WordArt style for the text in the text box by clicking one of the gallery's thumbnails (after using Live Preview to see how the new WordArt text style looks)

✦ **Text Fill** drop-down list button (the one with the A with a line drawn under it) to select a new fill color, gradient, picture, or texture for the text in the text box or to remove any existing fill color (by clicking No Fill option)

✦ **Text Outline** drop-down list button (the one with the pencil added to the A with the line drawn under it) to select a new color, line weight, or line style for the text in the text box or to remove its current outline (by clicking the No Outline option)

✦ **Text Effects** drop-down list button to select a new special effect such as a shadow, glow, or other 3-D effect for the text in the text box using the options and palettes available from its drop-down menu

When you first enter the text in a text box, Excel sets pretty scanty internal margins so that there's not a lot of white space between the text characters and the edge of the text box. If you're anything like me, one of the first things that you'll want to do is add decent margins to the text box.

To do this, open the Format Shape dialog box while the text box is selected by right-clicking the text box and then clicking Format Shape on its shortcut menu. Then, click the Text Box tab and enter the new values (in fractions of an inch) that you want to use in the Top, Bottom, Left, and Right text boxes in the Internal Margin section. Also, click the Resize Shape to Fit Text check box in the AutoFit section to put a check mark in it if you want Excel to automatically resize the text box to suit any formatting changes you make to its text (like increasing the font size, adding bold, or selecting a new text alignment).

Editing the text in a text box

You can edit the text in a text box as you would in any cell of the worksheet. To insert new text, click the insertion point at the appropriate place and start typing. To delete text, press the Backspace key to delete characters to the left of the insertion point or the Delete key to delete characters to its right. To delete an entire section of text, select it with the I-beam mouse pointer and then press the Delete key.

To spell check some or all of the text in the text box, select the text by dragging the I-beam mouse pointer through it and then click the Spelling button on the Review tab of the Ribbon (or just press F7).

To delete a text box from the worksheet, click its border to select the box (indicated by the solid outline) and then press the Delete key. Be sure that you don't click inside the box because this only selects the text (indicated by the dotted outline), in which case, pressing the Delete key doesn't get rid of anything but characters of text at the cursor's position.

Adding an arrow to a text box

When creating a text box, you may want to add an arrow to point directly to another graphic object or to the part of an embedded chart to which you're referencing. To add an arrow, follow these steps:

1. **Click the text box to which you want to attach the arrow in the chart or worksheet to select.**

   Selection handles appear around the text box and the Format tab on the Drawing Tools contextual tab is selected on the Ribbon.

2. **Click the Arrow command button in the Insert Shapes drop-down gallery at the very beginning of the Format tab.**

   The Arrow command button is the second from the left in the Lines section of Shapes gallery (with the picture of an arrow). When you click this button, it becomes selected in the gallery palette (indicated by the new color) and the mouse pointer assumes the crosshair shape.

3. **Drag the crosshair mouse pointer from the place on the text box where the end of the arrow (the one *without* the arrowhead) is to appear to the place where the arrow starts (and the arrowhead will appear) and release the mouse button.**

As soon as you release the mouse button, Excel draws two points, one at the base of the arrow (attached to text box) and another at the arrow-head. At the same time, the contents of the Shape Styles drop-down gallery changes to line styles.

4. **Click the More button in the lower-right corner of the Shape Styles drop-down gallery to display the thumbnails of all its line styles and then mouse over the thumbnails to see how the arrow would look in each.**

   As you mouse through the different line styles in this gallery, Excel draws the arrow between the two selected points in the text box using the highlighted style.

5. **Click the thumbnail of the line style you want the new arrow to use in the Shape Styles gallery.**

Excel then draws a new arrow using the selected shape style, which remains selected (with selection handles at the beginning and end of the arrow). You can then edit the arrow as follows:

✦ Move the arrow by dragging its outline into position.

✦ Change the length of the arrow by dragging the selection handle at the arrowhead.

✦ Change the direction of the arrow by pivoting the mouse pointer around a stationary selection handle.

✦ Change the shape of the arrowhead or the thickness of the arrow's shaft by clicking a thumbnail on the Shape Styles drop-down gallery or click-ing a new option on the Shape Fill, Shape Outline, and Shape Effects button on the Format tab of the Drawing Tools contextual tab or by opening the Format Shape dialog box (Ctrl+1) and then selecting the appropriate options on its Fill, Line Color, Line Style, Shadow, 3-D Format, 3-D Rotation, Picture, and Text Box tabs.

✦ Delete the arrow by pressing the Delete key.

Inserting WordArt

The WordArt gallery, opened by clicking the WordArt command button in the Text group of the Insert tab of the Ribbon, makes it a snap to add really artsy text to the worksheet. The only thing to keep in mind when adding WordArt is that, just as its name implies, this text is really a graphic (art) object that behaves just like any other Excel graphic object although it contains only text!

You can easily add this type of "graphic" text to your worksheet by following these steps:

1. **Click the WordArt command button on the Insert tab of the Ribbon or press Alt+NW.**

   Excel displays the WordArt drop-down gallery dialog box, as shown in Figure 2-8.

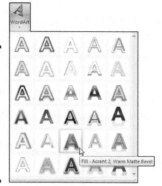

Figure 2-8: Selecting the text style for the new WordArt text from its drop-down gallery.

2. **Click the A thumbnail in the WordArt style you want to use in the WordArt drop-down gallery.**

   Excel inserts a selected text box containing `Your Text Here` in the center of the worksheet with this text in the WordArt style you selected in the gallery.

3. **Type the text you want to display in the worksheet in the Text text box.**

   As soon as you start typing, Excel replaces the `Your Text Here` text in the selected text box with the characters you enter.

4. **(Optional) To format the background of the text box, use Live Preview in the Shape Styles drop-down gallery on the Format tab to find the style to use and then set it by clicking its thumbnail.**

   The Format tab on the Drawing Tools contextual tab is automatically added and activated whenever WordArt text is selected in the worksheet.

5. **After making any final adjustments to the size, shape, or orientation of the WordArt text with the selection and rotation handles, click a cell somewhere outside of the text to deselect the graphic.**

Note that Excel automatically compresses the text to fill the shape and size of its text box. To put more space between the words and the characters in each word, make the text box wider by dragging the sizing handle on either side of the text box.

When you click outside of the WordArt text, Excel deselects the graphic, and the Drawing Tools contextual tab disappears from the Ribbon. (If you ever want this tab to reappear, all you have to do is click somewhere on the WordArt text to select the graphic.)

Figure 2-9 shows the name of my company, Mind over Media, Inc., after creating the text in the WordArt style called Fill – Accent 2, Warm Matte Bevel, selected on the WordArt gallery, and then formatting the text box with the style called Subtle Effect – Accent 1, selected in the Shape Styles gallery on the Format tab.

Figure 2-9:
The Mind over Media company name entered into a worksheet as a WordArt graphic.

Inserting SmartArt graphics

SmartArt represents a completely new breed of graphic object in Excel that gives the ability to quickly and easily construct fancy graphical lists and diagrams in your worksheet. SmartArt lists and diagrams come in a wide array of configurations that include a variety of organizational charts and flow diagrams which enable you to add your own text to predefined graphic shapes.

To insert a SmartArt list or diagram into the worksheet, click the SmartArt button on the Insert tab or press Alt+NM. Excel then opens the Choose a SmartArt Graphic dialog box (shown in Figure 2-10) and then click a category in the navigation pane on the left followed by the list's or diagram's thumbnail in the center section before you click OK.

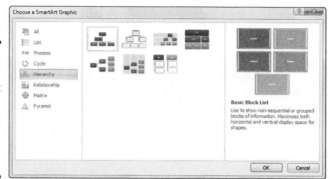

Figure 2-10: Select the SmartArt list or diagram to insert in the worksheet in this dialog box.

Excel then inserts the basic structure of the list or diagram into your worksheet along with a text pane (with "Type Your Text Here" on its title bar) containing a text outline to its immediate left. Here's where you enter the text for the various parts of the list or diagram (as shown in Figure 2-11). At the same time, the Design tab of the SmartArt Tools contextual tab appears on the Ribbon with Layouts and SmartArt Styles galleries for the particular type of SmartArt list or diagram you originally selected.

Filling in the text for a new SmartArt graphic

To fill in the text for the first section of the new list or diagram in the outline in the text pane that already contains the insertion point, simply type in the text. Then, press the ↓ key or click the next list or diagram section to set the insertion point there.

Don't press the Tab key or the Enter key to complete a text entry in the list or diagram as you naturally do in the regular worksheet — in a SmartArt list or diagram, pressing the Enter key inserts a new section of the list or diagram (at the same level in hierarchical diagrams such as an org chart) and Tab either indents the level of the current section on the outline (in hierarchical diagrams) or it does nothing except beep at you.

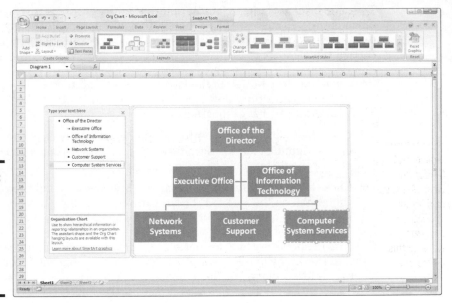

Figure 2-11:
Adding text
for a new
organiza-
tional chart
in the
SmartArt
text pane.

When you finish entering the text for your new diagram, click the close
button (with an X) in the upper right-hand corner of the text pane (you can
always re-open the text pane if you need to edit any of the diagram's text by
clicking the button that appears in the middle of the left side of the selected
list or diagram after you close the text pane).

If the style of the SmartArt list or diagram you select comes with more sections than you need, you can delete the unused graphics by clicking them to
select them (indicated by the selection and rotation handles around it) and
then pressing the Delete key.

Formatting a SmartArt graphic

After you close the text pane attached to your SmartArt list or diagram, you
can still format its text and graphics. To format the text, select all the
graphic objects in the SmartArt list or diagram that need the same type of
text formatting — remember you can select several objects in the list or
diagram by holding down Ctrl as you click them — and then clicking the
appropriate command buttons in the Font group on the Home tab of the
Ribbon.

To refine or change the default formatting of the graphics in a SmartArt list or diagram, you can use the Layouts, Change Colors, and SmartArt Styles drop-down galleries available on the Design tab of the SmartArt Tools contextual tab:

✦ Click the More button in the Layouts group and then click a thumbnail on the Layouts drop-down gallery to select an entirely new layout for your SmartArt list or diagram.

✦ Click the Change Colors button in the SmartArt Styles group and then click a thumbnail in the drop-down Change Colors gallery to change the color scheme for the current layout.

✦ Click the More button in the SmartArt Styles group and then click a thumbnail on the SmartArt Styles drop-down gallery to select a new style for the current layout, using the selected color scheme.

Figure 2-12 shows my fully formatted organizational chart after selecting Labeled Hierarchy in the Layouts gallery, Colorful – Accent Colors in the Change Colors gallery, and finally Inset in the SmartArt Styles gallery.

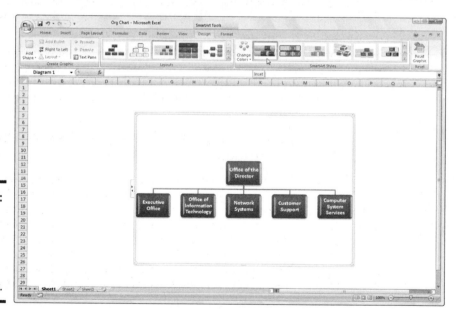

Figure 2-12: Worksheet with completed and formatted organizational chart.

Using Themes

With themes, Excel 2007 introduces a whole new way to uniformly format all the graphics that you add to a worksheet. You can select a new theme for the active worksheet simply by clicking the thumbnail of the theme you want to use in the Themes drop-down gallery opened by clicking the Themes command button on the Ribbon's Page Layout tab (or by pressing Alt+PTH).

Use Live Preview to see how the graphics you've added to your worksheet appear in the new theme before you click its thumbnail.

Excel Themes combine three default elements: the color scheme applied to the graphics, the font (body and heading) used in the graphics, and the graphic effects applied. If you prefer, you can change any or all of these three elements in the worksheet by clicking their individual command buttons in the Themes group at the start of the Page Layout tab:

✦ **Colors** to select a new color scheme by clicking its thumbnail on the drop-down palette — click Create New Theme Colors at the bottom of this palette to open the Create New Theme Colors dialog box where you can customize each element of the color scheme and save it with a new descriptive name.

✦ **Fonts** to select a new font by clicking its thumbnail on the drop-down list — click Create New Theme Fonts at the bottom of this list to open the Create New Theme Fonts dialog box where you can customize the body and heading fonts for both Latin and East Asian text and save it with a new descriptive name.

✦ **Effects** to select a new set of graphics effects by clicking its thumbnail in the drop-down gallery.

To save your newly selected color scheme, font, and graphic effects as a custom theme that you can reuse in other workbooks, click the Themes command button and then click Save Current Theme at the bottom of the gallery to open the Save Current Theme dialog box. Edit the generic Theme1 filename in the File Name text box (without deleting the .thmx filename extension) and then click the Save button. Excel then adds the custom theme to a Custom Themes section in the Themes drop-down gallery that you can apply to any active worksheet simply by clicking its thumbnail.

Book VI
Data Management

The 5th Wave   By Rich Tennant

"Unless there's a corrupt cell in our spreadsheet analysis concerning the importance of trunk space, this should be a big seller next year."

Contents at a Glance

Chapter 1: Building and Maintaining Data Lists

In This Chapter

✓ Understanding what goes into making a data list

✓ Adding data to a data list

✓ Editing records in a data list

✓ Finding records in a data list

✓ Sorting records on values in a data list

✓ Sorting a list on font color, cell color, or cell icons

✓ Subtotaling data in a data list

*I*n addition to its considerable computational abilities, Excel is also very accomplished at maintaining vast collections of related data in what are referred to as *database tables* or *data lists* (which is a little more accurate). This chapter covers all the basic procedures for creating and then maintaining different types of data lists in the Excel worksheet.

This basic information includes how to design the basic data list and then format it as a table so that you can add new data to the list without having to redefine it and can sort its data so that it's arranged the way you like to see the information. For data lists that contain numerical data, you also find out how to subtotal and total the data. For information on how to find data in the data list and produce subsets of the list with just the data you need, refer to Book VI, Chapter 2.

Data List Basics

In Excel, a data list or database is a table of worksheet data that utilizes a special structure. Unlike the other types of data tables that you might create in an Excel spreadsheet, a data list uses *only* column headings (technically known as *field names*) to identify the different kinds of items that the data list tracks. Each column in the data list contains information for each item you track in the database, such as the client's company name or telephone number (technically known as a *field* of the data list). Each row in the data list contains complete information about each entity that you track in the data list, such as ABC Corporation or National Industries (technically known as a *record* of the data list).

After you've organized your data into a data list that follows this structure, you can then use a variety of commands on the Ribbon's Data tab to maintain the data, as well as to reorder the information it contains. In data lists with numerical fields, you can also use the Subtotal command button to calculate subtotals and totals in the list when a certain field changes.

Designing the basic data list

All you have to do to start a new data list in a worksheet is to enter the names of the fields that you want to track in the top row of the worksheet, enter the first record of data beneath, and then format the two rows of data as a table (see Book II, Chapter 1 for details). When entering the field names (as column headings), be sure each field name in the data list is unique and, whenever possible, keep the field name short. When naming fields, you can align the field name in the cell so that its text wraps to a new line by clicking the Wrap Text command button on the Ribbon's Home tab after entering the name in its cell (Alt+HW). Also, you should not use numbers or formulas that return values as field names. (You can, however use formulas that return text, such as a formula that concatenates labels entered in different cells.)

When deciding on what fields you need to create, you need to think of how you'll be using the data that you store in your data list. For example, in a client data list, you split the client's name into separate title, first name, and last name fields if you intend to use this information in generating form letters and mailing labels with your word processor. That way, you are able to address the person by his or her first name (as in *Dear Jane*) in the opening of the form letter you create, as well as by his or her full name and title (as in *Dr. Jane Jackson*) in the mailing label you generate.

Likewise, you split up the client's address into separate street address, city, state, and ZIP code fields when you intend to use the client data list in generating form letters, and you also want to be able to sort the records in descending order by ZIP code and/or send letters only to clients located in the states of New York, New Jersey, or Connecticut. By keeping discrete pieces of information in separate fields, you are assured that you will be able to use that field in finding particular records and retrieving information from the data list, such as finding all the records where the state is California or the ZIP code is between 94105 and 95101.

To set up a new data list in a worksheet, you follow these steps:

1. **Click the blank cell where you want to start the new data list and then enter the column headings (field names) that identify the different kinds of items you need to keep track of.**

   After creating the fields of the data list by entering their headings, you're ready to enter the first row of data.

2. **Make the first entries in the appropriate columns of the row immediately below the one containing the field names.**

   These entries in the first row beneath the one with the field names constitute the first *record* of the data list.

3. **Click the Format as Table button on the Ribbon's Home tab and then click a thumbnail of one of the table styles in the drop-down gallery.**

   As soon as you click a table style in the drop-down gallery, the Format As Table dialog box appears listing the address of the cell range enclosed in the marquee in the Where Is the Data for Your Table text box, and the My Table Has Headers check box is selected.

4. **Click the OK button to close the Format As Table dialog box.**

Excel formats your new data list in the selected table format and adds AutoFilter (drop-down buttons) to each of the field names in the top row.

Figure 1-1 shows you a sample employee data list after formatting it as a table using Table Style Light 1. This data list begins in row 1 of this worksheet, which contains the names for the ten fields in this data list (ID No through Profit Sharing) all with AutoFilter buttons (thanks to the formatting as a table). Note that employees' names are divided into separate First Name and Last Name fields in this list (columns B and C, respectively). Note too, that the first actual record of the data list is entered in row 2 of the worksheet, directly under the row with the field names. When entering your records for a new data list, you don't skip rows but keep entering each record one above the other going down successive rows of the worksheet.

When you're entering the row with the first data record, be sure to format all the cells the way you want the entries in that field to appear in all the subsequent data records in the data list. For example, if you have a Salary field in the data list, and you want the salaries formatted with the Currency style number format without any decimal places, be sure to format the salary entry in the first record in this manner. If you have a ZIP Code field, format it with the Special Zip Code format or as Text so that Excel doesn't drop the initial zeros from codes that begin with them such as 00234. That way all subsequent records will pick up that same formatting for the salary field when you enter them with Excel's data form.

Creating calculated fields

When creating a new data list, you can make full use of Excel's calculating capabilities by defining fields whose entries are returned by formula rather than entered manually. The sample employee list introduced in Figure 1-1 contains just such a calculated field (shown on the Formula bar) in cell I2 that contains the first entry in the Years of Service field.

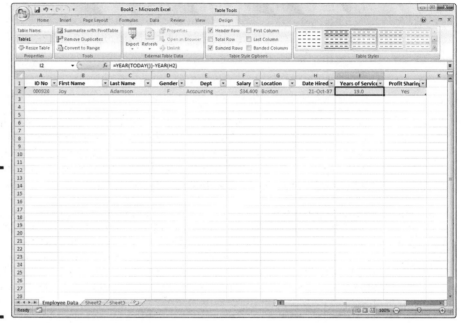

Figure 1-1: Creating an employee data list with the row of field names and first data record.

The original formula for calculating years of service in cell I2 is as follows:

```
=YEAR(TODAY())-YEAR(H2)
```

This formula uses the YEAR date function to subtract the serial number of the year in which the employee was hired (entered into the Date Hired field) in cell H2 from the serial number of the current year (returned by the TODAY function). After entering and formatting this original formula in cell H2, the data form picks up this formula and automatically copies it and applies it to any new record you add to the data list.

Modifying the structure of the data list

You may find after creating your data list that you need to modify its structure by adding or deleting some fields. To add a new field, you select the column (by clicking the column letter) where you want the field inserted, and then click the Insert command button on the Ribbon's Home tab to insert a new column. Replace the generic Column1 field name given to the new field in the top row with a descriptive name and then enter the entries for that field for each record in the data list. To delete an entire field from the data list (field name and entries), select its column, and then click the Delete command button on the Home tab.

To avoid losing data or disturbing the layout of data located outside of the data list caused by adding or deleting its fields, don't place any data tables or other entries in rows beneath the last row of the data list. In other words, always keep the rows used by the columns of the data list free for new records by locating all related data in columns to the right of the last field.

Add new records to a data list

After creating the field names and one record of the data list and formatting them as a table, you're ready to start entering the rest of the records in subsequent rows of the list. The most direct way to do this is to press the Tab key when the cell cursor is in the last cell of the first record. Doing this causes Excel to add an extra row to the data list where you can enter the appropriate information for the next record.

When doing data entry directly in a data list table, press the Tab key to proceed to the next field in the new record rather than the → key. That way, when you complete the entry in the last field of the record, you automatically extend the data list and add a new record and position the cell cursor in the first field of that record — if you press → to complete the entry, Excel simply moves the cell cursor to the next cell outside of the data list table.

Adding the Form button to the Quick Access toolbar

Instead of entering the records of a data list directly in the table, you can use Excel's data form to make the entries. The only problem with using the data form is that its command button is not found on the Ribbon: The only way to access the data form is by adding its command button as a custom button on the Quick Access toolbar. To do this, you must follow these steps:

1. **Click Office Button | Excel Options | Customize or press Alt+FIC.**

The Form command button you want to add is only available when you choose Commands Not in the Ribbon on All Commands in the Choose Commands From drop-down list.

2. **Click Commands Not in the Ribbon on the Choose Commands From drop-down list.**

3. **Click Form in the Choose Commands From list box and then click the Add button.**

   Excel adds the Form button to the very end of the Quick Access toolbar. If you wish, you can use the Move Up and Move Down buttons to reposition the Form button on this toolbar.

4. **Click OK to close the Excel Options dialog box and return to the worksheet with the data list.**

Using the data form

The first time you click the custom Form button you've added to the Quick Access toolbar, Excel analyzes the row of field names and entries for the first record and creates a data form that lists the field names down the left side of the form with the entries for the first record in the appropriate text boxes next to them.

Figure 1-2 shows you the data form that Excel creates for the sample Employee data list shown earlier in Figure 1-1. As you can see in this figure, the data form consists of a dialog box (whose title bar contains the name of the current worksheet file) that contains a vertical listing of each field defined for the data list.

When you click the custom Form button on the Quick Access toolbar to display the data form, Excel automatically displays the field entries for the first record entered (which just happens to be the only record in the list at this point). On the right side of the dialog box, the data form indicates the current record number out of the total number of records in the data list (1 of 1 in this case). This part of the form also contains a number of command buttons that enable you to add a new record, find a particular record for editing, or delete a record from the data list.

When the data form is displayed in the active document, you can use the scroll bar to the right of the fields to move through the records in the data list, or you can use various direction keys. Table 1-1 summarizes the use of the scroll bar and these keys. For example, to move to the next record in the data list, you can press the ↓ or Enter key or click the scroll arrow at the bottom of the scroll bar. To move to the previous record in the data list (assuming that there's more than one), you can press the ↑ key or Shift+Enter key or click the scroll arrow at the top of the scroll bar. To select a field in the current record for editing, you can click that field's text box or press the Tab key (next field) or press Shift+Tab (previous field) until you select the field (and its current entry).

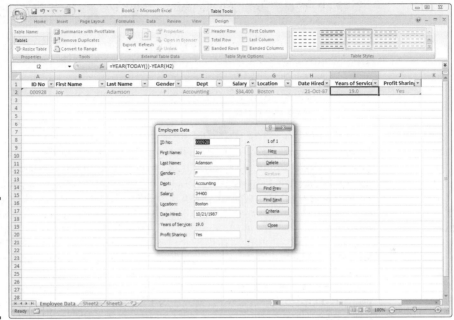

Figure 1-2:
Opening the data form in the new data list to add a new record.

Table 1-1	Techniques for Navigating the Data Form
Movement	*Keystrokes or Scroll Bar Technique*
Next record, same field in the data list	Press the ↓ or Enter key, click the downward-pointing scroll arrow, or click the Find Next command button.
Previous record, same field in the data list	Press ↑ or Shift+Enter, click the upward-pointing scroll arrow, or click the Find Prev command button.
Next field in the data form	Press Tab.
Previous field in the data form	Press Shift+Tab.
Move 10 records forward in the data list	Press PgDn.
Move 10 records backward in the data list	Press PgUp.
Move to the first record in the data list	Press Ctrl+↑ or Ctrl+PgUp, or drag the scroll box to the top of the scroll bar.
Move to the last record in the data list	Press Ctrl+↓ or Ctrl+PgDn, or drag the scroll box to the bottom of the scroll bar.
Move within a field	Press ← or → to move one character at a time, press Home to move to the first character and End to move to the last character.

Note that the data form does not allow you to select and edit calculated fields (such as the Years of Service field shown in Figure 1-2). Although calculated fields and their current entries are listed in the data form, the form doesn't bother to provide a text box for the fields for making editing changes. To modify the contents of a calculated field, you would need to modify the original formula in the appropriate field in the first record and recopy the edited formula down to the other existing records in the list.

Adding new records with the data form

To add a new record to the data list, you can either move to the end of the data list (by dragging the scroll box to the very bottom of the scroll bar or by pressing Ctrl+↓ or Ctrl+PgDn) or simply click the New command button. Any way you do it, Excel displays a blank data form (marked New Record at the right side the dialog box), which you can then fill out. After entering the information for a field, press the Tab key to advance to the next field in the record (be careful not to press the Enter key because this inserts the new record into the data list).

When you're making an entry in a new field, you can copy the entry from the same field in the previous record into the current field by pressing Ctrl+" (double quotation mark). You can use this keystroke shortcut, for example, to carry forward entries in the text box for the State field when you are entering a series of records that all use the same state.

When you've entered all the information you have for the new record, press the ↓ or Enter key or click the New button again. Excel then inserts the new record as the last record in the data list and displays a blank data form where you can enter the next record. When you finish adding records to the data list, press the Esc key or click the Close button to close the data form dialog box.

Editing records in the data form

The data form makes it easy to edit records in your data list. In a smaller data list, you can use the navigation keys or the scroll bar in the data form to locate the record that requires editing. In a larger data list, you can use the Criteria command button to quickly locate the record you need to change, as described in the next section.

When you've displayed the data form for the record that needs editing, you can then perform your editing changes by selecting the text boxes of the necessary fields and making your changes, just as you would edit the entry in its cell in the worksheet.

Finding records with the data form

You can use the Criteria button in the data form to find the records in your data list that you need to edit (or delete as described in the next section). When you click the Criteria button in the data form, Excel clears all the field text boxes so that you can enter the criteria to search for. For example, assume that you need to edit Sherry Caulfield's profit sharing status. You don't have her paperwork in front of you, so you can't look up her employee number. You do know, however, that she works in the Boston office and, although you don't remember exactly how she spells her last name, you do know that it begins with a C instead of a K.

To locate her record, you can at least narrow the search down to all the records where the Location field contains Boston and the employee's Last Name begins with the letter *C* (see Figure 1-3). To do this, you open the data form for the Employee data list, click the Criteria command button, and then enter the following in the Last Name field:

```
C*
```

Then, in the Location field you enter

```
Boston
```

When entering the criteria for locating matching records in the data form, you can use the question mark (?) and the asterisk (*) wildcard characters, just as you do when using the Excel Find feature to locate cells with particular entries. (See Book II, Chapter 3, for a review of using these wildcard characters.)

Figure 1-3: Entering the criteria to find records where Last Name starts with C and Location is Boston.

When you click the Find Next button or press the Enter key, Excel locates the first record in the data list where the last name begins with the letter *C* and the location is Boston. This is William Cobb's record, as shown in Figure 1-4. Then, to locate the next record that matches your criteria, you click the Find Next button or press Enter, which brings you to Sherry Caulfield's record, as shown in Figure 1-5. Having located Sherry's record, you can then change her profit sharing status by selecting the Profit Sharing text box and replacing No with Yes. Excel inserts the editing change that you make in the record's data form into the data list itself as soon as you close the Data Form dialog box by clicking the Close button.

Figure 1-4:
Locating
the first
matching
record for
William
Cobb.

Figure 1-5:
Locating
the next
matching
record for
Sherry
Caulfield.

When using the Criteria button in the data form to find records, you can use the following logical operators when entering search criteria in fields that use numbers or dates:

✦ **Equal to (=):** Finds records with the same text, value, or date you enter.

✦ **Greater than (>):** Finds records after the text characters (in the alphabet) or the date, or larger than the value you enter.

✦ **Greater than or equal to (>=):** Finds records the same as the text characters, date, or value you enter or after the characters (in the alphabet), after the date, or larger than the value.

✦ **Less than (<):** Finds records before the text characters (in the alphabet) or date or smaller than the value you enter.

✦ **Less than or equal to (<=):** Finds records the same as the text characters, date, or value you enter or before the characters (in the alphabet) or the date, or larger than the value.

✦ **Not equal to (<>):** Finds records not the same as the text, value, or date you enter.

For example, to find all the records where the employee's annual salary is $50,000, you can enter **=50000** or simply **50000** in the Salary field text box. However, to find all the records for employees whose annual salaries are less than or equal to $35,000, you enter <=35000 in the Salary field text box. To find all the records for employees with salaries greater than $45,000, you would enter **>45000** in the Salary field text box instead. If you wanted to find all of the records where the employees are female *and* make more than $35,000, you would enter **F** in the Sex field text box and >35000 in the Salary field text box in the same Criteria data form.

When specifying search criteria that fit a number of records, you may have to click the Find Next or Find Prev button several times to locate the record you want to work with. If no record fits the search criteria you enter in the Criteria data form, your computer will beep at you when you click the Find Next or Find Prev button.

To change your search criteria, select the appropriate text box(es) and delete the old criteria and then enter the new criteria. To switch back to the current record without using the search criteria you enter, click the Form button (this button replaces the Criteria button as soon you click the Criteria button).

Deleting records with the data form

In addition to adding and editing records with the data form, you can also delete them. To delete a record, you simply display its data form and then click the Delete button. Be very careful when deleting records, however, because you cannot restore the records you delete with Excel's Undo feature. For this reason, Excel displays an alert dialog box whenever you choose the Delete button, indicating that the record displayed in the data form is about to be permanently deleted. To continue and remove the record, you need to choose OK or press Enter. To save the current record, press the Esc key or click the Cancel button instead.

Keep in mind that although you can use the Criteria data form to locate a group of records that you want to delete, you can remove only one record at a time with the Delete button.

Eliminating records with duplicates fields

For the first time in Excel history, the program offers the Eliminate Duplicates feature that enables you to remove records from a list (or rows from a table) that contains duplicate records. This is a great feature especially when you're dealing with a really large data list in which several different people do the data entry and which should not have any duplicate records (such as client lists, personnel files, and the like).

To have Excel remove all duplicate records from a data list or table, you follow these simple steps:

1. **Position the cell cursor in one of the cells of the data list or table.**

2. **Click the Remove Duplicates command button on the Ribbon's Data tab or press Alt+AM.**

Excel selects all the cells in the data list while at the same time displaying the Remove Duplicates dialog box similar to the one shown in Figure 1-6.

Figure 1-6:
Using the
Remove
Duplicates
dialog box
to remove
duplicate
records
from a
data list.

When this dialog box first opens, Excel automatically selects all the fields in the list (by placing check marks in the check boxes in front of their names in the Columns list box). When all the fields are selected and you click OK in this dialog box, Excel deletes only complete duplicates (in other words, copies) of the records in the list.

If you want the program to remove records where there's any duplication of entries in particular fields (such as the SSN field or Record Number), you remove the check marks from all the columns except for whose duplication are sufficient reason for deleting the entire record (as described in Step 3). Otherwise, you proceed directly to Step 4.

3. **(Optional) Remove the check marks from all fields in the Columns list box except for those whose duplicates are reason for deleting the record.**

More about ascending and descending sort orders

When you use the ascending sort order on a field in a data list that contains many different kinds of entries, Excel places numbers (from smallest to largest) before text entries (in alphabetical order), followed by any logical values (FALSE and TRUE), error values, and finally, blank cells. When you use the descending sort order, Excel arranges the different entries in reverse: numbers are still first, arranged from largest to smallest; text entries go from Z to A; and the TRUE logical value precedes the FALSE logical value.

If only one or two fields out of many need to be selected in the Columns list box, click the Unselect All button to remove the check marks from all field check boxes and then individually click the fields that can't have duplicate entries.

4. **Click OK to have Excel close the Remove Duplicates dialog box and remove the duplicates records (rows) from the selected data list.**

Sorting Data

You can use the Sort & Filter command button on the Ribbon's Home tab and the AutoFilter buttons on the field names to quickly sort data. You can sort the records in your data list by sorting its rows, and sort the fields in the data list by sorting its columns.

In sorting, you can specify either ascending or descending sort order for your data. When you specify ascending order (which is the default), Excel arranges text in A-to-Z order and values from smallest to largest. When you specify descending order, Excel reverses this order and arranges text in Z-to-A order and values range from largest to smallest. When sorting on a date field, keep in mind that ascending order puts the records in oldest to newest order, while descending order gives you the records in newest to oldest date order.

Keep in mind that, although sorting is most often applied to rearranging and maintaining data list records and fields, you can use the Sort & Filter command button to reorder data in any worksheet table, whether or not the table follows the strict data list structure.

Sorting records on a single field

When you only need to sort the data list on one particular field (such as the Record Number, Last Name, or Company field), you simply click that field's

AutoFilter button and then click the appropriate sort option on its drop-down list:

✦ **Sort A to Z** or **Sort Z to A** in a text field

✦ **Sort Smallest to Largest** or **Sort Largest to Smallest** in a number field

✦ **Sort Oldest to Newest** or **Sort Newest to Oldest** in a date field

Excel then reorders all the records in the data list in accordance with the new ascending or descending order in the selected field. If you find that you've sorted the list in error, simply click the Undo button on the Quick Access toolbar or press Ctrl+Z right away to return the list to its previous order.

Excel 2007 shows when a field's been used in sorting the data list by adding an up or down arrow to its filter button. An arrow pointing up indicates that the ascending sort order was used and one pointing down indicates that the descending sort order was used.

Sorting records on multiple fields

When you need to sort a data list on more than one field, you use the Sort dialog box (shown in Figure 1-7). And you need to sort on more than one field when the first field contains duplicate values and you want to determine how the records with duplicates are arranged. (If you don't specify another field to sort on, Excel just puts the records in the order in which you entered them.)

The best and most common example of when you need more than one field is when sorting a large database alphabetically in last-name order. Say that you have a database that contains several people with the last name Smith, Jones, or Zastrow (as is the case when you work at Zastrow and Sons). If you specify the Last Name field as the only field to sort on (using the default ascending order), all the duplicate Smiths, Joneses, and Zastrows are placed in the order in which their records were originally entered. To better sort these duplicates, you can specify the First Name field as the second field to sort on (again using the default ascending order), making the second field the tie-breaker, so that Ian Smith's record precedes that of Sandra Smith, and Vladimir Zastrow's record comes after that of Mikhail Zastrow.

To sort records in a data list using the Sort dialog box, follow these steps:

1. **Position the cell cursor in one of the cells in the data list table.**

2. **Click Custom Sort on the Sort & Filter button's drop-down list on the Home tab or press Alt+HSU.**

   Excel selects all the records of the database (without including the first row of field names) and opens the Sort dialog box, as shown in Figure 1-7.

Figure 1-7:
Set up to
sort records
alphabet-
ically by
surname or
first name.

Note that you can also open the Sort dialog box by clicking the Sort command button on the Data tab or pressing Alt+AS.

3. **Click the name of the field you first want the records sorted by in the Sort By drop-down list.**

   If you want the records arranged in descending order, remember also to click the descending sort option (Z to A, Smallest to Largest, or Oldest to Newest) in the Order drop-down list to the right.

4. **(Optional) If the first field contains duplicates and you want to specify how the records in this field are sorted, click the Add Level button to insert another sort level and select a second field to sort on in the Then By drop-down list and select either the ascending or descending option in its Order drop-down list to its right.**

5. **(Optional) If necessary, repeat Step 4, adding as many additional sort levels as required.**

6. **Click OK or press Enter.**

   Excel closes the Sort dialog box and sorts the records in the data list using the sorting fields in the order of their levels in this dialog box. If you see that you sorted the database on the wrong fields or in the wrong order, click the Undo button on the Quick Access toolbar or press Ctrl+Z to immediately restore the data list records to their previous order.

By default, when you perform a sort operation, Excel assumes that you're sorting a data list that has a header row (with the field names) that is not to be reordered with the rest of the records in doing the sort. You can, however, use the Sort feature to sort a cell selection that doesn't have such a header row. In that case, you need to specify the sorting keys by column letter, and you need to be sure to click the My Data Has Headers check box to remove its check mark in the Sort dialog box.

Also, the Sort dialog box contains an Options button that, when clicked, opens a Sort Options dialog box, which contains options for doing a case-sensitive sort on fields that contain text. This dialog box also contains options for changing the orientation of the sort from the normal top-to-bottom order to left-to-right order when you want to sort columns in a list.

Figure 1-8 illustrates sorting the employee data list first in ascending order by location and then in descending order by salary. For this sort, the Location field is designated as the field (column) to sort on in the first level and the Salary field as the other field (column) as the second level. Also, to have the records within each location sorted from highest to lowest salary, I chose Largest to Smallest in the Order drop-down list to the right of the first Then By combo box.

After clicking OK in the Sort dialog box, you will note in Figure 1-8 how the records are now organized first in ascending order by the city listed in the Location field (Atlanta, Boston, Chicago, and so on) and within each city in descending order by Salary (38,900, 32,200, 29,200, and so on).

Sometimes, you may need to sort on a whole bunch of fields to get the desired order. For example, suppose that you are working with a personnel data list, and you want to organize the records in alphabetical order, first by department, then by supervisor, and finally by last name, first name, and middle name. To sort the records in this data list on these five fields, you have to define each of the columns as a separate level in the Sort dialog box as follows:

✦ First by Department field in A to Z order

✦ Then by Supervisor field in A to Z order

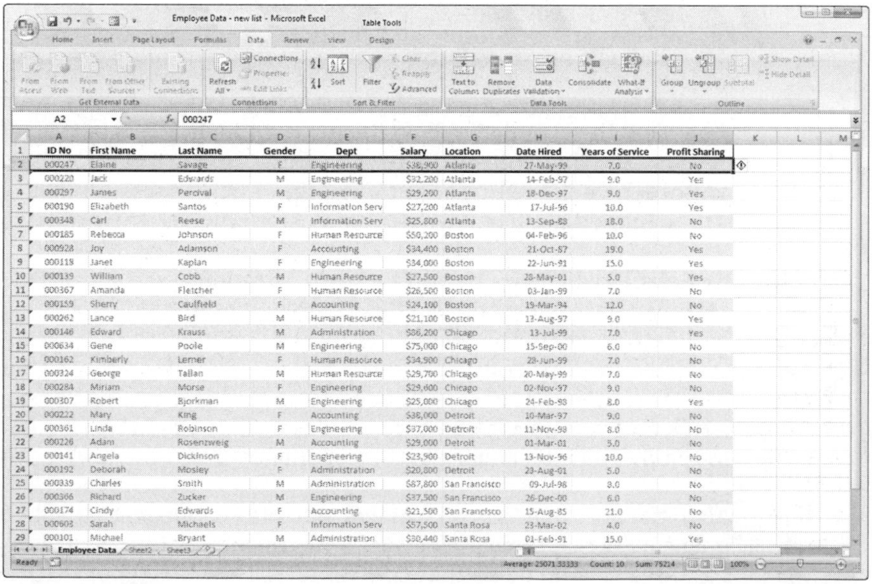

Figure 1-8:
Employee data list sorted by location and salary.

✦ Then by Last Name field in A to Z order

✦ Then by First Name field in A to Z order

✦ Then by Middle Name field in A to Z order

Figure 1-9 shows you the Sort dialog box after defining these as the columns on five separate levels on which to sort the personnel data list. Figure 1-10 shows you the result. As you can see after performing this sort operation, the records are now arranged in ascending order by department, then by supervisor within department, and finally by the last name, first name, and middle name under each supervisor.

Figure 1-9:
Sort dialog box with five levels of sorting keys for sorting the personnel data list.

Figure 1-10:
Personnel data list after sorting by department, supervisor, last, first, and middle names.

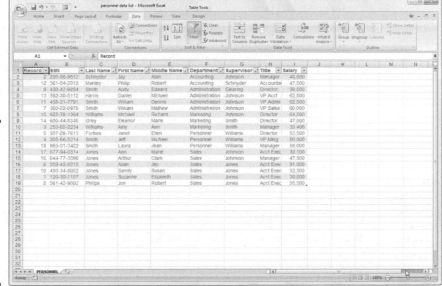

Sorting the columns of a data list

You can use Excel's column sorting capability to change the order of the fields in a data list without having to resort to cutting and pasting various columns. When you sort the fields in a data list, you add a row at the top of the list that you define as the primary sorting level. The cells in this row contain numbers (from 1 to the number of the last field in the data list) that indicate the new order of the fields.

Figures 1-11 and 1-12 illustrate how you can use column sorting to modify the field order of a data list in the sample Personnel data list. In Figure 1-10, I inserted a new row (row 1) above the row with the field names for this data list. As you can see, the cells in this row contain numbers that indicate the new field order. After the fields are sorted using the values in this row, the ID No field remains first (indicated by 1), the First Department field becomes second (2), Supervisor field third (3), followed by First Name (4), Middle Name (5), Last Name (6), Title (7), and Salary (8).

You can't sort data you've formally formatted as a data table in this manner until you convert the table back into a normal cell range, because the program won't recognize the row containing the column's new order numbers as part of the table on which you can perform a sort. In this example, to get around the problem, you take the following steps:

1. **Click a cell in the data table and then click the Convert to Range command button on the Design tab of the Table Tools contextual tab or press Alt+CTG.**

   Excel displays an alert dialog box asking you if you want to convert the table to a range.

2. **Click the Yes button in the alert dialog box to do the conversion.**

3. **Select all the records in the Personnel data list along with the top row containing the numbers on which to sort the columns of the list as the cell selection.**

   In this case, you select the cell range A1:H20 as the cell selection.

4. **Click the Sort command button on the Data tab (or press Alt+AS).**

   Excel opens the Sort dialog box. You can also open the Sort dialog box by clicking Custom Sort on the Sort & Filter button's drop-down list or by pressing Alt+HSU.

5. **Click the Options button in the Sort dialog box.**

   Excel opens the Sort Options dialog box.

6. Click the Sort Left to Right option button and then click OK.

7. Click Row 1 in the Row drop-down list in the Sort dialog box.

The Sort On drop-down list box should read Values and the Order drop-down list box Smallest to Largest.

8. Click OK to sort the data list using the values in the top row of the current cell selection.

Excel sorts the columns of the Personnel data list according to the numerical order of the entries in the top row (which are now in a 1 to 8 order). Now, you can get rid of the top row with these numbers.

9. Select the cell range A1:H1 and then click the Delete button on the Home tab.

Excel deletes the row of numbers and pulls up the Personnel data list so that its row of field names is now in row 1 of the worksheet. Now, all that's left to do is to reformat the Personnel data list as a table again so that Excel adds AutoFilter buttons to its field names and the program dynamically keeps track of the data list's cell range as it expands and contracts.

10. Click the Format as Table command button on the Home tab (or press Alt+HT) and then click a table style from the Light, Medium, or Dark section of its gallery.

Excel opens the Format As Table dialog box and places a marquee around all the cells in the data list.

11. Make sure that the My Table Has Headers check box has a check mark in it and that all the cells in the data list are included in the cell range displayed in the Where Is the Data for Your Table text box before you click OK.

Figure 1-12 shows the personnel data list after sorting its fields according to the values in the first row. After sorting the data list, you then delete this row and modify the widths of the columns to suit the new arrangement and reformat the list as a table before you save the worksheet.

When sorting the columns in a data list, you must remember to click the Options button and click the Sort Left to Right option button in the Orientation section of the Sort Options dialog box. Otherwise, Excel sorts your records instead of your columns, and in the process, the row of field names becomes sorted in with the other data records in your list!

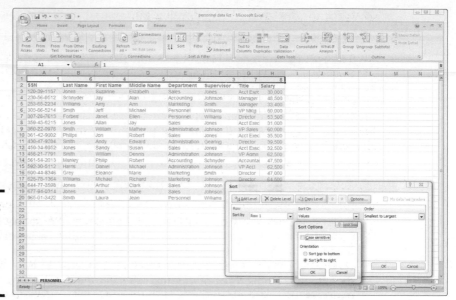

Figure 1-11:
Personnel
data list
before
sorting the
columns.

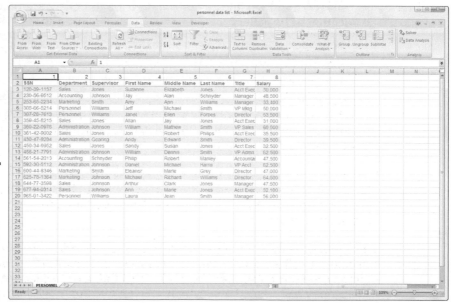

Figure 1-12:
Personnel
data list
after sorting
the columns
using the
values
entered in
the first row.

Sorting a data list on font and cell colors and cell icons

Although you normally sort the records of a data list or rows of a table on the values (entries) contained in one or more columns of the list or table, Excel 2007 also enables you to sort on the font or cell color or cell icons that you assign to them as well. These colors and icons are assigned by using Conditional Formatting to mark those values in the columns of a data list or table that are within or outside certain parameters with a distinctive font or cell colors or cell icon (see "Conditional Formatting" in Book II, Chapter 2 for details).

To sort a data list on a font color, cell color, or cell icon in a single field of the table, you click its AutoFilter button and then highlight the Sort by Color option on the drop-down menu. Excel then displays a continuation menu on which you click the font color, fill color, or cell icon to use in the sort:

✦ To sort the records so that those with a particular font color in the selected column — assigned with the Conditional Formatting Highlight Cell Rules or Top/Bottom Rules options — appear at the top of the data list, click its color swatch in the Sort by Font Color section on the continuation menu.

✦ To sort the records so that those with a particular cell color in the selected column — assigned with the Conditional Formatting Highlight Cell Rules, Top/Bottom Rules, Data Bars, or Color Scales options — appear at the top of the data list, click its color swatch in the Sort by Cell Color section on the continuation menu.

✦ To sort the records so that those with a particular cell icon in the selected column — assigned with the Conditional Formatting Icon Sets options — appear at the top of the data list, click the icon in the Sort by Cell Icon section of the continuation menu.

You can also sort the data list on more than one color or cell icon in the Sort dialog box opened by clicking the Custom Sort option on the Sort & Filter button's drop-down list on the Ribbon's Home tab or on the Sort by Color continuation menu.

When you want to sort the records in a data list on more than one font or cell color or cell icon, you select the field with the color or icon in the Column drop-down list, click Font Color, Cell Color, or Cell Icon in the Sort On drop-down list, and then click the color swatch or icon to use in the first level of the sort in the Order drop-down list.

Book VI Chapter 1

Building and Maintaining Data Lists

If you need to add another sort level, you click the Add Level button and then repeat this procedure of selecting the field in the Column drop-down list, selecting the Font Color, Cell Color, or Cell Icon in the Sort On drop-down list, and selecting the specific color or icon in the Order drop-down list. When you finish defining all the levels for the sort, click OK to have Excel go ahead and sort the list's records.

You can sort the records in the data list order by all the cell colors or cell icons assigned by applying the Conditional Formatting Color Scales and Cell Icons options. For each of three or five sorting levels you define in the Sort dialog box, the name of the field in the Column drop-down list button remains the same in all levels along with the Cell Color or Cell Icon option in the Sort On drop-down list button. Only the actual color or icon selected in the Order drop-down list button changes, reflecting the order in which you want to see the records appear in the sorted data list.

Subtotaling Data

You can use Excel's Subtotals feature to subtotal data in a sorted list. To subtotal a data list, you first sort the list on the field for which you want the subtotals, and then you designate the field that contains the values you want summed — these don't have to be the same fields in the data list.

When you use the Subtotals feature, you aren't restricted to having the values in the designated field added together with the SUM function. You can instead have Excel return the number of entries with the COUNT function, the average of the entries with the AVERAGE function, the highest entry with the MAXIMUM function, the lowest entry with the MINIMUM function, or even the product of the entries with the PRODUCT function.

To subtotal the salaries within each department in my example Employee Data list, first sort the list in A-to-Z order on the Dept column because Excel is to create a new subtotal at each change in the department entries within the list (Accounting, Administration, Engineering, and so on).

Excel does not allow you to subtotal a data list formatted as a table. Before you can use the Subtotal command button, you must first convert your table into a normal range of cells. To do this, click a cell in the table and then click the Design tab on the Table Tools Contextual tab on the Ribbon. Finally, click the Convert to Range command button in the Tools group followed by the Yes button in the alert dialog box asking you to confirm this action. Excel then removes the filter buttons from the columns at the top of the data list while still retaining the original table formatting.

Figures 1-13 and 1-14 illustrate how easy it is to use the Subtotals feature to obtain totals in a data list. In Figure 1-13, I sorted the sample Employee data list first by the Department field in ascending order and then by the Salary field in descending order. I then clicked the Subtotal command button on the Ribbon's Data tab to open the Subtotal dialog box shown in Figure 1-13.

Here, I selected the Dept field as the field for which the subtotals are to be calculated in the At Each Change In drop-down list box, Sum as the function to use in the Use Function drop-down list box, and the Salary check box as the field whose values are to be summed in the Add Subtotal To list box.

Figure 1-13:
Using the Subtotal dialog box to subtotal the salaries for each department.

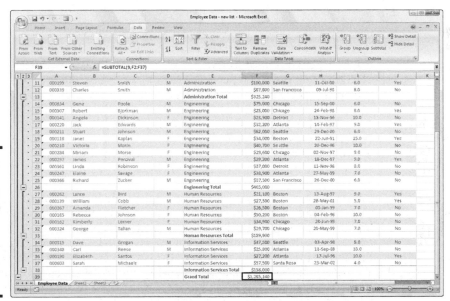

Figure 1-14:
Bottom of the data list showing the subtotals and grand total for department salaries.

Figure 1-14 shows the results I obtained after clicking OK in the Subtotal dialog box. Here, you see the bottom of the data list showing the salary subtotals for the Engineering, Human Resources, and Information Services departments along with the grand total of the salaries for all the departments. The grand total is displayed at the bottom of the data list because I left the Summary below Data check box selected in the Subtotal dialog box — if I hadn't wanted a grand total, I would have removed the check mark from this check box.

As you can see in Figure 1-14, when you use the Subtotal command, Excel outlines the data at the same time that it adds the rows with the departmental salary totals and the grand total. This means that you can collapse the data list down to just its departmental subtotal rows or even just the grand total row simply by collapsing the outline down to the second or first level. (Remember that you can toggle between showing and hiding the outline symbols at the left edge of the data list by pressing Ctrl+8.)

In a large data list, you may want Excel to insert page breaks (often referred to as a *break*) every time data changes in the field on which the list is being subtotaled (that is, the field designated in the At Each Change In drop-down list box). To do this, you simply click the Page Break between Groups check box in the Subtotal dialog box to put a check mark in it before you click OK to subtotal the list.

Chapter 2: Filtering and Querying a Data List

In This Chapter

✔ Understanding how to filter and query a data list

✔ Using AutoFilter to filter out unwanted data

✔ Filtering a list with custom criteria

✔ Filtering a list on font color, cell color, or cell icons

✔ Using Database functions to compute statistics from records that match your filter criteria

✔ Performing external data queries with text files, Web pages, and data files kept in other database sources

*I*t's one thing to set up a data list and load it with tons of data, and it's quite another to get just the information that you need out of the list. How you go about extracting the data that's important to you is the subject of this chapter. The procedure for specifying the data that you want displayed in an Excel data list is called *filtering* the data list or database. The procedure for extracting only the data that you want from the database or data list is called *querying* the database.

In addition to filtering and querying the data in your list, this chapter explains how you can use Excel's Database functions to perform calculations on particular numerical fields for only the records that meet the criteria that you specify. These calculations can include getting totals (DSUM), averages (DAVERAGE), the count of the records (DCOUNT and DCOUNTA), and the like.

Finally, this chapter introduces you to querying external databases in order to bring some of their data into the more familiar worksheet setting. These external databases that you query in Excel can be in other Windows database programs, such as Microsoft Access or dBASE, or in even more sophisticated, non-Windows database management systems, such as IBM's dB2 or Oracle Corporation's Oracle DBMS.

Data List Filtering 101

If you ever have the good fortune to attend my class on database management, you'll hear my spiel on the difference between data and information in the tables in a database (or *data list,* in Excel-speak). In case you're the least little bit interested, it goes like this: A data list or the tables that make up a database consist of a vast quantity of raw data, which simply represent all the stuff that everybody in the company wants stored on a given subject (employees, sales, clients, you name it). For example, suppose that you keep a data list on the sales transactions made by your customers. This data list can very well track such stuff as the customers' identification numbers, names, addresses, telephone numbers, whether they have a charge account with the store, the maximum amount that they can charge, the purchases that they've made (including the dates and amounts), and whether their accounts are due (or overdue).

However, this vast quantity of *data* stored in the customer data list is not to be confused with the *information* that particular people in the office want out of the data. For example, suppose that you're working in the marketing department and you're about to introduce a line of expensive household items that you want to advertise. You want to limit the advertising to those customers who have a charge account with the store and have purchased at least $5,000 of merchandise in the last six months. Use the *data* provided in the data list to supply the *information* to weed out the customers that you need from the list.

On the other hand, suppose that you work in the accounting department and you need to send out nasty notices to all the customers who have charge accounts that are more than 90 days past due. In this case, you want only the data identifying those customers whose accounts are overdue. You couldn't care less about what was actually purchased. All you care about is reaching these folks and convincing them to pay up. You again use the *data* provided in the data list to supply the *information* to weed out the customers that you need from the list.

From these simple examples, it should be clear that the data that supply information to one group in the company at a particular time are often not the same data that supply information to another group. In other words, for most people, the data list dispenses information only when you are able to filter out the stuff that you currently don't want to see, and leaves behind just the stuff that interests you.

Filtering Data

Filtering the data list to leave behind only the information that you want to work with is exactly the procedure that you follow in Excel. At the most basic level, you use the AutoFilter feature to temporarily hide the display of unwanted records and leave behind only the records that you want to see. Much of the time, the capabilities of the AutoFilter feature are all that you need, especially when your main concern is simply displaying just the information of interest in the data list.

You will encounter situations, however, in which the AutoFilter feature is not sufficient, and you must do what Microsoft refers to as *advanced filtering* in your data list. You need to use advanced filtering to filter the data list when you use computed criteria (such as when you want to see all the records where the entry in the Sales column is twice the amount in the Owed column) and when you need to save a copy of the filtered data in a different part of the worksheet (Excel's version of querying the data in a data list).

Using AutoFilter

Excel's AutoFilter feature makes filtering out unwanted data in a data list as easy as clicking the AutoFilter button on the column on which you want to filter the data and then clicking the appropriate filtering criteria on that column's drop-down menu.

If you open a worksheet with a data list and you don't find AutoFilter buttons attached to each of the field names at the top of the list, you can display them simply by positioning the cell cursor in one of the cells with the field names and then clicking the Filter command button on the Ribbon's Data tab or pressing Alt+AT.

The filter options on a column's AutoFilter drop-down menu depend on the type of entries in the field. On the drop-down menu in a column that contains only date entries, the menu contains a Date Filters option to which a submenu of the actual filters is attached. On the drop-down menu in a column that contains only numeric entries (besides dates) or a mixture of dates with other types of numeric entries, the menu contains a Number Filters option. On the drop-down menu in a column that contains only text entries or a mixture of text, date, and other numeric entries, the menu contains a Text Filters option.

Doing basic filtering by selecting specific field entries

In addition to the Date Filters, Text Filters, or Number Filters options (depending on the type of field), the AutoFilter drop-down menu for each field in the data list contains a list box with a complete listing of all entries made in that column, each with its own check box. At the most basic level, you can filter the data list by clearing the check box for all the entries whose records you don't want to see in the list.

This kind of basic filtering works best in fields such as City, State, or Country, which contain many duplicates, so you can see a subset of the data list that contains only the cities, states, or countries you want to work with at the time.

The easiest way to perform this basic type of filtering on a field is to first click the check box in front of the (Select All) option at the top of the field's list box to clear the check boxes, and then click each of the check boxes containing the entries for the records you do want displayed in the filtered data list. After you finish selecting the check boxes for all the entries you want to keep, you click OK to close the AutoFilter drop-down menu.

Excel then hides rows in the data list for all records except for those that contain the entries you just selected. The program also lets you know which field or fields have been used in the filtering operation by adding a cone filter icon to the column's AutoFilter button. To restore all the records to the data list, you can remove the filtering by clicking the Clear command button in the Sort & Filter group of the Data tab of the Ribbon or by pressing Alt+AC.

When doing this basic kind of list filtering, you can select specific entries from more than one field in this list. Figure 2-1 illustrates this kind of situation. Here, I want only the employees in the company who work in the Engineering and Information Services departments in the Chicago and Seattle offices. To do this, I selected only the Engineering and Information Services entries in the list box on the Dept field's AutoFilter drop-down menu and only the Chicago and Seattle entries in the list box on the Location field's AutoFilter drop-down menu.

As you can see in Figure 2-1, after filtering the Employee data list so that only the records for employees in either the Engineering or Information Services department in either the Chicago or Seattle office locations are listed, Excel adds the cone filter icon to the AutoFilter buttons on both the Dept and Location fields in the top row, indicating that the list is filtered using criteria involving both fields.

Keep in mind that after filtering the data list in this manner, you can then copy remaining records that make up the desired subset of the data list to a new area in the same worksheet or to a new sheet in the workbook where you can then sort the data (by adding AutoFilter buttons with the Filter command button on the Data tab), chart the data (see Book V, Chapter 1), analyze the data (see "Using the Database Functions" later in this chapter), or summarize the data in a pivot table (see Book VII, Chapter 2).

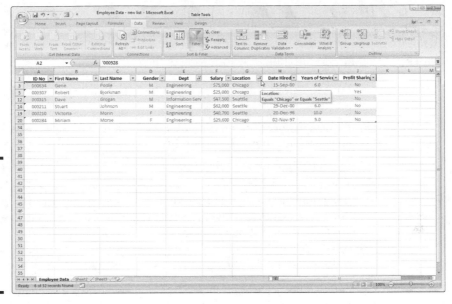

Figure 2-1:
Employee
data list
after
filtering the
Dept and
Location
fields.

Using the Text Filters options

The AutoFilter drop-down menu for a field that contains only text or a combination of text, date, and numeric entries contains a Text Filters option that when you click or highlight displays its submenu containing the following options:

✦ **Equals:** Opens the Custom AutoFilter dialog box with the Equals operator selected in the first condition.

✦ **Does Not Equal:** Opens the Custom AutoFilter dialog box with the Does Not Equal operator selected in the first condition.

✦ **Begins With:** Opens the Custom AutoFilter dialog box with the Begins With operator selected in the first condition.

✦ **Ends With:** Opens the Custom AutoFilter dialog box with the Ends With operator selected in the first condition.

✦ **Contains:** Opens the Custom AutoFilter dialog box with the Contains operator selected in the first condition.

✦ **Does Not Contain:** Opens the Custom AutoFilter dialog box with the Does Not Contain operator selected in the first condition.

✦ **Custom Filter:** Opens the Custom AutoFilter dialog box where you can select your own criteria for applying more complex AND or OR conditions.

Using the Date Filters options

The AutoFilter drop-down menu for a field that contains only date entries contains a Date Filters option that when you click or highlight displays its submenu containing the following options:

✦ **Equals:** Opens the Custom AutoFilter dialog box with the Equals operator selected in the first condition.

✦ **Before:** Opens the Custom AutoFilter dialog box with the Is Before operator selected in the first condition.

✦ **After:** Opens the Custom AutoFilter dialog box with the Is After operator selected in the first condition.

✦ **Between:** Opens the Custom AutoFilter dialog box with the Is After or Equal To operator selected in the first condition and the Is Before or Equal To operator selected in the second AND condition.

✦ **Tomorrow:** Filters the data list so that only records with tomorrow's date in this field are displayed in the worksheet.

✦ **Today:** Filters the data list so that only records with the current date in this field are displayed in the worksheet.

✦ **Yesterday:** Filters the data list so that only records with yesterday's date in this field are displayed in the worksheet.

✦ **Next Week:** Filters the data list so that only records with date entries in the week ahead in this field are displayed in the worksheet.

✦ **This Week:** Filters the data list so that only records with date entries in the current week in this field are displayed in the worksheet.

✦ **Last Week:** Filters the data list so that only records with date entries in the previous week in this field are displayed in the worksheet.

✦ **Next Month:** Filters the data list so that only records with date entries in the month ahead in this field are displayed in the worksheet.

✦ **This Month:** Filters the data list so that only records with date entries in the current month in this field are displayed in the worksheet.

✦ **Last Month:** Filters the data list so that only records with date entries in the previous month in this field are displayed in the worksheet.

✦ **Next Quarter:** Filters the data list so that only records with date entries in the three-month quarterly period ahead in this field are displayed in the worksheet.

✦ **This Quarter:** Filters the data list so that only records with date entries in the current three-month quarterly period in this field are displayed in the worksheet.

✦ **Last Quarter:** Filters the data list so that only records with date entries in the previous three-month quarterly period in this field are displayed in the worksheet.

✦ **Next Year:** Filters the data list so that only records with date entries in the calendar year ahead in this field are displayed in the worksheet.

✦ **This Year:** Filters the data list so that only records with date entries in the current calendar year in this field are displayed in the worksheet.

✦ **Last Year:** Filters the data list so that only records with date entries in the previous calendar year in this field are displayed in the worksheet.

✦ **Year to Date:** Filters the data list so that only records with date entries in the current year up to the current date in this field are displayed in the worksheet.

✦ **All Dates in the Period:** Filters the data list so that only records with date entries in the quarter (Quarter 1 through Quarter 4) or month (January through December) that you click on its submenu are displayed in the worksheet.

✦ **Custom Filter:** Opens the Custom AutoFilter dialog box where you can select your own criteria for more complex AND or OR conditions.

TIP

When selecting dates for conditions using the Equals, Is Before, Is After, Is Before or Equal To, or Is After or Equal To operator in the Custom AutoFilter dialog box, you can select the date by clicking the Date Picker button (the one with the calendar icon) and then clicking the specific date on the drop-down date palette. When you open the date palette, it shows the current month and the current date selected. To select a date in an earlier month, click the Previous button (the one with the triangle pointing left) until its month is displayed in the palette. To select a date in a later month, click the Next button (the one with the triangle pointing right) until its month is displayed in the palette.

Using the Number Filters options

The AutoFilter drop-down menu for a field that contains only number entries beside dates or a combination of dates and other numeric entries contains a Number Filters option that when you click or highlight displays its submenu containing the following options:

✦ **Equals:** Opens the Custom AutoFilter dialog box with the Equals operator selected in the first condition.

✦ **Does Not Equal:** Opens the Custom AutoFilter dialog box with the Does Not Equal operator selected in the first condition.

✦ **Greater Than:** Opens the Custom AutoFilter dialog box with the Is Greater Than operator selected in the first condition.

✦ **Greater Than or Equal To:** Opens the Custom AutoFilter dialog box with the Is Greater Than or Equal To operator selected in the first condition.

✦ **Less Than:** Opens the Custom AutoFilter dialog box with the Is Less Than operator selected in the first condition.

✦ **Less Than or Equal To:** Opens the Custom AutoFilter dialog box with the Is Less Than or Equal to operator selected in the first condition.

✦ **Between:** Opens the Custom AutoFilter dialog box with the Is Greater Than or Equal To operator selected in the first condition and the Is Less Than or Equal To operator selected in the second AND condition.

✦ **Top 10:** Opens the Top 10 AutoFilter dialog box so that you can filter the list to just the ten or so top or bottom values or percentages in the field (see "Making it to the Top Ten!" that follows in this chapter for details).

✦ **Above Average:** Filters the data list to display only records where the values in the field are greater than the average of the values in this field.

✦ **Below Average:** Filters the data list so that to display only records where the values in the field are less than the average of the values in this field.

✦ **Custom Filter:** Opens the Custom AutoFilter dialog box where you can select your own criteria for more complex AND or OR conditions.

Making it to the Top Ten!

The Top 10 option on the Number Filters option's submenu enables you to filter out all records except those whose entries in that field are at the top or bottom of the list by a certain number (10 by default) or in a certain top or bottom percent (10 by default). Of course, you can only use the Top 10 item in numerical fields and date fields; this kind of filtering doesn't make any sense when you're dealing with entries in a text field.

When you click the Top 10 option on the Number Filters option's submenu, Excel opens the Top 10 AutoFilter dialog box where you can specify your filtering criteria. By default, the Top 10 AutoFilter dialog box is set to filter out all records except those whose entries are among the top ten items in the field by selecting Top in the drop-down list box on the left, 10 in the middle combo box, and Items in the drop-down list box on the right. If you want to use these default criteria, you simply click OK in the Top 10 AutoFilter dialog box.

Figure 2-2 shows you the sample Employee Data list after using Top 10 AutoFilter to display only the records with the top ten salaries in the data list.

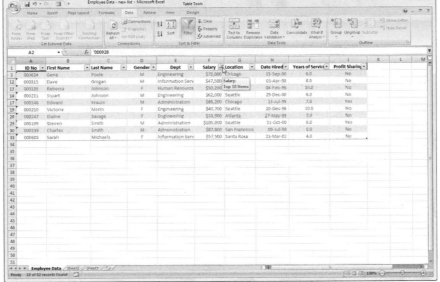

Figure 2-2:
Using the
Top 10
AutoFilter
dialog box
to filter out
all records
except for
those with
the top ten
salaries.

You can also change the filtering criteria in the Top 10 AutoFilter dialog box
before you filter the data. You can choose between Top and Bottom in the
leftmost drop-down list box and between Items and Percent in the rightmost
one. You can also change the number in the middle combo box by clicking it
and entering a new value or using the spinner buttons to select one.

Filtering a data list on a field's font and cell colors or cell icons

Just as you can sort a data list using the font or fill color or cell icons that
you've assigned with Conditional Formatting to values in the field that are
within or outside of certain parameters (see "Conditional Formatting" in
Book II, Chapter 2 for details), you can also filter the list.

To filter a data list on a font color, cell color, or cell icon used in a field, you
click its AutoFilter button and then highlight the Filter by Color option on
the drop-down menu. Excel then displays a submenu on which you click the
font color, cell color, or cell icon to use in the sort:

✦ To filter the data list so that only the records with a particular font color
   in the selected field — assigned with the Conditional Formatting
   Highlight Cell Rules or Top/Bottom Rules options — appear in the list,
   click its color swatch in the Filter by Font Color submenu.

✦ To filter the data list so that only the records with a particular cell color in the selected field — assigned with the Conditional Formatting Highlight Cell Rules, Top/Bottom Rules, Data Bars, or Color Scales options — appear in the list, click its color swatch in the Filter by Font Color submenu.

✦ To filter the data list so that only the records with a particular cell icon in the selected field — assigned with the Conditional Formatting Icon Sets options — appear in the list, click the icon in the Filter by Cell Icon submenu.

Custom AutoFilter at your service

You can click the Custom Filter option on a field's Text Filters, Date Filters, or Number Filters continuation menu to open the Custom AutoFilter dialog box, where you can specify your own filtering criteria by using conditions with the AND and OR logical operators (called AND and OR conditions for short). When you click the Custom Filter option, Excel opens the Custom AutoFilter dialog box, similar to the one shown in Figure 2-3.

Figure 2-3:
Using Custom AutoFilter to filter out records except for those within a range of salaries.

Here, you select the type of operator to use in evaluating the first and second conditions in the top and bottom drop-down list boxes and the values to be evaluated in the first and second conditions in the associated combo boxes. You also specify the type of relationship between the two conditions with the And or Or option button (the And option button is selected by default).

When selecting the operator for the first and second condition in the left-most drop-down list boxes at the top and bottom of the Custom AutoFilter dialog box, you have the following choices, depending on the types of entries in the selected field:

✦ **Equals:** Matches records where the entry in the field is identical to the text, date, or number you enter in the associated combo box.

✦ **Does Not Equal:** Matches records where the entry in the field is anything other than the text, date, or number you enter in the associated combo box.

✦ **Is After:** Matches records where the entry in the date field comes after the date you enter or select in the associated combo box.

✦ **Is After or Equal To:** Matches records where the entry in the date field comes after or is the same as the date you enter or select in the associated combo box.

✦ **Is Before:** Matches records where the entry in the date field precedes the date you enter or select in the associated combo box.

✦ **Is Before or Equal To:** Matches records where the entry in the date field precedes the date you enter or select in the associated combo box.

✦ **Is Greater Than:** Matches records where the entry in the field follows the text in the alphabet, comes after the date, or is larger than the number you enter in the associated combo box.

✦ **Is Greater Than or Equal To:** Matches records where the entry in the field follows the text in the alphabet or is identical, comes after, or is the same as the date, or is larger than or equal to the number you enter in the associated combo box.

✦ **Is Less Than:** Matches records where the entry in the field comes before the text in the alphabet, comes before the date, or is less than the number you enter in the associated combo box.

✦ **Is Less Than or Equal To:** Matches records where the entry in the field comes before the text in the alphabet or is identical, comes before, or is the same as the date, or is less than or equal to the number you enter in the associated combo box.

✦ **Begins With:** Matches records where the entry in the field starts with the text, the part of the date, or the number you enter in the associated combo box.

✦ **Does Not Begin With:** Matches records where the entry in the field starts with anything other than the text, the part of the date, or the number you enter in the associated combo box.

✦ **Ends With:** Matches records where the entry in the field ends with the text, the part of the date, or the number you enter in the associated combo box.

✦ **Does Not End With:** Matches records where the entry in the field ends with anything other than the text, the part of the date, or the number you enter in the associated combo box.

✦ **Contains:** Matches records where the entry in the field contains the text, the part of the date, or the number you enter in the associated combo box.

✦ **Does Not Contain:** Matches records where the entry in the field contains anything other than the text, the part of the date, or the number you enter in the associated combo box.

Note that you can use the Begins With, Ends With, and Contains operators and their negative counterparts when filtering a text field — you can also use the question mark (?) and asterisk (*) wildcard characters when entering the values for use with these operators (the question mark wildcard stands for individual characters and the asterisk stands for one or more characters). You use the other logical operators when dealing with numeric and date fields.

When specifying the values to evaluate in the associated combo boxes on the right side of the Custom AutoFilter dialog box, you can type in the text, number, or date, or you can select an existing field entry by clicking the box's drop-down list button and then clicking the entry on the drop-down menu. In date fields, you can select the dates directly from the date drop-down palette opened by clicking the box's Date Picker button (the one with the calendar icon).

Figure 2-3 illustrates setting up filtering criteria in the Custom AutoFilter dialog box that selects records whose Salary values fall within two separate ranges of values. In this example, I'm using an OR condition to filter out all records where the salaries fall below $35,000 or are greater than $75,000 by entering the following complex condition:

```
Salary Is Greater Than 75000 AND Is Less Than 35000
```

Using the Advanced Filter

When you use advanced filtering, you don't use the field's AutoFilter buttons and associated drop-down menu options. Instead, you create a so-called Criteria Range somewhere on the worksheet containing the data list to be filtered before opening the Advanced Filter dialog box.

If you use the Advanced Filter feature to do a query, you extract copies of the records that match your criteria by creating a subset of the data list. You can locate the Criteria Range in the top rows of columns to the right of the data list and then specify the Copy To range underneath the Criteria Range, similar to the arrangement shown in Figure 2-4.

To create a Criteria Range, you copy the names of the fields in the data list to a new part of the worksheet and then enter the values (text, numbers, or formulas) that are to be used as the criteria in filtering the list in rows underneath.

Filtering Data **625**

When setting up the criteria for filtering the data list, you can create either comparison criteria or calculated criteria.

After you've set up your criteria range with all the field names and the criteria that you want used, you click the Advanced command button on the Ribbon's Data tab (or press Alt+AQ) to open the Advanced Filter dialog box similar to the one shown in Figure 2-4. Here, you specify whether you just want to filter the records in the list (by hiding the rows of all those that don't meet your criteria) or you want to copy the records that meet your criteria to a new area in the worksheet (by creating a subset of the data list).

**Book VI
Chapter 2**

**Filtering and
Querying a Data List**

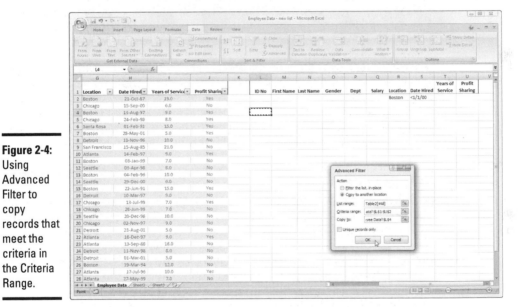

Figure 2-4:
Using
Advanced
Filter to
copy
records that
meet the
criteria in
the Criteria
Range.

To just filter the data in the list, leave the Filter the List, In Place option button selected. To query the list and copy the data to a new place in the same worksheet (note that the Advanced Filter feature doesn't let you copy the data to another sheet or workbook), you click the Copy to Another Location option button. When you click this option button, the Copy To text box becomes available, along with the List Range and Criteria Range text boxes.

To specify the data list that contains the data that you want to filter or query, click the List Range text box and then enter the address of the cell range or select it directly in the worksheet by dragging through its cells. To specify the range that contains a copy of the field names along with the criteria entered under the appropriate fields, you click the Criteria Range text box and then enter the range address of this cell range or select it directly in the worksheet by dragging through its cells. When selecting this range, be sure that you include all the rows that contain the values that you want evaluated in the filter or query.

If you're querying the data list by copying the records that meet your criteria to a new part of the worksheet (indicated by clicking the Copy to Another Location option button), you also click the Copy To text box and then enter the address of the cell that is to form the upper-left corner of the copied and filtered records or click this cell directly in the worksheet.

After specifying whether to filter or query the data and designating the ranges to be used in this operation, click OK to have Excel apply the criteria that you've specified in the Criteria Range in either filtering or copying the records.

After filtering a data list, you may feel that you haven't received the expected results — for example, no records are listed under the field names that you thought should have several. You can bring back all the records in the list by clicking the Clear command button on the Data tab of the Ribbon or by pressing Alt+AC. Now you can fiddle with the criteria in the Criteria Range text box and try the whole advanced filtering thing all over again.

Specifying comparison criteria

Entering selection criteria in the Criteria Range for advanced filtering is very similar to entering criteria in the data form after selecting the Criteria button. However, you need to be aware of some differences. For example, if you are searching for the last name *Paul* and enter the label **Paul** in the criteria range under the cell containing the field name Last Name, Excel will match any last name that begins with *P-a-u-l* such as Pauley, Paulson, and so on. To avoid having Excel match any other last name beside Paul, you would have to enter a formula in the cell below the one with the Last Name field name, as in

```
="Paul"
```

Only the unique need apply!

To filter out duplicate rows or records that match your criteria, select the Unique Records Only check box in the Advanced Filter dialog box before you start the filtering operation. You can remove the display of all duplicate records from a data list by selecting this check box and also removing all cell references from the Criteria Range text box before you click OK or press Enter.

When entering criteria for advanced filtering, you can also use the question mark (?) or the asterisk (*) wildcard character in your selection criteria just like you do when using the data form to find records. If, for example, you enter **J*n** under the cell with the First Name field name, Excel will consider any characters between *J* and *n* in the First Name field to be a match including Joan, Jon, or John as well as Jane or Joanna. To restrict the matches to just those names with characters between *J* and *n* and to prevent matches with names that have trailing characters, you need to enter the following formula in the cell:

`="J*n"`

When you use a selection formula like this, Excel will match names such as Joan, Jon, and John but not names such as Jane or Joanna that have a character after the *n*.

When setting up selection criteria, you can also use the other comparative operators, including >, >=, <, <=, and <>, in the selection criteria. See Table 2-1 for descriptions and examples of usage in selection criteria for each of these logical operators.

Table 2-1	The Comparative Operators in the Selection Criteria		
Operator	*Meaning*	*Example*	*Locates*
=	Equal to	="CA"	Records where the state is *CA*.
>	Greater than	>m	Records where the name starts with a letter after *M* (that is, N through Z).
>=	Greater than	>=3/4/02	Records where the date is on or after or equal to *March 4, 2002*.
<	Less than	<d	Records where the name begins with a letter before *D* (that is, A, B, or C).
<=	Less than	<=12/12/04	Records where the date is on or before or equal to *December 12, 2004*.
<>	Not equal to	<>"CA"	Records where the state is not equal to *CA*.

To find all the records where a particular field is blank in the database, enter = and press the spacebar to enter a space in the cell beneath the appropriate field name. To find all the records where a particular field is *not* blank in the database, enter <> and press the spacebar to enter a space in the cell beneath the appropriate field name.

Setting up logical AND and logical OR conditions

When you enter two or more criteria in the same row beneath different field names in the Criteria Range, Excel treats the criteria as a logical AND condition and selects only those records that meet both of the criteria. Figure 2-5 shows an example of the results of a query that uses an AND condition. Here, Excel has copied only those records where the location is Boston *and* the date hired is before January 1, 2000, because both the criteria Boston and <1/1/00 are placed in the same row (row 2) under their respective field names, Location and Date Hired.

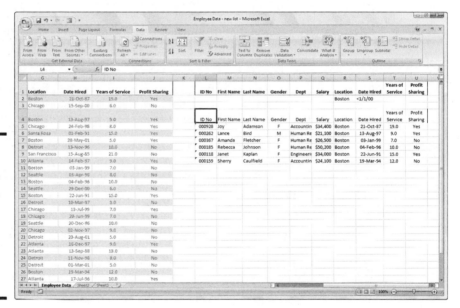

Figure 2-5: Copied records for the Boston location where the date hired is before January 1, 2000.

When you enter two or more criteria in different rows of the Criteria Range, Excel treats the criteria as a logical OR and selects records that meet any one of the criteria they contain. Figure 2-6 shows you an example of the results of a query using an OR condition. In this example, Excel has copied records where the location is either Boston or San Francisco because Boston is entered under the Location field name in the second row (row 2) of the Criteria Range above San Francisco entered in the third row (row 3).

When creating OR conditions, you need to remember to redefine the Criteria Range to include all the rows that contain criteria, which in this case is the cell range L2:U2 (if you forget, Excel uses only the criteria in the rows included in the Criteria range).

When setting up your criteria, you can combine logical AND and logical OR conditions (again, assuming that you expand the Criteria Range sufficiently to include all the rows containing criteria). For example, if you enter Boston in cell R2 (under Location) and <1/1/00 in cell S2 (under Date Hired) in row 2 and enter San Francisco in cell R3 and then repeat the query, Excel copies the records where the location is Boston and the date hired is before January 1, 2000, as well as the records where the location is San Francisco (regardless of the date hired).

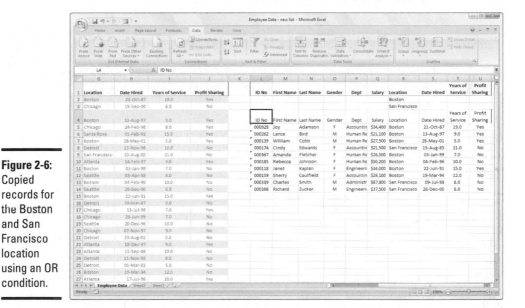

Figure 2-6: Copied records for the Boston and San Francisco location using an OR condition.

Setting up Calculated criteria

You can use calculated criteria when filtering or querying your data list. All you need to do is enter a logical formula that Excel can evaluate as either TRUE or FALSE in the Criteria Range under a name that is *not* used as a field name in the data list (I repeat, is *not* a field name in the data list). Calculated criteria enable you to filter or query records based on a comparison of entries in a particular field with entries in other fields of the list or based on a comparison with entries in the worksheet that lie outside the data list itself.

Figure 2-7 shows an example of using a calculated criterion that compares values in a field to a calculated value that isn't actually entered in the data list. Here, you want to perform a query that copies all the records from the Employee data list where the employee's salary is above the average salary. In this figure, cell V2 contains the formula that uses the AVERAGE function to compute average employee salary and then compares the first salary entry in cell F2 of the data list to that average with the following formula:

```
=F2>AVERAGE($F$2:$F$33)
```

Note that this logical formula is placed under the label Calculated Criteria in cell V2, which has been added to the end of the Criteria Range. Cell F2 is the first cell in the data list that contains a salary entry. The cell range, $F$2:$F$33, used as the argument of the AVERAGE function, is the range in the Salary field that contains all the salary entries.

To use this calculated criterion, you must remember to place the logical formula under a name that isn't used as a field name in the data list itself. (In this example, the label Calculated Criteria does not appear anywhere in the row of field names.) You must include this label and formula in the Criteria Range (for this query example, the Criteria Range is defined as the cell range L2:V2).

When you then perform the query by using the Advanced Filter feature, Excel applies this calculated criterion to every record in the database. Excel does this by adjusting the first Salary field cell reference F2 (entered as a relative reference) as the program examines the rest of the records below. Note, however, that the range reference specified as the argument of the AVERAGE function is entered as an absolute reference ($F$2:$F$33) in the criterion formula so that Excel won't adjust this reference but compare the Salary entry for each record to AVERAGE computed for this entire range (which just happens to be 40,161).

When entering formulas for calculated criteria that compare values outside the data list to values in a particular field, you should always reference the cell containing the very first entry for that field in order to ensure that Excel applies your criteria to every record in the data list.

You can also set up calculated criteria that compare entries in one or more fields to other entries in the data list. For example, to extract the records where the Years of Service entry is at least two years greater than the record above it (assuming that you have sorted the data list in ascending order by years of service), you would enter the following logical formula under the cell labeled Calculated Criteria:

```
=I3>I2+2
```

Most often, when referencing cells within the data list itself, you want to leave the cell references relative so that they can be adjusted, because each record is examined, and the references to the cells outside the database are absolute so that these won't be changed when making the comparison with the rest of the records.

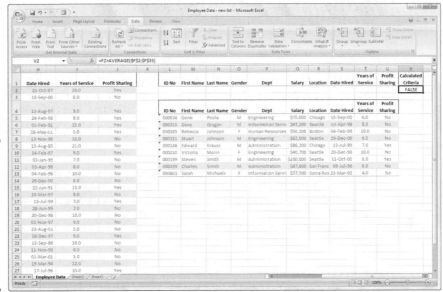

Figure 2-7: Extracted records for personnel whose salaries are above the salary average.

When you enter the logical formula for a calculated criterion, Excel returns the logical value TRUE or FALSE. This logical value applies to the field entry for the first record in the data list that you refer to in the logical formula. By inspecting this field entry in the database and seeing if it does, indeed, meet your intended selection criteria, you can usually tell whether your logical formula is correct.

Using the AND and OR functions in calculated criteria

You can also use Excel's AND, OR, and NOT functions with the logical operators in calculated criteria to find records that fall within a range. For example, to find all the records in the employee database where the salaries range between $55,000 and $75,000, you would enter the following logical formula with the AND function under the cell with the label Calculated Criteria:

```
=AND(F4>=55000,F4<=75000)
```

To find all the records in the Employee data list where the salary is either below $29,000 or above $45,000, you would enter the following logical formula with the OR function under the cell with the label Calculated Criteria:

```
=OR(F4<29000,F4>45000)
```

Using the Database Functions

Excel includes a number of database functions that you can use to calculate statistics, such as the total, the average, the maximum, the minimum, and the count in a particular field of the data list only when the criteria that you specify are met. For example, you could use the DSUM function in the sample Employee data list to compute the sum of all the salaries for employees who were hired after January 1, 2000, or you could use the DCOUNT function to compute the number of records in the data list for the Human Resources department.

The database functions, regardless of the difference in names (and they all begin with the letter *D*) and the computations that they perform, all take the same three arguments as illustrated by the DAVERAGE function:

=DAVERAGE(*database,field,criteria*)

The arguments for the database functions require the following information:

✦ *Database* is the argument that specifies the range containing the list and it must include the row of field names in the top row.

✦ *Field* is the argument that specifies the field whose values are to be calculated by the database function (averaged in the case of the DAVERAGE function). You can specify this argument by enclosing the name of the field in double quotes (as in "Salary" or "Date Hired"), or you can do this by entering the number of the column in the data list (counting from left to right with the first field counted as 1).

✦ *Criteria* is the argument that specifies the address of the range that contains the criteria that you're using to determine which values are calculated. This range must include at least one field name that indicates the field whose values are to be evaluated and one cell with the values or expression to be used in the evaluation.

Note that in specifying the *field* argument, you must refer to a column in the data list that contains numeric or date data for all the database functions with the exception of DGET. All the rest of the database functions can't perform computations on text fields. If you mistakenly specify a column with text entries as the field argument for these database functions, Excel returns an error value or 0 as the result. Table 2-2 lists the various database functions available in Excel along with an explanation of what each one calculates (you already know what arguments each one takes).

Table 2-2	The Database Functions in Excel
Database Function	*What It Calculates*
DAVERAGE	Averages all the values in a field of the data list that match the criteria you specify.
DCOUNT	Counts the number of cells with numeric entries in a field of the data list that match the criteria you specify.
DCOUNTA	Counts the number of nonblank cells in a field of the data list that match the criteria you specify.
DGET	Extracts a single value from a record in the data list that matches the criteria you specify. If no record matches, the function returns the #VALUE! error value. If multiple records match, the function returns the #NUM! error value.
DMAX	Returns the highest value in a field of the data list that matches the criteria you specify.
DMIN	Returns the lowest value in a field of the data list that matches the criteria you specify.
DPRODUCT	Multiplies all the values in a field of the data list that match the criteria you specify.
DSTDEV	Estimates the standard deviation based on the sample of values in a field of the data list that match the criteria you specify.
DSTDEVP	Calculates the standard deviation based on the population of values in a field of the data list that match the criteria you specify.
DSUM	Sums all the values in a field of the data list that match the criteria you specify.
DVAR	Estimates the variance based on the sample of values in a field of the data list that match the criteria you specify.
DVARP	Calculates the variance based on the population of values in a field of the data list that match the criteria you specify.

**Book VI
Chapter 2**

**Filtering and
Querying a Data List**

The Database functions are too rarely used to rate their own command button on the Ribbon's Formulas tab. As a result, to use them in a worksheet, you must click the Function Wizard (*fx*) button on the Formula bar and then click Database in the Or Select a Category drop-down list box and then click the function to use or type the Database function directly into the cell.

Figure 2-8 illustrates the use of the database function, DSUM. Cell B2 in the worksheet shown in this figure contains the following formula:

```
=DSUM(A3:J35,"Salary",E1:E2)
```

This DSUM function computes the total of all the salaries in the data list that are above $55,000. This total is $468,500, as shown in cell B2, which contains the formula.

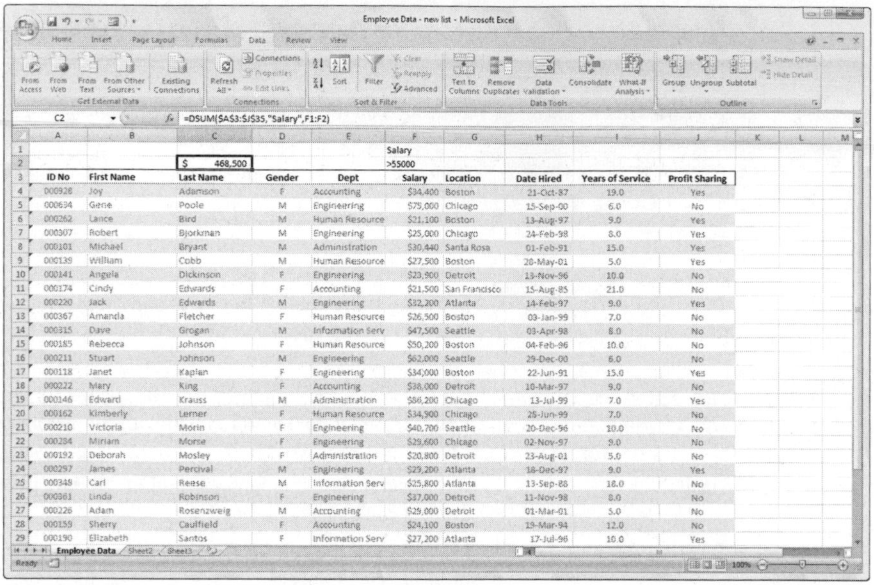

Figure 2-8:
Using the
DSUM to
total the
salaries
over $55,000
in the
Employee
data list.

To perform this calculation, I specified the range A3:J35, which contains the entire data list, including the top row of field names as the *database* argument (which Excel returned as an absolute range address). I then specified "Salary" as the field argument of the DSUM function because this is the name of the field that contains the values that I want totaled. Finally, I specified the range E1:E2 as the *criteria* argument of the DSUM function because these two cells contain the criteria range that designate that only the values exceeding 55000 in the Salary field are to be summed.

External Data Query

Excel makes it possible to query other external databases to which you have access and then extract the data that interests you into your worksheet for further manipulation and analysis. Excel 2007 makes it easy to acquire data from a variety of different data sources, including Microsoft Access database files, Web pages on the Internet, text files, and other data sources such as database tables on SQL servers, XML data files, and data tables following the OLEDB (Object Linked Embedded Database) and ODBC (Open Database Connectivity) specifications.

Retrieving data from Access database tables

To make an external data query to an Access database table, you click the From Access command button on the Ribbon's Data tab or press Alt+AFA. Excel opens the Select Data Source dialog box where you select the name of the Access database (using an *.mdb file extension) and then click Open. The Select Table dialog box then appears from which you can select the data table that you want to import into the worksheet.

After you click the name of the Access data table and click OK, the Import Data dialog box appears. This table contains the following option buttons from which to select:

✦ **Table** to have the data in the Access data table imported into an Excel table in either the current or new worksheet — see Existing Worksheet and New Worksheet entries that follow.

✦ **PivotTable Report** to have the data in the Access data table imported into a new pivot table (see Book VII, Chapter 2) that you can construct with the Access data.

✦ **PivotChart and PivotTable Report** to have the data in the Access data table imported into a new pivot table (see Book VII, Chapter 2) with an embedded pivot chart that you can construct with the Access data.

✦ **Only Create Connection** to create a connection to Access database table that you can use later to actually import its data.

✦ **Existing Worksheet** (default) to have the data in the Access data table imported into the current worksheet starting at the current cell address listed in the text box below.

✦ **New Worksheet** to have the data in the Access data table imported into a new sheet that's added to the beginning of the workbook.

Figure 2-9 shows you an Excel worksheet after importing the Orders data table from the sample Northwind Access database as a new data table in Excel. After importing the data, you can then use the Filter buttons attached to the various fields to sort the data (as described in Book VI, Chapter 1) and filter the data (as described earlier in this chapter).

Excel keeps a list of all the external data queries you make so that you can reuse them to import updated data from another database or Web page. To reuse a query, click the Existing Connections button on the Data tab (Alt+AX) to open the Existing Connections dialog box to access this list and then click the name of the query to repeat.

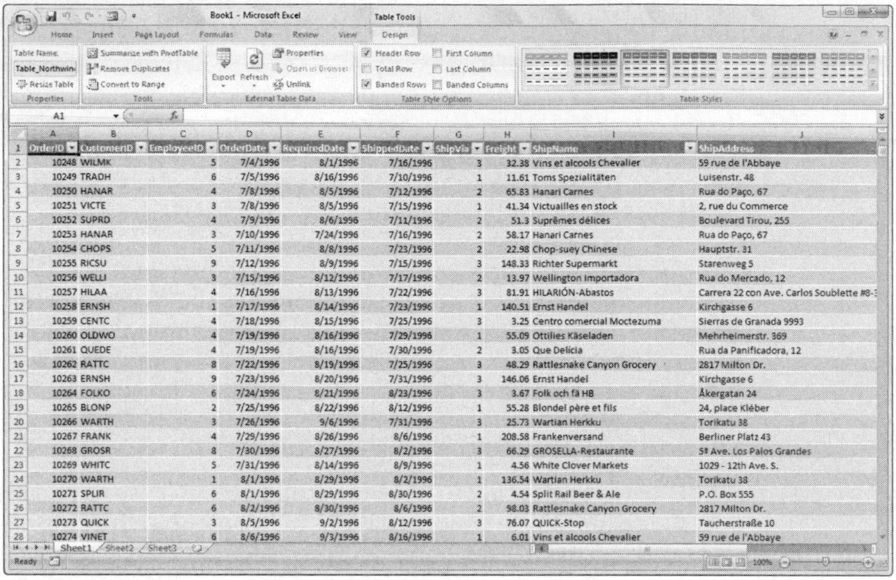

Figure 2-9:
Worksheet after importing an Access data table.

Retrieving data from the Web

To make a Web page query, you click the From Web command button on the Ribbon's Data tab or press Alt+AFW. Excel then opens the New Web Query dialog box containing the Home page for your computer's default Web browser (Internet Explorer 7 in most cases). To select the Web page containing the data you want to import into Excel, you can:

✦ Type the URL Web address in the Address text box at the top of the Home page in the New Web Query dialog box.

✦ Use the Search feature offered on the Home page or its links to find the Web page containing the data you wish to import.

When you have the Web page containing the data you want to import displayed in the New Web Query dialog box, Excel indicates which tables of information you can import from the Web page into the worksheet by adding a check box with an arrowhead pointing right. To import these tables, you simply click this check box to add a check mark to it (see Figure 2-10).

After you finish checking all the tables you want to import on the page, click the Import button to close the New Web Query dialog box. Excel then opens a version of the Import Data dialog box with only the Table option button available. Here, you can indicate where the table data is to be imported by selecting one of these two option buttons:

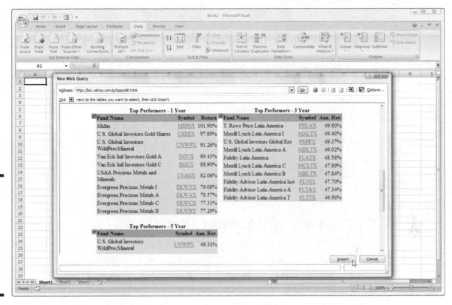

Figure 2-10:
Selecting
the data to
import on
the Yahoo
Finance
Web page.

✦ **Existing Worksheet** (default) to have the data in the Access data table
   imported into the current worksheet starting at the current cell address
   listed in the text box below.

✦ **New Worksheet** to have the data in the Access data table imported into
   a new sheet that's added to the beginning of the workbook.

After you click OK in the Import Data dialog box, Excel closes the box and
then imports all the tables of data you selected on the Web page into a new
worksheet starting at cell A1 or in the existing worksheet starting at the cell
whose address was entered in the text box in the Import Data dialog box.

Figure 2-11 shows the results of a Web query initiated in the New Web Query
dialog box shown in Figure 2-10. As you can see, Excel brings this data from
the Top Performers 1-Year, 3-Year, and 5-Year tables into the new worksheet
as cell ranges rather than as Excel tables. If you then want to be able to sort
or filter these imported data, you then need to select each range in turn and
click the Filter button on the Data tab of the Ribbon or press Alt+AFF to add
the requisite filter buttons.

You can only make Web queries when your computer has Internet access.
So, if you're using Excel on a laptop computer that can't connect to the Web
at the moment, you won't be able to perform a new Web query until you're in
a place where you can get online.

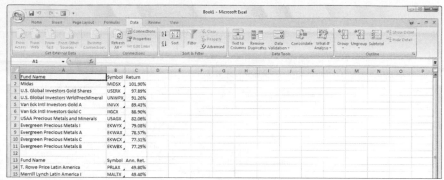

Figure 2-11:
New
worksheet
after
importing
the top 1-, 3-,
and 5-year
mutual fund
performers.

Retrieving data from text files

If you have a text file containing data you need to bring into your worksheet, you can import it by clicking the From Text command button on the Ribbon's Data tab (Alt+AFT) and then selecting the file to use in the Import Text File dialog box. After you select the text file containing the data you need to retrieve in this dialog box and click its Import button, Excel opens the first dialog box of the Text Import Wizard, which you can then use to tell Excel how to split up (or *parse*) its data into separate cells of the worksheet.

Most text files containing lists of related data use some sort of standard character to separate each data item (such as a comma or tab) in every line, just as it uses the character for the Enter key to mark the separation of each line of data within the file. Those text files that use the comma to separate data items are known as *CSV files* (for Comma Separated Values). Those that use tabs to separate the individual data items are known as *Tab delimited* files. Note that some programs use the generic term, *delimited files,* to refer to any text file that uses a standard character, such as a comma or tab, to separate its individual data items.

The Text Import Wizard uses these facts about text files to analyze the structure of incoming text files to help you to determine how to parse the data in the text file. Because the Text Import Wizard always imports the parsed text data into the current worksheet starting at the active cell and then uses as many subsequent columns and rows as necessary, you should always select an empty cell at the beginning of a blank region in the worksheet (or better yet, in a blank worksheet) before you invoke the Text Import Wizard. That way, you never run the risk of the incoming text file data wiping out existing data in the worksheet.

Figure 2-12 illustrates how the Text Import Wizard works and can help you to successfully import a text file that consists of a data list into an Excel worksheet. This figure shows the Text Import Wizard — Step 1 of 3 dialog box that first appears when you try to open a text file from the Import Text File dialog box.

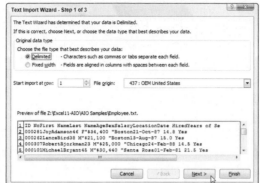

Figure 2-12:
First of three
Text Import
Wizard
dialog boxes
for parsing a
text file.

As this figure shows, Excel has analyzed the data and determined that it uses
some sort of delimiting character. If you're dealing with a text file in which
the data items all use the same number of characters (such as 11 spaces for
SSN and 10 spaces for ID number), click the Fixed Width option button.

The Text Import Wizard always assumes that you want to start importing the
data from the first to the very last line in the text file. If you don't need the
first line or lines imported (because they contain data, such as titles, that
you'd only have to eliminate from the worksheet if you did bring them in),
use the preview list box to determine the number of the first line to import
and then enter that number in the Start Import at Row text box or use its
spinner buttons to select this number.

Figure 2-13 shows the second Text Import Wizard dialog box that appears
when you click the Next> button in the Step 1 of 3 dialog box. As you can
see, the Text Import Wizard — Step 2 of 3 dialog box contains a Data Preview
section that shows your text data aligned (simulating their column arrangement in your Excel worksheet).

In the Step 2 of 3 dialog box, you need to select the delimiting character in
the event that the wizard selects the wrong character in the Delimiters section. If your text file uses a custom delimiting character, you need to click
the Other check box and then enter that character in its text box. If your file
uses two consecutive characters (such as a comma and a space), you need
to click their check boxes as well as the Treat Consecutive Delimiters As One
check box.

By default, the Text Import Wizard treats any characters enclosed in a pair of
double quotes as text entries (as opposed to numbers). If your text file uses
a single quote, click the single quote (') character in the Text Qualifier drop-
down list box.

Figure 2-13:
Second of
three Text
Import
Wizard
dialog boxes
for parsing
the text file.

Figure 2-14 shows you the third Text Import Wizard dialog box that appears
when you click the Next button in the Step 2 of 3 dialog box. In the Step 3 of
3 dialog box, you get to assign a data format to the various columns of text
data or indicate that a particular column of data should be skipped and
therefore not imported into your Excel worksheet.

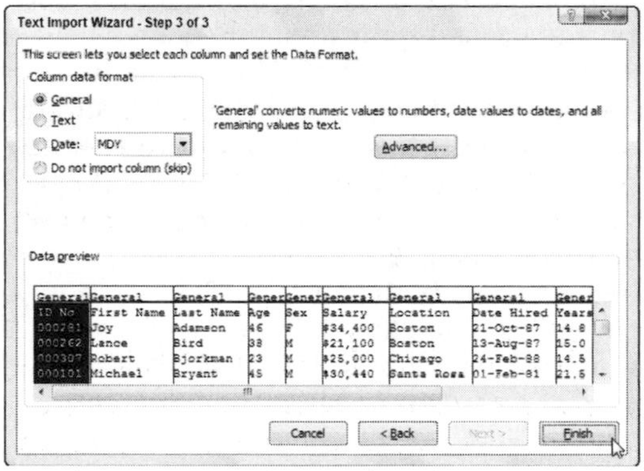

Figure 2-14:
Third of
three Text
Import
Wizard
dialog boxes
for parsing
the text file.

When setting data formats for the columns of the text file, you can choose
among the following three data types:

✦ **General** (the default) to convert all numeric values to numbers, entries recognized as date values to dates, and everything else in the column to text.

✦ **Text** to convert all the entries in the column to text.

✦ **Date** to convert all the entries to dates by using the date format shown
in the associated drop-down list box.

To assign one of the three data types to a column, click its column in the Data Preview section and then click the appropriate radio button (General, Text, or Date) in the Column Data Format section in the upper-right corner.

In determining values when using the General data format, Excel uses the period (.) as the decimal separator and the comma (,) as the thousands separator. If you're dealing with data that uses these two symbols in just the opposite way (the comma for the decimal and the period for the thousands separator), as is the case in many European countries, click the Advanced button in the Step 3 of 3 dialog box to open the Advanced Text Import Settings dialog box. There, click the comma (,) in the Decimal Separator drop-down list box and the period (.) in the Thousands Separator drop-down list box before you click OK. If your text file uses trailing minus signs (as in 100–) to represent negative numbers (as in –100), make sure that the Trailing Minus for Negative Numbers check box contains a check mark.

If you want to change the date format for a column to which you've assigned the Date data format, click its M-D-Y code in the Date drop-down list box (where *M* stands for the month, *D* for the day, and *Y* for the year).

To skip the importing of a particular column, click it in the Data Preview and then click the Do Not Import Column (Skip) option button at the bottom of the Column Data Format section.

After you have all the columns formatted as you want, click the Finish button to import and parse the text file data starting at the current cell. Figure 2-15 shows the rows of the imported and parsed text data that appeared in the new worksheet starting at cell A1 when I clicked the Finish button in the Text Import Wizard — Step 3 of 3 dialog box.

Querying data from other data sources

Database tables created and maintained with Microsoft Office Access are not, of course, the only external database sources on which you can perform external data queries. To import data from other sources, you click the From Other Sources button on the Data tab or press Alt+AFO to open a drop-down menu with the following options:

✦ **From SQL Server** to import data from an SQL server table.

✦ **From Analysis Services** to import data from an SQL Server Analysis cube.

✦ **From XML Data Import** to import data from an XML file that you open and map.

✦ **From Data Connection Wizard** to import data from a database table using the Data Connection Wizard that follows the OLEDB (Object Linked Embedded Database) standards.

✦ **From Microsoft Query** to import data from a database table using Microsoft Query that follows the ODBC (Open DataBase Connectivity) standards.

Book VI
Chapter 2

Filtering and
Querying a Data List

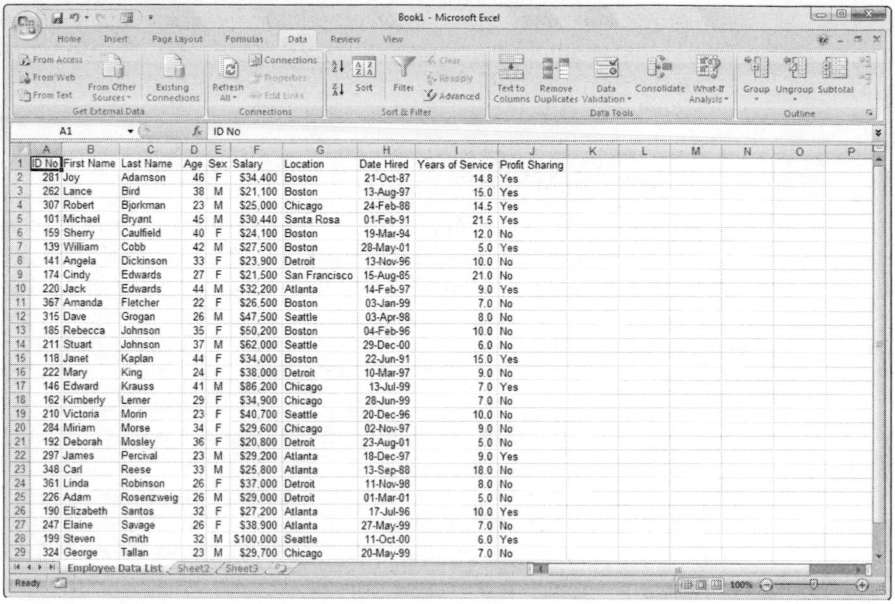

ID No	First Name	Last Name	Age	Sex	Salary	Location	Date Hired	Years of Service	Profit Sharing
281	Joy	Adamson	46	F	$34,400	Boston	21-Oct-87	14.8	Yes
262	Lance	Bird	38	M	$21,100	Boston	13-Aug-97	15.0	Yes
307	Robert	Bjorkman	23	M	$25,000	Chicago	24-Feb-88	14.5	Yes
101	Michael	Bryant	45	M	$30,440	Santa Rosa	01-Feb-91	21.5	Yes
159	Sherry	Caulfield	40	F	$24,100	Boston	19-Mar-94	12.0	No
139	William	Cobb	42	M	$27,500	Boston	28-May-01	5.0	Yes
141	Angela	Dickinson	33	F	$23,900	Detroit	13-Nov-96	10.0	No
174	Cindy	Edwards	27	F	$21,500	San Francisco	15-Aug-85	21.0	No
220	Jack	Edwards	44	M	$32,200	Atlanta	14-Feb-97	9.0	Yes
367	Amanda	Fletcher	22	F	$26,500	Boston	03-Jan-99	7.0	No
315	Dave	Grogan	26	M	$47,500	Seattle	03-Apr-98	8.0	No
185	Rebecca	Johnson	35	F	$50,200	Boston	04-Feb-96	10.0	No
211	Stuart	Johnson	37	M	$62,000	Seattle	29-Dec-00	6.0	No
118	Janet	Kaplan	44	F	$34,000	Boston	22-Jun-91	15.0	Yes
222	Mary	King	24	F	$38,000	Detroit	10-Mar-97	9.0	No
146	Edward	Krauss	41	M	$86,200	Chicago	13-Jul-99	7.0	Yes
162	Kimberly	Lerner	29	F	$34,900	Chicago	28-Jun-99	7.0	No
210	Victoria	Morin	23	F	$40,700	Seattle	20-Dec-96	10.0	No
284	Miriam	Morse	34	F	$29,600	Chicago	02-Nov-97	9.0	No
192	Deborah	Mosley	36	F	$20,800	Detroit	23-Aug-01	5.0	No
297	James	Percival	23	M	$29,200	Atlanta	18-Dec-97	9.0	Yes
348	Carl	Reese	33	M	$25,800	Atlanta	13-Sep-88	18.0	No
361	Linda	Robinson	26	F	$37,000	Detroit	11-Nov-98	8.0	No
226	Adam	Rosenzweig	26	M	$29,000	Detroit	01-Mar-01	5.0	No
190	Elizabeth	Santos	32	F	$27,200	Atlanta	17-Jul-96	10.0	Yes
247	Elaine	Savage	26	F	$38,900	Atlanta	27-May-99	7.0	No
199	Steven	Smith	32	M	$100,000	Seattle	11-Oct-00	6.0	Yes
324	George	Tallan	23	M	$29,700	Chicago	20-May-99	7.0	No

Figure 2-15: New worksheet with data after opening the parsed text file.

Retrieving external data with Microsoft Query

To retrieve data from an external database using Microsoft Query, you must complete two procedures. In the first procedure, you define the data source, that is, the database that contains the data you want to query. In the second procedure, you specify the data query itself, including all the columns of data that you want extracted along with the criteria for selecting particular records.

Creating a new data source definition

To perform the first procedure that creates the new data source, follow these steps:

1. **Click the From Other Sources command button on the Ribbon's Data tab or press Alt+AFO and then click From Microsoft Query on its drop-down menu.**

   The first time you do this, Excel displays an Alert dialog box stating that the Microsoft Query feature is not currently installed and asking if you want to install this feature now. Click Yes to have Excel install this feature (remember that you must have your Office 2007 DVD handy or be able to specify the path on your company's network where the necessary files are stored in order to do this).

After Microsoft Query is installed on your system, the Choose Data Source dialog box, shown in Figure 2-16, appears with the <New Data Source> item at the top of the list box on the Databases tab automatically selected.

2. **Click OK to accept the default <New Data Source> setting in the Choose Data Source dialog box.**

   This action opens the Create New Data Source dialog box where you need to name your new database query and specify the driver to be used in accessing the external database.

Figure 2-16: Using the Choose Data Source dialog box to create a new database query.

3. **Enter a descriptive name for the database query in the What Name Do You Want to Give Your New Data Source text box.**

   By naming the data source definition, you can reuse it without having to go through all these tedious steps for defining it. Next, you need to select a driver for your data source in the Select a Driver for the Type of Database You Want to Access drop-down list box. This list contains drivers for all the most popular PC databases, such as Access, dBASE, Paradox, and FoxPro, as well as an SQL driver for sophisticated database management systems, such as dB2 and an OBDC Oracle driver for querying an Oracle database (to name a few).

4. **Click the name of the driver to be used in the Select a Driver for the Type of Database You Want to Access drop-down list box.**

   Now you're ready to select the database to be accessed.

5. **Click the Connect button in the Create New Data Source dialog box.**

   This action opens a dialog box where you can select the database to be used. For example, if you select Microsoft Access Driver (*.mdb) as the driver in the Create New Data Source dialog box, Excel opens an ODBC Microsoft Access Setup dialog box.

6. Click the Select button, locate the folder that contains the database file that you want to query in the Select Database dialog box, and then click OK.

After you've selected the database to work with, you have completed the first major step of specifying the data source to use in your external query.

7. Click OK in the Setup dialog box for the type of database that you're accessing.

This action returns you to the Create New Data Source dialog box (shown in Figure 2-17), which now displays the name of the database that you selected. If you want, you can specify a default table to use in the database and, if you had to specify a user name and password to gain access to the database, you can have this information saved as part of the data source definition.

8. (Optional) Click the name of the default table in the Select a Default Table for Your Data Source (Optional) drop-down list box and click the Save My User ID and Password in the Data Source Definition check box to save this information.

Now you're ready to close the Create New Data dialog box and return to the Choose Data Source dialog box from which you can perform the second procedure of specifying your database query.

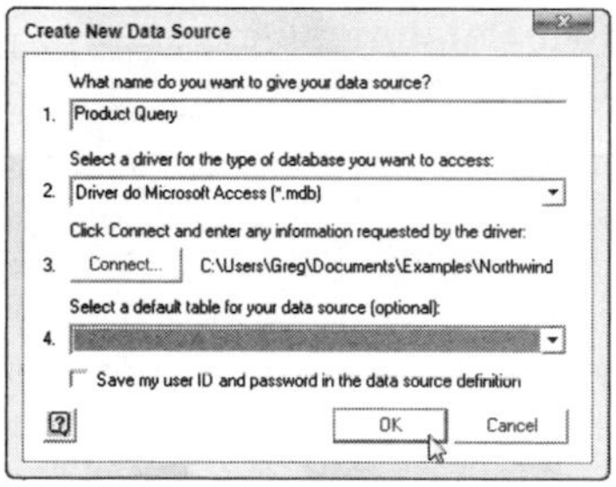

Figure 2-17:
Creating a
new data
source for
the external
database
query.

9. Click the OK button in the Create a New Data Source dialog box.

This action closes the Create a New Data Source dialog box, returning you to the Choose Data Source dialog box where the name that you've given to the data source definition that you've just completed appears selected.

Specifying the database query

Now that you've finished the data source definition, you can use it with the Query Wizard to specify which fields in the database to acquire. At this point, the Choose Data Source dialog box is still open and the name of your new data source definition is selected along with the Use the Query Wizard to Create/Edit Queries check box.

To perform the second procedure in which you specify the conditions of the query by using your new data source definition, follow these steps:

1. **Make sure that the name of your data source is highlighted on the Databases tab and the Use the Query Wizard to Create/Edit Queries check box has a check mark in it and then click OK in the Choose Data Source dialog box.**

This action closes the Choose Data Source dialog box and opens the Query Wizard — Choose Columns dialog box, similar to the one shown in Figure 2-18. This dialog box contains two list boxes: the Available Tables and Columns list box on the left side and the Columns in Your Query list box on the right side.

To select the fields that you want to acquire, click the Expand button (+) in front of the name of each table in the external database that contains fields that you want. Then, click the name of the field followed by the > button to copy the field name to the Columns in Your Query list box. To preview the data in that field, click the Preview Now button when the field name is selected in the Columns in Your Query list box.

Figure 2-18:
Specifying
the fields to
acquire in
the new
external
database
query.

Note that the order in which you add the fields determines their column order in your Excel worksheet. To change the order after copying the fields to the Columns in Your Query list box, click the field and then click the button to the right with the triangle pointing upward to promote the field in the list, or click the button with the triangle pointing down to demote it in the list.

2. **Select the fields that you want to use in the Available Tables and Columns list box on the left and then copy them to the Columns in Your Query list box on the right.**

After you finish selecting the fields to use in the query, you're ready to move on to the next dialog box in the Query Wizard where you specify how the data is to be filtered.

3. Click Next to open the Query Wizard — Filter Data dialog box.

To set up the criteria by which records are selected in the Filter Data dialog box (similar to the one shown in Figure 2-19), click the field for which you want to set criteria and then click the criteria to use in the drop-down list box on the left and the value to be evaluated in the combo box on the right.

Figure 2-19:
Specifying how the data are to be filtered in the new external database query.

The criteria available in the drop-down list boxes on the left are the same as those used with the Custom AutoFilter (see the "Custom Auto-Filter at your service" section previously in this chapter for details) with the exception of the "like" and "not like" and "is Null" and "is Not Null" operators, which are not available when setting criteria for the Custom AutoFilter ("like" refers to entries that sound like one that you enter in the associated combo box on the right and "Null" refers to empty entries in the field).

When entering the values to be evaluated in the associated combo boxes on the right side of the Filter Data dialog box, you can use the question mark (?) and asterisk (*) wildcard characters (question marks for single characters and the asterisk for multiple characters) in the text that you enter in these boxes. You can also select data entries in a field from which to compare to by clicking them in the drop-down list.

To set up an AND condition, make sure that the AND option button is selected when you specify the second and even third set of filtering criteria (remember that, in an AND condition, records are selected only when all sets of criteria are TRUE). To set up a logical OR condition, click the Or option button before you specify the second or even third set of criteria (remember that, in an OR condition, records are selected when any one of the sets of criteria are TRUE).

Note that if you want to acquire all data in a selected field, you don't specify any filtering criteria for that field in the Filter Data dialog box.

4. **Specify the filtering criteria, including any AND and OR condition, in the criteria drop-down list boxes on the left and evaluation combo boxes on the right for each field that should be filtered in the Column to Filter list box.**

   After you finish specifying the filtering to be used on the fields, you're ready to specify the order in which matching records are to be sorted.

5. **Click the Next button to open the Query Wizard — Sort Order dialog box.**

   To sort the data that you acquire in the external database query, click the name of the field in the Sort By drop-down list box and then select either the Ascending (default) or Descending option button (see Figure 2-20). To sort any duplicates in the field that you specify as the primary sorting key, you select the tie-breaking field for the secondary key in the Then By drop-down list box and then select between its Ascending (default) and Descending option buttons.

   You repeat this procedure to sort the incoming data on up to three fields. If you don't want the data sorted, click the Next button without selecting any fields as sorting keys.

6. **Specify the field or fields on which the external data is to be sorted and then click the Next button.**

   Clicking Next opens the Query Wizard — Finish dialog box shown in Figure 2-21. This dialog box contains several options that you can choose from in completing the query. You can return the data to the current or a new worksheet by leaving the Return Data to Microsoft Excel option button selected. You can view the data and/or edit the query in the Microsoft Query dialog box by clicking the View Data or Edit Query in Microsoft Query option button.

   You can also save your new query by selecting the Save Query button in the Query Wizard — Finish dialog box. When you do this, Excel saves it as a separate query file (indicated by the `.dqy` file extension) so that you can reuse the query from any workbook file. Note that Excel automatically saves the data source definition as a file (indicated by the `.dsn`) when you next save the current workbook but not the query.

7. **Click the Save Query button and then enter the filename for the new query file in the Save As dialog box before you click the Save button.**

   If you want to see the data and review your query before you bring it into your Excel worksheet, you click the View Data or Edit Query in Microsoft Query option button before you click OK in the Query Wizard — Finish dialog box. When you do this, Excel opens a Microsoft Query window similar to the one shown in Figure 2-22 where you can preview the way the acquired data will appear when you bring it into Excel. You can also edit the database query in this window.

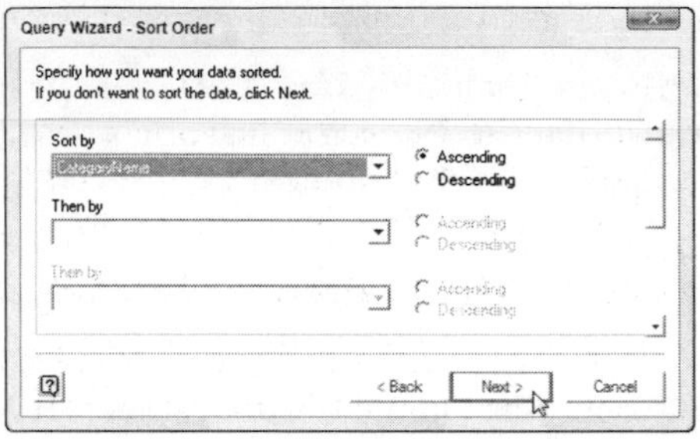

Figure 2-20:
Specifying how the data are to be sorted in the new external database query.

Figure 2-21:
Selecting the options in the Query Wizard — Finish dialog box.

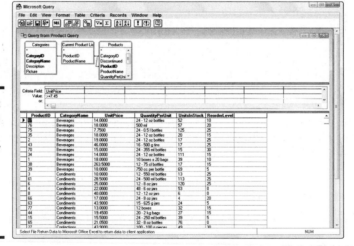

Figure 2-22:
Viewing the data to be acquired by the query in the Microsoft Query window.

8. **(Optional) Click the View Data or Edit Query in Microsoft Query option button and then click the Finish button to open the Microsoft Query window showing the fields and records to be acquired by the query along with the filtering criteria.**

After you finish viewing the data in the Microsoft Query window, you can click its Close button. Doing this opens the Import Data dialog box described in Step 9.

The Import Data dialog box is also displayed when you click the Finish button when the Return Data to Microsoft Excel option button is selected in the Query Wizard — Finish dialog box, which is described in Step 9.

9. **Click the Finish button in the Query Wizard — Finish dialog box.**

This action closes this dialog box and opens the Import Data dialog box (shown in Figure 2-23). Here, you indicate where you want to put the data acquired from the external database.

By default, the Table option is selected to import the data as a simple data list, the Existing Worksheet option button is selected, and cell A1 is designated as the start of this list's range. To import the external data as a new pivot table (see Book VII, Chapter 2), click the PivotTable Report option button. To import the data as a new pivot table and pivot chart , click the PivotChart and PivotTable Report option button. To change the starting cell, click it in the worksheet. To import the data into a brand-new worksheet in the current workbook, click the New Worksheet option button instead.

10. **Indicate how you want to view the data and where you want the data imported during the query and then click OK to start importing the data.**

As soon as you click OK, Excel executes the database query and acquires the data from the external database (see Figure 2-24). After the program finishes importing all the records that match your filtering criteria (when the Table option is selected), the program also displays the Table Tools contextual tab and selects its sole Design tab. You can use the command buttons on the Design tab to further format the table (by selecting a new table style in the Table Styles gallery), refresh the data by performing the query again (with the Refresh command button), or summarize the data list by creating a pivot table for it (with the Summarize with Pivot command button).

Figure 2-23:
Indicating
where to put
the queried
data in the
Import Data
dialog box.

After you've saved a data query, you can use it to connect to an external database and to acquire its data according to the query's parameters. To do this, click the Existing Connections command button on the Data tab of the Ribbon (or press Alt+AX) to open the Existing Connections dialog box and there click the descriptive name given to your query before you click the Open button.

After you perform an external query using Microsoft Query that extracts the data as a table, you can use the following command buttons on the Design tab of the Table Tools contextual tab:

✦ **Table Name** text box to change the name of the data table containing the external data.

✦ **Resize Table** command button to select a new data range for the data retrieved by the external query.

✦ **Summarize with PivotTable** command button to open the Create PivotTable dialog box that enables you to create a new pivot table using the data retrieved by the external query (see Book VII, Chapter 2).

✦ **Convert to Range** command button to convert the data table containing the external data into a regular range of data (which removes the Auto-Filter buttons and table formatting).

✦ **Export** command button to export the external data to a SharePoint list (see Book IV, Chapter 4) or a Visio diagram.

✦ **Refresh** command button to have Excel redo the query and automatically update the data table according to any changes made to the external database table(s).

✦ **Properties** command button to open the External Data Properties dialog box where you can change formatting and layout options for the data retrieved in the worksheet.

✦ **Open in Browser** command button to open the external data as a table in your computer's Web browser.

✦ **Unlink** command button to sever a link between the data retrieved in the worksheet by the external query and its original data source on a server so that the data are no longer automatically kept up-to-date.

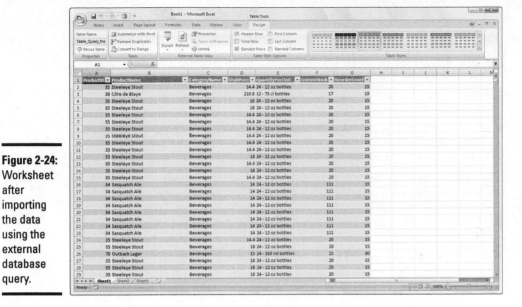

Figure 2-24:
Worksheet
after
importing
the data
using the
external
database
query.

Book VII
Data Analysis

The 5th Wave   By Rich Tennant

"I started running 'what-if' scenarios on my spreadsheet, like, 'What if I were sick of this dirtwad job and funneled some of the company's money into an off-shore account?'"

Contents at a Glance

Chapter 1: Performing What-If Scenarios

In This Chapter

✔ Doing what-if analysis in one- and two-variable data tables

✔ Creating and playing with different scenarios

✔ Performing goal seeking

✔ Using the Solver utility

*B*ecause electronic spreadsheets are so good at updating their results by automatically recalculating their formulas based on new input, they have long been used (and sometimes, misused) to create financial projections based on all sorts of assumptions. Under the guise of what-if analysis, you will often find the number crunchers of the company using Excel as their crystal ball for projecting the results of all sorts of harebrained schemes designed to make the company a fast million bucks.

As you start dabbling in this form of electronic fortune-telling, keep in mind that the projections you get back from this type of analysis are only as good as your assumptions. So when the results of what-if analysis tell you that you're going be richer than King Midas after undertaking this new business venture, you still need to ask yourself whether the original assumptions on which these glowing projections are based fit in with real-world marketing conditions. In other words, when the worksheet tells you that you can make a million bucks of pure profit by selling your lead-lined boxer shorts, you still have to question how many men really need that kind of protection and are willing to pay for it.

In Excel, what-if analysis comes in a fairly wide variety of flavors (some of which are more complicated than others). In this chapter, I introduce you to three simple and straightforward methods:

✦ *Data tables* enable you to see how changing one or two variables affect the bottom line (for example, you may want to know what happens to the net profit if you fall into a 45 percent tax bracket, a 60 percent tax bracket, and so on).

✦ *Goal seeking* enables you to find out what it takes to reach a predetermined objective, such as how much you have to sell to make a $20 million profit this year.

✦ *Scenarios* let you set up and test a wide variety of cases, all the way from the best-case scenario (profits grow by 20 percent) to the worst-case scenario (you don't make any profit).

At the end of the chapter, I introduce you to the Solver add-in utility, which enables you to find solutions to more complex what-if problems involving multiple variables. You can use the Solver to help you with classic resource problems, such as finding the correct product mix in order to maximize your profits, staffing to minimize your general costs, and routing to minimize transportation costs.

Using Data Tables

In an Excel spreadsheet, you can see the effect of changing an input value on the result returned by a formula as soon as you enter a new input value in the cell that feeds into the formula. Each time you change this input value, Excel automatically recalculates the formula and shows you the new result based on the new value. This method is of limited use, however, when you are performing what-if analysis and need to be able to see the range of results produced by using a series of different input values in the same worksheet so that you can compare them to each other.

To perform this type of what-if analysis, you can use Excel's Data Table command. When creating a data table, you enter a series of input values in the worksheet, and Excel uses each value in the formula that you specify. When Excel is finished computing the data table, you see the results produced by each change in the input values in a single range of the worksheet. You can then save the data table as part of the worksheet if you need to keep a record of the results of a series of input values.

When creating data tables, you can create a one-variable or a two-variable data table. In a one-variable data table, Excel substitutes a series of different values for a single input value in a formula. In a two-variable data table, Excel substitutes a series of different values for two input values in a formula.

Creating a one-variable data table

To create a one-variable data table, you need to set up the master formula in your worksheet and then, in a different range of the worksheet, enter the series of different values that you want substituted for a single input value in that formula. Figures 1-1 and 1-2 demonstrate how this is done.

In Figure 1-1, cell B5 contains a simple formula for computing the projected sales for 2008, assuming an annual growth rate of 1.75% over the annual sales in 2007. The 2008 projected sales in this cell are calculated with the following formula:

```
=Sales_07+(Sales_07*Growth_08)
```

This formula adds cell B2 (named Sales_07) to the contents of B2 multiplied by the growth rate of 1.75% in cell B3 (named Growth_08). Cell B5 shows you that, assuming an annual growth rate of 1.75% in the year 2008, you can project total sales of $890,312.50.

But what if the growth rate in 2008 is not as low as 1.75%, or what if the growth rate is even (heaven forbid) lower than anticipated? To create the one-variable table to answer these questions, you first bring forward the master formula in cell B5 to cell C7 with the formula = B5. Then, you enter the series of different growth rates as the input values in column B, starting in cell B8 (cell B7, at the intersection of the row with the master formula and the column with the input values, must be left blank in a one-variable data table). This series of input values for the data table can be created with the AutoFill feature (see Book II, Chapter 1 for details). In this example, a data series that increments each succeeding value by 0.5% percent is created in the cell range B8:B17, starting at 1 percent and ending at 5.5% percent.

After bringing the formula in cell B5 forward to cell C7 with the formula =B5 and generating the growth rate series in the cell range B8:B17, you then select the cell range B7:C17 and click the What-If Analysis command button in the Data Tools group on the Data tab and then click Data Table on its drop-down menu (or press Alt+AWT) to open the Data Table dialog box shown in Figure 1-1.

In this dialog box, you specify the row input cell in the Row Input Cell text box and/or the column input cell in the Column Input Cell text box. The cell that you designate as the row or column input cell in the Table dialog box must correspond to the cell in the worksheet that contains the original input value that is fed into the master formula.

In the data table in this example, you need to designate only B3 as the column input cell. (In the case of Figure 1-1, when you click this cell or use an arrow key to select this cell, Excel enters the absolute cell reference, as in $B$3.) You choose cell B3 because this is the cell that contains the growth rate value used in the master formula.

After indicating the row or column input cells, Excel computes the data table when you click the OK button. In this example, the program creates the data table by substituting each input value in the data series in the range B8:B17 into the column input cell B3. The value of cell B3 is then used in the master formula to calculate a new result, which is entered in the corresponding cell in the cell range C8:C17. After the program has finished calculating the data table, Excel returns the original value to the row or column input cell (in this case, 1.75% in cell B3).

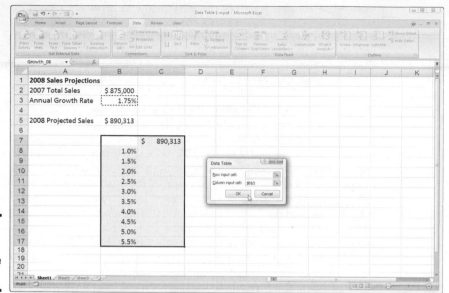

Figure 1-1:
Creating a
one-variable
data table.

Figure 1-2 shows the completed data table. Here, you can see at a glance how changing a half percentage point for the growth rate affects the projected sales for 2008. After creating the data table, you can then format the results and save the table as part of the worksheet.

If you want to see how using a different range of variables affects the results in the table, you only need to enter the new input values in the existing range. By default, Excel automatically recalculates the results in the output range of a data table whenever you change any of its input values. If you want to control when each data table is recalculated, while still allowing the formulas in the worksheet to be automatically recalculated, click the Automatic Except Data Tables option on the Options command button on the Formulas tab (Alt+MXE).

Excel computes the results in a data table by creating an array formula that uses the TABLE function (see Book III, Chapter 1, for more information on array formulas). In this example, the array formula entered into the cell range C8:C17 is as follows:

```
{=TABLE(,B3)}
```

The TABLE function can take two arguments, *row_ref* and/or *column_ref,* which represent the row input cell and column input cell for the data table, respectively. In this example, the data table uses only a column input cell, so B3 is the second and only argument of the TABLE function. Because Excel enters the results in a data table by using an array formula, Excel won't allow you to clear individual result cells in its output range. If you try to delete a single result in the data table, Excel displays an Alert dialog box, stating that you can't change part of a table.

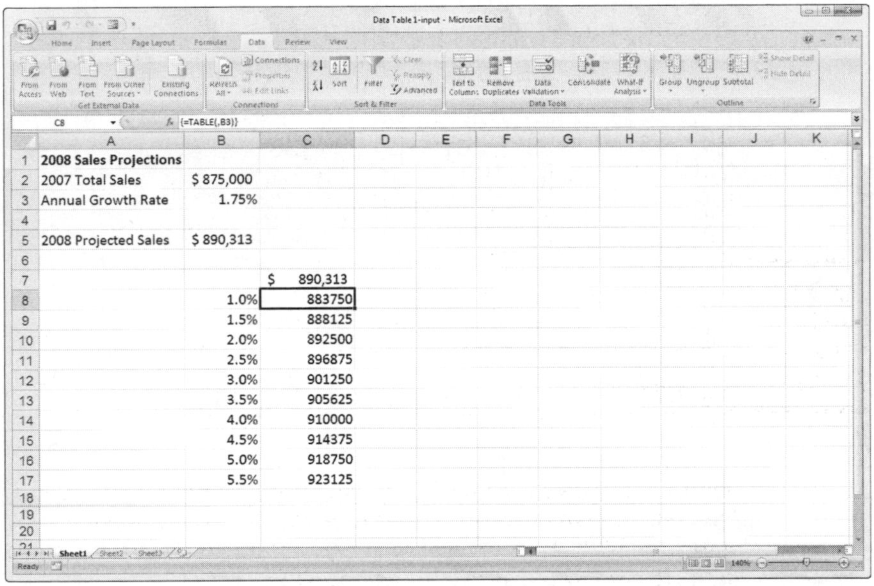

Figure 1-2: The completed one-variable data table.

	A	B	C
1	2008 Sales Projections		
2	2007 Total Sales	$ 875,000	
3	Annual Growth Rate	1.75%	
4			
5	2008 Projected Sales	$ 890,313	
6			
7			$ 890,313
8		1.0%	883750
9		1.5%	888125
10		2.0%	892500
11		2.5%	896875
12		3.0%	901250
13		3.5%	905625
14		4.0%	910000
15		4.5%	914375
16		5.0%	918750
17		5.5%	923125

If you want to delete just the results in the output range of a data table, you must select all the cells in the output range (cell range C8:C17, in the current example) before you press the Delete key or click the Clear All option on the Clear button's drop-down menu (or press Alt+HEA).

Creating a two-variable data table

When you have a master formula in a worksheet in which you want to see the effect of changing two of its input values, you create a two-variable data table. When you create a two-variable data table, you enter two ranges of input values to be substituted in the master formula: a single-row range in the first row of the table and a single-column range in the first column of the data table. When you create a two-variable data table, you place a copy of the master formula in the cell at the intersection of this row and column of input values.

Figure 1-3 shows the typical setup for a two-variable data table. This figure uses the projected sales worksheet shown previously in the section on a one-variable data table. Here, however, a second variable has been added to projecting the total sales in 2008. This worksheet contains a value in cell B4 (named Expenses_08) that shows the projected percentage of expenses to sales, which is used, in turn, in the master formula in cell B5 as follows:

```
=Sales_07+(Sales_07*Growth_05)-(Sales_07*Expenses_08)
```

Note that when you factor in the expenses, the projected sales at an annual growth rate of 1.75% falls in cell B5 from $890,312.50 to $864,062.50.

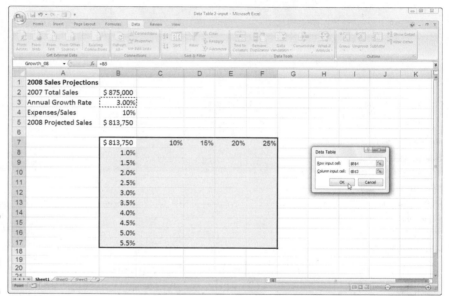

Figure 1-3:
Creating a
two-variable
data table.

To determine how changing both the growth rate and the percentage of expenses to sales will affect the projected sales for 2008, you create a two-variable data table. In setting up this table, you still enter the variable growth rates down column B in the cell range B8:B17. Then, you enter the variable expense rates across row 7 in the range C7:G7. This time, you bring forward the master formula by entering the formula **=B5** in cell B7, the cell at the intersection of the row and column containing the two input variables.

After setting up the two series of variables in this manner, you are ready to create the table by selecting the cell range B7:G17 and opening the Table dialog box, as shown in Figure 1-3. For a two-variable data table, you must designate both a row input and column cell in the worksheet. In this example, the row input cell is B4, which contains the original expense-to-sales percentage, while the column input cell remains B3, which contains the original growth rate. After these two input cells are entered in the Table dialog box, you are ready to generate the data table by clicking the OK button.

Figure 1-4 shows the completed two-variable data table with the results of changing both the projected growth rate and the projected expenses. As with a one-variable data table, you can save this two-variable data table as part of your worksheet. You can also update the table by changing any of the (two types) input variables.

	A	B	C	D	E	F
1	**2008 Sales Projections**					
2	2007 Total Sales	$ 875,000				
3	Annual Growth Rate	3.00%				
4	Expenses/Sales	10%				
5	2008 Projected Sales	$ 813,750				
6						
7		$ 813,750	10%	15%	20%	25%
8		1.0%	796250	752500	708750	665000
9		1.5%	800625	756875	713125	669375
10		2.0%	805000	761250	717500	673750
11		2.5%	809375	765625	721875	678125
12		3.0%	813750	770000	726250	682500
13		3.5%	818125	774375	730625	686875
14		4.0%	822500	778750	735000	691250
15		4.5%	826875	783125	739375	695625
16		5.0%	831250	787500	743750	700000
17		5.5%	835625	791875	748125	704375

Figure 1-4:
The completed two-variable data table.

The array formula entered in the output range (C8:G17) to create this two-variable data table is very similar to the one created previously for the one-variable data table, only this time the TABLE function uses both a *row_ref* and *column_ref* argument as follows:

```
{=TABLE(B4,B3)}
```

Remember that because this data table used an array formula, you must select all the cells in the output range if you want to delete them.

Exploring Different Scenarios

Excel enables you to create and save sets of input values that produce different results as *scenarios* with the Scenario Manager option on the What-If Analysis button's drop-down menu on the Data tab of the Ribbon. A scenario consists of a group of input values in a worksheet to which you assign a name,

**Book VII
Chapter 1**

Performing What-If
Scenarios

such as *Best Case, Worst Case, Most Likely Case,* and so on. Then, to reuse the input data and view the results that they produce in the worksheet, you simply select the name of the scenario that you want to use, and Excel applies the input values stored in that scenario to the appropriate cells in the worksheet. After creating your different scenarios for a worksheet, you can also use the Scenario Manager to create a summary report showing both the input values stored in each scenario and the key results produced by each.

Creating new scenarios

When creating a scenario for your worksheet, you create a spreadsheet that uses certain cells that change in each scenario (appropriately enough, called *changing cells*). To make it easier to identify the changing cells in each scenario that you create (especially in any scenario summary reports that you generate), you should assign range names to the variables in the spreadsheet with the Name a Range or Create from Selection command buttons on the Formulas tab of the Ribbon before you create your scenarios.

To create your scenarios with the Scenario Manager, follow these steps:

1. **Select the changing cells in the spreadsheet; that is, the cells whose values vary in each of your scenarios.**

   Remember that you can select nonadjacent cells in the worksheet by holding down the Ctrl key as you click them.

2. **Click the What-If Analysis command button on the Ribbon's Data tab and then click Scenario Manager on its drop-down menu or press Alt+AWS.**

   This action opens the Scenario Manager dialog box, similar to the one shown in Figure 1-5.

3. **Click the Add button in the Scenario Manager dialog box.**

   This action opens the Add Scenario dialog box, similar to the one shown in Figure 1-6. The Add Scenario dialog box contains a Scenario Name text box, where you give the new scenario a descriptive name such as *Best Case, Most Likely Case,* and so on. This dialog box also contains a Changing Cells text box that contains the addresses of the variable cells that you selected in the worksheet and a Comment box that contains a note with your name and the current date, so you'll always know when you created the particular scenario.

4. **Type a descriptive name for the new scenario in the Scenario Name text box.**

   Now, you should check over the cell references in the Changing Cells text box to make sure that they're correct. You can modify them if necessary by clicking the Changing Cells text box and then by clicking the cells in the worksheet while holding down the Ctrl key. You can also edit the note in the Comment box if you want to add more information about your assumptions as part of the new scenario.

Figure 1-5: Using the Scenario Manager to set up different sales forecast scenarios.

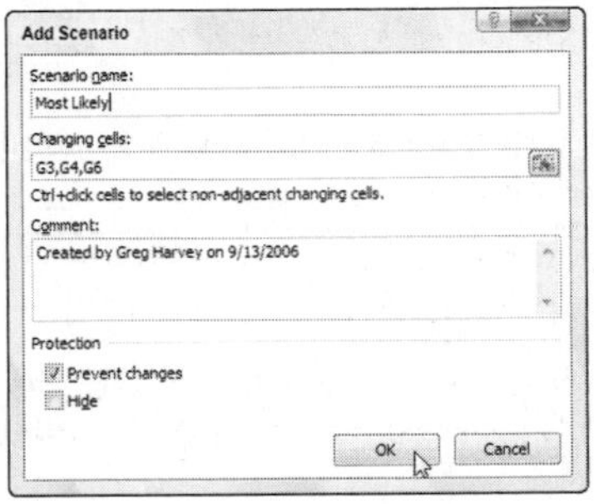

Figure 1-6: Adding a new Best Case scenario for the sales forecast.

By default, Excel protects a scenario from changes when you turn on protection for the worksheet (see Book IV, Chapter 1, for details) so that you can't edit or delete the scenario in any way. If you want Excel to hide the scenario as well when worksheet protection is turned on, click the Hide check box. If you don't want to protect or hide the scenario when worksheet protection is turned on, click the Prevent Changes check box to remove its check mark, and leave the Hide check box as it is.

5. **In the Protection section of the Add Scenario dialog box, choose what kind of scenario protection that you need, if any, with the Prevent Changes and Hide check boxes.**

Now you're ready to specify the changing values for the new scenario.

6. **Click OK in the Add Scenario dialog box.**

This action closes the Add Scenario dialog box and then opens the Scenario Values dialog box, similar to the one shown in Figure 1-7. The

Scenario Values dialog box numbers and shows the range name (assuming that you named each of the cells), followed by the current value for each of the changing values that you selected in the worksheet before starting to define different scenarios for your spreadsheet.

You can accept the values shown in the text box for each changing cell if it suits the current scenario that you're defining, or you can increase or decrease any or all of them as needed to reflect the scenario's assumptions.

7. **Check the values in each changing cell's text box and modify the values as needed.**

Now you're ready to close the Scenario Values dialog box, which completes the definition of the new scenario.

8. **Click the Add button in the Scenario Values dialog box.**

This action closes the Scenario Values dialog box and returns you to the Add Scenario dialog box, where you can define a new scenario name for the changing cells.

9. **Repeat Steps 4 to 7 to add all the other scenarios that you want to create.**

After you finish defining all the different scenarios you want to apply to the changing values in the spreadsheet, you can close the Scenario Values dialog box and then return to the Scenario Manager dialog box where you can use the Show button to see how using different sets of changing values affects your spreadsheet.

10. **Click OK in the Add Values dialog box and then click the Close button in the Scenario Manager dialog box.**

Figure 1-7:
Specifying
the
changing
values in the
Scenario
Values
dialog box.

When you return to the Scenario Manager dialog box, the names of all the scenarios that you added appear in the Scenarios list box. For example, in Figure 1-8, you see that three scenarios — Most Likely, Best Case, and Worst Case — are now listed in the Scenarios list box.

To show a particular scenario in the worksheet that uses the values you entered for the changing cells, you simply double-click the scenario name in this list box or click the name and then click the Show command button. Figure 1-8 shows the results in the sample forecast worksheet after showing the Best Case scenario.

If, after creating the scenarios for your worksheet, you find that you need to use different input values or you want to add or remove scenarios, you can edit the scenarios in the Scenario Manager dialog box. To modify the scenario's name and/or the input values assigned to the changing cells of that scenario, click the scenario name in the Scenarios list box and then click the Edit button so that you can make the appropriate changes in the Edit Scenario dialog box. To remove a scenario from a worksheet, select the scenario's name in the Scenarios list box and then click the Delete button. Note, however, that if you delete a scenario in error, you can't restore it with the Undo command. Instead, you must re-create the scenario by using the Add command button as outlined previously.

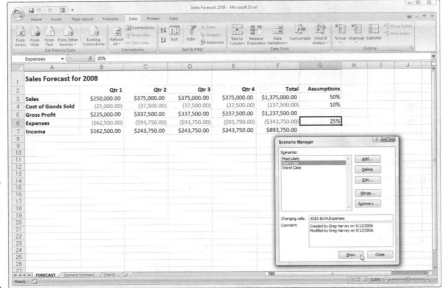

Figure 1-8:
Spreadsheet after showing the Best Case scenario.

**Book VII
Chapter 1**

Performing What-If Scenarios

You can also merge scenarios from other Excel workbook files that are open (of course, the workbooks should share the same spreadsheet layout and changing cells). To merge a scenario into the current worksheet from another workbook, click the Merge button in the Scenario Manager dialog box, and then select the workbook in the Book drop-down list box and the worksheet in the Sheet drop-down list box before you click OK. Excel then copies all the scenarios defined for that worksheet and merges them with any scenarios that you've defined for the current worksheet.

Producing a summary report

After creating the different scenarios for your worksheet, you can use the Summary button in the Scenario Manager dialog box to create a summary report that shows the changing values used in each scenario and, if you want, key resulting values that each produces. When you click the Summary button, Excel opens a Scenario Summary dialog box, similar to the one shown in Figure 1-9, where you may designate a cell selection of result cells in the Result Cells text box to be included in the report. After selecting the result cells for the report, click OK to have Excel generate the summary report and display it in a new worksheet window.

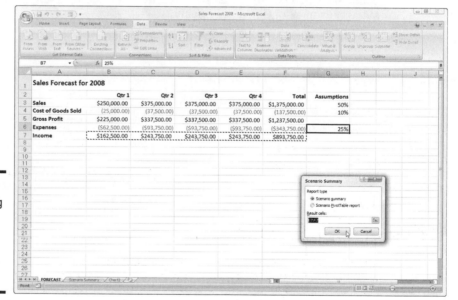

Figure 1-9: Designating the result cells in the Scenario Summary dialog box.

In the example shown in Figure 1-9, the cell range B7:F7, containing the projected income figures for the sales forecast, are designated as the result cells to be included in the summary report. Figure 1-10 shows the actual summary report generated for this sample worksheet in a new document window. Note that because all the changing and result cells in this worksheet are named, the summary report uses their range names in place of their cell references. Also, when the Scenario Manager generates a summary report, it automatically outlines the summary data, thus creating two vertical levels — one for the changing cells and another for the result cells.

After generating a summary report, you can save it by clicking the Save command button on the Quick Access toolbar (Ctrl+S) and/or print it by clicking the Quick Print command button (Ctrl+P).

Note that the Scenario Summary dialog box contains an option, Scenario PivotTable Report, which enables you to view the scenario results as a pivot table. See Book VII, Chapter 2, for details on the uses of pivot tables.

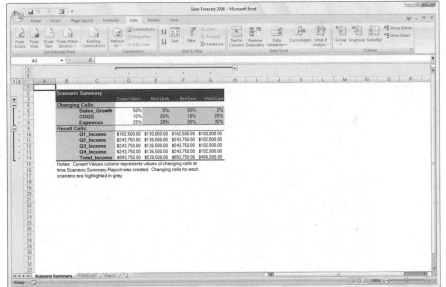

Figure 1-10:
Scenario
Summary
report
for the
scenarios in
the Sales
Forecast
table.

**Book VII
Chapter 1**

Performing What-If
Scenarios

Hide and Goal Seeking

Sometimes, you know the outcome that you want to realize in a worksheet and you need Excel to help you find the input values necessary to achieve those results. This procedure, which is just the opposite of the what-if analysis that I've been examining in this chapter, is referred to as *goal seeking*.

When you simply need to find the value for a single variable that will give the desired result in a particular formula, you can perform this simple type of goal seeking with the Goal Seek command. If you have charted the data and created a two-dimensional column, bar, or line chart, you can also perform the goal seeking by directly manipulating the appropriate marker on the chart. And when you need to perform more complex goal seeking, such as that which involves changing multiple input values to realize a result or constraining the values to a specific range, you can use the Solver command.

Performing goal seeking

To use the Goal Seek command, simply select the cell containing the formula that will return the result that you are seeking (referred to as the *set cell*), indicate what value you want this formula to return, and then indicate the location of the input value that Excel can change to return the desired result. Figures 1-11 and 1-12 illustrate how you can use the Goal Seek command to find how much sales must increase to realize first quarter income of $300,000 (given certain growth, cost of goods sold, and expense assumptions).

To find out how much sales must increase to return a net income of $300,000 in the first quarter, you first select cell B7, which contains the formula that calculates the first quarter income before you click Goal Seek on the What-If Analysis button's drop-down menu on the Ribbon's Data tab or press Alt+AWG. This action opens the Goal Seek dialog box, similar to the one shown in Figure 1-11. Because cell B7 is the active cell when you open this dialog box, the Set Cell text box already contains the cell reference B7. You then select the To Value text box and enter **300000** as the goal. Then, you select the By Changing Cell text box and select cell B3 in the worksheet (the cell that contains the first quarter sales).

Figure 1-12 shows you the Goal Seek Status dialog box that appears when you click OK in the Goal Seek dialog box to have Excel go ahead and adjust the sales figure to reach your desired income figure. As this figure shows, Excel increases the sales in cell B3 from $250,000 to $352,941.18, which, in turn, returns $300,000 as the income in cell B7. The Goal Seek Status dialog box informs you that goal seeking has found a solution and that the current value and target value are now the same (if this were not the case, the Step and Pause buttons in the dialog box would become active, and you could have Excel perform further iterations to try to narrow and ultimately eliminate the gap between the target and current values).

If you want to keep the values entered in the worksheet as a result of goal seeking, click OK to close the Goal Seek Status dialog box. If you want to return to the original values, click the Cancel button instead. If you change the value by clicking OK, remember that you can still switch between the "before" and "after" input values and results by click the Undo button on the Quick Access toolbar or by pressing Ctrl+Z.

To flip back and forth between the "after" and "before" values when you've closed the Goal Seek Status dialog box, press Ctrl+Z to display the original values before goal seeking and then Ctrl+Y to display the values engendered by the goal-seeking solution.

Figure 1-11:
Using goal
seeking to
find out how
much sales
must
increase to
reach a
target
income.

Figure 1-12:
Spreadsheet
showing
goal-
seeking
solution and
Goal Seek
Status
dialog box.

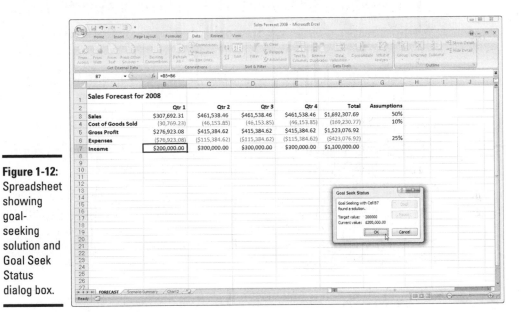

Using the Solver

Although the Data Table and Goal Seek commands work just fine for simple
problems that require determining the direct relationship between the
inputs and results in a formula, you need to use the Solver add-in when dealing with more complex problems. For example, use the Solver to find the
best solution when you need to change multiple input values in your model
and you need to impose constraints on these values and/or the output value.

The Solver add-in works by applying iterative methods to find the "best" solution given the inputs, desired solution, and the constraints that you impose. With each iteration, the program applies a trial-and-error method (based on the use of linear or nonlinear equations and inequalities) that attempts to get closer to the optimum solution.

When using the Solver add-in, keep in mind that many problems, especially the more complicated ones, have many solutions. Although the Solver returns the optimum solution, given the starting values, the variables that can change, and the constraints that you define, this solution is often not the only one possible and, in fact, may not be the best solution for you. To be sure that you are finding the best solution, you may want to run the Solver more than once, adjusting the initial values each time you solve the problem.

When setting up the problem for the Solver add-in in your worksheet, define the following items:

+ **Target cell:** The cell in your worksheet whose value is to be maximized, minimized, or made to reach a particular value.

+ **Changing cells:** The cells in your worksheet whose values are to be adjusted until the answer is found.

+ **Constraints:** The limits that you impose on the changing values and/or the target cell.

After you finish defining the problem with these parameters and have the Solver add-in solve the problem, the program returns the optimum solution by modifying the values in your worksheet. At this point, you can choose to retain the changes in the worksheet or restore the original values to the worksheet. You can also save the solution as a scenario to view later before you restore the original values.

You can use the Solver add-in with the Scenario Manager to help set up a problem to solve or to save a solution so that you can view it at a later date. The changing cells that you define for the Scenario Manager are automatically picked up and used by the Solver when you select this command, and vice versa. Also, you can save the Solver's solution to a problem as a scenario (by clicking the Save Scenario button in the Solver dialog box) that you can then view with the Scenario Manager.

Setting up and defining the problem

The first step in setting up a problem for the Solver to work on is to create the worksheet model for which you will define the target cell, changing cells, and the constraints.

REMEMBER

Keep in mind that the Solver is an add-in utility. This means that, before you can use it, you need to install and load the Solver add-in program. To do this, open the Add-Ins tab of the Excel Options dialog box (Alt+FI) and then click the Go button after making sure that Excel Add-Ins is displayed in the Manage drop-down list box to its immediate left. Then, click the Solver Add-in check box in the Add-Ins dialog box to put a check mark in it before you click OK to close the dialog box and install the add-in.

To define and solve a problem with the Solver add-in after you've loaded the add-in and have created your worksheet model, take the following steps:

1. **Click the Solver command button in the Analysis group at the end of the Ribbon's Data tab or press Alt+AY2.**

Excel opens the Solver Parameters dialog box, which is similar to the one shown in Figure 1-13.

2. **Click the target cell in the worksheet or enter its cell reference or range name in the Set Target Cell text box.**

Next, you need to select the Equal To setting. Click the Max option button when you want the target cell's value to be as large as possible. Click the Min option button when you want the target cell's value to be as small as possible. Click the Value Of option button and then enter a value in the associated text box when you want the target cell's value to reach a particular value.

**Book VII
Chapter 1**

**Performing What-If
Scenarios**

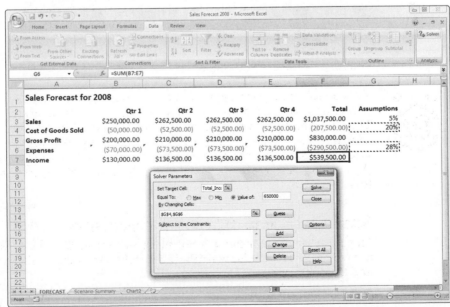

Figure 1-13:
Specifying the parameters to apply to the model in the Solver Parameters dialog box.

3. **Click the appropriate option button option in the Equal To section of the dialog box. If you select the Value To option button, enter the value to match in the associated text box.**

Next, designate the changing cells — that is, the ones Solver can adjust to reach your Equal To goal.

4. **Click the By Changing Cells text box and then select the cells to change in the worksheet or enter their cell references or range name in the text box.**

Remember that to select nonadjacent cells in the worksheet, you need to hold down the Ctrl key as you click each cell in the selection. To have Excel choose the changing cells for you based on the target cell that you selected, click the Guess button to the right of this text box.

Before having Solver adjust your model, you may add constraints for the target cell or any of the changing cells that determine its limits when adjusting the values.

5. **(Optional) Click the Add button to the right of the Subject to the Constraints list box in the Solver Parameters dialog box.**

This action opens the Add Constraint dialog box, similar to the one shown in Figure 1-14. When defining a constraint, choose the cell whose value you want to constrain or select the cell in the worksheet or enter its cell reference in the Cell Reference text box. Then choose the relationship (=, <=, >=, or *int* for integer or *bin* for binary) in the drop-down list box to the right, and (unless you chose int or bin) enter the appropriate value or cell reference in the Constraint text box.

Figure 1-14:
Adding a
constraint to
the target
cell in the
Add
Constraint
dialog box.

To continue adding constraints for other cells used by the Solver, click the Add button to add the constraint and clear the text boxes in the Add Constraint dialog box. Then, repeat Step 5 to add a new constraint. After you finish defining constraints for the target cell and changing values in the model, click OK to close the Add Constraint dialog box and return to the Solver Parameters dialog box (which now lists your constraints in the Subject to the Constraints list box).

6. **Click the Solve button to have the Solver solve the problem as you've defined it in the Solver Parameters dialog box.**

Solving the problem

When you click the Solve button, the Solver Parameters dialog box disappears, and the Status bar indicates that the Solver is setting up the problem and then keeps you informed of the progress in solving the problem by showing the number of the intermediate (or trial) solutions as they are tried. To interrupt the solution process at any time before Excel calculates the last iteration, press the Esc key. Excel then displays the Show Trial Solution dialog box, informing you that the solution process has been paused. To continue the solution process, click the Continue button. To abort the solution process, click the Stop button.

When Excel finishes the solution process, the Solver Results dialog box appears, similar to the one shown in Figure 1-15. This dialog box informs you whether the Solver was able to find a solution, given the target cell, changing cells, and constraints defined for the problem. To retain the changes that the Solver makes in your worksheet model, leave the Keep Solver Solution option button selected and click OK to close the Solver Results dialog box. To return the original values to the worksheet, click the Restore Original Values option button instead. To save the changes as a scenario before you restore the original values, click the Save Scenario button and assign a name to the current scenario before you click the Restore Original Values option and OK button.

Figure 1-15:
Solver
Results
dialog box
showing
that Solver
could not
find a
solution to
the problem.

Unlike when using the Goal Seek command, after clicking the Keep Solver Solution option button in the Solver Results dialog box, you can't use the Undo command button on the Quick Access toolbar to restore the original values to your worksheet. If you want to be able to switch between the "before" and "after" views of your worksheet, you must save the changes with the Save Scenario button and then select the Restore Original Values option button option. That way, you can retain the "before" view in the original worksheet and use the Scenario Manager to display the "after" view created by the Solver.

Changing the Solver options

For most of the problems, the default options used by the Solver are adequate. In some situations, however, you may want to change some of the Solver options before you begin the solution process. To change the solution options, click the Options button in the Solver Parameters dialog box. Excel then opens the Solver Options dialog box, shown in Figure 1-16, where you can make all necessary changes (refer to Table 1-1 for information on each option).

Figure 1-16: Modifying the solution options in the Solver Options dialog box.

After changing the options, click OK to return to the Solver Parameters dialog box; from here, you can then click the Solve button to begin the solution process with the new solution settings that you just changed.

Table 1-1	The Solver Option Settings
Option	*Function*
Max Time	Specifies the maximum number of seconds that the Solver will spend on finding the solution.
Iterations	Specifies the maximum number of times that the Solver will recalculate the worksheet when finding the solution.
Precision	Specifies the precision of the constraints. The number that you enter in this text box determines whether the value in a constraint cell meets the specified value or the upper or lower limit you have set. Specify a lower number (between 0 and 1) to reduce the time it takes the Solver to return a solution to your problem.
Tolerance	Specifies the integer tolerance. The number that you enter here is the maximum percentage of error allowed for integer solutions after you've constrained some of the changing cells to integers.
Convergence	Specifies the amount of relative change allowed in the last five iterations before Solver stops with a solution. The smaller the number you enter, the less relative the change allowed.

Option	Function
Assume Linear Model	Sets Solver to use the linear programming method by using the Simplex method when solving your problem. Selecting this option can greatly reduce the amount of time it takes for the Solver to return a solution to your problem when working on a linear problem.
Assume Non-Negative	Causes Solver to set 0 (zero) as the lower limit for all adjustable cells for which you have not already set a lower limit in the Add Constraint dialog box.
Use Automatic Scaling	Turns on automatic scaling for finding a solution to a problem where the magnitude of the changing cells differs greatly from the magnitude of the set cell and/or the constraint values.
Show Iteration Results	Pauses the Solver at each trial solution so that you can see the intermediate results in the worksheet.
Load Model	Displays the Load Model dialog box where you can select the reference of saved Solver parameters that you want to load as the current problem into the Solver (see Save Model that follows).
Save Model	Displays the Save Model dialog box where you specify the reference for storing the current Solver parameters that you want to save in the worksheet so that you can reuse them later. You need to use this option to save a problem model only when you've already defined at least one problem for the worksheet and want to save all the problems in the worksheet.
Estimates	Specifies the approach used to obtain initial estimates for the basic variables in each one-dimensional search. Click the Tangent option button to use linear extrapolation from a tangent vector. Click the Quadratic option button to use quadratic extrapolation (which can improve the results on highly nonlinear problems).
Derivatives	Specifies Forward differencing (the default) or Central differencing for estimates of partial derivatives. Central requires more worksheet recalculations but can help when the Solver dialog box displays the message indicating that the Solver could not improve the solution.
Search	Specifies either a (quasi-) Newton (the default) or Conjugate gradient method searching. Changing to Conjugate can be useful if, when stepping through iterations, you notice little progress between successive trial results.

Saving and loading a model problem

The target cell, changing cells, constraints, and Solver options that you most recently used are saved as part of the worksheet when you click the Save button on the Quick Access toolbar (Ctrl+S). When you define other problems for the same worksheet that you want to save, you must choose the

Save Model button in the Solver Options dialog box and indicate the cell reference or name of the range in the active worksheet where you want the problem's parameters to be inserted.

When you click the Save Model button, Excel opens the Save Model dialog box, containing a Select Model Area text box. This text box contains the cell references for a range large enough to hold all the problem's parameters, starting with the active cell. To save the problem's parameters in this range, click OK. If this range includes cells with existing data, you need to modify the cell reference in this text box before you choose OK to prevent Excel from replacing the existing data.

After you click OK, Excel copies the problem's parameters in the specified range. These values are then saved as part of the worksheet the next time you save the workbook. To reuse these problem parameters when solving a problem, you simply need to open the Solver Options dialog box, click the Load Problem button, and then select the range containing the saved problem parameters. When you click OK in the Load Model dialog box, Excel loads the parameters from this cell range into the appropriate text boxes in the Solver Parameters dialog box. You can then close the Solver Options dialog box by clicking OK, and solve the problem by using these parameters by clicking the Solve command button.

Remember that you can use the Reset All button whenever you want to clear all the parameters defined for the previous problem and return the Solver options to their defaults.

Creating Solver reports

You can create three different types of reports with the Solver:

+ **Answer report:** Lists the target cell and changing cells with their original and final values, along with the constraints used in solving the problem.

+ **Sensitivity report:** Indicates how sensitive an optimal solution is to changes in the formulas that calculate the target cell and constraints. The report shows the changing cells with their final values and the *reduced gradient* for each cell (the reduced gradient measures the objective per unit increase in the changing cell). If you defined constraints, the Sensitivity report lists them with their final values and the *Lagrange multiplier* for each constraint (the Lagrange multiplier measures the objective per unit increase that appears in the right side of the constraint equation).

✦ **Limits report:** Shows the target cell and the changing cells with their values, lower and upper limits, and target results. The lower limit represents the lowest value that a changing cell can have while fixing the values of all other cells and still satisfying the constraints. The upper limit represents the highest value that will do this.

Excel places each report that you generate for a Solver problem in a separate worksheet in the workbook. To generate one (or all) of these reports, select the report type (Answer, Sensitivity, or Limits) in the Reports list box of the Solver Results dialog box (as shown previously in Figure 1-15). To select more than one report, just click the name of the report.

When you click OK to close the Solver Results dialog box (after choosing between the Keep Solver Solution and Restore Original Values options), Excel generates the report (or reports) that you selected in a new worksheet that it adds to the beginning of the workbook (report sheet tabs are named by report type, as in *Answer Report 1, Sensitivity Report 1,* and *Limits Report 1*).

Chapter 2: Generating Pivot Tables

In This Chapter

✔ Understanding how pivot tables summarize data

✔ Using the PivotTable Wizard to create a pivot table

✔ Pivoting the elements in the data table

✔ Changing the summary function used in the pivot table

✔ Formatting a pivot table and changing the pivot table options

✔ Creating a pivot chart at the same time as your pivot table

The subject of this chapter is the *pivot table*, the name given to a special type of data summary table that you can use to analyze and reveal the relationships inherent in the data lists that you maintain in Excel. Pivot tables are great for summarizing particular values in a data list or database because they do their magic without making you create formulas to perform the calculations. Unlike the Subtotals feature, which is another summarizing feature (see Book VI, Chapter 1 for more information), pivot tables let you play around with the arrangement of the summarized data — even after you generate the table. (The Subtotals feature only lets you hide and display different levels of totals in the list.) This capability to change the arrangement of the summarized data by rotating row and column headings gives the pivot table its name.

Pivot tables are also versatile because they enable you to summarize data by using a variety of summary functions (although totals created with the SUM function will probably remain your old standby). When setting up the original pivot table — made really simple with the help of the PivotTable and PivotChart Wizard — you make several decisions: what summary function to use, which columns (fields) the summary function is applied to, and which columns (fields) these computations are tabulated with. You can also use pivot tables to cross-tabulate one set of data in your data list with another. For example, you can use this feature to create a pivot table from an employee database that totals the salaries for each job category cross-tabulated (arranged) by department or job site.

Creating Pivot Tables

To create a new pivot table, simply open the worksheet that contains the data list (see Book VI, Chapter 1) you want summarized by the pivot table, position the cell cursor somewhere in the cells of this list, and then click the PivotTable command button on the Ribbon's Insert tab or press Alt+NVT.

Excel then selects all the data in the list indicated by a marquee around the cell range. The program also opens the Create PivotTable dialog box shown in Figure 2-1. You can then adjust the cell range in the Table/Range text box under the Select a Table or Range option button, if the marquee does not include all the data to be summarized in the pivot table. By default, Excel builds the new pivot table on a new worksheet it adds to the workbook. If you want the pivot table to appear on the same worksheet, click the Existing Worksheet option button and then indicate the location of the first cell of the new table in the Location text box (just be sure that this new pivot table isn't going to overlap any existing tables of data).

Figure 2-1:
Indicate the data source and pivot table location in the Create PivotTable dialog box.

If the data source for your pivot table is an external database table created with a separate database management program such as Microsoft Access, you need to click the Use an External Data Source option button, then click the Choose Connection button and then click the name of the connection in the Existing Connections dialog box (see Book VI, Chapter 2 for information on establishing a connection with an external database table and retrieving its data through a query).

After you indicate the source and location for the new pivot table in the Create PivotTable dialog box and click its OK button, the program adds a placeholder graphic (with the text, "To build a report, choose fields from the PivotTable Field List") indicating where the new pivot table will go in the worksheet while at the same time displaying a PivotTable Field List task pane on the right side of the Worksheet area (see Figure 2-2).

This PivotTable Field List task pane is divided into two areas: the Choose Fields to Add to Report list box with the names of all the fields in the data list you selected as the source of the table preceded by an empty check box at the top and an area divided into four drop zones (Report Filter, Column Labels, Row Labels, and Values) at the bottom.

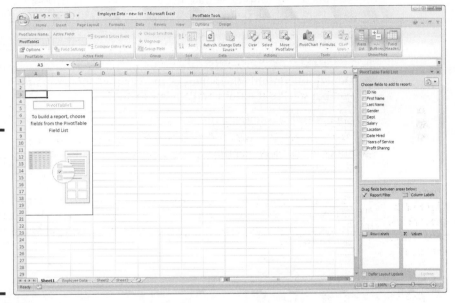

Figure 2-2:
New pivot table displaying the blank table grid and the PivotTable Field List task pane.

**Book VII
Chapter 2**

**Generating
Pivot Tables**

To complete the new pivot table, all you have to do is assign the fields in the Pivot Table Field List task pane to the various parts of the table. You do this by dragging a field name from the Choose Fields to Add to Report list box to one of the four areas (referred to as drop zones) in the Drag Fields Between Areas Below section at the bottom of the task pane:

✦ **Report Filter** for the fields that enable you to page through the data summaries shown in the actual pivot table by filtering out sets of data — they act as the filters for the report. So, for example, if you designate the Year Field from a data list as a Report Filter, you can display data summaries in the pivot table for individual years or for all years represented in the data list.

✦ **Column Labels** for the fields that determine the arrangement of data shown in the columns of the pivot table — their entries appear in the table's column headings.

✦ **Row Labels** for the fields that determine the arrangement of data shown in the rows of the pivot table — their entries appear in the table's row headings.

✦ **Values** for the fields whose data are presented in the cells in the body of the pivot table — they are the values that are summarized in the last row and column of the table (totaled by default).

To better understand how you can use these various areas in a pivot table, look at the complete pivot table in Figure 2-3. For this pivot table, I dragged these fields in the Employee data list to the following drop zones in the Drag Fields between Areas Below section in the PivotTable Field List task pane:

✦ **Gender** field contains F (for female) or M (for male) to indicate the employee's gender — to the Report Filter drop zone.

✦ **Dept** field contains the names of the various departments in the company — to the Column Labels drop zone.

✦ **Location** field contains the names of the various cities with corporate offices — to the Row Labels drop zone.

✦ **Salary** field contains the annual salary for each employee — to the Values zone.

As a result, this pivot table now displays the sum of the salaries for both the men and women employees in each department (across the columns) and then presents these sums by their corporate location (in each row).

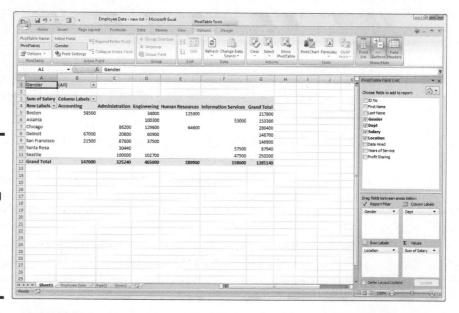

Figure 2-3: Completed pivot table after adding the fields from the employee data list to it various sections.

Changing the PivotTable Field List task pane display

By default, Excel displays the list of fields on top of the four drop zones — Report Filter, Column Labels, Row Labels, and Values — in the Pivot-Table Field List task pane. You can change this arrangement by clicking the Fields Section and Areas Section Stacked drop-down button (to the immediate right of the Choose Fields to Add to Report heading) and then clicking one of the following options on its drop-down menu: Fields Section and Areas Section Side by Side to place the list of fields in a column to the left of the four drop zones, Fields Section Only to list only the fields, Areas Section Only (2 by 2) to list only the drop zones in two columns, or Areas Section Only (1 by 4) to list only the drop zones in one column.

When you display only the four drop-zones in the PivotTable Field List task pane, you can click the drop-down buttons that appear to the right of the name of each field you add to the four zones to manipulate the fields: Move to Report Filter to move the field to the Report Filter drop zone, Move to Row Labels to move the field to the Row Labels drop zone, Move to Column Labels to move the field to the Column Labels drop zone, Move to Values to move the field to the Values drop zone, Remove Field to remove the field from its current drop zone, or Field Settings to open the Fields Settings dialog box where you can adjust the subtotals, filter, layout, and print settings for the field.

As soon as you create a new pivot table (or select the cell of an existing table in a worksheet), Excel selects the Options tab of the PivotTable Tools contextual tab added to the end of the Ribbon. Among the many groups on this tab, you find the Show/Hide group that contains the following useful command buttons:

✦ **Field List** to hide and redisplay the Pivot Table Field List task pane on the right side of the Worksheet area

✦ **+/– Buttons** to hide and redisplay the expand (+) and collapse (–) buttons in front of particular Column Fields or Row Fields that enable you to temporarily remove and then redisplay their particular summarized values in the pivot table

✦ **Field Headers** to hide and redisplay the fields assigned to the Column Labels and Row Labels in the pivot table

Formatting a Pivot Table

Excel 2007 makes formatting a new pivot table you've added to a worksheet as quick and easy as formatting any other table of data or list of data. All you need to do is click a cell of the pivot table to add the PivotTable Tools contextual tab to the end of the Ribbon and then click its Design tab to display its command buttons.

The Design tab on the PivotTable Tools contextual tab is divided into three groups:

✦ **Layout** group to add subtotals and grand totals to the pivot table and modify its basic layout

✦ **PivotTable Style Options** group to refine the pivot table style you select for the table using the PivotTable Styles gallery to the immediate right

✦ **PivotTable Styles** group contains the gallery of styles you can apply to the active pivot table by clicking the desired style thumbnail

Figure 2-4 shows the pivot table created for the Employee Data List in Figure 2-3 after applying the Pivot Style Medium 10 in the PivotTable Styles gallery to it. This style applies a light version of background color (rose) to the Gender Report Filter field and a darker version to the Values Label (Sum of Salary), Dept Column Labels, and Location Row Labels (so dark in fact, that Excel automatically reverses the label text to white).

Figure 2-4: New pivot table formatted with Pivot Style Medium 10 selected from the PivotTable Styles gallery.

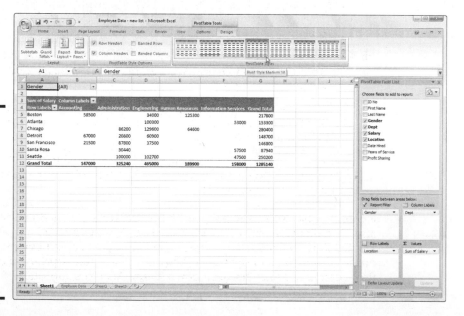

Refining the pivot table layout and style

After selecting a style from the PivotTable Styles gallery on the Design tab on the PivotTable Tools contextual tab, you can then refine the style using the command buttons in the Layout group and the check boxes in the PivotTable Style Options group.

The Layout group on the Design tab contains the following four command buttons:

✦ **Subtotals to** hide the display of subtotals in the summary report or have them displayed at the top or bottom of their groups in the report.

✦ **Grand Totals to** turn on or off the display of grand totals in the last row or column of the report.

✦ **Report Layout to** modify the display of the report by selecting between the default Compact Form and the much more spread out Outline Form (which connects the subtotals across the columns of the table with lines or shading depending on the table style selected) and Tabular Form (which connects the row items in the first column and the subtotals across the columns of the table with gridlines or shading depending on the table style selected).

✦ **Blank Rows to** insert or remove a blank row after each item in the table.

The PivotTable Style Options group contains the following four check boxes:

✦ **Row Headers to** remove and then re-add the font and color formatting from the row headers of the table in the first column of the table applied by the currently selected pivot table style.

✦ **Column Headers to** remove and then re-add the font and color formatting from the column headers at the top of the table applied by the currently selected pivot table style.

✦ **Banded Rows to** add and remove banding in the form of gridlines or shading (depending on the currently selected pivot table style) from the rows of the pivot table.

✦ **Banded Columns to** add and remove banding in the form of gridlines or shading (depending on the currently selected pivot table style) from the columns of the pivot table.

Figure 2-5 shows the original pivot table created from the Employee data list after adding the Years of Service field as a second row field and after selecting the Show in Outline Form option on the Report Layout command button's drop-down menu and the Insert Blank after Each Item option on the Blank Rows command button's drop-down menu. Also, the subtotals of the salaries for each department now appear at the bottom of the location group rather than at the top after selecting the Show All Subtotals as Bottom of Group option on the Subtotals command button's drop-down menu.

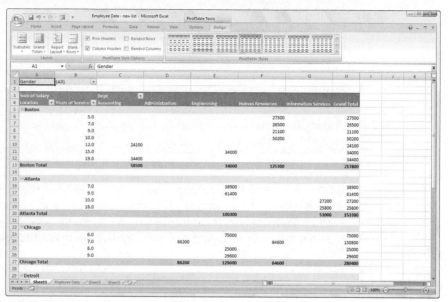

Figure 2-5:
Revised pivot table in the Outline Form with an extra blank row between each item in the pivot table.

Formatting the parts of the pivot table

Even after applying a table style to your new pivot table, you may still want to make some individual adjustments to its formatting, such as selecting a new font, font size, or cell alignment for the text of the table and a new number format for the values in the table's data cells.

You can make these types of formatting changes to a pivot table by selecting the part of the table to which the formatting is to be applied and then selecting the new formatting from the appropriate command buttons in the Font, Alignment, and Number groups on the Home tab of the Ribbon.

Applying a new font, font size, or alignment to the pivot table

You can modify the text in a pivot table by selecting a new font, font size, or horizontal alignment. To make these formatting changes to the text in the entire table, select the entire table before you use the appropriate command buttons in the Font and/or Alignment group on the Home tab. To apply these changes only to the headings in the pivot table, select only its labels before using the commands on the Home tab. To apply these changes only to the data in the body of the pivot table, select only its cells.

To help you select the cells you want to format in a pivot table, use the following Select items on the Options command button's drop-down list:

1. **Click a cell in the pivot table in the worksheet and then click the Options tab on the PivotTable Tools contextual tab.**

2. **Click the Select command button in the Actions group on the Options tab.**

Excel displays the Select submenu.

3. **On the Select submenu, you can do the following:**

- Click the Entire PivotTable option on the Select submenu to select all the pivot table cells including the Report Filter cells.

- Click the Labels option to select only the cells with the rows and column headings in the table.

- Click the Values option to select only the cells with values in the table.

- Click the Labels and Values option to select the cells with the row and column headings and those with the values in the table.

You can also use the following hot keys to select all or part of your pivot table:

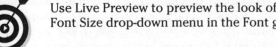

**Book VII
Chapter 2**

◆ **Alt+JTWE** to select the entire table, that is, all the cells of the pivot table including those with the Report Filter

◆ **Alt+JTWL** to select only the label cells with the row and column headings in the pivot table

◆ **Alt+JTWV** to select only the value cells with the values in the body of the pivot table

◆ **Alt+JTWA** to select the label cells with the row and column headings as well as the value cells with the values in the body of the pivot table

You can only use the Labels and Values, Values, and Labels select options on the Select button's drop-down menu and their hot key equivalents after you have selected the Entire PivotTable option to select all the cells.

Use Live Preview to preview the look of a new font or font size on the Font or Font Size drop-down menu in the Font group on the Ribbon's Home tab.

Applying a number format to the data cells

When you first create a pivot table, Excel does not format the data cells in the table that contains the values corresponding to the field or fields you add to the Values drop zone in the PivotTable Field List task pane and the subtotals and grand totals that Excel adds to the table. You can, however, assign any of the Excel number formats to the values in the pivot table in one of two manners.

In the first method, you select the entire table (Alt+JTWE), then select only its value cells in the body of the pivot table (Alt+JTWV), and then apply the desired number format using the command buttons in the Number group of the Home tab of the Ribbon. For example, to format the data cells with the Accounting number format with no decimal places, you click the Accounting Number Format command button and then click the Decrease Decimal command button two times.

You can also apply a number format to the data cells in the body of the pivot table by following these steps:

1. **Double-click the name of field in the table that contains the words "Sum of" followed by the name of the field whose values are currently summarized there to open the Summarize By tab of the Value Field Settings dialog box.**

   In my Employee example pivot table, this field is called Sum of Salary because the Salary field is summarized. Note that this field is located at the intersection of the Column and Row Label fields in the table.

2. **Click the Number Format button in the Value Field Settings dialog box to open the Number tab of the Format Cells dialog box.**

3. **Click the type of number format you want to assign to the values in the pivot table on the Category list box of the Number tab.**

4. **(Optional) Modify any other options for the selected number format such as Decimal Places, Symbol, and Negative Numbers that are available for that format.**

5. **Click OK twice, the first time to close the Format Cells dialog box and the second to close the Value Field Settings dialog box.**

Sorting and Filtering the Pivot Table Data

When you create a new pivot table, you'll notice that Excel automatically adds AutoFilter buttons to the Report Filter field as well as the labels for the Column and Row fields. These AutoFilter buttons enable you to filter out all but certain entries in any of these fields, and in the case of the Column and Row fields, to sort their entries in the table.

When you add more than one Column or Row field to your pivot table, Excel adds collapse buttons (–) that you can use to temporarily hide subtotal values for a particular secondary field. After clicking a collapse button in the table, it immediately becomes an expand button (+) that you can click to redisplay the subtotals for that one secondary field.

Filtering the report

Perhaps the most important AutoFilter buttons in a pivot table are the ones added to the Report Filter field(s). By selecting a particular option on the drop-down lists attached to one of these AutoFilter buttons, only the summary data for that subset you select is then displayed in the pivot table itself.

For example, in the example pivot table (Figure 2-3) that uses the Gender field from the Employee Data list as the Report Filter field, you can display the sum of just the men's salaries by department and location in the body of the pivot table simply by clicking the Gender field's filter button and then clicking M on the drop-down list before you click OK. Likewise, you can view the summary of the women's salaries by selecting F on this filter button's drop-down list — to later redisplay the summary of the salaries for all the employees, you then reselect the (All) option on this list before you click OK.

Excel then displays M in the Gender Report Filter field instead of the default (All) and replaces the standard drop-down button icon with a cone-shaped filter icon, indicating that the field is currently being filtered to show only some of the values in the data source.

Filtering individual Column and Row fields

The AutoFilter buttons on the Column and Row fields enable you to filter particular groups and, in some cases, individual entries in the data source. To filter the summary data in the columns or rows of a pivot table, click the Column or Row field's filter button and start by clicking the check box for the (Select All) option at the top of the drop-down list to clear this box of its check mark. Then, click the check boxes for all the groups or individual entries whose summed values you still want displayed in the pivot table to put back check marks in each of their check boxes before you click OK.

As when filtering a Report Filter field in the table, Excel replaces the standard drop-down button icon displayed in the particular Column or Report field with a cone-shaped filter icon. This icon indicates that the field is currently being filtered and only some of its summary values are now displayed in the pivot table. To redisplay all the values for a filtered Column or Report field, you need to click its filter button and then click (Select All) at the top of its drop-down list before you click OK.

Book VII Chapter 2

Generating Pivot Tables

Figure 2-6 shows the sample pivot table after filtering its Gender Filter Report Field to women by selecting F (for Female) and its Dept Column Field to Accounting, Administration, Engineering and Human Resources, and Information Services.

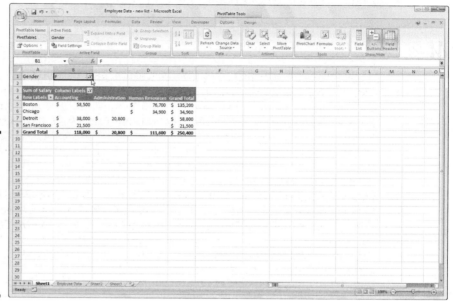

Figure 2-6: Pivot table after filtering the Gender Filter Report field and the Dept Column field.

Notice in Figure 2-6 that after filtering the pivot table by selecting F in the Gender Filter Report field and selecting Accounting, Administration, Engineering and Human Resources, and Information Services departments as the only Dept Column fields, the filtered pivot table no longer displays salary summaries for all of the company's locations (Santa Rosa, Seattle, and Atlanta locations are missing). You can tell the table's missing these locations because there are no women employees in the three selected departments and not as a result of filtering the Row field because the Location drop-down button still uses the standard icon and not the cone filter icon now shown to the right of the Gender Filter Report and Dept Column fields.

Sorting the pivot table

You can instantly reorder the summary values in a pivot table by sorting the table on one or more of its Column or Row fields. To re-sort a pivot table, click the AutoFilter button for the Column or Row field you want to use in the sort and then click either the Sort A to Z option or the Sort Z to A option at the top of the field's drop-down list.

Click the Sort A to Z option when you want the table reordered by sorting the labels in the selected field alphabetically, or, in the case of values, from the smallest to largest value, or, in the case of dates, from the oldest to newest date. Click the Sort Z to A option when you want the table reordered by sorting the labels in reverse alphabetical order (Z to A), values from the highest to smallest, and dates from the newest to oldest.

Modifying the Pivot Table

As the name *pivot* implies, the fun of pivot tables is being able to rotate the data fields by using the rows and columns of the table, as well as to change what fields are used on the fly. For example, suppose that after making the Dept Field the pivot table's Column Field, and the Location field the Row Field, you now want to see what the table looks like with the Location field as the Column Field and the Dept Field as the Row Field?

No problem: All you have to do is open the PivotTable Field List task pane (Alt+JTL) and then drag Dept from the Column Labels drop zone to the Row Labels drop zone and then drag Location from the Row Labels drop zone to the Column Labels drop zone. Voilà — Excel rearranges the totaled salaries so that the rows of the pivot table show the departmental grand totals and the columns now show the location grand totals. Figure 2-7 shows this new arrangement for the pivot table.

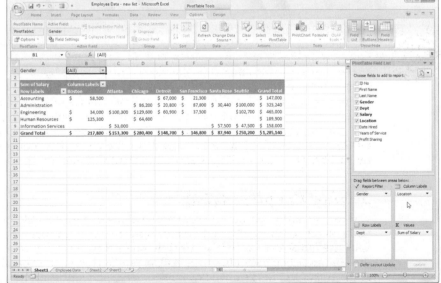

Figure 2-7:
Pivoting the table so that Location is now the Column Field and Dept the Row Field.

In fact, when pivoting a pivot table, not only can you rotate existing fields, but you can also add new fields to the table or assign more fields to the table's Column Field and Row Field areas.

Figure 2-8 illustrates this situation. This figure shows the same pivot table after making a couple of key changes to the table structure. First, I added the Profit Sharing field as a second Report Filter field by dragging it to the Report Filter drop zone in the PivotTable Field List task pane. Then, I made Location a second Row Field by dragging it from the Column Labels drop zone to the Row Labels drop zone. Finally, for this figure, I changed the setting in the Gender Report Filter from the default of All to M and changed the Profit Sharing Report Filter from Yes back to All.

As a result, the modified pivot table shown in Figure 2-8 now shows the salary totals for all the men in the corporation arranged first by their location and then by their department. Because I added Profit Sharing as a second Report Filter, I can see the totals for just the men or just the women who are or aren't currently enrolled in the profit sharing plan simply by selecting the appropriate Report Filter settings.

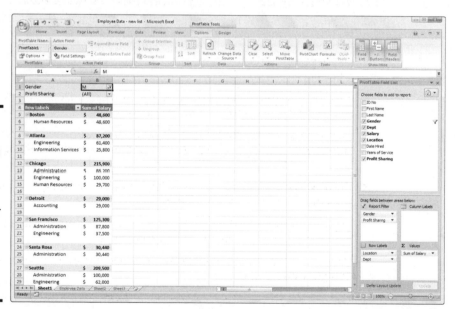

Figure 2-8: Pivot table after adding Profit Sharing as another Report Filter and making Location and Dept the Row Fields.

Changing the summary functions

By default, Excel uses the good old SUM function to total the values in the numeric field(s) that you add to the Values drop zone, thereby assigning them to the data cells in the body of the pivot table. Some data summaries require the use of another summary function, such as the AVERAGE or COUNT function.

To change the summary function that Excel uses, you open the Field Settings dialog box for one of the fields that you use as the data items in the pivot table. You can do this either by clicking the Value Field Settings option on the field's drop-down menu in the Values drop zone in the PivotTable Field List task pane (Alt+JTL) or by double-clicking the field's label or by clicking this label (this label is located at the cell intersection of the first Column and Row Field in a pivot table that has only one data field).

After you open the Value Field Setting dialog box for the field, you can change its summary function from the default Sum to any of the following functions by selecting it on the Summarize By tab:

+ **Count** to show the count of the records for a particular category (note that COUNT is the default setting for any text fields that you use as Data Items in a pivot table)

+ **Average** to calculate the average (that is, the arithmetic mean) for the values in the field for the current category and page filter

+ **Max** to display the largest numeric value in that field for the current category and page filter

+ **Min** to display the smallest numeric value in that field for the current category and page filter

+ **Product** to display the product of the numeric values in that field for the current category and page filter (all non-numeric entries are ignored)

+ **Count Numbers** to display the number of numeric values in that field for the current category and page filter (all non-numeric entries are ignored)

+ **StdDev** to display the standard deviation for the sample in that field for the current category and page filter

+ **StdDevp** to display the standard deviation for the population in that field for the current category and page filter

+ **Var** to display the variance for the sample in that field for the current category and page filter

+ **Varp** to display the variance for the population in that field for the current category and page filter

After you select the new summary function to use on the Summarize By tab of the Value Field Settings dialog box, click the OK button to have Excel apply the new function to the data presented in the body of the pivot table.

Adding Calculated Fields

In addition to using various summary functions on the data presented in your pivot table, you can create your own Calculated Fields for the pivot table. Calculated Fields are computed by a formula that you create by using existing numeric fields in the data source. To create a Calculated Field for your pivot table, follow these steps:

1. **Click any of the cells in the pivot table and then click the Calculated Field option on the Formulas command button's drop-down list.**

The Formulas command button is located in the Tools group on the Options tab.

Excel opens the Insert Calculated Field dialog box similar to the one shown in Figure 2-9. Note that you can also open this dialog box by pressing Alt+JTJF when any one of the cells in the pivot table is selected.

2. **Enter the name for the new field in the Name text box.**

Next, you create the formula in the Formula text box by using one or more of the existing fields displayed in the Fields list box.

3. **Click the Formula text box and then delete the zero (0) after the equal sign and position the insertion point immediately following the equal sign (=).**

Now you're ready to type in the formula that performs the calculation. To do this, insert numeric fields from the Fields list box and indicate the operation to perform on them with the appropriate arithmetic operators (+, -, *, or /).

4. **Enter the formula to perform the new field's calculation in the Formula text box, inserting whatever fields you need by clicking the name in the Fields list box and then clicking the Insert Field button.**

For example, in Figure 2-9, I created a formula for the new calculated field called Bonuses that multiplies the values in the Salary Field by 2.5 percent (0.025) to compute the total amount of annual bonuses to be paid. To do this, I clicked the Salary field in the Fields list box and then clicked the Insert Field button to add Salary to the formula in the Formula text box (as in =Salary). Then, I typed ***0.025** to complete the formula (=Salary*0.025).

When you finish entering the formula for your calculated field, you can add the calculated field to the PivotTable Field List task pane by clicking the Add button. After you click the Add button, it changes to a grayed-out Modify button. If you start editing the formula in the Formula text box, the Modify button becomes active so that you can click it to update the definition.

5. **Click OK in the Insert Calculated Field dialog box.**

This action closes the Insert Calculated Field dialog box and adds the summary of the data in the calculated field to your pivot table.

Figure 2-9:
Creating a
calculated
field for a
pivot table.

After you finish defining a calculated field to a pivot table, Excel automatically adds its name to the field list in the PivotTable Field List task pane and to the Values drop zone thereby assigning the calculated field as another Data item in the body of the pivot table.

If you want to temporarily hide a calculated field from the body of the pivot table, click the name of the calculated field in the field list in the PivotTable Field List task pane (Alt+JTL) to remove the check mark from its check box in the field list. Then, when you're ready to redisplay the calculated field, you can do so by clicking its check box in the field list in the PivotTable Field List task pane again to put a check mark back into it.

Changing the pivot table options

You can use the PivotTable Options dialog box (shown in Figure 2-10) to change the settings applied to any and all pivot tables that you create in a workbook. You open this dialog box by clicking the Options command button in the PivotTable Options group of the Options tab on the PivotTable Tools contextual tab or by pressing Alt+JTTT.

Figure 2-10:
Modifying
the pivot
table
options in
the
PivotTable
Options
dialog box.

The PivotTable Options dialog box contains the following five tabs:

✦ **Layout & Format** with options for controlling the various aspects of the layout and formatting of the cells in the pivot table

✦ **Totals & Filters** with options for controlling the display of the subtotals and grand totals in the report, and filtering and sorting the table's fields

✦ **Display** with options for controlling the display items in the table and the sorting of the fields in the PivotTable

✦ **Printing** with options for controlling print expand and collapse buttons when displayed in the pivot table, and print titles with the row and column labels on each page of the printout

✦ **Data** with options for controlling how the data that supports the pivot table is stored and refreshed

Perhaps the most important pivot table option is the Classic PivotTable Layout (Enables Dragging of Fields in the Grid) check box option on the Display tab. When you put a check mark in this check box, Excel lets you rearrange the fields within the pivot table simply by dragging their icons on the desired part of the table (Table Filter, Column Labels, or Row Labels). The program also lets you add fields to the pivot table by dragging them from the field list in the PivotTable Field List task pane and dropping them on the part of the table to which they are to be added.

Creating Pivot Charts

Instead of generating just a plain old boring pivot table, you can spice up your data summaries quite a bit by generating a pivot chart to go along with a supporting pivot table. To create a pivot chart from your pivot table, simply follow these two steps:

1. **Click the PivotChart command button in the Tools group on the Options tab attached to the PivotTable Tools contextual tab to open the Insert Chart dialog box or press Alt+JTC.**

Excel opens the Insert Chart dialog box where you can select the type and subtype of the pivot chart you want to create (see Book V, Chapter 1).

2. **Click the thumbnail of the subtype of chart you want to create in the Create Chart dialog box and then click OK.**

As soon as you click OK after selecting the chart subtype, Excel displays the following items in the same worksheet as the pivot table:

✦ **Pivot chart** using the type and subtype of chart you selected in the Insert Chart dialog box — you can move and resize this embedded chart as needed

✦ **PivotChart Filter pane** containing three drop-down lists — Report Filter, Axis Fields (Categories), and Legend Fields (Series) — along with a Values field at the very bottom listing the name of the field whose values are summarized in the chart

✦ **PivotChart Tools contextual tab** divided into four tabs — Design, Layout, Format, and Analyze — each with its own set of buttons for customizing and refining the pivot chart

Moving a pivot chart to its own sheet

Although Excel automatically creates all new pivot charts on the same worksheet as the pivot table, you may find customizing and working with the pivot chart easier if you move the chart to its own chart sheet in the workbook. To move a new pivot chart to its own chart sheet in the workbook, follow these steps:

1. **Click the Design tab under the PivotChart Tools contextual tab to bring its tools to the Ribbon and then click the Move Chart command button or press Alt+JCM.**

   Excel opens the Move Chart dialog box.

2. **Click the New Sheet option button in the Move Chart dialog box.**

3. **(Optional) Rename the generic Chart1 sheet name in the accompanying text box by entering a more descriptive name there.**

4. **Click OK to close the Move Chart dialog box and open the new chart sheet with your pivot chart.**

Figure 2-11 shows a clustered column pivot chart after moving the chart to its own chart sheet in the workbook.

Filtering a pivot chart

When you graph the data in a pivot table using a typical chart type such as column, bar, or line that uses both an x- and y-axis, the Row labels in the pivot table appear along the x- or category-axis at the bottom of the chart and the Column labels in the pivot table become the data series that are delineated in the chart's legend. The numbers in the Values field are represented on the y- or value-axis up that goes up the left side of the chart.

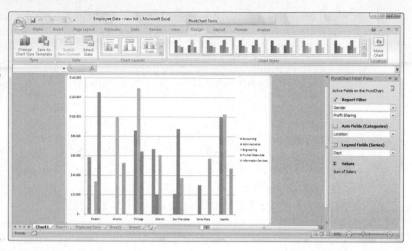

Figure 2-11:
Clustered
column
pivot chart
moved to its
own chart
sheet after
docking the
PivotChart
Filter pane.

You can use the drop-down list boxes in the PivotChart Filter pane to filter the charted data represented in this fashion like you do the values in the pivot table. Remove the check mark from the (Select All) or (All) option and then add a check mark to each of the fields you still want represented in the filtered pivot chart.

Click the following drop-down buttons to filter a different part of the pivot chart:

✦ **Axis Fields (Categories)** to filter the categories that are charted along the x-axis at the bottom of the chart

✦ **Legend Fields (Series)** to filter the data series shown in columns, bars, or lines in the chart body and identified by the chart legend

✦ **Report Filter** to filter the values charted along the y-axis on the left side of the chart

Formatting a pivot chart

The command buttons on the Design, Layout, and Format tabs attached to the PivotChart Tools contextual tab make it easy to further format and customize your pivot chart. Use the Design tab buttons to select a new chart style for your pivot chart or even a brand-new chart type. Use the Layout tab buttons to further refine your pivot chart by adding chart titles, text boxes, and gridlines. Use the Format tab buttons to refine the look of any graphics you've added to the chart as well as select a new background color for your chart.

To get specific information on using the buttons on these tabs, see Book V, Chapter 1, which covers creating charts from regular worksheet data — the Chart Tools contextual tab that appears when you select a chart you've created contains the same Design, Layout, and Format tabs with comparable command buttons.

Book VIII
Excel and VBA

The 5th Wave   By Rich Tennant

Well, obviously one of the cells in the navigational spreadsheet is corrupt!

Contents at a Glance

Chapter 1: Building and Running Macros

In This Chapter

✔ Understanding how macros do what they do

✔ Recording macros for instant playback

✔ Using the relative option when recording macros

✔ Running the macros you've recorded

✔ Changing the macro security settings

✔ Assigning macros to the Quick Access toolbar

Macros enable you to automate almost any task that you can undertake in Excel 2007. By using Excel's macro recorder to record tasks that you perform routinely, you not only speed up the procedure considerably (because Excel can play back your keystrokes and mouse actions much faster than you can perform them manually), but you are also assured that each step in the task is carried out the same way each and every time you perform the task.

Excel's macro recorder records all the commands and keystrokes that you make in a language called Visual Basic for Applications (VBA), which is a special version of the BASIC programming language developed and refined by the good folks at Microsoft for use with all their Office application programs. You can then use Excel's Visual Basic Editor to display and make changes to the macro's VBA code.

In this chapter, you find out how to use Excel's macro recorder to record, test, and play back macros that you use to automate repetitive tasks required when building and using your Excel worksheets and charts. In the next chapter, you find out how to use Excel's Visual Basic Editor to debug and edit the macros that you record, as well as to create complex macros that run custom functions and set up and run custom Excel applications, complete with their own pull-down menus and dialog boxes.

Macro Basics

You can create macros two ways:

✦ Use Excel's macro recorder to record your actions as you undertake them in a worksheet.

✦ Enter the instructions that you want followed in VBA code in the Visual Basic Editor.

Either way, Excel creates a special *module* sheet that holds the actions and instructions in your macro. The macro instructions in a macro module (whether recorded by Excel or written by you) are stored in the Visual Basic for Applications programming language.

You can then study the VBA code that the macro recorder creates and edit this code in the Visual Basic Editor, which you open by clicking the Visual Basic command button on the Developer tab (when this optional tab is displayed on the Ribbon) or by pressing Alt+F11.

Recording macros

With Excel's macro recorder, you can create many of the utility-type macros that help you to perform the repetitive tasks necessary for creating and editing your worksheets and charts. When you turn on the macro recorder, the macro recorder records all your actions in the active worksheet or chart sheet as you make them. Note that the macro recorder doesn't record the keystrokes or mouse actions that you take to accomplish an action — only the VBA code required to perform the action itself. This means that mistakes that you make while taking an action that you rectify won't be recorded as part of the macro; for example, if you make a typing error and then edit it while the macro recorder is on, only the corrected entry shows up in the macro without the original mistakes and steps taken to remedy them.

The macros that you create with the macro recorder can be stored either as part of the current workbook, in a new workbook, or in a special, globally available Personal Macro Workbook named PERSONAL.XLSB that's stored in a folder called XLSTART on your hard disk. When you record a macro as part of your Personal Macro Workbook, you can run that macro from any workbook that you have open (this is because the PERSONAL.XLSB workbook is secretly opened whenever you launch Excel, and although it remains hidden, its macros are always available). When you record macros as part of the current workbook or a new workbook, you can run those macros only when the workbook in which they were recorded is open in Excel.

When you create a macro with the macro recorder, you decide not only the workbook in which to store the macro but also what name and shortcut keystrokes to assign to the macro that you are creating. When assigning a name for your macro, use the same guidelines that you use when you assign a standard range name to a cell range in your worksheet. When assigning a shortcut keystroke to run the macro, you can assign

✦ The Ctrl kcy plus a letter from A to Z, as in Ctrl+Q

✦ Ctrl+Shift and a letter from A to Z, as in Ctrl+Shift+Q

You can't, however, assign the Ctrl key plus a punctuation or number key (such as Ctrl+1 or Ctrl+/) to your macro.

The Status bar at the bottom of the Excel 2007 program window contains a Record Macro button (the red dot on a worksheet to the immediate right of the Ready status indicator) that you can click to turn on the macro recorder. In addition, the Ribbon's View tab contains a Macros command button to which a drop-down menu containing the following three options is attached:

✦ **View Macros:** Opens the Macro dialog box where you can select a macro to run or edit.

✦ **Record Macro:** Opens the Record Macro dialog box where you define the settings for your new macro and then start the macro recorder the same as clicking the Record Macro button on the Status bar.

✦ **Use Relative References:** Uses relative cell addresses when recording a macro, making the macro more versatile by enabling you to run it in areas of a worksheet other than the ones originally used in the macro's recording.

And if this is not enough, Excel 2007 enables you to add a Developer tab to the Ribbon.

To add the Developer tab to the Excel 2007 Ribbon, follow these two steps:

1. **Click Office Button | Excel Options or press Alt+FI to open the Excel Options dialog box.**

2. **Click the Show Developer tab in the Ribbon check box on the Popular tab to select it and then click OK.**

When you turn on the macro recorder either by clicking the Record Macro button on the Status bar, clicking the Record Macro option on the Macros command button on the View tab (Alt+WMR), or clicking the Record Macro command button on the Developer tab (Alt+LR), the macro recorder records all your actions in the active worksheet or chart sheet as you make them.

To see how easy it is to create a macro with the macro recorder, follow along with these steps for creating a macro that enters the company name in 12-point, bold type and centers the company name across rows A through E with the Merge and Center feature:

1. **Open the Excel workbook that contains the worksheet data or chart you want your macro to work with.**

If you're building a macro that adds new data to a worksheet (as in this example), open a worksheet with plenty of blank cells in which to add the data. If you're building a macro that needs to be in a particular cell when its steps are played back, put the cell cursor in that cell.

2. **Click the Record Macro button (the one with a red dot on a worksheet) on the Status bar, or click the Record Macro option on the Macros command button on the View tab, or press Alt+WMR.**

The Record Macro dialog box opens, similar to the one shown in Figure 1-1, where you enter the macro name, define any keystroke shortcut, select the workbook in which to store the macro, and enter a description of the macro's function.

3. **Replace the Macro1 temporary macro name by entering your name for the macro in the Macro Name text box.**

Remember that when naming a macro, you must not use spaces in the macro name and it must begin with a letter and not some number or punctuation symbol. For this example macro, you replace Macro1 in the Macro Name text box with the name Company_name.

Next, you can enter a letter between A and Z that acts like a shortcut key for running the macro when you press Ctrl followed by that letter key. Just remember that Excel has already assigned a number of Ctrl+letter keystroke shortcuts for doing common tasks, such as Ctrl+C for copying an item to the Clipboard and Ctrl+V for pasting an item from the Clipboard into the worksheet. If you assign the same keystrokes to the macro that you're building, your macro's shortcut keys override and, therefore, disable Excel's ready-made shortcut keystrokes.

4. **(Optional) Click the Shortcut Key text box and then enter the letter of the alphabet that you want to assign to the macro.**

For this example macro, press Shift+C to assign Ctrl+Shift+C as the shortcut keystroke (so as not to disable the ready-made Ctrl+C shortcut).

Next, you need to decide where to save the new macro that you're building. Select Personal Macro Workbook on the Store Macro In drop-down list box to be able to run the macro anytime you like. Select This Workbook (the default) when you need to run the macro only when the current workbook is open. Select New Workbook if you want to open a new workbook in which to record and save the new macro.

5. **Click the Personal Macro Workbook, New Workbook, or This Workbook item on the Store Macro In drop-down list to indicate where to store the new macro.**

   For this example macro, select the Personal Macro Workbook so that you can use it to enter the company name in any Excel workbook that you create or edit.

   Now, you should document the purpose and functioning of your macro in the Description list box. Although this step is purely optional, it is a good idea to get in the habit of recording this information every time you build a new macro so that you and your coworkers can always know what to expect from the macro when they run it.

6. **(Optional) Click the Description list box and then insert a brief description of the macro's purpose in front of the information indicating the date and who recorded the macro.**

   Now you're ready to close the Record Macro dialog box and start recording your macro.

7. **Click OK to close the Record Macro dialog box.**

   When you do this, the Record Macro dialog box closes. The circular red icon on the Record Macro button both on the Status bar and the Developer tab changes into a square blue Stop Recording button.

   Click the Use Relative References option on the Macros command button on the View tab or the Use Relative References command button on the Developer tab (when it's displayed) when you want the macro recorder to record the macro relative to the position of the current cell. Doing this often makes a macro more versatile as it enables you to run the macro in areas in the worksheet other than the cells used in its original recording.

8. **(Optional) Click the Use Relative References option on the Macros command button on the View tab (Alt+WMU) or click the Use Relative References command button on the Developer tab (Alt+LU) if you want to be able to play back the macro anywhere in the worksheet.**

9. **Select the cells, enter the data, and choose the Excel commands required to perform the tasks that you want recorded just as you normally would in creating or editing the current worksheet, using either the keyboard or the mouse or a combination of the two.**

   For the example macro, all you do is type the company name and click the Enter button on the Formula bar to complete the entry in the current cell. Next, click the Bold button and then click 16 on the Font Size drop-down list on the Home tab. Finally, drag through cells A1:E1 to select this range and then click the Merge and Center button, again on the Home tab.

After you finish taking all the actions in Excel that you want recorded (See Figure 1-2), you're ready to shut off the macro recorder.

10. **Click the Stop Recording button on the Status bar or on the Developer tab of the Ribbon.**

The square blue Stop Recording button on the Status bar and the Developer tab change back into circular red Record Macro buttons, letting you know that the macro recorder is now turned off and no further actions will be recorded.

Figure 1-1:
Getting
ready to
record the
Company_
name macro
in the
Record
Macro
dialog box.

Figure 1-2:
Recording
the actions
for the
Company_
name in the
worksheet.

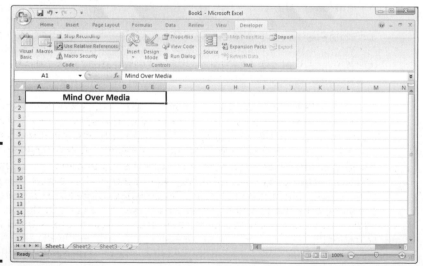

Running a macro

After recording a macro, you can run it by doing any of the following:

✦ Click the View Macros option on the Macros command button on the View tab or press Alt+WMV.

✦ Click the Macros command button on the Developer tab of the Ribbon when it's displayed or press Alt+LPM.

✦ Press Alt+F8.

Excel then opens the Macro dialog box, which is similar to the one shown in Figure 1-3. As this figure shows, Excel lists the names of all the macros in the current workbook and in your Personal Macro Workbook (provided you've created one) in the Macro Name list box. Click the name of the macro that you want to play and click the Run button or press Enter.

Figure 1-3:
Selecting the macro to run in the Macro dialog box.

If you assigned a shortcut keystroke to the macro, you don't have to bother opening the Macro dialog box to play the macro: Simply press Ctrl plus the letter key or Ctrl+Shift plus the letter key that you assigned and Excel immediately plays back all of the commands that you recorded.

Before testing a new macro, you may need to select a new worksheet, or at least a new cell range within the active worksheet. When recording cell references in a macro, the macro recorder always inserts absolute references in the macro sheet unless you click the Use Relative References button on the Developer tab before you start choosing the commands and taking the actions in the spreadsheet that you want recorded as part of the macro. This means that your macro enters its data entries or performs its formatting in the same area of the active worksheet (unless the code in the macro itself causes the macro to first select a new area or select a new sheet in the active workbook).

Book VIII Chapter 1

Building and Running Macros

If you run your macro in a worksheet that already contains data in the cells that the macro uses, you run the risk of having existing data and/or formatting overwritten during the macro's execution. Keep in mind that, although you can use the Undo feature to reverse the very last action performed by your macro, most macros perform a series of actions, so you may end up using multiple levels of Undo before you are able to successfully reconstruct your spreadsheet.

Macro Security

Excel 2007 uses a system called Microsoft Authenticode that enables developers to authenticate their macro projects or add-ins created with Visual Basic for Applications by a process referred to as *digital signing*. When you run a macro in your worksheet that's not saved in the trusted locations on your computer, such as the Templates and XLSTART folder in your user area on the computer, Excel checks to see if the macro is digitally signed and that the signature is both valid and current. The macro's developer must have a certificate issued by a reputable authority or is considered as a trusted publisher.

If the program cannot verify a macro's digital signature (perhaps because it doesn't have one) or the trustworthiness of its macro publisher, the program then displays a security alert on the message bar underneath the Excel Ribbon. This alert area contains an Enable Content and a Trust Center command button. You can then click the Enable Content button to ignore the alert and go ahead and run the macro, assuming that you can vouch for the macro's publisher and are sure that running the macro poses no security risk to your computer. You click the Trust Center command button in the security alert on the message bar to open the Trust Center dialog box where you can add to the trusted locations on your computer system and change the macro security settings.

You can also open the Macro Settings tab of the Trust Center dialog box by clicking the Macro Security command button on the Developer tab (Alt+LAS) or clicking the Trust Center Settings button on the Trust Center tab of the Excel Options dialog box (Alt+FIT) and then clicking Macro Settings in the dialog box's Navigation pane.

By default, Excel selects the Disable All Macros with Notification option button on the Macro Settings tab of the Trust Center. When this setting is selected, all macros that are not saved in one of the trusted locations are automatically disabled in the worksheet, but you do get a security alert each time you try to run one of these macros that enables you to ignore the alert and go ahead and run the macro by clicking the Enable Content button.

The Macro Settings tab of the Trust Center dialog box also contains these other option buttons you can select:

✦ **Disable All Macros without Notification** to disable all macros not saved in one of your computer's trusted locations and all security alerts so that you and the other users of the worksheet have no way to ignore the alert and run the macro. Select this option when you don't trust someone else's macros and want to make it impossible to run a macro carrying a computer virus.

✦ **Disable All Macros except Digitally Signed Macros** to automatically enable digitally signed macros from a publisher that you've indicated is trustworthy and to disable all macros that are not digitally signed without notification. When you select this option and you try to run a digitally signed macro that's not from a publisher you've indicated is trustworthy, Excel displays an alert in the message bar with a Trust All Documents from this Publisher button that you can select, thereby adding the publisher to the trusted list.

✦ **Enable All Macros (Not Recommended; Potentially Dangerous Code Can Run)** to throw all caution to the wind and allow all macros to run in any worksheet you open — this is one option you never ever want to select!

To change the trusted locations on your computer, you need to click the Trusted Locations tab in the Trust Center dialog box. You can then use these options to change the location settings:

✦ **Add New Location:** Use this command button to open the Microsoft Office Trusted Location dialog box where you select a new folder on your computer as a trusted location either by entering its directory path name in the Path text box or selecting it with the Browse button. Click the Subfolders of This Location Are Also Trusted check box to select it if you want all subfolders within the designated folder to be included as trusted locations.

✦ **Allow Trusted Locations on My Network (Not Recommended):** Select this check box so that you can designate folders to which you have access on your local network as trusted locations using the Add New Location command button (as described in the immediately preceding bullet point).

✦ **Disable All Trusted Locations, Only Files Signed by Trusted Publishers Will Be Trusted:** Select this check box to immediately disable all the folders currently designated as trusted locations and allow only macros from publishers designated as trustworthy to run in Excel.

**Book VIII
Chapter 1**

**Building and
Running Macros**

Assigning Macros to the Quick Access Toolbar

Instead of running a macro by selecting it in the Macro dialog box or by pressing shortcut keys you assign to it, you can assign the macro to a custom button on the Quick Access toolbar and then run it by clicking that custom button.

To assign a macro to a custom button on the Quick Access toolbar, you follow these steps:

1. **Click Office Button | Excel Options | Customize or press Alt+FIC to open the Customize tab of the Excel Options dialog box.**

2. **Click Macros in the Choose Commands From drop-down list box.**

Excel lists the names of the all the macros created in the current workbook and saved in the PERSONAL.XLSB workbook in the Choose Commands From list box.

3. **Click the name of the macro to add to a custom button on the Quick Access toolbar in the Choose Commands From list box and then click the Add button.**

4. **Click OK to close the Excel Options dialog box.**

After you close the Excel Options dialog box, a custom button with a generic macro icon (picturing a standard command flowchart icon) appears on the Quick Access toolbar. To see the name of the macro assigned to this custom macro button as a ScreenTip, position the mouse pointer over the button. To run the macro, click the button.

Keep in mind that you can also assign macros to the graphic objects you add to your worksheet, including shapes you draw, clip art, and pictures you import. To assign a macro to a graphic object, right-click it and then click the Assign Macro option on its shortcut menu. Then click the name of the recorded macro to run in the list box of the Assign Macro dialog box and click OK. Thereafter, when you position the mouse pointer over the graphic object, the pointer becomes a hand with a pointing index finger (just like when you assign a hyperlink to a graphic — see Book IV, Chapter 2), indicating that you can click it to run the macro.

Chapter 2: VBA Programming

The subject of this chapter is Visual Basic for Applications (usually known simply as VBA), which is the official programming language of Excel, and how you can use it to both edit the macros that you record (as described in Book VIII, Chapter 1) as well as to write new macros. The key to editing and writing macros in VBA is its editing program, the Visual Basic Editor (often abbreviated as VBE). The Visual Basic Editor offers a rich environment for coding and debugging VBA code with an interface that rivals Excel itself in terms of features and complexity.

VBA is a huge subject, well beyond the scope of this book. In this chapter, I simply introduce you to the Visual Basic Editor, and I explain how to use it to do basic macro editing. I also show you how to use the Visual Basic Editor to create custom Excel functions that you can then use when building formulas in your Excel spreadsheets. Custom functions (also known as *user-defined functions* or *UDFs*) work just like built-in functions except that they perform only the calculations that you define, by using just the arguments that you specify.

If this basic introduction to Visual Basic for Applications and using the Visual Basic Editor inspires you to go on and try your hand at real VBA project development in Excel, I recommend *VBA For Dummies,* 4th Edition, by John Paul Mueller (published by Wiley Publishing, Inc.) as an excellent next step. His book gives you the lowdown on all the ins and outs of VBA programming in that old, familiar, down-home *For Dummies* style that you've come to know and love.

Using the Visual Basic Editor

The first question that you may have is where the heck did they stick this Visual Basic Editor that you've heard so much about? Actually, the Visual Basic Editor is always ready to step forward whenever you press Alt+F11 or click the Visual Basic command button on the Developer tab or press Alt+LV when this optional tab is displayed on the Ribbon.

The Developer tab is not one of the permanent tabs on the Excel Ribbon. If your Ribbon doesn't have a Developer tab, this just means that you haven't yet added it to the Ribbon, something you definitely want to do when working with macros. To add the Developer tab, click Show Developer Tab in the Ribbon check box on the Popular tab of the Excel Options dialog box (Alt+FI) to select it.

Figure 2-1 shows the arrangement of the typical components in the Visual Basic Editor after you first open its window and open a new module sheet. As you can see, this window contains its own menu bar (with a few more menus than the regular Excel window uses). Beneath the menu bar, you find a Visual Basic Editor Standard toolbar. This toolbar, shown in Figure 2-2, contains a number of buttons that you may use when creating and editing VBA code.

Beneath the Standard toolbar in the Visual Basic Editor, you find a number of tiled windows of various sizes and shapes. Keep in mind that these are the default windows. They aren't the only windows that you can have open in the Visual Basic Editor (as though it weren't crowded and confusing enough), nor is this the only way that they can be arranged.

The two most important windows (at least, when you're first starting out using the Visual Basic Editor) are the Project Explorer window and the Code window. The Project Explorer window, which is located to the immediate left of the Code window (refer to Figure 2-1), shows you all the projects that you have open in the Visual Basic Editor and enables you to easily navigate their various parts. Note that in VBA, a *project* consists of all the code and user forms that belong to a particular workbook along with the sheets of the workbook itself.

The macros that you record in the workbook, as well as any that you write for it in the Visual Basic Editor, are recorded on module sheets to which generic names are assigned, such as Module1, Module2, and so forth. The actual lines of VBA programming code for the macro that are stored on a particular module sheet appear in the Code window when you select its module in the Project Explorer window (the Code window appears to the immediate right of the Project Explorer window).

Project Explorer window

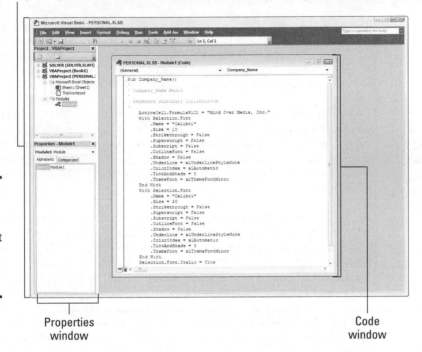

Figure 2-1:
The Visual
Basic Editor
window as it
appears
upon
opening.

Properties
window

Code
window

To open a module in the Code window, double-click its module icon in the Project Explorer or right-click the module icon and then click View Code at the top of its shortcut menu.

If you want to rename a module in your VBA project to something a little more descriptive than Module1, Module2, and so on, you can do this in the Properties window that appears immediately below the Project Explorer. Simply click and drag through the name (such as Module1) that appears after the label (Name) on the Alphabetic tab in the Properties window and replace it with a more descriptive name before you press Enter. When renaming a module, remember that you must use the same naming guidelines as when naming a range name in a worksheet: Begin the module name with a letter of the alphabet and don't put any spaces between words (use underlines instead).

Getting VBA help

Given the richness of the Visual Basic for Applications language and the sophistication of the Visual Basic Editor, you definitely want to become well acquainted with VBA online help as you begin to use the language and its editor to modify and refine your recorded macros and develop custom applications of your own. The VBA Help system works just like Excel's Help program (covered in Book I, Chapter 2).

**Book VIII
Chapter 2**

VBA Programming

Figure 2-2:
The buttons
on the
Visual Basic
Editor's
toolbar.

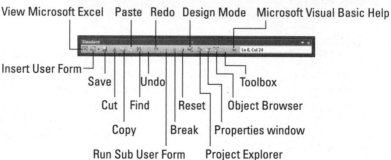

You can get help using Visual Basic for Applications by choosing Help⇨
Microsoft Visual Basic Help on the menu bar, pressing F1, or by clicking the
Microsoft Visual Basic Help button that appears near the end of the toolbar.
Excel then opens the Excel Help window with the Excel Developer Help and
How-to section containing the following links: Getting Started, What's New,
Concepts, How Do I...in Excel 2007, Excel Object Model Reference, and
Microsoft Graph Visual Basic Reference.

To get access to the topical information on Visual Basic, click one of the links
in the Excel Developer Help and How-to section or click the Show Table of
Contents button on the toolbar (the one with the closed book icon), then
click one of the books in the Navigation pane that appears on the left to
expand its topics, and then click one of its topical links to get detailed help
information.

You can also get help on a particular Visual Basic property by typing the command into the Search text box on the left side of the row immediately under the Help window's toolbar, and then clicking the Search button or pressing the Enter key. The Visual Basic Editor responds by displaying a list containing that property and others related to it that you can then click to obtain detail usage information.

In the Code window, when you need help with a particular property that appears in a line of your macro's VBA code, by far the best way to get help is to select the property with the I-beam mouse pointer and then click the Help button on the Standard toolbar or press F1. When you do this, the Visual Basic Editor opens an Excel Help window that lists the property. You can then click the link to display detailed information on the property including its syntax and examples of its usage.

By selecting unfamiliar statements in the code of the macros that you record and edit in the Visual Basic Editor and then opening a context-sensitive Excel Help window in this manner, you can quickly become familiar with the usage and syntax of the most commonly used statements and properties in the VBA language.

Editing recorded macros

After you've created a macro, you don't necessarily have to re-record it to change the way it behaves. In many cases, you will find it more expedient to change its behavior by simply editing its contents in the Visual Basic Editor. Note that if the macro you want to edit is stored in your Personal Macro Workbook (that `personal.xlsb` file in the XLSTART folder — see Book VIII, Chapter 1 for details), you *must* unhide this workbook before you edit it in the Visual Basic Editor.

To unhide the Personal Macro Workbook, follow these steps:

1. **Click the Unhide command button on the Ribbon's View tab or press Alt+WU.**

   Excel opens the Unhide dialog box showing the workbook, PERSONALB, in its Unhide Workbook list box.

2. **Click** PERSONALB **in the Unhide Workbook list box and then press Enter.**

   This action makes the Personal Macro Workbook visible and activates it so that you can now edit its macros in the Visual Basic Editor.

**Book VIII
Chapter 2**

VBA Programming

To open a macro for editing in the Visual Basic Editor, follow these steps:

1. **Click the View Macros option on the Macros command button on the View tab or press Alt+WMV or Alt+F8.**

   This action opens the Macro dialog box showing all the names of the macros that you've defined in the workbook and in your Personal Macro Workbook.

2. **Click the name of the macro that you want to edit in the Macro Name list box and then click the Edit button.**

   This action opens the Visual Basic Editor with the code for your macro displayed in the Code window unless you select the name of a macro saved in the Personal Macro Workbook and this workbook is still hidden. In that case, Excel displays an Alert dialog box telling you that you can't edit a hidden macro and informing you that you need to unhide this workbook. You then need to click OK in the Alert dialog box, press Escape to close the Macro dialog box, and then follow the steps for unhiding the Personal Macro Workbook immediately preceding these steps before you repeat these first two macro editing steps.

   After you have the lines of code for the macro displayed in the Code window in the Visual Basic Editor, you can edit any of its statements as needed. If you want to obtain a printout of the lines of code in your macro before you begin making changes, choose File⇨Print on the Visual Basic Editor menu bar or press Ctrl+P. This action opens a Print dialog box with the Current Module option button selected in the Range section and the Code check box selected in the Print What section so that you can go ahead and click OK to have Excel print all the statements in the macro.

   When editing the macro's commands, remember that you can use the Edit⇨Undo (Ctrl+Z) command to undo any deletion that you make by mistake. Also, remember that you can find out what a particular statement or property does in the macro by selecting it with the I-beam mouse pointer and pressing F1, or by clicking the Help button on the Standard toolbar to get help in the Help window.

3. **Edit the statements in the Code window of the Visual Basic Editor as needed.**

   After you finish editing the macro, you're ready to return to your spreadsheet where you can test out the modified macro and make sure that you haven't added some wacky, unwanted command to the macro or, even worse, crippled it so that it no longer runs at all.

4. **Click the View Microsoft Excel button at the beginning of the Standard toolbar or click the workbook's minimized button on the Windows taskbar.**

Select an appropriate or safe place in which to test your modified macro and then run it, either by pressing its shortcut keys or by pressing Alt+F8, clicking it in the Macro list box, and then clicking the Run button.

If something doesn't work as intended or if the macro doesn't work at all, you need to return to the Visual Basic Editor and find and correct your error(s). Click the Visual Basic command button on the Developer tab of the Ribbon (Alt+LV) to return to the Visual Basic Editor and have a try at editing the code one more time.

If everything checks out and runs as planned, you need to save your changes as outlined in Step 5.

5. Click the Save button on the Quick Access toolbar to save the changes to the modified macro if it's stored as part of the current workbook.

If you modified a global macro saved as part of the Personal Macro Workbook, you have to exit Excel in order to save your changes to the macro. When you click Office Button | Exit Excel or Alt+FX or Alt+F4, Excel displays an Alert dialog box asking if you want to save the changes you made to the `personal.xlsb` file. Click the Yes button to save your macro modifications as you close down Excel.

Keep in mind that Excel automatically hides the Personal Macro Workbook when you exit Excel if you don't click the Hide command button on the View tab or press Alt+WH when the `PERSONALSB` workbook is active sometime before exiting the program. This means that you must remember to click the Unhide command button on the View tab (Alt+WU) and select this personal macro workbook in the Unhide dialog box to make it visible before the next time you launch Excel and need to edit any of its macros during any subsequent editing session.

Finding and replacing code in the macro

You can use the Find feature in the Visual Basic Editor to quickly locate the statements or properties that need editing in your macro. You open the Find dialog box, shown in Figure 2-3, by choosing Edit⇨Find on the menu bar, clicking the Find button on the Standard toolbar, or by pressing Ctrl+F. This dialog box is very similar to the one you use when finding entries in your Excel spreadsheet. The main difference is that the Find dialog box gives you different choices for what to search for (in addition to the familiar options for finding whole words only and matching case):

✦ **Current Procedure option button** to search only the current programming procedure in the Code window.

✦ **Current Module option button** to search only the macros in the current module (the default).

✦ **Current Project option button** to search all the macros in all modules within the current project.

✦ **Selected Text option button** to search only the text that you've selected in the Code window (this option is not available unless you've selected a block of text in the current code).

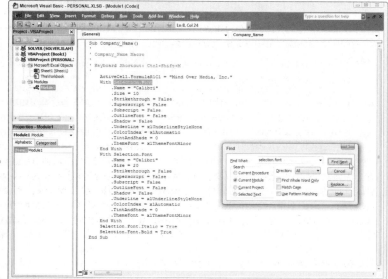

Figure 2-3:
Using the Find feature to locate the code to edit in the Code window.

After you enter the Visual Basic property or statement as your search string in the Find What text box, select the search options, and click the Find Next button, Excel attempts to locate its first occurrence in the code. When it does, the program highlights that occurrence in the current procedure, module, VBA project, or selected text block (depending on which Search option you use). To find the next occurrence, you can click the Find Next button in the Find dialog box again, or, if you closed this dialog box, by pressing F3.

If you have a number of occurrences throughout the macro that require the same type of updating, you can use the Replace feature to both find and replace them in the macro code. This is particularly useful when you decide to change a particular value throughout a macro (such as selecting the cell range named "income_08" for processing instead of the range "income_07"), and you want to make sure that you don't miss any occurrences.

To open the Replace dialog box, choose Edit⇨Replace on the Visual Basic Editor menu bar or press Ctrl+H. Note that you can open the Replace dialog box from within the Find dialog box by clicking its Replace button.

The Replace dialog box that appears is just like the Find dialog box, except that it contains a Replace With text box along with the Find What text box and has Replace and Replace All buttons in addition to the Find Next button. After entering the property or statement to find in the Find What text box and the one to replace it with in the Replace With text box, click the Find Next button to locate the first occurrence in the current procedure, module, VBA project, or selected text block (depending on which Search option you use). After this occurrence is selected in the Code window, you have it replaced with the replacement text by clicking the Replace button. Excel then locates the next occurrence, which you can then replace by clicking the Replace button or pass over to find the next occurrence by clicking the Find Next button.

Don't use the Replace All button to replace all the occurrences in your macro unless you're 100 percent sure that you won't be globally replacing something that shouldn't be replaced and possibly screwing up your macro big time. I once typed "selection.font.bold = ture" into the Replace With text box when I intended to enter "selection.font.bold = true" as the replacement text when searching for the property "Selection.Font.Bold = False" in the macro. I then clicked the Replace All button only to discover to my dismay that I introduced this error throughout the code! Of course, I then had to turn around and use the Replace feature to find all the instances of "selection.font.bold = ture" and replace them with "Selection.Font.Bold = true."

Changing settings for VBA properties

Even when you don't know anything about programming in VBA (and even if you aim to keep it that way), you can still get the gist of some of the more obvious properties in a macro that change certain settings, such as number format or font attribute, by experimenting with assigning them new values.

In the Company_name macro shown previously in Figure 2-3, for example, you can tell that the section of VBA commands between the line

```
With Selection.Font
```

and the line

```
End With
```

contains the procedure for assigning various font attributes for the current cell selection.

Going a step further, you probably can figure out that most of these attributes are being reset by making the attribute equal to a new entry or value, such as

```
.Name = "Calibri"
```

or

```
.Size = 12
```

or an attribute is being reset by turning it on or off by setting it equal to True or False, such as

```
Selection.Font.Bold = True
```

to make the text in the current cell selection bold.

Now, it doesn't require a programming degree (at least, not the last time I checked) to get the bright idea that you can make your macro behave differently just by — *carefully* — editing these settings. For example, suppose that you want the final font size to be 24 points instead of 12. All you have to do is change

```
.Size = 12
```

to

```
.Size = 24
```

Likewise, you can have the macro apply single underlining to the cell selection by changing

```
.Underline = xlUnderlineStyleNone
```

to

```
.Underline = xlUnderlineStyleSingle
```

Many times, the alternate settings allowed in a particular Visual Basic code, such as the Underline property, are anything but obvious (how's that for an understatement?). When you encounter such a property in the macro code and you want to know what kinds of values it will accept, simply look it up in the online Visual Basic Reference. Click the property in the Code window without selecting its current setting (such as selecting Underline rather than selecting Underline = xlUnderlineStyleNone) and then Press F1 to open the Excel Help window with links to information on that property. Usually the Example section at the bottom of this Help window gives you an idea of the different types of values that the property can take. Remember, too, that you can obtain a printout of this Help information by clicking the Print button on the Help window's toolbar.

Getting macro input by adding a dialog box

One of the biggest problems with recording macros is that any text or values that you have the macro enter for you in a worksheet or chart sheet can never vary thereafter. If you create a macro that enters the heading "Bob's Barbecue Pit" in the current cell of your worksheet, this is the only heading you'll ever get out of that macro. However, you can get around this inflexibility by using the InputBox function. When you run the macro, this Visual Basic function causes Excel to display an Input dialog box where you can enter whatever title makes sense for the new worksheet. The macro then puts that text into the current cell and formats this text, if that's what you've trained your macro to do next.

To see how easy it is to use the InputBox function to add interactivity to an otherwise staid macro, follow the steps for converting the Company_name macro that currently inputs the text "Mind Over Media" to one that actually prompts you for the name that you want entered. The InputBox function uses the following syntax:

```
InputBox(prompt[,title][,default][,xpos][,ypos][,helpfile,
    context])
```

In this function, only the *prompt* argument is required with the rest of the arguments being optional. The *prompt* argument specifies the message that appears inside the Input dialog box, prompting the user to enter a new value (or in this case, a new company name). The *prompt* argument can be up to a maximum of 1,024 characters. If you want the prompt message to appear on different lines inside the dialog box, you enter the functions, Chr(13) and Chr(10), in the text (to insert a carriage return and a linefeed in the message).

The optional *title* argument specifies what text to display in the title bar of the Input dialog box. If you don't specify a *title* argument, Excel displays the name of the application on the title bar. The optional *default* argument specifies the default response that automatically appears in the text box at the bottom of the Input dialog box. If you don't specify a default argument, the text box is empty in the Input dialog box.

The *xpos* and *ypos* optional arguments specify the horizontal distance from the left edge of the screen to the left edge of the dialog box and the vertical distance from the top edge of the screen to the top edge of the dialog box. If you don't specify these arguments, Excel centers the input dialog box horizontally and positions it approximately one-third of the way down the screen vertically.

The *helpfile* and *context* optional arguments specify the name of the custom Help file that you make available to the user to explain the workings of the Input dialog box as well as the type of data that it accepts. As part of the

Book VIII
Chapter 2

VBA Programming

process of creating a custom help file for use in the Excel Help system, you assign the topic a context number appropriate to its content, which is then specified as the *context* argument for the InputBox function. When you specify a help file and *context* argument for this function, Excel adds a Help button to the custom Input dialog box that users can click to access the custom help file in the Help window.

Before you can add the line of code to the macro with the InputBox function, you need to find the place in the Visual Basic commands where the line should go. To enter the Mind Over Media text into the active cell, the Company_name macro uses the following Visual Basic command:

```
ActiveCell.FormulaR1C1 = "Mind Over Media"
```

To add interactivity to the macro, you need to insert the InputBox function on a line in the Code window right above this ActiveCell.FormulaR1C1 statement, as follows:

1. **Position the insertion point in the Code window at the beginning of the ActiveCell.FormulaR1C1 statement and press Enter to insert a new line.**

Now that you've added a new line, you need to move the insertion point up to it.

2. **Press the ↑ key to position the insertion point at the beginning of the new line.**

On this line, you want to create a variable that supplies the *prompt* argument to the InputBox function. To do this, you state the name of the variable (InputMsg in this case) followed by its current entry. Be sure to enclose the message text on the right side of the equal sign in a closed pair of double quotation marks.

3. **Type the following code to create the InputMsg variable on line 7 and then press the Enter key to start a new line 9:**

```
InputMsg = "Enter the company name or title for this
      worksheet in the text box below and then click OK:"
```

Next, you create a variable named InputTitle that supplies the optional *title* argument for the InputBox function. This variable makes the text, "Spreadsheet Title" appear as the title of the Input dialog box. Again, be sure to enclose the name for the dialog box title bar in quotation marks.

4. **Type the following code to create the InputTitle variable on line 8 and then press Enter to insert a new line 10:**

```
InputTitle = "Spreadsheet Title"
```

Next, you create a variable name DefaultText that supplied the optional *default* argument to the InputBox function. This variable makes the text, "Mind Over Media," appear as the default entry on the text box at the bottom of the custom Company Name Input dialog box.

5. **Type the following code to create the DefaultText variable on line 9 and then press Enter to insert a new line 11:**

```
DefaultText = "Mind Over Media"
```

Next, you create a final variable named CompanyName that specifies the InputBox function as its entry (using the InputMsg, InputTitle, and DefaultText variables that you just created) and stores the results of this function.

6. **Type the following code to create the SpreadsheetTitle variable that uses the InputBox function on line 10:**

```
SpreadsheetTitle = InputBox(InputMsg, InputTitle,
    DefaultText)
```

Finally, you replace the value, "Mind Over Media," in the ActiveCell.FormulaR1C1 property with the SpreadsheetTitle variable (whose value is determined by whatever is input into the Spreadsheet Title Input dialog box), thus effectively replacing this constant in the macro with the means for making this input truly interactive.

7. **Select "Mind Over Media" on line 11 and replace it with SpreadsheetTitle (with *no* quotation marks).**

Figure 2-4 shows the Code window with the edited Company_name macro after adding the statements that make it interactive. Figure 2-5 shows the Spreadsheet Title dialog box in action in the worksheet. This input dialog box now automatically appears and prompts you for input whenever you run the edited and now fully interactive version of the Company_Name macro.

To go ahead and enter Mind Over Media into the current cell and then format it by using the rest of the macro commands, you just click OK in this custom dialog box. To enter and format the name of another company, you simply type the name of the company (which automatically replaces Mind Over Media in the text box) before you click OK.

Book VIII Chapter 2

VBA Programming

Figure 2-4:
Company_
name Code
window
after adding
variables
and the
InputBox
function.

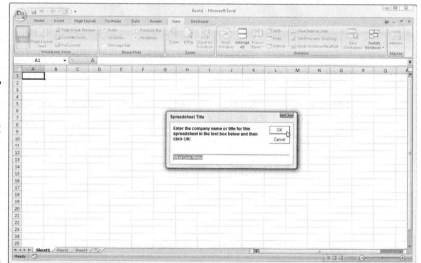

Figure 2-5:
The
Spreadsheet
Title dialog
box that
appears
when you
run the
Company_
name
macro.

Writing new macros in the Visual Basic Editor

After you have the skill in the VBA language, you can write new macros from
scratch in the Visual Basic Editor instead of just editing ones that you've previously recorded in your spreadsheet by using Excel's macro recorder. When
creating a macro from scratch in the Visual Basic Editor, you need to follow
these general steps:

Why not simply type in the arguments of the InputBox function?

The biggest reason for using the variables InputMsg, InputTitle, and PromptText to supply the *prompt, title,* and *default* arguments of the InputBox function — rather than just typing them into the function — is their length. If you typed in all three pieces of text within the parentheses of the InputBox function, you would end up with one of the longest (and hardest to read) lines of code in history. When you use variables to do the job, as in the example shown previously, you end up with lines of code that fit on one screen, thus making the lines of code easier to read and also making it possible to print them on a normal piece of paper. If you use the variables on other procedures in the macro, declaring them all together at the beginning of the code also makes it easy to update their values.

1. **Click the name of the VBA project in the Project Explorer window where you want to add the new macro.**

   If you want to write a macro just for the current workbook, click the VBAProject function that contains its filename in parentheses, as in VBAProject (My Spreadsheet). If you want to write a global macro in the Personal Macro Workbook, click VBAProject(PERSONAL.XLSB) in the Project Explorer window.

2. **Choose Insert⇨Module on the Visual Basic Editor menu bar.**

   Excel responds by opening a new, blank Code window in the Visual Basic Editor window and by adding another Module icon (named with the next available number) in the outline in the Project Explorer window under the appropriate VBA Project.

   Next, you begin your macro by creating a subroutine (all macros, even the ones you record in the spreadsheet, are really Visual Basic subroutines). To do this, you just type **sub** (for subroutine).

3. **Type sub and then press the spacebar.**

   Now, you need to name your new macro, which you do by naming your subroutine. Remember that in naming your new macro (or a subroutine), you follow the same rules as when naming a range name (begin with a letter and no spaces).

4. **Type the name of your macro and then press the Enter key.**

As soon as you press the Enter key, the Visual Basic Editor inserts a closed pair of parentheses after the macro's name, a blank line, and an End Sub statement on its own line below that. It then positions the insertion point at the beginning of the blank line between the lines with the Sub and End Sub statements. It's here that you enter the lines of code for the macro that you're writing.

5. **Enter the lines of VBA code for the macro in between the Sub and End Sub statements.**

   Before you begin writing the VBA statements that your macro is to execute, you should first document the purpose and functioning of this macro. To do this, type an apostrophe (') at the beginning of each line of this text to enter it as a comment (Excel knows not to try to execute any line of code that's prefaced with an apostrophe). When you press the Enter key to start a new line that begins with an apostrophe, the line of text turns green, indicating that the Visual Basic Editor considers it to be a comment that's not to be executed when the macro runs.

   After you document the purpose of the macro with your comments, you begin entering the statements that you want the macro to execute (which must not be prefaced by apostrophes). To indent lines of code to make them easier to read, press Tab. If you need to outdent the line, press Shift+Tab. For help on writing VBA code, refer to the VBA online help and Steve Cummings' excellent *VBA For Dummies*. When you finish writing the code for your macro, you need to save it before you test it.

6. **Choose File⇨Save on the Visual Basic Editor menu bar or press Ctrl+S.**

After you save your new macro, you can click the View Microsoft Excel button on the Standard toolbar to return to your worksheet where you can try it. To run the new macro that you've written, choose Tools⇨Macros or press Alt+F8 to open the Macro dialog box and then click the name of the macro that you just wrote before you click OK.

If Excel encounters an error when running the macro, it returns you to the Visual Basic Editor, and an Alert Microsoft Visual Basic dialog box appears indicating (in very cryptic form) the nature of the error. Click the Debug button in this dialog box to have the Visual Basic Editor highlight the line of code that it can't execute. You can then attempt to find the mistake and edit it in the line of code. If you do eliminate the cause of the error, the Visual Basic Editor removes the highlighting from that line of code, and you can then click the Continue button (which automatically replaces the Run button when the Editor goes into debug mode) with the blue triangle pointing to the right on the Standard toolbar to continue running the macro.

Creating Custom Excel Functions

One of the best uses of VBA in Excel is to create custom spreadsheet functions also known as *user-defined functions* (*UDFs* for short). User-defined functions are great because you don't have to access the Macro dialog box to run them. In fact, you enter them into your spreadsheets just like you do any of the other built-in spreadsheet functions, either with the Insert Function button on the Formula bar or by typing them directly into a cell.

To create a user-defined function, you must do four little things:

✦ Create a new module sheet where the custom function is to be defined in the Visual Basic Editor by selecting its project in the Project Explorer window and then choosing Insert⇨Module on the Visual Basic Editor menu bar.

✦ Enter the name of the custom function and specify the names of the arguments that this function takes on the first line in the Code window — note that you can't duplicate any built-in function names, such as SUM or AVERAGE functions, and so on, and you must list argument names in the order in which they are processed and enclosed in parentheses.

✦ Enter the formula, or set of formulas, that tells Excel how to calculate the custom function's result by using the argument names listed in the Function command with whatever arithmetic operators or built-in functions are required to get the calculation made on the line or lines below.

✦ Indicate that you've finished defining the user-defined function by entering the End Function command on the last line.

To see how this procedure works in action, consider this scenario: Suppose that you want to create a custom function that calculates the sales commissions for your salespeople based on the number of sales they make in a month as well as the total amount of their monthly sales (they sell big-ticket items, such as RVs). Your custom Commission function will then have two arguments — *TotalSales* and *ItemsSold* — so that the first line of code on the module sheet in the Code window is

```
Function Commission(TotalSales,ItemsSold)
```

In determining how the commissions are actually calculated, suppose that you base the commission percentage on the number of sales made during the month. For five sales or fewer in a month, you pay a commission rate of 4.5 percent of the salesperson's total monthly sales; for sales of six or more, you pay a commission rate of 5 percent.

To define the formula section of the Commission custom function, you need to set up an IF construction. This IF construction is similar to the IF function that you enter into a worksheet cell except that you use different lines in the macro code for the construction in the custom function. An ELSE command separates the command that is performed if the expression is True from the command that is performed if the expression is False. The macro code is terminated by an END IF command. To set the custom function so that your salespeople get 4.5 percent of total sales for five or fewer items sold and 5 percent of total sales for more than five items sold, you enter the following lines of code underneath the line with the Function command:

```
If ItemsSold <= 5 Then
        Commission = TotalSales * 0.045
Else
        Commission = TotalSales * 0.05
End If
```

Figure 2-6 shows you how the code for this user-defined function appears in the Code window for its module sheets. The indents for the IF...END IF statements are made with the Tab key and make differentiating the parts of the IF construction easy. The first formula, Commission = TotalSales * 0.045 is used when the IF expression ItemsSold <= 5 is found to be True. Otherwise, the second formula underneath the Else command, Commission = TotalSales * 0.05 is used.

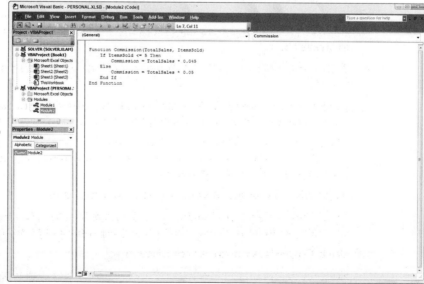

Figure 2-6:
Entering the Commission user-defined function in the Personal Macro Workbook.

After entering the definition for your user-defined function, you are ready to save it by choosing File⇨Save on the Visual Basic Editor menu bar or by pressing Ctrl+S. Then, you can click the View Microsoft Excel button on the Standard toolbar to return to the worksheet where you can try out your new custom function.

If you want to be able to use your user-defined function in any spreadsheet you create, be sure that you select VBAProject (personal.xlsb) in the Project Explorer window before you open a new module and define the custom function there.

Adding a description to a user-defined function

To help your user understand the purpose of your custom functions, you can add descriptions that appear in Insert Function and Function Arguments dialog boxes that help explain what the function does. To add this kind of description to your user-defined function, you use the Object Browser, a special window in the Visual Basic Editor that enables you to get information about particular objects available to the project that you have open.

To add a description for your user-defined function, follow these steps:

1. **Open the Visual Basic Editor from Excel by clicking the Visual Basic button on the Developer tab of the Ribbon or pressing Alt+LV or Alt+F11.**

   Now, you need to open the Object Browser.

2. **Choose View⇨Object Browser from the Visual Basic Editor menu bar or press F2.**

   This action opens the Object Browser window, which obscures the Code window.

3. **Click the drop-down list box that currently contains the value <All Libraries> and then click VBAProject on the drop-down list.**

   When you select VBAProject in this drop-down list, the Object Browser then displays your user-defined function as one of the objects in one of the Classes in the pane on the left.

4. **Right-click the name of your user-defined function.**

   This action selects the function and displays it in the Members pane on the right, while at the same time displaying the object's shortcut menu.

5. **Click Properties on the shortcut menu.**

   This action opens the Member Options dialog box for your user-defined function, where you can enter your description of this function, as shown in Figure 2-7.

6. **Type the text that you want to appear in the Insert Function and Function Arguments dialog box for the user-defined function in the Description text box and then click OK.**

Now, you can close the Object Browser and save your changes.

7. **Click the Close Window button to close the Object Browser and then choose the File⇨Save command.**

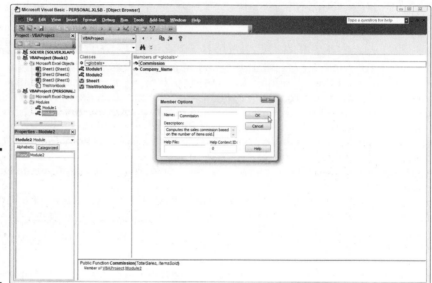

Figure 2-7:
Adding a description for the Commission user-defined function.

Using a custom function in your spreadsheet

The great thing about custom functions is that they can be inserted into your worksheets with your old friend the Insert Function button on the Formula bar. Figures 2-8 through 2-10 illustrate how easy it is to enter the custom Commission function in a worksheet with the Insert Function button.

Figure 2-8 shows a worksheet that contains a table with the April 2008 RV sales for three salespeople: Fred, Holly, and Jack. As you can see, the Automatic Subtotals feature (covered in Book VI, Chapter 1) has been used to compute both the monthly total sales (with the SUM function) and the number of sales (with the COUNT function) for each of these three salespeople.

To calculate the April monthly commissions for each salesperson in this table, you select the cell where you want the first commission to be calculated (Fred's commission in cell E5). Click the Insert Function button on the Formula bar and then click User Defined at the very bottom of the Or Select a Category drop down list. Doing this displays the PERSONAL.XLSB!Commission custom function in the Select a Function list box.

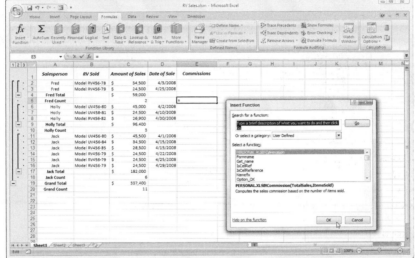

Figure 2-8:
Selecting a cell in the RV Sales spreadsheet into which to enter the Commission function.

When you click OK after selecting the PERSONAL.XLSB!Commission function in the Insert Function dialog box, the Function Arguments dialog box appears, shown in Figure 2-9. Here, you select cell C4 with Fred's total sales amount for April as the TotalSales argument and cell C5 with the number of sales made in that month as the ItemsSold argument.

When you click OK in the Function Arguments dialog box, Excel calculates Fred's commission by using the 4.5 percent commission rate because his two sales made in April are well below the five sales necessary to bump him up to the 5 percent commission rate used by the custom Commission function. Figure 2-10 shows the completed April sales table after calculating the monthly commissions for Fred, Holly, and Jack. In using the custom Commission function, both Fred and Holly fall into the 4.5 percent commission rate. Only Jack, the April RV sales king, gets paid the higher 5 percent commission rate for his six sales during this month.

Book VIII
Chapter 2

VBA Programming

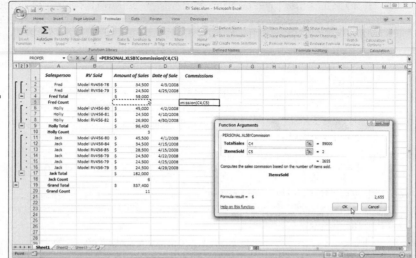

Figure 2-9: Specifying the TotalSales and ItemsSold arguments in the RV Sales spreadsheet.

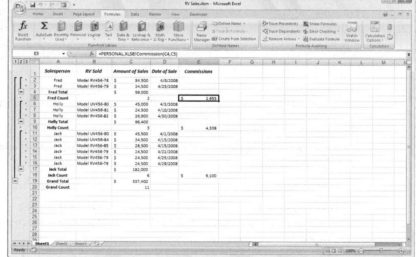

Figure 2-10: Completed spreadsheet for all sales people computed with the Commissions function.

Saving custom functions in add-in files

The only limitation to the user-defined functions that you save as part of a regular workbook file or the Personal Macro Workbook file is that when you enter them directly into a cell (without the use of the Insert Function dialog box), you must preface their function names with their filenames. For example, if you want to type in the custom Commission function that's saved in the Personal Macro Workbook, you enter the following formula:

```
=Commission(C9,C10)
```

Assuming that cell C9 contains the total sales and cell C10 contains the number of items sold, Excel returns the #NAME? error value to the cell. If you then edit the function to include the Personal Macro Workbook's filename as follows:

```
=PERSONAL.XLSB!Commission(C9,C10)
```

Excel calculates the sales commission based on the *TotalSales* in C9 and the *ItemsSold* in C10, returning this calculated value to the cell containing this user-defined function.

To be able to omit the filename from the custom functions that you create when you enter them directly into a cell, you need to save the workbook file that contains them as a special add-in file (for details on using add-ins in Excel, see Book I, Chapter 3). Then, after you've saved the workbook with your user-defined functions as an add-in file, you can start entering them into any worksheet sans their filename qualifier by activating the add-in in the Add-Ins dialog box (Alt+FIAA and then click the Go command button when Excel Add-Ins is displayed on the Manage drop-down list button).

To convert a workbook containing the user-defined functions that you want to be able to enter into worksheets without their filenames, follow these steps:

1. **Open the workbook in which you've saved your user-defined functions in Excel.**

   Make sure that each of the custom functions works properly.

2. **Press Alt+F11 or click the Visual Basic command button on the Developer tab or press Alt+LV if the Developer tab is displayed on the Ribbon.**

   This action opens the Visual Basic Editor window with the workbook file containing the user-defined functions selected in the Project Explorer window. Now you want to set up protection for this workbook so that no one but you can modify its contents.

3. **Choose Tools⇨VBAProject Properties from the Visual Basic Editor's menu bar.**

   This action opens the VBAProject — Project Properties dialog box with a General and a Protection tab, shown in Figure 2-11.

4. **Click the Protection tab and then click the Lock Project for Viewing check box.**

   Putting a check mark in this check box prevents other users from viewing the custom functions so that they can't make any changes to them. Next, you add a password that prevents them from removing the view protection status.

5. **Click the Password text box, enter the password there, and then click the Confirm Password text box and re-enter the password exactly as you entered it in the text box above before you click OK.**

   Now you're ready to return to the worksheet where you need to add a title and description for the new add-in file.

6. **Click the View Microsoft Excel button at the beginning of the Standard toolbar.**

   This action returns you to the worksheet in Excel. Before saving the workbook as an add-in, you should add a title and description of the user-defined functions that it contains (this information then appears in the Add-Ins dialog box whenever you select the add-in file).

7. **Click Office Button | Prepare | Properties or press Alt+FEP.**

   Excel opens the Document Information Panel at the top of the worksheet (similar to the one shown in Figure 2-12). Here you enter a brief name for the add-in in the Title field and a longer description of its custom functions.

8. **Click the Title text box and enter a descriptive title for the add-in, and then click the Comments text box and enter a description of its contents before you click the Close button (with the X) in the upper-right corner of the Document Information Panel.**

   Now you're ready to save the workbook file as a special add-in file.

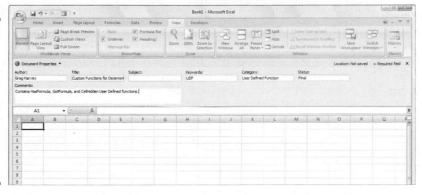

Figure 2-12:
Adding a title and description for the new add-in file in the Document Information Panel.

9. **Click Office Button | Save As or press Alt+FA.**

   This action opens the Save As dialog box, where you need to change the file type from Microsoft Excel Workbook (*.xlsx) to Microsoft Excel Add-In (*.xlam) and then specify the filename (to which Excel automatically appends the .xlam filename extension) under which to save it.

10. **Click the Save as Type pop-up button and then scroll all the way down to the bottom of the list and click Microsoft Excel Add-In (*.xlam).**

    This action selects the Add-Ins folder in the Save In drop-down list box showing the names of any add-in files that you've saved there.

11. **Click the File Name combo box and make any necessary changes to the filename (without changing the .xlam filename extension) before you click the Save button.**

    After saving your workbook as an add-in file, you're ready to activate the add-in so that you can enter its user-defined functions in any worksheet.

12. **Click Office Button | Excel Options or press Alt+FI and then click Add-Ins in the Navigation pane on the left.**

13. **Click the Go button near the bottom of the Add-Ins tab after checking to make sure that Excel Add-Ins is displayed on the Manage drop-down list button.**

    This action opens the Add-Ins dialog box showing the names of all the available add-ins. You must now add the name of your new add-in to this list.

14. **Click the Browse button in the Add-Ins dialog box.**

    This action opens the Browse dialog box that shows the contents of your AddIns folder.

15. **Click the name of your new add-in file in the Browse list box and then click OK.**

This action closes the Browse dialog box and returns you to the Add-Ins dialog box that now lists your new add-in file. Now all you have to do is make sure that the check box in front of the name of the new add-in (which displays the title and description you gave the add-in at the bottom of the Add-Ins dialog box) is selected before you click OK (see Figure 2-13).

16. **Click the check box in front of the name of the new add-in and then click OK.**

Figure 2-13:
Activating
the new
add-in file in
the Add-Ins
dialog box.

As soon as you click OK, Excel closes the Add-Ins dialog box and you can then start entering the custom functions that this add-in file contains directly into the cells of any spreadsheet without having to open the Insert Function dialog box.

Appendix: Using XML File Formats

*E*xcel 2007 supports the use of a new XML-based file format (which Microsoft officially calls the Microsoft Office Open XML format), which is touted as being more efficient in saving data, resulting in smaller file size and offering superior integration with external data sources (especially when these resources are Web-based ones supporting XML files). The basic XML-based file format carries the filename extension .xlsx and is the file format in which Excel automatically saves any new workbook you create. In addition, Excel supports the following file format extensions:

✦ .xlsm for macro-enabled XML workbook files

✦ .xltx for XML template files

✦ .xltm for macro-enabled XML template files

✦ .xlsb for non-XML binary workbook files

✦ .xlam for macro-enabled add-in files

The only problem with this new-fangled XML-based file format is that it's not one that earlier versions of Excel can open. This means that if everybody who needs to work with the workbook you've just created hasn't yet upgraded to Excel 2007, you need to save the new workbook in the earlier file format used in versions 97 through 2003 with the old .xls filename extension. To do this, click the Office Button, then highlight Save As and click the Excel 97-2003 Workbook option on the Save As submenu or press Alt+FF9 to open the Save As dialog box with the Excel 97-2003 Workbook (*.xls) selected as the file type. You can also select the Excel 97-2003 Workbook (*.xls) file type in the Save As Type drop-down list box if you open the Save As dialog box by clicking Office⇨Save As or pressing Alt+FA.

Keep in mind that filename extensions such as .xlsx and .xls do not appear as part of the filename (even though they are appended) in the File Name text box in the Save As dialog box unless you've removed the check mark from the Hide Extensions for Known File Types check box found on the View tab of the Folder Options dialog box in any Windows Explorer window such as Documents in Windows Vista and My Documents in Windows XP. To open the Folder Options dialog box from a Vista Explorer window, you click the Folder and Search option on the Organize button's drop-down menu. To open this dialog box from a Windows XP Explorer window, you click Folder Options on the Tool's pull-down menu.

The new binary file format called Office Excel 2007 Binary, or BIFF12 for short, that carries the .xlsb filename extension is designed for really huge spreadsheets that you create that have to be backwardly compatible with earlier versions of Excel.

Index

D

G

General number format
  as default, 95, 145
  overriding, 146
  trailing zeros, 94
General Options dialog box, 436–437, 439
Get a Digital ID dialog box, 476
GetPivotTable function, 64
Go To feature, 22, 130–131
Goal Seek dialog box, 668, 669
Goal Seek Status dialog box, 668, 669
goal seeking, in what-if analysis,
    655, 667–669
gradients, applying to cell selections,
    162, 163
graphic objects
  adding to charts, 559–585
  aligning, 565
  defined, 559
  deleting, 562
  drawing, 573–584
  grouping, 565–567
  illustrated, 560
  importing clip art, 568–571
  importing pictures, 568, 571
  layer issues, 562–565
  managing in Selection and Visibility
    task pane, 567–568
  manipulating, 561–562
  moving, 561–562
  overview, 560–568
  positioning, 561–562
  resizing, 561
  role of themes, 585
  selecting, 560
  showing/hiding, 71
  as worksheet backgrounds, 247–248
greater-than operator (>), 302, 304
greater-than-or-equal-to-operator (>=),
    302, 304

gridlines. *See also* Snap to Grid option
  vs. borders, 161
  changing color, 71
  for charts, 525
  customizing display, 537
  in printouts, 161
  removing, 71, 502–503
  showing/hiding, 71, 502–503
  in Workbook window, 161
Group and Outline command, Excel
    2007 equivalent to Excel 2003
    command, 36
[Group] indicator, title bar, 250–251
Group or Ungroup dialog box, 242–243
grouping graphic objects, 565–567
groups, as Ribbon component, 16

H

handheld calculator, Excel as, 300
Header and Footer command, Excel 2007
    equivalent to Excel 2003 command,
    33, 36–37
headers and footers
  custom, creating, 287–291
  custom, creating different even and odd
    page headers and footers, 287–291
  first-page, unique, 290
  overview, 284–285
  stock, adding, 285–287
Help button, 38, 40, 43, 47, 50
help information
  browsing related articles, 47–48
  expanding list of subtopics, 48
  Help Viewer, 47–49
  printing Viewer articles, 48
  searching Office Online for, 50–52
  Table of Contents pane, 49–50

J

U

V

Notes

Notes

Notes

Notes

Notes

Notes

Notes

Notes

Notes

Notes

Notes

Notes

Notes

INESS, CAREERS & PERSONAL FINANCE

0-7645-9847-3

0-7645-2431-3

Also available:
- Business Plans Kit For Dummies
  0-7645-9794-9
- Economics For Dummies
  0-7645-5726-2
- Grant Writing For Dummies
  0-7645-8416-2
- Home Buying For Dummies
  0-7645-5331-3
- Managing For Dummies
  0-7645-1771-6
- Marketing For Dummies
  0-7645-5600-2

- Personal Finance For Dummies
  0-7645-2590-5*
- Resumes For Dummies
  0-7645-5471-9
- Selling For Dummies
  0-7645-5363-1
- Six Sigma For Dummies
  0-7645-6798-5
- Small Business Kit For Dummies
  0-7645-5984-2
- Starting an eBay Business For Dummies
  0-7645-6924-4
- Your Dream Career For Dummies
  0-7645-9795-7

ME & BUSINESS COMPUTER BASICS

0-470-05432-8

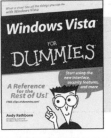

0-471-75421-8

Also available:
- Cleaning Windows Vista For Dummies
  0-471-78293-9
- Excel 2007 For Dummies
  0-470-03737-7
- Mac OS X Tiger For Dummies
  0-7645-7675-5
- MacBook For Dummies
  0-470-04859-X
- Macs For Dummies
  0-470-04849-2
- Office 2007 For Dummies
  0-470-00923-3

- Outlook 2007 For Dummies
  0-470-03830-6
- PCs For Dummies
  0-7645-8958-X
- Salesforce.com For Dummies
  0-470-04893-X
- Upgrading & Fixing Laptops For Dummies
  0-7645-8959-8
- Word 2007 For Dummies
  0-470-03658-3
- Quicken 2007 For Dummies
  0-470-04600-7

OD, HOME, GARDEN, HOBBIES, MUSIC & PETS

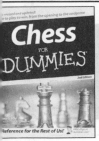

0-7645-8404-9

0-7645-9904-6

Also available:
- Candy Making For Dummies
  0-7645-9734-5
- Card Games For Dummies
  0-7645-9910-0
- Crocheting For Dummies
  0-7645-4151-X
- Dog Training For Dummies
  0-7645-8418-9
- Healthy Carb Cookbook For Dummies
  0-7645-8476-6
- Home Maintenance For Dummies
  0-7645-5215-5

- Horses For Dummies
  0-7645-9797-3
- Jewelry Making & Beading For Dummies
  0-7645-2571-9
- Orchids For Dummies
  0-7645-6759-4
- Puppies For Dummies
  0-7645-5255-4
- Rock Guitar For Dummies
  0-7645-5356-9
- Sewing For Dummies
  0-7645-6847-7
- Singing For Dummies
  0-7645-2475-5

TERNET & DIGITAL MEDIA

0-470-04529-9

0-470-04894-8

Also available:
- Blogging For Dummies
  0-471-77084-1
- Digital Photography For Dummies
  0-7645-9802-3
- Digital Photography All-in-One Desk Reference For Dummies
  0-470-03743-1
- Digital SLR Cameras and Photography For Dummies
  0-7645-9803-1
- eBay Business All-in-One Desk Reference For Dummies
  0-7645-8438-3
- HDTV For Dummies
  0-470-09673-X

- Home Entertainment PCs For Dummies
  0-470-05523-5
- MySpace For Dummies
  0-470-09529-6
- Search Engine Optimization For Dummies
  0-471-97998-8
- Skype For Dummies
  0-470-04891-3
- The Internet For Dummies
  0-7645-8996-2
- Wiring Your Digital Home For Dummies
  0-471-91830-X

parate Canadian edition also available
parate U.K. edition also available

able wherever books are sold. For more information or to order direct: U.S. customers visit www.dummies.com or call 1-877-762-2974.
customers visit www.wileyeurope.com or call 0800 243407. Canadian customers visit www.wiley.ca or call 1-800-567-4797.

SPORTS, FITNESS, PARENTING, RELIGION & SPIRITUALITY

0-471-76871-5

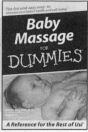
0-7645-7841-3

Also available:
- Catholicism For Dummies
  0-7645-5391-7
- Exercise Balls For Dummies
  0-7645-5623-1
- Fitness For Dummies
  0-7645-7851-0
- Football For Dummies
  0-7645-3936-1
- Judaism For Dummies
  0-7645-5299-6
- Potty Training For Dummies
  0-7645-5417-4
- Buddhism For Dummies
  0-7645-5359-3

- Pregnancy For Dummies
  0-7645-4483-7 †
- Ten Minute Tone-Ups For Dummie
  0-7645-7207-5
- NASCAR For Dummies
  0-7645-7681-X
- Religion For Dummies
  0-7645-5264-3
- Soccer For Dummies
  0-7645-5229-5
- Women in the Bible For Dummies
  0-7645-8475-8

TRAVEL

0-7645-7749-2

0-7645-6945-7

Also available:
- Alaska For Dummies
  0-7645-7746-8
- Cruise Vacations For Dummies
  0-7645-6941-4
- England For Dummies
  0-7645-4276-1
- Europe For Dummies
  0-7645-7529-5
- Germany For Dummies
  0-7645-7823-5
- Hawaii For Dummies
  0-7645-7402-7

- Italy For Dummies
  0-7645-7386-1
- Las Vegas For Dummies
  0-7645-7382-9
- London For Dummies
  0-7645-4277-X
- Paris For Dummies
  0-7645-7630-5
- RV Vacations For Dummies
  0-7645-4442-X
- Walt Disney World & Orlando
  For Dummies
  0-7645-9660-8

GRAPHICS, DESIGN & WEB DEVELOPMENT

0-7645-8815-X

0-7645-9571-7

Also available:
- 3D Game Animation For Dummies
  0-7645-8789-7
- AutoCAD 2006 For Dummies
  0-7645-8925-3
- Building a Web Site For Dummies
  0-7645-7144-3
- Creating Web Pages For Dummies
  0-470-08030-2
- Creating Web Pages All-in-One Desk
  Reference For Dummies
  0-7645-4345-8
- Dreamweaver 8 For Dummies
  0-7645-9649-7

- InDesign CS2 For Dummies
  0-7645-9572-5
- Macromedia Flash 8 For Dummies
  0-7645-9691-8
- Photoshop CS2 and Digital
  Photography For Dummies
  0-7645-9580-6
- Photoshop Elements 4 For Dummie
  0-471-77483-9
- Syndicating Web Sites with RSS Fee
  For Dummies
  0-7645-8848-6
- Yahoo! SiteBuilder For Dummies
  0-7645-9800-7

NETWORKING, SECURITY, PROGRAMMING & DATABASES

0-7645-7728-X

0-471-74940-0

Also available:
- Access 2007 For Dummies
  0-470-04612-0
- ASP.NET 2 For Dummies
  0-7645-7907-X
- C# 2005 For Dummies
  0-7645-9704-3
- Hacking For Dummies
  0-470-05235-X
- Hacking Wireless Networks
  For Dummies
  0-7645-9730-2
- Java For Dummies
  0-470-08716-1

- Microsoft SQL Server 2005 For Dumm
  0-7645-7755-7
- Networking All-in-One Desk Refere
  For Dummies
  0-7645-9939-9
- Preventing Identity Theft For Dummi
  0-7645-7336-5
- Telecom For Dummies
  0-471-77085-X
- Visual Studio 2005 All-in-One Desk
  Reference For Dummies
  0-7645-9775-2
- XML For Dummies
  0-7645-8845-1

LTH & SELF-HELP

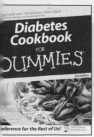

Diabetes Cookbook
0-7645-8450-2

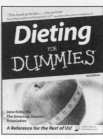

Dieting
0-7645-4149-8

Also available:
- Bipolar Disorder For Dummies
  0-7645-8451-0
- Chemotherapy and Radiation For Dummies
  0-7645-7832-4
- Controlling Cholesterol For Dummies
  0-7645-5440-9
- Diabetes For Dummies
  0-7645-6820-5* †
- Divorce For Dummies
  0-7645-8417-0 †

- Fibromyalgia For Dummies
  0-7645-5441-7
- Low-Calorie Dieting For Dummies
  0-7645-9905-4
- Meditation For Dummies
  0-471-77774-9
- Osteoporosis For Dummies
  0-7645-7621-6
- Overcoming Anxiety For Dummies
  0-7645-5447-6
- Reiki For Dummies
  0-7645-9907-0
- Stress Management For Dummies
  0-7645-5144-2

CATION, HISTORY, REFERENCE & TEST PREPARATION

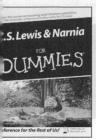

S. Lewis & Narnia
0-7645-8381-6

Genetics
0-7645-9554-7

Also available:
- The ACT For Dummies
  0-7645-9652-7
- Algebra For Dummies
  0-7645-5325-9
- Algebra Workbook For Dummies
  0-7645-8467-7
- Astronomy For Dummies
  0-7645-8465-0
- Calculus For Dummies
  0-7645-2498-4
- Chemistry For Dummies
  0-7645-5430-1
- Forensics For Dummies
  0-7645-5580-4

- Freemasons For Dummies
  0-7645-9796-5
- French For Dummies
  0-7645-5193-0
- Geometry For Dummies
  0-7645-5324-0
- Organic Chemistry I For Dummies
  0-7645-6902-3
- The SAT I For Dummies
  0-7645-7193-1
- Spanish For Dummies
  0-7645-5194-9
- Statistics For Dummies
  0-7645-5423-9

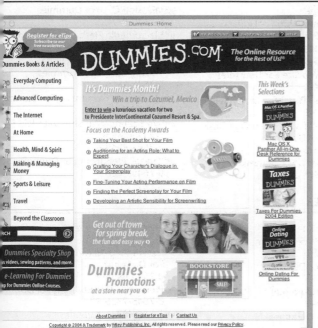

Get smart @ dummies.com®

- **Find a full list of Dummies titles**
- **Look into loads of FREE on-site articles**
- **Sign up for FREE eTips e-mailed to you weekly**
- **See what other products carry the Dummies name**
- **Shop directly from the Dummies bookstore**
- **Enter to win new prizes every month!**

e Canadian edition also available
U.K. edition also available

erever books are sold. For more information or to order direct: U.S. customers visit www.dummies.com or call 1-877-762-2974.
visit www.wileyeurope.com or call 0800 243407. Canadian customers visit www.wiley.ca or call 1-800-567-4797.